What's on the CD-ROM

The CD-ROM that accompanies this book contains security, software, and hacking tools to help you secure your network. The software packages are divided into the following categories:

- The Resources folder contains a generic policy document you can customize for your environment, and an HTML version of Appendix C you can use to click through to Web sites.

- The Hacking folder contains software written by or for hackers that you can use to test your defenses.

- The Security folder contains various security utilities and demo applications.

- The IE4 folder contains Microsoft Internet Explorer 4.0, one of the most popular and capable browsers available today. Copyright Microsoft Corporation, 1996. All rights reserved.

- The WinZip folder contains WinZip 6.3 from Nico Mak Computing, Inc. This zip utility will allow you to unzip many of the tools and applications on the CD-ROM.

- The Firewall folder contains demos of commercial firewall products.

 Do not install firewall demo products on production servers! They can restrict service to the machine so that you will not be able to log in correctly or use the machine for any other purpose.

NT Network Security

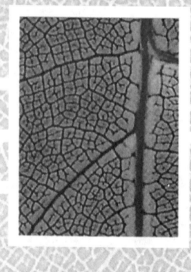

NT® Network Security

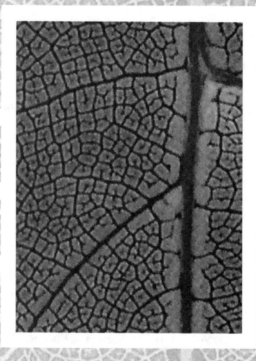

Matthew Strebe
Charles Perkins
Michael G. Moncur

San Francisco • Paris • Düsseldorf • Soest

Associate Publisher: Guy Hart-Davis
Acquisitions Manager: Kristine Plachy
Acquisitions & Developmental Editor: Neil Edde
Associate Developmental Editor: Maureen Adams
Editor: Vivian Perry
Project Editor: Shelby Zimmerman
Technical Editor: Jim Polizzi
Book Designer: Patrick Dintino
Graphic Illustrator: Andrew Benzie
Electronic Publishing Specialist: Kate Kaminski
Production Coordinator: Eryn Osterhaus
Proofreaders: Duncan Watson, Charles Mathews
Indexer: Nancy Guenther
Companion CD: Molly Sharp and John D. Wright
Cover Designer: Archer Design
Cover Photographer: The Image Bank

Screen reproductions produced with Collage Complete.
Collage Complete is a trademark of Inner Media Inc.

The CD Interface music is from GIRA Sound AURIA Music Library ©GIRA Sound 1996.

SYBEX, Network Press, and the Network Press logo are registered trademarks of SYBEX Inc.

TRADEMARKS: SYBEX has attempted throughout this book to distinguish proprietary trademarks from descriptive terms by following the capitalization style used by the manufacturer.

The author and publisher have made their best efforts to prepare this book, and the content is based upon final release software whenever possible. Portions of the manuscript may be based upon pre-release versions supplied by software manufacturer(s). The author and the publisher make no representation or warranties of any kind with regard to the completeness or accuracy of the contents herein and accept no liability of any kind including but not limited to performance, merchantability, fitness for any particular purpose, or any losses or damages of any kind caused or alleged to be caused directly or indirectly from this book.

Library of Congress Card Number: 97-80634
ISBN: 0-7821-2006-7

Manufactured in the United States of America

10 9 8 7 6 5 4 3 2 1

To Christy—*Matthew Strebe*
To Becky—*Charles Perkins*
To Laura—*Michael Moncur*

Acknowledgments

My wife has been a saint, patiently waiting for years now for me to finish writing so we can resume a normal life. Her support is the wind upon which I fly. I would also like to thank two of my oldest and dearest friends, Mike Moncur and Charles Perkins, without whom this book would have been much shorter. The people at Sybex work far harder on these books than do the authors. Thanks to Neil, Maureen, Guy, Shelby, Vivian, and Jim (and to Rodnay Zaks, author of the first computer book I owned, which still sits dog-eared and worn beside my own); perhaps they should be writing this acknowledgment. My family has always been a tremendous support, especially Roy and Carol, Lee and Donna, Terry and Sharee. Thanks also to my brothers and sisters: daan and Fukiko, Rachel and Kerry, Ruth and James, Chris and Phyllis, Jacqui and Bob, Duane, Gretchen and Paul, Susan and Jimmy, Victor, Doug and Colleen, Margaret and Richard, David and Debbie, Don and Christine, Sharon and Ken, Linda, Scott and LeAnn, Dennis, William and Kori, Rachelle, Brent, and LoraLee—*Matthew Strebe*

Thanks, Mike. This is all your fault. Thanks to my family and friends for keeping me sane. Thanks to the people at Sybex who haven't learned their lesson yet and keep letting me write things, and thanks to Henry J. Tillman for just being himself.—*Charles Perkins*

Thanks to Matthew and Charles for their help writing this book and for offering me the chance to participate. I'd like to thank the people at Sybex who helped produce this book, especially Neil Edde, Maureen Adams, and Shelby Zimmerman. I'd also like to thank Kate Kaminski, Eryn Osterhaus, Andrew Benzie, Molly Sharp, and Dale Wright for putting together the physical pages of the book, the rendered art, and the CD-ROM. Our editor, Vivian Perry, has been very helpful in making this book's explanations clear and correct. Jim Polizzi, the technical reviewer, provided many useful suggestions and prevented some embarrassing errors. I'd like to thank my wife, Laura, and my family: Mom, Dad, Kristen, Matt, Mel, and Ian. A special thanks to my grandmothers, Alice Moncur and Edna Tippets, for their love and support. Also, thanks to all of my friends: Matt and Christy, Chuck, Cory and Kathleen, Dylan and Joan, Robert, Curt, James, and Henry.—*Michael Moncur*

Contents at a Glance

Table of Contents

Introduction

Windows NT is rapidly becoming one of the most popular networking systems for all sizes of networks. One of the biggest concerns of system administrators is network security: Is your network safe from intruders or, for that matter, from your own employees?

This book is devoted to the full spectrum of network security for Windows NT networks, ranging from basic logon security to Internet security and firewalls. General security topics, such as encryption and human security, are also covered.

Who Should Read This Book?

This book is designed for network administrators who work with Windows NT networks or who plan to use Windows NT at some stage. Rather than being strictly a guide to Windows NT's security features, this book is intended as a guide to all aspects of security for Windows NT networks.

In this book, we take a serious look at Windows NT's security strengths and weaknesses, and provide recommendations for security ranging from the simple security measures required by small companies to the sophisticated measures required for large companies and government organizations.

This book will be useful for anyone who manages a Windows NT network, regardless of their experience level. However, we have made a few assumptions:

- You should be familiar with the basics of computers and have some familiarity with Windows NT, or at least Windows 95. This book does not explain how to install Windows NT, wire a network, or perform other basic tasks.

- You should have administrative access to a Windows NT network if you want to experiment with security or implement our suggestions. We do cover some aspects of security that apply to other network systems, but Windows NT is the main focus of the book.

How to Use This Book

The information in this book is organized into 22 chapters and four appendixes, beginning with an introduction to security and moving on to more advanced topics.

Chapter 1 Provides an introduction to the basics of security and the types of security you may wish to consider for your network.

Chapter 2 Explores *human security*: security problems caused by the actions of users.

Chapter 3 Explains how various encryption methods work, and how they can be used in your network security plan.

Chapter 4 Looks at the techniques and resources needed for successful security administration.

Chapter 5 Takes an in-depth look at the Windows NT security model and the components of NT security.

Chapter 6 Explains how to create, maintain, and assign rights to user accounts.

Chapter 7 Looks at system policies, which can be used to control access to individual functions within the operating system.

Chapter 8 Explains how file system security can be used to control access to files and directories.

Chapter 9 Looks at workgroups and shares, two simple but relatively nonsecure systems built into Windows NT.

Chapter 10 Explores domain security and trust relationships, Windows NT's secure solution for larger networks.

Chapter 11 Explains how fault tolerance methods—such as disk mirroring and backups—can prevent accidental data loss.

Chapter 12 Looks at security concerns related to the remote access service, which allows dial-up access to Windows NT networks.

Chapter 13 Is an overview of the security concerns you may need to deal with in a multivendor network, including UNIX, NetWare, and Macintosh security.

Chapter 14 Looks at the Internet and its local counterparts, intranets and extranets, and how they affect security.

Chapter 15 Looks at the TCP/IP protocol suite and the security risks associated with its protocols.

Chapter 16 Explores some of the ways security can be applied to client computers and applications.

Chapter 17 Looks at firewalls, devices used to control security between local networks and the Internet.

Chapter 18 Looks at the components of Microsoft BackOffice, such as Internet Information Server, and how they relate to security.

Chapter 19 Explores some high-level bugs and security holes that can be exploited by hackers and explains how to prevent attacks.

Chapter 20 Explains the security risks at the network and data link layers and how they can be prevented.

Chapter 21 Looks at various ways of securing Windows NT servers against local access.

Chapter 22 Explores the security concerns associated with the physical layer of the OSI model, such as wiretapping.

Appendix A Provides a document that shows what some typical security policies might look like.

Appendix B Takes a look at security tools.

Appendix C Covers online resources that are valuable in keeping up with developments that affect network security.

Appendix D Is an exhaustive glossary.

Although we would love it if you read this book cover to cover, it's also meant to be useful as a general reference. For example, when you're setting up user accounts, you can refer to Chapter 6, and when you decide to connect your network to the Internet, you can refer to Chapters 14 and 17.

Most of the chapters include three handy features:

Terminology These sidebars describe terms related to the chapter. See the glossary at the back of the book for additional definitions.

Policies These sidebars contain our suggestions for securing a particular aspect of your network.

Reality Check These sidebars are sometimes humorous personal accounts of real-world security problems we've run into. These stories provide you with an idea of the situations you might encounter with your network.

Keeping in Touch

The world of network security is constantly changing. The Internet, computer magazines, and even local newspapers include accounts of dangerous security risks—many of them inaccurate stories or outright hoaxes.

We've provided a list of online resources for up-to-date, accurate information about security in Appendix C. We are also maintaining a Web page to accompany this book, which includes links to new security items as well as additions and corrections to this book. Use this address to access our NT security page:

```
http://www.starlingtech.com/ntsecurity/
```

You can also reach us via e-mail. We'd love to hear your comments about the book and any interesting security-related stories you have to tell. You can also ask us questions about NT security, although we may not have time to answer all of them. Use this address:

```
ntsecurity@starlingtech.com
```

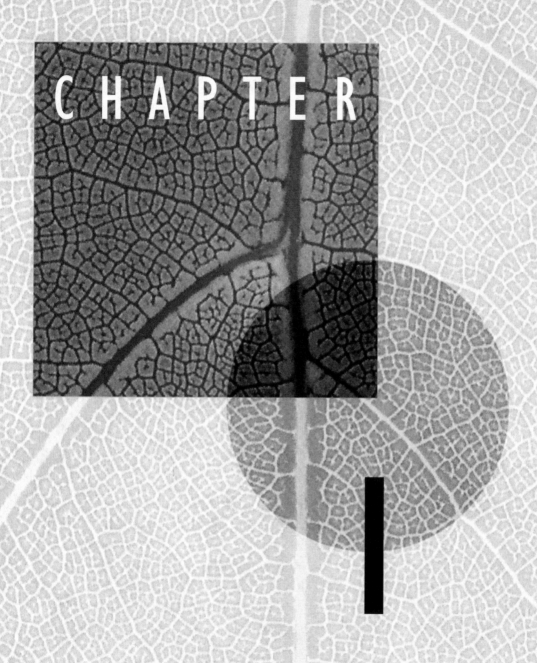

CHAPTER

1

Security Concepts and Terminology

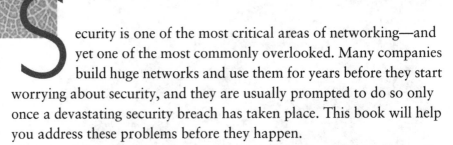

ecurity is one of the most critical areas of networking—and yet one of the most commonly overlooked. Many companies build huge networks and use them for years before they start worrying about security, and they are usually prompted to do so only once a devastating security breach has taken place. This book will help you address these problems before they happen.

In this chapter, we'll look at the basics of security and some common approaches to it. We'll also explain the policies your company should establish for dealing with security. Finally, we'll take a quick look at how the security features of Windows NT and other common operating systems compare.

Security Defined

When you hear the term *security*, you probably think of two basic ideas: protection and peace of mind. Network security is the sum of all measures taken to prevent loss of any kind, and when correctly implemented it ensures both protection and peace of mind. Securing your network requires coordination of a wide variety of security measures—from creating user accounts to hiring loyal employees to keeping the server in a locked room.

Security is a continual process. You cannot apply the security measures known at the time you install your Web server, lock it in a secure room, and assume that no one will ever find a bug in the operating system or server software that can be exploited. You must stay aware of new security issues that come up with the operating system and application software you use and then apply new security measures constantly. The following sections describe some basic categories of network security.

The security categories described in this chapter aren't necessarily the only components of network security. On the contrary, there are some extremely specific types of security that are complex enough to fill a book themselves. The following sections describe the basic types of security that apply to most networks.

Logon Security

In a secure network, the first thing a user encounters is a prompt for a user name and password. This is the network's first defense against security problems. To use a secure building as an analogy, this is like having a security guard or electronic lock at the building's door. While these measures don't prevent problems entirely, they do ensure that you'll know who was in the building (or the network) and when, and that unauthorized users can't enter.

Unfortunately, no logon security system is flawless. Users can choose easy-to-guess passwords, write their passwords down in obvious places, or share passwords. Windows NT provides various methods you can use to avoid these problems. We'll look at some of these issues in Chapter 2.

Terminology

- **Account:** A user name and password you create to give a user access to the network (or to a single machine). Along with the name and password, an account includes other information about the user, such as groups the user belongs to, and directories and files the user can access.

- **Hacker:** Someone who makes it their business to break into networks they have no right to access. Hackers range from teenagers looking for a challenge to foreign operatives looking for information. The word "hacker" originally referred to someone who was simply good with computers, but it is now much more widely used with this negative connotation.

- **Intruder:** This is a general term for anyone who attempts to log into a system without proper authorization. Intruders can be hackers, corporate spies, disgruntled former employees, or simply ordinary employees who've forgotten their passwords.

File System Security

Users log into a network for one main reason: to access files and directories on the server. *File system security* controls which files each user is able to access. Users can have rights to any number of files and directories, and each has a specific list of rights. For example, a user may have full rights in one directory (read files, create files, erase files, etc.) and read-only access in another directory.

In securing the files on the network, you should be sure to account for both files on the server and files on the local workstation. This is more difficult than it sounds. Many client operating systems, such as DOS and Windows 95, have few security features. The best solution is to encourage (and require) users to save their files on a server.

DOS, Windows 3.*x*, Windows 95, and Windows NT can all use the FAT file system. This system hasn't changed much since the early versions of DOS, and as you might expect, it isn't very secure. While there are ways of increasing the security of FAT files, the best approach is to use a more secure file system. Windows NT supports the *NTFS* (*NT File System*) system, which fully supports security.

Chapter 8 discusses file system security in detail.

Data Communication Security

Another aspect of security concerns data communication. Data traveling through the network includes sensitive information, such as confidential files. File system security isn't useful unless the network traffic between the workstation and the server is also secure.

It's possible to gain unauthorized access to information by monitoring the traffic through the network, unless care has been taken to secure the data. In addition to preventing unauthorized access to the wires and devices that make up the network, securing data also includes the use of encryption (encoding the data at one end and decoding it at the other to make it useless to anyone who intercepts it). Figure 1.1 illustrates how a secure communication system might work.

FIGURE 1.1

Secure data communication is accomplished by using encryption.

While communication security is a relatively minor issue on local area networks, it is more of a concern with larger networks. When a network is connected to the Internet, this type of security becomes critical.

We'll discuss data communication security in more detail in several chapters of this book, beginning with Chapter 3.

Administration

Another aspect of security is the administration of your network. If your network is small (one building and 50 or fewer users), chances are there's a single administrator. In this case, that one administrator will handle all aspects of security. In a larger network, which may include hundreds of users and span multiple locations, it's necessary to divide the workload. As well as giving a user access to files and network services, you can also give them the ability to act as an administrator.

There are many ways to distribute the administration duties for a network. As a simple example, you could assign an administrator for each company location. More complex arrangements can include naming specialized administrators, such as a file system administrator or Internet gateway administrator.

A large and complex network can have an entire hierarchy of administrators, and can even allow branch administrators to further subdivide administration by granting administration abilities to other users.

By default, Windows NT includes a user account called Administrator, which is given full administrative privileges. You can use this account to create other administrators.

Auditing

To take up where we left off with the building analogy, we might note that many companies use videotaped security cameras. While these can't prevent a problem when it happens, they are valuable after the fact: They give you a record of what happened, who did it, and when. In network security, *auditing* performs a similar monitoring function.

Windows NT's auditing feature can automatically log certain events when they happen. For example, you might want to know which users access a certain file. You can examine the log file later to determine if there is unauthorized access.

You can turn on auditing for various features with the User Manager for Domains utility's Audit Policy option. This dialog box is shown in Figure 1.2.

FIGURE 1.2

This dialog box in the User Manager for Domains utility allows you to control auditing.

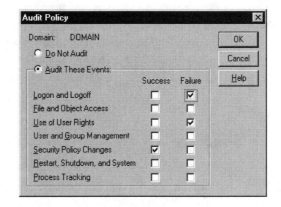

Depending on the level of security (and risk) in your network, you may wish to leave auditing turned on all of the time, or just depend on it for certain files, certain directories, or certain users. You can also turn on auditing after a security problem has occurred, in the hope of obtaining more information when the problem occurs again.

Physical Security

Of course, even the most secure server is only as safe as the building—and the room—it's in. Physical security means the security of the machines themselves. Your network's security can easily be compromised by a workstation or server left logged in and unattended, or even by someone physically stealing a machine.

There is one general rule when it comes to physical security: If someone can physically access your server, they can cause trouble.

Reality Check: Out in the Open

When I worked as a network consultant, I visited a company to train their IS department in managing and securing their NetWare server. I arrived to find that the server was stored inconspicuously next to the copier and coffee machine. The server console required a password to access, but that wouldn't stop a determined intruder. (Not to mention the potential consequences of spilled coffee.)

Human Security

Another important aspect of security deals with the most chaotic element in the network: the users. Human security encompasses many issues, from unauthorized break-ins to training users to avoiding security breaches.

Since users are the heart of the network, human security overlaps with many other types of security, and a network with a human security problem is not likely to be secure in other areas. Chapter 2 describes the aspects of human security in detail.

Planning a Security Approach

When you plan the security of your network, you can take one of two basic approaches:

- In the *optimistic approach*, you initially give all users access to everything, then explicitly deny access to critical information.

■ In the *pessimistic approach*, you initially restrict access to everything, then explicitly enable access to needed information.

Each of these approaches has its advantages, as you'll see in the following sections. Of course, you may use an approach that falls somewhere between these two, or use different approaches for different parts of the network. Following the discussion of the optimistic and pessimistic approaches, we'll look at security policies you should create to document your security approach.

The Optimistic Approach

The optimistic approach is the easiest way to go, at least from an administrative standpoint. At an extreme, you could use the ultimate optimistic approach: All users get access to everything. This requires very little administration; as a matter of fact, Windows NT defaults to this approach.

The disadvantages of too much optimism are obvious. In all but the smallest networks, it's hard to think of every conceivable problem when you set up a user. Therefore, this approach tends to result in *corrective security*; that is, each new security improvement is made to address a security breach that has already happened.

Network administrators who use the optimistic approach often fall into the trap of relying on *security through obscurity*. In other words, they assume that if a directory is buried a few levels deep in the file system, or if you need to know complex DOS or UNIX commands to access the information, the data is reasonably safe. Needless to say, it usually isn't. When a network's administration is that casual, there's a good chance that one of the users knows more than the administrator.

Another trap of the optimistic approach is to assume that users won't harm data unless they have a motive. Unfortunately, well-meaning users are just as capable of causing trouble as hackers and corporate spies.

Of course, it's possible to use the optimistic approach without going to extremes. If you have relatively few items that are confidential, this can be the best choice. For example, users in a small company wear many hats—the same secretary might need to access Accounts Payable, Accounts Receivable, and General Ledger data. In this situation, the optimistic approach works well. Most users need to access most areas, and critical areas—such as Payroll—can be secured.

The Pessimistic Approach

By contrast, the pessimistic approach requires a large amount of time and effort to administer. Each user starts out with no access, and you carefully add access for each specific need. Every time a user gains a new responsibility or changes jobs, you'll find yourself making changes to the account.

Obviously, this approach requires a commitment to administration; and since many IS departments are understaffed as it is, this is not a popular choice. However, it is widely used in situations where security is critical: by governments and by companies in highly-regulated industries such as banking and healthcare.

There is a distinct advantage to the pessimistic approach: It allows you to avoid most security problems, including problems you haven't thought of yet. This makes it a very appealing choice for anyone concerned with security. While a strict pessimistic approach may not be practical in your organization, you should consider using some elements of this approach, or using it for areas of your network that require high security.

One situation where you'll definitely want to use the pessimistic approach is in any system that is accessible through the Internet. While users in your company may not be obsessed with breaking your security, you can be assured that someone on the Net is.

Security Policies

Keeping a secure network requires organization—a sloppy approach will inevitably result in security holes. To ensure that the security on your network is effective, you should create a document that specifies the exact security features in use and their configuration. Ideally, you should plan and create a policy when you're planning and installing the network in the first place.

Your security policy should be clearly documented, and should be agreed upon by management and the IS department. You may even want to post it or distribute it to employees (perhaps on a company intranet) so everyone knows their role in the security of the company and its data.

A security policy should clearly state the following:

- Your organization's basic security approach (optimistic or pessimistic) and the portions of the network that are exceptions to the rule

- Details of all aspects of security, including physical and human security

- What access is required for each employee or group of employees

A network security policy should be part of a bigger plan that includes security for the building itself, the telephone system, and other aspects of the company.

Along with the policies you create to manage your company's security, there is another type of policy. Windows NT includes several options called *policies* that allow you to configure the basic rules for securing your network. For example, the Account Policy dialog box (see Figure 1.3) includes options for password requirements, minimum password length, and other items relating to user accounts. Your policy documentation should include values for each of Windows NT's policy options.

FIGURE 1.3

Windows NT's Account
Policy dialog box includes
options relating to user
accounts and passwords.

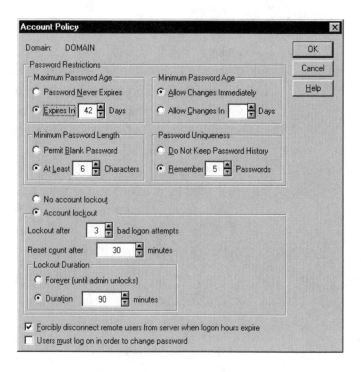

In each of the chapters that follows, we'll present suggested items you
should consider when creating a policy for that aspect of security. By
following the guidelines in this book, you should be able to create a
firm security policy that addresses all of the important issues. These
policies are summarized in Appendix A.

Security Problems and Their Consequences

Broadly speaking, the goal of any security policy is to avoid some kind of
loss. While a breach in a building's security can result in a loss of physical
merchandise, a breach in network security can result in loss of data, loss
of confidentiality, loss of service, or simply a loss of time on the part of
the network administrator and other employees.

In the following sections we'll take a quick look at the types of security breaches that can affect your network, and the losses that result from them. These are the consequences of an imperfect security policy—and all security policies are, to some extent, imperfect. By understanding the potential losses and deciding which would be most devastating to your company, you can focus your security policy to minimize risk.

Theft

While it is possible that a network server will be stolen, there are two more likely types of theft in network security:

- **Theft of data:** Unauthorized users can obtain copies of data stored on your network.

- **Theft of service:** If your network offers a service (as an Internet service provider does) unauthorized users can gain access and use the service without paying.

Unlike a physical theft, neither of these losses deprives you of the data or service, but both lose value quickly when they're available to unauthorized individuals. Confidential business data in the hands of a competitor can be devastating, and anyone who obtains a service offered by your network for free deprives you of a paying customer.

Unauthorized Disclosure

Another potential loss is the unauthorized disclosure of information. While corporate espionage is one possibility, this can also happen in less criminal—but often equally severe—ways. For example, if employees are able to access certain information, they may unwittingly disclose that information to a competitor. For this reason, it's best to restrict each employee's access to a "need to know" basis. For example, if a helpful employee is asked by a potential customer for references, he or she might simply fax them a customer list—not realizing that the caller is also a potential competitor.

In a less severe case, employees can obtain information not intended for them. For example, most companies would suffer a morale problem if employees were able to access salary information and compare what they and other employees earn. This also applies to communications between members of management, and even communications within a single department.

Information Warfare

A particularly devastating security loss can be caused by a malicious hacker. If hackers can break into a network to obtain information, they can also erase or modify the information. If you have a good backup system, data loss of this nature is usually not permanent—but it can waste some of your time, and sabotage your users' productivity. This kind of security breach is called *information warfare*.

On Internet-connected systems, two types of information warfare can be most damaging and time-consuming:

- **Denial-of-service attacks:** Various methods hackers can use to bring your network to a standstill, making it inaccessible to legitimate users. These methods typically involve opening and dropping TCP connections so quickly that the target server spends an inordinate amount of time dealing with connection overhead, or exploiting known bugs in software to crash servers or service applications.

- **Mail bombing:** The process of sending a very large quantity of electronic mail messages to a server, effectively crippling it. This attack is particularly easy to carry out—all you have to do is repeatedly send a huge file, or write a simple program to send small e-mail messages repeatedly. Depending on the size and utilization of the server, it could take between a thousand and several hundred thousand messages for this to happen.

Be warned: Unless you take extra precautions against them, these two types of attacks are actually easier for the hacker than breaking into your network. Bugs in otherwise-harmless network utilities can be exploited to cause denial-of-service, and any user with a mail program and a bit of patience can send a mail bomb. Fortunately, many hackers consider denial-of-service attacks and mail bombing to be juvenile and pointless, so they generally don't bother with them.

Accidental Data Loss

While it's glamorous to think that data disasters are often caused by malicious hackers, your company's data actually has a much more likely foe: its own employees. A disgruntled former employee may fall into the malicious category, but well-meaning employees can be every bit as dangerous.

If you take an optimistic approach to security, there's a good chance that users are able to delete files they didn't create. Of course, no competent user would make this mistake; but since many companies train employees using the "throw them in and see if they can swim" approach, you can't count on competence.

Reality Check: Attack of the Well-Meaning User

I once worked as network administrator at a company with a reasonably optimistic security approach. We were using several antiquated DOS accounting programs, and it was difficult to make them work without some flexibility in security. One of the users in the accounting department was responsible for creating reports using one of these programs. One day he noticed that the list of reports was long, and he didn't know what most of them were for.

Being an efficient, organized employee, he made it his task to examine each report and delete the ones he didn't use. Unfortunately, he didn't realize that this list included reports created by many other employees for many other departments. I began receiving complaints from all over the building that reports had vanished.

We were able to restore most of the reports from a backup tape, but one employee had spent the whole day creating several new reports, which had to be re-created. Needless to say, a bit of user training could have averted this disaster.

Taking a more pessimistic approach to security is one way to avoid disasters of this kind. Another often overlooked (and under-budgeted) approach is to provide computer training for the users. It's practically impossible to restrict access so much that users can't cause any trouble at all—so the best approach is to make sure the users know what they're doing. We'll look at these issues in more detail in Chapter 2.

Some companies with computer training programs tend to aim them at lower-echelon employees, such as secretaries and data entry clerks. This is a mistake—anyone who regularly uses a computer should be trained. As you may have noticed in your company, the title of Vice President doesn't ensure that a user knows anything about computers.

Operating Systems and Security

Of course, many of the security capabilities of your network depend on the operating system you're running it on. The operating systems available today for network servers and workstations have vastly different approaches to security—and vastly different features.

Because you're reading a Windows NT security book, you're probably most concerned with the security features of Windows NT. However, unless your network is very well-planned (or very small,) there's a good chance you're also running one or more other operating systems. To give you an idea of how they compare, the following sections briefly describe the security approach of today's common operating systems.

Windows NT

We'll start with the subject of this book: Windows NT. Although Windows NT was originally intended to replace Windows (and it still may someday), it's evolved into a platform for reliable network servers. Microsoft sells two versions of Windows NT:

- **Windows NT Workstation:** Intended as a general client OS (but more expensive and stable than Windows 95)

- **Windows NT Server:** Intended as a server operating system

There are many similarities between the two versions—as a matter of fact, the main difference is in what the software license allows you to do (and the price). Windows NT Server is usually the platform of choice for servers, so users expect more from it in terms of security.

Although Windows NT was designed with security in mind, it wasn't widely used for networking at first, and was plagued with security problems. Microsoft has improved its security significantly, but there are still security holes. Nevertheless, it is possible to run a very secure system using Windows NT; all it takes are the latest security fixes from Microsoft and the strategies outlined in this book.

Reality Check: An Unexpected Benefit from Hackers

At the time of this writing, Microsoft is getting some unwanted help in finding security flaws in Windows NT. It seems that several groups of hackers have devoted themselves to finding security holes in NT, and demonstrating them by attacking a rather popular Windows NT server: Microsoft's own Web server. I can't really say that this is a good thing—but then again, I've never seen Microsoft release security fixes so quickly in the past. Microsoft calls these updates "hot fixes," and they're available on the Web: http://support.microsoft.com/support/.

Windows 95

You may have noticed that there are no books on Windows 95 security. There's a simple reason for this: Any such book would consist of a few pages describing Windows 95's security features, and a few pages listing all of the reasons why you should use Windows NT instead.

Windows 95's operation is limited to the FAT file system, which does not include any security features to speak of. When Windows 95 files are shared across the network, they use a simple password scheme with limited security.

Because of these and other limitations, we do not recommend that you use Windows 95 for applications that require security. Of course, Windows 95 can be used for client workstations in a Windows NT network with little security risk—provided your users save their files on the server rather than a local hard drive, log out whenever they leave the console, and don't log in as a member of the Administrators group over the network.

UNIX

Like Windows NT, UNIX was plagued with security problems in its early days. UNIX wasn't really developed with security in mind. As a matter of fact, the creators of UNIX initially developed it so that they would have a platform to play games on. Despite its origins, UNIX is now the most widely used system for Internet servers, and it is widely considered secure.

The reason UNIX is considered more secure than Windows NT is simple: It's been around longer. UNIX was created in 1969, and since then has been the preferred victim for hackers everywhere. Because of this, developers of the various UNIX systems have rushed to keep up, plugging security holes as the hackers found them.

Despite its maturity, UNIX still has security problems. Although it's possible to make an extremely secure UNIX system by carefully configuring features and installing security fixes, many administrators don't have the time or budget to maintain a completely secure system.

UNIX systems are still the most commonly broken into systems on the Internet. While these incidents occasionally involve a newly discovered security flaw, the vast majority exploit the old security holes. Information on exploiting these holes is widespread in the hacker community, and it's common for hackers to attack machine after machine until they find one with an unplugged security hole.

NetWare

NetWare, from Novell Inc., was the original dedicated network operating system. Although it's rapidly losing ground to Windows NT, NetWare is still the most widely used network operating system. The latest version, NetWare 4.11, is included as part of Novell's IntranetWare package.

Unlike Windows NT, NetWare uses a vastly different operating system on the server than the one it uses on workstations. The NetWare server is a dedicated machine with a simple text-based user interface. Most of the administration can be performed from a DOS or Windows workstation.

NetWare has included security features from the beginning, and has been around nearly as long as UNIX. So as you might expect, it's one of the most secure systems. The latest version is comparable with Windows NT's level of security. Nevertheless, it does have its vulnerabilities.

One major security advantage of NetWare had been its use of the *Internetwork Packet Exchange (IPX)* protocol, which is not compatible with TCP/IP. The protocol incompatibility made it difficult to accidentally expose your server to the Internet without having your security set up correctly. The new version of NetWare, IntranetWare, fully supports TCP/IP and is now much easier to subvert from the Internet.

DOS and Windows 3.x

The first version of DOS was developed by Microsoft engineers working with only one goal: to finish an operating system before IBM came up with one of their own. DOS has evolved through the years, with version 6.22 the last official release. Microsoft has ceased further development of DOS as a distinct operating system, although Windows 95 is still based on a version of DOS.

DOS was never intended as a network operating system, of course, and security wasn't much of a concern. DOS uses the unsecure FAT file system, and isn't really equipped to deal with multiple users.

Windows 3.1x is a shell that runs on top of DOS, and doesn't really improve security. Although basic networking features are included (notably in the network-specialized version, Windows for Workgroups), these are fundamentally intended as client operating systems, and don't even attempt to be secure.

Summary

Security is one of the most critical areas of networking—and yet one of the most commonly overlooked. Securing a network basically means preventing unauthorized access and data loss. Security risks can come from hackers, competitors, and even well-meaning employees.

There are two basic approaches to security: optimistic and pessimistic. The optimistic approach requires the least amount of administration but is the least secure. The pessimistic approach is extremely secure but requires constant administration. You should decide on a firm security policy that defines this approach, as well as the specific security measures you will use in the network.

Security problems can result in losses, which can include theft of data or services; unauthorized disclosure of information; deliberate destruction of data or denial of service; and accidental loss of data.

Windows NT is one of the most popular operating systems for network and Internet servers, and includes many security features. By establishing a security policy and being aware of the security issues covered in this book, you can maintain a very secure Windows NT network.

CHAPTER

2

Human Security

People are the most likely breach in any security environment, including secure networks. Most breaches are completely accidental; few people actually set out to sabotage network security. In fact, most people never find out that they've compromised the network. Hackers routinely exploit weaknesses in network security caused by a lack of awareness among users.

Security is also breached intentionally. Intentional breaches range from naive to devious. By nature, humans select passwords that can be easily cracked, then write them down on Post-it notes so they don't forget them. Employees are enticed to provide information for favors, money, or higher-paying jobs. Traveling salespeople leave your office and head for the office of your competition with interesting tidbits of information to trade.

People take massive information containers called brains with them wherever they go. It's nearly impossible to control this source of information leakage out of your organization without damaging your coworker's ability to work at all. Despite the fact you can't necessarily control all aspects of human security, you must remain vigilantly aware that human security exists and that it is a very serious problem. You should consider human security lapses first when attempting to reconstruct how a specific breach occurred.

The Weakest Link

Of course it's not the intent of this chapter to leave you feeling that your coworkers and business associates cannot be trusted. The vast majority of them can, but it takes only one individual in your entire organization with access to your network to compromise its security intentionally or accidentally. People cause security problems because they:

- **Don't understand security.** Security is not an instinct—it must be taught. You cannot simply tell people to choose strong passwords and expect to have an impenetrable fortress. You must teach security to every person who participates in the secure environment.

- **Underestimate the threat.** Many people simply don't believe that much of a problem really exists. They've never met or known anyone affected by a hacker, and they've never seen a disgruntled worker cause serious problems. For them, security is an abstraction that simply isn't all that important. As a security manager, your job is to explain the threat clearly.

- **Fail to make security a work habit.** Many people simply don't change easily. They have old habits—and old passwords. It's hard to force people to form a security habit, so make it as simple for users as possible by implementing policies that don't rely on people to remember security; instead the policies are enforced by the network and by the work environment.

- **Forget about security outside the work environment.** Many people leave work at work—and security habits there too. They may take an employee list home and throw it in their trash. They may brag to a recent acquaintance about the importance of their job. They may write down their password on a sticky note and leave it in their Daytimer. These sorts of problems can only be dealt with by reminding people to leave work completely at work—not to talk about it except in vague references, especially items like user accounts, the structure of the network, software technologies in use, and other information that may be useful to an intruder. Also, they shouldn't transfer materials between work and home unless those materials do not contain trade secret material and do not contain information that may prove useful to someone attempting to gain access.

■ **Passively resist security measures.** Many people see security as an abridgment of their personal liberty and freedoms, or as an indication that they are not trusted. Remind them that they are free to live their lives as they please when they are not at work, but that as an employee they have a responsibility to safeguard proprietary information. Explain that security policies must deal with the lowest common denominator of trust by nature, and that security should not be viewed as an insult to any single individual.

Any book on network security probably seems pessimistic, but this chapter will seem especially so. These security issues directly involve the people who use your network—not just faceless hackers and soulless machines. These sorts of security breaches may seem more like grist for newspapers and espionage books than actual occurrences, but they happen all the time.

Promoting Good Security Practices

Human security is problematic because it is the only aspect of total network security not directly controlled by the information system staff. Unlike computers, your coworkers cannot simply be programmed with a strong security policy and put to work. They must be taught, reminded, and encouraged.

Your entire security policy manual will probably not pertain to most users, so consider putting together a pamphlet on human security issues that deal directly with most network users and is formatted for easy comprehension. For example, the U.S. Department of Defense publishes a series of security awareness posters that highlight a specific security concern and get the point across in a single sentence and image; they are posted randomly throughout all secure facilities.

You are likely to hear about major military spy cases and government security breaches in the media, but most commercial organizations are reluctant to make public the details of a security breach, even if it means letting the perpetrator get away with it to avoid publicity. Any organization with competition is a candidate for the sort of security compromises detailed in this chapter.

To protect your network completely, you should implement human security policies that may on the surface seem Draconian and perhaps unwarranted. Depending on the value of information on your network, they may indeed be unwarranted—only you and your organization can determine what level of human security is appropriate for the information you protect. Human security policies are probably the most invasive and cumbersome security policies. Choose carefully which policies you will implement and try to determine what the adverse effects of each policy will be on your coworkers.

The remainder of this chapter covers areas of human security that are vitally important, such as the use of passwords, sabotage, espionage, and infiltration. Many of these are well beyond the ability of a network administrator to control—which raises an important point.

There is no security without total security. Security is not simply a matter for the network administrator to deal with, it is a matter of policy for the company as a whole. This is why throughout the book we use the term *security administrator* rather than network administrator. Your job as a security administrator is to maneuver the rest of the company into a position of security awareness to the degree required—you alone may not have the authority to do this, in which case you should enlist the support of someone who does, such as your human resources director or the president of your company.

Speak, Friend, and Enter

Passwords are the easiest way to gain unauthorized access to a system. Why? Because your network is protected by passwords that average only six characters in length and are combinations of just 26 letters—this yields a mere 320 million possibilities. Since most passwords are real words, they are limited to a field of about 100,000 possibilities. Any modern computer can check that number of passwords against a password file in mere seconds (see *dictionary attack* in the Terminology sidebar that follows). Try typing your personal password into a word processor. If it gets no complaints from the spellchecker consider changing it.

Most of your network users may have strong passwords; it only takes one user with a poorly chosen password for a hacker to gain access to your network.

When guessing passwords, most hackers don't bother checking a large number of passwords against a single account—they check a large number of accounts against a few passwords. Where would they get a list of valid accounts on your network? Here's where:

- **E-mail addresses:** Are they the same as account names on your network? If so, you are publishing a list on the Internet.

- **Finger:** Many Internet systems provide support for the `finger` command, which will simply list the users of your network from any computer on the Internet. Issuing the `finger` command with an account name will reveal additional information about that user. Windows NT provides a finger command line utility (client), but does not include a finger server. Figure 2.1 shows the information provided by a typical finger server.

Terminology

- **Brute force attack:** The process of checking passwords in a password file against every possible password generated sequentially. This hack will reveal all the passwords of all users on your system, and takes approximately two days to run against Windows NT (with the default Lan Manager security provider installed) on a modern Intel Pentium-based computer. Also called a *keyspace attack*.

- **Dictionary attack:** The process of checking passwords in a password file against a list of words likely to be chosen as passwords, or against the entire language lexicon. This hack will reveal all passwords that are contained in the dictionary and takes less than five minutes to run against Windows NT on a modern computer.

- **Strong password:** A password that is difficult to guess. Strong passwords always include punctuation or numbers, and are longer than 10 characters.

- **Trojan horse:** A malicious software program (or an attachment to another benign program) designed to look harmless in order to entice a user to install it. Once installed, the Trojan horse software opens a vector for further attack, such as answering the modem or listening on a TCP/IP port and vectoring inbound data to the console.

- **Weak password:** A password that is easy to guess, such as a word or number relating to the account holder, a single letter, or words appearing in a word processor's spellcheck dictionary.

- **Voice-mail systems:** Many organizations include a directory of employees who have voice-mail boxes—typically the same employees who have expanded access to your network. Hackers can call your 800 number and simply write down a list of people who have accounts on your network.

FIGURE 2.1

Fingering an
Internet account

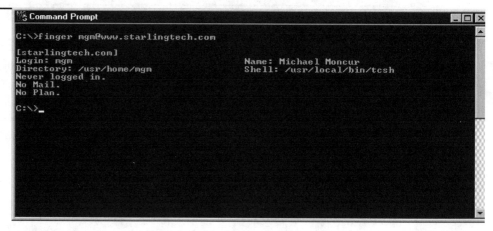

FIGURE 2.1

Fingering an
Internet account

- **Reconnaissance:** A quick jaunt through your building will reveal nameplates of people with offices who probably have more privileged accounts.

- **Trash:** Employee lists of phone numbers and responsibilities are thrown out every day. If your network account names are derived from employee names, you've just thrown away a list of network account names.

- **Calling:** By pretending to be employees of network service companies (especially Internet service providers), hackers have cajoled network account names and passwords over the phone from unsuspecting employees who merely think they're being helpful.

Passwords: Stick with the Unfamiliar

Passwords are generally chosen out of the information people have to remember anyway. This means that anyone with more than a passing familiarity with a network account holder stands a reasonable chance of guessing their password. Also consider that most people don't change their passwords unless they are forced to, and then they typically rotate among two or three favorite passwords. This is a natural consequence of the fact that people simply can't be expected to come up with and remember a unique new password regularly.

Common sources of passwords include:

- Names of pets or close relatives (a huge problem—nearly a third of all computer account holders use spouses', children's, or pets' names as passwords)

- Slang swear words (these are the easiest to guess)

- Birthdays or anniversaries

- Phone numbers and social security numbers

- Common passwords (one letter, "password," the name of the company, the account name, the account name backwards, the initials of the account holder repeated to the minimum password length, the names of a deity, and other blatantly obvious passwords)

Most people also tend to use the same account names and passwords on all systems. For instance, a person may choose to use their network account name and password on an online service or on a membership Web site. That way they don't have to remember a different account name and password for every different service they use. It also means that a security breach on a system you don't control can quite plausibly yield account names and passwords that work on your system.

Random passwords tend to be difficult for people to remember. Writing passwords down is the natural way for users to solve that problem—thus making their datebook a codebook for network access.

Plugging Administrative Holes

One major hole in many network systems is the initial password problem: How does a security administrator create a number of new accounts and assign passwords to all of them that people can use immediately? Usually, by assigning a default password like "password" or the account name itself as the password and then requiring that the user change the password the first time they log in. This is fine, except that out of 100 employees, typically only 98 them actually log on and change it. For whatever reason, two of them don't actually need accounts because they don't have computers, or they're the janitors, or whatever. This leaves 2 percent of your accounts with easily hacked passwords just waiting for the right hacker to come along.

Many membership-based Web sites don't take measures to encrypt the transmission of account names and passwords while they are in transit over the Internet, so an interception can also provide valid account names and passwords on your network.

A membership Web site is any Web site where you must log in with an account to gain access. Typically, these are subscription Web sites that perform some useful service, such as Microsoft's Developer's Network.

Lastly, there exists the slight possibility that a membership Web site may be set up with the covert purpose of gleaning account names and passwords from the public at large to provide targets of opportunity for hackers. The e-mail address you provide generally indicates exactly which network that account name and password will work on, too.

Setting Up an Account Password Policy

Password policy in Windows NT is set through the User Manager or the User Manager for Domains. Figure 2.2 shows the Account Policy window of the User Manager.

Reality Check: Passwords and Post-It Notes

When the authors were budding security experts in high school (read: *hackers*), we noticed that one of the counselors kept a 3 x 5 card taped to his monitor with a matrix of all the codes, function keys, and passwords required to enter and modify student grades. So while one of us sat down with the counselor and talked at length about future goals, another sat behind him and copied the codes down on his hand.

We also noted that this specific sort of terminal used telephone line cord to connect the keyboard. We procured a keyboard of the correct type, some phone cord, and a phone line splitter which we stored in the drop ceiling above the counselor's office (we were wiring a ceiling fan in the meeting room next door as we were also vocational electronics students). We planned to wait for a moment of opportunity to drop the cord and splitter and plug them into the back of the terminal. Through the ceiling, we could then change our grades at will assuming we didn't make any typing mistakes (because we couldn't see the screen).

The keyboard and line-cord were found in the ceiling before we could actually modify our grades—but that was merely a coincidence. The school's security policy was nonexistent, and the administration failed to make the connection between the keyboard and the 3 x 5 card of codes, which may remain there still.

Reality Check: Easily Guessed Passwords

I was once asked to gain access to an accounting system that had been password-secured by a former employee. The circumstances of his dismissal were such that he would not reveal the administrative password for the system. The accounting files were encrypted using the password as a key, so there was no way to extract the accounting data without knowing the password. Faced with the prospect of using the key-space hack (see the *Policies: Passwords* section) that would require weeks to run if I couldn't guess the password, I began asking questions about the employee. After about 40 incorrect attempts, I hit using the name of the employee's dog. This information was common knowledge to everyone in the office, and was known to salespeople who did business with the firm.

Policies: Passwords

- Set network password policy to force long passwords (at least 10 characters).

- Force periodic password changes about every 30 days.

- Run a dictionary hack against your own network, and request that users with weak passwords change them. Appendix B shows how to use various dictionary hack tools against your own network.

- Have users include punctuation marks in their passwords to keep them from being exposed by dictionary hacks or password guessing.

- Change the name of the administrative account. Chapter 6 discusses user accounts and account passwords.

- Inform users of the dangers of using their network account names or passwords on other systems.

- Make sure your servers don't respond to `finger` requests on the Internet.

- Use account names that aren't simply hashes of the user's name.

- Set up e-mail accounts using the employee's real name instead of the account name.

- Set up a security/recycling policy that requires printouts to be thrown away in special security/recycling containers.

- Give employees two separate trash cans: one for printouts and one for trash. Destroy printouts.

- Make sure everyone knows that no one legitimate will ever call to ask for their password.

Policies: Passwords

- For each facility in your organization, assign a security administrator whose job is to assign passwords, implement security policy, and even run attacks against other facilities as a simulated hacker. Security can be a corollary duty for any trusted employee with another primary job. Make finding security holes a contest with a specific reward.

- Implement a secure method to assign initial passwords, for example, by having employees report directly to the network administrator to have their passwords set.

To set the account policy follow these steps:

1. Launch the User Manager or the User Manager for Domains by choosing Start ➢ Programs ➢ Administrative Tools.

2. Open the Account Policy window by choosing Policy ➢ Account.

3. Set each of the input boxes according to your company's security policy. The input boxes are:

- **Maximum Password Age:** Consider using no more than 60 days as a maximum password age, and avoid accounts with passwords that never expire.

- **Minimum Password Age:** This setting is used to prevent hackers from using a Trojan horse to change a password, exploit the system, and then cover their tracks by changing it back to the original setting. This sort of attack is rare, however.

- **Minimum Password Length:** Longer is better. Use passwords at least eight characters in length, and never allow blank passwords.

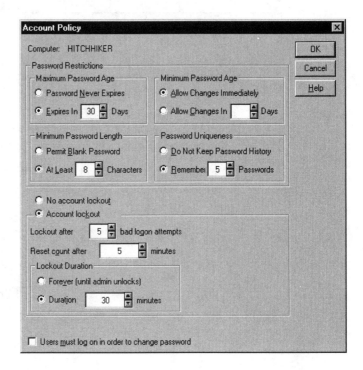

F I G U R E   2.2

The Account Policy
window

- **Password Uniqueness:** This setting forces users to rotate among a larger number of favored passwords, rather than simply rotating between the same two every time they are forced to change their password by the maximum password age policy. More is better for security, worse for the user's sanity.

- **Account Lockout:** This setting determines how accounts are frozen when an attempt to hack a user's password is detected. Always use an account lockout; they prevent automated brute force keyspace attacks on account passwords from the Internet or local network.

- **Lockout After:** This setting determines the number of times a legitimate user is allowed to mistype their password before locking their account. Most users can be relied upon to type their password correctly within three attempts.

- **Reset Count After:** This setting determines the time frame during which consecutive attempts are considered together. Five minutes is sufficient to obviate brute force attacks, and allows employees a coffee break if they've blown their password twice and don't want to lock their account.

- **Lockout Duration:** This setting allows you to specify how long the account is locked out until the user can again log on normally. If you want to track any brute force attempts and don't mind inconveniencing users, set this to "forever" so the user will have to inform you every time their account is unavailable. This ensures that you are immediately informed of brute force attacks that occur overnight, for instance, because the legitimate user is denied the use of their account until you unlock it. If you tend to check your security log as often as you should, or have users that blow their passwords often, consider setting it to a reasonable time long enough that a hacker will lose interest but your users won't be seriously hampered.

- **Forcibly Disconnect Remote Users from Server When Logon Hours Expire:** Checking this setting causes Windows NT to log users off even if they are still using their computers when their logon hours expire, rather than simply not letting them log on during the expiration period. This allows you to perform backups at night without users attached and keeps users from simply staying logged in permanently.

- **Users Must Log In to Change Password:** Checking this setting forces users to have the administrator set their password if it expired while they were on vacation. There's little security need for this setting, but it is useful if you like to make people grovel for a new password regularly.

Love, Money, and Revenge

This section is about espionage, sabotage, and other words of French origin ending in *age* (except *fromage,* which is covered in the chapter on workgroup networking). This section may seem especially alarmist, and probably doesn't really apply to most businesses. The tactics and problems discussed here only apply to businesses that deal with information that is extremely valuable, such as trade secrets for large market products, defense industrial secrets, or any product with exceptionally high profit margins, such as popular software. Most information on your network doesn't warrant this sort of attention, and most hackers don't use these tactics because they are expensive and they take a lot of time. Hackers tend to select targets of opportunity, and are not likely to direct their attacks against specific organizations unless they perceive some unusual threat, insult, or challenge.

Who does have the time, money, and interest to use these tactics? Believe it or not, these tactics are usually engaged against high technology businesses by foreign governments. Many high technology businesses are young and naive about security, making them ripe for the picking by the experienced intelligence agencies of foreign governments. These government agencies already have budgets for spying, and taking on a few medium-sized businesses to extract technology that would give their own corporations an edge is commonplace.

Low Pay and Wide Access Spell Trouble

Nearly all high-level military spy cases involve individuals who have incredible access to information, but as public servants don't make much money. This is a recipe for disaster. Low pay and wide access is probably the worst invitation to a security breach you could have if you think your competition might actually take active measures to acquire information about your systems.

For some, loyalty is bought, and it goes to the highest bidder. Would someone at your company who makes $10 an hour think twice about selling their account name and password for a hundred thousand dollars? Money is a powerful motivator, especially to those with crushing debt problems.

Many spies are also recruited from the ranks of the socially inept using love, sex, or the promise thereof. Think about the people who work with you—would every one of them be immune to the charms of someone who wanted access?

Remember that these sorts of attacks are not generally perpetrated by your domestic competition, but by the governments of foreign competitors. Domestic competitors prefer the time-honored (and legal) method of simply hiring away those individuals in your company who created the information your network stores. There's very little that can be done about this sort of security breach, unless you already have in place, as a condition of employment, agreements that stipulate noncompetition when employees leave the company.

Reality Check: Hiring Talent Away

Many have accused Microsoft of being a talent-sucking vortex, hiring away high-profile technical experts from their competition with regularity. The Windows NT kernel was designed by a people hired away from Digital Equipment Corporation who had also designed the core technology for DEC's premier operating system. Not surprisingly, the systems are very similar.

In another incident, a recent high-level suit involving two major software vendors centered around the fact that an employee hired away took a wealth of information about the company's software products with him.

The Care and Feeding of Employees

Disgruntled employees are perhaps the most dangerous security breach of all. An employee with an ax to grind has both the means and the motive to do serious damage to your network. These sorts of attacks are difficult to detect before they happen, but some sort of behavioral warning generally precipitates them. Overreacting to an employee who is simply blowing off steam by denigrating management or coworkers is a good way to create a disgruntled employee, however. So be cautious about the measures you recommend to prevent damage from a disgruntled employee.

Also remember that out-sourced network service companies may put in place policies that make them hard to replace if you decide you no longer wish to retain their services. Disgruntled small companies tend to behave a lot like disgruntled employees. There's very little that can be done about attacks that come from people with an intimate knowledge of your network, so you should either choose your service providers wisely and exercise a lot of oversight, or require that they are escorted by a trusted employee at all times.

Obviously, a security administrator alone cannot implement many of these policies—for instance, you (probably) cannot give a coworker a raise. What you can do is act as a security liaison to those who can. Alert them to any changes you feel are warranted in the security status of a coworker.

Privacy and security are continually at odds with one another. While we recommend monitoring the work patterns and usage of employees considered security risks, you should realize that monitoring can seriously strain employee relations. Legally, companies have the right to monitor any activities that make use of company resources such as computers or networks—but exercising that right can backfire if it's done without sensitivity to the user's privacy.

Policies: Employee Relations

- The company should try to foster loyalty by making the workplace as pleasant as possible for employees. This may seem difficult, but a secure workplace does not have to become an Orwellian nightmare of control and restriction. For instance, despite years of research, there appears to be no correlation between suits and productivity—relaxing dress codes, especially for employees with no physical contact with customers, is an easy and free morale booster. Positive reinforcement will help employees make a habit of security without adversely affecting their attitudes.

- Employees should be paid commensurate with their value to your organization—and their value to your competition.

- Access to information should rise with pay and with proven loyalty.

- Restrict sensitive data available to new and low-paid employees.

- Try to be sensitive to personal problems that might make employees easy targets for recruitment by your competition. These include debt, drug use, loneliness, and animosity towards the company.

- Look for sudden changes in demeanor that might indicate an external factor at work in the employee's life. For instance, a person saddled with debt who arrives in a new car may have a new and lucrative source of income. Ask them about it. Ideally, the company should help the employee resolve the issues that make them targets for recruitment. If that's not possible, consider restricting access to information in extreme cases.

- Watch for signs of animosity towards the company or coworkers in network users. You can use audit policy (see Chapter 6) to begin monitoring the behavior of suspect individuals without alerting them to the fact that they are under observation. Track the files that they delete, and look for evidence that the employee is browsing through the network looking for ways to do damage.

Policies: Employee Relations

- Consider obtaining permission to monitor the contents of suspect employee's company e-mail. Because many people consider e-mail private, your company should promulgate a policy warning to employees that monitoring e-mail is open to the company.

- If the audit policy monitoring reveals that the employee is a risk, begin restricting access to sensitive information.

- Require an employee escort for all out-sourced service personnel.

- Demand a list of former customers in the area from out-sourced network service providers. Contact everyone on the list and interview him or her about the service contractor's performance. Be alert for instances of sabotage or less than helpful behavior at the end of the contractor's service contract.

- Require documentation of all contract user accounts, passwords, and network configuration information on a periodic basis.

- Do not allow out-sourced service personnel to have administrative accounts on your network. Rather, have a trusted employee escort service personnel and log in for them. The trusted employee does not have to know anything about Windows NT—their purpose is only to retain control of the administrative accounts.

Spies Like Us

Spies? Get real. Who would actually pay someone to go to work at another company on the off chance that they might find useful information after they've infiltrated the company for a period of months? As you probably suspected, this sort of spying is so rare that it really doesn't need to be discussed in detail. For the most part, if a competing organization were willing to foot the bill for this sort of intrusion, there would be little you could do about it anyway, even if you performed background investigations on all your employees.

Far more common, however, is the back channel of information that flows among businesses of the same type in the same region. The businesses your organization deals with on a daily basis form this back channel. These organizations work with all the businesses of your type in your market. They typically include:

- Subcontractors

- Consultants

- Distributors/resellers

- Salespeople

- Temps and short term contract employees

- Out-sourced service agencies

- Service organizations, clubs, and chambers of commerce

So why would these organizations and individuals talk about your company to your competition? For many reasons: to curry favor, to win a bid, or for a commission. In short, it all adds up to making money.

But what could they possibly know about your organization that might be of value to your competition? Personal information about your employees might yield clues to what sort of password that employee might select. Out-sourced organizations may have very expanded access to your network, especially if you outsource your network services. In essence, your network security lies in the hands of another company—a company whose employees you know very little about.

Another major problem that fits into this category is that of physical penetration of the premises. Hackers are notoriously nonchalant, and they have on numerous occasions simply walked into a business, sat down at a local terminal or network client, and begun setting the stage

---

Reality Check: Corporate Spying

While in the employ of a network cabling firm, I walked into a cubicle and found a trusted salesperson who had worked among all the cabling contractors in the area for years sitting at a computer that had been left logged on. He was calmly printing out our proprietary bid and design documents for a $150,000 installation.

When I questioned him about his activities, he claimed he just wanted to keep the design "for his files" because we had specified his company's cable. He claimed also that an employee had given him permission to take the files. That employee had not given him permission to copy the documents, so they were confiscated and he was told never to return. The company's bid success rate rose noticeably following the incident.

---

for further remote penetration. (See Chapter 22 for more on this topic.)

In large companies, there's no way to know everyone by sight, so an unfamiliar worker in the IS department isn't uncommon or suspicious at all. In companies that don't have ID badges or security guards, it isn't anybody's job to check credentials, so penetration is relatively easy. And even in small companies, it's easy to put on a pair of coveralls and pretend to be with a telephone or network wiring company, or even to be the spouse of a fictitious employee. With a simple excuse like telephone problems in the area, access to the server room is granted (oddly, these are nearly always colocated with telephone equipment). If left unattended, a hacker can simply create a new administrative user account. A small external modem can be attached and configured to answer in less than a minute, often without even rebooting your server.

Using Security Classifications

If security is a very serious concern at your organization, you may find it helpful to implement a security classification system to help people

---

Policies: Premises Security for Physical Control

- Employ a security officer or an "attack receptionist" to guard your front desk, and don't allow nonemployees to have access beyond that point.

- Require security check in/check out and security badges if you have any sort of proprietary information.

- Don't allow nonemployees to move through the premises unescorted.

- Don't offer more information to salespeople, consultants, and outsourced service personnel than they need in order to perform their jobs.

---

determine what information can be accessed by whom and in what manner. You may find these classifications useful. They are adapted for corporate use from the classifications used by the Department of Defense:

- **Unclassified:** Distribution of this material is not limited. This includes marketing information, sales materials, and information cleared for release to the public. Any material not marked with a classification is assumed to be unclassified.

- **Sensitive:** Disclosure of this information may cause some individuals measurable harm. Information of this nature includes salary and benefits information, personal information about anyone, employee review results, test results, etc. Special care should be taken to safeguard sensitive material.

- **Confidential:** Disclosure of this information could cause measurable damage to the organization as a whole, and includes market strategies, plans for marketing campaigns, bid documents, or other factors that could cause the loss of an individual contract or customer. Confidential material should be safeguarded at all times, but trusted employees are permitted to take it home.

- **Secret:** Disclosure of this information would cause serious damage to the organization as a whole, and includes trade secrets, blueprints or schematics for proprietary equipment, or information that if released to competitors could cause the loss of many contracts or customers. Secret material should not leave the company facilities or be left unattended in an open space.

- **Top Secret:** Disclosure of this information would cause grave and irreparable harm to the organization as a whole, and includes legal documents, high-level strategies, proprietary secrets upon which the company is based, and any information which if released to competitors could cause the downfall of the organization. Top Secret information should be controlled using distribution lists, sign-out sheets, and inventories.

Under this system, all printed material should be marked with its classification, and software systems should make clear the classification of materials viewable on screen. Any compilation of classified material from multiple sources is classified the same as the highest classified component material.

Beware Geeks Bearing Gifts

The Internet is a phantasmagoria of information and software, most of it for free. You can find information on nearly anything and download a software utility to perform nearly any task. You can also unwittingly download a Trojan horse that returns account information to hackers or opens a communications channel using ports that your firewall passes to it. Figure 2.3 shows how such an attack might happen.

This sort of attack happens all the time because it's easy to propagate. A hacker need only release a useful little utility and wait for it

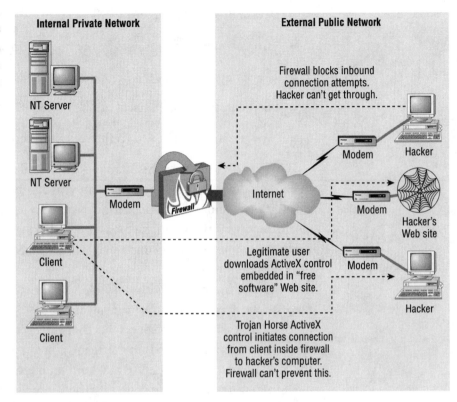

FIGURE 2.3

Through a Trojan horse
attack outsiders can gain
access to your system

to report back when it's reached a Windows NT server attached to
the Internet. Only one in a hundred copies will ever reach just the
right server environment to get back to the hacker's computer with
any information, but that's not important. Most hackers are not
looking for specific information, they are looking for targets of opportunity. By using a utility that contains a Trojan horse, your server
becomes a literal beacon of opportunity to these hackers.

Be especially wary of utilities designed for use by the administrator—
these are the most likely homes of Trojan horses because NT's defenses
are down when the administrator is logged in. While logged in as an
administrator:

- Device drivers can be installed.

- Virii can embed themselves in the boot process.

- The registry can be searched and modified.

- The operating system itself can be modified.

- New users can be added to the security accounts database.

If a Trojan horse or virus manages to install while you are logged in as the administrator, the only way you can be sure you've gotten rid of it is to reinstall the operating system to a different location and delete the operating system that was infected. You may also have to rewrite the boot sector using a utility like the MS-DOS fdisk utility to eliminate a virus.

Users also unwittingly cause problems by installing their own software on work computers. Something as simple as taking work home on a floppy disk can bring back a virus that the user's child accidentally downloaded from the Internet while installing a game. Some virii, like the Word macro virus, operate at a very high level and can quickly permeate an entire network in spite of strong security measures. These virii tend to be more annoying than damaging, but they still require a considerable amount of effort to eradicate.

Reality Check: Virus Outbreaks

A major computer virus outbreak occurred in a Navy shipboard network when some unscrupulous users installed, on the ship's LAN, pirated software that they had purchased in Singapore. After several failed attempts to eliminate the problem, the ship's commanding officer ordered a ship-wide seizure of all floppy disks. The IS staff then spent the next week systematically virus scanning over 5,000 floppy disks. Thirty-five instances of four different computer virii were detected. All floppy disk drives were then permanently removed from computers attached to the network except for the supervisor's computer, which was locked in a secured room.

Policies: Software

The following policies will reduce your risk from software installation-related attacks:

- Purchase all software installed or used on your server from reputable sources. Do not install software downloaded from the Internet or a bulletin board service.

- Do not log in as a member of the administrators group unless you are actually administering the network. Do not make your typical logon account an administrator equivalent.

- Require that all administrative logons occur from the server's console only. Do not allow remote administration.

- Do not allow users to install software on their own computers. You may wish to take removable media drives like floppy, CD-ROM, and Zip drives out of client computers since all authorized software installations can occur over the network.

- Carefully review your company's work-at-home policy in light of the security breaches that sharing removable media can cause. Consider providing laptop computers to employees that work at home with the stipulation that they cannot be connected to the Internet or used by any family member other than the employee. Employees should use their own computers at home for entertainment or personal interests.

- Never install pirated software or "cracked" demo software.

Summary

Human security is both the most difficult type of security to control and the most likely source of a security breach in an otherwise well-secured network, because it lies outside the direct control of security and network professionals. How well you choose policies and train network users for security will directly impact the success of your human security efforts.

Human security lapses happen for many reasons, most purely accidental. A number of direct dedicated lapses can occur, but they are far less common than those caused by simply not being aware of security problems and threats.

Strong human security policies can be implemented that prevent most human security lapses at the cost of convenience, efficiency, and human comfort. A good human security policy for your organization balances the need for security against the efficiency and well-being of users. First, select those policies with the least impact on ease of use and efficiency, then implement more stringent policies as your needs dictate.

CHAPTER

3

Encryption

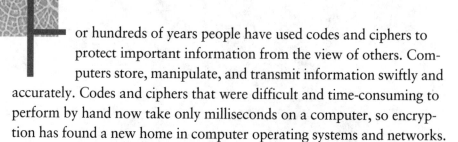

or hundreds of years people have used codes and ciphers to protect important information from the view of others. Computers store, manipulate, and transmit information swiftly and accurately. Codes and ciphers that were difficult and time-consuming to perform by hand now take only milliseconds on a computer, so encryption has found a new home in computer operating systems and networks.

This chapter will first examine what encryption is and how it has developed from a tool for spies and diplomats to become an integral part of modern communications. Next, you'll see how computer networks use encryption to secure your files, keep out unauthorized users, provide a secure channel for communications, and identify trusted computers or users. Finally, you'll be introduced to the several kinds of encryption and the strengths of and uses for each. In addition, you'll be given a glimpse of how a network intruder might attempt to circumvent encryption measures on your network.

How to Keep a Secret: Encryption

The primary purpose of encryption is to keep secrets. It has other uses, which you'll explore later in this chapter, but encryption was first used to protect messages so that only the person knowing the "trick" to decoding the message (or the *key* in the jargon of cryptographers) could read the message. History is full of clever codes and ciphers used by kings and princes, spies, generals, business people, and inventors. As you read through this chapter, you'll see examples of historical codes and ciphers, and learn how the concepts illustrated by those examples are used in computers today.

Terminology

- **Cipher:** Protects a message by permuting its text (by rearranging it or performing modifications to the encoding, rather than the meaning, of the message.)

- **Code:** An agreed-upon way of keeping a secret between two or more individuals.

- **Codebook:** Contains meanings assigned to words; a code word replaces the word that it stands for.

- **Decryption:** The process of turning ciphertext into plaintext using a cipher and a key.

- **Encryption:** Keeping a secret by transforming it so that only someone with a *key* can read it.

- **Key:** A bit of information that is required to decrypt a message. Also, a value (usually a number or a string of characters) that is used with a cipher to encrypt a message. The key must be kept secret in order for the message to remain private.

- **Substitution cipher:** Replaces each character (or other minimal unit such as a byte) of the message with a different character (or byte) according to the cipher algorithm.

- **Transposition cipher:** Rearranges the text of the message according to the cipher algorithm.

One simple code is used by children around the world. If today is "backwards day" (the key to the code is knowing whether it is backwards day or not) then up is down, right is left, true is false, and enemies (parents, usually) are confused. This is a code, not a cipher. Some words in the message are replaced with other words, and the recipient of the message must know which words to replace and what the replacement words are.

Grown-up versions of backwards day are the codebooks used by the military and intelligence agencies around the world. When you see a code word in the body of the message, you look up the word in the codebook (you have to know which codebook to use, of course) to see what the code word actually refers to.

The strength of this kind of code is that if you keep the codebooks secret, it is incredibly difficult to crack the code. Even if some code words are compromised, other parts of the message may remain secure. The weakness of this kind of code is that the codebook must anticipate all of the kinds of messages you may need to send. If you need to send a message about the Sultan of Oman, and your codebook doesn't have an entry for him, then you're out of luck.

The ABCs of Ciphers

A cipher used by children around the world is pig Latin (no offense is intended towards pigs or aficionados of Latin). The secret is simple— the first consonant is moved to the end of the word and the "ay" sound is appended to it. If the word begins with a vowel, simply append "ay." Thus: "Isthay isay anay iphercay orfay implesay essagesmay."

Many dialects of the pig Latin cipher exist; you could use the keys "oi" or "ah" instead. What makes this cipher different from the backwards day code is that you can encode any message in pig Latin. This ability to encode any message (or plaintext, as unencrypted messages are called) regardless of subject is a common feature of all ciphers. This is not a feature of codebooks. Codebooks operate by obscuring the meaning of words in messages, and are limited to the words in the book, whereas ciphers obscure which words are being used regardless of what the words actually are.

A cipher almost as simple as pig Latin that is being used on the Internet and on computer bulletin boards around the world today is the Rot(13) cipher. If you've seen an e-mail or newsgroup message that looks like a jumble of random letters and has <rot13> at the top, then you have seen a message using this cipher. The trick to decoding it (the trick is called the *algorithm* in the jargon of cryptographers) is to rotate each letter through the alphabet 13 places. For example, *A* would be replaced with *N*, *B* would be replaced with *O*, *W* would be replaced with *J*, and *M* would be replaced with *Z*. Abg n irel pbzcyvpngrq pvcrpe. This is a simple *substitution cipher*, so called because each letter of the alphabet is replaced with a substitute letter. The key is to know which letters are replaced with which other letters—in this case, the letter 13 letters away from it. (It doesn't matter if you rotate backward or forward, because there are 26 letters in the English alphabet.) Figure 3.1 shows how the Rot(13) substitution cipher works.

FIGURE 3.1

In the Rot(13) substitution cipher the plaintext is rotated 13 characters for encryption into ciphertext, and then rotated 13 characters back into plaintext for decryption.

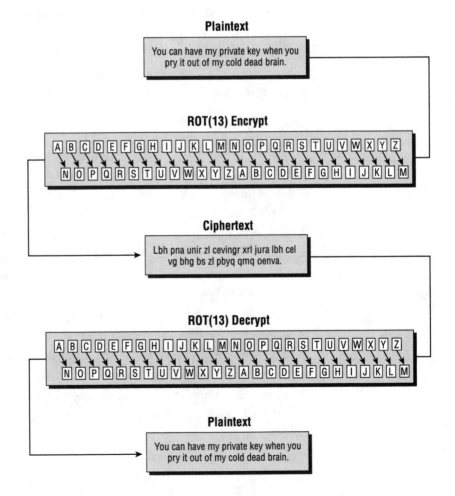

Rot(13), like pig Latin and backwards day, is not very hard to figure out. Any message encoded with a simple substitution cipher that is long enough (25 characters is enough for most messages) can be decoded simply by counting the frequency of each letter. The letter *E*, for example, is the most common English letter and will probably be the one at the top of the frequency list. Common two-and three-letter combinations of letters are also clues to the hidden identity of substituted letters.

More Complex Ciphers

Simple substitution is clearly not good enough for important secrets like troop movement orders and the food preferences of foreign leaders. Over time, people with secrets to hide and communications to keep private have made many improvements to the simple substitution cipher.

One improvement (used in the Duchy of Mantua in 1401) is the homophonic substitution cipher, in which each cleartext letter (or letter contained in the original unencrypted document, which is also called the plaintext) can be replaced by one of several ciphertext letters (the ciphertext is the resulting encrypted message). This changes the frequency of ciphertext letters, and thereby makes it more difficult to guess which ciphertext letters correspond to cleartext letters.

For example, consider the message "The rain in Spain falls mainly in the plain" which has six occurrences of the letter *I* in it. With a simple substitution cipher, all of the *I* letters would have to be replaced with the same ciphertext letter. You could replace them all with *J*, or the number 1, or the asterisk punctuation mark, according to which cipher alphabet you chose.

With the homophonic substitution cipher on the other hand, you could replace the first occurrence with a *J*, the next one with the number 1 or the asterisk, and so on, because all of the substitutions represent the same letter *I*. In other words, it is more difficult to decipher the ciphertext without knowing the code because there are more possibilities for substitutions for the same letter.

The polyalphabetic substitution cipher (invented in 1568 by Leon Batista) uses a different simple substitution cipher for each successive letter in the message. This kind of cipher has a *period*, which is the number of letters that can be encoded before the first simple substitution cipher (or alphabet) is used again. Polygram substitution ciphers encode several letters together (such as *AA* might encode to *SXZ* while *AB* encodes to *ORT*) and running key ciphers use the letters in one plaintext to select which of several codes is used to encode the letters in another plaintext.

Another kind of cipher is the *transposition cipher*. Instead of replacing the letters in a message, this kind of cipher rearranges them. Imagine writing the letters of a message in the squares of a piece of graph paper. You would then copy the message to another sheet of paper, but instead of taking the letters from left to right you would take them from top to bottom. To decipher the message, you would put the letters back on graph paper from top to bottom and then read them from right to left, as usual.

A weakness of ciphers is that if someone knows the cipher you are using and the key you have chosen (say you are using the cipher PigLatin97 with the secret key "chu") then everything you send or have sent with that cipher and key can be read by that person. This makes it very important to choose a cipher that is difficult to crack and a key that is difficult to guess.

Keeping Secrets Automatically

Encryption and decryption take a long time to perform by hand, and when your computing tools are limited to a pencil and paper (and, of course, the substitution alphabets or codebook) you can only use the simplest of ciphers. For hundreds of years the manual process was the only way, until the advent of the Industrial Revolution and the invention of calculating machines.

The various national governments of the 1920s developed rotor machines to automate the encryption and decryption process of cryptographic substitution. The ability to send secure and lengthy messages from the headquarters of the various armed forces to remote locations over a medium that anyone could eavesdrop on (the newly invented radio) proved to be a crucial aspect of modern warfare. Secure communications often meant victory, and broken codes often meant defeat. The most popular encryption machines had rotors and were primarily mechanical.

Each machine contained a number of rotors, and each rotor was wired to replace one letter with another letter. The rotors would rotate at different rates, so a machine with rotors that had 26 positions (one for each letter of the English alphabet) would have a period of 26 times the number of rotors. This means that a rotor machine with three rotors would encode the same letter with the same encrypted value every 78 letters of the message. The Enigma machine used by the Germans in the late '30s was the most famous rotor machine of the time and was fiendishly difficult for British cryptanalysists (people whose profession is to break codes) to crack.

Keeping Secrets Electronically

The development of electronics and computers gave code makers and code breakers a whole new arsenal to work with. They were able at last to develop ciphers that were much too complex to perform by hand. They could also program computers to automatically try many different combinations of keys and ciphers much more quickly than a human being was able to. Many ciphers were developed in secret, and only governments or large corporations had the computing power necessary to use or break the codes.

One algorithm that was developed in secret but then released for use by the public as well as the government (but only for "Unclassified but Sensitive" information) is the *Data Encryption Standard*, or *DES*. It is a symmetric algorithm, which means the same key is used for encryption and decryption, and uses a 56-bit key. DES is widely used in commercial software and in communication devices that support encryption. There is lingering suspicion, however, that the DES algorithm might contain a weakness that could allow the National Security Agency

(NSA), which has a vested interest in maintaining its ability to decrypt communications and which cooperated in the development of DES, to more easily break messages encrypted with DES.

RSA (which was named after its inventors) is an algorithm that was not developed by a government agency. Its creators—Rivest, Shamir, and Adleman—exploited the computationally difficult problem of factoring prime numbers to develop a nonsymmetric, or public key algorithm, which can be used for both encryption and digital signatures. RSA has since become a very popular alternative to DES. RSA is used by a number of software companies, including Microsoft, Digital, Sun, Netscape, and IBM, that produce products that must negotiate secure connections over the nonsecure Internet (such as Web browsers) .

The NSA and the executive branch of the U.S. government has developed a new encryption technology and is attempting to convince the rest of the government and private industry as well to use it. First called "Clipper," and then "Capstone," the encryption scheme uses hardware that embodies a classified algorithm (called the "Skipjack" algorithm). The algorithm uses a secret key in combination with an escrow key or keys. The escrow keys are meant be given to a pair of government or other escrow key agencies. Authorized law enforcement officials can then obtain the keys to the hardware device and decrypt any messages encoded by that device. The ostensible purpose is to make further digitally encrypted communications devices wiretappable.

The Clipper and Capstone efforts have gained very little support from the private sector because they are viewed as a threat to privacy.

The ciphers described here are not the only ones available for use in computers and networks today—other governments (such as the former USSR) were just as active as the United States in developing codes and ciphers, and many private individuals (especially in the last decade) have made contributions to the field of cryptography. GOST was developed in the former USSR, FEAL was developed by NTT Japan, LOKI was developed in Australia, and IDEA was developed in Europe. Most of these ciphers use patented algorithms which must be licensed for commercial use, but there are some (such as Blowfish, which is described later in this chapter in the *Symmetric Functions* section) which are not. Each cipher has strengths and weaknesses, some of which will be explored later in this chapter.

All of the ciphers described in this section have the same weakness: If you know the cipher being used to encode a message but not the key, there are a number of attacks you can use to attempt to decode the message, including the "brute force" method of trying all of the possible keys.

The purpose of ciphers, after all, is to hide information. Hiding information would not be a useful activity (especially for war-time governments that have other pressing areas to spend time and money on) if no one were interested in the information being hidden. The converse of hiding information is attempting to discover what is hidden, and advances in breaking codes (or deciphering codes without the key) have progressed hand-in-hand with developments in creating codes. The practice of attempting to break codes is called *cryptanalysis,* and the people who break codes are called *cryptanalysists.*

Key discovery methods other than brute force cryptanalysis have been developed by cryptographers. *Differential* and *linear cryptanalysis* are two examples of the esoteric art of breaking codes; they are complex mathematical analyses that would each take a book to explain. Some ciphers are more vulnerable to these two methods of cryptanalysis than others are. Some ciphers use a longer key than others (a longer key contains more bits) and therefore require more time or compute power to go through all of the possible keys; some ciphers can accept a variable number of bits in the key (you can choose how strong you want the encryption to be). Once the key is discovered, however, all of the messages encrypted using that cipher with that key are compromised.

Terminology

- **Ciphertext:** An encrypted message that requires a cipher and a key to decrypt.

- **Cleartext:** The message to be sent from the sender to the receiver. This is what must be protected from being intercepted and understood. (See also plaintext.)

- **Cryptanalysis:** The examination of codes and ciphers.

- **Cryptographer:** An individual who studies codes and ciphers. (See also cryptologist.)

- **Cryptography:** The study of codes and ciphers.

- **Cryptologist:** An individual who studies codes and ciphers. (See also cryptographer.)

- **Plaintext:** The message to be sent from the sender to the receiver. This is what must be protected from being intercepted and understood. (See also cleartext.)

The Almost Perfect Cipher

There is one encryption cipher—the *one-time pad*—which cannot be compromised if you do not have the key, even with all the time left in the universe and all the compute power that is theoretically possible. It is not simply improbable that the key would be discovered or the message retrieved using brute force; it is impossible. Unfortunately, the requirements of the cipher make it impractical for use in anything but certain kinds of low-bandwidth communications.

A one-time pad uses a key exactly as long as the message being encoded. The key must be completely random (anything less than random leaves your message open to certain kinds of cryptographic analysis) and no portion of it can be reused without compromising the security of your message. Each letter (or byte) of your message is combined mathematically with an equal-sized portion of the key (often by the XOR mathematical function or addition with modulus mathematical function) which results in the ciphertext and uses up the key.

The reason that the one-time pad is so secure is that from the ciphertext being decoded, any resulting plaintext (of the same length) and associated key is equally likely. For example, "henryjtillman" encoded with the one-time pad key "lfwpxzgwpoieq" results in the ciphertext "tkkhsjafbavfe." While the ciphertext decoded with the correct key produces the original message, the ciphertext can also be decoded using the possible key "swgpnmquypciq" resulting in the message "andrewjackson" or using the key "gbywrvwcmlkwz" resulting in the message "milkandcookie." The attacker has no way of knowing which key and resulting plaintext is correct.

The problem with the one-time pad is that it requires a key as big as the message being sent, and both the sender and the receiver must have the same key. If you needed to encrypt a 10Mbps Ethernet link you could use up a CD-ROM worth of key data in just 10 minutes!

Clearly, the one-time pad is best used in cases where communication is infrequent or uses very little bandwidth, such as e-mail messages that must have the most secure encryption possible.

Encryption in Your Network

The previous section took a look at how cryptography developed and how it works in a cursory manner. The next section, *A Conspiracy of Cryptographers,* will examine the world of cryptography in greater detail and explore the advantages and disadvantages of specific algorithms, as well as give you a glimpse of how they can be broken. This section focuses on how you can use encryption in your network.

After all, what good is a secret decoder wheel if you have no secrets to keep? You can use encryption to protect the following types of network data:

- Private communications

- Secure file storage

- User or computer authentication

- Secure password exchange

Figure 3.2 illustrates places in your network where security can be enhanced by encryption. Let's examine each of these types of network data in detail.

F I G U R E   3.2

Encryption can secure communications, file storage, and password exchange, as well as authenticate users and messages.

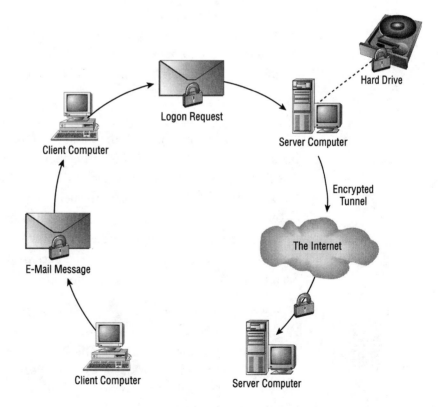

Hard Drive

Logon Request

Server Computer

Client Computer

Encrypted Tunnel

The Internet

E-Mail Message

Client Computer

Server Computer

Policies: Encryption

- Encrypt any communications containing sensitive or proprietary information that go over a nonsecure medium such as radio, a telephone network, or the Internet.

- Use file system encryption to protect sensitive data when operating system features are not effective (when the hard drive has been removed or the operating system has been replaced).

Private Communications

The most common use for encryption with computers is to protect communications between computer users and between communications devices. This use of encryption is an extension of the role codes and ciphers have played throughout history. The only difference is that instead of a human being laboriously converting messages to and from an encoded form, the computer does all the hard work.

E-Mail

Many e-mail packages include the capability to encrypt an e-mail message before sending it. Even those programs that do not can include encrypted text that comes from a separate encryption program, such as Pretty Good Privacy (PGP). When you receive an encrypted e-mail message you can have the e-mail package decrypt it for you (if your e-mail supports encryption—basic LAN e-mail products such as Microsoft Exchange and CC:Mail often don't, but advanced packages such as Microsoft Exchange Server do) or you can use an external program to decrypt the message.

You can download the Pretty Good Privacy software at no charge for individual (noncommercial) use. The PGP software can be used with most e-mail packages, including CC-Mail, Pegasus Mail, and Microsoft Exchange. You can learn more about PGP at the company's Web site: http://www.pgp.com.

In order to encrypt or decrypt a message you must have the key to the message. You'll usually use the same key for messages to the same person, so if you regularly exchange encrypted mail with a lot of people you'll have a lot of keys to keep track of. Your e-mail package or your encryption package can make keeping track of keys easier by storing your keys in key rings (files on your disk drive that keep track of your keys for you). The key rings are, of course, encrypted and protected by a key as well. The benefit of this is that you only have to remember one key.

Communications Links

Encryption can protect the communication between network devices as well as between computer users. Any time two network devices are communicating over an *nonsecure* medium (that is a medium that an intruder can listen in on) you should consider encrypting the communication. For example, you might encrypt the data transferred over a microwave link between buildings if sensitive data flows over the link.

If you regularly log on to your network remotely via a laptop and a cellular phone, you should encrypt the serial link so that no one can eavesdrop on the radio signals and intercept account names, passwords, or data such as e-mail messages, spreadsheets, or word processing files.

Encryption can be expensive, however, either in terms of the processing power required to encrypt or decrypt data, or in terms of the cost of specialized hardware to do the same thing. The more data there is to encrypt (the greater the bandwidth of the encrypted link), the more processing power is required. So while any modern personal computer can encrypt a 56 Kbps modem link without slowing down the user's applications all that much, encrypting a 100Mbps Fast Ethernet link will tax even the most powerful RISC and Pentium processors.

Dedicated encryption hardware also costs much more than regular unencrypted communications devices like Ethernet adapters and

modems. For these reasons you probably would only encrypt those portions of your network that are exposed in a way that they are accessible
to an eavesdropper.

Secure File Storage

Encryption isn't just for communication. It can also be used to protect
data in storage, such as data on a hard drive. Windows NT has many
sophisticated security features. You may have configured it to allow
only authorized users to access files while the operating system is running, but when you turn your computer off all those security features go
away and your data is left defenseless. An intruder could load another
operating system on the computer, or even remove the hard drive and
place it in another computer that does not respect the security settings
of the original computer.

There is a file system driver for DOS and Windows 95 called NTFSDOS
that will allow those operating systems to read NTFS volumes. You can
find it on the companion CD-ROM.

Encryption Utilities

You can use encryption software to encrypt specific files that you want
to protect, and then decrypt them when you need access to them. The
encryption and decryption process can be cumbersome, however, and
you may end up having to remember a lot of encryption keys. Using
encryption in this manner can also leave behind temporary files or files
that are erased but still present on the hard drive and contain sensitive
information. This is obviously not what you want.

Encrypted File Systems

A better approach to security is to have the operating system encrypt
and decrypt the files for you. You can get encrypted file systems for
Windows NT (and Windows 95 and DOS as well) that will encrypt all

the files on your hard drive, even temporary ones created by the applications you use.

Check out `http://softwinter.bitbucket.co.il/` for an example of disk encryption software.

You must supply the cryptographic key when you start your computer, but otherwise you can treat the files on your hard drive as regular, unencrypted files. This doesn't protect your files from being accessed while the operating system is running—that is what the operating system security features are for—but it does keep the data safe even if someone steals the hard drive.

Reality Check: Serious Encryption

While working for a network services company as a network integrator, I received a request for help from a government contractor who had been hired to decrypt the contents of a hard disk that had been seized by a federal law enforcement agency. There are two kinds of encryption in common use on computers today: encryption that will keep coworkers out of your files and encryption that will keep everyone out of your files.

An examination of the contents of the hard drive revealed that this drive (which contained an encrypted NTFS volume protected by a pass phrase that we did not have) used the latter kind of encryption. I had to inform the contractor that our organization did not have the resources that would be required to break the encryption, and it was likely that no organization did.

User or Computer Authentication

In addition to keeping secrets (either stored or transmitted), encryption can be used for almost the opposite purpose—to verify identities. It's used to authenticate users logging on to computers, it's used to ensure that software you download from the Internet comes from a reputable source, and it's used to ensure that the person who sends a message is really who they say they are.

Logon Authentication

You may not know it, but your operating system already uses encryption. When you log on to a Microsoft operating system such as Windows 95 or Windows NT, the operating system does not compare your password to a stored password. Instead, it encrypts your password using a one-way cryptographic function, and then compares the result to a stored result. Other operating systems such as UNIX and OS/2 work the same way.

This seems a round-about way of verifying your identity when you log on, but there is a very good reason for the operating system to do it this way. By only storing the cryptographic hash of your password, the operating system makes it more difficult for a hacker to get all of the passwords in your system when they gain access to the system. One of the first things a hacker goes for in a compromised system (that is, one where the hacker has gotten at least one password) is that computer's password list, so that the hacker can get account names and passwords that may be valid on other computers in your network.

With a one-way cryptographic function, it's easy to generate a hashed value from the password, but it's difficult or impossible to generate the password from the hashed value. Since only the hashed values are stored, even a hacker that has complete access to the computer can't just read out the passwords. The best the hacker can do is to supply passwords one by one and see if they match any of the hashes in the password list. The hacker can run a program to do this instead of typing them all in by hand, but it can take a while if the users of the computer have chosen good passwords. (See Chapter 2 for more on choosing passwords).

Digital Signatures and Certificates

One problem with Internet e-mail is that it was not designed with security in mind. Messages are not protected from snooping by intermediate Internet hosts, and you have no guarantee that a message actually came from the person identified in the e-mail's From: field. Internet newsgroup messages have the same problem: You cannot really tell who the message actually came from. You can encrypt the body of the message to take care of the first problem, and digital signatures take care of the second.

Digital signatures are useful because while anyone can check the signature, only the individual with the private key can create the signature. The difference between a digital signature and a certificate is that you can check the authenticity of a certificate with a certificate authority.

In Chapter 2 you read about the danger in downloading files from the Internet. Hackers can (and do) upload programs and utilities that contain Trojan horses, which can leave your network wide open to intrusion. One way to make sure that those programs and utilities are safe to download is to only download files that have certificates signed by a reputable certificate authority.

A software company can transmit a certificate, along with a file you download, that certifies that the file is free of virii and Trojan horses. You can check the certificate with a certificate authority you trust (VeriSign is the certificate authority that Microsoft uses) and hackers cannot forge the certificates. Certificates and digital signatures are explained in more detail later in this chapter.

Secure Password Exchange

When you log on to your network file server, or when you connect to your Internet service provider, you supply a user name and password. These two pieces of information control your access to the network and represent your identity on the network. They must be protected from eavesdropping.

Most network operating systems (Windows NT included) protect your user name and password when you log on, by encrypting the user name and password before sending them over the network to be authenticated. The file server (or ISP host) checks the encrypted user name and password against the list of legitimate users and passwords. The host can check the password either by decrypting it and checking the database of passwords stored in the clear, or it can encrypt the stored password and check the result against what has been sent from the client over the network.

To keep the same encrypted data from being sent every time, the client can also include some additional information, such as the time the logon request was sent. This way your network credentials are never sent unprotected over your local LAN or over the telephone system. Windows NT does accept unencrypted passwords from older LAN Manager network clients, however, so you should be careful about allowing older clients on your network.

Not every authentication protocol encrypts the user name and password. SLIP, for example, does not. Telnet and FTP do not. PPP may, if both the dial-up client and server are configured that way. Windows NT by default requires encrypted authentication.

A Conspiracy of Cryptographers

Cryptography is the study of codes and ciphers. Like any other group of specialists, cryptographers have a language of their own to describe what they do. You don't have to be a theoretical mathematician to evaluate and use cryptography in your network, but it helps to have a general understanding of encryption when you are evaluating cryptography options for your network.

The rest of this chapter covers cryptographic theory in detail. The algorithms that form the foundation of encryption are covered, as are the various protocols used for secure exchanges and the attcks that encryption is vulnerable to.

Terminology

- **Block cipher:** A cipher designed to operate on fixed-size blocks of data.

- **Breakable:** A cipher that, given a reasonable amount of time and resources, can be compromised by a competent cryptanalysist.

- **Computationally secure:** A cipher that, given all the computational power that will be available to the most powerful governments over the next hundred years, is unlikely to be compromised.

- **Secure:** A cipher that, even given a reasonable amount of time and resources, most likely cannot be compromised by a competent cryptanalysist.

- **Stream cipher:** A cipher designed to operate on a continuous stream of data.

- **Strong:** A cipher that, given the computational power that may reasonably be brought to bear on it any time in the near future, is unlikely to be compromised.

- **Unconditionally secure:** A cipher that, given an unlimited amount of time and an infinitely powerful processor, cannot be compromised.

Algorithms

When you encode a message (transform a plaintext into a ciphertext) you must perform a series of steps. For example, to encode a message using the PigLatin93 cipher, you do the following:

1. Take the first word of the plaintext.

2. Replace each vowel in the word with "ra" followed by that vowel.

3. Write the modified word down (this is the ciphertext).

4. If you have words left, take the next word of the plaintext and then go to step 2. Otherwise, you're done.

A set of instructions, like the steps outlined above, is an *algorithm*. Ciphers are algorithms that describe how to encode or decode messages; therefore ciphers are *cryptographic algorithms*. Not every algorithm is a cipher, of course—algorithms are used for many other things, especially in computers. In fact, everything that computers do is detailed in an algorithm of one sort or another.

Algorithms can be performed by people (recipes are algorithms) but the all-time-champion algorithm followers are computers. This, combined with the fact that most ciphers are meant to be performed by a computer, means that most ciphers are detailed in computer languages such as C rather than in English steps like the example above. The following is an example of a cipher in C:

```
/*
ROT(n)
Usage: rot [e|d] number inputfile outputfile
The number should be between 0 and 26, exclusive
Assumes a contiguous linear character encoding (i.e. ASCII)
*/

#include <stdio.h>
#include <string.h>
```

```
int do_rotate( char isencrypt, int key, int thechar ){
  if(isencrypt=='d')
    key *= -1;
  if( thechar >= 'A' && thechar <= 'Z'){
    thechar+=key;
    if(thechar>'Z')
      thechar-=26;
  }
if( thechar >= 'a' && thechar <= 'z'){
    thechar+=key;
    if(thechar>'z')
      thechar-=26;
  }
  return(thechar);
}

void main(int argc, char *argv[]){
  FILE *infile,*outfile;
  int thischar, keyval, isencrypt;

  isencrypt=(char)argv[1];
  keyval = atoi(argv[2]);
  if(keyval>0&&keyval<26&&(isencrypt=='e'||isencrypt=='d')){
    if((infile = fopen(argv[3], "rb")) != NULL){
      if((infile = fopen(argv[4], "wb")) != NULL){
        while((thischar = getc(infile)) != EOF) {
          putc(do_rotate(isencrypt,keyval, thischar),
outfile);
        }
      }
    }
  }
}
```

If you examine the above cipher, you will notice that there are two basic parts to it: the main part that takes care of opening, reading, stepping through, and writing files, and the do_rotate part that performs a specific function (in this case, adding or subtracting the key value) to a portion of the file (in this case, one character). This is the function that is performed by the cipher. (It is also defined as a function written in the C programming language, but that's beside the point. If it were written in BASIC it might be called a subroutine, but it still performs a cryptographic function.)

You can implement other ciphers by replacing the do_rotate function with a different function, such as one that performs an XOR on the character with a specific key. You would then be implementing an XOR cipher instead of a ROT cipher. There are many different ciphers that you can implement in this manner, each performing a specific mathematical function on input text (plaintext) with a key to produce the output text (the ciphertext).

Terminology

- **Algorithm:** Detailed steps for performing a function.

- **Keyspace:** The range of all possible keys for a cipher. A cipher with a large keyspace is harder to crack than one with a smaller keyspace because there are more keys (numbers or combinations of letters) to try.

- **Restricted algorithm:** An algorithm that is kept secret to make it more difficult to break.

- **Symmetric algorithm:** An algorithm in which the same key is used for encryption and decryption.

Symmetric Functions

If the same key can be used to encrypt or decrypt the message (as in the ROT example in the *Algorithms* section), then the cipher uses a symmetric function. Both the sender and receiver must have that same key. Good symmetric ciphers are fast, secure, and easy to implement using modern microprocessors. Figure 3.3 illustrates how symmetric functions work.

FIGURE 3.3

Symmetric functions use the same key for encryption and decryption.

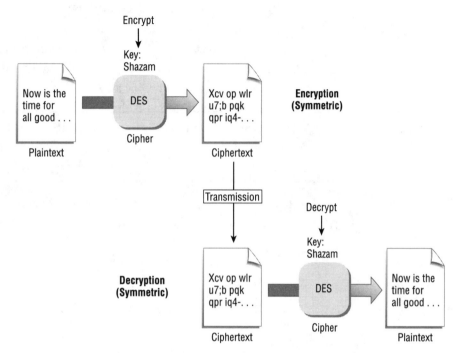

Some ciphers are more secure than others. The XOR cipher, for example, is not very secure. (An XOR is a simple mathematical function that computers can perform quickly.) A competent cryptanalysist can decode an XOR-encoded message in short order. There are two general features of a symmetric algorithm that make it secure:

- The algorithm produces ciphertext that is difficult to analyze.

- The algorithm has a sufficiently large keyspace.

Cryptanalysists test ciphertext for correspondences in the text, an uneven distribution of instances of numbers, and essentially anything that differentiates the ciphertext from a series of truly random numbers.

A good algorithm will produce a ciphertext that is as random-seeming as possible. This is where the XOR cipher fails miserably—an XORed message has a lot in common with a regular ASCII text message. Cryptographers will exploit these commonalties to recover the key and decode the whole message.

A cryptanalysist who cannot exploit nonrandomness in the ciphertext has little choice but to simply try all the possible key combinations to decode the message. This is a lot like the hacker trying to guess the password to your system—if they don't know that the password is a birthday or the name of your dog, then they must try all the possible passwords.

Just as a longer password is safer than a shorter one, a longer key is more secure than a shorter key.

There are a number of symmetric ciphers used in both software and hardware. You can get a feel for what is available by comparing the following three ciphers.

DES

IBM and the U.S. National Security Agency cooperated to develop this cipher (see the *How to Keep a Secret* section earlier in this chapter). It has been designed to be resistant to differential cryptanalysis, but has been shown to be susceptible to linear cryptanalysis (linear and differential cryptanalysis are described later in this chapter in the section *Attacks on Ciphers and Cryptosystems*). Its key length is only 56 bits, which makes it increasingly easy to perform a brute-force examination of all of the possible keys for an encrypted ciphertext. DES is in common use in encryption hardware and software. It is an ANSI standard.

IDEA

This cipher has a key length of 128 bits—considerably more than DES uses. While a sufficiently motivated and financed organization can break a DES-encoded message, the large key space makes a brute force attack on IDEA impractical. IDEA was designed to be immune to linear and differential cryptanalysis, and you can reasonably be assured that not even the NSA can decode an IDEA-encrypted message without the key. IDEA is patented both in Europe and United States.

Blowfish

This cipher can use a key with from 32 to 448 bits, allowing you to select how secure you want to make your message. It was designed to be immune to linear and differential cryptanalysis. Its developer, Bruce Shneider, has not sought a patent on the algorithm so that a good, freely implementable algorithm would be available to both private individuals and the public sector.

One-Way Functions

When you type your password to log on to Windows 95 or Windows NT, it is encrypted and compared against the stored encrypted value of your password (see *Logon Authentication* earlier in this chapter). The reason the password is stored using a one-way function (also called a hash, trap-door, digest, or fingerprint) is so that it will be difficult for a hacker or other network intruder to determine your password even if the hacker has gained access to the operating system's stored settings. Figure 3.4 illustrates a one-way hash function.

FIGURE 3.4

One-way functions produce a hash of the original message that may be much shorter than the original message.

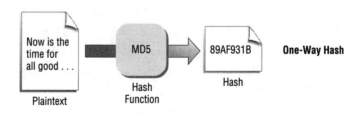

Hash functions can also used for other purposes. You can use a hash to "fingerprint" files (create a digital fingerprint, or hash, that is unique to that file), for example. A hash function can produce a result that is much smaller than the input text: A hash of a multimegabyte word-processor document, for example, may result in a 128-bit number. A hash (or fingerprint) is also unique to the file that produced it—it is practically impossible to create another file that will produce the same hash value. You might use this kind of hash to make sure that your Internet-distributed software product is delivered free of virii and other malicious modifications. You can allow your customers to download the software, and then tell them what the hash value for the software files is. Only your unmodified software files will hash to the same value.

One feature of a hash function (especially one that produces short hashes) is that any hash value is equally likely. Therefore it is practically impossible to create another file that will hash to the same value.

Some hash functions require a key, others do not. Anyone can calculate a hash that does not use a key; this kind of hash is good for distributing software or making sure that files have not been changed without you noticing. A hash function with a key can only be calculated by someone (or something) that has the key.

Public Key Encryption

While symmetric ciphers use the same key to encrypt and decrypt messages (that's why they're called symmetric), public key encryption (or a public key cipher) uses a different key to decrypt than was used to encrypt. This is a relatively new development in cryptography, one that solves many longstanding problems with cryptographic systems, such as how to exchange those secret keys in the first place.

The problem with symmetric ciphers is this: Both the sender and the recipient must have the same key in order to exchange encrypted messages over a nonsecure medium. If two parties decide to exchange private messages, or if two computers' network devices or programs must establish a secure channel, the two parties must decide on a common key. Either party may simply decide on a key, but that party will have no way to send it to the other without the risk of it being intercepted on its way. It's a chicken-and-egg problem: Without a secure channel, there is no way to establish a secure channel.

In 1976, Witfield Diffie and Martin Hellman figured out a way out of the secure channel dilemma. They found that by using a different key, the one-way function could be undone. Their solution (called public key cryptography) takes advantage of a characteristic of prime and almost prime numbers: specifically, how hard it is to find the two factors of a large number that has only two factors, both of which are prime. Since Diffie and Hellman developed their system, some other public key ciphers have been introduced. The difficulty of determining quadratic residues (a subtle mathematical construct that few people other than mathematicians and cryptologists really understand) for example, has been exploited to make a public key cipher.

The mathematics of these ciphers is a matter for theoretical mathematicians and programmers, not network administrators—unless you are *really* paranoid and don't trust any cryptographic tool you didn't write yourself. What you should understand, however, is what these ciphers can do for you.

With a public key cipher, one key (the public key) is used to encrypt a message, while the other one (the private key) is the only key that can decrypt the message. This means that you can tell everyone your public key, even complete strangers and NSA agents. Anyone who has your key can encrypt a message that only you can decrypt. Even the NSA agent who has your public key cannot decrypt the message. Figure 3.5 illustrates public key cryptography.

One problem that plagues secure public key ciphers is that they are slow—much slower than symmetric ciphers. You can expect a good public key cipher to take 1,000 times as long to encrypt the same amount of data as a good symmetric cipher. This can be quite a drag on your computer's performance if you have a lot of data to transmit or receive.

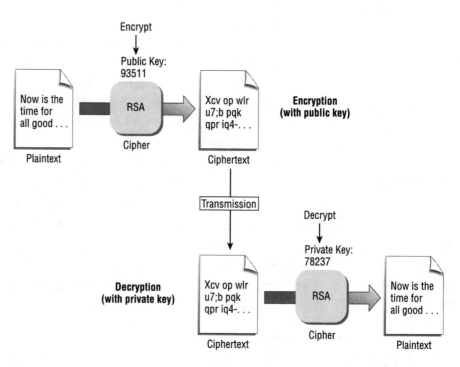

Terminology

- **Attack:** An attempt to discover the key or plaintext of a ciphertext.

- **Private key:** The key in public key encryption that is kept private.

- **Public key:** The key in public key encryption that is made public.

- **Public-key algorithm:** An algorithm in which a different key is used for encryption than for decryption.

Although it is much slower than symmetric systems, the public key–private key system neatly solves the problem that bedevils symmetric cryptosystems. When two people (or devices) need to establish a secure channel for communication, one of them can just pick a secret key and then encrypt that secret key using the other's public key. The encrypted key is then sent to the other party, and even if the key is intercepted, only the other party can decrypt the secret key, using the private key. Communication may then continue between the two parties using a symmetric cipher and that secret key. A system that uses both symmetric and public key encryption is called a *hybrid cryptosystem*.

Protocols

There is a lot of mathematics in cryptography, and to be a good cryptographer you almost have to be a theoretical mathematician, but there is more to cryptography than mathematics. There is even more to cryptography than ciphers that use math. The ciphers all by themselves are merely a computational curiosity—they only become useful when secure communications systems are built using them.

Communications systems are built out of protocols. Protocols, in turn, describe how the entities in a communications system (such as the computers in a network) interoperate. Protocols also perform the same function in human terms. *Robert's Rules of Order*, for example, contains the protocols for people communicating in a meeting or assembly, including who may speak at any particular time and how to excuse yourself from the meeting.

For a computer, the protocols describe who will transmit when, what will be transmitted, how it will be formatted, and what (and who) will transmit next. A protocol is very much like an algorithm, but while an algorithm describes the steps for one computer to take, a protocol describes the steps that two or more communicating computers must take.

The parts of a protocol that one computer performs make an algorithm. You can think of a protocol as a set of algorithms that communicating computers use.

Every time you log on to your network or connect to the Internet you use protocols. The Internet uses TCP/IP, which is a set of protocols that all communicating Internet computers use. Windows NT uses the Net-BIOS protocol along with either the TCP/IP, NWLink, or NetBEUI protocols to provide access to shared files and printers. These are general-purpose protocols that allow networked computers to communicate, and they are designed more for efficiency and scalability than for security.

Cryptographers have a very narrow view of protocols—sure, a cryptographer will consider such aspects as the computation time required for a protocol, or whether or not it is feasible for a 1,000,000 computers to use it, but the cryptographer is more concerned with whether the protocol is susceptible to such network malfeasance as the man-in-the-middle attack (see the *Attacks on Ciphers and Cryptosystems* section).

The following is a simple protocol for two people (let's call them Alice and Bob, in the tradition that real cryptographers follow) to establish a symmetrically encrypted communications channel using public key encryption. Here are the steps:

1. Alice sends Bob her public key (or Bob gets Alice's public key from a public key directory).

2. Bob selects a secret key for use with a symmetric cipher, encrypts it using Alice's public key, and then sends it to Alice.

3. Alice decrypts the secret key using her private key.

4. Alice and Bob use the secret key and the symmetric cipher to send private messages to each other.

However, this protocol has a problem. We'll explore this problem in the next section.

Attacks on Ciphers and Cryptosystems

Throughout history, cryptography has been a race between those trying to keep secrets and those trying to find out what those secrets are. (The code makers and the code breakers are often the same people.) It's no different today. If you are really serious about keeping information private using cryptography, you should be aware of what others may do to ferret out that private information. Cryptographers call these attempts *attacks*, and they come in two forms: cryptanalysis and protocol subversion.

Cryptanalysis

Cryptanalysis is the process of examining encrypted information to try to determine what the encrypted message is, or what the key that encrypted the message is (which, of course, gives you what the message itself is). There are a number of different techniques a cryptanalysist can use, including:

- **Keyspace search:** This is the hard way to crack an encrypted message. A keyspace search involves checking all of the possible keys that might have been used to encrypt the message. This is like trying all of the possible combinations on a bank vault in order to open it. A keyspace search is only feasible when there are not very many possible keys. A cryptanalysist might use this technique if the key length is 32 or 48 bits, and perhaps if it were 56 bits and the message were really worth the millions of dollars worth of hardware that would be required. Keyspace searches of larger keyspaces are impractical at the present level of computing technology.

- **Known plaintext:** A cryptanalysist can reduce the number of possible keys to be searched for many ciphers if the cryptanalysist already has the plaintext of the encrypted message. (Why would the cryptanalysist want the key if the message is already out? Perhaps there is another message encrypted with the same key.) If even a portion of the message is always the same, especially at the beginning of the message, (for example, the headers in an e-mail message are always the same), your ciphertext may be vulnerable.

- **Linear and differential cryptanalysis:** A cryptanalysist may also look for mathematical patterns in collections of ciphertexts that have all been encrypted with the same key. Some ciphers (not all) are vulnerable to either or both of these kinds of analysis and a cryptanalysist may then have a much smaller range of keys to search.

Protocol Subversion

Just choosing a good cipher doesn't make your network safe. Recall the protocol example in the previous section with Alice and Bob. They both used a pretty good public key encryption system to exchange a secret key that they then used with a very secure symmetric cipher. That wasn't enough to ensure their privacy, though, because their protocol was weak. Consider the following scenario, with a determined and powerful adversary, Mallet:

1. Alice sends Bob her public key.

2. Mallet intercepts Alice's public key and sends Bob his own public key (alternatively, Mallet intercepts Bob's request for Alice's public key from the directory and substitutes his own).

3. Bob selects a secret key for use with a symmetric cipher, encrypts it using Mallet's public key (which he thinks belongs to Alice), and then sends it to Alice.

4. Mallet intercepts Bob's response. He then encrypts the secret key he received from Bob with Alice's own public key and sends it to her.

5. Alice decrypts Mallet's secret key using her private key.

6. Mallet maintains the illusion that Alice and Bob are talking to each other rather than to him by intercepting the messages and retransmitting them.

F I G U R E   3.6

A man-in-the-middle attack interposes Mallet between Bob and Alice's communications.

Bob sends his public key.

Mallet substutiutes his own public key.

Mallet decrypts the secret key, re-encrypts it with Bob's public key, then sends it to Bob.

Alice sends a secret key encoded with Mallet's public key.

Obviously, the above scenario, called a *man-in-the-middle attack*, requires that Mallet be able to intercept messages and substitute his own. This is possible in some media (such as the Internet) and not others (such as radio). A protocol can be modified to be resistant to man-in-the-middle attacks. Consider the following modification (called the Interlock Protocol and invented by Ron Rivest and Adi Shamir) and how it affects Alice and Bob's negotiation of a secure key:

1. Alice sends Bob her public key.

2. Bob sends Alice his public key.

3. Alice selects a secret key and sends Bob a message encrypted with that secret key. Neither Bob nor Mallet can read the message, since neither of them have the secret key.

4. Bob selects a secret key and sends Alice a message encrypted with that secret key. Neither Alice nor Mallet can read the message, since neither of them have the secret key.

5. Alice encrypts her secret key with Bob's public key and then sends it to Bob. Bob can then read Alice's message.

6. Bob encrypts his secret key with Alice's public key and then sends it to Alice. Alice can then read Bob's message.

7. Bob and Alice continue to communicate, using the secret keys they have established.

The above protocol is not perfect, but it does make it much more difficult for Mallet to impersonate Alice and Bob. Mallet cannot read Alice's message until step 5, and cannot read Bob's message until step 6. In both cases, it is too late for Mallet to change the message already sent to the other party. In order for Mallet to subvert this protocol he must correctly guess what is being sent in steps 3 and 4 in order to create a convincing counterfeit.

Digital Signatures

In the above examples using public key encryption, the message is encrypted with the public key and decrypted with the private key. You can also do it the other way—encrypt with the private key and decrypt with the public key.

Why would you want to encrypt a message that anyone can decrypt? That seems a bit silly but there is a good reason to do so—only the holder of the private key can encrypt a message that can be decrypted with the public key. It is in effect a digital signature, proving that the holder of the private key produced the message.

Since the purpose of a digital signature is not to conceal information but rather to certify it, the private key is often used to encrypt a hash of the original document, and the encrypted hash is appended to the document or sent along with it. This process takes much less processing time to generate or verify than does encrypting the entire document, and it still guarantees that the holder of the private key signed the document.

Stenography

Cryptography can be very effective at keeping a secret. With a sufficiently powerful cipher and a sufficiently long key, even major world governments cannot read your diary. What if you don't want people to know that you're keeping secrets, though? After all, an encrypted file or an encrypted hard drive is pretty strong evidence that you're hiding something. *Stenography* is the process of hiding those encrypted files where it is unlikely that anyone will find them.

Encrypted files look like random numbers, so anything that also looks like random numbers can be used to hide an encrypted message. In graphics images that use many colors, the low-order bit for each pixel in the image doesn't make much difference to the quality of the image. You can hide an encrypted message in a graphic file by replacing the low-order bits with the bits from your message. The low-order bits of high-fidelity sound files are another good place for encrypted data. You can even exchange encrypted messages with someone surreptitiously by sending graphics and sound files with those messages hidden in them.

Random Sequence Generation

Most cryptographic systems manage the selection of keys and the negotiation of protocols for you. Systems that do this must be able to select keys that are not easily guessed, because one way to attack a cryptographic system is to predict the keys that might be used in the system. These keys are selected by generating random numbers.

It is difficult for a computer to generate good random numbers. Computers, by their very nature, are extremely predictable, and hundreds of thousands of engineers have labored (collectively) millions of years to make them more so. If you run a computer program twice and give it the same input the second time as you did the first, you will get the same output the second time as you did the first. Since the whole point of a truly random number is not to be able to guess the output based on the input, computers (unassisted) make lousy dice-throwers.

The best that computers can do by themselves is good *pseudorandom numbers*. These are numbers that have many of the characteristics of truly random numbers, including incompressibility, good distribution (each number is equally likely), and nonrepetition over a reasonable amount of numbers. However, if you start a pseudorandom number generator (or program) with the same initial state (or *seed*) it will produce the same series of random numbers as before. A cryptosystem that uses pseudorandom numbers therefore relies on having a good seed value.

Terminology

- **Pseudorandom:** Numbers created by a deterministic means (that is, given identical starting conditions, identical numbers will be produced). Good pseudorandom numbers have a long periodicity and satisfy the other conditions of random numbers, such as incompressibility and having an even distribution.

- **Random**: Unpredictable (a series of random numbers cannot be produced, even from identical starting conditions). Truly random numbers also satisfy other criteria, such as incompressibility and having an even distribution.

In order to get a good random number (to use as a seed value, for example) the computer must look outside itself. There are many sources of randomness in the real (noncomputer) world—the weather, ocean waves, lava-lamp wax gyrations, the times between one keystroke and the next—and a computer can measure these events and use them to generate random numbers. Keystroke timing is commonly used to generate secret keys. Another way is to ask the user to type in a paragraph or two of text; there are no published algorithms that will predict arbitrary user input (yet).

If a random number is going to be used as a seed for pseudorandom numbers, it should have enough bits to make it difficult to guess. For example, you don't want to protect a 128-bit cryptosystem that uses IDEA with a password of 8 characters or less for a seed—this is effectively only about 48 bits of security if you just use printable ASCII characters in the password.

> ### Reality Check: Why Lots of Bits Are Better
>
> A little while after Netscape introduced Secure Socket Layer encryption for their Web browser, they were embarrassed by some hackers who exploited a weakness in the browser encryption software. (Netscape promptly provided a security fix for its software.) The Web browser used a strong cipher, and its key length was enough to deter most efforts at decryption (but not all—it was limited to 40 bits so that the software could be exported from the United States).
>
> What the hackers exploited, however, was a weakness in key generation. An examination of Netscape's software revealed that the key was generated using the computer's current time, which effectively limited the bit length of the seed to 12 bits, which similarly limited the keyspace of the cipher.

Summary

Important secrets throughout history have been encrypted in one manner or another. The codes and ciphers used have steadily gotten more difficult to break as technology has improved and our understanding of the mathematics behind encryption has deepened. Encryption has left the realm of generals and spies, and joined the adding machine (now a spreadsheet) and the typewriter (now a word processor) as an important business tool.

There are a number of places you can use encryption in your Windows NT network. You can use it to protect both the communications between individuals (e-mail) and the communications between devices (network protocols such as Ethernet or TCP/IP). You can use it to protect file storage even when the operating system is unavailable or has been subverted. You can use it to confirm the identity of a user logging on, the organization that produced software you have downloaded, or the true sender of e-mail or Usenet news.

The study of encryption is the study of mathematical problems. The harder the problem, the better cryptographers like it, because hard mathematical problems (such as factoring large numbers, or traversing lattices) make for good ciphers. Cryptographers make ciphers, which encode and decode information (the plaintext). Ciphers are used in protocols, which govern the interaction of two or more communicating entities (computers, usually).

Cryptanalysis is used to find the weaknesses of ciphers and protocols, and to develop attacks that exploit those weaknesses. Brute force attacks mainly depend on the length of the key and become impractical when larger key lengths are used. Linear and differential analysis can be used to narrow the key space and, sometimes, reveal the key used to encrypt a message. Not all ciphers are vulnerable to this kind of analysis. Protocol attacks, such as the man-in-the-middle attack, exploit weaknesses in the communication protocols rather than in the ciphers themselves.

Symmetric encryption requires that the same key be used by the sender and the receiver, while public key encryption allows separate keys to be used. A public key can be used to encrypt a message that only the private key can decrypt. Public key encryption typically requires more processing power than does symmetric encryption, so often public key encryption is used to exchange private keys for continued secure communication using a symmetric cipher. Public key encryption also can be used to create certificates and digital signatures. Any form of automatic encryption (symmetric or public key) requires a good source of random numbers for key generation.

How you use encryption in your network depends on how important it is that your data remains private. Very few networks require encryption to protect their data—the effort required to protect the data to the maximum degree is not warranted by the actual value of the data. If you determine that your data does require the maximum degree of protection, you should consider encrypting the file systems of your file servers, encrypting communications links that traverse nonsecure media (such as radio or the Internet), and using encrypted authentication protocols to ensure that only authorized users can access your network.

CHAPTER

4

Successful Security Administration

ecurity isn't something that can be set up and forgotten—
rather, it is the continual process of discerning potential
threats and taking new measures to prevent those threats
from materializing. But how can you easily recognize what threatens
security? How can you effectively manage those things that must
remain somewhat nonsecure to be useful? Although these questions are
difficult to answer, and the responses to them often run counter to the
efficiency of the system, there are a few axiomatic approaches to security that always work well.

This chapter will outline the process of security administration, providing a step-by-step method for identifying vulnerabilities and securing
your system against them. The remainder of this book explores in detail
the measures you should take against known threats and discusses possible vectors of attack in detail—this chapter will help you apply that
information usefully.

Security administration is work that is continually performed to keep
a system as free from the threat of loss as is practicable. As a security
administrator, it is your job to determine which security measures need
to be taken and if those security measures have been properly executed.

Although the task is daunting, it can be broken down into discreet
steps that can be methodically executed. The following steps can also be
seen as a perpetual security cycle (see Figure 4.1), that is, safeguards
and processes you must continually implement. The process of security
administration is defined in the following steps:

 1. Identify potential vulnerabilities.

2. Evaluate vulnerabilities to determine how they can be effectively nullified.

3. Determine which countermeasures can be effectively employed against the vulnerabilities.

4. Deploy those measures.

5. Test measures for effectiveness by simulating an attack.

6. Monitor logs, intrusion detection software, and border systems for evidence of security breaches.

7. Investigate any indications of a breach to determine the progression of the breach and identify new potential vulnerabilities.

8. Study public security sources for news of newly discovered security vulnerabilities.

9. Start over.

We'll discuss each of these steps in the following sections.

F I G U R E 4.1

The security cycle

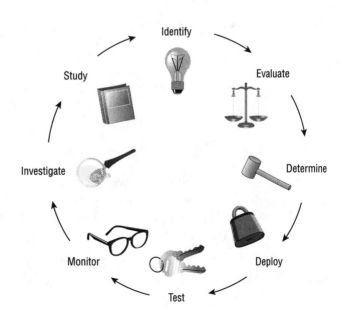

Identifying Potential Vulnerabilities

Vulnerabilities are relatively easy to identify if you set aside for the moment the evaluation of how much of a threat each vulnerability actually poses. External vulnerabilities are any service connected in any way to your secure system that listens for and accepts connections from outside the secure system. All external security threats must attach to your system; therefore, a vector that listens for and answers connection attempts is required. The following is a list of potential vulnerabilities:

- A keyboard and console

- The server service of an NT machine

- Web service

- A fax server

- Dial-up modem banks or a remote access service

- E-mail service

- An employee

- Remote access software

- Remote control software

- Voice-mail

- The front door

The common denominator in the above list is that each of these resources waits for a connection attempt and then responds, in some way allowing access to information. Therefore, each represents a potential vulnerability in your secured system.

Terminology

- **Attack:** Measures taken to undermine the security of a system either to force a denial of service or to gain unauthorized access.

- **Border:** A security perimeter formed by a natural or logical boundary that can only be passed at defined locations called border gateways.

- **Border gateways:** Routers that attach a private network to the Internet. They are usually used in a system as security checkpoints that force all traffic into and out of a secured system through a single point of access control. Traffic passing through the border gateways is security tested before being passed through to the secure system. Firewalls are an example of border gateways.

- **Breach:** A loss of security due to a successful attack.

- **Countermeasures:** Actions taken to eliminate security vulnerabilities.

- **Denial of service:** An attack that attempts to eliminate or reduce the ability of a system to provide a service. A *denial-of-service attack* is far easier to perform than an *unauthorized access attack* because access to the system is not required, and because far more vectors exist.

- **External security:** Measures taken to prevent intrusion from outside the security perimeter of the system.

- **Internal security:** Measures taken to prevent unauthorized access from inside the security perimeter of the system.

- **Vector of attack (vector):** A method (or a point of entry) used to exploit vulnerability.

- **Vulnerability:** A specific weakness in a system that can be exploited to gain unauthorized access to a system.

Evaluating Vulnerabilities

Admittedly, some of the vulnerabilities presented in the list in the previous section are a bit outlandish, which makes the case for evaluating vulnerabilities. Some are not likely to be threats at all, whereas others, which appear harmless, may in fact enable deep penetration into your network. It can be difficult to tell at first glance which vulnerabilities can actually turn out to be serious security threats.

To evaluate vulnerabilities, you must determine exactly how they are connected to your secure system. For instance, a fax machine is probably not connected at all, and is therefore not a threat. But a fax server is connected, so it does allow a possible vector for attack and should be considered. Voice-mail may not be connected, but new integrated voice-mail servers that read your e-mail to you and allow your voice-mail to be routed to your desktop machine certainly do provide a potential vector.

For the vulnerabilities you identify, determine how exactly they are connected to your system. Then determine what it would take to exploit that vulnerability. The more access the vulnerability provides and the easier it is to exploit, the more dangerous it is. Vulnerabilities that do not allow access to servers or are difficult to exploit may not be a big deal in your security environment.

Internal Security

Imagine the worst-case attack against your network. It would come from within your firewall. The perpetrator would know the architecture of the network hardware and software. The perpetrator would know valid account names and the software running on the servers. The perpetrator would be an employed administrator of your network.

If you didn't know the administrative account password on your network, would you be able to get in? If so, your network is not secure.

How many of your coworkers freely offer their passwords while you work on their computers because they can't be bothered to type them in? Have you ever given out the administrative password to keep from walking to another building? Although these examples sound pretty lax, they are quite common.

The employees who work for an organization, including typical users and network administrators, have direct access to the network, and their motivations may not always align precisely with those of the organization. All the people who have accounts on your network are potential security threats, and they have the potential to be the most serious threats.

People tend to trust those they work with. This trust (although good for interpersonal relationships) is bad for security. No one expects a coworker to act against the interests of the organization, but personal motivations override the organizational good all the time. Trusted coworkers can suddenly become your biggest security problem.

This means network security isn't simply Internet security or security against hackers. Far more common are attacks from inside your own network. Internal attacks might include everything from the merely curious employee snooping for files, to budding computer experts flexing their newfound computing skills, to an employee trying to cover his tracks when a mistake is made, to outright theft of information.

Of course we don't recommend taking a hard line against computer access. Remember that security is the appropriate balance between useful efficiency and requisite security. Appropriate security restrictions vary widely between organizations.

Hackers have on occasion manipulated their way into a position to attack the network from the inside. These hackers may actually be employees or contractors, students (in an academic environment), or very courageous thieves. In reality these kinds of attacks are rare, but strong internal security can keep them from happening at all.

Policies: Internal Security

- Install the latest security packs as they become available. Service packs for Microsoft software are available for download from the Microsoft Web site (`http://www.microsoft.com`). Installation is self-explanatory.

- Maintain strong NTFS file permissions on your servers, and periodically test access from accounts that shouldn't have permission to access certain areas. Maintaining strong NTFS permissions means that you give permission to access files only when necessary. Of course, it means removing the "everyone" access to all hard disk partitions at the very least. You'll find it easiest to remove the "everyone" permission when a disk has very few files. NTFS file permissions are covered in Chapter 8.

- Force password changes often. Passwords should be valid for no longer than 30 days at a stretch. Use the User Manager for Domains Account Policies window to set and enforce password lengths and restrictions. User accounts and account policy are covered in Chapter 6.

- Make sure coworkers understand that no one else ever needs to know their password. If files are stored securely on a server, with proper group accounts set up to allow coworkers access to the same files, there should never be a need for users to supply their passwords for use when they are absent. If your users have to have a specific individual's password to access something, you haven't set up account security correctly. Passwords are discussed in detail in Chapter 2.

- Restrict users to logging in from certain machines in their area. See Chapter 6 for more information on user account restrictions.

- Disallow administrative logon from the network for servers. Travel to your servers to administer them. Disallow local access on servers for all nonadministrative accounts. Never use a server or domain Administrative account on another machine. User rights are covered in Chapter 6.

- Remove the keyboard and monitor from servers if possible. They can be reattached when you need to administer the server. Certain mouse devices will not reset properly when reattached, so you should leave those attached. Server physical and peripheral security is covered in Chapter 21.

- Make certain all servers are located in locked and secure rooms. Restrict access to administrative personnel. Ideas on how to do this are given in Chapter 21.

- Maintain a normal user account for yourself. Use it rather than your administrative account except when you actually need to log in as the administrator. User accounts are covered in Chapter 6.

- Never give out an administrative password for the sake of convenience.

- Change all affected account passwords immediately when you suspect a compromise has occurred. You can change passwords for any user with the User Manager for Domains, as discussed in Chapter 6.

- Restrict logon access to the network to the computers that an employee normally uses. This makes it impossible to exploit an account name and password from anywhere other than the user's regular computer. This is covered in Chapter 6.

Identifying Countermeasures to Vulnerabilities

Once you have prioritized your list of vulnerabilities, identify actions you can take to reduce or eliminate the threat of an attack through that vector. This may include strong passwords, closing down a service on a server, encryption, blocking a service using a firewall, or requiring an identification number to check voice-mail. Successful countermeasures significantly reduce the threat of intrusion without significantly reducing the efficiency or usefulness of the system.

Determining countermeasures often means looking for hardware or software products like dead bolts or firewalls that will solve the problem for you. Sometimes, it means implementing a human security policy such as adding a security guard or classifying documents.

Deploying Security Measures

Putting a security measure in place may be as simple as enabling a software service or it may be as difficult as creating photo identification tags for all the employees in your company—and getting those employees to wear them. Obviously, a network administrator alone doesn't have the authority to employ many security measures, so you may have to simply make security recommendations to those who do have the authority to implement them.

Each of the policy statements in this book proposes a security measure you can employ to strengthen your network against attack.

You can significantly improve your chances of using security measures effectively by teaching users why the security measures exist and what the security threats actually are. People naturally tend to passively resist restrictions that don't come with explanations. Security training will help users feel like they are an integral part of the security program, rather than prisoners in a high-security environment.

You must also convince management that security is worth spending money on and that the restrictions are worthwhile. The easiest way to do this is usually by arranging a demonstration of how easy it is for a hacker (you) to gain access to the system in an unauthorized manner. Compromising your Web server from the Internet is usually pretty easy; or you can direct the participant's Web browser to a security Web site that will show them their passwords. If management doesn't understand the threats, how easy certain systems are to exploit, or that some loss of efficiency is a necessary part of security, then you probably won't get the resources you need to secure your network.

Employing external security is the most chaotic facet of a total security policy. New security holes are found nearly every week, and the sheer volume of hacking activity on the Internet makes it the most probable source of attack.

Firewalls are the only effective solution to the problem—there is no good alternative. But they are not the only thing you need. Some machines, like Web and mail servers, must provide service to the public Internet, so these machines must either exist outside the firewall or open a security hole through it.

Machines outside your firewall must have strong security settings of their own, like disabled NetBIOS bindings, packet rejection from untrusted domains, and security logging. Figure 4.2 shows how you would place public servers in a single firewall configuration.

FIGURE 4.2

Protecting an internal network while providing public services

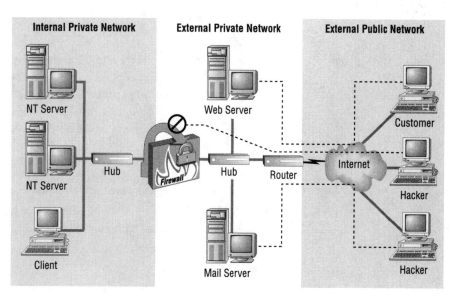

Policies: External Security

- Use the NWLink IPX transport for your internal network (unless you can't because you also use NetWare servers). Install TCP/IP only on those workstations that need access to the Internet and those servers that serve data to the Internet (and exist outside your firewall). Servers that aren't running TCP/IP are reasonably secure against Internet attacks.

- Set up your own firewall. Place Web and FTP servers outside it, and mail servers on the inside. Pass only SMTP and POP3 traffic from external sources. Run no other services or software on mail, Web, FTP, or firewall servers.

- Unbind NetBIOS from all servers outside the firewall. Set the TCP/IP stacks on those machines to accept connection only on ports for services you intend to provide with that specific machine.

- Never publish a list of user names on your Web site. Publish job titles instead.

- Use different e-mail names than you use for network account names.

- Log all public access to servers, and check your logs often. Use alerting software to detect hacking attempts against your exposed machines.

- Use a port scanner periodically (about once a month) from outside your network to check the status of your firewall, packet filter, and NetBIOS bindings. This is especially important when servers are maintained by more than one person or when retaining outsourced security services. Shareware port scanners are included on the companion CD-ROM and discussed in Appendix B.

- Make a serious attempt to hack into your network from a remote site at least once a year using the new tools and methods that have been developed in that year.

Attacking Your Own Network

Attacking your own network may seem a little silly when you first consider it, but periodic attempts to gain access without proper clearance are necessary to ensure that your security measures work. Finding security holes yourself is immeasurably better than having hackers find them for you. Attacking your own network is especially important if you rely on the services of a third party to defend your network.

Of course, you have to be a reasonably good hacker to simulate reasonably good hackers, but after you've read this book you'll know nearly everything they know about getting into your network. So simply apply the tactics you use to secure your network from the other perspective. There are very few good hackers—the vast majority simply download the tools written by the few good hackers and try them out against sites that are particularly vulnerable. With a little practice, you'll at be least as good as these hackers.

Although we recommend downloading and using hacker tools to test them against your network, you must remain diligently aware of the possibility that a Trojan horse may be embedded in the code. Never install software created by hackers on an operating system partition you use for any purpose other than attacking your own network. You should disconnect your Internet connection while attacking your own network to prevent any hidden software from contacting the outside world while it is in use (see the *Hacking Tools* section). Many of these tools are included on the companion CD-ROM and discussed in Appendix B.

Set up a workstation inside your own network to simulate internal attacks (generally, you can use your administration station) and a workstation outside your firewall to simulate external attacks. You can use the same computer if you can conveniently change its location or the way it is attached to your network. Load Windows NT in its own partition, and if you feel comfortable with Linux, load that on a partition too. Install all the hack tools you'll use on these partitions. Boot these partitions only when you are actively attempting to attack your own network.

Reality Check: Filtered Packet Services

A client of mine uses a filtered packet service from their Internet service provider because they cannot yet afford the cost of a true firewall. When the service was set up, I verified that I could not attach to the network via NetBIOS from the Internet (the filtered service passed only HTTP, FTP, NNTP, SNMP, and POP3). The filtered packet service worked correctly.

A few months later during a routine security scan of their network from my site, I was shocked to find the NetBIOS ports open and receiving connections. I mapped a drive from my site and logged in, exposing the contents of their server over the Internet. After I informed my client about the unexpected failure of the filtered packet service, we called the Internet service provider and demanded an explanation. The ISP verified that the filter had been shut off for my client, but could not explain why. They turned it back on (and accidentally blocked HTTP and mail traffic for a few hours) the next morning.

My client's site had been exposed to the Internet without the protection of a firewall for an unknown period, and if I had not routinely scanned their site, they probably would never have known that the filtering had gone down.

Hacking Tools

Hacking tools are very similar to third-party security tools and can in many cases be used legitimately for increasing the security of your site. They are different however, in that they serve primarily as attack tools rather than defense tools, and in that they generally come from individuals rather than from software companies. As such, their interfaces are usually primitive, and their functionality is generally somewhat limited to the specific task at hand. General categories of hacking tools are discussed in the following sections, and an in-depth look at specific tools is provided in Appendix B.

Hacking tools targeted towards network administrators are the perfect carriers for a Trojan horse. Be especially alert for unusual behavior in any software of this nature, and run it only from limited-use test machines—never from your servers or work computers.

Password Cracking Tools

Password cracking tools like L0phtCrack (which is provided on the companion CD-ROM) or NT Crack can be used to determine whether or not passwords on your network are strong enough to be "hacker proof." These tools work by extracting the encrypted password lists from the primary domain controller's registry, and then running a high-speed brute force comparison of the entire Windows NT or LAN Manager password keyspace with the encrypted passwords in the database.

Although the encryption hash used by Windows NT cannot be reversed to reveal the password, it's a simple matter to encrypt a test password the same way you would an ordinary password and compare the resulting hash to the hash stored in the primary domain controller's registry. If the two hashes match, the source is equal to the password.

These tools simply run through the entire allowed set of characters for passwords on an NT system against all the accounts on the server, slowly revealing each account's password as the attack progresses. When the job is finished after a few days, the resulting list contains all the passwords to every account on your network.

These tools must be run from an Administrator account, so they are not really considered a security vulnerability because a hacker would already have had to gain access as the administrator to run the tools. You can use these utilities to inspect the passwords chosen by account-holders on your network and make sure they are strong enough to be hacker-proof.

Automated Logon Software

Automated logon tools are the engines upon which hacking is largely based. Their mission is simple: Automated logon tools attempt to log onto network accounts again and again using successive candidates from a list of potential passwords. These tools typically perform about one logon attempt per second, but hackers can run many simultaneous sessions from a single machine thanks to TCP/IP multiplexing and Windows 95 and NT's multitasking. Running through the majority of words in the English language would take approximately 10,000 seconds at 10 attempts per second, or about three hours.

Reality Check: Automated Logon Software

While I was writing this book, a client asked me to check the security on their Windows NT-based Web server. I ran a port scan against it and noted that the SMB logon port was open. After connecting as an anonymous user and determining that the Administrator account had not been renamed, I ran a dictionary attack against the server over the Internet. After just 48 minutes, I had discovered the Administrator's password and was able to map a drive with full access permissions from my machine at my office. Scary, isn't it?

Hackers will typically use lists of common passwords, first names, and linguistic word lists such as dictionaries. Clever hackers may adapt their word lists to suit the organization in question; for instance, if attacking a Web site run by an Islamic organization, they may distill a word list from an electronic copy of the Koran.

If users' passwords on your network are names or real words, there's a very strong possibility that they could be hacked by these tools. The built-in Windows NT Administrator account is especially vulnerable because it cannot be locked out due to successive failed attempts.

The Administrator account is the natural object of dictionary attacks by hackers since it cannot be locked out and it provides complete control over the machine.

Bug Exploitation Software

Just as typos exist in all books of significant length, bugs exist in all non-trivial software. There is simply no way to perfectly validate all the code that goes into a complex software system like Windows NT. There are many ways to reduce the probability that a software bug will seriously affect the operation of a system, and Microsoft has done an excellent job with Windows NT in that respect. Although hundreds of bugs are known to exist in Windows NT, it is very likely that you will never be affected by any of them due to Windows NT's modular and protected kernel architecture.

However, with the thousands of hacking hours that go into searching for and exploiting security-related bugs, it's inevitable that bugs are found and exploited. In the summer of 1997, a serious flaw was exploited by a Russian security expert which allowed any Windows NT account, regardless of security restrictions, to execute a program as the administrator, which in turn could be used to give that account administrative permissions. Simply by running the example program that was provided with an explanation of the flaw, then logging out and logging back in, any user of a Windows NT computer could become a full-fledged member of the Administrators group. Windows NT security is based entirely on the sanctity of the Administrator accounts, which means this was the ultimate security breach.

Tempering the gravity of the flaw is the fact that the hacking software must be run on the machine for which administrative control is desired, so it doesn't work over a network or the Internet. If your Primary Domain Controller is physically secure (that is, locked up), your network is safe. However, in combination with other hacking tools, this program is still very dangerous. Microsoft has released a patch that is available at their tech support Web site. However, now that a flaw of this nature has been found, other hackers are actively looking for similar flaws. This means you may be hearing about these types of attacks for quite some time.

Stay up to date on service packs and software revisions. They fix many flaws that vendors never make public, so you can prevent quite a few types of security intrusions by staying current. If you don't, you're leaving a number of well-known back doors open to hackers and thieves. Appendix C contains current Web site addresses and instructions for finding this and other Web sites and mailing lists of interest.

Linux and Samba

Linux is a 32-bit version of UNIX developed entirely on the Internet by computer scientists who believed that a free operating system should be available to break the Microsoft hegemony on the architecture of the PC. Linux began life as a multitasking kernel created by a young Finnish programmer named Linus Torvalds. He released a stable multitasking kernel on the Internet for free, which quickly supplanted a few other efforts to develop the same thing. Other packages, such as TCP/IP networking stacks, X windowing systems, and drivers for different hardware that had already been created for other operating systems were quickly recompiled to work with Linus' kernel, and the Linux distributions were born.

NetBSD is a UNIX operating system very similar to Linux available for free on the Internet. NetBSD is simply Berkeley UNIX without a copyright. Many packages for Linux are available for NetBSD or can be recompiled for it.

The most important thing about Linux from a security standpoint is that it is given away for free with the complete source code for the operating system. These two factors make it readily available to hackers, and easy to modify for a specific purpose.

Samba is a NetBIOS/SMB package for UNIX. Samba adds the ability to log into NetBIOS operating systems like Windows for Workgroups, OS/2, Windows 95, and Windows NT.

Linux and Samba provide all the tools necessary for hackers to search for and exploit very esoteric security loopholes in Windows NT. Because they have an operational SMB client to work with, they can simulate other operating systems, create automated high-speed network logon attacks, and launch numerous other similar attacks. For this reason, many Windows NT attack tools are based on the Linux operating system.

But Linux is not just a tool for hackers. A user who downloads a Linux distribution can set up all these functions inside your network without your knowledge, thus opening an attack vector without you knowing about it. Linux can also be used for any of the following network services for your Windows NT network:

- **Router:** As with any TCP/IP-based network operating system, you can use Linux as a router. However, you may find it far more difficult to find card drivers for non-Ethernet cards, and you can probably forget about finding high-speed card drivers until they become commonplace. Linux has far less overhead than Windows NT and can be optimized to perform the routing function only. This makes it a faster router than the Windows NT multiprotocol router.

- **Bridge:** Experimental (read: beta quality) software exists that allows Linux to operate as an Ethernet bridge/switch, moving packets between network adapters independent of any specific protocol. Acting as a bridge, a computer could move TCP/IP, IPX, NetBIOS, or any other network protocol among different network segments. Bridging can only be achieved using adapters that operate in special "promiscuous" modes that allow them to respond to all network traffic irrespective of addressing.

- **Proxy:** Proxy servers are essentially Internet caches. They sit between a network and the Internet. Clients inside the network make all HTTP requests to the proxy server, which retrieves the Web page from the Internet on behalf of the client and returns it to the client. It then caches the Web pages, usually storing them based on how often they are requested or for a specific timeout period.

- **IP Masquerade:** IP masquerades are similar to proxy servers. Sitting between a network and the Internet, they make all the TCP/IP sockets appear to be coming from a single IP address, effectively hiding the presence of the other machines inside the network. Proxy servers and firewalls often act as IP masquerades.

- **Web server:** As are all UNIX operating systems, Linux is especially well suited as a Web server. However, Windows NT is generally much easier to configure as a Web server than Linux, and it provides the latest support for technologies such as Active Server Pages.

- **FTP server:** Linux can also serve any of the less often used TCP/IP protocols such as FTP and Gopher, but if you already use Internet Information Server with Windows NT, you should consider using it for these services.

- **Firewall:** Firewalls combine any of the services of a proxy server, IP masquerade, packet filter, and many other security-based services. Using a firewall as the sole gateway to the Internet gives you one point at which all external security measures can be controlled. Linux can operate as a host for firewall software.

Linux is very difficult to use and configure for those not already familiar with UNIX. For this reason, you should not even attempt to use Linux for security-based services unless you already know UNIX very well. The risk of accidentally leaving a security hole open in an unfamiliar operating environment is too great.

Policies: Attacking Your Own Network

- Run regular hacking attempts (at least monthly) from the Internet by dialing in and, from inside your network, using the methods you discover by frequenting hacking Web sites.

- Maintain a machine (or at least an operating system installation in its own partition) that is used exclusively for the installation of hacking tools. Do not use this operating system installation for any other purpose, and do not run untrusted software on any other machine. This machine should be a laptop, if possible, to facilitate its relocation around your network.

- Run port scans against all internal clients to be certain you know exactly which TCP/IP ports are exposing which services on which machines. Maintain a log, and be especially alert for changes in service ports that may indicate a user has installed Internet service software or an alternate operating system like Linux on a client machine. Be alert for the TCP/IP port addresses of remote control software, as these products are especially insecure.

Monitoring Your Network for Signs of Attack

How would you know if a hacker had attacked your network? There won't be any muddy footprints. However, there will probably be an unusually high number of logon attempts from the Internet, and if you've set up your monitoring and logging tools correctly, you'll be able to tell when you check them. Appendix B highlights some real-time security monitoring tools available on the companion CD-ROM.

Being alerted to attacks in progress is important both so you can catch the party perpetrating the attack and discover vulnerabilities you may not have been aware of. Therefore, it is beneficial to let an attack proceed once you've discovered that it's in progress—but to keep a vigilant watch on the progress of the attack to make sure the perpetrator can't gain access to sensitive information if they get in.

There are two reasons to let an attack proceed: to discover the identity of the perpetrator and to identify undiscovered vulnerabilities in your system. Hackers tend to be a few days ahead of even the best security administrators, so they may know something you don't about Windows NT security. And, you may find the attack is progressing from inside your security perimeter, in which case you'll want to know which employee is the perpetrator and determine what information they are going after.

Determining the identity of the perpetrator isn't as difficult as it might seem. All attacks coming in from the Internet have a source IP address you'll find in your logs. You can use reverse address resolution to determine who the organization or Internet service provider is, and then contact that organization to determine who is logged on to their network with the IP address you've found. If you tell them an attack (for which they could potentially be liable) is in progress, they will almost always assist you in determining the identity of the hacker.

If the attack is coming from inside your network, you'll get the name of the logged-on user in your logs. Perhaps the most difficult vectors to trace are dial-up phone lines, because you have to enlist the support of your phone company, and finding your phone company's fraud detection unit can be difficult.

Policies: Attack Detection

- Use security monitoring software that is capable of detecting attempts of intrusion against your network, and have it send a page to a pager that is passed around among network support personnel. Appendix B details the installation and use of software that supports intrusion monitoring.

- Respond immediately to intrusion attempts when they are detected. Collect as much information about the attacker as possible. Use their IP domains to determine who the higher-level service providers are.

- Prosecute individuals identified as intruders in your secure systems. This may mean filing criminal or civil charges, contacting the FBI, or consulting with Human Resources, depending on who the perpetrator is, where he or she is located, and whether he or she is an employee.

- Gather contact information for your telephone companies as soon as possible so that it is on hand if dial-up hacking attempts are discovered.

Testing security requires software tools. Some tools are the basic utilities provided with Windows NT itself, such as the Event Log viewer and the Performance Monitor. Third-party security software vendors provide some very compelling software packages that are specifically geared towards security. Finally, as we discussed earlier in this chapter, you can use the tools hackers create to make certain your network is not vulnerable to them, and to test your logging and alarming systems.

This chapter provides general information on many utilities. Refer to Appendix B for specific information on the installation and use of tools that you choose to use on a regular basis.

Windows NT Security Tools

Windows NT provides a basic set of tools to secure your network. These tools are geared towards administration rather than security, so they lack many of the automated alarm features that set professional security tools apart. Few of these tools are capable of automatically alerting you to changing conditions, so they must be checked regularly.

- **The Event Log Viewer:** One of the most important security tools you can use. In conjunction with Windows NT Auditing, the Event Log Viewer shows you the types of security breaches that are being attempted against your network. Look for numerous failed logon attempts, repeated object access failures, and other such indications of unauthorized access attempts.

- **Crystal Reports for Internet Information Server (IIS):** Makes searching through the logs created by Internet Information Server easy. These logs are complex and filled with details you probably won't need on a daily basis for alarming and security purposes. So a tool like Crystal Reports, which comes with IIS, makes it easy to spot trends in usage or unusual activity. The details presented in IIS logs can be crucial in tracking down a suspected security intruder, since it logs the IP addresses of all connected users.

■ **The Performance Monitor:** Can be used to measure a number of network security-related factors, such as failed logon attempts, network bandwidth usage, number of logon attempts in a given time period, and so forth. Unlike the other built-in tools, the Performance Monitor is capable of immediately alerting you to a threatening condition by running a program when its counters pass certain thresholds. You can use this capability to send e-mail alerts, launch a utility to send a page, or pop up a message on administrative consoles. Figure 4.3 shows the Performance Monitor configured to detect intrusion attempts. The following section gives a step-by-step explanation of how to configure the Performance Monitor in this way.

FIGURE 4.3

Using the Performance Monitor to detect intrusion attempts

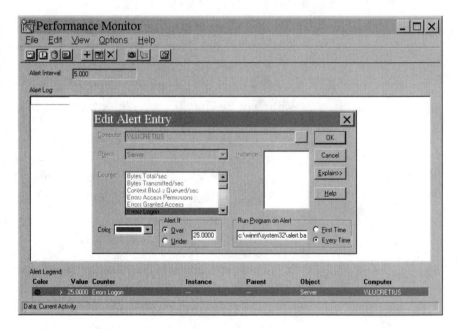

Configuring the Performance Monitor to Detect Intrusion

To configure the Performance Monitor to detect intrusion attempts, follow these steps:

1. Open the Performance Monitor.

2. Select View ➤ Alert, and then select Options ➤ Alert.

3. Check Switch to Alert View, and then check Log Event in Application Log.

4. Check Send Network Message.

5. Enter **Administrator** (or your normal logon name) in the network name input box.

6. Enter 300 in the Periodic Update input box. (Alerts more frequent than every five minutes can become quite cumbersome). Click OK.

7. In the Alert view, select Edit ➤ Add to Alert.

8. Select Server in the object pick list.

9. Select Errors Logon in the Counter pick box.

10. Enter 25 in the Alert If Over input box.

11. Enter **C:\winnt\system32\Alert.bat** (or any other program you desire) in the Run Program on Alert input box.

12. Select First Time in the Run Program on Alert input box. Use First Time for cumulative counters like logon errors and Every Time for momentary counters.

When the Performance Monitor indicates that 25 failed logon attempts have occurred, it will send a message to your logon account name and launch the `alert.bat` command file, which you can use to run any alerting program, including software that will page you directly. Figure 4.4 shows the network alert sent by the Performance Monitor when an automated logon attempt is detected.

You must leave the Performance Monitor running if you want to use it as a security monitor. The Performance Monitor cannot detect security events unless it is running.

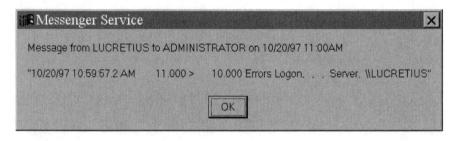

F I G U R E 4.4

The Performance
Monitor has detected
excessive logons.

Third-Party Security Tools

Third-party security tools go further than the utilities provided by Windows NT to secure your network because they are specifically designed for that purpose. These tools usually take one of two forms: security analysis tools and security monitors. Try out the demonstration editions provided on the companion CD-ROM.

NT Security Analysis Tools

A number of third-party security analysis tools exist which test Windows NT servers for various known security loopholes. Invariably, these tools run a suite of tests based on security loopholes known to have existed earlier; in other words, they break no new ground and won't uncover security vulnerabilities that haven't already been exploited by hackers. But they are very valuable for simply documenting the security status of servers and for making certain you've closed all the obvious doors. Examples of this sort of software are contained on the companion CD-ROM.

Security Monitoring Software

Security monitors use the performance counters built into Windows NT to look for "hacker-like" activity, such as a high level of network logon attempts, a sudden appearance of a large number of bad packets which may indicate a failed attempt at packet forgery, and so forth. These security monitoring tools usually have very sophisticated methods of alerting security and network administrators, including e-mail and paging, and they may be able to perform some initial investigation into the incident or provide some automatic response, such as automatically rejecting logon attempts from that domain. Examples of this sort of software are contained on the companion CD-ROM.

Visiting Security and Hacking Sites

If you intend to secure your site against intrusion from the Internet, you must keep abreast of developments in security for your software. This is true whether you use Windows NT, NetWare, UNIX, or any other networked system. There is no substitute for studying new reports of flaws in your system software. Hackers and security experts are constantly exposing (and exploiting) new-found security flaws in operating systems and in Internet service software like mail or Web service.

Even if you've locked down your site securely today, new methods and attacks will certainly be developed, which in turn will be patched and plugged by software vendors. This cycle of measure versus countermeasure repeats indefinitely, and will never cease. To date, no software has been "proven" secure scientifically, and due to the complexity of software and the enormity of that task, any software that is provably secure is likely to be obsolete before its release.

Current software development practices simply do not support provably secure software development because the time required to prove software secure would make it obsolete before it reached the market. For example, to prove that Windows NT Server is secure would probably take Microsoft about four times the effort that it took to create it, meaning it would reach the market in about 20 years.

How do you stay on top of security developments? Traditional media such as newspapers and books (like this one) take far too long to publish to claim any sort of immediacy in the area of security developments. The Internet itself is by far the best source of security news and developments because its time to publication is mere hours rather than weeks. It is also easier to search than printed matter. Finally, hackers use the Internet themselves to trade security information, and you can infiltrate their sites and societies to obtain this same information.

Web Sites and Security Information

Web sites are the best source of edited, timely information about hacking and Windows NT security. In sum, these sites represent nearly all that is known about Windows NT security, TCP/IP security, and network security in general. There are three different types of security Web sites maintained by three distinct groups: operating system vendors, security software vendors, and hackers. Each of these represents a different perspective and a different motivation in the publication of security-related material.

Operating System Vendors

As the creators of network operating systems and security software, vendors generally keep abreast of security issues regarding their software; however, they are generally not the first to know about new issues, and they tend to whitewash the seriousness of security issues in their press releases. They will usually post patches to fix blatant security problems as soon as they possibly can.

As the vendor of Windows NT, Microsoft responds to security breaches in a few different ways. In many cases, they claim the breach isn't serious because Windows NT can be configured to deal with it, even though the automatic security settings set by default when you Install Windows NT don't deal with it.

For serious breaches, Microsoft generally releases a "hot fix," which is beta-quality code designed to plug a specific hole. You should avoid using hot fixes unless you perceive an immediate danger to your site, because hot fix code has not been properly validated and may crash your servers. Finally, Microsoft periodically releases service packs, which are a series of bug and security fixes for problems that have been identified and resolved since the last service pack. A list of Windows NT vendor Web sites is presented in Appendix C.

Security Software Vendors

Security software vendors write software to secure Windows NT. Their Web sites generally have white papers about security and downloadable demos of software used to improve the security of your network. Security software vendors tend to make a big deal about any security flaw—no matter how slight—as soon as they find out about it, because it represents an opportunity for them to sell software. A list of security vendors' Web sites is also presented in Appendix C.

Hackers

Hackers maintain Web sites to trade information, to express their opinions, to rant against the state of the software industry, and to brag about their hacking accomplishments. As such, the sites are generally light on information and heavy on attitude. In addition, you can usually count on hackers to use vulgar language and to attack people or organizations they feel have wronged them or hackerdom in general. On the up side, however, these sights are where security loopholes break first, and where attack tools to break into Internet sites are posted. Many hackers are somewhat altruistic in nature and publish information specifically to help administrators secure their networks against intrusion. A list of Web sites frequented by hackers is presented in Appendix C.

Newsgroups

Newsgroups are a reasonably good source of breaking news about Windows NT and security in general. However, they are time sensitive in nature and news messages are only available for a limited time, so they require real dedication to keep on top of. Also, newsgroups are usually unarbitrated, so idiots can and do post. About 80 percent of all traffic on newsgroups these days seems to consist of new users pleading for help or information on a relatively simple topic they could just buy a book about, or rants and raves from subscribers to the list about the topic of the day.

For most security administrators, there simply isn't enough time in the day to stay on top of and filter through the volume of traffic presented by newsgroups.

Mailing Lists

Mailing lists are probably the most convenient way to stay on top of breaking security news. Once you subscribe, they come to you automatically. They are edited by real security experts, so there's very little to filter through.

Policies: Security Administration

- Make a list of Web sites maintained by software vendors for each software package you run on your servers.

- Visit Web sites of software vendors at least once a month. Search on security topics if there is no specific security discussion.

- Subscribe to newsgroups related to security and your specific software. Check them at least monthly.

Start Over

The cyclical nature of security cannot be stressed enough (take a look back at Figure 4.1). Unlike a vault, which is static through time and suffers from only a few well-known vulnerabilities, computer networks are not static—they change constantly. Every new addition, be it software or hardware, must be evaluated in the context of security to determine if it will add a new vulnerability to the system.

The methods used by hackers to gain access to a system must be continually researched, and system software must be updated as new security fixes are released. Network security is like walking on a treadmill—you have to keep moving just to stay in place. As time goes by, new vectors of attack will be discovered and your network will become less secure even if no changes are made to it.

Policies: Changing Network Configurations

■ Evaluate every new piece of software and every new type of hardware device attached to your network for potential security vulnerabilities.

■ Provide periodic security training for new and established employees alike. Even if you don't have any new information, a periodic refresher keeps users aware of security problems.

Summary

Security administration is the continual process of identifying vulnerabilities and securing them against exploitation. The folowing make up the cycle of security administration:

1. **Identify potential vulnerabilities:** All software and hardware systems that provide a communication channel with the outside world are potential vulnerabilities.

2. **Evaluate vulnerabilities to determine how they can be effectively nullified:** This will give you a list of candidate countermeasures.

3. **Evaluate each countermeasure to determine which measures should employed:** Some countermeasures have a more drastic effect on productivity than others. Use those countermeasures that are both effective and have the least impact on productivity.

4. **Deploy measures:** Deployment may be simple or it may be difficult, depending upon how centrally controlled the measure is.

5. **Test measures for effectiveness by simulating an attack:** Use the same methods used by hackers.

6. **Check monitors, logs, and border systems for evidence of security breaches:** There's usually no other way to tell if your security has been compromised.

7. **Explore any indications of a breach to determine the breach progression and identify new potential vulnerabilities:** When security fails, the failure exposes a new vector that can then be secured against.

8. **Check public security sources for news of newly discovered security vulnerabilities:** Stay abreast of security news and issues for all the software and hardware in your system.

9. **Start over:** Security administration is a perpetual cycle since security diminishes with time in a dynamic system.

Network security is like walking on a treadmill—you have to keep moving just to stay in place.

CHAPTER

5

The Windows NT Security Model

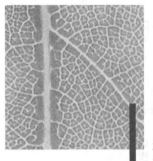

I f you want to keep a building secure you need to know what kinds of locks are where, which of the people who use the building have keys to those locks, and what other security mechanisms (motion detectors, timed or electronic locks, and so forth) are in place. Similarly, if you want to keep your network secure you need to know how your network operating system implements security.

With the knowledge of Windows NT security details you've already gained, you won't be surprised by some of the quirks of NT security. When you discover (or hear about) security loopholes you'll understand what is being exploited to create the loophole, and you'll be able to implement an effective counter to it. You can create a secure network environment that still allows network users to easily access the network.

The purpose of this chapter is not to give you specific instructions on how to arrange the security in your network; instead, its purpose is to describe how security works in your network so that you can make the best use of the information in the rest of this book.

This chapter will explore Windows NT security piece by piece, as follows:

- Computer security requirements

- Accounts

- Logging on

- Objects and permissions

- Security reference monitor

- Rights versus permissions

Computer Security Requirements

The object of computer security, like any other kind of security, is to control who has access to what. The *who* in the case of computer security are network users to whom you wish to give access, and everyone else to whom you wish to restrict access. The *what* that you want to control access to are the resources on your network, including files, directories, printers, tape backup units, and so on.

It's the job of the operating system to control user access to resources. A computer operating system that has good security mechanisms does the following:

- Keeps track of individual users with an account name and password for each

- Allows you to keep track of security by creating groups of users

- Applies the security granted to the user to all of the programs that the user runs

- Relaxes or restricts what the user may access depending on the location or mode of access of the user (such as logging on interactively or over the Internet)

- Keeps track of the owners of files and directories

- Allows users to control who may access files and other resources belonging to them

- Differentiates the types of accesses allowed to a file or other object (Read, Delete, and so on)

- Establishes operations that may be performed by the user on the operating system as a whole (rather than individual objects such as files and printers)

- Has an extensible security system that can be used over a network as well as locally

Operating systems differ on which of the preceding security functions they implement, to what degree, and how. DOS, for example, has none of the functions in this list. Windows 95 allows you to specify a logon password and allows you to password-restrict shares, but otherwise provides very little security. Most versions of UNIX do almost all of the above (managing intracomputer security in a UNIX network is not always seamless, however). Windows NT provides all of the above functionality, and more.

Computer security is based on keeping track of computer users, as described in the next section.

Managing User Accounts

Security in a Windows NT network starts with the user accounts. When you log on to a Windows NT or Windows 95 computer you are confronted with a logon prompt, where you must supply a user name and a password. The purpose of the logon prompt is so the computer can identify you and give you access to things you should be able to use (such as the files in your home directory) and deny you access to things you shouldn't (such as the files in the home directory of your boss). The logon prompt is the gatekeeper to your Windows NT computer (see Figure 5.1).

In Windows 95 the default configuration allows the user to disregard the logon prompt, but if the user does so they will not be able to access Windows NT domain resources. You can make logging on to the domain mandatory by establishing a computer system policy for that computer (see Chapter 7).

FIGURE 5.1

The logon prompt identifies you to the computer and protects your network from unauthorized access.

Chapter 6 shows you how to work with user and group accounts. This chapter describes accounts only to the degree necessary for you to see their role in the Windows NT security mechanisms.

Every user should have an individual account that is only for that user. Accounts are easy to set up and manage, and you can assign permissions for resources to groups of users. Even when a group of people do the same thing (such as data entry), you should give each person their own account. This is so that when one user violates security you can track the violation back to the user rather than just to a group of people who use the same account.

You can create group accounts (see Chapter 6) for groups of users that need the same access permissions. For example, you may create a group for everyone in the sales department of your company and then give that group access to the Sales Projections and Prospective Clients directories. This way everyone that is a member of that group will have access to the directories, and you can assign the sales department's permissions a new account just by adding the account to the group. You can add new permissions (or remove existing permissions) for everyone in the group by adding (or removing) the permissions for the group account.

There are user accounts and group accounts which are only valid for a single Windows NT computer (these are called local user and group accounts), and there are also user and group accounts that are valid for all the Windows NT computers that are participating in a Windows NT domain (these are called global or domain user and group accounts). Local user and group accounts are maintained by the computer for which they are valid; each Windows NT computer has its own list of local user and group accounts.

Terminology

- **Group account:** A record, maintained by Windows NT, of user accounts that are assigned access permissions as a group.

- **Global account:** A user or group account that is defined on the Windows NT Server Primary Domain Controller and may be used from all computers that are participating in the Windows NT domain.

- **Local account:** A user or group account that only exists on the local Windows NT computer.

- **User account:** A security record maintained by Windows NT that records your user name, password, logon permissions, home directory, and other information pertaining to your individual use of the computer and the network.

The Windows NT computer need go no further than its own data structures to resolve security questions concerning local users and groups. Global user and group accounts are maintained by the Primary Domain Controller (PDC) and are backed up by the Backup Domain Controller (BDC); so a domain security question is resolved by referring to data maintained by the PDC or BDC.

Fortunately, accesses involving domain accounts do not always require mediation by the PDC because of the way Windows NT keeps track of security permissions, as you will see in the following sections.

Logging On to Windows NT

There are two ways to access a Windows NT account: directly from the Windows NT console or over the network from another computer (Windows NT, Windows 95, OS/2, MacOS, or DOS can all be network clients to a Windows NT computer). In either case, you'll provide a user name and password. If you have logged on interactively (say, from the Windows NT console) the Windows NT computer will perform object accesses (directory reading, file opening, printer writing, and so on) directly.

If the user has logged on to the Windows NT computer over a network from the client computer, the Windows NT computer will perform the object accesses on behalf of the client computer. Even in the case of remote access, it is the Windows NT computer containing the resource (file, printer, or directory) that will check to see if the user has permission to perform the operation, and will disallow the operation if the user does not have permission to access the resource. This way client computers that don't have elaborate security mechanisms, such as Windows 95, the MacOS, or DOS, can still benefit from Windows NT security.

The user account is contained in a database on the Windows NT computer (either the local computer, if it is a local account, or the PDC, if it is a domain account). In addition to the information that you can view using the User Manager program (the user name, the password settings, the full name, the description, and many more settings described in Chapter 6), the account contains some information that you cannot directly see such as the access token which is the information primarily used to keep Windows NT secure.

When the WinLogon process (which logs you on and sets up your computing environment for you) needs to refer to the security database it communicates with the Security Accounts Manager (SAM), which is the Windows NT operating system component that controls the account information. If the information is stored locally on the Windows NT computer, the SAM will refer to the database and return the information to the WinLogon process. If the information is not stored locally (for example, it pertains to a domain account) SAM will query the PDC (or a BDC if the PDC is busy or down) and then return the information to the WinLogon process.

Understanding Security Identifiers

One important piece of information contained in the user account database is the user's Security Identifier, or SID. The SID uniquely identifies the user account to the operating system. When you create an account using the User Manager program, a new SID is always created. This is true even if you use the same account name and password as an account that has existed before (but that you must have deleted, because Windows NT won't let you create two accounts with the same name). The SID will remain with the account for as long as the account exists. You may change any other aspect of the account, including the user name and password, but you cannot change the SID, because to Windows NT the SID *is* the account. You can imagine the SID as your key for locks that are set to open when your account accesses them.

A group accounts also has a SID, which is a unique identifier that is created when the group is created. You can make any change to a group except changing the SID, because to Windows NT, the SID identifies the group. The only way to get a new group SID is to create a new group. You can imagine the group SID as the key for locks that are set to open when any member of the group accesses them.

When you log on to the computer (either directly from the console or remotely over the network) you are communicating with the WinLogon process. The purpose of the process is to check your user name and password to see if you should be allowed to access the network. If the account is valid and the password is correct, the WinLogon process will create an access token for you (see Figure 5.2). The access token contains your Security ID and all of the Security IDs of the groups that your user account is a member of. (It also contains a Locally Unique

Identifier, or LUID, which will be described in the section on *Rights versus Permissions*). You can imagine the access token as the key ring containing your personal key (your SID) and all the group keys (group SIDs) you can use.

FIGURE 5.2

The WinLogon process queries the Security and Accounts Manager in order to create an access token for you.

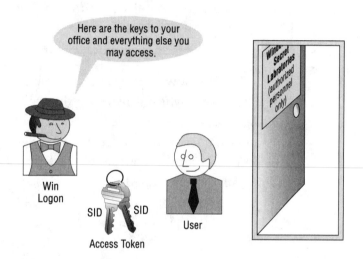

An access token is created each time you log on to Windows NT. This is why you must log off and then log back on again after making changes to your user account—you need a new access token that will reflect the changes you have made.

There are some special Security Identifiers that are automatically placed in access tokens by the WinLogon process. These SIDs represent the special groups of Windows NT. Every access token receives the Everyone special group SID. Access tokens for users that log on via the Windows NT console get the SID for the Interactive special group, while access tokens for users that log on via the network get the Network SID.

> ## Terminology
>
> - **Access token:** The combined Security Identifiers for a user account and the group accounts that the user is a member of, along with the LUID for the user.
>
> - **Security Identifier (SID):** A unique identification number for a user or group account.

The Windows NT Service Pack 3 created a new SID for Authenticated Users, which is placed in the access token when you successfully log on. A special SID called the SECURITY_LOGON_IDS_RID is created and included in your access token each time you log on. This SID is only valid for the duration of one logon session and makes sure that certain objects created in one logon session cannot be accessed from other sessions.

One SID that will be placed in a user's access token only in unusual circumstances is the System SID. This is an SID that Windows NT system services (such as the scheduler service) have, and which give these system services permission to do things that a regular user account (even the Administrator account) cannot do. Operating system services are started by the Windows NT Kernel, not the WinLogon process, and they receive the System SID from the kernel when they are started.

The Authenticated Users SID closes a security loophole that predated Service Pack 3. That loophole was called the "Red Button" security breach, and it allowed any user (authenticated or not) to access portions of the Windows NT registry. Make sure you have the latest version of the Windows NT Service Pack installed to close this and other security holes. Refer to Appendix B for information on how to find this and other software resources on the Internet.

Processes and User Logon

Logging on (typing in a user name and password) identifies the user to the computer, and security identifiers specify what the user can and can't do, but it is the computer programs the user runs that actually do all the work for the user in the operating system.

The user doesn't personally reach into the file system and manipulate files; it is a program that performs these operations for the user. A program, though, is a static thing—it is just a set of instructions for the computer to execute, like a theater script is a set of lines and directions for actors to perform. A program that is being executed is called a *process*, and it is a dynamic and changing thing that occurs over a period of time, much as a script that is being performed is a play.

In a play, different actors may play a single part on different days and a different director may direct them from the same script, leading to entirely different performances. Similarly, different users on different computers may cause a program to be executed, leading to different results (because one user might have access to different files than another).

Terminology

- **Process:** An executing program.

- **Program:** Instructions that the computer performs to accomplish a task.

- **WinLogon process:** The process that presents the logon window to the user, and that coordinates the logon authentication and the user's logon process creation.

Since processes perform actions on the behalf of the users (you can think of them as your agents that go and do things for you in the computer). The processes must be given the same permissions to access things that are stored in the user accounts. Processes also have to come from somewhere, and another function of the WinLogon process is to ask the Win32 subsystem of Windows NT to create your logon process (the first process you get when you log on) for you.

The access token created by the WinLogon process, from the account SID and various group SIDs, is given to the logon process belonging to the user account. When a process attempts to access an object on the user's behalf (you'll learn more about objects in the next section), the operating system checks the SIDs attached to the process to see if the process belongs to a user or group that has permission to access the object.

One nice benefit of how Windows NT associates the access token with the processes is that, after you log on and the WinLogon process creates the access token, the Windows NT computer doesn't have to access the SAM database to check your security permissions—it already has a list of SIDs. In comparison, if it did not have the SIDs and you were using a domain account, every file read or write operation would require negotiation over the network with the Primary Domain Controller, which would slow down your computer tremendously.

Inheriting Access Tokens

Another feature of Windows NT is that you can have many processes running at the same time on the Windows NT computer, each one performing a different function for you. If you log on to the Windows NT computer directly, you can have one process running a word-processor program, another downloading files off the Internet, and a third keeping you entertained with a solitaire program. One of the things a process can do is start other processes, and this is exactly what the logon process does when you use your computer. The logon process starts the other processes that you use (when you log on to the Windows NT computer directly), including the Desktop Explorer process, which you can use to start even more processes, such as your spreadsheet, word processor, or Web browser.

When you log on to a Windows NT computer over the network, the access token generated by the WinLogon process on the server is not sent back to your client computer. Instead the access token goes to the Server service on the Windows NT computer, which maintains a connection to your client computer and performs the actions on the server (opening files, writing data, printing documents, and so on) for the client computer. Since the access token never leaves the Windows NT computer, there is no chance it will be intercepted on your LAN, and it cannot be modified by a malicious program on an insecure operating system such as Windows 95.

When a process starts another process, the Win32 subsystem (which is responsible for creating new processes, among other various and sundry operating system functions) gives the new process a copy of the access token of the old process (see Figure 5.3). This way the new process will have the same permission to access resources as its parent process did. All of your processes then inherit the permissions that are established for you when you log on to Windows NT.

The Win32 subsystem doesn't actually create the new processes (the Windows NT operating system kernel does that), but it is the interface for 32-bit Windows processes to all operating system functions, including process creation.

Logging On and Security

The process Windows NT goes through to log a user on is lengthy, but each step is necessary to create an environment that is secure and in which the user can still perform useful work. A computer that is turned off, after all, is very secure, and a computer without a network connection is very secure from network attacks. If you want to be able to run programs on the computer, and you want to be able to access network

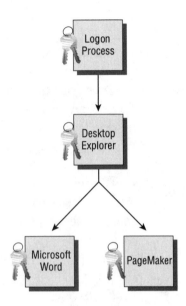

resources, Windows NT must log you on to that computer and onto the network. The steps that Windows NT goes through to log a user on are a little different if you are logging on to the Windows NT computer over the network. The steps for logging on directly are as follows:

1. The user presses Ctrl+Alt+Del, which causes a hardware interrupt that is captured by the operating system. The operating system activates the WinLogon process.

2. The WinLogon process presents the user with the account name and password logon prompt.

3. The WinLogon process sends the account name and encrypted password to the Local Security Authority. If the user account is local to that Windows NT computer, the LSA queries the Security and Accounts Manager of the local Windows NT computer. Otherwise the LSA establishes a secure channel via the NetLogon service and then queries the SAM of the Primary Domain Controller or

Backup Domain Controller (if it is a global account) to authenticate the logon request.

4. If the user has presented a valid user name and password, the LSA creates an access token containing the user account SID and the group SIDs for the groups that the user is a member of. The access token also gets a Locally Unique Identifier, or LUID, (which is described later in this chapter in *Rights versus Permissions*). The access token is then passed back to the WinLogon process.

5. The WinLogon process passes the access token to the Win32 subsystem along with a request to create a logon process for the user.

6. The logon process establishes the user environment, including starting the Desktop Explorer and displaying the backdrop and Desktop icons.

If you are logging on to a Windows NT computer (presumably a server) over the network, the following steps will occur:

1. The user enters the user name and password into the logon window of the network client software.

2. The network client software opens a NetBIOS connection to the NetLogon service on the server.

3. The network client software encrypts the password and sends the logon credentials to the WinLogon process on the server.

4. The WinLogon process on the server sends the account name and encrypted password to the Local Security Authority. If the user account is local to that Windows NT computer, the LSA queries the Security and Accounts Manager of the local Windows NT computer. Otherwise the LSA establishes a secure channel via the NetLogon service and then queries the SAM of the Primary Domain Controller or Backup Domain Controller (if it is a global account) to authenticate the logon request.

5. If the user has presented a valid user name and password, the LSA creates an access token containing the user account SID and the group SIDs for the groups that the user is a member of. The access token also gets a Locally Unique Identifier, or LUID (which is described later in this chapter in *Rights versus Permissions*). The access token is then passed back to the WinLogon process.

6. The WinLogon process passes the access token to the Server service of Windows NT, which associates the access token with the NetBIOS connection opened by the client computer.

Any further actions (file reads, print requests, and so on) that are sent over that NetBIOS connection are performed on the server with the credentials established by that access token.

Unlocking the Meaning of Objects and Permissions

Users have access tokens that identify them and the groups they belong to. In order for Windows NT to enforce security for these users, there need to be some rules about what resources each user may access in the computer. That's what this section is about—objects (the resources) and permissions (the rules). The two previous sections about accounts and logging on showed you how Windows NT establishes your user identity and associates that identity (including which groups your account is a member of into a Security Identifier) with the programs you run (the processes).

In the physical world, keys unlock things that you want to protect, such as a filing cabinet containing confidential papers. In the computer world, SIDs are the keys. In a computer you want to protect files, directories, printers, and other resources that might be altered, destroyed, consumed unfairly or inappropriately, or that might contain information that you don't want made public. The locks that protect these resources in the Windows NT operating system are called *objects*, and they prevent access, just like the lock on a filing cabinet.

In the strange world of Microsoft terminology, an object is both a resource and the lock that protects that resource. This is because security is built into every Windows NT resource.

These objects are much more sophisticated than the physical locks that you may be used to, however. As you'll see shortly, Windows NT associates an object with just about anything you can think of, but file and directory objects are the objects that network administrators are most concerned with. Objects in Windows NT include (but are not limited to):

- Directories
- Symbolic links
- Printers
- Processes
- Network shares

- Ports
- Devices
- Windows
- Files
- Threads

Processes, which contain access tokens and manipulate objects, are also themselves objects. This is because processes can manipulate other processes by starting them, stopping them, increasing or decreasing their priority, and so on. Processes belonging to one user must be protected from other users' processes, so processes are objects, too.

Services: What Objects Do

There are many things a process (your agent in the computer, remember?) can do to a file if it has *permission*. It can read the file, write to it, or delete it. The things a process can do with an object are called the object's *services*. For example, for a file they include the following:

- Open
- Clos
- Read
- Write
- Delete

- Change
- Take ownership
- Change permissions
- No Access
- Full Control

These operations should be familiar to you because they are the Windows NT File System permissions that you can set on files and directories in an NTFS volume. Different kinds of objects often have different services. The services associated with a printer object, for example, are as follows:

- Print

- Manage documents

- No access

- Full control

There are two permissions which are associated with all objects, regardless of type: *No Access*, which is described later in this chapter, and *Full Control*, which grants the user the ability to use any of the object's services.

The object also contains other information about itself, including its name (the file name in the case of a file object, or the printer name in the case of a printer object), the object data (the contents of the file if it is a file), and an access control list that describes the users and groups that may use the object's services. Figure 5.4 illustrates a file object's type, services (permissions), and attributes.

F I G U R E 5.4

A file object has a type, services, and attributes.

Storing Security Information

The security information for an object is contained in the object's Security Descriptor. The Security Descriptor has four parts: Owner, Group, Discretionary Access Control List, and System Access Control List. See Figure 5.5 for an illustration of a Security Descriptor. Windows NT uses these parts of the Security Descriptor for the following purposes:

- **Owner:** This part contains the SID of the user account that has ownership of the object. The object's owner may always change the settings in the Discretionary Access Control List (the permissions) of the object.

- **Group:** This part is used by the POSIX subsystem of Windows NT. Files and directories in UNIX operating systems can belong to a group as well as to an individual user account. This part contains the SID of the group of this object for the purposes of POSIX compatibility. This field is not used by Windows NT for any other purpose.

- **Discretionary Access Control List:** The DACL contains a list of user accounts and group accounts that have permission to access the object's services. The DACL has as many Access Control Entries as there are user or group accounts that have specifically given access to the object.

- **System Access Control List:** The SACL also contains Access Control Entries, but these ACEs are used for auditing rather than for permitting or denying access to the object's services. The SACL has as many ACEs as there are user or group accounts that are specifically being audited.

FIGURE 5.5

The Security Descriptor contains the object's Owner, Group, Discretionary Access Control List, and Security Access Control List.

Security Descriptor
Owner SID
Group SID
DACL:
ACE
ACE
SACL:
ACE
ACE

Each Access Control Entry in the Discretionary Access Control List and System Access Control List consists of a Security Identifier followed by an access mask. The access mask in the DACL identifies those services of the object which the SID has permission to access (that's why those services are commonly called permissions.) There is also a special type of ACE called a *deny ACE*. This type of ACE indicates that all access to the object will be denied to the account identified by the SID. The deny ACE comes before all other ACEs, and the deny ACE is how Windows NT implements the No Access permission.

The permissions in the DACL for the user account and for the group accounts are cumulative. This is an important feature. Let's say, for example, that an object has an ACE granting the user account SID read permission, an ACE granting a group SID write permission, and an ACE granting another group SID change ownership permission. Let's also assume that those two group SIDs are in the access token with the user account SID. Then processes that have that access token may read from, write to, and change ownership of that object.

There is one exception to the cumulative rule: If there is a Deny ACE permission (representing the No Access permission) in the object with an SID that also exists in the access token, no access to the object will be permitted to the process with that access token.

One way to think of the DACL is as a chain of locks, each of which is opened by a specific SID. When you open a lock with an SID you can perform the operations that the access mask allows. Each access control entry that matches an SID allows the account represented by that SID to perform the function indicated by the access mask of the access control entry (see Figure 5.6).

FIGURE 5.6

Opening a lock with an SID

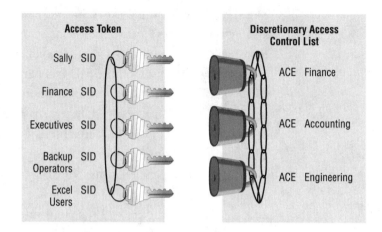

The Access Control Entries in the SACL are formed the same way as the ACEs in the DACL (they are composed of a SID and an access mask) but the access mask in this case identifies those services of the object for which the account will be audited.

Not every object has a DACL or an SACL. The FAT file system, for example, does not record security information, so file and directory objects stored on a FAT volume lack DACLs and SACLs. When a DACL is missing, any user account may access any of the object's services. This is not the same as when an object has an empty DACL; in that case, no account may access the object. When there is no SACL for an object, that object may not be audited.

Enforcing the Rules: The Security Reference Monitor

The access tokens and the access control lists are the "rules" by which processes may access objects. How are those rules enforced? That's the role of the *Security Reference Monitor*—it's the watchdog of the Windows NT operating system.

Terminology

- **Access mask:** Identifies the services of the object which the account identified by the SID of the Access Control Entry may access.

- **Discretionary Access Control List (DACL):** Lists services that users are permitted to access.

- **Object:** A Windows NT resource that may be shared and which has a list of services that user accounts may be permitted or denied access to.

- **Permissions:** The object services that a user or group account may access.

- **Security Descriptor:** The portion of the object containing the Owner, Group, and Access Control List information.

- **System Access Control List (SACL):** Lists services for which user access will be audited.

Your processes do not access objects such as files, directories, or printers directly. The Windows NT operating system (specifically, the Win32 portion of it) accesses the objects on the behalf of your processes. The primary reason for this is to make programs simpler—the program doesn't have to know how to directly manipulate every kind of object, it can just ask the operating system to do it. Another important benefit, especially from the security point of view, is that since the operating system is performing the operations for the process, the operating system can enforce object security.

When a process asks the Win32 subsystem to perform an operation on an object (such as reading a file), the Win32 subsystem checks with the Security Reference Monitor to make sure that the process has permission to perform the operation on the object. The Security Reference Monitor compares the access token of the process with the Discretionary Access Control List of the object.

Terminology

- **Security Reference Monitor (SRM):** The portion of the Windows NT operating system that checks each object access made by a process to ensure that that access is allowed in the object's DACL. It initiates an audit event if that access is being audited in the object's SACL.

The Security Reference Monitor compares the access token with the DACL by checking each SID in the access token (the SID of the user account as well as the SIDs of all of the groups that the account is a member of) against the SIDs in the DACL. If there is an ACE (access control entry) with a matching SID that contains an access mask that allows the operation, and there is no ACE with a matching SID that denies all access to the object, then the Security Reference Monitor will allow the Win32 subsystem to perform the operation.

At the same time the Security Reference Monitor is checking permissions it also checks to see if that object access is being audited and should be reported in the Windows NT security and event log. It checks for auditing the same way it checks for permissions—by comparing each SID in the access token with each access control entry's SID. If it finds a match it checks to see if the operation (or service) being performed is one of those services indicated in the access mask. If it is, and the result of the security check against the DACL matches the kind of auditing being performed (the access failed and failure is being audited, or the access succeeded and the success is being audited, or both) then the audit event is written to the event log.

See Figure 5.7 for a view of how a process accesses an object.

File and object accesses will only be audited if you enable file and object auditing in the User Manager or User Manager for Domains program.

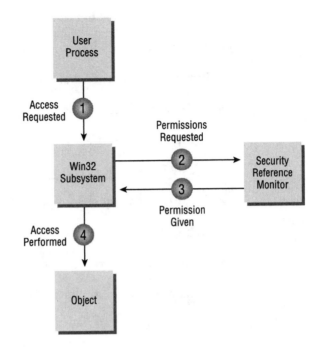

FIGURE 5.7

The Win32 subsystem performs object accesses for processes, and the Security Reference Monitor informs the Win32 subsystem whether an access may be performed.

Rights versus Permissions

As you learned earlier, the object services that a user or group account may access are called permissions. However, there are a number of things that a user may want to do that do not apply to any specific object, but instead apply to a group of objects or to the operating system as a whole. An example is shutting down the operating system—that's an operation that affects every object in the system! Operations of this nature require the user to have user rights to perform the operation. Some user rights are as follows:

- Access this computer from network

- Act as a part of the operating system*

- Add workstations to domain

- Back up files and directories

- Bypass traverse checking*

- Change the system time

- Create a pagefile*

- Create a token object*

- Create permanent shared objects*

- Debug programs*

- Force shutdown from a remote system

- Generate security audits*

- Increase quotas*

- Increase scheduling priorities*

- Load and unload device drivers

- Lock pages in memory*

- Log on as batch job*

- Log on as a service*

- Log on locally

- Manage auditing and security log

- Modify firmware environment values*

- Profile single process*

- Profile system performance*

- Replace a process-level token*

- Restore files and directories

- Shut down the system

- Take ownership of files or other objects

The items marked with an asterisk (*) in the preceding list are advanced user rights. You seldom have reason to change how Windows NT assigns these user rights.

The section about logging on earlier in this chapter mentioned that the Local Security Authority includes a Locally Unique Identifier when it creates an access token. The LUID describes which of the user rights that particular user account has. The LUID is created by the Local Security Authority from security information in the Security and Accounts Manager database. The SAM database keeps track of which users and which groups have which rights.

The LUID is a combination of the rights of that specific user account along with the rights of all of the groups that the account is a member of. For example, the account BOB has the Add Workstations to Domain right for a Windows NT Server computer and is also a member of the Backup Operators group, which has the Back Up Files and Directories right as well as the Restore Files and Directories right. Bob may both add workstations to the domain as well as back up and restore files on that computer.

Rights take precedence over permissions. That's why the Administrator account can take ownership of a file to which the owner of the file has given the No Access to Everyone permission: The Administrator has the Take Ownership of Files or Other Objects right. The Windows NT operating system checks the user rights first, and then (if there is no user right specifically allowing the operation) the operating system checks the ACEs stored in the DACL against the SIDs in the access token.

One right that a user account has (even in the case of a No Access permission) is to read or write to an object that the user account owns. A user account may also change the permissions to an object that is owned by that user account.

Summary

The security model used by Windows NT borrows the best security concepts and mechanisms of other, older operating systems, especially the VMS operating system developed by Digital. As with VMS, objects are protected by access control lists, accounts have tokens and group membership, and a central security mechanism ensures that permissions are not violated. Windows NT neatly integrates these security features into its domain networking environment, giving users the ability to log on to a single Windows NT computer or onto the network as a whole.

Security starts with the logon prompt, which is displayed by the WinLogon process when you press Ctrl+Alt+Del. The account name and password that you enter there is passed to the local security authority, which queries the local Security Accounts Manager if the account is a local one, or which queries a domain controller (via a secure channel created by the NetLogon service) to determine if the log on is valid. If it is valid, the SAM returns security information (SIDs for user identity and group membership, as well as user rights for the LUID) from which the LSA creates an access token. The access token is returned to the WinLogon process, which passes it to the Win32 subsystem with a request that the Win32 subsystem create a logon process for the authenticated user.

The access token is associated with all of the processes controlled by the user. When a process attempts to access an object on the behalf of the user, the Win32 subsystem performs the access for the process. The Win32 subsystem checks with the Security Reference Monitor to make sure that the process is allowed to perform the action.

The Security Reference Monitor checks the Security Identifiers in the access token against the access control entries in the Discretionary Access Control List. If there are no No Access ACEs found for the access token's SIDs and there are ACEs with SIDs that match those in the access token and that have access masks that allow the requested operations, then the access to the object is allowed to proceed. So long as the No Access permissions are absent for the access token, ACE permissions for the user account and for groups of which the account is a member are combined.

Some user accounts and group accounts have rights that supersede the permissions recorded in objects. These rights may affect the operation of the operating system as a whole, or they may affect operations on groups or classes of objects. User rights take precedence, even over the No Access permission. All user accounts have the right to read from, write to, or change the permissions of objects that have their SID in the owner field of the object's security descriptor.

CHAPTER

6

User Accounts

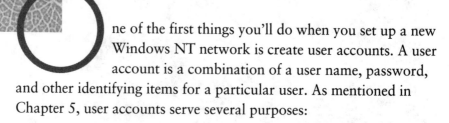

ne of the first things you'll do when you set up a new Windows NT network is create user accounts. A user account is a combination of a user name, password, and other identifying items for a particular user. As mentioned in Chapter 5, user accounts serve several purposes:

- As a first defense against network intrusion. Hopefully, users who have no right to access the network have not been assigned a password.

- To uniquely identify each user. You can then assign file system and other rights to specific users or groups of users.

- To provide an audit trail—the user name can be used in auditing, as well as to stamp files created or modified by the user.

Creating new user accounts is a simple process, but there are many potential security holes that you can inadvertently fall into. In this chapter we'll start with a review of the process of creating user accounts, then move on to specific properties and policies you should use to avoid these pitfalls.

This chapter covers security issues associated with user accounts under Windows NT. Many of the security risks of user accounts relate to the users themselves. See Chapter 2 for more details about those types of security problems.

User Account Basics

In this section, we'll take a look at the basics of user accounts. We'll start with an introduction to the logon process, then consider the settings you can use when creating a new account. We'll also look at policies you can use to make user accounts more secure.

Mandatory Logon

The foundation of Windows NT security is the mandatory logon. Unlike some networking systems, there is no way to do anything in Windows NT without a user account name and password. The logon screen is always displayed when a Windows NT machine boots, so even direct access to the server requires a password.

One thing you may have noticed about Windows NT's logon procedure is the message "Press Ctrl+Alt+Del to logon." Since this is a keystroke that traditionally (under DOS and Windows 3.1*x*) causes a warm boot of the machine, many users think a trick is being played on them when they first see this screen.

Although it's not the most user-friendly of keystrokes, there's a very good reason Windows NT requires this step to log in, and it's one of the reasons Windows NT is considered secure. Because the Ctrl+Alt+Del keystroke is handled by the BIOS as a hardware interrupt, there's literally no way to for a clever programmer to make the keystroke do something else without literally rewriting the operating system.

Without this feature, a hacker would be able to write a program that displayed a fake logon screen, collecting passwords from unsuspecting users. However, since the fake screen wouldn't be able to include the Ctrl+Alt+Del keystroke, few users would be fooled.

Creating Accounts

When you create an account for a new user, you can specify a variety of options, many of which are related to security. We'll now take a close look at the process of creating user accounts. You create user accounts using the User Manager for Domains utility, shown in Figure 6.1.

If you are working with Windows NT Workstation, or Windows NT Server configured with a workgroup rather than a domain, you'll use the User Manager utility. It includes many of the same options as User Manager for Domains, but lacks security features that require a domain system.

FIGURE 6.1

User Manager for Domains allows you to create and manage user accounts.

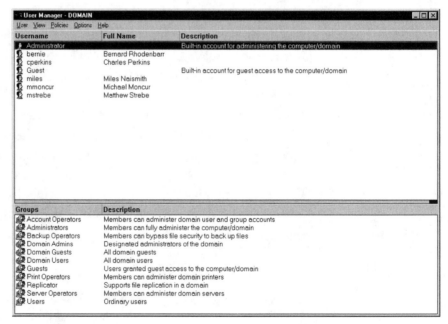

To create a new user, select New User from the User menu. The initial New User dialog box, shown in Figure 6.2, is displayed. In this dialog box you can enter the required information for a new user. In addition, the following options are included:

- **User Must Change Password at Next Logon** provides you with an easy way to allow users to choose their own passwords. You can create the account with no password or a default password; the user is forced to change the password when they log in.

- **User Cannot Change Password** overrides the previous option and prevents the user from changing passwords at all. This is most useful for accounts used by more than one user.

- **Password Never Expires** overrides the normal expiration of passwords, which you can configure with the Account Policy dialog box (explained later in this chapter). This option is a security compromise, and should only be used with select accounts, such as guest accounts with few privileges.

- **Account Disabled** disables the account entirely. This is useful for temporarily disabling the account of a user who is not currently allowed to access the network.

F I G U R E   6.2

Enter the required information to create a new user.

The buttons at the bottom of the New User dialog box are used to display related dialog boxes, which are discussed in the following sections.

Terminology

- **Administrator:** Any user who is able to perform administrative tasks, such as creating or modifying other user accounts. By default, Windows NT includes an account called Administrator with these privileges.

- **Authentication:** The process used by Windows NT to recognize a user and grant privileges based on user account name and password. The authentication process is designed to avoid storing passwords as text or sending them over the network.

- **Hash:** An algorithm that converts a string of text (such as a password) to a number. If the number can be converted back to the original text, it is referred to as a two-way hash. In a one-way hash, such as that used by Windows NT's password authentication process, the number cannot be converted back to text.

Group Memberships

The first thing you'll want to do when assigning a new user is put the user into one or more groups. This is an easy way to give the user the rights they need. For example, if a user will be an administrator, adding them to the Administrators group assigns the necessary rights.

You can assign groups using the Group Memberships dialog box, which is accessed by clicking the Groups button in the New User dialog box. This dialog box is shown in Figure 6.3. To keep the network secure, follow these guidelines when assigning groups to a user:

- Assign as few groups as possible—never make a user a member of a group "just in case."

- It can be tempting to add a user to a group with too many rights. For example, in creating an account for an assistant network administrator, assigning the Administrators group seems like a simple task, but this may include many rights the user shouldn't really have. A more secure approach is to create a group with limited rights and assign the user to that group instead.

- Be sure you're familiar with the file system and administrative rights each group membership includes.

By default, a user is assigned to a single group: Domain Users. In many cases this is sufficient.

FIGURE 6.3

The Group Memberships dialog box allows you to assign a user to groups.

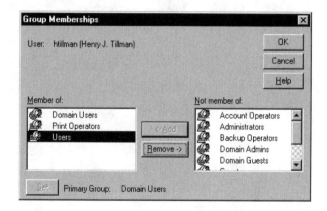

 Groups are often assigned file system rights, and you should be aware of these rights when assigning a user to groups. See Chapter 8 for details about file system rights.

Environment Settings

Clicking on the Profile button in the New User dialog box displays the User Environment Profile dialog box, shown in Figure 6.4. This dialog box allows you to select a profile path, which will be used to store preferences for the user. You can also choose a home directory for the user, and specify a logon script to be executed when the user logs in.

You might think that these settings have little effect on security—and you're right. None of these settings grants any particular rights to the user—in fact, you'll need to give the user file system rights to access the home directory, profile, and logon script.

Restricting Hours

You can limit the hours and days of the week a user is allowed to access the network. The Logon Hours dialog box, shown in Figure 6.5, is displayed when you press the Hours button in the New User dialog box. This dialog box displays a grid consisting of 24 columns, representing the 24 hours in a day, and 7 rows representing the days of the week. Highlight a time period and use the Allow or Disallow buttons to control whether logon is allowed at that time.

FIGURE 6.5

Select the hours the user
is allowed on the system.

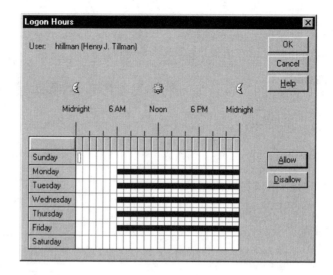

While this is feature can make life difficult for the administrator if overused, it greatly increases the security of user accounts. As an extreme example, if all employees worked during the typical hours of 8:00 am to 6:00 pm, you could restrict all user accounts except Administrator to this time period. This would make things difficult for a hacker—the only time to attack the network would be during business hours, when the administrator is on duty.

Of course, you probably don't need that level of security on your network, and the employees of the company probably don't work schedules that are that strict. Nevertheless, you can usually prevent intruders to some extent with this feature. For example, if the building is always locked between midnight and 6:00 am, it makes sense to disallow most employees access during this time.

Restricting Workstations

The Logon To button in the New User dialog box displays the Logon Workstations dialog box, shown in Figure 6.6. This dialog box allows you to specify a list of workstations the user is allowed to access.

Normally, the User May Log On to All Workstations option is selected, which allows the user to log in anywhere.

FIGURE 6.6

Select the workstations
the user is allowed to
log on to.

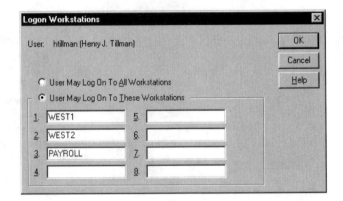

When you select the User May Log On to These Workstations option, you can specify up to eight workstations that the user will be allowed access to. These are the Windows NT computer names shown in Network Neighborhood.

While this is another feature that can lead to administrative nightmares—every time a user needs to log in and happens to be visiting a different location or building, or manning someone else's desk, they'll need your help to log in. However, if your users frequently use the same workstations (or are required to), this option can greatly reduce the risk of an intruder gaining access.

Account Expiration

The Account button in the New User dialog box displays the Account Information dialog box, shown in Figure 6.7. The most important security feature in this dialog box is the Account Expires option. This allows you to enter a date when the account will become disabled. You should specify an expiration date for any account that you consider temporary: temporary employees and guests such as auditors.

F I G U R E   6.7

Select an expiration date
and other options for
the account.

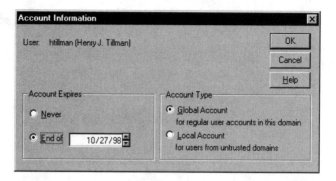

If an account expires and you need to re-enable it, you can simply uncheck the Account Disabled option in the User Properties dialog box and specify a later expiration date, or choose the Never Expires option.

Don't confuse account expiration with password expiration, which we'll discuss later in this chapter. An expired account must be re-enabled by the administrator; an expired password simply means that the user is required to select a new password.

Controlling Dial-Up Access

The final button in the New User dialog box is labeled Dialin, and displays the Dialin Information dialog box, shown in Figure 6.8. This dialog box allows you to grant the user permission to dial into the network remotely (using RAS). You can also specify options for callback, which is an increased security measure because it calls the user back to establish a connection.\

Allowing dial-up access to the network creates many security issues. We've devoted Chapter 12 to these topics.

FIGURE 6.8

Configure the account for
dial-up access.

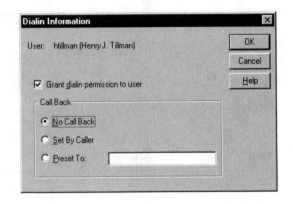

Account Policy

You should now have an idea of the sort of parameters you have control over for each individual user account. In addition, there are a number of features that apply collectively to all user accounts. These are listed in the Account Policy dialog box, which you can access by selecting Policies ➢ Account in User Manager. This dialog box is shown in Figure 6.9.

All of the Account Policy options have to do with security. Your security policy should include all of these items, and you should enforce them with this dialog box. The first set of options are grouped in a box labeled Password Restrictions. Policy guidelines for using these options were given in Chapter 2.

User Rights Policy

Selecting User Rights from the Policies menu in User Manager displays the User Rights Policy dialog box, shown in Figure 6.10. This dialog box allows you to control a number of specific rights, each of which can be assigned to a number of users or groups.

The vast majority of these rights are assigned to the Administrator account by default only, and have little effect on security. The Show Advanced User Rights option enables the display of a larger list of

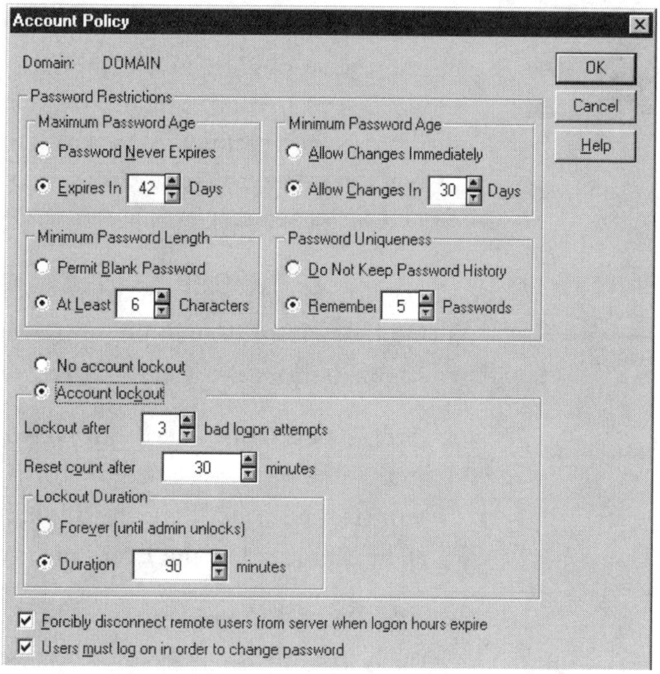

FIGURE 6.9

FIGURE 6.9

The Account Policy dialog box includes a variety of options to make accounts more secure.

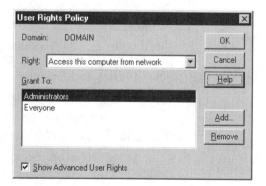

FIGURE 6.10

The User Rights Policy dialog box allows you to assign rights to groups.

rights. While many of these are obscure and only useful to programmers, some deserve the attention of network administrators.

As with other types of rights, it's a good idea to avoid assigning these rights to users directly unless a user has a unique need. Otherwise, it's best to assign rights to a group.

In some situations you may wish to assign rights to the Everyone group, a virtual group that automatically includes all users; be aware that this can be a security risk, since even the Guest account is a member of Everyone. The Everyone Group is explained in the *Plugging Potential Security Holes* section, later in this chapter.

The following are some of the rights you should be aware of in securing the network, including those shown with the Show Advanced User Rights option:

- **Access This Computer from Network** is simply the right to log on to the domain (or the workstation in a nondomain setup) from a workstation other than the domain controller. By default, this right is granted to the Everyone group.

- **Add Workstations to the Domain** allows users to connect previously unknown workstations to the domain. Since the workstation gains access to the domain's list of users and global groups, this can be a security risk. By default, no groups appear in the list for this right; however, it is implicitly granted to members of the Administrators and Account Operators groups.

- **Back Up Files and Directories** gives users the ability to access files on the domain controllers for backup purposes. This is a dangerous right, because it grants read access to all files without regard to the file system rights you've assigned. By default, this right is granted to the Administrators, Backup Operators, and Server Operators groups.

- **Bypass Traverse Checking** is normally granted to the Everyone group. This allows users to navigate into a directory even if the directory is made inaccessible by file system rights. Since the user can do little but see that a directory exists, this right doesn't present much of a threat to security.

- **Change the System Time** is granted to Administrators and Server Operators by default. This right allows users to change the time in the internal clocks of the domain controllers. Although the ability to set the time is not a great security risk, synchronized time is important to a smooth-running network, so you should avoid granting this right to additional users.

- **Force Shutdown from a Remote System** allows a user to shut down the system remotely—at least in theory. In reality, this right isn't implemented in Windows NT 4 or previous versions. This dubious privilege is granted to the Administrators and Server Operators groups by default.

- **Log On as a Service** is an advanced right. This right allows a user to register with the operating system as a service. Obviously, normal users have no business doing this. This right is used by special-purpose accounts, such as those used by Internet Information Server or used for data replication. This right is not granted to anyone by default.

- **Log On Locally** allows users to log in at the domain controller itself, or at a workstation in a workgroup system. You may need to grant this right in a small network where the domain controller can also be used by users. This right is normally granted to the Administrators group and all of the Operators groups.

- **Manage Auditing and Security Log** allows users to control auditing of file system objects. This right is normally granted to the Administrators group. Users with this right are *not* given access to the Audit Policy dialog box described in the next section.

- **Restore Files and Directories** is a complement to the Backup Files and Directories right, and allows a user to restore files. Since this basically allows a user to overwrite any file on the system without the corresponding file system rights, it can be dangerous. It is granted to the Administrators, Backup Operators, and Server Operators groups by default.

- **Shut Down the System** allows a user to access the Shut Down option on the Start menu. (In a domain system, this applies only to the domain controllers; users can shut down workstations without restrictions.) This right is granted by default to the Administrators group and all of the Operators groups.

- **Take Ownership of Files or Other Objects** allows a user to become the listed owner of files and other objects. This is useful if the original owner of the files is a deleted or disabled user account. This right is granted to the Administrators group by default.

Auditing

The final policy available in User Manager for Domains is the Audit Policy dialog box, shown in Figure 6.11. To view this dialog box, select Policies ➢ Audit. When you select the Audit These Events option, you can select events to include in auditing. You can audit events that succeed, fail, or both; for example, you may wish to audit failed logon attempts. The events you can audit include the following:

- **Logon and Logoff** includes all attempts to log in or out of the network. This is useful to keep track of who was online when a problem occurred.

- **File and Object Access** logs access to files and other objects. You can control the individual files that auditing applies to from the Security tab in the Properties dialog box for a drive, directory, or file.

- **Use of User Rights** logs an entry whenever a user makes use of one of the privileges discussed in the previous section.

- **User and Group Management** logs changes to users and groups, usually something only administrators are allowed to do.

- **Security Policy Changes** logs changes to the three Policies options in User Manager, including the Audit Policy dialog box itself.

- **Restart, Shutdown, and System** logs system events: shutdown, restart, and critical errors.

- **Process Tracking** logs the individual processes involved in running a program (windows opening, thread execution, etc.) and is useful for debugging.

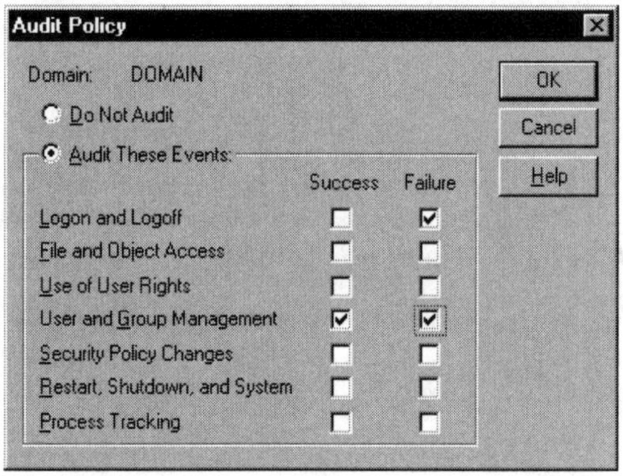

FIGURE 6.11

The Audit Policy dialog box allows you to select criteria for auditing.

Making Passwords Secure

Of course, the security of your network is only as strong as the passwords chosen by the users. In this section we'll look at the process Windows NT uses to authenticate passwords, then discuss the various methods of assigning passwords. Finally, we'll look at the process a hacker might use to obtain valid passwords on your network.

Unlike the passwords on some systems, the passwords in Windows NT are case-sensitive. If a user has trouble getting a password to work, there is a good chance the case was different when the password was initially entered.

The Authentication Process

When a user logs in to a workstation or domain, Windows NT uses a process called *authentication* to identify the user based on the user name and password they provide. If you consider what happens in the background when a user logs in, you probably imagine something like this:

1. User enters name and password.

2. Server compares stored password with entered password.

3. User is allowed access if passwords match.

This approach was actually used by some early computer systems—but that was long before Windows NT was around. While this basic approach sounds logical, it has two major problems. First, the passwords for all users are stored in a file—anyone who obtained access to that file could look up all passwords. Second, the password entered by the user is sent over the network, and could easily be obtained by a snooper using packet sniffing.

Thankfully, Windows NT uses a more complex approach. This is accomplished through encryption. The password you enter to log in is encrypted using an algorithm, or *hash*. This is a one-way system: The password is converted into a series of bytes, but there is no way to convert these bytes back into a password—at least in theory. We'll look at some ways a hacker can get around this later in this section.

For details about hashing and other forms of one-way and two-way encryption, see Chapter 3.

Using this approach, only the hashed value is sent across the network. The hashing algorithm is also used to encrypt the password assigned to the user in the first place, and the encrypted value is the only value stored in the file system. Here's the actual authentication process used by Windows NT:

1. User enters name and password.

2. User's machine encrypts password with one-way hash.

3. User name and hash are sent over the network.

4. Domain controller compares hashed password in database with hashed password entered by user.

5. If encrypted passwords match, user is issued an access token. This token is sent with all requests during the logon session and includes encrypted information about the access available to the user.

Windows NT Service Pack 3 includes a fix called SYSKEY that improves the encryption of password hashes. Be sure to install this service pack for maximum security.

Reality Check: What's My Password?

When I worked as a network administrator, one of the most common questions posed to me by users was, "I've forgotten my password. Can you tell me what it is?" Of course, due to the one-way encryption used by Windows NT and other secure systems, there's no way for the administrator to look up a password, so I was forced to inform them that I would have to change their password instead. One such user responded by asking if there was any way to avoid this, since he had really liked his original password. Apparently he just didn't like it enough to remember it...

Assigning Passwords

One major source of security holes is the way passwords are initially assigned. For example, when a user is asked to choose a password, they might write the password down or even ask a coworker for password ideas. In this section, we'll look at the two methods you can use to assign passwords: user-chosen and administrator-assigned. We'll also look at the importance of regular password changes.

User-Chosen Passwords

The simplest approach is to allow users to choose their own passwords. This method is moderately secure if done correctly, and is the most comfortable method for users. When you create the user's account, you can check the User Must Change Password option and leave the password field blank. The user logs in with no password, and is immediately required to enter a password. Here are some guidelines for keeping this method secure:

- It's a good idea to watch the user log in for the first time to ensure that they choose a password immediately (and quietly).

- If you're not sure when the user will first log in, you may wish to assign a default password rather than a blank password. This provides a measure of security until the user changes the password.

- Inform the user of the basic password guidelines: Don't use an obvious choice, write it down, or share it with other users.

There are some potential security holes when users are allowed to choose passwords. The main problem is the users themselves—as we said earlier in the book, users often make the mistake of choosing obvious passwords such as birth dates, children's names, and even their own names or initials.

One way to prevent obvious passwords is to mandate the format that passwords must follow. A simple example of this is the options in Windows NT's Account Policies to require passwords, and to require a minimum password length. A more complex system can make passwords more secure. For example, you might require that all passwords fit these criteria:

- Must be six characters long or longer

- Must include at least one numeric character

- Cannot be the user's first name, last name, or initials

Although Windows NT does not have a built-in provision for requirements like this, you can enforce it manually by forcing users to contact an administrator to change their password. In addition, there are a number of third-party utilities that can be used for formatted password changes.

Reality Check: Bears vs. Windows NT

When Americans think of the Super Bowl, the last thing they connect with it is computer security—but it's more related than you think. A number of years ago when the Chicago Bears were one of the two finalists for the game, a number of hackers in the Chicago area realized that "Bears," player names, and other team-related words were becoming popular passwords. One administrator spent a few minutes testing his own system and was able to quickly obtain access to several accounts, including one with administrative privileges. Situations like this are a good reason to enforce complex passwords.

Assigning Random Passwords

For even greater security, you may wish to prevent users from choosing their own passwords at all. You can use randomly chosen passwords, which eliminate any possibility that the passwords will be easy to crack. While this is not a built-in feature of Windows NT, there are several utilities that can choose random passwords. One of these, PASSPROP.EXE, is included with the Windows NT 4 Resource Kit from Microsoft.

If you use randomly chosen passwords, you should be aware of two main concerns. First, you need to ensure that the passwords are distributed securely. As an absurd example, if you chose random passwords and informed the user by reading them over the public address system, there would be very little security advantage.

Reading the password over the phone to the user is secure enough in most cases. Methods such as fax, printed memo, and e-mail are generally not considered safe—unless you're sure only the intended recipient will read the password. On the other hand, if your e-mail system is equipped with encryption, it may be even safer than a phone call.

The second major concern about randomly chosen passwords is that if the user didn't choose the password, they're not likely to remember it. This can cause administrative problems as users will frequently need to have passwords changed. In addition, many users will solve the problem themselves by writing the password down at their desk.

If you do choose to use randomly assigned passwords, be sure you can make the distribution secure, and be sure users are trained not to write passwords down or otherwise compromise their security. With proper enforcement, this makes for a very secure network.

Changing Passwords

Any password security policy should also provide for regular password changes. These ensure that if an intruder does obtain one or more passwords, they'll be useless after a certain period of time. You can enforce periodic password changes by setting the Maximum Password Age parameter in the Account Policy dialog box.

To choose how frequently to require password changes, you'll have to make a compromise between two extremes:

- If you allow too much time between password changes, intruders will have plenty of time to use information they have. In addition, the longer a user has a single password, the more likely it is that it's been shared with another employee for some reason.

- If you require password changes too frequently, users will have trouble remembering them. This invariably results in passwords written on sticky notes, or a user reciting their password audibly over and over to commit it to memory.

You'll need to choose a value that fits the level of security (and level of administration) of your network. For many reasonably secure systems, 90 days is a good compromise. A period of 30 days provides for even more security. Smaller numbers than that are generally only useful for high-security applications.

Recognizing Password Security Holes

As you should know by now, nothing is 100 percent secure, and passwords are no exception. While techniques such as formatted passwords and random passwords improve password security, a dedicated hacker can still find out what the passwords are. Luckily, few companies are the objects of truly dedicated hackers—but you should still have an idea of the potential risk.

Basic Attacks

As you learned in Chapter 3, there are two basic methods of password hacking.

The *brute force attack* is the one you've probably seen used by fictional hackers in movies and television. While it's popular there, it's actually considered a last resort by most hackers. In this method, passwords are chosen and tried sequentially, usually by a computer program. The passwords tried will look like "aaaaaa," "aaaaab," and so on.

Suppose you're a hacker trying to break into a network. If the system requires six-character passwords, and if we assume that they're all lowercase and use only alphabetic characters, there are a total of 387,420,489 possible passwords. Assuming that you have to get about halfway through the list before finding a match and that you're using a very fast program that can try 100 passwords per second, it will still take 538 hours—a little over 22 days—to break in. If you're a typical hacker, you're probably not that patient.

By contrast, the *dictionary attack* uses a list of English words (or the appropriate language for the country the server is in). A reasonably comprehensive dictionary of common English words includes somewhere near 25,000 words. The largest desktop paper dictionaries include as many as 300,000 words. Even if you used a list of 500,000 words for a dictionary attack, it would take less than an hour for the program to find a password—provided it was an English word.

Intelligent Attacks

An intelligent hacker can avoid either of the above methods. With a bit of knowledge about a user, passwords are often easy to identify. If the hacker is a former employee or knows an employee, it may be a simple matter of trying such personal items as children's names, nicknames, and names of favorite sports teams. More sophisticated hackers can use social engineering—contacting users under false pretenses—to obtain information (often including the passwords themselves).

Don't forget that a hacker may even be a current employee of the company. Such a person could easily know personal information about other employees, and could casually check offices and desks for written passwords.

Hacker Techniques

Of course, in order to try to break in with any of the above methods, a hacker will need to repeatedly try passwords. If your network has dial-up access or is connected via the Internet, the hacker can attempt to log in remotely. If the network has no remote access, the hacker will need to actually enter the building and sit at a terminal, which becomes a matter of building security.

Rather than staying connected for long periods of time, the hacker may try to obtain a copy of the password list. While the passwords are stored in encrypted form, the list is still very useful to a hacker—it becomes a simple matter of running the dictionary words through the same encryption scheme, trying to find a matching hash code.

The actual password file is stored with the file name SAM in the \\WINNT\SYSTEM32\CONFIG directory. This file is readable by all users, but is held open by the system at all times and is therefore inaccessible. However, backup copies are created with .SAV extensions in this directory. There is also a backup copy in the \\WINNT\REPAIR directory, that is created when Windows NT is installed.

A hacker's usual technique will be to log in with an easy-to-obtain password, such as Guest or an obvious one chosen by an employee, then to obtain access to one of the password files, download it, and use it to attempt to obtain the Administrator password. If you restrict access to those directories, you can force hackers to make their attempts manually—a much more time-consuming process.

WARNING If you created an emergency repair disk when installing Windows NT, this disk also includes a backup of the password file. You should keep the disk in a locked drawer when not in use.

If a hacker obtains access to a single ordinary user account, they can make the process of finding the administrator and other important accounts easier. The command NET USER displays a list of users on the domain, and NET LOCALGROUP Administrators displays a list of members of the Administrators group.

Plugging Potential Security Holes

You should now have an understanding of the basics of user accounts and passwords, and the many properties and policies you can set to improve user account and password security. In this final section, we'll look at some often-overlooked security holes relating to particular user accounts, such as Administrator, and groups, such as Everyone.

Reality Check: Don't Write It Down

I once worked in the IS department of a mainframe-based company. The management was concerned about a recent security breach, and asked us to do what we could to crack down on potential security problems. After most employees had gone home at the end of the day, I took a quick tour of the various desks and offices and returned with a wide variety of paper notes—all containing passwords. Some employees had even jotted down other employees' passwords, including those of some members of management. Needless to say, this problem could have been avoided with proper user training.

The Administrator Account

The Administrator account is the hacker's ultimate goal—and ironically, it is often the easiest account to break into. With most user accounts, the hacker must determine the user name and then the password. With Administrator, the user name is given—and is the same on almost every Windows NT system. Breaking in becomes a simple matter of finding the password.

There's one obvious solution to this problem: Use a long, complex, non-English word as the Administrator password. Don't write it down anywhere, and don't give the password to anyone under any circumstance. Change it frequently, just in case.

Another solution is to edit the Administrator account to limit its rights, and to create an account with a different name to use for most administrative purposes. Windows NT does not allow you to remove Administrator from the Administrators group or delete it entirely, but you can reduce the rights of the Administrators group and create an alternate group that has the real power. This also prevents the hacker from simply displaying the members of the Administrators group, as mentioned earlier in this chapter.

Regardless of which account you use for administration, never leave it logged in if you're not actively using it. For one thing, users could walk up to your workstation and obtain access. Also, the hacker can display a list of logged-in users to narrow down the list of potential administrators.

When you're using these or other methods to secure the Administrator account, be careful that you don't lock yourself out of the network. It's a good idea to assign an alternate administrator account and test it before modifying the main Administrator account.

The Everyone Group

The Everyone group is a built-in group that automatically includes all users on the network. This means that certain rights are given to all users, and it's easy to compromise security by assigning rights and privileges to this group.

One example of a default assignment to the Everyone group that you should definitely change lies in the file system. When you create and format an NTFS volume, the Everyone group is given Full Control privileges on the volume. This essentially means that any user can do anything to any file, basically rendering file system security invalid. This is the first thing you should change when creating a volume.

some ways a hacker can get around this later in this section.

Chapter 8 describes this and other file system security risks in detail.

Guest and Anonymous Accounts

The final accounts you should be concerned with are guest and anonymous accounts. The Guest account is created automatically when Windows NT is installed. In Windows NT 4, this account is disabled by default; in previous versions, it was enabled by default. You may be required to enable the Guest account in certain situations, such as when running some Internet server products. Internet Information Server also creates an anonymous account when installed, and this account can be a security risk as well.

While you can't always delete these accounts entirely, you can at least check to make sure that they don't have significant file system rights or other rights. The best way to test this is to log into the account and see what damage you can cause.

Policies: User Accounts

- Keep the Administrator account secure.

- Limit the rights of the Administrators group, and create a separate group with full access.

- Don't leave the Administrator account logged in.

- Remove default assignments to the Everyone group.

- Limit the rights of Guest and Anonymous accounts.

Summary

User accounts are combinations of user names, passwords, and other identifying items for users of the network. These accounts act as a first defense against network intrusion, identify users uniquely, and provide a record of who uses the network at what times.

User accounts are only as secure as their passwords. You should enforce a password policy to ensure that passwords are as secure as you need them to be. In addition, be careful of security holes, such as those involving the Administrator and Guest accounts.

CHAPTER

7

System Policy

Computer and network security traditionally divides people into two groups: those you trust and have given accounts on your network, and those you don't trust, who don't have accounts on your network and who might, in fact, try to break into it. But what of those computer users who you only trust a little bit, who need access to your network but shouldn't have access to everything? Some user accounts you might want to limit include:

- Temporary worker computers and accounts
- Accounts for consultants
- Student network accounts
- Guest accounts and accounts for anonymous access

Another situation where you might wish to limit the ability of users to make changes in a computer is when the computers are for general purpose use, rather than being assigned to just one individual. You would probably prefer these computers to keep the same background, have the same applications, and have the same resource settings (workgroup membership, printer connections, and so on) after a person has finished using the computer. So environments like the following are good reasons for you to limit the abilities of users:

- Computers dedicated to a specific purpose or program
- Student computer-lab computers in a university network
- General use computers
- Public use computers in libraries or coffee shops

For these kinds of users you need a mechanism for limiting the resources available to the user accounts. You also need a way to limit the changes that can be made to public-use computers. The System Policy Editor is the tool you use to limit these accounts. This chapter introduces you to this tool and describes changes you might want to make in your network to enhance the security of your network. The system options you can modify with the System Policy Editor are arranged in a tree structure. Each branch of the tree modifies some specific behavior of Windows NT or Windows 95. Some options have more impact on the security of a Windows 95 or Windows NT computer than other options do.

In order to present the full picture (many important security options are buried in otherwise innocuous branches of the policy tree), and because you never know what features you might want to restrict, this chapter will give you an exhaustive view of the System Policy trees for Windows 95 and Windows NT. First, however, you'll get a look at how to use the System Policy Editor to load, edit, store, and make active system policies for Windows 95 and Windows NT.

Using the System Policy Editor

System policies are specific behaviors of Windows NT or Windows 95 computers that a network administrator can control via a system policy file. Whether or not the user may change the Desktop settings is one example of a system policy; the required length of a password is another. The administrator uses the System Policy Editor to manage system policies. You'll find the System Policy Editor by choosing Start ➤ Administrative Tools on your Windows NT Server Desktop. There you'll also find the other tools you use to administer your network: the User Manager for Domains, the Disk Administrator, the Performance Monitor, and so on.

> You must use the Administrator account (or an account that is a part of the Administrators or Domain Admins group) to use the System Policy Editor to make changes in your system's registry.

This section covers the following aspects of using the System Policy Editor to implement computer and user policies on your network:

- Policies and the System Policy Editor

- Opening policy files or opening the registry

- Computer policies versus user or group policies

- Putting policies into effect

- Windows 95 policies versus Windows NT policies

Following this section are detailed sections on which registry settings you can manage with the System Policy Editor. Further along in the chapter we'll discuss computer policies for Windows NT and Windows 95, as well as user and group policies for the same operating systems.

Understanding Policies and the System Policy Editor

The System Policy Editor is an important part of your toolkit, especially if you manage a large network. Before you can use the System Policy Editor effectively, however, you will need to know what the Windows NT and Windows 95 registries are, you must understand what a policy is, and you must know what the System Policy Editor does.

Registry Settings

The Windows NT Registry contains keys (named locations) that hold values that affect how the operating system functions. (The same holds true for the Windows 95 Registry, as well.) One such key is the

`HKEY_LOCAL_MACHINE\SOFTWARE\Microsoft\Windows NT\CurrentVersion\`
`Winlogon\ShutdownWithoutLogon`, and its default value is 0 for Windows NT Server computers, but 1 for Windows NT Workstation computers. This means that this computer will present the WinLogon prompt with the Shutdown option grayed out. A user of the computer will have to log on successfully before the operating system will allow them to shut down the computer.

You can modify the behavior of your computer by changing the value of the key. If you want users of your workstations to log on before they shut the computer down, you can change the key to 1. If you want to allow anyone to shut down your server computers without logging on to the console first, change the value of the key to 0.

System Policies

If you have a number of registry settings that you change on Windows NT and Windows 95 computers—settings that restrict what users can do and that make administration easier for you—you could call those setting changes a "policy." Such an arrangement would fit Microsoft's definition of a policy. With the System Policy Editor, you can set up policy files that apply to specific computers, to specific users, to groups of users, or to all the users in your network.

Conventional use of the word *policy* can be a bit confusing. A policy can refer to a specific registry setting configured with the System Policy Editor. A policy can also refer to the collection of registry configuration settings collected into a Windows NT or Windows 95 policy file.

The System Policy Editor doesn't do anything for you that you can't do yourself (with a little more effort) using the Registry Editor of Windows NT or Windows 95. The System Policy Editor simply provides a more structured interface and gives you some guidelines for appropriate values to be placed in the registry keys.

Terminology

- **Policy:** 1) A specific Windows NT or Windows 95 registry setting configured with the System Policy Editor, for example, the Windows NT Logon Banner policy. 2) The registry settings that are collected in a single Windows NT or Windows 95 system policy file and that are applied to user accounts when the user logs on to the network.

- **Registry:** The Windows NT operating system database that contains security and configuration settings for the operating system and for service and application software that uses the registry API.

For example, if you wanted to set a Windows NT user's background pattern to `winnt256.bmp`, you could create a policy for that user in the System Policy Editor and then specify the `winnt256.bmp` wallpaper in the Desktop portion of that user's policy (see Figure 7.1). You could also directly make the change in that user's profile in the registry, identified by that user's SID in the HKEY_USERS key of the registry. (See Figure 7.2.) Incidentally, if that user were to log on and change the background using the display Control Panel, the Control Panel would just make the same change in the same place.

You should note that there are many more entries for each user in the registry than are represented in the System Policy Editor or the Control Panel programs. You will find no reason to edit most of these settings (such as the WaitToKillAppTimeout, shown in Figure 7.2) but they must be there for the operating system, and you should know about them.

When you make changes directly to the Windows NT Registry you have to know which changes to make and where to make them. For example, you have to know which SID (Security Identifier) corresponds to which user, because the information about users is stored by SID, not user name.

F I G U R E   7.1

The System Policy Editor
allows you to make
changes to the registry
that are shown in the
Policies tab.

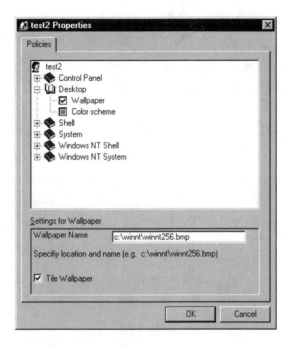

The Control Panel programs store the locations of the various registry keys as a part of their programs. They also give you a choice of values that make sense for the keys they help you edit. (For example, they will give you a list of bitmap files to choose from for the background.) Similarly, the System Policy Editor gives you menus and value choices, but the System Policy Editor is even more flexible than the Control Panel programs—the System Policy Editor draws its list of keys and valid choices from .ADM text files (see Figure 7.3). You can extend the System Policy Editor by extending these .ADM files.

One difference between making a policy change for a user in the System Policy Editor and making the change directly via the Registry Editor or the Control Panel is that the change made with the System Policy Editor may not necessarily take effect immediately. Instead, if you are using the Policy Editor to edit policy files (.POL files) rather than using the editor to edit the registry directly, then the changes take effect after the policy is saved in the appropriate location and the user logs on using that account.

F I G U R E   7.2

You can also make changes directly to the registry.

F I G U R E   7.3

The System Policy Editor programs are configured to edit the registry from .ADM files.

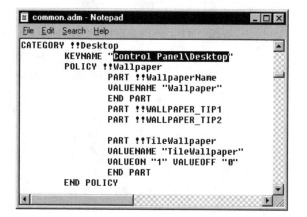

NOTE A system policy takes effect every time the user logs on. For example, a system policy may set the background to `winnt256.bmp`. The user may change the background to something else using the control panel, but the background will be changed back to `winnt256.bmp` the next time the user logs on. This is one important difference between a system policy and a user's profile.

Opening Policy Files or Opening the Registry

Before you can add or edit policies you have to do one of the following (each can be done from the File menu of the System Policy Manager program):

- Create a new policy file

- Open an existing policy file

- Open the local registry

- Connect to the registry of a remote computer

Opening the registry or connecting to the registry of a remote computer does what you might expect; the changes you make using the program are reflected in the registry of the computer as soon as you select File ➤ Close.

This works great if you are changing settings for an individual computer or for an individual user account—but what if you want to make the changes effective for a number of computers, or an entire group of users, not all of whom may be turned on/logged in at the moment? Also, what if you want to make several sets of changes (several policies), and you would like to be able to switch between them without making all those changes each time?

With the System Policy Editor you can create policy files (files with names ending with the .POL extension) that contain just the registry key and value changes. Those changes will then be applied to the registry of the computer when the user logs on to the server or when the computer attaches to the server containing the policy file. (The policy file must be stored in the appropriate location in order for the computer to apply the policy, though.) You can also have multiple policy files and copy the appropriate policy file to the proper location in order to change policies.

Computer Policies versus User or Group Policies

Once you have created or opened a policy file, or connected to the registry of a computer, you can edit two kinds of policies: computer policies and user or group policies. (A group policy is exactly the same as a user policy except that it applies to more than one user. The registry keys you can edit are identical.)

The difference between computer policies and user policies is that the settings controlled by a computer policy affect all of the users of that computer, regardless of who the user is or which groups that user belongs to. User policies, on the other hand, control settings that affect only the user or group of users that the policy was created for. Figure 7.4 shows icons representing computer, user, and group policies.

F I G U R E   7.4

Computer policies affect all of the users of the computer, while user and group policies affect only the users they were created for.

WARNING Don't edit the Default Computer or the Default User policies unless you are sure of what you are doing. Instead, create specific computer and user or group policies for the computers and the users in your network. Once you make restrictive changes to the default policy accounts, you may find that you can't change the policies back. This is because these default policies are put in effect if there is no more specific policy for the operating system to apply to that computer or user.

You can add, remove, and copy policies in a policy file using the Edit menu in the System Policy Editor. If you are directly editing the registry, however, you can't create or copy policies. You can only edit the policies for the local computer and the local user; this is because policies are put into effect by having the logon process make the changes to the registry at the time the user logs on.

Putting Policies into Effect

Once you have created a policy file that contains computer, user, and group policies for your Windows NT domain (or individual Windows NT computer) you must save it in a location where the computer(s) will find them when a user logs on.

The standard location for policy files is in the netlogon share of the Primary Domain Controller (winnt\system32\repl\export is the usual location of the netlogon directory share). You must also give the policy file the file name the operating system is looking for: NTConfig.pol in the case of Windows NT, and Config.pol in the case of Windows 95.

You don't necessarily have to save the policies in the netlogon share nor do you have to give the files those specific names (NTConfig.pol and Config.pol). Of course, you can change the location of the files, or change the names that the operating systems will search for them under, by editing the registries of the computers.

The registry key HKEY_LOCAL_MACHINE\System\CurrentControlSet\ Control\Update may contain the entries NetworkPath and Update-Mode. If the UpdateMode entry contains the numeric value 1, then the operating system will check in the default location (the netlogon share) for the policy file. If you change the value to 2, however, the operating system will instead look to the location you enter in the NetworkPath field. You must change this registry key for every computer that will look for its policy file in a nonstandard location. The NetworkPath field should contain a UNC path in the form of *computername*\ *sharename**filename*.pol, because the policy file may reside on a remote computer (typically, the primary domain controller).

You can make that registry change using the registry editor (you may have to add the NetworkPath key), or you can use the System Policy Editor to do it for you. You can open the registry on your computer using the File ➤ Open Registry option (or open the registry of another computer on your network using the File ➤ Connect... option).

Once you have opened a registry you will find the settings you need to change in the Network section of the Local Computer icon. Follow these steps:

1. Open the Network book, and then open the System Policies Update book.

2. Check the Remote Update check box. The bottom of the window will show you your update options, including the update mode and the path for a manual update. (This is where you type your alternate location.)

3. Click the OK button in the Local Computer Properties window.

4. To finish up, select File ➤ Close. Click Yes when asked if you want to save the changes to the registry.

Windows 95 versus Windows NT Policies

The policies you create using the System Policy Editor take effect in the registry of the computer that the individual uses to connect to the network. If the user connects from a Windows NT Workstation, or logs on directly to a Windows NT Server console, then the changes take effect in the Windows NT registry of that computer. If the user logs on from a Windows 95 computer, however, the registry changes are made to the registry of that Windows 95 computer, and the Windows 95 computer needs a different policy file than the Windows NT computer uses.

The distinction between Windows 95 and Windows NT policy files is important because the structure of the Windows 95 registry differs from that of Windows NT. Many more security options can be modified in the Windows NT registry, and some security options are implemented differently in Windows 95 from the way they are implemented in Windows NT.

The default file name for Windows 95 policy files is `Config.pol`. The policy file is normally stored in the same place as Windows NT policy files (the `netlogon` directory) but you can change where Windows 95 computers will look for policy files the same way you redirect Windows NT.

You will find the Windows 95 Policy Editor on the Windows 95 installation CD-ROM in the `ADMIN\APPTOOLS\POLEDIT` directory. The file that contains the locations of registry settings for Windows 95 is called `Admin.adm`. You can use the `Admin.adm` file with the Security Policy Editor that comes with Windows NT (select Options ➤ Policy Templates and you can remove the two default templates and add `Admin.adm`), but it's easier just to use the Windows 95 POLEDIT program for your Windows 95 clients and the Windows NT System Policy Editor for Windows NT computers. Otherwise, you would have to switch the template files you are using every time you switch the platform you are configuring.

You can run both the Windows NT System Policy Editor program and the Windows 95 POLEDIT program on your Windows NT Server computer.

Working with Windows NT Computer Policies

Before you begin on your tour through the possible policy settings, you should understand that you don't necessarily have to use all of the settings available to you. Many of the settings won't really make your network any more secure—some just make the administrator's job easier when there are a large number of computers and computer users to administer. You should just select those policies that fit the specific circumstances of your particular network, and leave the default settings for the rest.

When you create a new policy file there is one computer policy created by default for you: the Default Computer policy. You can create additional computer policies by selecting Edit ➢ Add Computer (you will be asked for a computer name for the new policy). Once you install the policy file on your Primary Domain Controller, any computer that logs on to the server will first look for a computer policy with a name that matches that of the connecting computer. If it finds a matching name, it applies that policy to the registry of the computer. Otherwise, it applies the Default Computer policy.

The status of each policy setting is one of the following:

- **Checked:** This policy option is in effect. You may have to enter data in information fields at the bottom of the properties window.

- **Clear:** This policy option is not in effect.

- **Gray:** This policy option will not be changed from the state already stored in the registry of the connecting computer.

The Default Computer and the Default User policies are created with all of the options in the third state (grayed out) so that none of the registry settings will be changed when a client computer connects to your Windows NT Server computer. New computer and user or group policies are also created with all of the settings in the gray state.

Once you have made the changes for one computer policy, you can copy that policy as many times as you like. The copies will retain all of the same settings that you established in the original policy. You can then customize the copies for the specific circumstances of a particular computer. Since Windows NT does not provide group accounts for computers (it only provides them for users) you can't create a policy that will apply to a group of computers on the network.

The policy settings are organized in a tree structure, with the name of the policy at the top of the tree. Each section of the tree is represented by a book icon. By opening the book icon, you see subsections (also represented by book icons) or the policy settings, each with a check box to indicate its state. See Figure 7.5 for a view of a Windows NT computer policy tree.

FIGURE 7.5

The Windows NT computer policies have a tree structure.

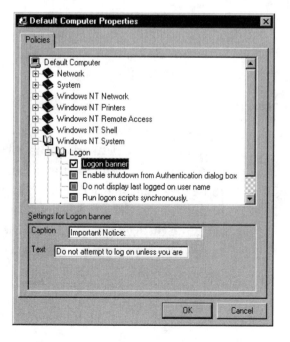

The following sections walk you through each of the options that you can specify using a Windows NT computer policy.

Network: System Policies Update and Remote Update

The Remote Update key governs where the Windows NT operating system will look for the Config.nt file. This is the setting you must change if you store the policy files in a nonstandard location. The settings for this key are as follows:

- **Update Mode:** Automatically instructs the operating system to look in the default location for the policy files (the Netlogon share of the PDC). Manual instructs the operating system to look in the location indicated by the path field, below.

- **Path for manual update:** This is the manual location for the policy file. You enter a UNC path here (in the form *server**share**file*.pol).

- **Display error messages:** Checking this option instructs the operating system to report if there are errors accessing the policy file.

- **Load balancing:** Checking this option allows the operating system to load the policy from a domain controller other than the primary domain controller when the PDC is heavily loaded.

System

This section of the computer policy contains two keys: SNMP, which governs how the network error and status portion of Windows NT interoperates with Internet management tools, and Run, which lists those programs that will run when the computer starts up. The SNMP settings govern who may access the SNMP component for administration, and the Run settings can be used to activate security software that must start when the system starts.

SNMP

SNMP stands for Simple Network Management Protocol, and it is how devices based on Internet technology (including file servers and clients that use TCP/IP) report error conditions and their operational status. The SNMP service must be installed for you to use this option in your computer.

Communities SNMP devices can be organized into communities, which may be administered as a group. The Communities button allows you to add entries for the SNMP communities that this computer will be a part of.

Permitted Managers You can restrict who can manage the SNMP service. The Permitted Managers button presents you with a list that you may add managers to.

Traps for Public Community You may elect not to configure the SNMP service as part of a community. The Public community list identifies recipients of trap messages in this case. Click the Trap Configuration button to edit the list of destinations for trap messages when communities are not in effect for this computer.

Run: Run

This key lists the programs that the computer will run when it starts up. The programs you add to the list can perform almost any security or administrative function, from scanning for virii to resetting the contents of the hard drive to a preset state. Click the Items to Run at Startup button to edit the list of programs that will start automatically when the operating system starts.

Policies: Virus Scanner

- Install virus scanner software in all of the computers on your network. Use the Run Security Policy setting to require all computers to run the virus scanner on startup.

Windows NT Network: Sharing

These two keys control hidden shares in Windows NT. The hidden drive shares make it easier for administrators to connect to and manipulate the hard drive partitions of Windows NT computers—but hackers target hidden shares.

Create Hidden Drive Shares (Workstation)   Checking this option instructs Windows NT Workstation computers to create the C$, D$, and other volume hidden shares, as well as the admin$ hidden share. Clearing this option inhibits the creation of these shares.

Create Hidden Drive Shares (Server)   Checking this option instructs Windows NT Server computers to create the C$, D$, and other volume hidden shares, as well as the admin$ hidden share. Clearing this option inhibits the creation of these shares.

Policies: Clear Hidden Drive Shares

- Clear the Create Hidden Drive Shares options for your computers unless you have a specific need for these shares, such as an administrative tool that relies on the existence of the shares. If you have such a tool, consider replacing the tool with another tool that doesn't rely on the existence of the shares, because these shares are often exploited by hackers.

Windows NT Printers

The Security Policy Editor has three options for printers, only one of which (that option is Disable Browse Thread) has an impact on network security.

Disable Browse Thread on This Computer   Checking this option instructs the computer not to inform network browsers of the existence of printers that are connected to this computer. In order for other computers to print to a printer on this computer you must type the UNC path to the printer directly rather than selecting it from a browse list. The security risk of a browsable printer is minimal—you should only enable this option if you are concerned about misuse of the printers connected to the computer.

Scheduler Priority   This option affects the performance of the print service, not the security of your computer or your network. You can set the print scheduler priority to above normal (enhancing printing speed at the cost of application performance) or below normal (enhancing application performance at the expense of printing speed).

Beep for Error Enabled   By checking this option you instruct the computer to beep every 10 seconds while there is an error on a print server.

Windows NT Remote Access

The first option in this section of the computer policy tree directly affects the security of your network; the other two are optimization settings. You will want to evaluate these options for each of the computers that have the Remote Access Service installed.

Max Number of Unsuccessful Authentication Retries   This is the number of times a caller can attempt to type a user name and password. It is important to have a low number of retries, because a common network attack is to guess passwords. When the attacker must dial your RAS server repeatedly the attack will take longer and you are more likely to discover that your RAS server is under attack.

The number of retries defaults to 2, which allows 3 total attempts to log on per connection.

Policies: RAS Connect Retries

- Although the default setting for the number of unsuccessful authentication retries is 2, you should also make it a policy for RAS servers that the number of retries be 2. By checking the option and making it a policy, you are making sure that even if the setting is changed in the computer's registry through some other means, the number of retries will be set back to 2 the next time the computer connects to the server.

Max Time Limit for Authentication   This setting tells the operating system how long to wait for the user to type in a user name and password. The user is given two minutes by default. You may want to reduce this setting if your modems are in frequent use. The Length in Seconds defaults to 120.

Wait Interval for Callback   This is how long the RAS server will wait before calling back an RAS client that has callback enabled (callback enhances security by requiring that the client computer be at a specified phone number). You might extend the interval if your modem line takes a while to reset; you might reduce it if your system will support it. Length in Seconds defaults to 2.

Auto Disconnect   This feature keeps users from monopolizing the RAS connections—after a set number of minutes you can have RAS automatically drop the connection. This feature does not enhance the security of your network. Disconnect After (Minutes) has no default setting.

Windows NT Shell: Custom Shared Folders

With the System Policy Editor you can customize the locations of Desktop components in your Windows NT computers. Changing these settings will not significantly increase the security of your network.

Custom Shared Programs Folder   Path to the location of shared Programs items—the default is `%SystemRoot\Profiles\All Users\Start Menu\Programs`.

Custom Shared Desktop Icons   Path to the location of shared Desktop icons. The default is `%SystemRoot\Profiles\All Users\Desktop`.

Custom Shared Start Menu   Path to the location of shared Start menu items. The default is `%SystemRoot\Profiles\All Users\Start Menu`.

Custom Shared Startup Folder   Path to the location of shared Startup items. The default is `%SystemRoot\Profiles\All Users\Start Menu\Programs\Startup`.

Windows NT System

The Windows NT System section allows you to modify some aspects of logging on to Windows NT and some details of file system behavior. Of these configuration settings, displaying the logged-on user name is the most pertinent to computer security. The other settings are more appropriate for optimizing the performance of your Windows NT computer at the expense of compatibility with older programs.

Logon

Logon characteristics you can modify include the banner, the authentication dialog box, and how scripts are run, as follows:

Logon Banner   The purpose of this setting is to inform users of the proper use of computers in your network when they log on. You can include legal warnings, computer-use assignments, or organization identification in the logon banner text.

- **Caption:** This field contains what will be shown in the banner title.

- **Text:** This is the body of the message that will be displayed to the user when they log on.

Enable Shutdown from Authentication Dialog Box   It may appear that a shutdown option in the logon box reduces security because anyone can select it, but think about it. Anyone can also simply turn off the computer or unplug it. A methodical shutdown, even from the logon window, is much safer for the data stored on the computer than just turning the computer off.

Do Not Display Last Logged On User Name   Enabling this option increases security in your network because one objective of network intruders is to collect valid user names. The convenience of not having to type your user name in again if you used the computer last is not worth the security risk.

Policies: Disable Last User Name Display

- Enable the Do Not Display Last Logged On User Name option so that valid account names won't be seen by unauthorized individuals.

Run Logon Scripts Synchronously   Enabling this option increases compatibility at the expense of performance. It does not measurably enhance security.

File System

The three file-system options primarily enhance the performance of your system at the expense of older programs that expect a file system to conform to the restrictions of older versions of MS-DOS. You should only enable these options if you are sure that your older programs will work properly in the new environment.

Do Not Create 8.3 File Names for Long File Names   Older programs often expect file names to have no more than eight letters in the name with an extension of just three letters. Windows 95 and Windows NT both allow you to have file names up to 254 characters in length. If this option is disabled, Windows NT must maintain two file names—a longer one for new programs and a shorter one for older programs. Enabling this option causes Windows NT to respond only to the longer file names.

Allow Extended Characters in 8.3 File Names   File names in MS-DOS and Windows are limited to a subset of the ASCII characters. Windows NT supports a much wider range of characters, encoded in UNICODE. Selecting this option enables the use of UNICODE characters in older, 8.3 file names.

Do Not Update Last Access Time   In comparison with the other two file system options, enabling this option will give you the greatest performance gain. By default, after every access, even a read access, NTFS will update the time of last access for the file. This update takes a considerable amount of time. High security environments should leave this setting enabled.

Windows NT User Profiles

The user profile options primarily increase the performance of Windows NT when the user is logging on to a network file server over a slow network link. You never know; perhaps some hacker will find a way to exploit cached copies of roaming profiles, so you'll want to delete them.

Delete Cached Copies of Roaming Profiles   Enabling this option will cause the Windows NT client computer to delete the user profile after the user logs off. This saves disk space, especially when there are a large number of users that use the same computer, such as in a college computer lab.

Automatically Detect Slow Network Connections   This option enables the operating system to detect whether or not the logon is occurring over a slow dial-up link or a fast network connection.

Slow Network Connection Timeout   If downloading the profile is taking too long (the timeout has been exceeded) then the download will be canceled and a stored or default profile will be used instead. The time default value is 2000 milliseconds.

Timeout for Dialog Boxes   If the profile dialog boxes are ignored, the process will proceed without user intervention. The time default is 30 seconds.

Working with Windows 95 Computer Policies

Windows 95 is a different operating system internally than Windows NT, and the Windows 95 computer policies reflect those differences. Many of the options are similar, however.

There are only two top-level sections, Network and System, and the policy options they allow you to set are as follows (see Figure 7.6).

Network

The Network section of a Windows 95 computer policy contains the lion's share of policy options. You'll find settings similar to those in Windows NT in the Logon, SNMP, and Update keys. You'll also find more settings that apply to network security in the Windows 95 computer policies, because Windows 95 does not have any other method of enforcing computer security.

Access Control: User-Level Access Control

Windows 95 does not maintain its own security structures for users and groups, but it can refer to the security databases of a network server to control access to some resources (and to network shares, in particular).

- **Authenticator Name:** This is the name of the server that maintains the security database for the network.

- **Authenticator Type:** Your two options are a Windows NT domain or a NetWare 3.*x* or 4.*x* server.

Policies: Windows 95 User-Level Access

- In networks that must be secure from internal as well as external threats, you should require user-level access control for Windows 95 resources.

Logon

Windows 95, like Windows NT, can present you with a logon banner when you first log on to the computer. A more useful feature from the security viewpoint is to require that the user log on to a network before they are allowed to use the Windows 95 computer.

Logon Banner   This banner, like the banner for Windows NT, can contain any message you want to put there. You may want to display in the text a legal message, a company welcome message, or a message about the use that the particular computer should be dedicated to.

- **Caption:** This is the title of the logon message.

- **Text:** This field contains the body of the message that will be displayed when the user logs on.

Require Validation by Network for Windows Access   When you enable this option the user will be required to log on to the network before they can use the resources of the Windows 95 computer.

Policies: Require Network Validation

In order to make sure that only authorized individuals use the computers on your network, enable the Require Validation option. This will keep people from bypassing security by selecting the Close or Cancel button in the Windows 95 logon screen.

Microsoft Client for NetWare Networks

Windows 95 comes with client software for connecting to NetWare networks, and that client software is installed and configured by default when you install networking.

Preferred Server   Windows 95 can connect to NetWare 3.12 networks, as well as those running NetWare 4.1 and later versions. How you present the server name depends on the kind of network you are connecting to. A simple server name will suffice for NetWare 3.12 networks or 4.1 networks with bindery emulation enabled. The Server Name field is a simple text field that should contain the name of the server or the NetWare server context.

Support Long File Names   Windows 95 can provide support for long file names in networks that do not natively support them. NetWare 4.1 and later versions of NetWare support long file names natively. The Support Long File Names option presents you with two choices of platforms for long file names: all NetWare servers that support long file names, or NetWare 3.12 and above.

Search Mode   You can select the search mode of Windows 95 for NetWare networks with this option. The Search Mode option is a numeric value with a default of 0.

Disable Automatic Netware Logon   Windows 95 will attempt to automatically log on to a NetWare network if there is one present and the Client for NetWare redirector is present on the client computer. This can present a security problem.

Policies: Disable Automatic NetWare Logon

- Disable the automatic NetWare logon on your network if you don't have a NetWare server on your network. It is conceivable for a computer to masquerade as (or actually be) a NetWare server on your network in order to gain access to user names, passwords, and other sensitive information.

Microsoft Client for Windows Networks

If you have Windows NT Servers on your network (and if you don't, why are you reading this book?) then you will most likely have Microsoft Client for Windows installed on your Windows 95 computers. There are three policy options for the client software for Windows.

Log On to Windows NT   This is the information that governs the domain membership of the Windows 95 computer. The options are:

- **Domain Name:** This should contain the name of the domain.

- **Display Domain Logon Confirmation:** This presents the logon information to the user when the user logs onto the domain.

- **Disable Caching of Domain Password:** This keeps the Windows 95 computer from keeping the password that was used to log on to the Windows NT Server computer.

> ### Policies: Disable Caching of Domain Password
>
> ■ Select the Disable Caching of Domain Password option on all your Windows 95 computers. Otherwise, it is too easy for a hacker to get hold of a password file on a Windows 95 computer and then use password dictionaries to crack the password.

Workgroup   This is the group of computers that the Windows 95 computer will consider as peers for file and print sharing. The Workgroup Name field may contain any valid workgroup name.

> ### Policies: Set Workgroup Name
>
> ■ Set the workgroup name as a policy so that it will be reset to the correct value every time the computer logs on. Since changing the workgroup name requires a reboot, this (along with requiring network authentication) will ensure that the workgroup is not changed by a user.

Alternate Workgroup   In the event that the regular workgroup is not accessible, this workgroup may be joined. The Workgroup Name field may contain any valid workgroup name.

File and Printer Sharing for NetWare Networks: Disable SAP Advertising

In larger networks, especially networks with bridges or routers that are configured to route SAP traffic, you should disable SAP advertising on all computers that are not actually hosting a network resource (such as a shared printer or network file share) in order to reduce traffic and broadcast storms.

Passwords

Password settings are always very important in network security because the password is the gateway to the network. Until thumbprints and retina scans become commonplace, the password will continue to confirm the identity of the user.

Hide Share Passwords with Asterisks   Under the default setting for Windows 95 computers, anyone is able to see what password is being required for a Windows 95 share simply by examining the shares for that computer (from that computer, of course).

Disable Password Caching   By default, Windows 95 keeps passwords in password files on the computer's hard drive so that users do not have to type the password each time they attempt to access a network resource.

Require Alphanumeric Windows Password   This setting guarantees that a password will not be found in a dictionary or other common word list.

Policies: Passwords

- Select the Hide Share Passwords with Asterisks in order to keep share passwords from being seen by casual users of a computer or by passers-by.

- One reason to disable password caching is so that passwords do not accumulate on the computer and become a target for hackers. What this costs in convenience (you may have to type some passwords each time you access a resource) is outweighed by the increase in security.

- You should require alphanumeric Windows passwords so that a hacker cannot quickly determine the password to a user account simply by performing a "dictionary scan."

Minimum Windows Password Length   Short passwords are easier to guess than long ones, and are more quickly discovered in a brute force attack on your network. The default value for length is three characters. Increase the minimum password length to at least seven characters in order to make it harder for hackers to discover a user's password.

Dial-Up Networking: Disable Dial-In

This option prevents users from dialing in to a Windows 95 computer if it has a modem attached.

Policies: Disable Dial-In Networking

- Disable dial-in networking, except in the cases of trusted individuals or to special computers, because dial-in networking can bypass regular network security.

Sharing

One of the strengths of Windows 95 is its ability to share files and printers with other computers in a workgroup. In most LAN environments the benefits of peer-sharing outweigh the security risk. In untrusted environments, such as college computer labs or public-access computers in coffee shops, file sharing can be exploited to circumvent network security.

Disable File Sharing   This option prevents Windows 95 from sharing directories from its hard drives.

Disable Print Sharing   This option prevents Windows 95 from sharing printers that are attached to it.

SNMP

The SNMP section of the policy tree for Windows 95 is very similar to the SNMP section for Windows NT.

Communities   Clicking this button takes you to a list of communities that this computer is a member of.

Permitted Managers   Clicking this button lists those who may manage the SNMP service.

Traps for Public Community   Clicking this button lists destinations for SNMP traps when communities are not specified for this computer.

Internet MIB (RFC1156)   This field accepts the contact information required for RFC1156 compliance. The fields are as follows:

- **Contact Name:** The individual responsible for the SNMP service (the administrator responsible for the Windows 95 computer)

- **Location:** Where the administrator can be reached

Update: Remote Update

The Update fields for Windows 95 are exactly the same as they are for Windows NT:

- **Update Mode:** This can be automatic (the default setting) or manual.

- **Path for Manual Update:** If the update mode is manual, this is where the computer will look for the file.

- **Display Error Messages:** If there are error messages, this setting informs the operating system to display them to the user.

- **Load Balance:** This setting allows the computer to retrieve the policy file from a BDC if the PDC is busy.

System

The system section of the Windows 95 computer profile governs how Windows 95 starts up. It contains several settings that are not necessarily designed with security in mind but can certainly be used to increase security in your network.

Enable User Profiles

While they are a requirement in Windows NT, user profiles are an option in Windows 95. If this option is disabled, then all of the users of the Windows 95 computer will share the same user profile. That means that changes one user makes to the background, start menu, sounds, and so forth will affect the other users of the computer. Enabling user profiles will give each user their own profile, just like in Windows NT.

Policies: Enable Windows 95 User Profiles

■ Enable Windows 95 user profiles so that you can give specific users and groups their own security settings that reflect their level of trust in the network.

Network Path for Windows Setup

The Network Path for Windows Setup option locates the Windows 95 setup program, which can be used to fix a damaged Windows 95 installation or reinstall Windows 95 on your computer. The path can be a UNC location on the network.

Network Path for Windows Tour

The Windows Tour gives new users an introduction to Windows 95. This entry must end in TOUR.EXE.

Run

Windows 95 maintains a list of programs to run whenever you log on. There are many programs you can use (virus scanners, especially) that can run in the background and protect your computer while you are doing other things with it. The Items to Run at Startup button presents you with a list of programs that will be executed when the system starts.

Policies: Run Virus Scanner

- Use the Run option to run a virus scanner whenever a user logs on to the computer.

Run Once

This option probably won't help you much. Installation programs use the Run Once feature to continue the installation process once the computer reboots. The Items to Run Once at Startup button presents you with a list of programs that will run the next time the computer is started, but which will then remove themselves from the Run Once list.

Run Services

Services are parts of the operating system that perform special functions, such as hosting WWW files. Services persist through logon sessions. You should have no reason to change Run Services settings. The Services to Run at Startup button presents you with a list of services that will be executed when the system starts.

Working with Windows NT User or Group Policies

A computer policy affects a single computer or (in the case of the default computer policy) all computers that do not have a specific computer policy defined for them. User policies are similar to computer policies—if there is no specific user policy for a user who logs on, then the Default User policy is applied.

But wait, there's more! If the user belongs to a group for which a policy is defined, then that policy is also applied.

Since a user can belong to more than one group, there may be more than one policy that may apply to that user. In the Options menu of the System Policy Editor you can establish priority among the groups; when policy settings conflict, the group policy with the highest priority will take precedence.

As with computer policies, you can create new user and group policies from the Edit menu of the System Policy Editor. The policies that are created will be blank: No options will be selected in the policy trees. Once you have made policy changes in a policy file, however, you can copy that policy and those changes will be in effect in the new policy. See Figure 7.7 for a view of a Windows NT user policy.

The six sections of the Windows NT user and group policies will be described in more detail in the section that follows.

Control Panel: Display: Restrict Display

The Control Panel policy options in Windows NT are primarily concerned with display settings. Since Windows NT adequately controls who may make changes to the display hardware without requiring the

FIGURE 7.7
Windows NT user
policies have six sections:
Control Panel, Desktop,
Shell, System, Windows
NT Shell, and Windows
NT System.

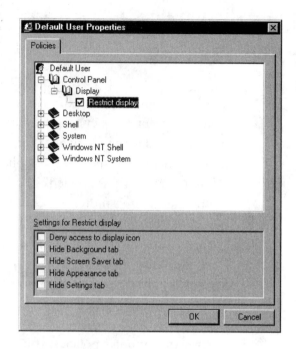

intervention of the System Policy Editor, these settings simply enforce a consistent environment and make administration easier for the administrator. The following settings are available:

- **Deny Access to Display icon:** Denies all access to the display control panel item.

- **Hide Background tab:** Keeps the user from changing the background.

- **Hide Screen Saver tab:** Keeps the user from changing the screen saver.

- **Hide Appearance tab:** Keeps the user from modifying the appearance settings.

- **Hide Settings tab:** Keeps the user from accessing the hardware configuration settings.

Desktop

The Desktop settings, like the display settings, enforce conformity on the network. The settings you can lock down are for the wallpaper and the color scheme.

Wallpaper

This option sets the bitmap that will appear as the screen background.

- **Wallpaper Name:** This should specify a `.bmp` file. It may refer to another computer via a UNC path.

- **Tile Wallpaper:** This option causes the image to be tiled (repeated) instead of centered with a border.

Color Scheme

The color scheme defines the colors and Desktop object characteristics, such as font size and selection. The Scheme name may be any of the schemes defined in the Windows NT Colors control panel.

Shell: Restrictions

This section and the next (*System: Restrictions*) contain the user policy settings that have the most impact on security. You should be careful when applying these options because you can quickly render a Windows NT computer unusable with them, and then not be able to change the settings back.

Policies: Enable Shell Restrictions

- Enable the shell restrictions for accounts that serve a particular purpose, such as public e-mail accounts, public word-processing accounts, process control, and so on.

Remove Run Command from Start Menu   This option makes the Run start menu item go away—making it more difficult for the user to start a program not found in the start menu.

Remove Folders from Settings on Start Menu   This option keeps the user from modifying computer settings and adding or removing printers.

Remove Find Command from Start Menu   A clever user could use the find command to locate a program, and then execute the program. This option removes the find command from the start menu.

Hide Drives in My Computer   A user can click on programs in drive windows that are displayed. This menu option removes access to the drives.

Hide Network Neighborhood   The Network Neighborhood can show you remote shares containing programs that the user can execute. It can also show the user printers and other resources that the user can map to. This option removes the network neighborhood from the Desktop.

No Workgroup Contents in Network Neighborhood   You may wish to allow network browsing but only of network shares covered by domain security—in that case you might want to disallow browsing of workgroup contents that may have shares secured by the less stringent Windows 95 security model.

Hide All Items on Desktop   This option removes everything from the Desktop. You would enable this option if you are dedicating the user account to run just one program (such as a data entry or process control application).

Disable Shutdown Command   This option prevents the user from shutting down the computer. Since Windows NT can be shut down remotely, you might want to make that an administrative function for computers dedicated to a particular purpose.

Don't Save Settings on Exit   This option preserves the Desktop settings as they were when the user logged on—any changes are transient and are gone when the user logs off.

System: Restrictions

These two system restrictions can go a long way toward securing a network against hacking from internal sources. Once a hacker has access to a computer on your network, he or she will need access to the registry and to hacking tools in order to exploit the information stored on the computer.

Disable Registry Editing Tools   This setting keeps the user from running the Registry Editor, the System Policy Editor, or any other registry editing tool.

Policies: Disable Registry Editing Tools

- Disable the registry editing tools for all users except system administrators.

Run Only Allowed Windows Applications   This option can be even more restrictive than disabling certain tools. You can use this option to restrict the user to only certain allowed programs—all others will not run. You can then make sure that the allowed programs (such as a word processor, spreadsheet, and Web browser) are safe to run.

The List of Allowed Applications button shows you a list of the programs that Windows NT will allow this user to run.

Policies: Restrict Applications

- Use the Run Only Allowed Windows Applications option to restrict the programs that can be run by users who are security risks.

Windows NT Shell

You can customize the appearance and function of the Windows NT shell for particular groups of users. You might, for example, want to provide members of the Engineering group one set of programs that show up on the Desktop or in the Start menu, and members of the Finance group a different set of programs that are shared by members of their group. The option to choose the location of the custom folders gives you a mechanism for giving each group a different environment in which you can specify the Desktop and Start menu programs.

Custom Folders

The custom folders options describe the locations of the directories that will contain the new items, icons, and menus. These directory locations should already exist.

Custom Programs Folder   Path to the location of program items; the default is %USERPROFILE%\Start Menu\Programs.

Custom Desktop Icons   Path to the location of Desktop icons; the default is %USERPROFILE%\Desktop.

Hide Start Menu Subfolders   If you have a custom programs folder for Desktop items, select this option as well so that the original subfolders will not appear.

Custom Startup Folder The path to the location of startup items—the default is blank. This directory contains the items that will be started when the user logs on.

Custom Network Neighborhood The path to the location of Network Neighborhood items—the default is blank. This directory contains the items that will show up in the Network Neighborhood. You can configure this folder to contain only those resources you want the user to have access to.

Custom Start Menu The path to the location of Start menu items; the default is %USERPROFILE%\Start Menu.

Restrictions

The shell restrictions work in addition to the above settings, as follows.

Only Use Approved Shell Extensions This keeps users from extending the shell or replacing it in an insecure manner (it disables third-party shell extensions that may contain a Trojan horse).

Remove Common Program Groups from Start Menu This option leaves only the individual program groups in the Start menu, which may either be the default program groups or program groups as defined in the previous section, *Custom Folders*.

Windows NT System

The two options in the Windows NT System section of a user policy govern what happens just after the user logs on to the account.

Parse Autoexec.bat When the user first logs on Windows NT must establish the user environment. Windows NT by default will not parse and execute commands in the autoexec.bat file, but by enabling this option you can configure it to do so.

Run Logon Scripts Synchronously   This option requires Windows NT to wait for logon scripts to complete before it starts the user's shell. That way any logon script effects (including abnormal termination) will be communicated to the user's shell.

Working with Windows 95 User or Group Policies

Just as there are quite a few differences between Windows NT and Windows 95 computer policies, there are also quite a few differences between Windows NT and Windows 95 user and group policies. However, Windows 95 policies behave the same as Windows NT policies: If there is no policy that specifically applies to a user, the Default User policy will take effect. Group policies are also applied to the user account and are applied in order of group priority. See Figure 7.8 for a view of Windows 95 user policy settings.

Since Windows 95 has no other security mechanisms to speak of, you should be particularly careful about how you configure security in the Windows 95 security policy for users and groups. There are five Windows 95 user policy sections, which are explained in detail in the following section.

Control Panel

In contrast to what you saw in the Windows NT Control Panel policy options, there is quite a lot for you to do in the Control Panel policy tree for Windows 95. This is where you control access to the display, to network configuration, to passwords, to printers, and even to the System Control Panel.

FIGURE 7.8

Windows 95 user settings
differ from those of
Windows NT.

Display: Restrict Display Control Panel

This option is very much like the Windows NT Display Control Panel option. It offers the following options:

- **Disable Display Control Panel:** Removes the user's access to any display options.

- **Hide Background Page:** Removes the ability to change the background.

- **Hide Screen Saver Page:** Removes the ability to change the screen saver.

- **Hide Appearance Page:** Removes the ability to change the colors, font size and choice, and so on.

- **Hide Settings Page:** Removes the ability to change the display hardware settings.

Policies: Hide Windows 95 Display Settings

- In mischief-prone settings (such as computer labs or public terminals) hide the Windows 95 display settings page from everyone except administrators.

Network: Restrict Network Control Panel

The network control panel governs how the Windows 95 computer connects to the domain. The following options are available:

- **Disable Network Control Panel:** Removes all access to network settings.

- **Hide Identification Page:** Keeps the user from changing which network the computer will connect to.

- **Hide Access Control Page:** Keeps the user from changing the share settings for the computer.

Policies: Disable Network Control Panel

- Disable the network control panel for all users except administrators and trusted, knowledgeable users.

Passwords: Restrict Passwords Control Panel

The passwords control panel is another sensitive location in Windows 95. Most users have no reason to modify remote administration or user profile settings. The following options are available:

- **Disable Passwords Control Panel:** Keeps users from making any changes to passwords, remote access, or user profiles.

- **Hide Change Passwords Page:** Keeps users from changing passwords.

- **Hide Remote Administration Page:** Keeps users from changing remote administration settings.

- **Hide User Profiles Page:** Keeps users from deleting profiles.

Policies: Hide Remote Administration and User Profiles Pages

- Hide the remote administration page and the user profiles page for all users except administrators. As we've mentioned earlier in the book, you should allow users to change their own passwords often.

Printers: Restrict Printer Settings

Printer settings are not usually a security issue, but they can become a nuisance issue if you have users that are prone to mischief. Using the following settings can make your life easier:

- **Hide General and Details Pages:** Keeps users from changing printer settings for individual printers.

- **Disable Deletion of Printers:** Keeps users from removing printers.

- **Disable Addition of Printers:** Keeps users from connecting to printers without permission.

Policies: Hide Printer Pages

- If you are concerned about users making mischief, you should do the following for printers in your network: hide the general and details pages, disable deletion of printers, and disable the addition of printers.

System: Restrict System Control Panel

The system control panel contains settings that can compromise the security of the Windows 95 computer or cause the computer to fail to operate properly. The System option allows you to restrict access to the following parts of the system control panel:

- **Hide Device Manager Page:** Keeps users from adding and removing devices.

- **Hide Hardware Profiles Page:** Keeps users from changing the hardware environment that the computer boots to.

- **Hide File System Button:** Keeps users from modifying the operation of the file system (enabling 16- or 32-bit access, for example).

- **Hide Virtual Memory Button:** Keeps users from changing the location, amount, and method of operation of virtual memory.

Policies: Enable System Control Panel Policy Options

- Enable all of the options in the system control panel policy of Windows 95 for all users except administrators.

Desktop

The Desktop settings for Windows 95 are the same as for Windows NT.

Wallpaper

This option sets the bitmap that will appear as the screen background.

- **Wallpaper Name:** This should specify a `.bmp` file. It may refer to another computer via a UNC path.

- **Tile Wallpaper:** This option causes the image to be tiled (repeated) instead of centered with a border.

Color Scheme

The color scheme defines the colors and Desktop object characteristics, such as font size and selection. The scheme name may be any of the schemes defined in the Windows NT colors control panel.

Network: Sharing

Windows 95 does not provide the same level of control over file and print sharing that Windows NT does. File and print sharing makes many kinds of computer collaboration much easier than it might be, however. You must balance the need for security on your network with the need to facilitate the user's work.

Disable File Sharing Controls   This option removes the ability to share directories from the hard drives of the Windows 95 computer.

Disable Print Sharing Controls   This option removes the ability to share printers that are attached to the Windows 95 computer.

Shell

The shell section of a user policy allows you to configure how the Desktop appears in Windows 95 for that user or group of users. The shell restrictions for Windows 95 are more important than they are for Windows NT because the Windows NT and NTFS security structures provide much of the required security in Windows NT. The ability to change the location of the custom folders gives you a mechanism for giving each group a different environment.

Custom Folders

The custom folders options describe the locations of the directories that will contain the new items, icons, and menus. These directory locations should already exist. The options are the same as for Windows NT; refer to the *Custom Folders* section for Windows NT earlier in this chapter for a description of each option.

The shell restrictions for Windows 95 are the same as the shell restrictions for Windows NT. See *Shell: Restrictions* in the Windows NT user and group policy section for a description of the restrictions' options.

System: Restrictions

The first two system restrictions are the same for Windows 95 as they are for Windows NT. Windows 95 adds two more, however, that have to do with the running of MS-DOS applications.

Disable Registry Editing Tools   This setting keeps the user from running the Registry Editor, the System Policy Editor, or any other registry editing tool.

Policies: Disable Registry Editing Tools

- Disable the registry editing tools for all users except system administrators.

Run Only Allowed Windows Applications   This option can be even more restrictive than disabling certain tools. You can use this option to restrict the user to only certain programs—all others will not run. You can then make sure that the allowed programs (such as a word processor, spreadsheet, and Web browser) are safe to run. The List of Allowed Applications button shows you a list of the programs that Windows 95 will allow this user to run.

Disable MS-DOS Prompt   This denies the user the ability to launch programs from the DOS prompt. If you wish to limit which programs the Windows 95 user can use, you should disable the MS-DOS prompt.

> ### Policies: Restrict Applications
>
> - Use the Run Only Allowed Windows Applications option to restrict the programs that users who are security risks may run.

Disable Single-Mode MS-DOS Applications   One way around Windows 95 security is to leave Windows 95 behind and reboot to MS-DOS only. A hacker could then run any DOS-mode tools that can be loaded from a floppy disk, and since the computer is most likely connected to your network, that could include packet sniffers or alternate operating systems. This option removes the user's ability to reboot to MS-DOS.

> ### Policies: Disable MS-DOS
>
> - If you are concerned about hackers gaining physical access to your computers or you are concerned about general mischief, disable single-mode MS-DOS applications on your Windows 95 computers. In the BIOS, you should also disable booting from the A: drive and apply a password requirement to keep the user from using a DOS boot floppy.

Summary

The System Policy Editor is a powerful tool for establishing a secure network environment. You can make all of the changes that the System Policy Editor makes piecemeal using the Registry Editor, but the System Policy Editor is much easier to use and ensures that you make valid changes to the registry.

Because Windows NT and Windows 95 have different registry structures, there are two policy editor programs: POLEDIT for Windows 95, and System Policy Editor for Windows NT. Each uses different .ADM files to configure how the Policy Editor edits the respective registries.

The System Policy Editor can make changes directly to the registries of computers, or it can make the changes to policy files (files with the .pol extension), which then must be saved in an appropriate location (such as the netlogon share) in order for the policies to take effect. The file name for Windows NT policies is NTConfig.pol and the file name for Windows 95 policies is Config.pol.

There are two kinds of policies: computer policies and user or group policies. If a computer (or user) can't find a policy that specifically references that computer (or user) then that computer (or user) will use the Default Computer (or Default User) policy. User accounts also apply the options set in the group policies that correspond to groups that the user is a member of. When group policies conflict, the policies take effect in order of priority.

CHAPTER

8

File Systems

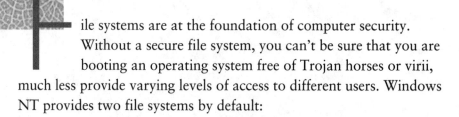

ile systems are at the foundation of computer security. Without a secure file system, you can't be sure that you are booting an operating system free of Trojan horses or virii, much less provide varying levels of access to different users. Windows NT provides two file systems by default:

- **FAT (File Allocation Table)** for backwards compatibility, small volumes, and workstations that must dual boot.

- **NTFS (New Technology File System)** for security, fault tolerance, performance, and convenience.

Each file system has its appropriate place and function, but on a secure Windows NT server, only one should appear on your hard disk drives: NTFS. With the solitary exception that some RISC microprocessors must boot from a FAT volume, there's no valid reason why a secure computer should use the FAT file system on its hard disk drives.

Until the release of Windows NT 4, Windows NT supported HPFS (High Performance File System) for the purpose of dual booting OS/2. This driver will still work on NT 4 systems that have been installed as upgrades to NT 3.5 servers, but is no longer included in the standard installation. Windows NT does not support security on HPFS, so it should not be used on Windows NT servers.

The following sections will compare the FAT and NTFS file systems, explore security from a file system perspective, look at the security issues raised by file systems, and explore a number of ways to solve them.

The Big FAT Security Problem

The File Allocation Table (FAT) file system developed by Microsoft for MS-DOS in the early '80s is by far the simplest file system still supported by modern computers. In fact, due to its age and simplicity, it is supported by every modern personal computer operating systems, including:

- MS-DOS

- Windows 95

- Windows NT

- OS/2

- Macintosh OS

- UNIX (all common variants)

This portability makes the FAT file system very convenient for data transfer but also highly nonsecure. A FAT-formatted hard disk can be removed from a Windows NT server, attached to nearly any computer on the planet, and read from directly, without the need for any special software.

The low-level structure of the FAT file system is common knowledge and better discussed in books about file systems. For the purpose of security and administration, the FAT file system has the following advantages:

- **Extremely small size and computation overhead:** FAT is implemented as a single slightly redundant linked list from an allocation table and directory name space to linked lists of clusters that make up a file. This low overhead makes it perfect for small media such as floppy disks or removable cartridge hard disks and for computers with limited processing power.

- **Portability across operating systems:** FAT has been implemented for every significant microcomputer operating system, so it is the natural choice for disks that must be used by more than one operating system.

And the FAT system has a much longer list of disadvantages:

- **Corruptibility:** Lack of error recovery techniques means that the FAT file system becomes corrupted every time the computer crashes or is improperly shut down. This manifests as dangling pointers, and requires the frequent use of disk consistency checking software.

- **Single user:** The FAT file system was developed for single-user operating systems like MS-DOS, so it retains no ownership information about files and does not implement any security measures beyond a few simple global attributes like hidden and read-only, which are easy to circumvent.

- **Nonoptimal update strategy:** The FAT file system keeps its directory information in the first sectors of a disk. Since the FAT must be updated constantly as a file is changed, the disk drive must seek across the surface of the disk constantly. When copying multiple small files, this overhead becomes very obvious.

- **No optimization to protect against fragmentation:** The FAT file system simply assigns space on a first available sector basis, which tends to increase fragmentation, and therefore access time, as files are added and deleted over time.

- **Limited file name sizes:** FAT file names consist of only eight characters with a three-letter extension. This is usually not enough space to provide meaningful file names. Modern extensions to the FAT file system hack around this limitation using extra directory entries that are coded with an invalid attribute set so they won't confuse older versions of DOS.

- **Size limitations:** FAT volumes are limited to 2GB under MS-DOS and Windows 95. Windows 95 OSR/2 uses an extended version of the FAT file system, FAT 32, which allows larger file sizes and cluster suballocation, but that version is not compatible with any other operating system. FAT volumes under Windows NT were limited to 4GB prior to NT 4, and are now limited to 16GB. Why Microsoft increased the drive size support for a file system they don't recommend using for disks over 200MB is a mystery.

WARNING Windows 95 Operating System Revision 2 (available only on new computers purchased since 1997) has a new variant of the FAT file system that supports clusters suballocation and volumes larger than 2GB. This variant of the FAT file system is not compatible with any version of Windows NT and probably never will be.

Windows NT relies strongly upon file system security to implement security throughout the Windows NT operating system. Without file system security, there's no way to stop someone with any access to the operating system from installing Trojan horses and virii, deleting files inappropriately, or gaining access to sensitive information. Essentially, without file system security, a system cannot be locally secured.

Network security can still be provided through share-level security, but that security won't apply to services that provide a gateway to a local account the way the Internet Information Server (IIS) anonymous user account does. Essentially, anonymous users are logged on locally to the IIS server, which means that they have unsecured access to the hard disk drive of the IIS server if it is FAT formatted.

WARNING Never use the FAT file system for the boot partition of a server, especially if it's attached to the Internet. The lack of file system security makes it an open house for hackers.

Policies: FAT File System

- Never use the FAT file system on the hard disk of a Windows NT computer when security is a concern.

Terminology

- **Cluster:** The basic unit of allocation in a file system, equal to a number of sectors fixed when the volume is formatted.

- **File system:** A combination of a driver and a structure used to store data in named capsules, called files, on a storage device.

- **Format:** The process of creating a volume in a partition.

- **Partition:** A distinct space on a physical storage device that can contain a volume.

- **Sector:** The basic unit of physical storage on a mass storage device.

- **Volume:** The logical structure of a file system.

NTFS in a (Rather Large) Nutshell

Security in Windows NT depends upon the security of the file system. Without a secure file system there's no way to guarantee that any number of security breaches have not or cannot occur. An early requirement for Windows NT when it was being developed was security, so the designers knew they would need a file system that went beyond what FAT and HPFS (the operating system included with OS/2 and which Microsoft had the right to use) could give them.

So they developed NTFS from the ground up to be secure and fault tolerant. While they were at it, they threw in nearly every other feature they could think of (with the notable exception of encryption). The major categories of features of NTFS include:

- Fault tolerance

- Performance

- Security

- Compatibility

- Convenience

Understanding NTFS security requires an understanding of the features of NTFS in general. The next few sections elucidate those features.

NTFS Fault Tolerance Features

Windows NT implements a number of fault tolerance features that in combination virtually guarantee that your disk volumes won't be corrupted. They are: transaction logging, hot fixing, disk mirroring, and disk striping with parity.

Terminology

- **Application Programming Interface (API):** A set of related procedures built into Windows NT that are called by applications to perform a specific function.

- **Checkpointing:** The process of moving transactions from the transaction log to their permanent location on disk.

- **Disk mirroring:** A fault tolerance feature that maintains two exact duplicates of the same data in case one fails.

- **Hot fixing:** The automatic detection, recovery, and out-of-use marking of bad disk sectors.

- **Parity:** Extra information used to recover data when portions are missing.

- **Roll back:** The process of regressing to a consistent error-free prior state.

- **Striping:** An optimization feature that apportions data in a volume equally across a number of physical disks so they can be accessed in parallel.

- **Transaction:** A write-to-disk operation.

Transaction Logging

NTFS is a log-based file system, which means that it records changes to files and directories as they happen and also records how to undo or redo the changes in case of a system failure. This feature makes the NTFS file system much more robust than other PC file systems. Transaction logging allows NTFS to recover from system crashes and abnormal shutdowns gracefully.

Whenever data is written to an NTFS volume, it is recorded as a transaction in the system log file. As time is available, transactions in the transaction log file are written to the disk and removed from the log file. This process is called *checkpointing*.

When a transaction is written, NTFS records both redo and undo information for that file in the transaction log file (don't confuse this with the event log—they are completely different). If for some reason NTFS cannot complete the transaction, the state of the file is "rolled back" to its previous state using the undo information in the transaction log.

When Windows NT is shut down properly, the transaction log is emptied and the final checkpoint status is set. Before mounting a

volume during the boot process, the status of the last checkpoint is verified to make sure the volume was dismounted properly. If the status of
the last checkpoint indicates that all transactions were not written
because the computer crashed or was otherwise shut down improperly,
the NTFS volume is in an unknown state.

Windows NT uses the transaction log to restore the opened files in
the NTFS volume to a consistent state using the following three-phase
process:

1. An analysis phase NTFS uses to determine how to restore each
   opened file.

2. A redo phase that attempts to correct data to the state the user last
   updated it to. Files can be rolled forward if a redo entry in the
   transaction log exists for that file.

3. An undo phase that attempts to correct data back to the last
   known good state. Files can always be rolled back because the
   transaction log is updated before the file is actually opened.

Transaction logging guarantees that the file system will remain in a
stable, consistent state. It does not guarantee that data won't be lost
in the event of a sudden crash.

Hot Fixing

Hot fixing allows NTFS to tolerate the normal aging process of magnetic media without losing data. NTFS will automatically detect when a
sector write fails, mark the failed cluster out of use, and write to a new
cluster. On SCSI disks that support it, NTFS will also use low-level
sector sparing instead of cluster remapping, which basically does the
same thing in hardware.

If a cluster returns an error when NTFS writes to it, the address of
the errant cluster is recorded in the bad cluster file and a new cluster is

used to store the data instead. No error message is returned to the user. This process is called cluster remapping, or soft hot fixing.

Hard hot fixing, or sector sparing, is only implemented on SCSI drives that support hot fixing in hardware. On these drives, Windows NT will perform a hardware operation to retrieve a spare sector rather than implementing cluster remapping. The net result is essentially the same.

Disk Mirroring

Disk mirroring allows NTFS to tolerate the complete failure of one hard disk drive in your system. NTFS allows you to designate two partitions of identical size as a mirrored volume, storing the same data to both locations. If either fails, its mirror is used until the failed partition has been replaced. Obviously, the mirror partitions must be on separate hard disks.

Disk mirroring is set up using the Disk Administrator, and is only available in Windows NT Server. Disk mirroring can be used on the boot and system partitions because the system can simply boot off one drive until the NTFS driver is loaded and recognizes the mirror. If the boot drive fails, you can set the computer to boot the mirror in hardware or software as appropriate for your computer.

Disk Striping with Parity

NTFS will allow you to create stripe sets across multiple hard disks such that all hard disks are accessed simultaneously. One hard disk's worth of storage contains a mathematical sum of the data stored on the remaining hard disk space, which can be used to recalculate the data contained on any one failed hard disk in the stripe set. This means that in a multidisk environment, any one hard disk can fail without bringing down the system. Disk striping with parity is available only in Windows NT Server and is set up using the disk administrator. Disk striping cannot be used on the boot or system partitions because the NTFS driver must be loaded before it can recognize stripe sets.

NTFS Performance Features

NTFS also implements a number of features that improve performance, such as lazy writing (write-back caching), simultaneous mirror reads, disk striping, and file compression.

Lazy Writing

NTFS implements an automatic write-back cache, which means that writes to your disk are stored in a cache until it becomes convenient for NTFS to write them to disk. Since the system logs transactions, this will not cause inconsistency if the computer loses power before the cache is written. It will cause data loss, however.

Simultaneous Mirror Reads

If you've set up a disk volume as a mirror set, Windows NT will automatically read from both mirrors simultaneously, cutting access time in half.

Disk Striping

NTFS stripe sets are read from simultaneously, so if you have six disks in a stripe set, you could see disk performance improve by 600 percent (assuming no other bottlenecks, of course). The system and boot partitions cannot be part of a stripe set (but they can be part of a mirror set, which can double read throughput).

Compression

Since NT 3.51, NTFS has supported built-in file-level compression as a speed optimization. Compressed files usually take up about half the space as a regular file, so they also take only half as long to load. Since your processor usually isn't all that busy during disk reads, those spare CPU cycles are put to work decompressing the file as it comes in, providing an improvement both in disk space and load speed. Application servers that are really busy will see a speed drop due to compression.

TCompression cannot be set on volumes with cluster sizes greater than 4KB.

NTFS Security Features

NTFS implements a number of security features, including permissions based on user and group accounts, auditing, ownership, secure file erasure, and last-access time stamp.

Permissions

NTFS keeps track of which users and groups can access certain files and directories, and it provides different levels of access for different users. NTFS permissions are a complex topic covered in more detail in a section later in this chapter.

Auditing

Windows NT can record NTFS security-related events to a security log for later review using the Event Viewer. The system administrator can set what will be audited and to what degree of detail.

Ownership

NTFS also tracks the ownership of files. A user who creates a file or directory is automatically the owner of it and has full rights to it. An administrator, or other individual with equivalent permissions, can take over ownership of a file or directory.

Secure File Erasure

NTFS will not return the data stored in disk sectors that are not allocated; rather, it will return zeros. This prevents the use of low-level access to the disk for retrieving portions of deleted files.

Secure file erasure is implemented through the Windows NT API (Application Programming Interface). Whenever low-level access to a disk cluster is requested, the Windows NT API checks to see if that cluster is part of a file. If it is not, all zero data is returned no matter what the sector actually contains. This keeps users from being able to recover fragments of deleted files. However, the data on the disk is still vulnerable to direct access from other operating systems, so the system must be physically secure for this security measure to remain useful.

Last-Access Time Stamp

NTFS records the time the file was last opened for any access. This can be important when you are trying to assess the extent of an intrusion into your system. It does cause a slight performance hit however, so you may want to disable it using the System Policy Editor if it's not important to you.

NTFS Compatibility Features

And finally, there are a few features that support compatibility with a wide range of other operating systems and platforms: POSIX compliance and multiplexed data streams.

POSIX Compliance

NTFS supports file name case sensitivity and hard links (two directory entries to the same file) so that POSIX-compliant software can be ported quickly from UNIX to Windows NT.

NTFS preserves the case of files to maintain POSIX compliance, but none of the application subsystems (VDM, WOW, OS/2, and Win32) are case sensitive. The effect of this is that it is possible for the following three files to exist in the same directory at the same time:

```
Readme.txt
README.txt
README.TXT
```

It's not possible however to use any of the tools that come with Windows NT to reliably determine which file an operation will work with or whether it will report an error. Technically, this problem can only occur if the files are created by a POSIX-compliant application subsystem. You must use POSIX-compliant tools for Windows NT to correct this problem if it ever occurs.

Multiplexed Data Streams

NTFS supports the presence of multiple independent streams of data inside a file. This feature isn't used by any of the application subsystems, but it is used by the Services for Macintosh service to store the resource and data forks of a Macintosh file. In the future, multiplexed data streams might be used to implement binary code for different microprocessors to support true platform independence. Multiplexed data streams is sometimes called multithreading by those unaware that the term *multithreading* already refers to something else.

Convenience Features

Finally, Windows NT supports a number of features that improve the usability and convenience of the operating system: volume sets and long file names.

Volume Sets

NTFS allows you to concatenate all the disks in your computer into one big virtual disk called a *volume set*. This is especially handy when your server starts flaking out because it's running out of disk space and you don't feel like reinstalling on a larger disk. You can simply drop in another disk, add it to the volume set, and violà! You've got a bigger disk. Volume sets don't improve performance, and they reduce fault tolerance because any one failed disk will bring down the volume set. Since the NTFS driver must be running to recognize a volume set, you cannot use them for the boot or system partitions.

Long File Names

Like the VFAT-extended version of the FAT file system that ships with Windows 95 and HPFS, NTFS supports long file names up to 255 characters in length (although you can only refer to file names less than 253 characters from the command prompt). The difference is that NTFS supports them natively, and it also creates an 8.3 hash for operating systems like DOS that don't get along well with long file names. You can use the system policy editor to turn off 8.3 name mangling to improve performance if you don't need that support.

Disadvantages of NTFS

As you can see, the list of features in NTFS is truly impressive. There are, however, always some trade-offs; so in the interest of fairness, here's what NTFS doesn't do well: floppy disks, small volumes, and disk quotas.

Floppy Disks

NTFS has too much overhead for volumes as small as floppy disks. You cannot use NTFS to format a volume smaller than 5MB.

High Overhead

Microsoft doesn't recommend using NTFS on partitions smaller than 200MB due to the space overhead. However, you can use NTFS file compression to compensate for space lost due to overhead—and still come out megabytes ahead compared to the FAT file system—so that's really not much of a disadvantage. With compression, NTFS remains effective down to about 50MB.

Disk Quotas

Disk quotas allow system administrators to designate how much space users are allowed to use on a volume, thus preventing heavy users from dominating the storage space with files better stored elsewhere. Most network operating systems, including NetWare and UNIX, support disk quotas, but Windows NT does not. Certain low-level structures in NTFS indicate that support for quotas may exist, but there's no way to implement them. There are third-party tools that add quota support to NTFS.

Security and File System Permissions

Windows NT implements file system permissions based on user and group accounts. For each file, directory, and volume, there exists a list of permissions called an *access control list* that enumerates which users or groups have which type of access to that resource. Individual entries in the access control lists are called access control entries (no surprise there) and they constitute a combination of an access attribute and the security identifier of the user or group allowed access. The specific access attributes will be discussed in detail later in this section.

Older file systems, such as FAT, do not have a rich enough set of file and directory attributes to implement security on a file or directory basis, so file system permissions are not available for FAT volumes. The server service implements share permissions to secure access to file systems that do not implement security.

File system permissions are only available for NTFS volumes, not FAT volumes. You cannot properly secure servers without using file system permissions. FAT volumes are inherently insecure.

Modern file systems such as NTFS implement detailed security control over the sharing of information with file system permissions, which are assigned to individual files and directories using file system attribute bits that are stored in the directory tables of the file system.

Consequently, file system permissions work on the local machine, and do not rely upon a network service to allow or deny access. For instance, if Jane creates a directory and assigns permissions for only herself, then no one else can access that directory (except administrators who take ownership of the directory) even if they are logged on to the same machine.

File system permissions can also be used to restrict which files are available to resource shares. Therefore, even though share permissions may allow access to a directory, file system permissions can still restrict it. Table 8.1 shows the effect of directory permissions.

T A B L E 8.1 Directory Permissions	Permission	Effect
	No Access	Prevents any access to the directory and its files.
	List	Allows viewing of file names, browsing of directories. Does not allow access to files unless overridden by other file or directory permissions.
	Read	Allows opening files and executing applications.
	Add	Allows adding files and subdirectories even when the user does not have read access.
	Change	Incorporates Add and Read permissions and adds the ability to delete files and directories.
	Full Control	Incorporates change plus taking ownership and assigning permissions.

Setting Secure NTFS File Permissions on an Existing Server

Setting up proper security permissions on a server isn't always easy—especially if the server already exists. Overhauling existing security permissions might take some time. So be prepared for a little bit of effort on your part, and for the reactions of perplexed users when they suddenly find they can't access certain parts of the server anymore. Use these steps to properly secure a production server:

1. Open a command prompt.

2. Type the following at the C:\ prompt, which will remove the Everyone permission from all directories and files on the disk:

```
CACLS *.* /T /E /C /R EVERYONE
```

3. On your boot partition, type the following (replace \WINNT with the name of your Windows NT system directory):

```
CD \WINNT\SYSTEM32
CACLS *.* /E /C /P "Domain Users:C
CD \WINNT\SYSTEM32\CONFIG
CACLS *.* /E /C /P "Domain Users:R
CD \WINNT\SYSTEM32\DRIVERS
CACLS *.* /E /C /P "Domain Users:R
CD \WINNT\SYSTEM32\SPOOL
CACLS *.* /E /C /P "Domain Users:R
CD \WINNT\SYSTEM32\REPL
CACLS *.* /E /C /P "Domain Users:R
CD \WINNT\SYSTEM32\REPL\IMPORT
CACLS *.* /E /C /P "Domain Users:R
CD \WINNT\USERS
CACLS *.* /E /C /P "Domain Users:R
CD \WINNT\USERS\DEFAULT
CACLS *.* /E /C /P "Domain Users:C
CD \WINNT\WIN32\APP
CACLS *.* /E /C /P "Domain Users:R
CD \WINNT\TEMP
CACLS *.* /E /C /P "Domain Users:C
```

4. For each directory to which normal domain users should have unabridged access (to it and its child directories), type the following:

```
CACLS *.* /T /E /C /P "Domain Users:C
```

5. The remainder of your directories (to which special permissions should be set up) are unaffected by this change.

The preceding procedure can be automated using the securing setting batch files on the companion CD.

Policies: File Permissions

- Implement strong permission-based security for all files stored on your server.

- For low to medium security installations, replace the default Everyone, Full Control permission with a Domain Users, Change permission on all drives except the system and boot volumes.

- For high security installations, remove all instances of the Everyone, Full Control permission. Do not set a default permission to replace it. Add permissions only where specifically required.

- Create groups based on natural associations in your organization. Assign file permissions by groups. Make user accounts members of the groups that need access to certain files.

- Use the No Access permission only when necessary to override other permitted access.

- Use third-party permissions auditing software to manage permissions in complex environments.

Conflicting Permissions

With the myriad of shares, groups, files, and directories that can be created in a network environment, some resource permission conflicts are bound to occur. When a user is a member of many groups, some of those groups may specifically allow access to a resource while other group memberships deny it. Also, cumulative permissions may occur. For example, a user may have Read access to a directory because he's a domain user and also have Full Control because he's a member of the Engineers group. Windows NT determines access privileges in the following manner:

- Administrators always have full access to all resources. However, access will be denied if the administrator does not appear in the access control list until the administrator takes ownership.

- File system permissions are combined to allow the most permissive access to a user based on that user's specific access and group memberships.

- A specific denial (the No Access permission) always overrides specific access to a resource.

- When resolving conflicts between share permissions and file permissions, Windows NT chooses the most restrictive. For instance, if the share permission allows full control but the file permissions allow read-only, the file is read-only.

When a user or program requests permissions to access a resource, either all of the permissions requested are granted or none of them are. For example, if a user requests Read and Write access to a directory, and the user has only Read access, no access will be granted. The user may request access only for resources that he or she has permission to access.

Viewing Permissions

You can view the permissions for a file or directory by selecting that file's icon and then selecting File ➤ Properties, or by right-clicking once on the file's icon and selecting the Properties item in the pop-up menu. When the file's Properties window appears, select the Security tab and then click the Permissions button. The Directory (or File) Permissions window will display the names of the users and groups that have access to the file (or directory). Figure 8.1 shows a File Permissions window.

FIGURE 8.1

The File Permissions window lists the names of users and groups that have access to the file.

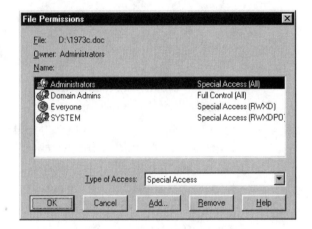

Using the Permissions window for a directory you can specify additional permissions for subdirectories and files stored in the directory. Figure 8.2 shows a Directory Permissions window.

A user that is not explicitly listed in the File or Directory Permissions window may still have access to the file or directory, because the user may belong to a group that is listed in the window. In fact, as we've mentioned in earlier chapters, you should never assign access to files or directories to individual users. Instead, you should create a group, give access permissions to the group, and then assign users to that group. This method allows you to change access rights for whole groups of users without having to modify each individual user account.

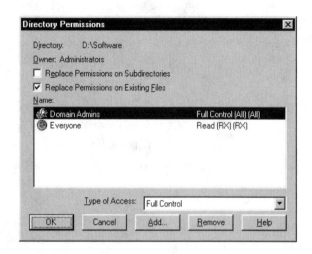

NTFS defines access permissions based on file system operations. Because useful permissions usually require more than one file system operation, the file system permissions you can assign are actually combinations of permitted file system operations. Table 8.2 shows the file system operations that are allowed, and Table 8.3 shows the combinations that are used to create actual permissions. The question marks in the Special Access row of Table 8.3 indicate that special access provides a way to create your own combinations of file system operation permissions to create complex special accesses.

T A B L E 8.2

File System Operations

Operation	Description
R	Read or display data, attributes, owner, and permissions.
X	Run or execute the file or files in the directory.
W	Write to the file or directory or change the attributes.
D	Delete the file or directory.
P	Change permissions.
O	Take ownership.

TABLE 8.3 Access Permissions	Permission	R	X	W	D	P	O
	No Access						
	List (Directory only)	X	X				
	Read	X	X				
	Add (Directory only)		X	X			
	Add & Read (Directory Only)	X	X	X			
	Change	X	X	X	X		
	Full Control	X	X	X	X	X	X
	Special Access	?	?	?	?	?	?

Each access permission can perform a specific set of operations on the file or directory, except for Special Access, which can allow or disallow any combination of tasks.

There is no specific right for the capability to compress or decompress files. This capability is carried along with the Write permission for files and directories.

The File Permissions and Directory Permissions windows are similar but not exactly the same. The permissions for users and groups listed in the Directory Permissions window have two sets of parentheses after the description (such as Full Control (All) (All)). The first set of parentheses describes the permissions for that directory and subdirectories of that directory. Changing the Special Directory Access (see Figure 8.3) controls these permissions.

FIGURE 8.3

The Special Directory Access window contains special permissions for directories.

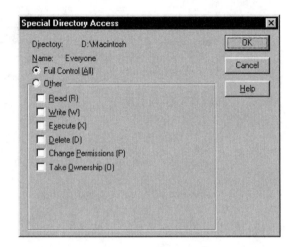

The second set of parentheses describes the permissions to be set for the current files in the directory and any new files. Changing the options selected in Special File Access (see Figure 8.4) controls these permissions.

FIGURE 8.4

The Special File Access window contains special permissions for files.

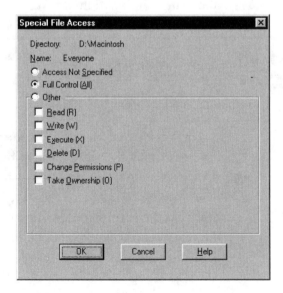

Changing Permissions

To change permissions for a file or directory, you must meet one of the following three conditions:

- You have Full Control access to the file or directory.

- You have the Change Permission permission.

- You are the owner of the file or directory.

You set permissions for directories and files graphically from the Directory (or File) Permissions window. Here's how to change the Dir_1 directory to add permission for June to access the directory and remove the permission for Everyone to access the directory. (This assumes that the C: drive on your Windows NT computer is an NTFS partition. If your C: drive does not use NTFS, substitute a drive that does.) Follow these steps:

1. Open the My Computer icon on your Desktop.

2. Open the (C:) icon (or the icon for the NTFS partition in your computer) in the My Computer window.

3. Click the Dir_1 icon in the (C:) window (or other directory in the window corresponding to the NTFS drive on your computer) to select it.

4. Select File ➤ Properties. Select the Security tab in the Properties window.

5. Click the Permissions button. Select the Everyone group in the Directory Permissions window, and then click Remove.

6. Click Add. Click the Show Users button. Select June. Click Add, and then click OK.

7. Click OK in the Directory Permissions window, and then OK in the Properties window to return to the Desktop.

You can also use command line utilities like CACLS.EXE to change permissions for batches of files, or you can use third-party utilities to automate the process.

Default Permissions

The default permissions setting for a newly formatted NTFS partition is Full Control to the group Everyone. This setting makes an NTFS volume behave much like a FAT or an HPFS volume because any user can make any modification to any file. You should restrict access to the NTFS volume by removing the Everyone group and assigning access permissions to a group with a more restricted set of users. You should, of course, make sure that the Administrators group has Full Control of the partition by setting permissions on the root directory.

WARNING The Everyone, No Access permission will deny access to an object for every user account. Usually, the administrator intends to deny access only to those accounts whose only qualification for access is membership in the Everyone group, so the Everyone, Full Control access control entry should be removed, not set to No Access.

Default permissions for a Windows NT boot partition are set during the initial Windows NT installation. These permissions are designed to keep nasty uninvited guests like Trojan horses and virii from propagating themselves into files that boot when Windows NT loads, and they are quite effective.

There is a security snag, however. If you use the command line utility CONVERT.EXE to change your boot partition from FAT to NTFS (because you read this chapter and got nervous), the default permissions will not be set for you—the Everyone group will have full control of the boot partition. To make matters worse, you can't simply change the permissions to restrict access to members of the Administrator group, because many of the services in your server depend on users being able to access certain boot files in a controlled fashion.

Copying and Moving Files with Permissions

When you copy a file (or a directory) from one directory to another on an NTFS partition, the file inherits the permissions and owner of the receiving directory. In other words, moving a file or directory from one directory to another does not change the permissions and owner of that file or directory.

The difference between copying and moving files is that when you copy a file, the original file still resides in its original location. You are essentially creating a new file in the new location that contains the same data as the old file. The new file (the copy) will have the receiving directory's New File permissions.

When a directory is copied, it receives the directory and default New File permissions of its new parent directory. As the new files are created within the new directory, they receive the New File permissions of this directory.

Moving a file or directory, instead of copying it, merely changes pointers in the directory structure on the NTFS partition. The file or directory disappears from the old location and appears in the new location but does not physically move on the hard disk. The permissions and ownership of the file or directory remain the same. A file can be moved in this manner only between directories on the same NTFS partition.

Some programs perform a move command by actually copying the file or directory to the new location and then deleting it from the old location. In this case the file obtains new permissions from the receiving directory, just as it would in a regular copy operation. People who feel the need to name things call this the *container effect*.

Ownership

By default, the creator of a file or directory has ownership of that file or directory. On an NTFS partition, Windows NT keeps track of the owners of files and directories. The owner has full control of the file or directory and can change any of its permissions.

The Owner dialog box (see Figure 8.5) shows the current owner and allows you to take ownership of the file if you have the permissions to do so. An administrator always has the permission to take ownership of a file or directory, even when the owner has restricted those rights.

FIGURE 8.5

The Owner dialog box allows you to take ownership of a file if you have permission.

No user can *give* ownership of a file or directory to another user. You must *take* ownership to become the owner. For users other than the administrator, however, the owner must allow the user the permission to take ownership of the file or directory.

Circumventing NTFS Security

Despite all the wonderful security features built into Windows NT, there are a few problems:

- NTFS can't automatically decide what security permissions are appropriate—you must.

- NTFS can't safeguard your data if Windows NT isn't running.

- NTFS can't keep applications with Read and Delete access from changing permissions automatically.

- Permissions aren't applied to backup tapes.

- Backup operators essentially have full Read access to all files.

Of course there are ways to deal with all these problems, and they are explained in the following sections.

Bad Permission Settings

Bad permissions are the number one cause of security failure in Windows NT systems. Simply put, the administrator either doesn't understand how to set security properly, or users have stored data that should be kept secure in nonsecure areas. As a security administrator, you need to be vigilant about security settings. Make sure you remove the default Everyone, Full Control permission from every location where it is not absolutely necessary. Even a permission like Domain Users, Full Control is vastly better because it denies access to guest and anonymous users.

Create a coherent and easy-to-follow secure directory structure, and make sure users are familiar with it. Test your security settings periodically from accounts that shouldn't have access to be sure permissions are configured the way you think they should be. If you can afford to, use automated security scanning software to identify security problems with your permissions structure.

The Need for Physical Security

If the hard disk of a Windows NT computer is removed and installed in another NT machine, the administrative accounts on that other machine will have full access to the NTFS files regardless of their security settings. This happens somewhat by design—data recovery is frequently more important than data security, so Microsoft chose to allow administrative accounts the ability to take ownership and assign rights regardless of the NTFS security settings. For this and other reasons, there is no such thing as data security on an NTFS drive that is not physically secured. Your hard disk and server must be secure from theft and removal in order for file security to be absolute. Chapter 21 discusses physical security in more detail.

Alien Operating Systems

Nothing prevents low-level access to an NTFS-formatted volume by another operating system if the disk is directly attached to the alien operating system. You could, for instance, boot DOS and then use a disk editor to patch together the contents of a file that would otherwise be secure.

Even worse, software exists (some of which is included on the companion CD-ROM) that will allow you to mount NTFS volumes under MS-DOS or Linux. This allows direct read-only access to the entire NTFS volume so you can use other MS-DOS tools to copy the data to another volume irrespective of NTFS permissions. Obviously, this represents a very serious security problem.

To make this more difficult, you can use stripe sets (which make it more difficult to write a driver to access the NTFS data in another operating system) and compression (which makes the data nonobvious and difficult to interpret with a direct sector editor). Neither of these "security through obscurity" methods will work against software specifically designed to crack NTFS security through an alien operating system. For that, you need encryption. For a detailed look at this area, see Chapter 3.

WARNING   A Windows NT computer that is not physically secure is not secure. There are no exceptions to this rule.

Avoid putting a dual-booting DOS partition on any computer where security is a concern. Having one just makes it easy to sidestep NT security through direct disk access. Turn off Floppy Disk Booting in the BIOS setup page, and use a strong BIOS password. Make them rip your server apart if they want access to your data! And speaking of that, put your server in a small safe with holes only for the power and network cables. You'll be the envy of all your security-conscious friends.

Reality Check: Computer Vaults

In case you're thinking that last recommendation was facetious, I've actually worked on military computer systems inside room-sized vaults that had holes only for power and network cables, and the locked vault door.

Stupid Software Tricks

Some software applications will circumvent file system permissions for you, without any effort on your part at all. All versions of Microsoft Word before Word 97, for instance, create a temporary file when you open a document. Changes are made to the temporary file, and when you close the file you've changed, the original file is deleted and the temporary file is renamed with the original file name.

This is great for crash protection (a real problem on Microsoft operating systems other than NT), but it's also great for resetting security to the defaults for that folder and for changing the document ownership to whomever last modified the file. Microsoft's official solution is to store those documents in a folder that has matching permissions for the files to inherit, not to care who owns it, to save the file with a different file name, or (of course) upgrade to Word 97.

Microsoft isn't the only company that suffers from this sort of software myopia. Any application that creates backup copies isn't likely to copy file permissions correctly unless the application is NT aware.

Tape Backup

The vast majority of network administrators routinely circumvent all the security measures they've put in place to protect data on their Windows NT servers. In fact, they do it every day by backing up all their secure, encrypted data to nonsecure, nonencrypted tape. Many administrators even carry these tapes to nonsecure facilities like their houses to make sure one tape is kept off site in case a meteor hits their primary facility. Good habits from a safety perspective, but a total security short circuit.

The default NT backup program is not secure. Restricting access to the tape provides a rudimentary form of security, but the administrator of any NT machine can overcome that restriction. Although NT Backup stores file and directory permissions on the tape for restoration, the tape itself is protected only by an administrative password. And that password is only checked if the file is restored using NT Backup. Any other software, including software that simply dumps the contents of the tape to a file, can ignore the password and proceed directly to the information stored on it. Since most servers can be completely backed up on one tape, every backup tape you make can be a nonsecure copy of all your data.

Needless to say, you should keep your backup tapes in a vault. Besides being secure, vaults are usually fireproof, earthquake resistant, and waterproof, so you'll actually be able to recover your data when you need it. Better yet, use third-party commercial backup software that encrypts the data being written to the tape based on a large key. Of course, forgetting the key makes the tape worthless, but hey, nobody said security was easy.

Another security loophole comes under the guise of tape support. Any user with the Backup Files/Directories right will be able to bypass all Windows NT security permissions when backing up files. Theoretically, this right could be exploited by software pretending to be backup software in order to gain access to any files on the machine. Practically,

---

Reality Check: Backup Tape Security

When commissioned to recover data from a Windows NT server that had been seized in a criminal investigation, I was disheartened to find that most of the data was contained in a file system that had been encrypted by a third-party encryption utility. I had neither the key nor the compute power or software to decrypt it using brute force.

I was about to call with the bad news that I would not be able to recover the data on the machine, when I noticed that the machine had a 4mm DAT tape drive. I pushed the eject button, and sure enough, a tape popped out. After determining that the tape had indeed been written by NT Backup, I restored it to a fresh Windows NT installation on a new machine (it didn't even have a password) and proceeded to take ownership of all the files, including those needed for the government's case.

---

this can be exploited simply by creating a backup tape on the server and restoring the files on another machine where the user has administrative privilege.

Policies: Server Security

- Make certain your servers are stored in an area that is secure from physical compromise under all reasonable circumstances. Make sure all nonsecurity personnel have an escort when they are in the room.

- Store backup tapes in a waterproof, flameproof safe in the server room. If tapes must be moved off site, be certain security measures are in place to prevent their being compromised while off site.

- Test software applications that create backup files to be certain files are created with appropriate permissions assigned.

Encrypted File Systems

Encrypted file systems close the one loophole NTFS leaves open: direct disk access by an operating system other than Windows NT. Using on-the-fly encryption for sensitive data effectively eliminates the risk of that data being decrypted, so long as the password or key is sufficiently long as to make a brute-force decryption impractical. Encryption is covered in detail in Chapter 3.

Encrypted file systems work in one of three ways:

- **Volume encryption:** The encryption software uses low-level disk access to encrypt the contents on a sector-by-sector basis.

- **Simulated volume encryption:** The encryption software creates a simulated volume or partition in space allocated to a single large file. This provides much greater flexibility at the cost of a small performance penalty.

- **File encryption:** The encryption software encrypts on a file-by-file basis based on a stored key that must be password activated and an extended attribute bit (much like NTFS compression) or a simple command. This is more difficult to manage, but provides somewhat greater inherent fault tolerance and selectivity.

None of these methods allows the operating system boot and system volumes to be encrypted since the operating system must be running in order to encrypt and decrypt files. This normally is of no real consequence, since a vanilla Windows NT installation isn't very secret. You can encrypt all of your data, and that is what's most important.

Of these three methods, creating a simulated volume or partition in the space allocated to a single large file is by far the most popular. It provides great advantages in flexibility and administration, and when mounted it acts just like a hard disk drive. Unlike file-by-file encryption, there's never any question as to what is encrypted and what isn't—if it's stored on the encrypted drive, it's encrypted. So when the government seizes your computer, they'll be faced with the daunting task of a brute-force decryption in order to bring any substantial charges against you.

To maintain cosmic balance, there have to be some tradeoffs. The disadvantages of encryption are:

- **Increased compute burden:** Depending upon the algorithm and the key, cryptography can guzzle CPU cycles. If your server is already heavily loaded, you'll need either more or beefier processors or dedicated cryptography disk controllers with processors on board. Consider throwing a bunch more RAM in for disk buffering if you use encrypted file systems.

- **Encrypted volumes can't mount themselves:** You've got to be there when the computer boots to provide the key or password. Storing it on the computer defeats the purpose. This makes the computer vulnerable to denial-of-service attacks that work by crashing the computer and relying on the boot to hang while waiting for action from an administrator.

- **Third-party driver software:** File system drivers run inside Windows NT's kernel space, which means that bugs in them can freeze your machine solid. You'll think blue screens are downright friendly after walking up to an NT server with a frozen cursor that isn't about to reboot. Normally, it helps to be able to curse Microsoft when NT crashes, but you'll lose that comfort when you install encryption file systems. Weigh stability versus security before installing an encrypted file system.

Time heals all problems, especially where computer power and software stability are concerned. In a few years, these disadvantages will seem quaint. Strong encryption will probably be built into NTFS, come straight from Microsoft, and will be installed by default because there's no reason not to. Either that or it will be illegal. You decide.

Policies: Disk Encryption

■ If your server's physical security could be compromised in any way, and the data on the disk warrants protection, use file system encryption.

■ Test file system encryption candidates for robust operation with voluminous file copies of complex files. Test the encrypted file system's performance characteristics. Familiarize yourself with the encryption technique used, and try to find out from the vendor what method is used to generate random numbers. Avoid encryption techniques that use the real-time clock as random number seeds, as these are frequently far less secure than they seem.

Summary

Microsoft provides two file systems with Windows NT to address different problems: FAT for floppy disks, and NTFS for everything else. From a security standpoint, you should never use the FAT file system unless there's no other option. NTFS provides a number of fault tolerance and security features that make it virtually impenetrable under a system running Windows NT.

NTFS provides file and directory security according to user and group membership. Individual access control lists enumerate the permissions; different accounts have to operate on files and directories. While Windows NT is running, there is no way to circumvent NTFS security unless a user is logged in as the administrator and takes ownership of the secured objects.

Physical security is a necessary component of NTFS security, however, because the file system can be exploited by other operating systems. Direct access to the hard drive containing an NTFS partition will reveal useful information. Encryption can be used to prevent low-level exploitation of an NTFS volume, if available and appropriate considering the hardware and user environment.

CHAPTER

9

Workgroups and Share-Level Security

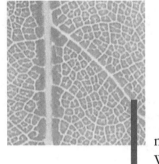

I n the next few chapters, we'll be looking at various aspects of Windows NT network security, ranging from the simple to the complex. At the simple end of the spectrum are the subjects of this chapter:

- *Workgroups*, which are simple peer-to-peer networks.

- *Shares*, which are directories or volumes made available to the network by a workstation.

Although you can set up a reasonably secure small network with workgroups and shares, these techniques don't really scale well for larger networks and high-security applications, and there are many security holes in these systems. We'll cover all you need to know about workgroups and shares in this chapter, including how to choose whether these are the appropriate solutions for your application.

Chapter 10 moves on to domain security, which is suitable for large, high-security applications.

Networking with Workgroups

As you probably know, there are two basic types of networks:

- *Server-based networks* include a dedicated server and client workstations. The server is used for all file sharing, printer sharing, and other services. A typical server-based network is illustrated in Figure 9.1.

■ *Peer-to-peer networks* consist only of workstations. Workstations can share files and printers, and make them available to other workstations. See Figure 9.2 for a diagram of a typical small peer-to-peer network.

FIGURE 9.1

In a server-based network, one or more dedicated servers provide file and print services.

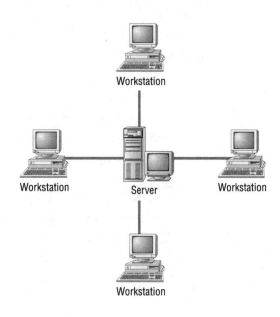

FIGURE 9.2

In a peer-to-peer (workgroup) network, no one computer is dedicated to serving files.

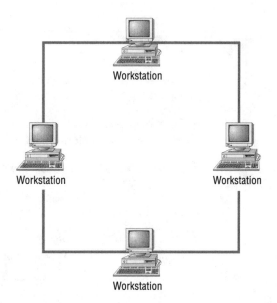

Historically, most networks have been of the server-based variety. Peer-to-peer networks are a more recent development, and are generally considered less robust—and therefore more appropriate for smaller networks than for larger ones. One of the first popular peer-to-peer systems was the networking subsystem built into Windows for Workgroups, Microsoft's network-ready version of Windows 3.11. This peer-to-peer system was refined, and a much-improved version is included with Windows 95.

Microsoft's term for a peer-to-peer network is *workgroup*. A workgroup is comprised of a small group of computers (and users), that are related in some way—they're usually in the same department or the same building. It's possible to set up a network with several separate workgroups. A simple one-workgroup network is sufficient for many small companies.

Windows NT also supports peer-to-peer networking with workgroups, and includes security features not found in Windows 3.1*x* or Windows 95. In the following sections we'll look at the ins and outs of configuring and working with workgroups, beginning with a discussion of which networks should use this system and which should use the more complex domain system, Windows NT's server-based solution.

Terminology

- **Domain:** A type of network that uses a dedicated server, or *domain controller*.

- **Peer-to-peer:** A type of network that uses interconnected workstations and no dedicated server.

- **Server:** A machine dedicated to sharing files and other services across the network.

- **Share:** A directory that has been made available across the network.

- **Workgroup:** Microsoft's implementation of peer-to-peer networking, found in Windows for Workgroups, Windows 95, and Windows NT.

Choosing Workgroups or Domains

The workgroup system is easy to set up and requires no dedicated server, but it's not for everyone. There are a variety of factors to consider in choosing whether to use the workgroup or domain model, but you can use a simple rule in most cases: The workgroup system works well with small networks of 10 users or less. If you have more users than that, or if your network spans multiple locations, you should seriously consider the domain system.

Even with a small network, the workgroup model can make life difficult for the administrator. As we'll see later in this section, you may need to create several user accounts for each user to arrange access to resources on various workstations in the workgroup.

Security is a final consideration. The workgroup model is really not meant for high-security applications, and so if you have critical data, you may wish to choose the domain system even for a smaller network. We'll look at the security holes in the workgroup system later in this section.

There's no automatic way to convert a workgroup network into a domain network. If you change between the two, you'll need to move all of the shared resources to a server, create new domain accounts for each user, and set up a security system to match the original security of the workgroup. Since this is a major effort, you may wish to choose the domain model if you anticipate that the network will grow beyond 10 users in the near future.

WARNING If you have 20 users, you might be tempted to divide them into two 10-user workgroups. While this might work, it is still as difficult to manage as a single 20-user workgroup. In addition, there is very little security between workgroups, and users may be able to access data not meant for their group.

Configuring a Workgroup

One good thing about a workgroup-based system is that it's extremely easy to configure—there's no server to install, and no need to actually create the workgroup. All you have to do is choose a name for the workgroup, and assign that workgroup name to one or more workstations. All workstations with the same workgroup name are considered part of a single workgroup.

Workstations in a workgroup can use Windows 95, Windows NT Workstation, or Windows NT Server. However, using Windows NT in a workgroup requires a bit of planning. When you install Windows NT, you are asked whether the computer will be a primary domain controller (PDC), backup domain controller (BDC), or standalone server. Choose the standalone server option; you can then configure the computer to join a workgroup as explained below.

WARNING Although you can change a standalone server's workgroup after the installation, or choose whether it is part of a domain or a workgroup, you can't change between domain controller and standalone server without reinstalling Windows NT. Be sure you know which type of network you'll use before beginning the installation.

Once you've determined the name for the workgroup, you'll also need to choose computer names for each workstation. You can use any names you wish, but they must be unique within the workgroup. You should choose names that are meaningful and easy to remember, since users may need to use these names when referring to a shared resource.

Configure each workstation to join the workgroup by following these steps:

1. Right-click on the Network Neighborhood icon on the Desktop, and select Properties.

2. Select the Identification tab. The current workgroup information is displayed, as shown in Figure 9.3.

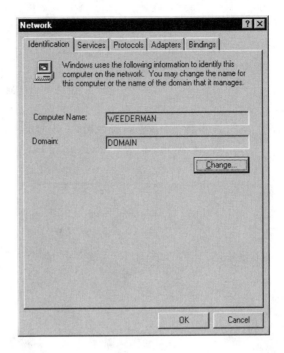

3. Click the Change button. Select the Workgroup option. (If this option is not present, your installation is not a standalone server.)

4. Enter the computer name and the workgroup name.

5. Click the OK button. The changes will take effect when you restart the computer.

The steps given here are for Windows NT. However, you can configure a Windows 95 workstation to join a workgroup using the same steps. The only difference is that you won't need to select the Workgroup option, since Windows 95 defaults to a workgroup configuration.

Creating User Accounts

Although it's easy to configure a few workstations to join a workgroup, there's another task you must perform. Unless all of the data you'll be sharing will be made available to all members of the workgroup, you'll need to set up security for the user accounts.

Since there is no central workgroup database for user accounts, your work is cut out for you: Each user needs an account for each workstation they'll be accessing nonpublic data on. In an extreme situation, this might mean you'll need to set up user accounts for all 10 of your users on each of 10 workstations—a total of 100 accounts. As you might imagine, this is why we don't recommend workgroups for networks of more than 10 users. Figure 9.4 provides an example of the user accounts that might be needed in a complex workgroup.

FIGURE 9.4

In a complex workgroup, you'll need to create several accounts for each user.

Workstation 1

Users:
FJONES
RJENSEN
HTILLMAN
JKEPLER

Workstation 2

Users:
JSMITH
FJONES
RJENSEN
HTILLMAN

Workstation 3

Users:
JSMITH
FJONES
RJENSEN
HTILLMAN

Workstation 4

Users:
FJONES
RJENSEN
HTILLMAN

See Chapter 6 for details about creating and securing user accounts.

Workgroup Security Holes

As you might have guessed from the simplicity of the workgroup system, this setup has more than a few security holes. As mentioned earlier, you should definitely consider a domain-based system for higher security. Here are some of the most glaring security problems with the workgroup system:

- Since each workstation controls its own list of user accounts, there is no easy way for the administrator to see who is logged in to which workstation.

- There's no protection from walk-up access to a workstation that holds shared data.

- As you learned earlier in this section, it's very easy to add a workstation to the workgroup—in fact, it's so easy that anyone can do it. A workstation can be hooked to the network and, given the workgroup name, can be made a member of the workgroup without so much as a password.

- Users from other domains and workgroups can access data you've made public to the workgroup by navigating to the workgroup from the Network Neighborhood window. There's no way to enforce security between workgroups.

- The users are the biggest security risk. A user can easily access the administrative utilities and control access to his or her own workstation. While you can restrict this somewhat, you still can't stop the user from causing trouble—a user could simply turn the workstation off when going home for the day, making the shared data inaccessible.

If you do use a workgroup system, you can use system policies to prevent users at the workstations from accessing some options, such as the Network control panel, that could affect the workgroup's access to data. See Chapter 7 for details.

Policies: Workgroups

- Have a strict rule (such as a 10-user limit) as to when to use workgroups and when to use domains.

- Use workstation user accounts and system policies to prevent individual users from controlling the security of their workstations.

- Try to arrange data so that as few user accounts as possible are required for users to access it.

- Make sure that building security is adequate to prevent walk-up access to workstations.

- Train users to prevent mishaps by doing things such as turning off a workstation that holds shared data.

Using and Securing Shares

The main reason to set up a workgroup—or most networks, for that matter—is to share files. Any directory on any workstation in the workgroup can be set up as a shared directory, or *share*. Although shares don't have the same level of security as NTFS directories on a dedicated server, Windows NT does provide a simple set of security features for shared directories.

NOTE Although it's often associated with the workgroup model, you can also share files from workstations within a domain. In order to do this the Server service must be running. Also, as is the case in the workgroup system, the user must have an account on the sharing server.

The basic share system in Windows NT is similar to the one found in Windows 95, although Windows NT adds a set of permissions for shares similar to the NTFS file permissions. In this section, we'll look at the process of creating and accessing shares, permissions for use with shares, and some security issues you should be aware of.

Creating a Share

You can create a share with any volume or any directory within a volume. You can create shares in either NTFS or FAT partitions, although shares in NTFS partitions can be made more secure. To create a share, right-click a drive or directory in an Explorer window and select the Sharing option. The Sharing Properties dialog box, shown in Figure 9.5, is displayed.

FIGURE 9.5

Select options to share a file or directory.

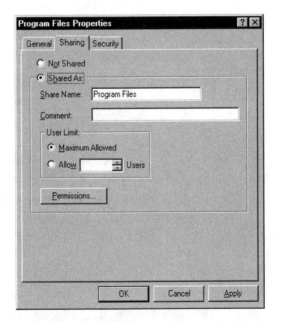

From this dialog box you can specify these options:

- **Not Shared/Shared As:** Specify whether the volume or directory should be shared.

- **Share Name:** Choose a name for the share. This name will appear as a directory name when users view a directory listing for the server. If the share will be accessed by users running Windows 3.*x*, or if your users use DOS applications, be sure to use a DOS-compatible name for the share.

- **Comment:** Enter a description of the share's purpose, or other information. (This is optional.) The contents of this field are displayed in the Explorer window to the right of the share name if the user selects the Details view.

- **User Limit:** If Maximum Allowed is selected, the number of users accessing the share is limited only by the Windows NT license. If a number is specified, only that many concurrent users can access the share.

- **Permissions:** Clicking this button displays a dialog box that allows you to change permissions for the share, as described later in this chapter.

When a directory or drive is shared, it is listed in the Explorer with a special icon that shows a hand underneath the drive or folder icon, as if to suggest an unseen hand reaching from across the network to steal items from the folder. (Microsoft probably didn't mean it this way, but this is a good way to picture just how secure shares are.)

Accessing Shares

Although a server might have several shares configured—some entire volumes, some directories several levels deep—they all appear to users as a single listing under the server's name. Users can navigate to the server name using the Network Neighborhood icon, then open it to display a list of shares.

As an example, suppose we created several shares, including VOL_F for an entire NTFS volume, and IE4 for the \Program Files\Plus!\ Microsoft Internet directory. A user who navigated to the server through Network Neighborhood would see a flat list of shares, as shown in Figure 9.6. (Notice the comment fields mentioned in the previous section.)

FIGURE 9.6

Shared directories and
volumes appear over the
network as a flat list of
directories.

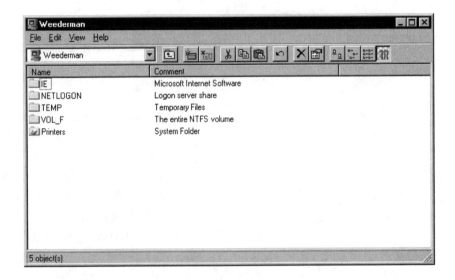

To make access to shares more convenient for users in the workgroup, you can create Desktop shortcuts to particular directories. You can also map a drive letter on the workstation to the share. This method has the benefit of fooling not only users, but also DOS and Windows applications that otherwise might not support network access. To map a drive to a share, right-click the Network Neighborhood icon and then select Map Network Drive. The dialog box shown in Figure 9.7 will be displayed.

To use this dialog box, choose a local drive letter, then choose a server name and path to map the drive to. The window at the bottom of the dialog box displays a list of servers and shares. Select the Reconnect at Logon option to have the drive mapped each time the user logs on.

FIGURE 9.7

Users can map
a local drive to a
shared directory for
convenient access.

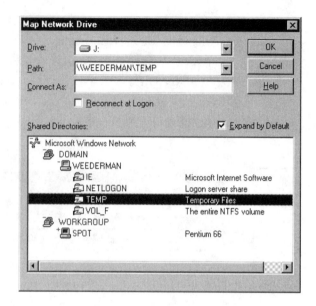

As an administrator, you have another option for displaying a list of shares on a server. The Server Manager utility includes a feature that allows you to list shares, add or remove shares, and monitor users who are currently accessing shares. To run this utility, go to the Start menu and select Administrative Tools ➢ Server Manager. Highlight a server and select Computer ➢ Shared Directories. A dialog box lists the server's available shares, as shown in Figure 9.8. From this dialog box you can add shares, edit the properties for an existing share, and remove (disconnect) existing shares.

FIGURE 9.8

The Shared Directories
dialog box accessed from
the Server Manager utility
can be used to list and
manage shares on servers.

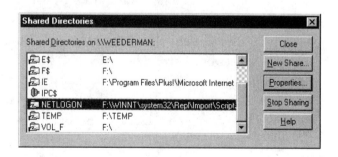

You can also access a different set of features by double-clicking a server name within Server Manager or selecting Server from the Control Panel, then clicking the Shares button. The Shared Resources dialog box, shown in Figure 9.9, is displayed. From this dialog box you can view the number of users currently accessing a share, list the users accessing it, and disconnect individual users.

F I G U R E   9.9

The Shared Resources
dialog box displays
information about user
access to shares.

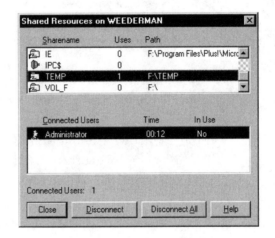

Default Shares

In the Server Manager dialog boxes shown earlier, you may have noticed several shares with names ending in a dollar sign: D$, E$, ADMIN$, and so forth. These are *administrative shares*—shares automatically configured by Windows NT, and accessible only to administrators and the operating system itself. These shares are used for remote administration and communication between systems.

Each drive is automatically given an administrative share, with the share name being the drive letter followed by a dollar sign. The ADMIN$ share is connected to the \WINNT directory on each server. There is also an IPC$ share, used for interprocess communication between Windows NT servers, and a PRINT$ share, which shares printer information between servers.

As you've probably noticed, these shares don't appear in the browse lists that you can view from the Explorer. The only way to list them is with Server Manager, which was described in the previous section.

You can create your own "administrative" shares. Any share name ending with a dollar sign ($) will be hidden from browse lists. Users (administrators or not) can access the share if they know its exact name.

Administrative shares present a potential security risk. A hacker who has gained access to the Administrator account on a single workstation in the workgroup can access the system drives of other workstations, effectively allowing administrator-level access to the entire workgroup.

You can improve security by disabling the administrative shares. You can remove the shares from each drive's Properties window, or use the Server Manager utility's Stop Sharing option. It's best to disable all of these, and then add a share for any specific drives or directories that need to be available across the network.

Share-Level versus File-Level Security

Windows NT's file sharing system includes its own level of security, called *share-level security*. This type of security allows you to set permissions for a share, either for groups or individual users. This is similar to file system security, but not nearly as sophisticated (or as secure.)

There is one significant advantage of share-level security: It works with any shared directory, whether it's on an NTFS or FAT volume. This is the only way to assign permissions to FAT directories. However, the share permissions you set only affect remote users. Users logged onto the machine locally can access anything on a FAT volume, shared or not.

If you're sharing files on a FAT volume, you can't use file-level security. Share-level security provides an alternative, but can be cumbersome. For example, suppose you wanted to share an entire volume but restrict users' access to certain directories. Using only share-level security, you would have to share the volume, then share each individual directory with restricted permissions. (The permissions of lower-level directories override those given to higher-level ones.)

On the other hand, if you have the luxury of using NTFS on the volume, you can simply add a single share for the volume with full access for Everyone, then use file-level security to restrict some directories.

File-level security is more sophisticated and more complex than share-level security. File-level security is explained in detail in Chapter 8.

Share Permissions

As mentioned above, share-level security uses a simple list of permissions. To set permissions for a share, click the Permissions button in the Sharing Properties dialog box. The Access Through Share Permissions dialog box, shown in Figure 9.10, will appear.

FIGURE 9.10

Set permissions to control user and group access to the share.

Access Through Share Permissions

Access Through Share: E_DRIVE
Owner: |
Name:

Everyone   Full Control

Type of Access: Full Control

OK   Cancel   Add...   Remove   Help

By default, the Everyone built-in group is given Full Control access to the share—in other words, share security is not implemented by default. The first thing you should do to secure a share is remove Everyone from the list. You can then add any number of users or groups, and give them specific permissions. The following are the permissions available for shares:

- **Read:** Allows users to list contents of the directory, open and read files, and execute programs.

- **Change:** Allows users to create, delete, or modify files, as well as the Read permissions.

- **Full Control:** Allows all Read and Change permissions. In addition, users can change permissions and change file ownerships.

- **No Access:** Disallows access entirely. This is useful in subdirectories, where it can be used to override access given at a parent directory.

Since share permissions are not as powerful as file-level permissions for NTFS volumes, you should use file-level security for NTFS volumes. Share permissions are most useful for FAT volumes, which would otherwise have little security.

Spotting Share Security Holes

Shares are often used in a workgroup environment, and thus have the security holes of workgroups described earlier in this chapter. In addition, be aware of the following potential security problems:

- If the share is on a FAT volume, there's no protection at all from local access. (Of course, as you learned in Chapter 8, using the FAT system is a security hole in itself.)

- Another concern about FAT volumes is that users can easily create additional shares and make them available over the network. This may be useful, but also may lead to information being made available to the entire network (when perhaps the user meant to simply share it with one coworker).

- If you're setting up a complex sharing arrangement using share-level security, there's no easy way to view the big picture, and it's easy to forget to restrict access to a key directory or two.

- If you use shares with dollar signs ($) at the end of their names to create hidden shares, be aware that this isn't an entirely secure practice, since it basically amounts to security through obscurity. Avoid this except where security isn't critical.

Policies: Share Security

- Use NTFS volumes for file sharing whenever possible, and use file-level security rather than share-level security when possible.

- To make administration easier and leave less possibility for error, use several shares on one workstation, if possible, rather than scattering them among several workstations.

- If you're using sharing on FAT volumes, be aware of the possibility of local access.

- Instruct users to avoid inappropriate local access and creating or modifying shares.

- Try to grant permissions for a share to a specific group or set of users, rather than using the Everyone group and attempting to restrict users at the subdirectory level.

Summary

Workgroups are peer-to-peer networks where workstations can share files, and where no computer is dedicated as a server. Workgroups are most suitable for networks with 10 users or less, and situations where high security is not a requirement. Workstations can be added to the workgroup without any security checks. Administration can be difficult, since you need to create user accounts for each user on each server with a share the user needs to access.

Shares are directories or volumes made available from a workstation or server for access by other computers in the network. Shares can be publicly available, or can be given a list of users or groups with permission to access. Shares use share-level security, which allows you to control permissions for individual shared directories. File-level security is superior to share-level security, but can only be used on NTFS volumes.

CHAPTER

10

Domain Security and
Interdomain Trust Relationships

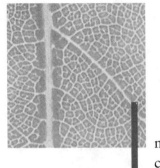

I n the previous chapter you learned about workgroups, which can be used for peer-to-peer networking and are recommended for networks of 10 users or less. In this chapter we'll look at the domain model, which uses dedicated servers in a single domain to support larger numbers of users. You can also set up a system of trusted domains to support many thousands of users.

We'll start with a basic look at the domain model and its advantages and a discussion of how domain security works. We'll then take a look at security for multiple domains. Finally, we'll look at the Active Directory, which will provide multiple-domain security in Windows NT 5.

Domain Basics

As demonstrated in the previous chapter, the workgroup model doesn't work well with large, complex networks. Since the database of user accounts is separate for each machine, you end up creating accounts for each user on each machine he or she needs to access. In a network with 100 workstations and 100 users, each needing to access an average of 10 machines, you would need to create a total of 1,000 user accounts. Needless to say, we don't recommend the workgroup model for such a network.

The domain model provides an alternative. By using dedicated servers called *domain controllers*, this type of network uses a single, shared security database. You can create a user account once for the domain, and the user can log in from any workstation to access data on the domain controller and other servers. A domain-based network can support large networks—up to 100,000 users—without creating administration difficulties.

Terminology

- **Domain:** A type of network that uses a dedicated server, or *domain controller.*

- **Domain controllers:** Machines that supervise the domain and provide user authentication. These include primary and backup domain controllers (PDCs and BDCs).

- **Member server:** A server that acts as part of a domain, but is not a domain controller.

- **Replay attack:** Copying a valid session key and attempting to reuse it.

- **Trust:** A relationship between domains that allows users of one to access the other without separate authentication.

Domain Server Roles

In a workgroup, all of the workstations and servers have the same role: to act as points of access for users and as servers for shared data. In the domain model, workstations and servers have more clearly defined roles. The domain model supports four basic server roles:

- **Primary domain controller (PDC):** This server acts as the main security checkpoint for the domain, and stores the main copy of the security database.

- **Backup domain controllers (BDCs):** These servers serve two purposes: to store replicas of security information as a backup for the PDC and to authenticate users without slowing down the PDC. If the PDC goes down, one of the backup domain controllers will automatically assume the primary role temporarily.

- **Member servers:** These are servers that are members of the domain and may store shared data, but don't act as domain controllers.

- **Standalone servers:** These servers are not members of any domain. They can be used as standalone machines or can participate in a workgroup.

These are explained in more detail in the sections that follow.

Be sure that you understand these server roles before installing any machines in the network, since you must choose the role a server will take when you install Windows NT. In most cases, you cannot change the server role after installation. The one exception to this rule is that PDCs can become BDCs, and vice versa.

Primary Domain Controller

The primary domain controller is the most important machine in the domain. There can be exactly one PDC per domain, although you can have multiple domains on the network. When a user attempts to log on to the domain, the PDC authenticates the user name and password, providing an access token for future use.

The PDC should be the first server installed on the network. When you install it, you will be asked for a name for the domain. This can be changed later, but the server role can't. The security account database is created when the PDC is installed and is used from that point forward.

Backup Domain Controllers

Backup domain controllers act, not surprisingly, as backups for the PDC. They periodically contact the PDC and obtain a copy of the security account database. This database can then be used to authenticate users, just as the PDC can; however, the database on a BDC can't be changed. To make changes to user accounts, you must be able to reach the PDC.

If the PDC is unavailable for a period of time, the BDCs on the network contact each other and hold an election to determine which machine will assume the duties of the PDC. This machine can then act as primary controller and allow changes to user accounts. When the real PDC comes back online, it will take over again and update its database with changes made while it was down.

You can promote a BDC to a PDC permanently. See the *Promoting Backup Domain Controllers* section, later in this chapter.

Member Servers

The simplest type of servers on a domain are member servers. These machines don't store a copy of the domain's security database at all and cannot authenticate users. You can use these servers to store shared data or as application servers; however, users will need to authenticate with a domain controller before they can access this server.

Standalone Servers

Finally, standalone servers are not configured to join a domain at all. These can be used as standalone machines, requiring a local login to obtain access. You can also use them as members of a workgroup, as described in Chapter 9. Users at these servers can't authenticate with the domain without changing their configuration.

Adding Member Servers to a Domain

As you may recall from the previous chapter, it's easy to add computers to a workgroup—a bit too easy, since you can do it without any authentication or permission from other machines. The process of adding machines to a domain is much more secure.

If you installed the machine as a primary or backup domain controller, it is configured automatically. Follow these steps to add a member server to a domain:

1. Be sure the server is connected to the network.

2. Log on to the domain as Administrator.

3. Right-click the Network Neighborhood icon on the Desktop, and select Properties.

4. Select the Identification tab. The current domain information is displayed.

5. Click the Change button to change the domain information. The Identification Changes dialog box, shown in Figure 10.1, is displayed.

F I G U R E   10.1

The Identification Changes dialog box allows you to change domain membership settings.

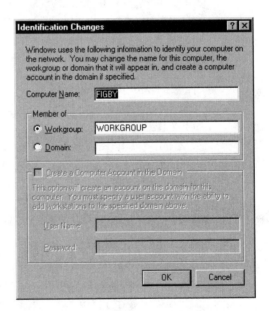

6. Select Domain, and enter the name of the domain to join. Also, be sure the computer has been assigned a unique name.

7. Check the Create a Computer Account box. Enter the domain's Administrator user account and password.

8. Click OK.

9. Exit the Network Properties dialog box. Restart the computer to join the domain.

This process creates an account on the PDC corresponding to the computer's name. Thus, the PDC has complete control over which servers are members of the domain, and it's impossible to add a member without a valid administrator account for the domain.

Promoting Backup Domain Controllers

You can promote a backup domain controller to a primary domain controller if the PDC is permanently unavailable or if you need to transfer the primary database to a better or faster machine. Follow these steps to promote a domain controller:

1. Run the Server Manager utility from the Administrative Tools menu. Be sure you are using Server Manager for Domains, which is provided with Windows NT Server.

2. A list of servers is now displayed, as shown in Figure 10.2.

3. Highlight the BDC you wish to promote.

4. Select Promote to Primary Domain Controller from the Computer menu.

5. Click OK to exit and save the changes.

You may have noticed that there is no demote option. Promoting a controller will not result in two PDCs on the network. Instead, the PDC (if currently available) is automatically demoted when you promote a BDC.

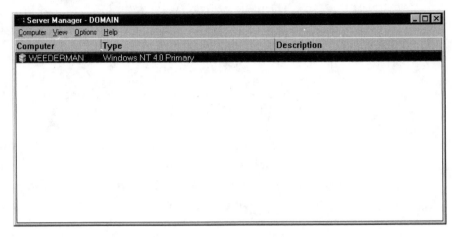

FIGURE 10.2

Use the Server Manager utility to promote a backup domain controller.

Domain User Accounts

The advantage of a domain is that there is only one list of user accounts. This list is stored on the PDC and backed up by the BDCs. Although each workstation or server in the domain still has its own security database, this applies only to local access to the machine. Domain user accounts are stored on the domain controllers and provide authentication for the entire domain.

As with standalone machines, the Administrator account on the PDC is the default administrator for domains. This account is created when you install the primary domain controller.

You can create domain user accounts using the User Manager for Domains utility, shown in Figure 10.3. The process is identical to creating an account on a local machine. The main difference is that a domain has two types of groups:

- Local groups have access to the local computer only. Each machine has a separate list of local groups.

- Global groups apply to the entire domain. A single list of global groups is kept for the entire domain.

FIGURE 10.3

Use the User Manager for Domains utility to create domain user accounts.

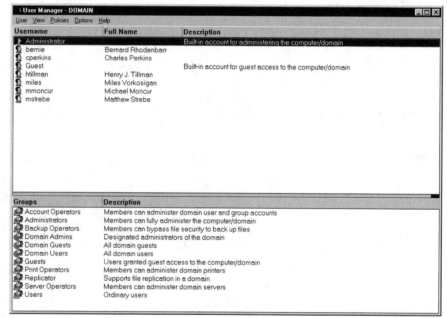

See Chapter 6 for more information about user accounts and the User Manager for Domains utility.

Policies: Domain Security

- Keep the domain controllers physically secure.

- Don't leave an account (particularly Administrator) logged in at PDCs or BDCs.

- Add trust relationships between domains only when access is needed by several users.

- Follow the instructions in Chapter 6 to keep domain user accounts secure.

Securing Multiple Domains

The domain security model used by Windows NT does not sufficiently address the needs of large organizations, especially those with many offices. Microsoft recognized this early on, and implemented the concept of trusting domains to allow authorized users of one domain access to another. Domain administrators can establish trust relationships between domain controllers to give very specific access to members of other domains.

Multiple domain security is merely an extension of domain security. As such, at the time of this writing there are no known bugs or security exploits that specifically target the trust relationship nature of domain security. Therefore, multiple domain security is deemed as reliable as domain security.

There are two participants in any trust relationship. They behave as follows:

- The trusting party has faith that any users from the trusted party are authorized users, and will allow them access to its resources contingent, of course, upon their presence in the access control lists of the objects.

- The trusted (the trustee, or the recipient of trust) domain controls the account security of the users involved in the trust relationship, and provides the user's credentials to the trusting domain.

Trust relationships simply provide a way to give users access to foreign domains without having to have a separate account in every domain. It is possible to create a user account for each user in every domain, and modern clients like Windows 95 and Windows NT will automatically log a user on when access is created. Trust relationships merely shortcut the domain account process by allowing users of one domain to access other domains that trust their domain. If you think of the trust relationship process this way, you'll have no problem keeping the intricacies of the process straight.

Trust Relationships

Trust relationships are established between domains using the User Manager for Domains utility. The establishment of a trust relationship involves two steps:

- On the domain controller of the trusted domain, you must add the new trusting domain to the list of *trusting* domains.

- On the domain controller of the trusting domain, you must add the new trusted domain to the list of *trusted* domains.

These steps can be performed in either order, but in this order the relationship is established immediately. If you do this in the reverse order, there is a delay of about 15 minutes while the domains are synchronized. A basic trust relationship is illustrated in Figure 10.4.

Trust relationships are unidirectional—that is, when one domain trusts another, the reciprocal relationship is not assumed. To initiate a bidirectional trust, you just establish two trust relationships. Add the foreign domain to both the trusting and the trusted domains lists at the same time and then perform the reciprocal operation on the other domain controller. Figure 10.5 shows an example of a bidirectional trust.

FIGURE 10.4

A trust relationship allows resource access across domains.

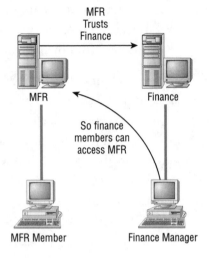

FIGURE 10.5

In a bidirectional trust, two domains trust each other.

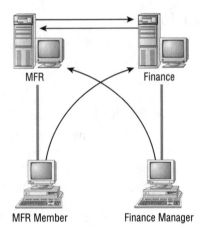

Groups and Accounts

Establishing trust between domains does very little to provide access to users, however. The only group membership that is automatically changed by trust relationships is membership in the Everyone group. Everyone automatically contains all interactive users and all network users, which implicitly includes members of trusted domains. Other than this, no automatic group memberships are assumed. If you've followed our advice so far, you've eliminated the presence of the Everyone group in all your shares and access permissions anyway, so this is of little help.

Each global group can be considered to automatically contain the name of the domain from which the group comes—for instance, the Domain Admins group on the Finance domain should be thought of as FINANCE\DOMAIN ADMINS rather than as Domain Admins. In this light, it's obvious that FINANCE\DOMAIN USERS is not the same thing as MANU-FACTURING\DOMAIN USERS.

This means, of course, that you must now add the FINANCE\DOMAIN USERS global group to every share or NTFS folder that you want finance users to have access to inside the MANUFACTURING domain. Since Windows NT doesn't allow global groups to contain global groups, the FINANCE\DOMAIN USERS global group cannot be added to the MANUFAC-TURING\DOMAIN USERS global group. The reasons for this are complex and have to do with the possibility of creating circular security lookups that would never resolve.

There is no easy or good way to automate the process of giving specific permission to users of other domains. You simply have to add the domain global group permission to each resource those users should have access to. Consider the domain model shown in Figure 10.6 and think about the myriad of permissions that would have to be implemented to properly secure this network.

Centralized Multiple Domain Security

One of the fundamental security axioms is that of simplification: The simpler a security problem is, the easier it is to control. For instance, vaults have only one door. This means they need only one lock, which requires only one key, the distribution of which can be tightly controlled. More doors equals more keys equals more complex distribution problems and more opportunity for failure.

FIGURE 10.6

A complex trust model

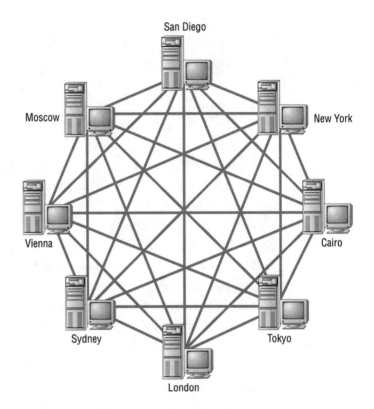

Microsoft's trust relationship model suffers from poor design and a lack of consideration for the large customer's need for centralized administration and authority. The original intent—single logon to domain resources—is a very solid idea. Trust relationships violate the original intent of the single logon to domain resources because they assume all domains are equal peers; there is no established authority over all domains the way a primary domain controller is the established authority over all domain member servers. For this reason, a hierarchical group structure that can be noncircular is not available, so administration and security are made more complex.

Having a single authentication authority promotes security by simplifying the problem. The complexity allowed by numerous trust relationships makes it far more likely that you will accidentally incorrectly implement security permissions. To contain the security problem effectively, there must be some way to centralize account management and trust relationships. Of course there is, otherwise this section wouldn't be here.

You can use the trust relationship model to implement your own central authentication authority, referred to as the *master domain*. In the master domain concept, all user accounts are created in one domain. That domain's primary domain controller is dedicated to the task of domain control and logon authentication, and should be used for no other purpose.

All other domains (referred to as resource domains) share resources and files as required by your organization. They do not implement user accounts of their own—rather, they trust the master domain for user account information. Now, since all of your users are members of a single domain, you can add share permissions for MASTER\DOMAIN USERS rather than simply DOMAIN USERS on each of your resource domains. Then, when you install the PDC for the various resource domains and set up security for the resources it provides, you can establish the trust relationship between the resource domain and the master domain, and implement correct and simple permissions. You also have the added benefit of being able to centrally administer all account management. Figure 10.7 shows the master domain concept in action. It's simple and reasonably effective.

To make the process work correctly over wide area networks, simply establish a backup domain controller for the master domain in each major location (those having more than 25 or so users; fewer users probably won't benefit much from a dedicated BDC).

Active Directory

The domain security model will change completely with the release of Windows NT 5. Because the current domain model does not scale well past 100,000 users, and because complex new network

FIGURE 10.7

The Master Domain
security concept

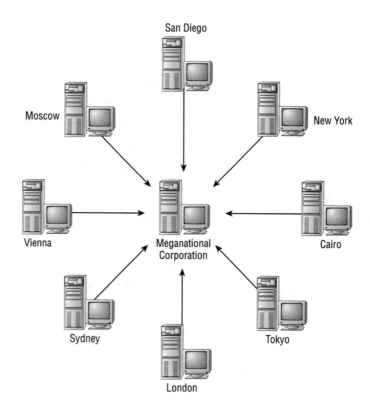

relationships exist between vendors and customers over the Internet, the standard NT security model is not sufficient. At the time of this writing, Windows NT 5 is expected to adopt a new centralized security and resource management paradigm called *Active Directory*.

Active Directory is based on the existing standards embodied in the lightweight directory access protocol and the Kerberos trust encryption standard developed by the Massachusetts Institute of Technology with corporate sponsors. It will actually be based on the Microsoft Exchange Server service platform and index mechanism and will:

- Use Lightweight Directory Access Protocol (LDAP) rather than a proprietary protocol.

- Allow interoperation in X.500 environments like Novell NetWare NDS (NetWare Directory Services).

- Use DNS (rather than WINS and browsing) as a locator service; eliminate WINS, which never really worked well, and browsing, which doesn't scale well.

- Provide a managed hierarchy for the management of all network objects—file shares, groups, e-mail users, Web pages, printers, etc.

- Partition administration and security into organizational units (subdomains), domains, and trees of domains.

- Scale to 10 million users (up from about 100,000 with NT's current domain model) per domain, with domain linking (trust relationships, but way farther out).

- Replace the registry-based Security Accounts Manager with security objects stored on Exchange Server-based Active Directory servers. This will increase the speed of authentication in large environments.

- Implement MIT's Kerberos authentication based on private key encryption that is far more secure than NT's LanManager or NT network authentication.

- Support public key encryption for logon authentication of business partners and clients.

- Emulate NT 3.*x*/4.*x* directory services for backward compatibility. However, domains that are emulating older security models cannot be added to a domain tree.

Of course, this remains a wish list on Microsoft's part until the actual software is released. How much of the above functionality is included in the product that is finally released cannot yet be known at the time of this writing. Microsoft has hinted that it may release an Enterprise addition with the full set of features and a small business edition with a more limited feature set. (You can probably guess which version will become available first.)

The Kerberos Authentication System

Kerberos authentication, an Internet standard for user authentication, is the basis for the new security features that will be available with Windows NT 5. Like the Windows NT domain model, Kerberos is a trusted authentication system, meaning all the servers in the domain hierarchy use (and trust) the same system.

Kerberos does not rely upon a secure network, the physical security of network clients, or the host's IP address for security. Kerberos was designed from the ground up with the assumption that traffic on the network could be read, written, and changed at will by a theoretically perfect hacker who would understand all of the security-related issues in the network and the Kerberos system. In other words, Kerberos does not rely on security through obscurity at all.

Kerberos keeps a database of the private keys of its clients. Those clients may be users or network services. If the client is a user, that private key is an encrypted password. In this respect, the system behaves very much like NT security.

Kerberos authentication is described in detail by Internet Request for Comments (RFC) 1510, available at: `http://www.globecom.net/ietf/rfc/rfc1510.shtml`.

Once a Kerberos client has been authenticated by the Kerberos system, the Kerberos server generates unique session keys that two clients (the user and the service being used) use to authenticate messages between one another. Kerberos supports three levels of encryption security:

- **Authentication:** "Proves" to each client that the other is who it says it is initially, but provides no further identification mid-stream.

- **Message signing:** Includes an encrypted signature with each communiqué (packet) of data, proving to each client that the message originates from the other client and is not a forgery. Message signing is sometimes referred to as *safe messages*.

- **Encryption:** Makes the contents of each packet indecipherable to parties other than the clients engaged in the conversation. These are called *private messages*. They are used by the Kerberos system for the transmission of passwords over the network.

In most Kerberos systems, any or all of these methods can be used for any session, depending upon the level of security required and the amount of load that the system can tolerate for the encryption process.

Kerberos is based on DES encryption. DES (Data Encryption Standard) was developed by the U.S. government for public use. That being the case, many people have theorized that the government may have some method for decrypting the contents of DES-based systems that is faster than a simple brute force attack. This has not been shown to be true, and no statistical evidence has implied any abnormal weakness in DES security. Kerberos is not dependent upon DES encryption, and it is not clear whether or not Microsoft will use DES encryption in its implementation.

See Chapter 3 for details about DES and other forms of encryption.

Kerberos session keys have a short valid lifetime. If an intruder gains access to a session key, it's only useful until it expires. If your session key lifetime is set to a reasonably short value, for instance one day, even if compromised it can only be used for that day. Copying a valid session key and attempting to reuse it is called a *replay attack* (because the session key, although not decrypted, is simply used again by a third party to gain access). Most Kerberos implementations attach a time-stamp to each message that must be valid to within a few minutes or the message is assumed to be an attempt at a replay attack.

Reality Check: Play It Again

Replay is a common encryption exploitation technique. One example of this technique is a recently discovered security hole in Internet Explorer. When you log into a Web site from Windows NT running Internet Explorer, the remote server can request your user name and password to identify you on that system. Your encrypted password is transmitted over the network to the remote server. Your password does not need to be decrypted by a third party to be exploited—they can simply pass the encrypted data to the server to gain access as you.

Kerberos authentication and the new security features of Windows NT 5 will dramatically change the face of security in Windows NT environments. Perhaps the next edition of this book will be much thinner!

Summary

The domain model allows for greater security and easier administration than the workgroup model. In a domain, there is one list of user accounts. The domain can include a primary domain controller (PDC), one or more backup domain controllers (BDCs), and any number of member servers, which provide no authentication.

In a large network, multiple domains provide for greater security and convenience. By assigning trusts between domains, you can create a complex security model for access throughout the network. Trusted domains don't allow you to administer the network as one giant domain, however; you must log in to each domain to assign trusts.

The domain security model will change completely with the release of Windows NT 5. The new system is called *Active Directory* and supports a more unified approach for managing large networks. Active Directory will easily support networks larger than 100,000 users and will provide better support for Internet standards.

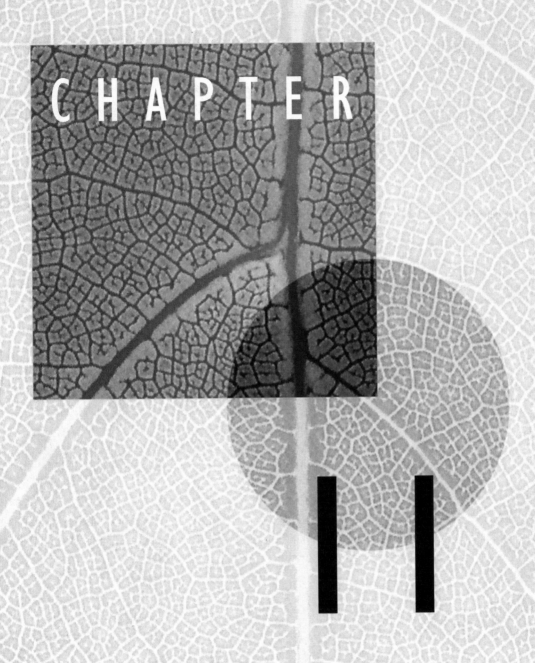

CHAPTER

11

Fault Tolerance

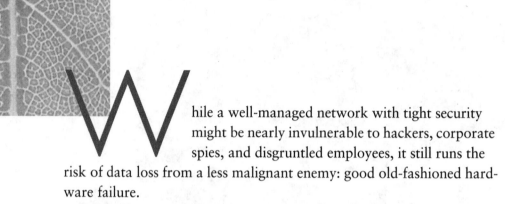

hile a well-managed network with tight security might be nearly invulnerable to hackers, corporate spies, and disgruntled employees, it still runs the risk of data loss from a less malignant enemy: good old-fashioned hardware failure.

While disk crashes, virii, and backup strategies are often overlooked when discussing the subject of security, these issues can cripple a network as completely as the deepest security hole. In this chapter we'll look at ways to keep your data safe from hardware failures, ranging from simple measures such as backups to complex, expensive solutions such as duplicate servers.

This type of security is referred to as *fault tolerance*. The key word here is *tolerance*: there's no way to prevent hardware problems with absolute certainty. What you can do is build measures into your network to tolerate—and quickly recover from—these problems.

In addition to protecting drives with fault tolerance measures, be sure the data within those drives is safe from prying eyes. Chapter 8 discusses file system security.

Disk Mirroring and Duplexing

Two of the most commonly used—and useful—fault tolerance measures are disk mirroring and duplexing. Both of these involve using two separate disk drives to store the same data. When one drive fails, the other can take over. We'll look at the basics of these techniques and the differences between them, then move on to practical instructions for creating mirrored and duplexed drives.

Mirroring versus Duplexing

Disk mirroring and disk duplexing are very similar—in fact, Windows NT considers them to be the same thing, and uses the term *mirroring* to describe both. The differences between the two are described in the following sections.

While mirroring or duplexing increases fault tolerance, it's no substitute for regular backups. Be sure to set up a backup strategy, as described later in this chapter.

Disk Mirroring

In *disk mirroring,* two disk drives (or partitions within larger drives) are linked together as a *mirror set*. A mirror set is treated by Windows NT as a single volume. For example, two 200MB partitions on separate drives can be combined to create a single mirror set with a 200MB capacity. Figure 11.1 illustrates a mirror set.

Reads and writes are handled differently on mirror sets than with a single drive:

- Writes are performed simultaneously to both of the drives in the mirror set. This can cause a slight decrease in speed, but is not usually an issue with good drives and controllers.

- Reads are performed from one drive. Since either drive can be used equally well for a read operation, the decrease in write speed is coupled with a dramatic increase in read access speed.

Of course, the main purpose of disk mirroring is redundancy. Since it's rare for two drive crashes to happen at the same time, data is quite safe from most drive failures.

FIGURE 11.1

In a mirror set, two partitions on different drives store the same data.

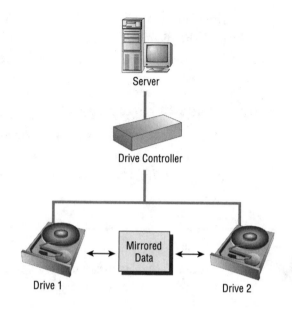

When a crash makes one volume inaccessible, Windows NT informs the administrator with an alert message at the server. The drive is still accessible from the second copy, although a new second drive should be added to the mirror set as soon as possible.

Don't confuse mirror sets with volume sets. A volume set is a combination of two or more partitions used as a single volume; since the volume is spread among different drives, this actually reduces fault tolerance.

Disk Duplexing

There's one serious deficiency in disk mirroring. When a hard drive becomes inaccessible, it doesn't always indicate a problem in the drive: Sometimes the hard disk controller is at fault. On top of that, when certain disk drive problems occur, the controller might lock up and make the remaining drive inaccessible.

Disk duplexing addresses this problem by duplicating not only the drive, but the drive controller as well. With two separate controllers attached to two separate drives, there's very little possibility that both drives will become inaccessible at once. Figure 11.2 illustrates disk duplexing.

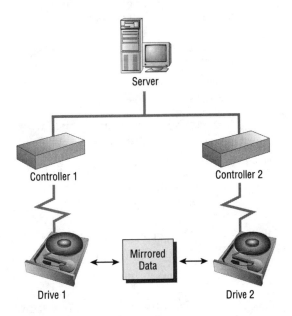

Duplexing is more reliable than disk mirroring, but today's drive controllers are quite reliable, and you may not need duplexing. However, using multiple drive controllers may increase performance, so duplexing can be a side benefit.

Windows NT treats mirroring and duplexing as the same thing. To set up duplexing, simply install two drives with separate controllers and proceed with the installation of a mirror set, as described later in this section.

> ### Reality Check: Mirroring Doesn't Solve Everything
>
> During the time I worked as a network consultant, a client called to report that they had lost several crucial files on their server—despite the duplexed drives we had installed. I investigated and found that the directory on the volume had somehow become corrupt, causing some of the files to overwrite each other.
>
> Of course, as the errors occurred and compounded, they were automatically and efficiently duplicated on the second half of the mirror set. We had to reformat the volume, but were able to save most of the files and restore the rest from a backup.

Hardware Requirements

In order to create a mirror set, you'll need at least two disk drives. They should be set up in the following way:

- One drive contains a partition with a volume already created in it. The volume may be FAT or NTFS formatted, and it may already contain data.

- The other drive has free (unpartitioned) space equal to or greater than the size of the formatted volume.

- If you wish to use duplexing, the drives should be connected to separate drive controllers. However, you can install an additional controller later to convert from mirroring to duplexing.

You can set up disk partitions and volumes using the Disk Administrator utility, available from the Administrative Tools menu in Windows NT.

As an example, Figure 11.3 shows the Disk Administrator display before mirroring. The PAYROLL volume on Disk 0 (Drive E) will be mirrored; Disk 1 contains enough free space to hold the mirrored volume.

FIGURE 11.3

Disk Administrator shows the status of volumes before mirroring.

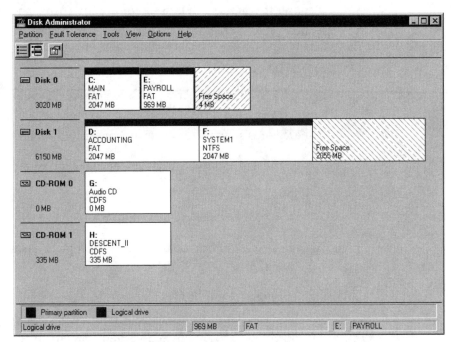

You can create a mirror of the system or boot drive. However, if the main drive fails, the mirror copy will not boot until it has been made active. Be sure you have a boot disk for this purpose.

Drive Types for Mirroring

SCSI drives are traditionally recommended for mirrored sets, and particularly for duplexing. IDE drives can be used, but there are two potential problems: Installing two IDE controllers may cause a conflict, and many IDE controllers aren't able to be accessed at the same time.

If you do use IDE, use controllers specifically intended for mirroring. Cards are available with two controllers in a single card for this purpose. If you use SCSI, use high-quality cards, and be sure they support bus mastering—this allows two controllers to work simultaneously.

The RAID Standard

RAID (Redundant Array of Inexpensive Disks) is a standard for disk mirroring and fault tolerance. This standard defines a series of numbered levels. Three of these are supported directly by Windows NT:

- Level 0 refers to striped sets without parity, described later in this chapter.

- Level 1 is disk mirroring (or duplexing).

- Level 5 refers to striped sets with parity, described later in this chapter.

Although these RAID levels are supported in software by Windows NT 4, the RAID standard is usually used to describe hardware devices. Controller cards are available that implement RAID entirely in hardware, requiring no support from the software.

The main advantage of hardware fault tolerance measures is speed: Since all of the logic for writing to multiple drives and reading from a mirror set is handled by the card, there is no system slowdown when mirroring is implemented this way.

The main disadvantage of these devices is cost. While a typical high-end SCSI controller usually costs between $200 and $300, RAID controllers often cost well above $800.

It is unclear at the time of this writing whether Windows NT 5 will support software RAID. If you choose to use it, you may need to delay upgrading until you've installed a hardware solution.

Creating a Mirror Set

If you have a volume to be mirrored and enough free space on a separate drive, you're ready to create a mirror set.

The Disk Administrator utility can destroy data if not used carefully. Be sure to read all the steps carefully before beginning this process. If you make any mistakes, exit without saving the partition information—no changes are made to the disk until you exit or select the Commit Changes Now option.

To create a mirror set, follow these steps:

1. In the Disk Administrator utility, locate and select the partition you wish to mirror. It should already be formatted.

2. Hold down the Ctrl key to allow multiple selections. Select an area of free space on another drive to hold the mirrored partition. The free space must be equal to or greater than the size of the formatted partition.

3. Select Fault Tolerance ➣ Establish Mirror.

4. If you are mirroring the boot drive, you are shown a notice reminding you that a boot floppy is needed to boot from the mirrored drive in the event of a crash. Click OK.

5. Select Partition ➣ Commit Changes Now.

6. Click OK.

7. You will need to restart the machine to begin the mirroring process.

After you have established the mirror, the system will begin to copy data from the formatted volume to the new volume on the second drive. You can begin to use the mirrored drive immediately. Figure 11.4 shows the Disk Administrator display of the volumes in the earlier example after mirroring.

FIGURE 11.4

Disk Administrator
shows the status of
volumes after mirroring.

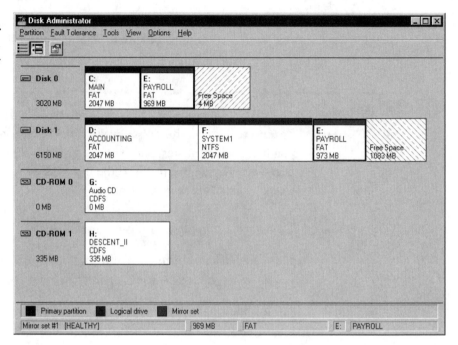

The space on the mirrored volume may be slightly larger than that on
the original volume, because a few megabytes of overhead are used in
the mirroring process.

Repairing a Mirror Set

If one of the drives in a mirror set fails, you can easily install a new
drive and reestablish the mirror set. Follow these steps to repair a
mirror set:

1. In Disk Administrator, select the failed drive. Select Fault Tolerance ➤ Break Mirror Set.

2. Shut down the computer. Remove the drive that failed and replace it with the new drive. Restart the computer.

3. When you run Disk Administrator, NT will inform you that a new drive has been detected. Click OK.

4. Select the undamaged portion of the mirror set.

5. Hold down the Ctrl key, and select an area of free space on the new drive equal to or larger than the size of the volume.

6. Select Fault Tolerance ➤ Establish Mirror.

7. If the failed drive was the boot drive, make sure the new partition is active and bootable.

8. Exit Disk Administrator and restart the server.

Terminology

- **Backup:** A copy of files on a network written to a storage device, usually a tape drive.

- **Disk duplexing:** A fault tolerance mechanism that uses two drives connected to separate controllers, with data copied between them.

- **Disk mirroring:** A fault tolerance mechanism that uses two drives hooked to the same controller.

- **RAID:** A standard for fault tolerance, often implemented in hardware. There are several levels of RAID protection.

- **Replication:** Any system that duplicates data between servers. This can include simple replication, supported by Windows NT, or full server replication via third-party software.

- **Virus:** A malicious program that copies itself between computers and occasionally damages data.

Using Stripe Sets

A *stripe set* is created from a number of equal-sized partitions on different drives. Basic stripe sets are defined by RAID level 0. Unlike mirror sets, stripe sets store different data on each of the partitions. When data is written to a stripe set, it is interwoven between the disks.

The main advantage of stripe sets is speed: Since data is written to several drives at once, both reading and writing speed are greatly improved. The down side is fault tolerance. Since each file is spread between two or more drives, the failure of a single drive could make all files inaccessible.

Windows NT provides a fault-tolerant alternative to stripe sets: A *stripe set with parity* uses part of the available space on each drive to store parity information, created by applying an algorithm to the actual data. When a drive in the set fails, the parity information on the remaining drives can be used to recreate that drive's data. Striped sets with parity are equivalent to RAID level 5.

As with mirroring, a stripe set can be vulnerable to disk controller problems if the drives share a controller. Providing each drive with a separate controller makes a striped set with parity as secure as disk duplexing.

Creating a Stripe Set with Parity

As with mirroring and duplexing, you can create a striped set using the Disk Administrator utility. Since basic stripe sets actually decrease fault tolerance, we'll focus on stripe sets with parity here.

Before creating a stripe set, you should have free space on each of the drives you will use. For a stripe set with parity, you will need at least three drives. Follow these steps to create a stripe set with parity:

1. In Disk Administrator, select the area of free space on one of the drives. Hold down the Ctrl key and select the remaining areas of free space.

2. Select Fault Tolerance ➤ Create Stripe Set with Parity.

3. Enter the size of the stripe set. The number you specify will be divided among the drives to create a partition on each one.

4. Click OK.

5. Select Partition ➤ Commit Changes Now.

6. Click OK. You will need to restart the computer to begin using the new volume.

Repairing a Stripe Set with Parity

When one member of a stripe set with parity fails, Windows NT automatically removes it from the stripe set. A new drive should be added as soon as possible because a parity stripe set with a failed drive is no more reliable than a regular stripe set.

When the drive fails, an alert message is displayed at the server and logged in the system event log. Follow the steps below to repair the stripe set:

1. Shut down the server.

2. Remove the failed drive and install the new drive.

3. Restart the server.

4. When you start Disk Administrator, you are informed that a new drive has been detected.

5. Highlight the stripe set, and then hold down the Ctrl key and select the available space on the new disk.

6. Select Fault Tolerance ➤ Regenerate.

Windows NT will repair the stripe set in the background. Depending on the size of the volume and the other usage of the server, this may take from several minutes to several hours.

Using Server Replication

One step above mirroring, duplexing, and stripe sets is server replication—keeping an entire redundant server. This provides a dramatic amount of fault tolerance, since you're protected from any disaster up to and including the complete destruction of the server.

Windows NT provides an extremely basic service for data replication between servers. We'll examine it in the sections below, and also introduce two third-party alternatives with more sophisticated features.

The server replication techniques here deal only with files and directories on the servers. Be sure you've configured your backup server as a backup domain controller, so it can also keep a copy of the user authentication database and serve as a login server. See Chapter 6 for details.

Windows NT Replication

Windows NT's data replication feature is called the Directory Replicator service. This service supports the copying of files and directories between servers, with some limitations:

- This service can't copy open files.

- It only copies files—it doesn't compare versions between the servers and synchronize them.

- It can only replicate one directory path at a time.

If you have replication needs that fit within these limits, this can be a handy feature. Follow the steps below to set up the directory replicator service:

1. Create a user for the replication service, and make the user a member of the Replicator and Backup Operators groups.

2. From the Services control panel, select Directory Replicator.

3. Click Startup. The Service dialog box, shown in Figure 11.5, is displayed.

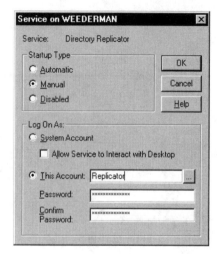

4. Select Automatic, select This Account, and enter the name of the user you created in step 1.

5. Click OK.

6. Select Start ➤ Programs ➤ Administrative Tools ➤ Server Manager.

7. Highlight the server, and select Computer ➤ Properties.

8. Click Replication. The Directory Replication dialog box, shown in Figure 11.6, is displayed.

9. Select the directory to replicate, and select one or more servers to export it to or import it from.

10. Click OK, and exit the Server Manager utility.

FIGURE 11.6

Select directories and servers for replication.

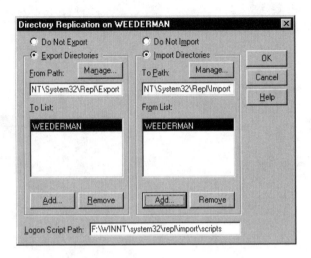

Third-Party Alternatives

Since Windows NT's built-in data replication service isn't very impressive, third-party vendors have stepped in to provide sophisticated server replication products. Two of the most popular products are described here.

Vinca Corporation

Vinca makes StandbyServer for NT, a server replication system that uses a dedicated network link between two servers to handle the mirroring traffic. It installs as a device driver, so from Windows NT's point of view, you're simply creating a mirror set—one of the partitions just happens to be in another machine.

Since it uses (and requires) its own network link, this product doesn't increase network traffic. StandbyServer also has the ability to automatically switch the backup machine into place when the main server goes down.

Vinca can be reached on the Web at `http://www.vinca.com/`.

Octopus Technologies

Octopus Technologies, a division of Qualix Group, currently produces two server replication products for Windows NT:

- Octopus DataStar allows you to create mirror copies of NT volumes, or selected files, on one or several servers across the network.

- OctopusHA+ is an enhanced version that provides the same data replication capabilities, but also has the ability for a backup server to automatically take over when the original server goes down.

Octopus Technologies can be reached on the World Wide Web at `http://www.octopustech.com/`.

Backups and Virus Protection

The most complex and expensive RAID system available may not help you in the event of a fire or earthquake, or even if a user manages to replace several critical files with copies of his Excel spreadsheet. In these cases backups invariably come to the rescue.

A good backup strategy can save your network, and can even be helpful in the event of an IRS audit. In this section, we'll look at backup devices and the software and policies you should use with them. We'll also take a quick look at virii, another danger from which data replication will not protect you.

Backup Devices and Software

The most common device for backups is a tape drive. Tapes vary in capacity from a few megabytes to several gigabytes, and the cost seems to vary exponentially with the capacity. Other devices, such as removable hard disk drives, offer increased speed but usually have lower capacities and cost more.

In determining the best backup device for your network, you should first determine the amount of data you will need to back up. If you are selective in your choices, you may be able to use a lower-cost backup media.

For example, you should definitely include directories where users save files in the backup. You may not need to back up directories containing applications, since it might be just as easy to reinstall them.

You'll also need backup software. Microsoft provides a simple utility with Windows NT called Backup. This utility is shown in Figure 11.7 and can be found in the Administrative Tools menu. You can use Backup for simple backup and restore operations, but it isn't very sophisticated.

FIGURE 11.7

A simple backup application is included with Windows NT.

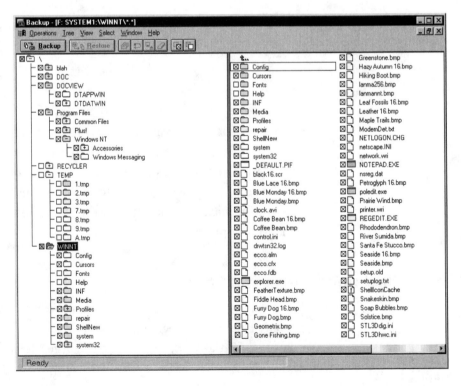

Third-party backup software provides a much larger array of features than Microsoft's Backup. Look for these features in a third-party product:

- Support for your chosen tape device

- Choice of full or incremental backups

- Ability to schedule backups daily

- Management of tape rotation

- Ability to back up open files

- Support for any database applications you use, such as SQL Server or Exchange Server, so their files can be backed up properly

- Ability to back up open files

- Application-specific backup (SQL Server/Exchange Server), so that it is able to back up the data from these services without them having to be shut down

You also have a choice between local or networked tape backup. In a single-server network, a tape drive in the server works well. In a large network with many servers, you may wish to dedicate a server to handling backups, and use backup software that supports backup over the network.

Some backup software can even back up files at client workstations. While this sounds like a neat feature, it's best to avoid using it—allowing users to store files at their workstations opens up a whole new can of worms, and the network traffic to back up all of the clients could be enormous. It's best to remind users to store all important files on the server in a directory that will be backed up frequently.

Creating a Backup Policy

Whether your backups are done automatically by software or painstakingly by an underpaid employee, you should create a backup policy to specify when backups will be performed, what they will contain, and what will be done with the tape.

Your policy should specify which type of backup will be used: full, incremental, or differential. In addition, it should specify which tapes will be used and how they are rotated. These specifics are explained in the sections below.

Whichever backup strategy you choose, be sure you test the backup by restoring the first backup tape you make, and periodically test another tape. Be sure you don't find out about the problems with your backup software when a critical file needs to be restored.

Reality Check: What Backup?

When visiting a new client as a network consultant, one of my first questions is, "What's your backup policy?" Unfortunately, the answer is often a blank stare.

One client responded by proudly leading me to a back room, opening a box, and removing a backup tape. Upon closer examination it turned out that the tape had been created by the consultant who installed the network in the first place, and it was nearly seven years out of date. Needless to say, I sold the client new backup software.

Full Backups

In an ideal world, everyone would make full backups every day. In simple terms, a full backup contains all of the files on the server, or at least all of the ones you consider crucial. This strategy has a clear advantage: You always have a current backup of all of the files, and you can restore any file from that tape.

Unfortunately, full backups aren't for everyone. For one thing, it may be difficult to find—or afford—a backup device with the capacity of your network if you have a large amount of storage. You can use multiple tapes, but someone will have to be there to put each new tape into the machine.

Another issue is the amount of time it takes to perform a backup; since you'll usually schedule backups to run in off hours, the available time is limited. If your company has multiple shifts, there may be only a 3- to 4-hour period when no users are logged in. (Some backup software is able to back up open files, which solves this problem.)

Incremental Backups

An incremental backup backs up all of the files that have changed since the previous backup. This means a much smaller space is required on the backup tape—even in large networks, it's rare for 1GB or more of data to be changed in a day.

An incremental backup strategy still requires a full backup occasionally. It's best to make a new full backup regularly—say, once a week—and then make incremental backups during the week.

The FAT and NTFS file systems include a file attribute called the *archive bit*, which indicates that a file has been changed. Backup software can use this feature to back up only the changed files and reset the archive bits after the backup.

There's a definite down side to incremental backups. If you need to restore a single file, you may not know which tape it's on, and if you need to restore a number of files in a directory, they may have wound up on several different tapes. In addition, tiny changes to a large file (such as a database) can cause the whole file to be included on each tape.

Luckily, some backup software packages are able to take the guesswork out of incremental backups by keeping a catalog of when files are backed up and to which tape. The software can then tell you which tapes are needed to restore a file or group of files. Backup software that directly supports your database files can back up only the records that have changed, saving space on the tape.

Differential Backups

Differential backups are a compromise between full and incremental types. A differential backup includes all of the files that have changed since the last full backup. Thus, restoring always requires a maximum of two tapes: the most recent full backup and the most recent differential backup.

Backup software can use the time stamps that are built into the FAT and NTFS file systems to determine the files that have changed since the date and time of the last full backup. Since this is a complex process, not all backup software supports this type of backup.

One down side of differential backups is that they require more space than incremental backups. Each day's differential backup is bigger than the one before, and you may have to increase the frequency of full backups to prevent the differential backups from becoming too large.

Tape Rotation

The final item you should include in your backup policy is a plan for tape rotation. Since you probably don't intend to buy a new tape for each day's backup, you can reuse (rotate) the tapes.

The simplest tape rotation strategy for full backups uses two tapes, alternated each day. The tape that isn't being used each day should be stored off-site in case of disaster. One easy way to do this is to assign an employee to take the tape home (although this can be a security risk as well).

Another common method uses a weekly set of tapes. A full backup is made one day each week, and an incremental backup the remaining days. With this strategy you always have a current backup of all files.

Depending on your needs, you may wish to expand this strategy. Four-week rotations are popular; some companies even archive one of the tapes each week for accounting purposes.

Avoiding Virii

Computer virii are one of the most feared causes of data loss—but, as it turns out, they have more of a reputation than they deserve. Despite the media attention devoted to virus attacks, you're much more likely to lose data due to a disk crash than to a virus.

Nevertheless, you should be aware of the potential for damage by virii. These malicious programs are usually spread in two ways: on floppy disks (such as those an employee might bring to work to install a favorite game) and in downloaded files. (For details about some of the ways virii are introduced into networks, see Chapter 2.)

The good news is that, first of all, the companies that make virus protection software have a much larger budget than the virus creators, and so installing and continuing to update a good software package can prevent any trouble.

Second, due to its inherent security, Windows NT is immune to most virii. However, NT is vulnerable to some virii, such as macro virii (see below). In addition, files stored on a Windows NT server and manipulated by users can be a breeding ground for DOS and Windows virii.

In the following sections, we'll take a quick look at the three main types of virii. Be sure the software you choose is able to detect all of these.

Boot Sector Virii

The oldest and most common virii live in the boot sector of a hard disk and spread through the boot sectors of floppy disks. If you turn on your PC with a floppy in the drive, there's a good chance it will attempt to boot the floppy before the hard drive, and this is often how a virus moves onto a new hard disk.

The BIOS in most new computers includes a virus protection option that prevents software from writing to the boot sector of a disk. If turned on, this prevents the spread of these virii entirely.

BIOS boot sector protection may cause conflicts with some software. Ironically, the software that most often causes conflicts is virus protection software.

Executable File Virii

A slightly more sophisticated type of virus attaches itself to executable files. The virus then runs whenever the file is executed, and is able to spread to any other executable files it can find.

These virii most often affect DOS executables. Windows NT applications are unaffected, and even Windows 3.1 applications are relatively immune to virii. Preventing write access to executable files on a server can stop these virii from spreading across the network.

Macro Virii

Macro virii are the latest craze among virus programmers. These virii are written in a higher-level language, such as the macro language built into Microsoft Word. These virii are attached to documents and can spread to other documents that are saved after opening the infected one.

Luckily, macro virii are relatively harmless, and Microsoft has worked to close the security holes in the Word macro language (the most common macro virii are specific to Word). Most virus protection software also handles the known types of macro virus.

Policies: Fault Tolerance

- Use disk mirroring or duplexing for critical data. Use duplexing when possible.

- If you have three or more drives, use a stripe set with parity for added speed and reliability.

- Consider using hardware RAID, which is faster and is independent of the operating system.

- Repair damaged drives in mirror or stripe sets as soon as possible.

- For extreme fault tolerance, consider using a third-party server replication system.

- Create a backup strategy and test backups regularly.

- Use virus protection software, and train users to avoid introducing virii into the network.

Summary

Fault tolerance is the area of security that deals with data loss due to hard drive crashes and other disasters. While disasters are inevitable, you can quickly recover from them when they happen.

Measures for fault tolerance include disk mirroring and duplexing, which duplicate a volume on two separate drives; stripe sets with parity, which distribute a volume among several drives and keep check-sums in case of a drive loss; and server replication systems, which keep an entire server aside for emergencies with a copy of all data.

Your network's fault tolerance policy should also include regular backups, tape rotation, and an up-to-date backup stored off site. You may also want to consider virus protection software to protect files on the network.

CHAPTER

12

Remote Access

Remote access allows network users to attach any computer to your network using the public telephone network and modems. Remote access is the enabling technology for the "work-at-home revolution" and for the Internet—nearly all home connections to the Internet use remote access technology to dial into UNIX or NT servers or into terminal servers on an IP network.

Without remote access, the Internet would still simply be an interesting educational and scientific network of universities and high-tech businesses.

Remote access is still the method used most often by hackers to intrude into private networks. (The Internet will pass remote access sometime in 1998 as the most popular method of intrusion.) You must consider using remote access just as carefully and just as suspiciously as Internet connections on your network. Putting together a physically secure network with a robust firewall means nothing if a hacker can let his fingers do the walking around it.

The advent of low-cost high-speed modems has made a reality of remote access for graphical user interface operating systems like Windows 95 and Windows NT. Features like adaptive speed leveling let users make the most of whatever connection they have, be it from home, a hotel room, or over a cellular radiotelephone. Remote control software makes modems even more useful than slow LAN connections because it can respond nearly as quickly as a local user's computer; since massive files are not transferred over the link—only keystrokes, mouse movements, and drawing commands are.

This chapter outlines the risks associated with remote access, provides brief coverage of the hardware and software used to achieve various types of remote access, and then covers the various methods you can use to keep your network secure without restricting it to local use.

Reach Out and Hack Someone

The hacker's love affair with the telephone networks used by remote access technology predates personal computers and local area networks. Since the mid-1970s, hackers have been using tone generators, modified telephones, and custom dialers to route their own phone calls and usurp billing accounts. This lets them use long distance trunks without paying for the time, and helps them cover their tracks by making calls difficult, if not impossible, to trace.

Like the Internet, the public phone system was put together without concern for security. After all, in the 1960s when these systems were designed and implemented, no one could possibly afford the expensive equipment required to generate custom tones just to get free long distance Figure 12.1 shows how the public switched telephone network transmits a telephone call between two telephones. Note that there may be only one telephone company involved for local phone calls, and more than two for long distance.

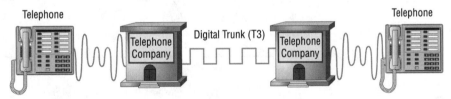

Phreaking

Of course, the phone company was very surprised by the semiconductor and the personal computer. Personal computers with sound capabilities and modems made it possible to generate all the tones used by the phone company to control DTMF (dual-tone multifrequency, or touch tone) switching equipment, allowing phreakers to route their own calls, redirect charges, and gain administrative control over phone switches. It took about a decade to lock down the national telephone system to make it reasonably hack-proof.

This lock-down pushed phreakers away from the public network and into private ones—not because the public telephone network is 100 percent hack-proof, it's just harder to hack than private exchanges that usually aren't secured properly.

Although the phone companies had secured their equipment, private companies still used equipment based on the same old technology. By dialing the toll-free number of a major company, then entering codes reserved for traveling sales personnel, phreakers could route calls back out of the Private Branch Exchange (PBX) with the corporation picking up the entire bill. Of course smaller phone companies that use dial-up codes and calling card companies are big phreaking targets, too.

Reality Check: Corporate Phreaking

American Express's 1-800-THE-CARD phone number is probably the most hacked exchange of all time. As of 1994, the company had lost millions in illegal telephone calls routed through their exchange. In the face of such relentless hacking attempts, most companies change their phone number (the phone companies require such a change in order to monitor hacking attempts against the original number), but American Express had far too much advertising effort invested to make that an option.

If your company has a PBX, it's likely that your remote access lines pass through it. You may use dial-back to control who can access your network from the telephone system. Dial-back requires the calling party to provide their telephone number and then hang up. The system then calls back to the number provided it's on a list of phone numbers that are authorized for callback. In this way, your network can't be called from just anywhere.

Hackers who can gain control of your PBX can very likely figure out how to bypass lines that are designated for dial-back and those that aren't because they originate inside your internal telephone network (a remote office coming in on a WAN link, for instance). For instance, you may not require dial-back on phone lines usually reserved for sales-people or for numbers that you don't provide to employees (because other servers use the numbers to establish wide area network connec-tions). Once they figure out how to dial into your PBX, they can quickly determine how to further exploit the system to gain access without being impeded by your dial-back security settings.

Familiarize yourself with the PBX and make sure that it isn't pro-viding an easy way onto your network. When you attach modems to internal lines coming from a PBX, you make it possible for someone who controls the PBX to reassign which outside line telephone numbers attach to specific modems—this can potentially circumvent your dial-back security settings. The best approach is to make no exceptions for internal users. Treat all remote access to your network with the same level of security.

Policies: Telecommunications Security

- Make telecommunications security an integral part of your network security if your network can be accessed via modems.

- Don't allow special access to inside lines or telecommunication lines that originate from remote offices. Treat all inbound telephone lines the same regardless of their origin.

War Dialing

But how would hackers get your remote access phone number anyway? If you restrict the distribution of remote access phone numbers, you'll be safe, right?

Wrong—hackers have a lot of time on their hands. Most hackers are high school or college students, or are underemployed. It's very common for hackers to use automated software to have their computers simply dial random numbers or all numbers in a series (all night while they sleep) looking for computers that answer their calls. This is called

---

Terminology

- **Cellular:** Radiotelephony that works by establishing a radio link with a "cell site," or fixed radio transceiver connected to the telephone network. This radio link can be handed off to other closer cell sites as the radiotelephone moves, thus enabling (in theory, anyway) truly mobile permanent telephone connections.

- **PCS:** Personal Communication Service. Digital cellular that digitizes the radio signal in the radiotelephone to allow lower transmission powers, light encryption, and loss-less transmission.

- **Phreaking:** Hacking telephone systems, whether by computer or other means. The term comes from "phone freak."

---

war dialing. When a computer answers, the software simply logs the number and hangs up. This almost never triggers an alarm, since misdialed numbers are so common.

An overnight war dialing session usually yields about 10 phone numbers for modems that answer the phone, excluding fax machines. The hacker will then explore these phone numbers by dialing in with terminal software like HyperTerminal, which comes with Windows 95 and NT. Computers that give the telltale signs of an easily hacked system become targets, while computers that put up some serious resistance are usually ignored.

The vast majority of the computers that answer the phone are used by public or private wide area networks and Internet service providers like AOL, TymeNet, SprintNet, and CompuServe. A hacker looking for a private network will ignore these and keep looking. UNIX or NT machines make for more interesting targets because they are generally located on private local area networks.

War dialing also refers to the process of automated dial-up code guessing in an attempt to gain access to a telephone network owned by a long distance provider, calling card provider, or corporation. By repeatedly dialing the access number and then a random number, the computer can detect when access is allowed and record the successful number. That code number can then be used to get free long distance service. Say, for example, that a hacker doesn't want to pay for long distance. The hacker sets up their computer to dial AT&T's phone card access number (1-800-CALLATT), sends the touch tones to get to the calling card section, and then just sends random numbers of the correct length. About 1 percent of the time, the call will go through, so the hacker's computer records that number as a valid AT&T calling card number that they are then free to exploit whenever they want.

Reality Check: War Dialing

When the authors were nascent security experts (teenage hackers), we occasionally set our computers up to war dial alternate access telephone companies (for the sole purpose of collecting statistics for later use in this book, of course). A solid week of war dialing provided surprisingly good results—about 60 valid phone card numbers. But a 12-year-old friend who illegally used one taught us all a valuable lesson when the FBI raided his house, confiscated his computer, and held his parents liable for a $20,000 telephone bill.

Policies: Alarming Software

- Use alarming software to detect numerous attempts at password guessing over dial-up networks. You can use the standard performance monitor to detect this activity, or purchase third-party alarming software.

Cellular Security Risks

Cellular phones are the ultimate extension to the remote access network. Using cellular radiotelephones, you can dial into your network from literally anywhere in the United States—even from a moving vehicle if necessary. Traveling salespeople, marketers, and executives use them all the time to access their networks from the road. Usually, using a cellular radiotelephone with a computer requires a special modem or a dial-tone adapter.

Hackers love analog cellular phones, which are by far the most common variety. Their signals are easy to pick up with a scanning radio receiver and are not encrypted at all. By feeding the audio output into a standard modem, a hacker can log all the computer information that goes over the air on that connection. That data includes the cellular phone's ESN (electronic serial number, which identifies the phone to the cellular network), the telephone number being called, clear text passwords, account names, and all the other data that travels over a remote access connection. A dial-back from a secure remote access server even provides the telephone number of the cellular phone.

Scanning is done using a specially built radio receiver (called a *scanner*) to automatically tune through the radio spectrum looking for interesting signals—much the way you would tune through the radio bands looking for a good radio station. Scanners merely perform the seek function much faster than a normal radio and are capable of scanning through the entire useful radio spectrum. They can easily pick up cellular phone signals.

Hackers don't know when someone will pass through their area on a cellular link. But an enterprising hacker can sit in his car in the airport parking lot and choose between two or three simultaneous cellular remote access connections. The remote telecommuter's corporate network just became a target for that hacker.

Cloning is another common cellular phone hack. Hackers program cellular phones (usually stolen ones) with identification numbers they get from their scanners when you pass near while using your cellular phone. They then begin racking up cellular bills on your account, and are able to answer when your phone rings—for instance, when your remote access server calls back! Figure 12.2 shows how cellular remote access connects to the public switched telephone network.

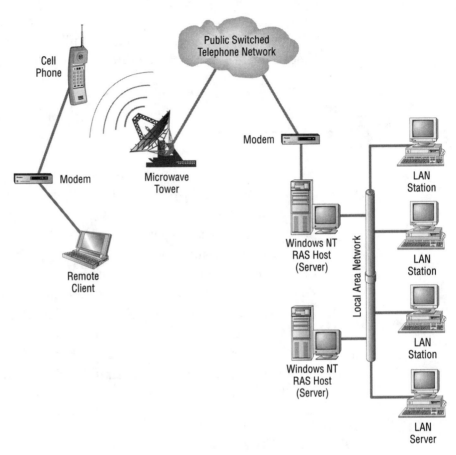

FIGURE 12.2

Overview of cellular remote access

WARNING
If you use your analog cellular phone for remote access to your network, you are exposing yourself to considerable risk. It takes only a serial cable, the jack from your phone's charger, and a PC to clone most analog phones, and complete instructions are available on the Internet.

Digital cellular radiotelephones (also called PCS) are far more secure than analog cellular phones—but their simple encryption scheme has already been cracked. PCS cellular providers have backed down from claiming that PCS is secure to claiming that PCS is more secure than analog technology. The security difference between them is currently very significant, however—it takes very dedicated hackers to crack PCS encryption, and PCS cellular phones still have not been cloned, which means there's (currently) no threat of a misdirected call back over PCS.

PCS is a far better medium than analog for modem traffic due to its clarity and noise immunity.

Finally, billions of dollars worth of laptop computers are stolen every year, usually from airports and hotels. Since many remote users use scripts to automate the tedious and error-prone process of logging in remotely, you've got the makings for another big security hole when a laptop is lost. A stolen laptop can become a key into your network from anywhere on the planet. Hackers can decrypt the password files stored on laptops to obtain the account names and passwords of everyone who has attached to your network with that machine.

Most employees, loathe to admit the loss of an expensive piece of equipment, may spend days searching before reporting the theft of a laptop to the network security staff. During that time, your network has been an open book for a thief.

In through the Out Door

Many corporations are turning to the Internet as a cheap way to route data long distances because there are no distance-based charges. It is far less expensive than paying for toll charges on dedicated telephone lines.

Rather than dialing directly into a corporate network some distance away, users dial a local Internet service provider and then attach to the organization's secure server using some sort of encryption tunneling software, usually the Point-to-Point Tunneling Protocol software provided free with Windows NT. This method of attaching to a remote server is reasonably secure, but it does cause the potential problem that anyone who gets hold of an account name and password could log on. With a standard account lockout policy (where users are locked out after missing five or so passwords), that shouldn't be a problem.

Policies: Laptop Computers

- Carefully consider the wisdom of providing cellular telephones and modems for use with laptop computers. This technology isn't usually justified considering the relatively modest increase in productivity compared to the cost and the security risk of a lost laptop.

- Limit the number of employees who use laptops to those that absolutely need them to perform their jobs. Corporate laptop usage should not be considered a perk, due to the inherent security risk and the cost of replacement.

- Foster an environment where users are not afraid to come forward immediately when a laptop is missing, and emphasize the importance of an immediate warning to the staff in charge of network security. Generally, this means creating a policy where users won't be held personally responsible for the loss.

So goes the thinking. Unfortunately, there is a major security problem with many home computers logged onto the Internet. One-third of all Internet home users who use Windows 95 to attach to the Internet have file sharing turned on, and have no passwords assigned to restrict access. This means that any hacker with a home user's IP address can map that user's hard disk and rifle through its contents looking for password list files (.PWL), public key texts, e-mail contents, corporate files, or anything else the remote user stores on their computer. Figure 12.3 shows how a hacker can gain access to an Internet client computer

How do hackers target a specific user and determine their IP address when it's dynamically assigned? They don't. This is a target of *opportunity hack*. Hackers will simply IP scan an entire IP domain looking for computers with TCP/IP port 139 (NetBIOS session) open and port 135 (browser) closed. These are the fingerprints of a Windows 95 computer with file sharing enabled.

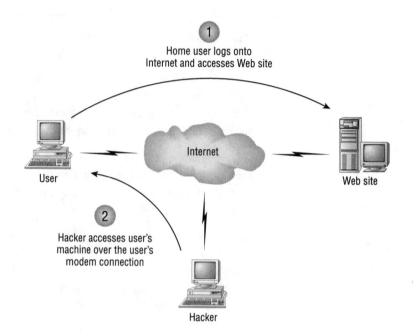

FIGURE 12.3

The security risk of
Internet connections

Reality Check: Thanks for (File) Sharing

To come up with meaningful statistics for this book, I used IP address-scanning software to check the responses from other computers attached to my Internet service provider. (This software is provided on the companion CD-ROM.) About 70% of the computers scanned were Windows 95 machines with file sharing turned on. Half of those had no password to protect access to their hard drives, making it easy to map their hard disk and rifle through its contents. Shocked by this result, I expanded the breadth of my scan to include other ISPs and enough clients for a reasonably accurate statistic. While I performed this scan, fully one-third of all the computers active on the Internet (via the remote access connections of Internet service providers rather than a direct Internet connection) were open to intrusion in this manner.

The hacker then maps all the drives that are not password-protected, and then rifles through the contents of your employee's hard drive downloading .PWL files and anything else that might be of use to gain access to your server directly. If enough information exists on the home user's hard disk, they might find the address of your server, an account name, and a password. Armed with this information the hacker makes your corporate server a target.

How do hackers map drives over the Internet? It's easy: All versions of Windows support this, and Windows NT makes it really easy. Simply right-click on Network Neighborhood, select Map Network drive, enter two backslashes followed by the IP address, type another backslash followed by the share name (usually C or C$ for the C drive), and click OK. A new network drive shows up in My Computer just as if it were a server on your local network.

Policies: Internet Access

- Do not allow attachment of clients over the Internet, even when using IP-encrypted tunnels. Encrypted tunnels only provide security for the socket between the home user and your server—they do not protect the home user from attack. Force home users to dial in directly despite the cost.

- If you chose to allow attachment via the Internet, be absolutely certain that home users who attach via the Internet do not have file sharing turned on. Use automatic scanning software across the range of IP addresses attached to your network to make sure that no clients respond on TCP/IP port 139. Appendix B shows you how to scan your network for excess services.

- For distant telecommuters, consider a constantly connected 56K frame relay as an alternative to long-distance ISDN. Frame relay has a fixed monthly cost, and it is available to home users in many metropolitan areas.

Profile of a Hacker

Just who are these hackers, and why do they hack?

Hackers almost invariably start out as curious teenagers who have recently mastered the basics of their computers and are looking for a challenge. They begin hacking because it's technically challenging and because it's thrilling both to gain access to a system and to rifle through other people's stuff.

Teenage hackers that eventually outgrow the habit constitute about 90 percent of all hackers and about 20 percent of the threat to security. Hackers nearly always start in their teens because accumulating the sheer volume of trivial computer knowledge required to successfully hack most systems takes more time than a usefully employed adult can afford to spend on it.

Teenagers usually spend their time working up to the big hack that will gain them respect among their peers and vault them into real hackerdom (grand prize: a Web page that people actually visit). Most teenage hackers graduate from hackerdom the day they graduate from high school or college. They then get real jobs where their knowledge of hacking makes them pretty good at network security.

Real hackers (and the real security threat) are those teenage hackers who, for whatever reason, aren't able to acclimate to the social reality of the adult world and for that reason are underemployed. They usually hold "pay the rent" jobs or grunt programming jobs that have no future and don't occupy much of their minds. This lack of material success usually causes feelings of resentment against the establishment, which they frequently refer to as "BigGov" and "BigBiz."

Real hackers are frequently associated with various "patriot" groups like militias, and spend their time trying to embarrass various government and law enforcement agencies.

These real hackers, as opposed to the wannabes, are the products of a combination of high intelligence, low utilization of skills, failure to bind to the establishment, and membership in a social group where their hacking exploits bring them the esteem of their peers. These hackers are the ones who find new vulnerabilities and write the tools that exploit them. They rarely have a specific agenda and usually don't cause any real harm. There exists in hackerdom a "leave no trace" ethic that most adhere to because denial-of-service attacks don't accomplish anything and don't win respect from their peers, and because they don't want to get caught. Most of these hackers will continue to hack for their entire lives.

Although most hackers frequently break laws (especially software piracy laws), they aren't actually out to cause damage. Most often, they are attempting only to show their hacking prowess and to embarrass Microsoft (or the BigBiz *du jour*). The risk posed by these hackers is that they occasionally get pissed off at someone and join the ranks of the criminal hacker.

Despite the common perception that hackers are social outcasts and loners, they rarely actually work alone—and never in a vacuum of information. Hackers use Internet Web pages, Usenet newsgroups, and mailing lists to disseminate information. They form hacking cadres to trade exploits and information.

Hackers even hold a convention yearly in New York and Las Vegas. This convention is attended in nearly equal numbers by hackers and members of federal law enforcement and federal espionage agencies. It's a surreal environment, to say the least.

Finally, the last category of hackers is those hackers who are actually criminals. Criminal hackers use their powers for evil. They may be paid to perform their tasks or they may be seriously antisocial, but, in any case, their objective is true destruction and exploitation for profit or revenge. There is a persistent myth in hackerdom that governments and major businesses recruit hackers to perform their dirty work. The authors know of no substantiated instance of this type of activity by a U.S. government agency or a corporation.

Lest you think badly of the teeming hordes of teenagers and real hackers who are not actually criminals, remember this: Were it not for them, the criminal hackers would have free reign in virgin unhacked territory. Most other people would simply assume this territory was secure because no one exploited it routinely. The millions of hackers at work out there find security problems for us, and force (through embarrassment and bad press) vendors to fix the problems that otherwise would be easy for them to simply dismiss.

Remote Accessories

Remote access technology is built largely upon one device: the modem. Various incarnations of this device fulfill all of the different functions required for complete remote access, both on the client side and the server side. In addition to modems, direct digital ISDN adapters are popular. ISDN is the only other dial-up technology that competes with regular analog phone lines. All other telephone circuits and alternative access methods are constantly connected and therefore fall under the category of wide area network connections.

On the server side of remote access, some rather complicated devices are used to manage the array of modems that are required by multiple simultaneous remote access users. ISDN has a great benefit on the server end: No complicated hardware is required to support multiple ISDN remote users. High-speed primary-rate ISDN adapters can answer numerous lower speed ISDN connections without external equipment to segregate the signals, convert them to analog, back to digital, and then multiplex them again into an aggregate stream.

Terminology

- **Adaptive speed leveling:** A modem technology that allows modems to attempt a change in the bit rate at which data is transmitted to optimize for changing telephone line conditions. For instance, a connection initially made at 33.6Kbps might drop to 28.8Kbps if the error rate exceeds a certain threshold that indicates a transient line problem.

- **Dial-up connections:** Network connections (analog or digital) that can be made to any receiving station in the world by specifying (dialing) the receiver's unique address.

- **(Digital) key system:** Small switches that usually use proprietary digital telephones to provide internal switching of inbound telephone lines (rather than trunks) to internal extensions. Generally used in installations with between 10 and 100 internal extensions and less than 24 outside lines.

- **ISDN:** Integrated Services Digital Network. A completely digital dial-up network available in most parts of North America and Europe.

- **Modem:** Modulator/Demodulator. A device used to convert serial data streams (usually RS-232) to analog signals that can be transmitted over public telephone networks.

- **PBX:** Private Branch eXchange. A PSTN telephone switch owned and operated by a private corporation other than a telephone company (telco). PBXs allow large corporations to use trunk lines directly from the telephone company rather than individual telephone lines, and to pay for telephone service at wholesale prices by switching telephone extensions themselves. Generally used only in installations with 100 or more internal telephone extensions and 24 or more inside lines.

- **PSTN:** Public Switched Telephone Network. An industry acronym referring to standard analog telephone service. POTS (Plain Old Telephone Service) is another common reference.

- **Trunk, dedicated circuit, WAN link:** All these synonymous terms refer to the digital high-speed circuits that aggregate individual telephone lines for transport between telephone company central offices (CO) and PBXs.

- **T0, DS0:** The basic digital telephone trunk that carries a single voice conversation at a data rate of 56Kbps (64Kbps in Europe, Central and South America). DS refers to the data rate; T refers to the trunk itself. Also commonly used as a low speed dedicated connection to an Internet service provider.

- **T1, DS1:** A high-speed circuit that multiplexes 24 DS0 circuits onto a single 1.5Mbps circuit. These circuits are also commonly used as a medium speed connection to Internet service providers.

- **T3, DS3:** The next most common high-speed trunk, it aggregates 30 T1 lines onto a single 45Mbps circuit. Also commonly used as a high-speed transport to Internet service providers.

- **X.25, frame relay:** Two similar telephony protocols which allow the routing of digital trunk circuit data over the telephone network in a manner similar to packet-switched networks like IP over the Internet (they are in fact frame-switched). X.25 is a more robust older protocol that provides more error correction and addressing for the establishment of temporary circuits. Frame relay simply provides for virtual permanent circuits with various levels of guaranteed service referred to as Committed Information Rates (CIRs).

Modems

Modems convert serial streams of digital information into analog signals that can be transmitted over standard telephone lines. The word *modem* is an abbreviation for modulator/demodulator. Originally, modems were slow and cumbersome. Before the breakup of AT&T, the telephone company would not allow the attachment of modems directly to phone lines, so modems had to operate through acoustic couplers attached to telephone handsets. This inefficiency kept modems operating below 300 baud.

After the telephone company breakup, attachment to the telephone networks fell under the jurisdiction of the FCC, which allowed direct attachment of modems to telephone lines. Modem bandwidth doubled about every two years as technology improved, in the following denominations: 300, 1200, 2400, 9600, 14.4Kbps, 28.8Kbps, 33.6Kbps, and finally "x2" 56Kbps modems.

Modems that are sold as "x2" 56Kbps modems currently actually peak at about 53Kbps for reception and 33.6Kbps for transmission. They only achieve those rates when the server to which they are attached uses a pure digital transport rather than modems for its connection to the network.

The theoretical maximum possible transfer rate over telephone lines in the United States is 56Kbps. Modems cannot transfer more information than the 56Kb DS0 digital transports that are used to carry the analog signal between telephone switches because the digitization process will simply lose information beyond its digital resolution when the information is digitized. The theoretical limit in Europe and South America is 64Kbps.

Most computers today come with a modem. The availability, reasonable price, and ease of use of modems make them the first choice for most remote access and Internet users.

The Trouble with Modems

The widespread availability of modems means that many of the computers on your network likely have modems installed. Those modems give your users the option of dialing directly out of their own computer and onto the Internet if they feel the need to bypass your corporate firewall. A byproduct of this activity is that they open an unprotected vector into your network. It also allows them to dial into their home computer to transfer a file furtively.

The worst of all threats is the possibility that a user might install remote control software on their client so they can work from home. Software like pcAnywhere on a client creates a gaping hole in your network security because anyone can dial in and drive the client computer to access your entire network from the inside. Although the software is usually protected by a password, it is outside the normal security control systems on your network and therefore less secure. It's likely that the user who sets up the software will either not set a password or never change the one they originally set. Consider also the fact that they are likely to use the same password they use on your network and on other systems.

This threat is made more serious by easy-to-use remote control software because there is no way you can control its use or distribution inside your network, and because there's no real way to forensically determine what exactly happened after an intrusion has occurred. In addition, there's no good way to tell if an intrusion has occurred, because it will appear to be standard access from inside your network—no alarms will sound.

You can remove all the internal modems from client computers on the network, but there's the additional threat that anyone can attach an external modem to a free serial port on the computer. To completely secure your network from this threat, you should disable unused serial ports in the computer's BIOS and use a strong password on the BIOS to prevent users from re-enabling the port.

This leaves one final common modem threat, that of a PCMCIA modem in a laptop. Unfortunately, there isn't anything you can do to keep a user from adding a PCMCIA modem to a laptop. But since laptops typically move out of the office anyway, laptop users should have stronger security indoctrination than other users.

ISDN

Integrated Services Digital Network (ISDN) adapters are the second most common method used to attach to networks over the public telephone system. ISDN adapters rely upon special digital telephone lines rather than analog phone lines to transmit digital information without

---

Policies: Modems and Remote Control Devices

- Remove all modems and other alternative access devices from client computers. Each client computer should have one—and only one—possible connection to any data network.

- Disable unused serial ports in the BIOS of client computers. Put strong administrative passwords in the BIOS setup pages of client computers to maintain central control of network security.

- Disable all unused I/O ports, especially parallel ports that are not attached to printers, since many alternate access devices are capable of attaching through the printer port.

- Make certain that all users understand the security risks of intentionally circumventing security for the sake of convenience, and the risks of intrusion posed by the uncontrolled proliferation of remote control software on secure networks.

---

the loss involved in the analog modulation and demodulation processes. In addition, ISDN allows multiple phone lines to be "bonded" or "multilinked" into a single communication stream. Most ISDN services provide two 64Kbps digital telephone lines over four wires, which are bonded into a single 128Kbps data stream.

You must order ISDN service specially from your local telephone company, and ISDN lines cannot be used with normal telephones. The telephone company will convert existing telephone lines in your building to ISDN lines, and you must then purchase special digital telephones or ISDN adapters to use the lines.

ISDN can be ordered in many different data rates—for instance, it is possible to get 23 bonded ISDN lines for nearly 1.5Mbps of dial-up connectivity. These lines are very expensive, however.

With the advent of 56Kbps modems, which are nearly as fast as a single line ISDN connection and far less expensive in most cases, the future of ISDN is cloudy. Once the designated heir of the modem, ISDN still has not been adopted universally and is not available in many rural areas. With the advent of packet-switched networks like the Internet, most people only dial one number anyway, that of their Internet service provider, so there's little reason not to use dedicated circuits or constantly connected alternate carriers like cable television or satellite ISPs. Finally, ISDN is extremely expensive for long distance connections since the user is billed by the minute, making dedicated circuits or frame relay (for which the user pays a flat monthly rate) less expensive under normal circumstances.

Policies: ISDN and Frame Relay

- Promote the use of ISDN for remote access connections within your local toll area. ISDN equipment is far less prevalent than modems are, so it provides a measure of security through obscurity.

- Use frame relay dedicated circuits for telecommuters outside your local toll area. Frame relay connections are very secure.

Alternative Remote Access

The goal of remote access is to attach users away from the office to their company's network. In some areas, alternative remote access options through the Internet are available.

Since Internet connections can be made literally over any type of data link, you don't have to worry about matching the network technology at the office to the technology used at home. For instance, your office might have a T1 line connected to the Internet, but you might have a high speed cable modem at home. Since they are both attached to the Internet, you can access your office from home without worrying about what type of network technology is actually used to make the connection.

High-speed cable modems are very compelling, since the cable television provider's coaxial connection into your house is by far the highest bandwidth connection you can get.

Typically operating at 10MBps from the cable service provider to the home and some fraction of that from the home to the cable service provider, cable modems can allow telecommuters to access corporate networks at a speed that rivals that of regular Ethernet.

Of course there are security problems endemic to opening up remote access service over the Internet, but the jump in productivity can be worth it, and the security problem can be contained with strong monitoring.

Other alternative access providers include small local telephone companies and digital satellite television providers. Satellite providers usually use the satellite signal to send you Internet data and a modem for you to send data back—which is fine for consuming information but no better than a regular dial-up connection for producing it. Some cable television ISPs also operate in this manner.

Connection through alternative access providers almost always means connecting over the Internet, so the security risks and problems involved are the same as those presented earlier in this chapter and in Chapter 14.

Point-to-Point Tunneling Protocol

The Point-to-Point Tunneling Protocol, which comes with Remote Access Server, allows private connection through the public Internet. PPTP encrypts all the data between two Internet hosts, and then subsumes it into the policy and control mechanisms of RAS, which allows a very secure mechanism for connection over the Internet.

Many other software packages provide the tunneling service—the most secure are those integrated with your firewall software. See Chapter 17 for more information about encrypted tunneling software.

Policies: Remote Access Alternatives

■ If low-cost, high-speed alternative access, such as cable modems, is available for telecommuters in your area, consider using it (along with a high-speed dedicated circuit to the Internet from your corporate site) as the sole method of remote access to your network. This of course opens an Internet security problem, but it closes the problems raised by dial-up remote access. The Internet problem can be contained with strong firewall policy, encrypted tunnels, security awareness, and constant monitoring.

■ To simplify security administration, allow only one method of remote access into your network.

Policies: Tunneling Encryption

■ Use the Point-to-Point Tunneling Protocol for all Internet connections you allow into your network, or use some third-party software that performs the encrypted tunnel function in concert with your firewall.

■ Tunneling encryption software does not protect the server and client from other connections coming in from the Internet. Be certain no client attaching from the Internet is listening for connections on any port.

Modem Banks

Internet service providers and corporations with a large number of remote access users provide dial-up access to their networks using devices called *modem banks*. Modem banks are exactly what they sound like—a bank of modems attached to telephone lines.

Often, these telephone lines come in digitally on a single T1 or larger trunk line and are then broken out using devices called codecs (coder/decoders) which convert the digital signal into multiple analog phone lines, which are then turned back into RS-232 serial streams using modems. These serial streams are either converted directly into network traffic by terminal servers or received into standard servers that have multiport serial boards. In either case, the individual modem connections can now be routed and processed like any other network connection. Figure 12.4 shows a modem bank.

FIGURE 12.4

Modem banks and multiport serial adapters

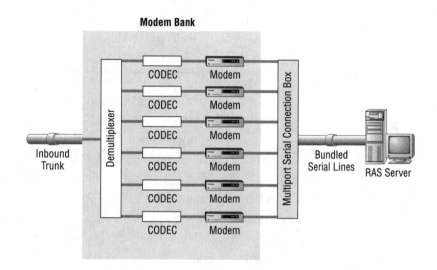

Modem Bank

Multiport Serial Adapters

Your computer probably has two COM ports. That allows you to answer two remote access modems without adding additional hardware. What if you wanted to answer eight or 16? Installing that many internal modems in a computer not only doesn't make sense, it's not really possible because PC architecture doesn't allow that many distinct interrupts.

Multiport serial boards solve that problem by providing a large number of discreet RS-232 serial communications ports using a single interrupt and a single slot adapter. Usually, a high pair-count cable is used to attach a serial port break-out board or a modem bank, thus providing a unique serial port for each inbound modem. Windows NT supports up to 256 serial ports with the use of multiport serial adapters. Figure 12.4 shows a multiport serial adapter attached to a modem bank.

Terminal Servers

Terminal servers provide perhaps the best solution to the service side of remote access by obviating the need for the server entirely. Terminal servers are dedicated server computers that simply route inbound serial connections (from modems or modem banks) onto a high-speed network connection like Ethernet. They usually come in densities of eight ports, 16 ports, or 32 ports.

Since they attach directly to Ethernet networks, there's no need for special software or even other servers if all you intend to do is route them directly onto the Internet. And, you can attach as many terminal servers to an Ethernet network as you need under normal circumstances because serial connections don't load an Ethernet network much. Most ISPs use terminal servers to answer inbound dial-up connections (see Figure 12.5). Think of terminal servers as high-count serial to Ethernet (or other high-speed protocol) routers.

Modems attached via terminal servers don't need to use the services of RAS—remote access software is built into the terminal servers. Terminal servers answer PPP (or SLIP) connections and route the TCP/IP traffic embedded in the PPP (or SLIP) frames onto the network. Higher level traffic like PPTP is embedded inside the TCP/IP packets so the terminal server just routes it through to the end server.

From a security standpoint, the various software packages used in terminal servers can be a problem, because the security for each specific terminal server is configured differently. Be certain to use extra caution and to familiarize yourself with the specific security features of your terminal server before attaching them to your network. You may consider putting terminal servers outside your firewall and treating them as you would any other inbound Internet connection.

FIGURE 12.5

Terminal servers on an
intranet

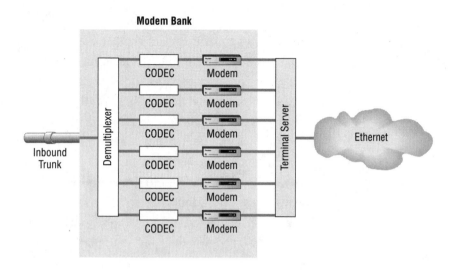

Multiport Serial Tunnels

There is a new and rather strange method to attach a large number of
remote access users to your network: multiport serial tunnels. These
devices are similar to terminal servers in appearance—in fact, they can
look exactly the same. But they are not servers as they have no computational hardware and run no software.

Policies: Servers and Computing Devices

- Be certain you are familiar with the security management of all server
  devices on your network. Terminal servers are servers in their own
  right, that run operating systems and have their own security settings
  outside those of your Windows NT servers.

- Limit the number of computing devices (those that actually contain
  microprocessors which run an operating system) on your network to
  the extent possible.

They simply take the inbound serial traffic, encapsulate it in network frames, and transmit it out the network port (usually an Ethernet network) to a server running a special driver that understands the proprietary transport protocol used for the Ethernet tunnel. That server then demultiplexes the serial traffic from the multiport serial tunnel and presents it as a serial communications port on that server (a COM port)—thus mimicking the functionality of a multiport serial board without the extra adapter. The serial ports are controlled by a standard server, which must be running remote access software like RAS in order to answer inbound connections.

From a security standpoint, multiport serial tunnels are better than terminal servers for the following reasons:

- A single server running well-known and secure RAS software can control them all (up to 256 ports), creating a single point of control and management.

- They do not create routable traffic on your network so there's no possibility of bypassing your security firewalls or routing onto wide area networks.

- Setting them up incorrectly does not result in unknown security holes (however, RAS must be configured correctly on the recipient server).

- They are not protocol dependent and can be used with any transport protocol supported by the RAS server.

- Traffic does not need to be transmitted on your network at all if the RAS server is capable of fulfilling network requests from remote users—for instance, if it is a server for thin clients.

In addition to all that, multiport serial tunnels are easier to set up, requiring very little vendor-specific knowledge, and they are considerably less expensive than terminal servers. In sum, you should consider using multiport serial tunnels rather than terminal servers if possible.

There are some down sides to multiport serial tunnels. They do require the use of a third-party driver on your server. This can be cause for some concern because the drivers are supposedly less thoroughly debugged than Microsoft code, and since they execute inside the protected operating space they can therefore crash the operating system. However, Microsoft's own track record with Windows NT drivers and code is only marginally better than that of third-party providers, so there is very little real cause for concern.

Multiport serial tunnels also basically ensure that all serial traffic appears on your Ethernet twice: inbound to the RAS server for processing, and outbound (assuming your RAS server isn't the only computer on your network) from the RAS server to the server actually being addressed by the remote client. It may make sense to simply dedicate an Ethernet adapter in your RAS server to your multiport serial tunnels to avoid this problem. Figure 12.6 shows a multiport serial tunnel.

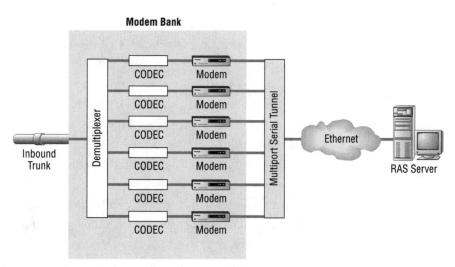

FIGURE 12.6

A multiport serial tunnel sends encapsulated serial traffic to an NT RAS server.

Policies: Multiport Serial Tunnels

■ Multiport serial tunnels are inherently more secure than terminal servers because they concentrate the management problem on your Windows NT servers. Use them rather than terminal servers whenever possible.

Remote Access versus Remote Control

Remote access refers to the establishment of network connections over dial-up circuits. These remote access links work just like any permanent circuit or network technology: The client requests data from the server, which transmits the data for processing on the remote client. This is the method used by most Internet protocols, such as WWW, FTP, and Gopher, as well as Internet file systems like NFS and NBT.

On the other hand, *remote control* means controlling another computer (be it single or multiuser) from a remote location. By sending keyboard and mouse commands, and by receiving and displaying video information, remote control users can perform the same work as a remote access connection but without consuming the bandwidth required to transmit large files.

Both of these remote use methods have their security advantages and drawbacks. Remote access uses all the same familiar security protocols you are used to working with for the rest of your network. Remote control on the other hand usually relies upon having a constantly logged-on local computer available for the remote user. That remote user has the security permissions of the user logged in on the local machine. This provides a back door secured only by the scheme provided by the remote control software—and it is usually far less secure than NT's network security.

On the other hand, remote control doesn't really give full access to files from the remote location. For instance, although a user could work on a file remotely, they can't necessarily copy that file to the remote computer. Also, database information can be extracted over remote access applications but remains secure over a remote control connection, because the remote control connection exposes only as much data as the user is using at the time, not the entire file or database.

The next two sections explore each type of remote use methodology in detail.

> ### Terminology
>
> - **Remote access:** A suite of related technologies that allow the extension of private networks over dial-up circuits.
>
> - **Remote control:** Software that allows remote users to control the functionality of a distant computer over a low bandwidth connection.
>
> - **Thin client:** A computer designed to remotely control a user session on a more powerful multiuser computer.

Remote Access Service

Remote access service consists of service software and network drivers for modems. Once a dial-up session is established, the RAS server acts as a router for network traffic to and from the dial-up circuit. Remote access allows you to treat modem connections as regular (albeit slow) LAN connections.

Windows NT comes with some of the best remote access support ever released as part of an operating system. Using RAS and the RAS security manager you can control how access to your network is provided and over which protocols. You can determine whether RAS traffic is routed over the network or is local to the answering machine. And, you can specify which users are allowed to dial in to the server.

Remote Control

Terminals and mainframes were the first remote control computers. Terminals provided a remote keyboard and character terminal for a user session that occurred on a multiuser mainframe. The terminal itself had no processor—it simply controlled a user session remotely on the mainframe. With the advent of the PC, it no longer made sense to have all the computing power in one place, so distributed LANs became more popular. With LANs, each user has their own computer, and the central computers merely serve files or provide other network services.

Policies: Remote Access and the Network

- If you must have remote access to your network, an RAS server provides the most secure method. Choose it over all other remote access methods.

- Never allow client computers on your network to answer remote access connections. Organize all remote access servers in a centrally controlled location.

- Remove the remote access and dial-up connection services from clients on your network. There should be no need for remote access outbound connections from computers on networks that are connected to the Internet.

Unfortunately for the remote user, LANs rely on very high-speed network connections—at least 10MB of bandwidth is required to provide reasonable responsiveness for modern applications and files. So software developers responded with remote control software that allowed a home user to dial into their computer at work and use the home computer as an extension of the work computer. This got around the problem of low-speed connections for the most part.

It then became obvious that network computers could be made very cheaply if they didn't need the latest microprocessors and large hard disks to operate, because they could use the disk and compute resources of a more powerful central computer. These computers are referred to as *thin clients,* because they remotely control a powerful multiuser central computer—much the same way terminals control user sessions on a mainframe. The servers driven by thin clients are multiuser computers.

The Windows NT Kernel supports multiuser applications, but the Desktop Explorer is a single-user application. No support for multiple users currently ships with Windows NT 4, but Windows NT 5 for the Enterprise will ship with a multiuser interface that is currently code-named "Hydra."

Remote Loss of Control

Third-party companies currently provide all remote control software. Each software package is different, and all use proprietary methods to provide remote control of a network. For instance, some transmit compressed raw video, while others transmit GDI device calls that are executed on the remote computer. Each has advantages and disadvantages.

One major security problem caused by remote control software is the fault of security managers. It's easier to administer a network directly from the primary domain controller—but PDCs are usually inconveniently located in computer rooms or distribution closets. So administrators put a copy of pcAnywhere on their servers and then just dial in or connect via IP to manage their servers easily. Of course, this establishes a major breach of security. Now anyone can dial into the modem attached to your PDC and manage your network remotely. And since most dial-up software doesn't provide the sophisticated security and monitoring functions available to remote access connections, you can't control the security of these remote control connections.

Policies: Thin-Client and Remote Access Software

- Thin-client and remote control software can be more secure than remote access software in certain circumstances. For instance, an entire database could be copied down using remote access software, but that same data would be extremely difficult to extract using remote access software configured to disallow file transfers. Consider the nature of your security problem when deciding which manner of remote use you will allow.

- Control the distribution of remote access software on your network. Never allow client computers to run remote control software. If remote control software is necessary, run the software from centrally controlled computers or thin-client servers.

- Use external modems that have on/off switches for those machines that have remote access software installed. Only turn on a modem when a user calls in and requests a remote control connection (and, of course, you must have a secure method of verifying the identity of the requester).

Thin-Client Software

In the drive to reduce the cost of corporate networking, the concept of the thin client has come to the fore. Thin clients are simple computers containing (usually) only lower power processors, a small amount of RAM, video adapters and monitors, a keyboard and mouse, and a network connection. They may boot from hard disks or they may boot remotely over the network.

These computers run only client software that allows them to attach to a multiuser server that provides the computational power and the hard disk space required for running their applications. Currently, this functionality is provided by a software package from Citrix called Win-Frame; it will be included in the next release of Windows NT as part of the operating system.

Securing Remote Access

Windows NT has a very secure remote access system built in. On top of all the normal security features of Windows NT, the Remote Access Server (RAS) provides additional security features that reduce the risk of dialing in. These security features can be mixed and matched to provide a security environment closely tailored to your needs.

The next few sections show you how to secure RAS on your Windows NT servers. These security features are set up either by using the Remote Access Admin tool in the Administrative Tools folder of the Start menu or by clicking the Remote Access Server service in the Services tab of the networking control panel program.

> **Policies: Remote Access Server**
>
> - If remote access is required only occasionally, set the Remote Access Server service to start manually, then use the services control panel to start the service when needed and stop it when it is no longer in use.
>
> - If possible, use external modems to answer RAS connections. They can be powered off when no RAS activity is anticipated, and they allow you to manually disconnect users if necessary.

Callback Security

With callback security, the user sends a telephone number to the server and then hangs up. The server uses that number to return the telephone call. The server logs the telephone number in the RAS security log. Alternatively, the administrator can hard code a telephone number to make sure the network can only be accessed from specific locations.

Of the RAS-based security measures, callback security is the most important. With a strong callback security policy, you can prevent virtually all unauthorized access to your network through remote access. The only possible way to circumvent hard-coded callback security is for the hacker to somehow reassign their own phone number to one on the list, or to gain physical access to a telephone line that is on the list.

The first is impossible (with the exception of cellular telephone cloning, and even that can't necessarily be made to answer correctly). The second is a reasonably serious concern in certain circumstances. If your network is an espionage target and your primary facility is physically secure, callback remote access can make the homes of your coworkers targets for physical intrusion because they become the weakest link in your total security policy. Consider this callback method carefully in the context of your total security policy.

As a convenience to users, callback security has the side effect of charging the bulk of the telecommunications charges to the organization. For accounting and compensation purposes, this makes remote access very convenient. However, in situations where the user should be responsible for telecommunications charges, you will not be able to use callback security.

With transmitted telephone number callback security, the RAS server simply logs the telephone number and then allows access. This provides the security administrator with a complete log of all the phone numbers that have accessed the network. This makes it easy to track down unauthorized logon attempts using CD-ROM-based telephone directories that support reverse lookup if the intruder calls from a private telephone.

Unfortunately, serious intrusion attempts are likely to come from public or semi-public (such as hotels or other businesses open to the public) telephones, making tracking them down rather difficult. Figure 12.7 shows the dialog box for setting callback security on a per user basis in the Remote Access Admin utility. Using the Remote Access utility is covered in depth in Appendix B.

FIGURE 12.7

Callback security settings

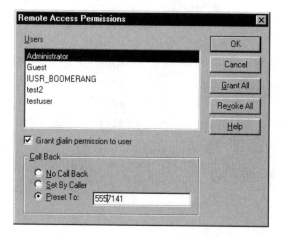

> **Policies: Callback Security**
>
> - Use callback security. Without callback security, tracing RAS-based intrusion attempts is very difficult.
>
> - Use hard-coded callback security for all remote users who don't normally travel, to prevent their account from being exploited from unknown locations.

Protocol Selection

Protocol Selection allows you to determine which protocols will be supported for RAS connections and which won't, independently of those present on your network. You can specify any or all of the following three protocols:

- **TCP/IP:** The protocol of the Internet, UNIX, and the rest of the known universe

- **IPX (NWLink):** The protocol of NetWare

- **NetBEUI:** The original protocol of IBM and Microsoft networks

Both the server and the client must have one protocol in common. For instance, if the server is configured to answer NetBEUI and TCP/IP, and the client is configured with IPX and NetBEUI, the connection will use NetBEUI. If no common protocol exists, the connection attempt will fail.

Consider the protocols you allow on the server side in the context of security. For instance, if your entire network is based on IPX rather than TCP/IP, you won't have to worry about hacking attempts from the Internet except for those machines that have the TCP/IP stack installed. If your servers don't respond to TCP/IP, they cannot be hacked from the Internet.

Installing TCP/IP only on clients that need access to the Internet makes those clients the only Internet-based security risk. By selecting protocols carefully in consideration of security, you can significantly reduce your risk of intrusion and isolate the damage done when intrusions do occur. Figure 12.8 shows the protocol selection options available in the RAS service options of the Network control panel program.

F I G U R E   12.8

Selecting Protocols to use with RAS

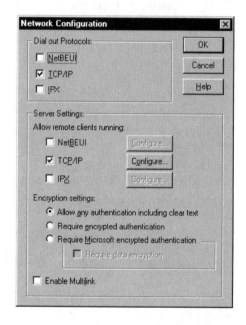

Policies: Protocols

- To limit the extent of intrusions on your network, consider using only the NetBEUI protocol for remote access.

- Limit the number of protocols in use throughout your network to the extent possible.

Gateway Isolation

Using gateway isolation you can decide whether connections for each protocol will be limited to the answering server or gated onto the remainder of your network. By limiting access to the answering server only, you reduce the risk of a remote access penetration spreading to the rest of your network. Unfortunately, you also limit your intentional users to the resources available on the remote access server.

Enabling network access essentially turns the remote access server into a router, much the same way as an Internet service provider provides a gateway to the Internet. Figure 12.9 shows the gateway options available in the RAS service options of the Network control panel program.

FIGURE 12.9

RAS Gateway isolation options for TCP/IP

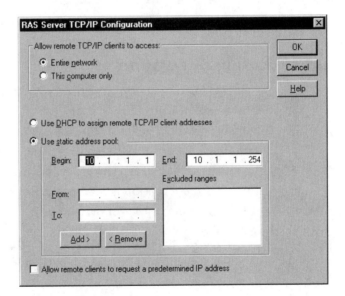

IP Address Assignment

IP address assignment allows you to determine exactly how IP addresses will be assigned to dial-in users independently of how they are assigned to network users. This gives you the flexibility to apply firewall security for remote users that's different for internal users, because they'll be in a different address range. Figure 12.9 shows the IP address assignment options in the RAS service configuration option of the Network control panel program.

Policies: Gateway Isolation and IP Address Assignment

- Consider using gateway isolation if the services required by your users can be made available from a single machine.

- You can use IP address assignment, in combination with an internal firewall and IP selection on servers, to further control and partition the access allowed to remote users.

Authentication Encryption

Authentication encryption allows you to determine how passwords will be accepted from remote users and to prevent them from being sent unencrypted. When passwords are transmitted without encryption, anyone between the transmitting client and the recipient server with a packet sniffer can retrieve the password without difficulty. Obviously, password encryption is an important part of network security.

RAS supports the following authentication methods:

- **Allow any authentication including clear text** allows clients to connect using the Password Authentication Protocol, a nonsecure plaintext password authentication protocol. It is included for compatibility with non-Microsoft applications that require it, but it is disabled by default. You may need to use PAP to support connection by older UNIX-based SLIP Internet hosts—but you should consider upgrading your client software rather than disabling server-side security protocols.

- **Require Encrypted Authentication** allows clients to authenticate using any supported encrypted authentication method, including

Shiva PAP (a version of PAP implemented by Shiva in its remote client software), Data Encryption Standard (DES, the encryption protocol designed by the National Bureau of Standards), Challenge Handshake Authentication Protocol (CHAP), or MS-CHAP (a Microsoft version of RSA Message Digest 4 is the default RAS server challenge and reply protocol; this authentication protocol can negotiate encryption and use the RC4 algorithm to encrypt communications between the host and client). All of these encryption algorithms encrypt passwords.

- **Require Microsoft Encrypted Authentication** forces clients to authenticate using MS-CHAP, the strongest RAS security setting, but it will only work with Microsoft client software. This setting can also be used to encrypt the communication stream so that even if wiretapped the data is worthless to an intruder.

Figure 12.8 shows the authentication encryption settings of RAS service in the Network control panel program.

Policies: Passwords

- Do not allow clear text-password authentication.
- Use Microsoft encryption when possible.

Data Encryption

Data encryption allows you to encrypt the remote access links, making them invulnerable to wiretapping. With Windows NT's Remote Access Server, you can enable data encryption when you use Microsoft password encryption. This data encryption is the same encryption used when passwords are Microsoft encrypted. Encryption does require a bit more CPU power than a clear transmission, but remote access servers generally have heavy I/O loads and light CPU loads anyway.

Port Usage

Port Usage allows you to control whether remote access servers will initiate RAS sessions or listen for them, or both. Servers listen for connections and clients initiate them by dialing out. You can use the Port Usage setting to make certain that Windows NT clients don't accidentally answer the phone and open a back door onto your network. Figure 12.10 shows the dialog box you can use to specify port usage in the Remote Access Server service of the Network Control Panel program.

FIGURE 12.10

Specifying dial-in and
dial-out port usage

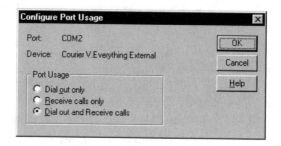

Policies: RAS Encryption and RAS Port Usage by Computer Role

- Data encryption over standard telephone lines is necessary only for companies that might be an espionage target. It is easy to implement as an extra security measure, but limits the types of clients that can attach to your network. This limitation may provide in itself an extra measure of security in homogenous networks.

- Clients should not be allowed to answer dial-in security connections.

- Client computers should not be allowed to use any sort of remote access software.

- Servers have no need to originate dial-out connections (except when using telephone lines as low-cost WAN connections, but these connections should be relatively permanent).

Disconnection

Disconnection allows you to disconnect a specific user—without affecting other RAS users—if you determine that an attack is in progress. With the disconnection feature of the Remote Access Administrator, you can selectively disconnect any remote access user at any time. Typically, this is a last resort against an intrusion in progress. You would generally need some sort of alarming software in place (which you can set up using the performance monitors alarming feature as shown in Appendix B) to determine that an attack is in progress in time to disconnect it.

Dial-in Permission

User-based dial-in permission allows you to specify exactly which users are allowed to dial in and allows you to set callback policy on a per-user basis. With specific dial-in permission, you can enable dial-in access only for those users that require it. Figure 12.7 shows the RAS dialog box for specifying user-based dial-in permissions in the Remote Access Administrator.

Policies: Connection Monitoring and Dial-In Permissions

- Use connection-monitoring software like the Performance Monitor to alert you to potential intrusion attempts.

- Tightly control user-based remote access permissions. Allow only those users who have an immediate need to log in remotely.

- Revoke dial-in permissions for users during periods when they are not necessary, and invoke them when the user is away from the office or working from home for a period.

- Encourage an easy-to-use (but secure, of course) method for users to indicate when they need remote access, for how long, and to which phone number. Base your dial-in permissions on these requests. Always verify the request verbally with the user to ensure that it's not a spoof.

Alternate Remote Methods

A myriad of less popular remote access methods exist, ranging from voicemail software that encapsulates messages into e-mail and conversely reads voicemail messages over the phone, to "3D" fax software that can be used to transmit images that represent executable files over standard fax machines. All of these methods are designed for convenience—and usually by software companies that have little or no security expertise.

WARNING Carefully consider any method of remote access that provides for the execution of software or access to potentially secret information in an uncontrolled manner.

Problems can be created by software in the name of efficiency. For instance, you may have a fax server that sits on your network and receives fax images, which are then encapsulated in e-mail messages and mailed to the appropriate user. That fax server runs a computer operating system, and many of the less-expensive models simply use freely available versions of UNIX or DOS which might be likely to answer an inbound modem connection and provide an IP gateway to an intruder.

Remember that every device or service in your organization that listens for a connection should be seriously scrutinized for its potential to open an unintentional door into your network. Also remember that nearly everything that makes life easier in a network creates a security hole.

Summary

Remote access provides a very powerful and convenient extension to your network. As with everything powerful and convenient, it causes very serious security problems. With proper security management, however, remote access can be secure.

Dial-up intrusion attempts are still very common. Hackers use numerous methods to detect networks with remote access software and to intrude. Security measures such as dial-back security make remote access far more secure than it would be if it allowed anyone to dial in an attempt to log in to your network.

Remote control software is an alternative form of remote access that provides a connected user interface rather than a connected file system, so that remote users can "drive" a local computer that is directly attached to your network. Usually this is the most responsive and convenient way to work from remote locations. However, it also provides a convenient back door for hackers into your network.

Windows NT's Remote Access Server provides a number of security measures beyond those provided by the standard secure operating system. Careful consideration and implementation of these measures will allow you to take advantage of the efficiency of remote access without exposing your network to significant additional risk.

CHAPTER

13

Security in a Multivendor Network

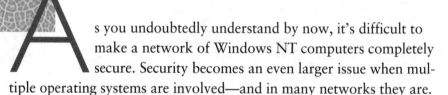

As you undoubtedly understand by now, it's difficult to make a network of Windows NT computers completely secure. Security becomes an even larger issue when multiple operating systems are involved—and in many networks they are.

In this chapter we'll take a brief detour from basic Windows NT security to look at three types of systems you may also have on your network: NetWare, UNIX, and Macintosh. We'll examine the basics of securing each of these systems, describe how they can be integrated with Windows NT, and look at the security holes that these systems may bring to your network.

NetWare Security

Despite Windows NT's rapidly increasing market share, Novell NetWare is still the most widely used network operating system. Although many NetWare networks have been upgraded to Windows NT, NetWare and Windows NT work surprisingly well together. In this section we'll look at the basics of NetWare security and describe the ways that NT and NetWare can be connected. We'll also examine some potential security holes in NetWare and in NT-NetWare connectivity.

Three versions of NetWare are in wide use at this writing:

- NetWare 3.12, released in 1993, is still in use in many networks.

- NetWare 4.1, introduced in 1994, was aimed mainly at wide area networks and includes features for managing large networks.

Novell later marketed this version as an all-purpose upgrade to earlier versions.

■ IntranetWare, released in 1996, is NetWare's contribution to the growing Internet and intranet markets. This package includes an updated version of NetWare (4.11) as well as Web, FTP, and other servers.

Introducing NetWare Security

NetWare has been a popular network operating system for over 10 years, and Novell has continued to improve its security features with each new version. The latest version, 4.11, is comparable in security to Windows NT. NetWare has some particular security advantages:

■ The NetWare server uses a proprietary operating system, and it can't be used for client applications. This is a limitation, but it also means that NetWare servers can be locked in a secure room without limiting their use.

■ NetWare 4.*x* includes NDS (NetWare Directory Services), a global database of user accounts, groups, servers, printers, and other network resources. The entire network can be managed in one directory tree, which makes for easy administration and less chance of security problems. Version 3.12 and earlier use a database called the Bindery for these functions, using separate Binderies for each server.

■ In a Windows NT server with a FAT file system, anyone with access to the server can boot DOS and access the files, unimpaired by security. The file system on a NetWare server is proprietary, although it is designed to emulate the DOS FAT file system at the client level. Because of this, booting DOS at the NetWare server doesn't provide access to any files.

We will now take a look at the basics of securing a NetWare network. There are two main components of NetWare security: NDS security and file system security. We'll examine these in the sections below, and then look at the process of NetWare administration.

File System Security

The NetWare file system is similar to NTFS in that it is structured similarly to the FAT system but includes additional security features. By default, NetWare supports DOS-style names, but loading an optional driver allows support for long file names similar to those used in Windows 95 and NT.

NetWare uses a pessimistic security approach by default: No users have any access to files unless you specifically grant it. A user, group, or other NDS object that has access to a file or directory is called a *trustee*. Trustees can be assigned a number of different rights, similar to the permissions in NTFS security. The rights available are summarized in the table below.

	Symbol	Name	Description of Right
T A B L E 13.1 File System Rights in NetWare	[R]	Read	Read data from existing files
	[W]	Write	Write data to existing files
	[C]	Create	Create new files or subdirectories
	[E]	Erase	Delete existing files or directories
	[M]	Modify	Rename files or change file attributes
	[F]	File Scan	List files in a directory
	[A]	Access Control	Grant rights to a file to other trustees
	[S]	Supervisor	A combination of all of the above rights

The NetWare file system supports a system of inheritance for these rights: A trustee with rights for a parent directory has the same rights to subdirectories. The rights inherited at subdirectories can be limited by the Inherited Rights Filter (IRF), which lists rights that can be inherited for each subdirectory.

NDS Security

NDS manages all of the non-file resources of the network in a single directory: users, groups, organizations, servers, and even printers. These are stored as NDS *objects*. The objects in the NDS database are organized in a tree-like structure, as shown in Figure 13.1.

FIGURE 13.1

A simple NDS tree structure

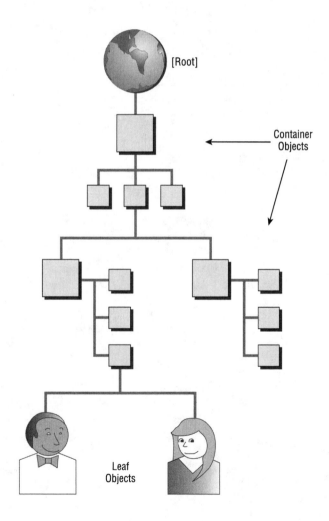

The NDS database is stored on one of the servers in the network in a *master replica*, and other servers store backup replicas. This is similar to Windows NT's system of primary and backup domain controllers.

> With the Active Directory, to be introduced in Windows NT 5, Windows NT will have a way to organize resources in a tree structure, similar to NDS. See Chapter 10 for details.

NDS Objects   Objects are categorized as *container objects*, used to organize resources, and *leaf objects*, which represent the resources themselves. Table 13.2 shows some of the common NDS objects.

	Object Name	Object Type	Description
T A B L E 13.2 Common NDS Objects	[Root]	container	The object at the root of the NDS tree that contains all other objects.
	Country	container	The highest-level container object; divides resources by container. Rarely used.
	Organization	container	Defines an organization. The highest-level object in most networks.
	Organizational Unit	container	Divides an organization into departments or locations.
	User	leaf	Defines a network user.
	Group	leaf	Defines an arbitrary group of users, not necessarily from the same container.
	Organizational Role	leaf	Defines a role that can be assigned to a user.
	Server	leaf	Represents a NetWare server.
	Volume	leaf	Represents a NetWare volume (disk partition).

	Object Name	Object Type	Description
TABLE 13.2 (cont.) Common NDS Objects	Printer	leaf	Represents a printer (NT calls this a print device).
	Print Queue	leaf	Represents a queue for printing documents (NT calls this a printer).

NDS Rights   NDS security is used to grant users (or groups or other trustees) the right to create, delete, or manage users and other NDS objects. Trustees can be granted several rights, similar to the file system rights. These rights are listed in Table 13.3.

	Right	Description
TABLE 13.3 Available NDS Rights	Browse	Allows the user to browse through the NDS tree
	Create	Allows creation of new objects
	Rename	Allows renaming of existing objects
	Delete	Allows deletion of existing objects
	Supervisor	A combination of the above rights

As with the file system, NDS rights are inherited to subdirectories in the NDS tree, and the IRF (Inherited Rights Filter) controls this inheritance.

Administration

In NetWare 3.12 and earlier versions, user administration tasks are performed using DOS-based utilities; the main utility, SYSCON, is shown in Figure 13.2. NetWare 4.1 introduced NWADMIN (NetWare Administrator), a Windows-based utility for managing NDS objects.

F I G U R E   13.2
The SYSCON utility is used to manage users in NetWare 3.12.

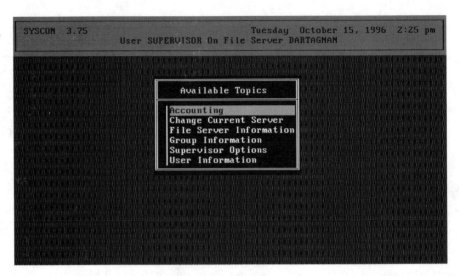

NWADMIN displays NDS objects in their tree structure and allows you to add, delete, or change the properties of objects. A typical NWADMIN window is shown in Figure 13.3.

NetWare versions 3.12 and earlier use the SUPERVISOR account as a default administrator, and versions 4 and later call the account ADMIN. In version 4.*x*, the ADMIN account can be limited and replaced by separate administrator accounts.

Connecting NetWare and Windows NT

Despite the competition between Novell and Microsoft, both companies have made reasonable efforts to allow connectivity between these two networking systems. In the sections below we'll look at four Microsoft services included with Windows NT for use with NetWare:

- **NWLink** is a set of protocols compatible with NetWare's IPX and SPX protocols.

- **Client Services for NetWare** (CSN) allows Windows NT machines to act as NetWare clients.

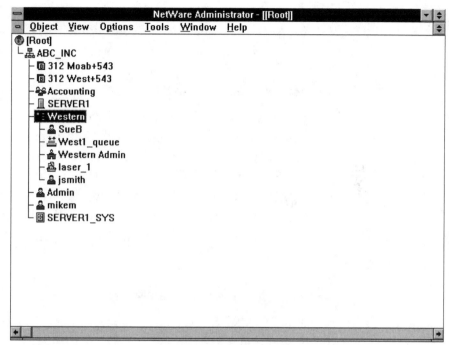

FIGURE 13.3

NWADMIN is used to manage users and other objects in NetWare 4.1.

- **Gateway Services for NetWare** (GSNW) allows a Windows NT machine to act as a gateway to NetWare resources.

- **Microsoft Services for NetWare** allows NetWare clients to access Windows NT shares and printers.

NWLink (IPX/SPX Protocols)

NetWare uses a proprietary set of protocols called IPX (Internetwork Packet Exchange) and SPX (Sequenced Packet Exchange). Although NetWare servers can also support TCP/IP and other protocols, IPX and SPX are the standards.

NWLink is Microsoft's implementation of these protocols, and is installed when you install Gateway Services for NetWare or Client

Services for NetWare (explained below). Although it's mainly intended for NetWare compatibility, you can use NWLink as a general-purpose transport protocol for NT networks.

Client Services for NetWare

Client Services for NetWare is the client for NetWare servers included with Windows NT Workstation. This client redirects NetWare file and print services and makes them accessible as if they were Windows services.

CSN can be added from the Services tab in the Network control panel. Once it is installed, the Network Neighborhood window will include an entry for the NetWare network, with subentries for each NetWare server. Shared files and printers can be browsed just like NT shares.

Gateway Services for NetWare

Windows NT Server includes Gateway Services for NetWare (GSNW). In addition to the features of CSN, this software also allows a Windows NT server to act as a gateway to the NetWare network.

GSNW can be added from the Services tab in the Network control panel. Once it's installed, a GSNW option becomes available in the Control Panel. Select this icon to display the Gateway Service for Net-Ware dialog box, shown in Figure 13.4.

Once the gateway service is installed and configured, users on the same network as the Windows NT server can access NetWare resources as shares, without loading the NetWare client software.

GSNW has a useful side effect: The gateway server requires only one user name and password for the NetWare network. This means that an unlimited number of Windows clients can access the NetWare network without buying a multiple-user NetWare license. (This can also create security problems, as mentioned later in this section.)

FIGURE 13.4

Use this dialog box to configure Gateway Services for NetWare.

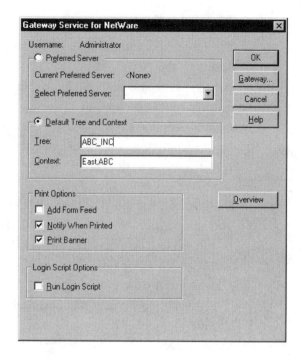

Microsoft Services for NetWare

The final service in our list of available services is Microsoft Services for NetWare. This is an add-on product for the NetWare server that allows workstations running NetWare client software to access the resources of the Windows NT network. In other words, basically it's the opposite of GSNW.

NetWare Security Holes

NetWare is a reasonably secure system, but it does have potential holes. Most of these are related to physical access to the server, so it's important to locate the server in a secure room. The following sections describe potential security problems with NetWare and NT-NetWare connectivity.

Access to the Server

The largest potential threat for intrusion of a NetWare server is physical access to the server. Although this is a risk for any server, it's particularly problematic with NetWare because it's possible for a hacker to quickly obtain an administrator password and return the server to normal—in one case, it doesn't even need to be taken down.

The following are several ways a hacker can compromise a NetWare server, given physical access.

Password Change Utilities   If you call NetWare to complain that you've lost your ADMIN password, they will (after asking you for proof of a legitimate NetWare license) send you a utility called CHANGEPW .NLM on a floppy disk. This disk is customized for your particular server, and it only works once.

Unfortunately, there are modified versions of this utility floating around the hacker community that limit these restrictions. Given access to the server and its floppy drive, a hacker can quickly change the administrator password.

The easiest way to remedy this is to load the MONITOR utility at the server and use its Lock Server Console option. This will make the administrator password a requirement for access to the console.

Disk Editors   As mentioned earlier, NetWare uses a proprietary disk format that can't be accessed from DOS. However, it's possible to access the data in the NetWare partition with a sector-based disk editor. Novell teaches its Certified Novell Engineers a way to change the ADMIN account password using this loophole.

This technique is a bit complicated. First, the server is taken down and rebooted with a DOS diskette. The sector editor is then used to access the directory of the partition and change the name of several critical files: the Bindery or NDS database.

After this is done, the server is restarted. Since the database files are effectively missing, the server acts like a new installation, meaning that the ADMIN or SUPERVISOR account has no password. The hacker can then log into the server, rename the files back to what they were before, and change the ADMIN password.

Most hackers scoff at this method because it's long and complex, and because it's hard to get away with bringing the server down without someone noticing. To prevent this from working, try to prevent unauthorized reboots of the server. One way to do this is to use a boot floppy and keep it locked up. There's one problem with this method: If the power goes out, someone will have to go in to restart the server.

The Debugger   The reason hackers don't usually mess with the method described in the preceding section is simple: There's an easier way. Both 3.1*x* and 4.*x* versions of NetWare include a built-in assembly-level debugger for programmers. It can be accessed with a single keystroke, although you may need three hands to perform the keystroke: Alt+Left Shift+Right Shift+Esc.

Once in the debugger, it's a simple matter (if you know what you're doing) to disable the password-checking routine. In NetWare 3.12, for example, this can be done with three commands. The hacker can then log on with the SUPERVISOR or ADMIN account from a workstation. The debugger can then be used to undo the changes, leaving no trace.

This method is particularly elegant because the hacker can create a new account rather than changing the password of the existing administrator, and it can be hard to detect the intrusion. The only way to prevent these attacks will also prevent the others described earlier: Keep the server under lock and key.

Packet Sniffing and Spoofing

A more complex method of NetWare hacking involves listening to network packets with a packet sniffer. Since IPX packets are sent to every machine on the network, you can monitor packets intended for other machines.

Reality Check: How Did You Do That?

I worked as a NetWare consultant during the days when 3.12 was the most popular version. On one occasion I accompanied another CNE to a client's site, where he was making a call because they had lost their SUPERVISOR password.

My colleague was prepared to use the disk editor method to change the password—or worse, to reinstall NetWare. I walked up to the server and used the debugger method, which I had learned from the hacker community. We had access within a minute, and it then took me 20 minutes to explain how what I had done was possible.

The simplest exploit using this method begins with access to an ordinary user's account. The hacker then listens to network packets, ideally hoping to catch an administrator logging on. Although passwords are sent in encrypted form, the encrypted password can be captured and used in a modified login program to obtain access.

If an administrator is logged in, it's also possible to monitor packets on the network until that machine is identified. The hacker can then send packets modified to appear to come from that machine. This is difficult, though, and usually requires custom hardware.

Holes in NetWare-NT Connectivity

The utilities provided by Microsoft for NetWare and Windows NT connectivity are generally quite secure, and there are no gaping security holes in these systems. Here are some areas where there is a potential for security problems, though:

- Since many networks use the same passwords for NT and NetWare accounts, all of the potential security holes in NT's user accounts (described in Chapter 6) apply.

- Since GSNW is usually used with one powerful NetWare account and left logged in, a hacker with physical access to this machine can easily access NetWare files.

- Since a large number of NT clients can access the NetWare server through GSNW, the NetWare server's user-level auditing is effectively bypassed, and there is no way to audit access to individual NetWare files or directories from the NT server.

Policies: NetWare and Windows NT

- Keep the NetWare server physically secure.

- Lock the NetWare console using the MONITOR utility.

- Consider booting the NetWare server with a floppy disk to avoid unauthorized rebooting.

- Always use a complex password for administrative accounts.

- Never leave the ADMIN or SUPERVISOR accounts logged in.

- Keep the Windows NT server that runs GSNW physically secure.

- When creating an account for GSNW, give it only the NetWare access that is specifically needed by NT network users. Resist the temptation to use the ADMIN account.

Terminology

- **Client Services for NetWare:** Microsoft's service, included with Windows NT Workstation, that allows access to NetWare servers.

- **Gateway Services for NetWare:** An expanded NetWare client included with Windows NT Server. The server acts as a gateway and can allow NT and Windows 95 clients to access the server without the use of NetWare client software.

- **Microsoft Services for NetWare:** Software for NetWare servers that allows NetWare clients to access Windows NT services.

- **NDS (NetWare Directory Services):** NetWare's directory of network resources, stored as NDS objects. NDS keeps a single database for the entire network, and allows single-logon access.

- **NFS (Network File System):** The UNIX standard for file sharing.

- **Services for Macintosh:** The service, included with Windows NT Server, that allows Macintosh clients to share files on a Windows NT server.

- **Trustee**: In NetWare, a user (or other object) that has been given access to a file, directory, or NDS object.

UNIX Security

Unix is an operating system originally developed by Bell Labs and available in a wide variety of versions (ranging from free to very expensive) for just about every computer made today. UNIX has many security holes—not because it's basically insecure, but because it's complex and has long been a favorite target for hackers. To complicate this, UNIX machines are often connected to the Internet, making them even more vulnerable.

Basics of UNIX Security

In this section we'll take a brief look at the components of UNIX security. This is only a quick overview, since UNIX security is a complex subject. The main areas of UNIX security are users and groups, and the file system.

Users and Groups

Like Windows NT, UNIX uses user names and passwords to recognize users. Each user is assigned to one group, and users and groups can be given access to files and directories. This is really all there is to UNIX security: In order for a user to be able to create other users, that user is simply granted write access to the password file.

The File System

The file system in UNIX is organized in a hierarchical structure, similar to that used in Windows NT. File names can be long and are case sensitive. Each file has a simple set of permissions. Permissions are either on or off for three categories of user: the owner of the file, the group that owns the file, and users in other groups. The available permissions for each of these include the following:

- **Read (R):** Allows users to read existing files. If this right is granted for a directory, it allows the directory's contents to be read.

- **Write (W):** Allows users to write to existing files. If granted for a directory, the user is allowed to create new files in the directory.

- **Execute (X):** Allows programs (executable files) to be run. If granted for a directory, this permission allows users to switch to that directory.

UNIX and Windows NT

UNIX networks can interoperate with Windows NT networks, although not as transparently as NetWare networks. Windows NT includes the TCP/IP protocol, which is used on UNIX systems; this means that NT and UNIX machines on the same network can communicate. In this section we'll look at how NT and UNIX can be combined in a network.

Securing TCP/IP

UNIX uses the TCP/IP protocol suite, also available in Windows NT. This protocol suite is complex, and can include everything from basic network transport to World Wide Web services. Not surprisingly, TCP/IP has a few security holes of its own. We discuss these in Chapter 15.

Remote File Systems

Although a common network protocol exists, UNIX and Windows NT file and print services are vastly different, and special software is required to share files between the two. The most common type of software is NFS (Network File System). This is the UNIX standard for shared files, and is supported on Windows NT by several third-party software packages.

UNIX Security Holes

As with Windows NT, the passwords in the UNIX password file are stored in encrypted form. However, in older UNIX versions the password file is a simple ASCII file (found in `/etc/passwd` on most UNIX systems). Since this file is often readable by all users, a hacker can run a list of common passwords through the encryption and see if any of them matches one in the file. A wide variety of security holes in particular UNIX systems and utilities allow access to this file. Newer versions of UNIX store user information in the main password file, and they use a separate file called the *shadow password file* for the encrypted passwords. This file is never readable by all users.

One of the most important tasks in securing a UNIX system is to apply all of the available patches for the UNIX kernel and for all software packages used. To keep track of the security holes that have been found, see the Web pages described in Appendix C.

Policies: UNIX and Windows NT

- Use complex passwords for root and other powerful accounts.

- Restrict file permissions to limit unauthorized access.

- Use a version of UNIX that supports shadow password files, and keep the password file secure.

- Follow the guidelines in Chapter 14 for securing Internet services.

- Follow the guidelines in Chapter 15 to secure the TCP/IP protocol.

- Consider using a firewall, as described in Chapter 17.

Macintosh Security

Macintosh computers were the first to include built-in networking. Macintosh networking uses the AppleTalk protocol for network communication, and the AppleShare protocol for file and print sharing.

Mostly due to their proprietary nature, Macintosh computers are considered extremely secure. They have never been favored by hackers, and have no known significant security holes. In this section we'll take a quick look at the basics of Macintosh security, and look at how NT and Macintosh networks can be interconnected.

Macintosh Security Basics

Macintosh computers each store their own database of users and groups, and file and printer sharing can be restricted to particular users or groups. We'll look at these aspects of Macintosh security in the following sections.

Users and Groups

To manage the list of users and groups on a Macintosh, choose Control Panels from the Apple menu, then double-click Users and Groups. A list of users and groups is displayed. You can add or delete users, create groups, and add users to groups from this dialog box.

The database of users and groups is separate for each Macintosh, and access to one does not grant you access to any other. This makes unauthorized access difficult.

File and Print Sharing

Any Macintosh on the network can share files or printers. To access these options, highlight the folder or printer to be shared, and select File ➤ Sharing. You can specify a user or group to share the item with, or select the Everyone option to grant access to the whole network.

You can list shared directories by selecting Control Panels from the Apple menu, and choosing File Sharing Monitor. This utility lists the currently shared directories, and also displays a list of currently attached users.

NT-Macintosh Connectivity

Windows NT Server includes Services for Macintosh (SFM), a service that provides support for Macintosh-style file and print services. Using this service, NT directories and printers can be shared with Macintosh clients. Since SFM directly emulates an AppleShare server, no additional software is required on the client.

To support this feature, Macintosh clients must have System 6.07 or later as their operating system. They must also have a protocol in common with the NT network; since Ethernet (EtherTalk) is included on most modern Macintoshes, this shouldn't be a problem.

To install Services for Macintosh, follow these steps:

1. Choose the Services tab from the Network control panel.

2. Select Add. A list of available services is displayed, as shown in Figure 13.5.

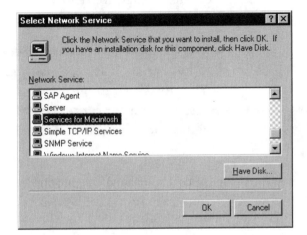

3. Select Services for Macintosh.

4. Click OK to install the service.

5. Restart the server to make the new service available.

Once SFM is installed, shared files can be accessed by Macintosh clients. Macintosh files can only be stored on NTFS partitions. In addition, Macintosh clients can only access Macintosh-accessible volumes within the partition. You can create these volumes using the Server Manager utility.

Security Holes

As mentioned above, Macintosh computers are quite secure. In fact, using SFM to store Macintosh files on an NT server greatly decreases the security of the files, since Windows NT has its share of security holes. Aside from the general file-system security problems noted in Chapter 8, there are no additional security holes when SFM is installed.

Summary

In this chapter, we've looked at three non-Microsoft operating systems that can be integrated with Windows NT networks:

- NetWare uses dedicated servers and provides sophisticated file and print sharing. It's a reasonably secure system, and NDS (NetWare Directory Services) provides a secure database of users and other resources for the entire network. Windows NT includes several utilities for NetWare connectivity.

- UNIX systems are available from a variety of vendors. These systems are reasonably secure when the latest patches are applied, and only trusted software is run. Windows NT networks and UNIX networks can be interconnected with the TCP/IP protocol, but third-party software is required for file or printer sharing.

- Macintosh computers include peer-to-peer networking functions. Each computer stores its own list of users and groups, and can be used for file or printer sharing. Windows NT Server includes Services for Macintosh (SFM), which allows Macintosh clients to access files and printers on the NT server.

CHAPTER

14

Internet Security:
Barbarians at the Gateway

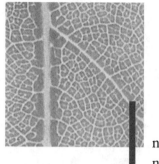

In order for someone to break into your network, that person needs a way to get at your network. A small number of people (employees, mostly) can walk up to computers on your network and attempt to use them. A larger number of people (anyone who can get the phone number) can dial up your network and attempt to get in if you have RAS with modems installed.

That may seem like a lot of people, but it's peanuts compared to how many can attempt to get into your network if you connect it to the Internet. The Internet, as an information superhighway, is used by hackers just as well as by students, shoppers, workers, researchers, and writers. Potential network intruders may be physically located anywhere around the world—the Internet makes it as easy to test your security from Norway as it is from down the street. When you secure your Internet-connected network, you're not just protecting your network from network users or from people who know your dial-up number; you're protecting your network from *everyone*.

This chapter describes the risks in connecting your network to the Internet. In the first section, *Can't Live With It, Can't Live Without It,* we provide a brief overview of what the Internet is, and how intranets and extranets relate to it. We cover in greater detail where the Internet came from and how the Internet works in the following section, *The Internet Protocols: Broken As Designed.* Finally, in the last section, *Connection Methods,* you get an idea of what options you have and what the security concerns are in connecting your network to the Internet.

Can't Live with It, Can't Live without It

You hear about the Internet everywhere. There are TV commercials, seminars, magazine articles, and radio spots about it. What is the big deal about the Internet, and why would anyone want to connect to it if the Internet is such a big security risk? Also big news today are those new offshoots of the Internet—intranets and extranets. What are they all about? Our goal in this section is to give you some answers to those questions.

The Internet

The Internet is the biggest thing to come along and affect how computers are used since the personal computer was invented. It's also the most pernicious security threat to your computing environment since the invention of the modem. The Internet connects buyers to sellers, researchers to information, remote offices to central ones, and similarly interested people to each other all over the world. The Internet provides businesses with a new way to sell to the more affluent segments of society, and it provides a mechanism for professionals to keep in touch and up to date.

The great appeal of the Internet to businesses is that it facilitates electronic commerce. Electronic commerce is not just Web pages you can use to order things (although that is a significant aspect of it on the Web today); electronic commerce refers to the many kinds of business transactions (ordering, specification, contract negotiation, product tracking, invoicing, and so on) that are performed electronically over a network instead of in person or through the mail using forms printed on paper. Electronic commerce speeds up business transactions, and can have a large impact on how responsive a company can be (and therefore how profitable that company is).

Before the wide-scale adoption of the Internet, many businesses did business electronically using private wide area networks, or WANs. The WANs themselves, as well as the electronic commerce software developed for them, performed the specific functions they were designed for, but they were not flexible systems—they were designed to fill a specific networking need. A WAN that linked Boeing with its many aerospace parts suppliers could certainly allow Boeing to order parts and track suppliers' inventory levels, but it would not do the same for Ford and Ford's automotive parts suppliers. A manufacturer that provided both aerospace and automotive parts might be required to participate in two or even more networks, and that manufacturer couldn't use those networks to conduct business with the raw materials suppliers that it relied on.

Before the adoption of the Internet, WANs were expensive propositions, both in terms of hardware and communications (each WAN had dedicated communications circuits that were used only for that WAN), but also in terms of software. Each WAN application (such as a parts inventory program, a specification document exchange system, or a bidding system) had to be crafted for the specific users of the program. Only the largest companies could afford them. Before the Internet came along, WANs allowed companies to exchange information, but each company needed its own WAN. With the Internet, a company can connect to an Internet service provider and use the same network links that other companies (and individuals) use (see Figure 14.1).

Any bookstore, bicycle manufacturer, or aerospace behemoth can attach to the Internet. A Web browser is the universal front-end for electronic commerce tasks such as ordering, inventory tracking, group messaging, document transfer, bidding, pricing and requests for pricing, contract negotiation, and publication of technical specifications. With a bit of customization, Web servers such as Internet Information Server can provide the back-end service for all of the above tasks.

The Internet has rapidly become an essential business tool, like the fax machine and the telephone. A salesman must have an e-mail

FIGURE 14.1

The Internet can take the place of several WANs.

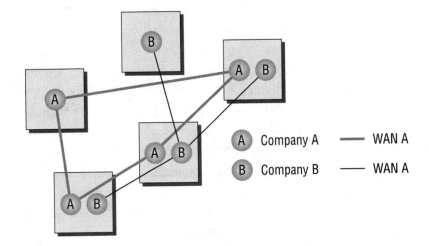

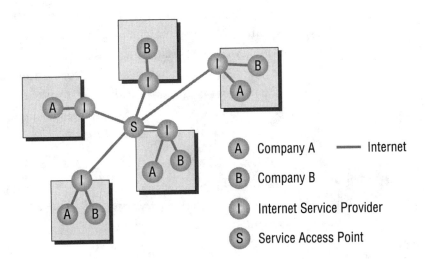

address, engineers must be able to FTP files to and from colleagues, the public relations department must have a Web page, and the service and support team must be able to put up drivers and other configuration files for customers to download.

Just because anyone can access your network doesn't mean that you should allow everyone to access it. If your company sells medical diagnostic equipment, you want the attention of medical professionals, not teenage pranksters or rival companies. Unless your company produces something hackers want (software, for instance) the biggest threat to your network from the Internet is not from individuals specifically interested in the information on your network; instead, the biggest threat is from hackers who would like to use computers in your network as a staging point for attacks on other networks and as a dumping ground for pirated software or pornography.

Another problem that organizations with high-profile Internet sites (such as the CIA, NASA, and the FBI) face is vandalism of their Web pages. Hackers break into these Web sites and change the contents to parody or denigrate the organizations. The vast majority of companies are far too boring to hackers to make this a significant threat, however.

Although hackers are not financially motivated as a rule, some of them are looking to make a fast buck. Those that break into networks for money can cause an inordinate amount of damage. Any organization that keeps financial or credit information on a network connected to the Internet is at risk of intrusion from the Internet. Companies that accept credit card numbers for purchases made over the Internet are common targets for this kind of attack.

Because the Internet is a security risk, financial institutions still maintain their own private WANs. To banks and mutual fund firms, the advantages of the Internet over private networks are simply not worth the risks inherent to them.

Intranets

Many of the tools developed for the Internet can be of use elsewhere, as well. (This is true of Web browsers, FTP clients, HTML and FTP servers, NetNews readers and servers, Internet Relay Chat clients and servers, and so on.) With a little customization, Internet tools can be used to replace very expensive custom-designed programs that would otherwise be used in a dedicated WAN. Many large companies are keeping the WAN (or large internal corporate network) and throwing away their custom-designed tools in favor of the Internet tools.

When you use Internet tools to create organizational data systems (such as shared databases, message boards, tracking systems, and inventory management tools), you probably won't want the public at large accessing these resources. You can, fortunately, use these tools on a private network that the general public can't access.

A private network that uses Internet tools is called an intranet. An intranet Web or FTP site is just as easy to set up as an Internet one, but the intranet site has an additional advantage: Only participants on the private WAN or campus network can access the intranet site. This makes the task of securing the site against attack significantly easier (see Figure 14.2).

An intranet can use all the same networking technology as the Internet, including TCP/IP, routers, DNS servers, and so on. The difference between the Internet and an intranet is that an intranet is either protected from the Internet by a firewall or other security mechanism, or an intranet is completely separated from the Internet (this separation is the defining characteristic of an intranet). If an intranet site is accessible from the Internet, then the intranet is really just a part of the Internet that is mostly used by individuals in your organization.

Policies: Internet and Intranet Services

- Divide the services you want to provide using Internet tools into public services and private (organizational) services. Place the public services on an Internet server (or servers) external to your Internet firewall and provide the private services on an intranet server (or servers) on your protected LAN. (See Chapter 17 for more information on how to protect your LAN using firewalls and other boarder security tools.)

FIGURE 14.2

An intranet uses the same tools as the Internet, but it resides on a private network.

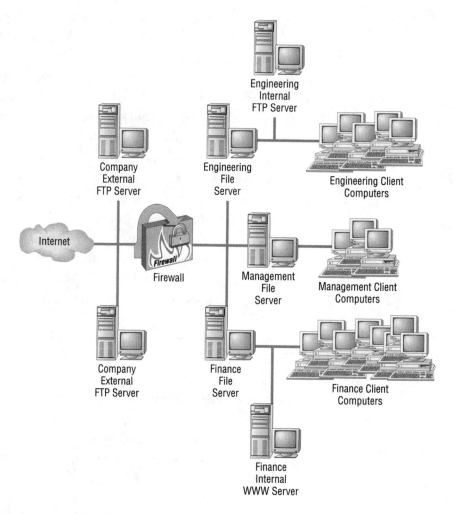

Engineering
Internal
FTP Server

Company
External
FTP Server

Engineering
File
Server

Engineering Client
Computers

Internet

Firewall

Management
File
Server

Management Client
Computers

Company
External
FTP Server

Finance
File
Server

Finance Client
Computers

Finance
Internal
WWW Server

Extranets

Because your intranet servers reside on your local network, the intranet neatly protects your internal Web and FTP sites from attack from the Internet (so long as your private network itself is adequately protected from the Internet). In many cases, however, you don't want to deny everyone outside your network access to your organizational data—you just want to protect it from the general public. Strategic partners, suppliers, customers, and other company affiliates may have a legitimate reason to access information on the Web sites and FTP servers you maintain.

A TCP/IP network shared by affiliated organizations in a particular industry is called an *extranet.* You can think of an extranet as a "members-only Internet" that is restricted to similar companies or organizations with a specific relation to yours. See Figure 14.3 for a view of how an extranet might be set up.

FIGURE 14.3

An extranet is a "members-only" TCP/IP network with services provided using standard Internet tools.

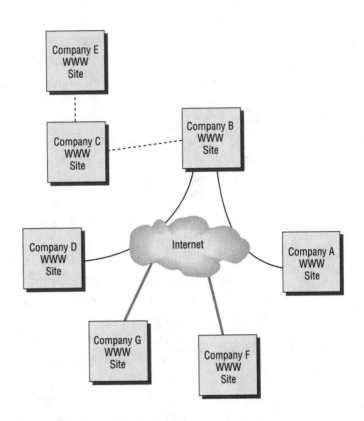

Internet Connection

Virtual Private Network Link

Leased Line

Sites in companies A through E are part of a private extranet; sites in companies F and G are part of the Internet.

The Internet Protocols: Broken As Designed

The Internet was not designed to be secure. It was designed to be flexible, scalable, and complete. The designers could not foresee the immense popularity their protocols and tools would enjoy, nor could they anticipate the wide variety of uses to which they would be put.

The Internet was born in 1969 as a research project of the Department of Defense's Advanced Research Projects Agency. ARPA funded an experiment with a new kind of networking technology—one that divided messages into packets to be sent over a multinode network piecemeal rather than using the standard procedure of first establishing a circuit for the message and then sending the message whole.

Up until 1969, computer networks created circuits (complete electrical paths) between the sending and the receiving computer, much the way older (analog) telephone systems created an analog circuit between the dialing and the ringing telephone. Once the circuit was established, the two computers could use the circuit for whatever they wanted. When the computers were through with the circuit, they broke the connection (just as a caller does by hanging up the phone after a telephone conversation).

The question ARPA sought to answer was simple: Instead of requiring an electrical circuit to be routed from the source to the destination through intermediate network nodes, could the message just be forwarded from one node to the next, broken up if were too large and reassembled at the other end? The answer was "yes," and to demonstrate how it might be done, four universities' research center computers were linked with a prototypical internetwork protocol. The experiment was a success. Other university computer centers joined in on the fun, the protocols were fine-tuned into the TCP/IP stack, and before anyone knew what was happening, the experiment became the basis of a new national information infrastructure.

How the Internet Works

The Internet is based on the TCP/IP transport protocol described in Chapter 15. TCP/IP is sufficiently flexible to link together a few computers in a single LAN or link together millions of computers across the world. In terms of the networking protocol, each of the computers is the same, and what the protocols convey (the data) is irrelevant.

The Internet is more than just a common transport protocol, however—the transport protocol links the computers together, but the character and utility of the Internet comes from the application layer services that use the protocol to transmit data. In terms of service, computers are not equal; server computers, which are also called hosts or sites, provide services (such as HTML, FTP, and Gopher) to Internet client computers which view or download the data for the user.

Internet Clients and Servers

The client/server relationship on the Internet is like the client/server relationship in a LAN. A single file server in a LAN provides file and print services to a number of client computers in the network. The server uses a protocol to provide the service to the clients: Windows NT uses NetBIOS to provide file and print services to Microsoft networking clients, for example. Several file servers can coexist in the same LAN, each dedicated to a specific purpose, such as storing engineering documents or financial transaction data. However, there are usually many more client computers in the LAN than there are servers, and the servers usually have greater capacity (in disk space, networking bandwidth, and memory) than client computers do.

Similarly, on the Internet, an Internet server, or host, provides services to which client computers can connect. Each service that an Internet server provides has a protocol associated with it that the server uses to communicate with the client for that service. A host providing Web service to a Web browser on a client computer would use the HTTP protocol, while a host (perhaps the same one) providing FTP service to an FTP tool on a client computer would use the FTP protocol.

One big difference between the Internet and a private LAN is that on the Internet everybody's Internet client computers and server computers are all connected together, and any client can reach any server. This is very good for electronic commerce, but very bad for security, as described in the next section *Intrinsic Internet Security Problems*. See Figure 14.4 for a comparison of LAN and Internet clients and servers.

Internet Services and Protocols

Imagine that the Internet is like the telephone system. (That shouldn't be difficult since Internet connections are made using leased telephone lines.) The TCP/IP transport protocol can be compared to the lines connecting one telephone to another, and the computers on the Internet can be compared to the telephones. Now, imagine that you want to call someone to order a pizza, and there is no one anywhere that will answer the phone. That is how the Internet would be without services—all the computers would be connected together, but there would be nothing to do with the connections.

A Web browser requests an HTML page in much the same way you order a pizza (except the pizza isn't usually delivered over the phone). You dial the number of the pizza parlor and begin a conversation with the order-taker. The conversation has an established format—you are placed on hold, you specify the kind of pizza you want, the order taker confirms the price, you confirm your location, and the order taker tells you how long it will take for the pizza to arrive.

The Web service is like the order taker—it accepts connections and satisfies requests. The HTTP protocol might be compared to the conversation format—the protocol describes how the Web page is requested just as the conversation format governs how a pizza is ordered. Different services have different protocols just as a conversation in which you order flowers differs from one in which you order pizza. A flower shop may ask for a credit card number, a delivery address different from your own, and perhaps a message. Very few pizza parlors routinely expect a note to be sent with the pizza.

FIGURE 14.4

Any client can access any
server on the Internet.

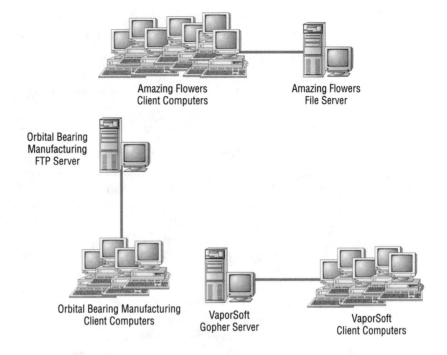

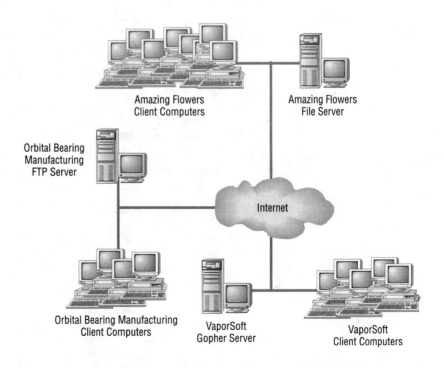

FIGURE 14.4

Any client can access any
server on the Internet.

There are services on the Internet supporting just about any computing task you can think of. The most common Internet services (and the protocols they use) are defined in the Terminology sidebar.

Terminology

- **Web (HyperText Transport Protocol):** This is the service that most people use over the Internet today. Web browsers on client computers display the data stored on Web server computers. The introduction of the graphical interface of the World Wide Web made the Internet accessible to nontechnical people. The Web is also the basis of most electronic commerce on the Internet. The Web is a relatively recent addition to the Internet though—before 1990 there was no such thing as the World Wide Web.

- **Telnet (Telnet):** UNIX computers can provide a command-line interface to remote computers using the Telnet protocol and program. Other operating systems (Windows NT included) can also be Telnet hosts. A Telnet client on a client computer will allow the user of the client computer to run command-line programs on the remote server computer.

- **FTP (File Transfer Protocol):** You can use this service to transfer files to and from remote computers over the Internet. Internet file archives often provide FTP access to the files. The FTP client software on the client computer enables uploading files to, as well as downloading files from, an FTP server on the Internet.

- **Gopher (Gopher):** Gopher is a hypertext system that predates the World Wide Web. Gopher has hypertext menus that refer to other menus or to regular text or binary files. Gopher is not as visually rich as the Web. Gopher client software on the client computer displays information, over the Internet, that is stored on Gopher server computers.

- **E-mail (Simple Mail Transfer Protocol and Post Office Protocol):** Electronic mail is forwarded from one e-mail server computer to the next over the Internet using SMTP. Using SMTP or POP, e-mail software on the client computers can access the host computers to retrieve mail in an individual e-mail account. The e-mail server can also transform the mail so that a LAN e-mail package, such as Microsoft Exchange or CC:Mail can access it (an e-mail server that converts the e-mail to another format is called an e-mail gateway).

- **Chat (Internet Relay Chat):** Using IRC, people can engage in real-time conversations with other Internet users (by typing rather than speaking). IRC client software connects to IRC servers that distribute the conversation to all other IRC clients.

- **Usenet News (NNTP):** Usenet is a global electronic bulletin board system where people with similar interests, expertise, or problems can exchange messages. News servers exchange Usenet messages via the NNTP protocol, and news reader software on client computers can read and post messages to the servers using the same protocol.

- **Domain Name Service (DNS):** This service is used by networking software to translate textual Internet names into numeric IP addresses.

Don't confuse the *World Wide Web* with the *Internet*. The World Wide Web uses the Internet to connect Web browsers with Web servers, but the Internet can also connect FTP clients with FTP servers, and Usenet readers to NNTP hosts.

One computer can provide any of the Internet service protocols, or more than one. Windows NT with Internet Information Server provides WWW, FTP, and Gopher services, for example. You can install additional software that will turn your NT server into an IRC host or an e-mail gateway as well.

Intrinsic Internet Security Problems

In the previous section there was no mention of how security on the Internet works—because it doesn't really. The transport protocol the Internet uses (TCP/IP) was not designed with security in mind. The lack of intrinsic security mechanisms leads to haphazard security mechanisms implemented by the upper-level services described in *Service-Level Insecurity*.

No Intrinsic Encryption, Identification, or Access Control

TCP/IP was created as an experiment in packet-based networking, not an experiment in positive user identification, secure message exchange, network use accounting, or controlled user access. If the Internet is a freeway system (as the common comparison goes), then it is a freeway with a few deficiencies, including the following:

- There are no licenseplates on the cars: A packet can come from anywhere and the return address can easily be forged.

- There are no driver's licenses: Anyone can connect a computer to the Internet.

- There is no highway patrol: Packet redirection (also called connection hijacking) is relatively easy to do if someone has the right tools.

- There are no speed limits: Anyone can send as much data as they want, denying other users the bandwidth they need.

The need for encryption, identification, and access control within a network depends on the perceived value of the information contained in the network and the perceived value of the commerce conducted over it. In addition, a private network may have relaxed internal security because "outsiders" are not expected to have access to it.

The Internet was initially a networking experiment shared by a closed community of researchers, and commerce over it was not allowed. So the perceived value of the information contained in the network was low (it's just research data, after all, and it will be published in the next issue of the *Journal of Obscure Computer Information Systems Research* anyway).

Since strong mechanisms for encryption, identification, and access control were left out of the TCP/IP layer, they must be provided by the services that use TCP/IP. The next section describes service-level security, or the lack of it, on the Internet.

Service-Level Insecurity

On the Internet, each service must implement its own security mechanisms. Some services, NFS for example, use elaborate challenge-and-response authentication and encrypt the password exchange, while other services (such as SMTP) do nothing at all to authenticate the user or ensure that the use of the service is authorized. Most services fall somewhere in the middle, providing some security, but not enough to foil a determined attacker.

Telnet is an example of security that is almost good enough. It at least requires a user name and password for access to restricted systems, but the user names and passwords are transmitted without encryption from the client computer to the server computer. Since they are transmitted in the clear, any eavesdropping computer on any intervening network can "capture" and use those passwords.

Other protocols don't even provide that much security—with only the built-in operating system tools any user can connect to an SMTP server and forge e-mail that appears to come from, for example, Henry J Tillman, President of Tillman World Enterprises. A wily hacker or disaffected employee can cause havoc in an organization that relies on the authenticity of electronic mail.

Another weakness of SMTP mail is that by default all of the mail is transmitted across the Internet unencrypted and is readable by supervisor-level accounts in intermediate SMTP servers. In fact, when there is a problem with an SMTP message, it is often directed into the inbox of the SMTP supervisor account—something to keep in mind the next time you send a romantic e-mail message to your paramour or an e-mail with confidential bid information to a subcontractor. Some unscrupulous network administrators live for that sort of thing—they have search tools that find messages with specific words and phrases in them, and they delight in sharing the best parts of those messages.

Reality Check: Not-So-Private E-Mail

One morning the head of the personnel department burst into my office and asked if I could stop an e-mail message. One person in the organization had sent a congratulatory message to another—about an award that that individual was not yet aware he would be receiving.

While a coworker stalled the award recipient to keep him from checking his mail, I logged on to the mail server and used a software tool to search the files stored there for specific text contained in the message. Once the file containing the message was identified, I removed that specific file from his inbox. He was surprised with the award at the meeting later that afternoon, and a number of people were reminded just how private their e-mail *wasn't*, both under company policy and due to the software used to implement the e-mail system.

Since TCP/IP does not provide network security, the service protocols must provide it instead. Secure HyperText Transfer Protocol (SHTTP) provides security for Web page transmission by encrypting the data exchanged between a Web browser and a Web server. Many Web servers support Secure Socket Layer (SSL) communications, which also encrypt HTTP communications. SSL, unlike SHTTP, can be used for more than just Web traffic; some Telnet and FTP servers support connections from client software via SSL.

Comparing Internet Security to Windows NT Domain Security

The fact that there are many different security mechanisms that provide different levels of security makes it more difficult to secure a computer that hosts a number of services over the Internet than it is to secure a Windows NT server that hosts NetBIOS resources in a LAN. Windows NT with NetBIOS is easier to secure because there is one security mechanism for all of the resources hosted by Windows NT computers in a domain: That mechanism is the Windows NT security model (described in Chapter 5).

In the domain security model, the user must be authenticated by a domain server before they can access resources in the domain—even resources that are made available to the Everyone special group. All user authentication, no matter which service is requested (file storage, printing, or SQL database access, for example), is satisfied by the Security and Accounts Manager using the NetBIOS authentication protocol. The specific allowable services (permissions) may differ from one kind of object to another, but how the administrator controls the permissions does not change, and the same auditing mechanism is used for all of the SAM-controlled objects.

In contrast, each Internet service must provide its own security mechanisms, and many Internet services do not even try. Each security mechanism must be administered separately, and the auditing and reporting mechanisms (if they exist) all go to different places and report in different formats. Some implementations of Internet services use the mechanisms of the host operating system to maintain security (the WWW, FTP, and Gopher services of IIS use the security mechanisms of Windows NT), while other services create their own security mechanisms. (The WWW service of Netscape Enterprise Server, for example, uses LDAP to manage its own separate list of users and groups.)

Security Weaknesses of Internet Services

Each protocol has its own security weaknesses and strengths. Many protocols are obsolete or are not relevant to the majority of Windows NT networks connected to the Internet, but the following services are all popular and should be evaluated carefully:

- **World Wide Web:** The problem with the World Wide Web is its very flexibility. A WWW site can be very secure or very nonsecure depending on how the server software and Web pages are administered. Clients can connect anonymously, authenticate using cleartext, or (at least with IIS) use encrypted authentication. Improperly written CGI scripts or ISAPI applications can open holes in your network security. WWW clients in your network can betray user name and password information to malicious Web sites on the Internet, and it is very easy to download software, such as Trojan horses, that will entirely compromise your network security (by transmitting the password file of the client computer to a remote host, for example).

- **Telnet:** This service is very insecure. User names and passwords are not encrypted, so any computer on the Internet between the client and the host may eavesdrop on the communication and capture the account information. The connection established via Telnet is not encrypted, so any actions taken by the user (such as viewing sensitive information on that host or logging on to a third host via the remote host) may also be observed by "sniffing" the communications stream. A hacker can also insert additional information into a Telnet session and cause the remote computer to divulge information or compromise security, or the session may actually be hijacked by a network attacker.

- **File Transfer Protocol:** The big issue with FTP is not the protocol or the service software, but rather the way FTP is used. A user name and password can be required, but many organizations use FTP to make files available to anonymous users over the Internet. The identity of anonymous users cannot be verified by the FTP software. So if uploads are allowed, even to a read-only directory, the FTP server can be misused to store inappropriate material or even brought down without the administrator being able to tell who did it. Authenticated FTP access is also not secure against playback and man-in-the-middle attacks, and the data transmitted between the FTP server and client is not encrypted.

- **Gopher:** This service is similar to the World Wide Web and has been mostly eclipsed by it due to the Web's more graphical nature and its client-side extensibility. However, many academic and government sites still make information available via the Gopher protocol. Since Gopher servers are extensible in a manner similar to most WWW servers, the primary concern is making sure that the external programs that Gopher servers use do not compromise security.

- **E-mail (SMTP):** The primary security problem with this protocol is that it does not authenticate the sender of mail. It is trivial for any user with access to the SMTP port of a mail server to forge e-mail from any user or to any user. E-mail is also not encrypted when sent via SMTP, therefore intermediate hosts and computers on the same network segments as an SMTP server can eavesdrop on SMTP-transferred e-mail. There are additional security problems with the mail server software, rather than with the protocol. E-mail software is complex and requires access to system services at the administrative level. Therefore e-mail software is both hard to debug and capable of opening up the e-mail hosting system to a wide variety of attacks if a bug is found and exploited.

- **E-mail (POP):** The security issue with the Post Office Protocol is that the user name and password for the e-mail account are not encrypted before being sent to the remote mail server, and therefore are easily intercepted. E-mail is also not encrypted when retrieved via POP, therefore intermediate hosts and computers on the same network segments as a POP server or client can eavesdrop on POP-transferred e-mail.

- **Internet Relay Chat:** By itself, this protocol is harmless enough, but many IRC client software packages allow the user to open up the client computer to externally generated commands.

- **Usenet News:** The NetNews Transfer Protocol does not pose much of a security risk to a network because the information exchanged using the protocol is usually forwarded around the world anyway. NNTP does not, however, verify the identity of message posters, so impersonation is a risk. Also, if an organization uses NetNews to implement private local newsgroups, improper administration of an NNTP server could make the internal newsgroups available externally. The biggest problem with NNTP occurs if an NNTP server is left accessible to the entire Internet. Such a server can easily be overloaded by having too many unauthorized clients connect to it.

- **Domain Name Service:** This protocol cannot be used to gain direct control of a computer. But the majority of Internet programs rely on DNS, so the transmission of false DNS data to a computer is often the first step in compromising that computer. DNS data exchanges are automatic and seldom logged with the identity of the computer requesting DNS data. Received DNS data is seldom checked for validity by the client computer. A DNS server can also reveal more about your network (computer identities, operating systems, and roles, for example) than most administrators would like outsiders to know.

Policies: Internet Services

- Do not use clear text authentication for WWW accounts that are also accounts on your Windows NT server.

- Limit the use of external programs and scrutinize their application in Web site and Gopher site development.

- Educate network users on safe and unsafe WWW browsing practices.

- Educate network users on safe and unsafe IRC practices.

- Use Secure Socket Layer encryption for sensitive HTTP traffic.

- Have a separate SMTP server on your firewall that forwards mail to and from an internal, trusted SMTP server.

- Do not use e-mail to send proprietary or sensitive information over the Internet without first encrypting it.

- Do not use POP to connect to a mail server over the Internet.

- Restrict who may place files for download on your FTP server.

- Make any FTP upload directories write-only.

- Require FTP, Telnet, POP, and other Internet service account names and passwords to be different from Windows networking account names and passwords.

- Deny NNTP connections from all hosts external to your network except the host providing your NNTP feed.

- Limit the amount of local DNS information available to computers external to your network.

Connection Methods

With a clear understanding of the benefits and risks of connecting the computers in your network to the Internet, you can evaluate the ways you can go about making that connection. As illustrated in Figure 14.5, you have three options:

- Don't connect to the Internet.

- Make temporary connections to the Internet from client computers.

- Make a permanent continuous connection to the Internet via a router.

FIGURE 14.5

Your organization has three basic options for dealing with the security threat posed by the Internet.

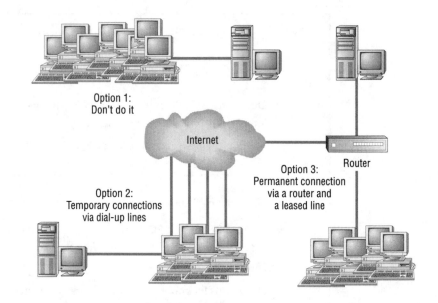

If you select a permanent connection there are several ways you can go about it. These methods include installing a firewall, installing a separate network, allowing the clients to access only the Internet, installing packet filters and proxies, and properly configuring Windows security.

Don't Do It

Your first option is simply not to connect to the Internet. For a number of organizations this is the best option—not everyone needs to connect to the Internet, and the decision to connect or not should always be made on the evaluation of the benefit versus the costs and risks involved in being connected. There are two reasons for not connecting to the Internet:

- **You don't need it:** The purpose of an Internet connection is to allow people in your network to exchange data with others over the Internet. If the nature of your business is such that people in your company don't need to exchange data with outside agents in order to get their work done, then the Internet may be more of a distraction than a help.

- **You can't risk it:** Organizations that maintain valuable or private data on their own networks may risk too much by placing their computers on the Internet, even temporarily or at a reserve. Often, these are also organizations that create their own wide area networks when they need to link remote sites. Banks, medical records repositories, and intelligence agencies are examples of this sort of organization.

Temporary Connections

It is difficult for hackers to get into your system via the Internet if you are seldom connected to the Internet. Temporary connections for client computers via modems and dial-up lines are more than just a cheap way to get online: They also narrow the window of opportunity for network attacks.

The modem line is like a draw-bridge. While the drawbridge is down anyone can try to get across, but while it is up your castle is safe. In a similar way, if the modem is connected hackers may try to get in while you are connecting to the outside, but when the modem is offline the hackers are stymied.

WARNING Be careful about allowing these computers to answer the phone line—some hackers still remember how to use a modem. In 1996, more network intrusions were reported to have occurred over dial-in modems than over the Internet.

Temporary connections do limit the presence you can establish for your organization on the Internet, however, and temporary Internet connections made from client computers without the knowledge of the network administrator can put the network at risk.

The first Internet connections in a network are usually made from client computers via a modem and a dial-up line, often without the knowledge of the network administrator by people on the LAN who install their own modems on their computers. Because of the file-sharing and network routing capabilities of many network client computers, the temporary connections can leave your network defenseless to Internet attacks for as long as the user is logged on to the Internet service provider. Most network users don't have sufficient knowledge to protect their computers (and by extension your network) from Internet attacks.

A few simple precautions taken with the client computers, however, can make this one of the safest ways of connecting to the Internet. Simply do not bind the file sharing protocols to the Internet connection, and disable TCP/IP routing from the Internet connection to the local network. The client computer will still be vulnerable to Trojan horse attacks in the form of downloadable files or Web browser controls, but the only way to protect your network against that kind of attack is by educating network users.

The drawbacks of this kind of Internet connection are the reduced bandwidth of each Internet connection (modern analog modems are limited to a maximum speed of 56Kbps) and the limited number of connections possible (one for each computer with a modem and an open phone line). Although initially cheap, this kind of Internet connection can get expensive when there are a large number of computers with modems and phone lines—your company must pay for those phone lines whether they are being used or not.

A third drawback of only connecting to the Internet when your clients dial out is that it prevents you from maintaining your own Internet presence from your LAN. If your organization wants a Web or FTP site, you'll need to have the site hosted elsewhere. In addition to providing your network connection, most Internet service providers will host your site for you as an additional service. But you have less control over the management and the content of the site when you rely on someone else to administer it for you. Internet mail will also reside on an external host until your client computers access it, but this is less of a security concern because the Internet mail has traversed the Internet unprotected already.

Policies: Dial-up Internet Connections

- Disable file sharing to the RAS connection and routing to computers on your network from the network connection, for client computers that connect to the Internet.

- Closely control dial-in access to client computers.

Permanent Connections

It makes sense to get a dedicated line from your network to an Internet service provider if you want to maintain your own Internet sites rather than relying on your ISP to do it for you, if you need the greater bandwidth that a leased line can provide, or if you have a large number of client computers to connect to the Internet.

That permanent connection is like a permanent bridge over the moat into your castle. It may be wider and stronger than the little drawbridge, but it is always there for attackers to try to cross by subterfuge (Trojan horses or impersonation) or by brute force (password attacks, denial-of-service attacks, and so on). The measures you take to protect your castle from Internet barbarians can include one or more of the following forms:

- Naked Internet

- Packet filter

- Firewall

- Proxy

- Client Internet access only

- Separate network for Internet

- Windows security

Naked Internet

The easiest thing to do is nothing at all: Just connect the leased line to your internal router and forget about it. This is not the recommended solution. Even if you believe your networked computers have no information on them that would be valuable to anyone outside your network, you could still fall prey to vandalism, and your network always has one thing the Internet barbarians prize: space. Before you know what's happening, your file server could be stuffed full of pirated software and scanned images of dubious merit.

Packet Filters

One of the simplest—and most effective—things you can do to get the greatest security benefit for the least administrative effort is to install a packet filter between your network and the Internet. The packet filter won't stop all kinds of Internet attacks in a complicated network environment (see Chapter 17), but it does allow you to limit access to your network based on the following criteria:

- Specific kinds of packets such as IP, ICMP, ARP, and RARP

- Packet flags such as Fragmented, Source Routed, and ACK

- Source and destination IP addresses

- Source and destination TCP ports

Packet filters allow you to establish rules based on the above criteria to allow or deny packets to pass. Packet filters perform no more than a cursory examination of the data contained in IP packets—the packet filter is primarily concerned with what kind of packet it is and what kind of header information it has (its source, destination, status, and so on).

If your Internet needs are simple (you just want to pass HTTP and e-mail traffic through your Internet connection, for example) a packet filter may be sufficient for your network security. Otherwise, you should install a firewall between the Internet and your network.

Firewalls

Firewalls are more complicated than packet filters because firewalls examine the data portions of packets, as well as the headers, in an attempt to control the data transferred in the packets as well as the sources and destinations of the packets. The firewall can only control the data portion for protocols that the firewall understands, so the additional security provided by a firewall only applies to the most commonly used Internet services. For new, experimental, or proprietary protocols, a firewall is no more useful than a packet filter.

A firewall can detect, for example, that a connection coming into your network from an allowed external mail server does not conform to the syntax used by the SMTP service. A properly configured firewall will then disallow access from the (presumably) compromised external computer and alert the administrator to an unauthorized access attempt on the network. Similarly, a firewall would detect non-NFS data coming through an NFS-allowed port, or non-HTTP data coming from an allowed HTTP port.

Firewalls are usually used in conjunction with packet filters and with proxy servers, which provide greater service-level functionality.

Proxy Servers

A proxy server for a service will access Internet services for client computers on your network. The proxy access has two benefits: It hides the identity of the computers on your network, which gives attackers from the Internet less information about your network, and it can cache commonly accessed resources so that many client requests are satisfied much faster than they could be without the proxy.

A proxy server also makes firewall and packet filter configuration easier because all external connections to the services mediated by the proxy will go to the proxy server computer. Any other external connections can be explicitly denied. Proxy servers also can "condition" the data going through the proxy so that, for example, data flowing through an FTP proxy conforms to the data exchange formats for FTP. This makes it more difficult for a hacker to use an open port for a purpose other than that intended by the network administrator.

Dedicated Internet Servers

You should not use your file and print server as an Internet server; instead, you should place a dedicated machine outside your firewall to host WWW, FTP, and Gopher services. This limits the extent that security will be compromised if the Internet server is broken into. Because the firewall must examine every packet that crosses its barrier, using a dedicated machine also reduces the load placed on the firewall if you host a popular Internet site.

Client Internet Access Only

Network intruders hope to compromise the network file server because that's where you store the important data on your network, where network passwords are found, where a pirate may store stolen software, and where the security for your network is controlled. You can make it much harder to get at your servers (but not impossible; hackers are notoriously clever) by not allowing the servers to connect to the Internet.

In order for the client computers on your network to access the Internet they must have the TCP/IP transport protocol installed. Your router must route TCP/IP, and your packet filter and firewall must pass TCP/IP packets. Your network clients and file server don't have to use TCP/IP for file and print services, though, and it is a good idea to use either NetBEUI or NWLink instead of TCP/IP for that purpose.

If your file server does not have TCP/IP installed, an external attacker cannot use weaknesses in TCP/IP to get at your server. Nor can the attacker use a compromised client computer to tunnel TCP/IP into and out of your network to attack the server (in the case that your firewall merely blocks access to your server's IP address). Instead, the attacker must be able to remotely control the client computer so that it will perform the file access itself, or the attacker must install software on the compromised client that will perform a protocol conversion, which is not an easy thing to do.

WARNING Do not allow anyone to install remote control software on client computers on your network. If *you* install such software, make sure that it can't be abused.

Separate Network for Internet Access

For organizations that simply cannot accept the risk of local network intrusion from the Internet but still want access to the Internet, there is only one solution: Create two networks, one for secure local storage and the other for Internet access. This solution is sometimes called the "sacrificial goat" form of network security because computers on the vulnerable network may be compromised without risking data on the secure network.

In fact, the computers on the sacrificial network may intentionally be left with substandard security and then closely monitored to determine (when the clients show evidence of being hacked) that the organization is under attack. Figure 14.6 shows a private and public network configuration.

FIGURE 14.6

A separate network allows Internet access while eliminating the possibility of intrusion on a separate private LAN.

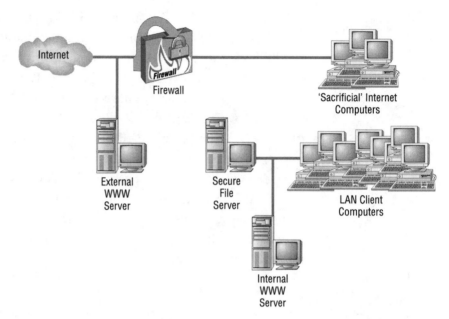

The problem with this sort of Internet connection is that to be truly effective no computer can be on both networks at the same time. Network users must physically move to a station that is connected to the Internet in order to access it, and information retrieved from the Internet must be physically moved from the Internet stations to the stations on the LAN.

Windows Security

Regardless of the Internet security implemented at the border between your network and the Internet, you should have strong Windows NT domain security in your LAN. After a hacker penetrates your Internet security, the Windows NT security may still protect your data if you have set up the security properly.

Policies: Permanent Internet Connections

- Install a packet filter, a firewall, and proxy servers between your LAN and the Internet.

- Use dedicated computers outside your firewall to provide Internet services such as WWW, FTP, and Gopher.

- Do not use the TCP/IP transport protocol on internal file servers.

- If your network requires greater security, use a separate network for computers attached to the Internet.

- Implement strong Windows NT security on your network.

Summary

The problem with the Internet is that it is too useful to dismiss and too dangerous to turn your back on. Soon no company will be able to compete without an Internet presence (a Web site) or at least an Internet connection for e-mail and Web access. A network administrator must be careful when setting up an Internet connection and vigilant while managing it.

Internet connections are difficult to secure because the Internet was not designed with security in mind. There are no intrinsic encryption, authentication, or access control mechanisms in TCP/IP; therefore security must be implemented by the services that use TCP/IP. Each service implements security differently, making security administration difficult and creating security weaknesses that can be exploited in network attacks.

The network administrator has three basic options for connecting client stations to the Internet: choosing not to do it at all, connecting clients individually via dial-up lines, or connecting the LAN to the Internet via a leased line. The permanently connected LAN must be protected from network intruders; packet filters, firewalls, and proxy servers can stand between the LAN and the Internet.

Additional measures administrators can take include dedicating Internet servers, allowing only client computers to connect to the Internet, and creating a separate network for connecting to the Internet. Internet security should always be supplemented with Windows NT network security.

CHAPTER

15

A Condensed TCP/IP Reader

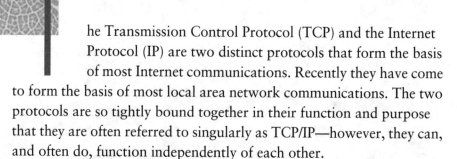

he Transmission Control Protocol (TCP) and the Internet Protocol (IP) are two distinct protocols that form the basis of most Internet communications. Recently they have come to form the basis of most local area network communications. The two protocols are so tightly bound together in their function and purpose that they are often referred to singularly as TCP/IP—however, they can, and often do, function independently of each other.

In common usage, the entire suite of Internet protocols is referred to as the TCP/IP protocol suite. Those protocols include low-level protocols like IP, ARP, UDP, and TCP, as well as higher-level protocols like HTTP and FTP, which rely upon the services of the lower-level Internet protocols. This chapter is concerned only with the low-level protocols. Higher-level protocols and their related security issues are discussed in Chapter 18.

TCP/IP is the communications medium between computers on the Internet. Understanding security on the Internet requires a thorough understanding of TCP/IP and routing. Before we delve into the security issues surrounding TCP and IP, we will discuss exactly how each of the low-level Internet protocols function, and its intended use. We will then explain how these protocols can be exploited and what you can do to avoid exploitation.

The Internet Protocol

The Internet Protocol (IP) is the foundation upon which all other high-level Internet protocols operate. IP provides the basic mechanism for the forwarding of data between two computers on separate networks. IP can fragment packets if they are too large for some older networks to forward, but this feature is largely obsolete because all routers built during the past decade are able to pass large IP packets.

IP packets are simply handed from computer to computer until they reach their destination. The computer sending the packet and the computer receiving the packet are called *end systems* because they are at the ends of the communication session. The computers between the end systems are called *intermediate systems*. Intermediate system is a generic and more theoretical term for computers more commonly called *routers, gateways,* or *multi-homed hosts*.

Services of IP

IP provides the functions of addressing and fragmentation only to support packet forwarding—no other functionality is presumed or implemented. Therefore:

- IP cannot guarantee that a packet will reach its destination.

- IP has no ability to perform flow control.

- IP performs no error correction.

- IP performs no error detection for the data payload.

- IP does not guarantee that packets will arrive in order and does not order them sequentially.

IP relies on the data link (such as Ethernet or frame relay) to transmit data in an error-free condition and does not attempt to provide any guarantees of service. Other protocols, which are transported within IP packets, add information such as packet serial numbers and error-correction codes. The destination system can check to see if all the packets have arrived, arrange them in the correct order, and request that any missing packets be sent again based on this additional information. (TCP performs all these functions, as explained in the next section.)

IP treats each packet as if it existed alone and were not related to any other packet being transmitted. For this reason, IP packets are often referred to as *datagrams*, which, like a telegram, implies a short but complete transmitted message. IP does not have logical or virtual connections, circuits, sockets, or any other mechanism to provide associations between packets. These functions are all provided by higher-level protocols like TCP (or occasionally lower-level protocols like ATM).

IP does not perform error correction. IP does, however, implement limited error checking to verify that the header information is correct; damaged header information could result in the packet being forwarded to the wrong address. If a router on the path between the sending computer and the receiving computer detects at any time that an IP packet's address header has become damaged (by comparing the header with the header's checksum), the router will simply discard the packet without notification of any kind. Again, higher-level protocols will determine what data is missing and generate a request for retransmission. This header checksum does not detect errors that may have crept into the data portion of the packet—that function is also left up to higher-level protocols.

Whenever you see the term *router* used in a generic sense, remember that the device could be any intermediate system, such as a gateway or a multi-homed host.

IP does include information about how long a packet is to be kept "alive" in a system. Every IP packet contains a *time-to-live indicator* that is decremented each time a router forwards the packet or whenever one second of real time elapses. The time-to-live counter usually starts at around 64, but 128 is the maximum possible value. When a packet's time-to-live counter reaches zero the packet is discarded. This event can occur in three (rare) cases:

- When the network is too busy to forward packets in a timely manner

- When a circular route exists and packets are simply being passed around it

- When the route between two computers is simply too long to be useful

In all three cases, the route is not usable so communications should not continue.

Internet Protocol is defined in RFC 791. Appendix C tells you where to find RFCs on the Web.

Internet Addresses

All computers attached to an IP network (such as the Internet) are uniquely identified by a 32-bit number, usually expressed in decimal notation and with each byte separated by a period. Because each portion of the address specifies 8 bits, the decimal range is between 0 and 255 for each of the 4 bytes. For example:

10.191.31.10

You'll often see bytes referred to as *octets* in other network documents. In this book, a byte is always 8 bits long and an octet is eight singing barbers.

This address must be unique to the specific computer to which it is assigned—no other computer can have this address if it is attached to the same network (that is, the Internet). If two computers ever do have the same address, unpredictable routing errors will result. IP addresses are analogous to house addresses in that no two are ever the same and each element (in the case of house addresses, elements would be states, cities, streets, and numbers) is increasingly specific—they become more specific as you read to the right.

Waterfront Property in Cyberspace

Due to the limited number of Internet addresses available (there are only slightly more than 4 billion addresses in a 32-bit number) and the somewhat wasteful manner in which the IP network number and the client address are assigned, InterNIC is running out of unique Internet addresses. In a few years, it will be nearly impossible to get large batches of IP addresses to assign to your computers.

IPV6, IP version 6 (alias IPNG, IP Next Generation) has a larger address space that is a superset of the IP address space. The specification requires that all TCP/IP software for hosts and intermediate systems be rewritten to support it, so it's not likely we'll see it implemented any time soon.

In the meantime, IP masquerades provide a working solution to the problem by converting internal IP addresses to a single fixed IP address (or more than one, if necessary) at the border gateway between the private network and the public network. This effectively allows you to extend the address space of IP to include the 16-bit port number—however, since each IP socket requires a port number, you're really addressing IP sessions rather than IP hosts. A single masquerade can effectively manage about 2,000 internal hosts—more than enough for most networks.

In fact, IP masquerades are so effective that they may forestall the need to switch to IPV6 indefinitely if most medium to small networks implement them at their borders and request only a single "public" IP address. IP masquerades are discussed in detail in Chapter 17.

Network Numbers

IP addresses contain two elements of data: the network number and the host number. The network number is the unique code assigned to your network. This number functions much the way a ZIP or postal code functions for routing mail—it gets the packet to the general area: the network. The host (or station) number determines the specific host on that network to which the packet is addressed. This is similar to your street address.

The following example explains how IP addresses are assigned and how networks are *subnetted*, or divided into IP networks. Let's say that BT&T, a telephone company and Internet service provider, has been assigned the 10 address range. Within that range, BT&T is able to split up and sell ranges of IP addresses. BT&T's network number is 10, and the client numbers for routers on this network are 3 bytes long.

Now let's say that American Internet, a regional ISP that serves the East Coast, purchases from BT&T high-capacity network connections and the right to act as a second-tier Internet service provider. BT&T assigns the 191 range of its 10 address range to American Internet, which is now free to assign any addresses more specific than 10.191. American Internet's network number is 10.191, leaving 2 bytes to assign to client addresses.

You may see network numbers shown as either 10.191 or 10.191.0.0. Both are equal. The zero placeholders are used to make it obvious that the number is used by IP.

Digital Widgets, a small company that makes a digital version of the ubiquitous widget and has 200 computers, leases a T1 service and the ability to assign its own IP addresses within the company, from American Internet. American Internet gives Digital Widgets the 64 address range so that Digital Widgets is free to assign any IP address more specific than 10.191.64 to their own computers. Digital Widget's network number is 10.191.64 and they have 1 byte to assign to client addresses.

Classes

Internet addresses were originally segmented on byte boundaries. Large networks on which the first byte specifies the network number and the last 3 bytes specify the local addresses are called *Class A domains*. Medium-size networks on which the first 2 bytes specify the network number and the last 2 bytes specify the local addresses are called *Class B domains*. Smaller networks on which the first 3 bytes specify the network number and the last byte specifies the local addresses are called *Class C domains*. In the preceding example, BT&T has a Class A domain, American Internet has a Class B domain, and Digital Widgets has a Class C domain.

Classless Addressing

This example is fairly simple; it is also possible to subnet at any point within the 32 bits of the IP address—not just on byte boundaries. This method of dividing network numbers from local addresses is known as *classless addressing*.

Originally, most Internet addresses were segmented on byte boundaries simply because it was easy, but as IP addresses became scarce, the more conservative practice of segmenting based on the actual estimated size of a network became more common.

To explain this system, let's say Digital Widgets has 1,000 computers rather than just 200. Since you can't fit 1,000 IP addresses into the 254 allowed addresses of the last 8 bits of an IP address, American Internet has to provide a larger subnet to its customers.

If you thought 8 bits could provide 256 addresses (because 2 to the 8th power is 256), you'd be right. But in this case two addresses in every subnet are reserved. The "all zeros" address is used to specify the entire subnet. 10.191.61.0 specifies Digital Widget's entire network; 10.191.0.0 specifies American Internet's network; and 10.0.0.0 specifies BT&T's network. The "all ones" (binary "11111111" = 255) address is used to specify an IP broadcast, so sending an IP packet to 10.191.61.255 means that all computers should receive it. Therefore, to calculate the number of available addresses in a subnet, you raise 2 to the number of bits in the subnet portion of the address and then subtract 2.

Each additional bit of address space doubles the number of hosts allowed on a network, but divides the number of possible networks in half. So by adding 1 bit to an 8-bit subnet, we can address 510 computers (2^9 = 512–2=510) Adding another bit doubles that to 1,022 (2^{10} = 1,024–2=1,022), which is large enough to cover the required number of computers. But 1,022 possible client addresses leaves very little room for growth, so another bit is added to provide room for expansion, resulting in an 11-bit subnet that can accommodate 2,046 computers.

Subnet Masks

Every IP address has two portions:

- The network number

- The local host address

Because both numbers are contained in the same 32 bits and because the size of the network varies greatly from organization to organization, some method is required to determine which part of the IP address is the network number and which is the host's unique identifier.

The subnet mask determines which portion of the IP address is the network number and which portion is the local host address. The subnet mask is a 32-bit number—consisting of all ones to the left and all zeros to the right—that specifies how large the network number is. The switch between ones and zeros occurs at the bit size of the network. In the preceding example 11 bits of address space are needed to address all the current and future hosts in Digital Widget's network. The following subnet mask supports this division:

```
11111111.11111111.11111000.00000000 = 255.255.248.0
```

The ones mean that the network number is 21 bits long, and the zeros mean that an 11-bit range is available for host addresses.

The subnet mask determines whether the destination computer and the source computer reside on the same local network or whether the transmission will require routing. When a computer creates an IP packet, it masks off the host address of the destination computer, leaving only the network number. It compares this network number to its own network number, and if the two are equal, the computer transmits the packet directly to the destination computer because the two computers are on the same local data link. If the two numbers are not equal, the client transmits the packet to its default gateway. The default gateway performs a similar comparison. This process continues until the packet eventually reaches the data link to which it is local and is finally received by the destination computer. Figure 15.1 shows how the subnet mask forms the boundary between the network address and the host address.

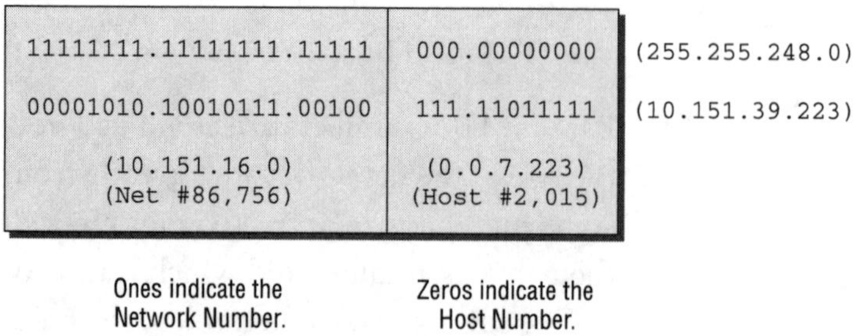

FIGURE 15.1

The host number is used to derive both the network number and the host number from an IP address.

```
11111111.11111111.11111   000.00000000   (255.255.248.0)

00001010.10010111.00100   111.11011111   (10.151.39.223)

    (10.151.16.0)          (0.0.7.223)
    (Net #86,756)         (Host #2,015)
```

Ones indicate the
Network Number.

Zeros indicate the
Host Number.

Routing

Routers, gateways, and multihomed servers perform the *routing* function. Routing is the process of forwarding packets among intermediate systems between two end systems. Routers forward datagrams

Terminology

- **Checksum**: The result of a mathematical function applied to a data payload which will remain the same as long as no errors have crept into a datagram between end systems.

- **Class A domain**: Large networks on which the first byte specifies the network number and the last 3 bytes specify the local addresses.

- **Class B domain**: Medium-size networks on which the first 2 bytes specify the network number and the last 2 bytes specify the local addresses.

- **Class C domain**: Smaller networks on which the first 3 bytes specify the network number and the last byte specifies the local address.

- **Classless addressing**: A subnet mask that splits the network number and the host number without regard for byte boundaries.

- **Data link**: A hardware protocol used to connect computers. Usually Ethernet in local area networks or frame relay in leased telephone line connections.

- **Datagrams**: Individually addressed chunks of data.

- **End System**: A host that either initiates or receives a datagram.

- **Gateway**: General-purpose computers that are used as routers and perform no other function.

- **Host**: Any computer attached to the Internet with at least one unique IP address.

- **Intermediate system**: A host that forwards datagrams between networks but is not interested in the content.

- **Multihomed host**: General-purpose computers that perform some other function in addition to routing packets, such as file service or Internet site hosting.

- **Packet**: A datagram.

- **Router**: Specially designed computers optimized for routing packets.

- **Subnet mask**: A number associated with an IP address that indicates which portion of the address is the network number and which portion is the host number.

- **Time-to-live indicator**: A metric used to determine when a packet should be discarded.

received on one network to another network that is closer to the destination. This process repeats until the datagram reaches its destination. Consequently, routers must be attached to both networks and have an Internet address that is local to each network. (Obviously, the devices need more than one IP address.)

IP addresses are assigned to each network interface, not to each computer. If a server has two network interfaces, each attached to a different network, then it is a multihomed server. Since most clients have only one network interface, clients have only one IP address and can be referred to by that IP address. Multihomed servers, routers, and gateways all require more than one address; they are generally referred to by the IP address of the adapter through which the default gateway for that multihomed host is reached.

You may see the term *host* used to describe either a server or a client. Host means any computer attached to the Internet—either client or server.

Figure 15.2 shows a small portion of a very large Internet. Each interrupted circle represents a network. The network number portion of that network is shown in boldface, and the host number portion is shown next to each host. The complete IP address for a host is formed by appending the host number to the network number—for instance, host number 1.3 on network number 10.191 has an IP address of 10.191.1.3.

FIGURE 15.2

An IP network showing
the path between two
hosts

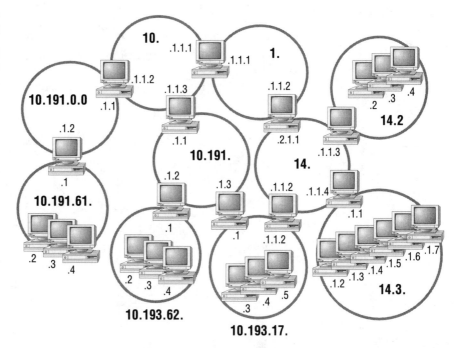

The computers that sit between two networks are multihomed hosts
acting as routers—they have more than one IP address. Notice the following about Figure 15.2:

- Multihomed computers have an IP address for each network to
  which they are attached.

- Multihomed hosts connect the networks by forwarding data
  between them.

- Bottom-tier networks have a larger network number, usually 3
  bytes long. Hosts on these networks are only 1 byte long.

- Medium-tier networks have 2-byte network numbers and 2-byte
  host identifiers.

- Top-tier networks have 1-byte network numbers and 3-byte host identifiers.

- Multihomed hosts are usually attached to networks with somewhat similar network numbers, but this is not a requirement.

- More than one path can exist between any two-end systems.

A trace route using the `tracert.exe` utility from host `10.191.61.4` to host `14.3.1.7` would produce the following IP address list:

`10.191.61.4`

`10.191.1.2`

`10.1.1.2`

`1.1.1.1`

`14.2.1.1`

`14.3.1.1`

`14.3.1.7`

This trace shows that seven routers are involved between the two end systems—an average size for any typical Internet connection. Routers are shown by the port that the packet travels out of, not by the port that the packet travels into.

The Default Route

In the absence of more specific routing information, the default route specifies which router to send packets to. A router may have any number of network interfaces, and for each interface the router will maintain lists of routes, called *routing tables*, about the network to which that interface is attached and the networks that are reachable from that network. The router will forward a packet to the network port (and therefore, the network) that is closest to that packet's destination.

If there is no information in a router's routing tables that tells it where a packet should specifically go, the router sends the packet to a default gateway. This route is called the *default route,* because data with no better addressing information is forwarded there. The default route can be followed until the packet reaches a high-level router that has no default route because it is at the top of the routing hierarchy. The final router either knows where to route the packet or the packet is dropped and the route is unreachable.

Due to an obscure bug, Windows NT allows you to specify a default route for every adapter installed in a multihomed server but uses only the default route established for the first bound network adapter. If the first bound adapter is not the network interface on the same data link as the router that connects to the Internet, your server will not route packets to the Internet. Never specify more than one default route for a multihomed computer. Assign a default gateway only for the adapter on the same data link as the router that routes to the Internet.

Routing Update Protocols

Routing update protocols are used to exchange information among routers (also known as *Internet gateways*) about routes, their availability, and their relative congestion. This information provides each router with enough information about its own network environment to make routing decisions for packets. For instance, a router may determine that a certain link is not functioning correctly, and send packet traffic to another router attached to a working link. The various routing protocols have evolved through time into two basic groups:

- **Interior Gateway Protocols,** which are good at managing small-to-medium-scale networks

- **Exterior Gateway Protocols,** which are used on the Internet backbone for sophisticated traffic management.

Four common routing protocols are in use today:

- Routing Information Protocol (RIP)

- Border Gateway Protocol (BGP)

- Open Shortest Path First protocol (OSPF)

- External Gateway Protocol (EGP)

Windows NT currently supports only RIP, because it is designed for small-to-medium-scale networks of the sort Windows NT was designed to support, and because it is the most commonly implemented of all routing protocols. As Windows NT scales up into the Enterprise, Microsoft may begin including support for BGP or OSPF.

Routing Information Protocol

Routing Information Protocol (RIP) is an Internet protocol that routers, gateways, and multihomed hosts use to trade routing information. RIP was originally developed by Xerox for the Xerox Networking System and adapted for use in IP networks. On UNIX systems, RIP is implemented by the *routed daemon.*

RIP is a distance vector protocol, meaning that a router sums the distance cost metrics programmed into each routing interface and selects the route with the lowest sum. A *cost metric* is simply a number assigned by a security administrator that indicates the resources necessary to use that route. Usually, it's just "1", meaning one hop. The metric assigned to each interface could be assigned based on the cost of a leased line, the expected congestion, speed, or any other factor the administrator wishes to use.

Periodically, routers send RIP messages to all directly attached routers informing them of their current routing costs. For each route, routers typically remember only the minimum cost seen in RIP updates for that route. Whenever a shorter route is seen in a RIP update, this new route replaces what was formerly the shortest route.

A router may transmit a change in its own cost metric that is higher than its former value, and, in this case, the routers will increase the cost associated with that route. If a router is not heard from in some period of time, that router and the routes associated with it will be invalidated, so another route will be automatically chosen. The router, of course, will be automatically added when it again begins sending RIP updates. This provides a modicum of fault tolerance in case a router fails.

RIP is built into Windows NT 4 and can be added to Windows NT 3.51 by installing the Multi-Protocol Router package on the Windows NT 3.51 Service Pack CD-ROM. With RIP for IP installed and more than one network adapter, your Windows NT server can act as a fully functional multihomed host by automatically updating its routing tables based on information received from other routers.

RIP has a number of important limitations:

- By design RIP is limited to covering 15 hops.

- Circular routes can cause RIP to consume inordinate amounts of bandwidth and time trying to resolve a path.

- RIP relies upon programmed metrics involving an administrator's judgment of routing cost rather than real-time metrics such as current load, capacity, delay, or reliability. This virtually ensures that in a large network, routing will not be optimal.

- RIP has no security mechanisms to prevent bogus updates.

RIP unfortunately allows anyone to send RIP updates to your router. Denial-of-service attacks have already occurred due to bad RIP updates (albeit by accident) and have taken down large portions of the Internet. Using RIP, anyone could use a router, multihomed server, or custom IP stack to essentially reprogram your router.

It is theoretically possible to spoof a router into routing to a different location, but the spoofed location would have to be within the same IP network as your Internet service provider in order to provide a connected route, making it extremely difficult to accomplish to useful effect. Denial of service is the primary security problem with automated routing protocols.

Reality Check: Rest in Peace

A well-intentioned network administrator on the East Coast of the United States decided to use a batch program to automatically update a list of routing tables in his office router. He started the program, which unbeknownst to him had an improperly coded terminal condition resulting in an infinite loop—the program ran forever. His router dutifully received the data directly through a Telnet connection, updated its tables, and transmitted RIP broadcasts to the routers to which it was attached.

This process continued until the buffers on routers in the area began to overflow because they ran out of memory. This overflow condition crashed the operating systems of most of the routers, caused others to restart, and others to overwrite their valid routing tables. This cascaded into a general Internet outage as routers all over the East Coast and in parts of Europe lost their routing tables or shut down.

Policies: Routing Protocols

- Do not use RIP or other automated routing protocols. Statically assign your routing tables and disable RIP updates unless your network is too large to manage manually. This makes them impervious to RIP-based denial-of-service or spoofing attacks.

- Use your firewall to filter out RIP updates from the Internet. If you have only one connection to the Internet, you can hard code that connection in the router connected to your service provider's network. You can then use RIP or other automated routing protocols to manage routing inside your network.

Routing Protocols Not Supported by Windows NT

RIP is the most common routing protocol implemented on the Internet, and most routers support it. To round out your knowledge of routing protocols you should know a little about the following protocols even though they aren't directly supported by the routing mechanism in Windows NT. Your Internet service provider most likely uses one or more of these protocols, and a denial-of-service attack involving them directly affects you.

Open Shortest Path First Protocol   OSPF is an internal gateway protocol designed for use in medium-sized autonomous networks and designed as a replacement for RIP. Unlike RIP, OSPF is a link-state algorithm capable of quickly selecting new routes around failed links or other traffic problems. RIP is capable only of changing routes after considerable delay, and suffers from problems propagating change messages throughout the routed network.

OSPF was designed specifically for TCP/IP networks, whereas RIP is an adoption of a more general routing algorithm to IP networks. OSPF can quickly recalculate link costs to respond to link failure, and is capable of using more than one route to transmit IP packets if the route costs are the same. In addition, OSPF routing update exchanges are authenticated, so they are more difficult to spoof. OSPF also generates less traffic dealing with router updates than RIP.

Exterior Gateway Protocol   Exterior Gateway Protocol is implemented by the *gated daemon* on UNIX gateways, and is obsolete. It may be in use in the backwaters of the Internet somewhere, but it is no longer in wide circulation. It does not compare favorably to other automated routing protocols.

Border Gateway Protocol   Border Gateway Protocol is used to connect the networks of Internet service providers. Its updates are transmitted via TCP rather than IP or ICMP, so there's no problem with missing updates except in a failure state. BGP is somewhat similar to OSPF in its operation, but it is not a link-state protocol and does not react as quickly to peer failure. The BGP specification does not specify an authentication mechanism, so it can be subject to spoof attacks.

Transmission Control Protocol

Transmission Control Protocol (TCP) provides a reliable connection using an unreliable transport mechanism by supplying the services that IP is missing. Those services are:

- **Reliable delivery:** TCP will request lost packets until the transmission is complete or will return a valid and useful error message. TCP guarantees that as long as a data path exists between two end systems, a reliable stream of data can be transmitted.

- **Sequencing:** TCP will put out-of-order packets back in order so a sequential stream of data is maintained.

- **Constant connection:** TCP makes data streams act somewhat like files that can be opened, read from, and closed. It abstracts the packet-based protocol away from the user's application.

- **Error detection and correction:** TCP adds a checksum to the data payload. If the checksum shows that a packet is damaged, it is discarded and retransmitted automatically.

- **Flow control and handshaking:** TCP implements mechanisms to adapt to the reliability of lower-level systems and improve throughput based on current data link conditions.

- **Multiplexing:** TCP uses the concept of sockets and ports to create many simultaneous streams of data between the end systems.

TCP does not need any guarantees of service from lower-level protocols. It can use any packet-switched or connection-oriented network protocol, as long as two-way communication actually exists between the two end systems. The ability to provide a reliable stream of communication between two systems from an unreliable packet-based transport makes TCP the perfect foundation for higher-level services that require error-free communications.

The TCP specification also provides a modicum of security, but those security mechanisms are obsolete (because they don't really work), so they are not discussed here. Encryption services that work above the TCP layer provide true security by reimplementing the socket services with encryption. These services are collectively referred to as *tunnels* and at the TCP layer they make up the Secure Socket Layer (SSL). SSL is described in more detail following the section on TCP.

TCP is defined by RFC 793.

Ports and Sockets

As mentioned earlier, TCP provides a multiplexing mechanism to allow multiple data streams to be transmitted between end systems. This multiplexing feature is implemented through ports, sockets, and connections. The ability of a computer to provide different services, such as Telnet service, FTP service, Web service, and NetBIOS service, is dependent upon this multiplexing ability. Without multiplexing, a server could not tell the difference between different higher-level protocols connecting from the same client computer.

A *port* is a TCP connection number. TCP has 16 bits for port numbers, so two end, systems may establish up to 65,535 simultaneous separate communications streams. A *socket* is a port, and the IP (or other protocol) address of the end system necessary to form a complete path to data; it is usually specified in the form 10.191.61.2:80, where the first 4 bytes are the IP address and the number after the colon (:) is the port. A matched pair of sockets between a client and a host forms a connection.

The transmission and reception ports are not the same in a connection. For instance, when a connection to port 80 on a server is established, the client may inform the server to respond to port 15543 on the client. This allows the same client to connect to the same service on the same server multiple times.

Once a connection is established, data can be transmitted between systems bidirectionally until the connection is closed. TCP connections are full duplex, or bidirectional.

Well-Known Ports

When you attach your Web browser to an Internet host, the Web browser knows which port to use because the developers of the HTTP service agreed to use the same port number for HTTP servers and clients. This is known as the convention of *well-known ports*.

The well-known port convention specifies that Internet servers of a certain type should "listen" on a certain TCP port for connection requests from client software. The various server software components (such as the Internet Information Server component services) simply open up their socket (local IP address + well-known port for that service) and wait for connection attempts from remote clients. Table 15.1 lists some common (and some silly) services and the well-known port that each service uses.

	PORT	SERVICE	FUNCTION
TABLE 15.1 Some Well-Known Ports	17	Quote	Quote of the Day
	21	FTP	File Transfer Protocol
	23	Telnet	Telnet
	25	SMTP	Mail transfer

	PORT	SERVICE	FUNCTION
T A B L E 15.1 (cont.) Some Well-Known Ports	37	Time	Time
	53	DNS	Domain Name Server
	67	BOOTP	BootP Server
	70	Gopher	Gopher
	80	HTTP	World Wide Web
	110	POP3	Post Office Protocol 3
	135	BROWSE	NetBIOS Browsers
	139	NBSession	NetBIOS Session

Many well-known ports are in use, but the majority of them are of little consequence except in special systems. Those listed in Table 15.1 are general in nature and used by most Internet hosting systems.

The Internet Assigned Numbers Authority of the Internet Engineering Task Force assigns all well-known port numbers below 1024. Port numbers above 1024 are available for public use in any manner. Users of some nonofficial protocols, like Internet Relay Chat (IRC), have simply chosen their own port numbers (in this case, :8000). By convention, everyone knows to use port 8000 for IRC, so it has become a de facto standard. After all, this type of usage is how the well-known port numbering system came to be.

Internet Assigned Numbers are defined in RFC 1700.

Secure Socket Layer

Secure socket layer is a seamless encryption protocol for TCP/IP networks that creates a connection between Internet hosts that is secure from eavesdropping. Netscape communications developed SSL and released it to the Internet community; it is currently a draft RFC. SSL is not included with Windows NT, but it can be used to add encryption to many Windows NT TCP/IP services. SSL encrypts data at the session layer between the transport layer (TCP) and the application layer (HTTP, FTP, and so on).

SSL is a public encrypted tunneling protocol. Its purpose is merely to obscure the contents of an encrypted stream of data between a client and a server. Although SSL includes support for user authentication, it is usually used between anonymous users and public servers. In this case, the identity of the client is not important; it is only important that the communication channel be secured. Internet commerce requires this level of security to ensure that financial transactions are not compromised or forgeable. For example, without some sort of encryption, hackers would be able to extract credit card numbers from TCP/IP sessions between shoppers and online catalog stores.

SSL is not specific to a higher-level protocol—any higher-level protocol (HTTP, FTP, Telnet) can be encapsulated in SSL tunnels so long as both the client and the server understand SSL. Currently, only Web services commonly use SSL connections.

A similar standard, HTTPS (the S is for Secure), can also be used to encrypt HTTP connections, but since it's limited to a single protocol it has been obviated by the more general services of SSL.

Both the client and the server must understand SSL: All modern Web browsers do, so this isn't a problem on the client end. Most HTTP servers either directly support SSL or have modules that add support for SSL.

Either host may initiate the challenge to establish an SSL connection. Upon receipt of the challenge, the hosts initiate a handshaking session during which they agree upon a mutually supported encryption protocol (for instance, DES) and, optionally, a compression protocol. Upon completion of the handshake, both hosts have established an SSL session using the agreed upon encryption and compression methods. When encryption services are no longer required, the SSL session is dropped and a new TCP session can be initiated.

SSL uses the reliable transport services of TCP over IP. This means that SSL connections can be redirected, and that SSL servers are subject to the same sort of denial-of-service attacks that any normal TCP/IP host is subject to.

Terminology

- **Default route:** The router to which a host (end or intermediate system) will forward packets if its routing table has no better information.

- **Flow control:** The handshaking signals to moderate the speed at which data is transmitted to make the best of data link conditions.

- **gated daemon:** An early UNIX routing service. Gated is no longer in widespread use.

- **Hijacking:** A hack wherein an established TCP session is redirected in mid-communication to an unauthorized host.

- **Port:** A TCP connection number used to determine which service a specific datagram should be sent to on a host.

- **Route:** The list of intermediate systems between two specified end systems.

- **routed daemon:** A UNIX routing service that uses the Routing Information Protocol (RIP).

- **Routing:** The process of forwarding datagrams among end systems to read a specified end system.

- **Routing Tables**: Lists of routes maintained by a router to determine which router is the next closest in the route to a specific end system.

- **Tunnels**: Secure encrypted links created over non-secure public mediums like the Internet.

- **Well-known ports**: Common port assignments for services that listen for public connections. Well-known ports are used when no prior information about how to connect to a specific host is known.

Dynamic Host Configuration Protocol

The Dynamic Host Configuration Protocol (DHCP) makes implementing a TCP/IP network considerably easier than it used to be. In the dawn of time, it was necessary to manually install a unique TCP/IP address, subnet mask, and default gateway (at least) for every computer on a network. It was easy to unintentionally reuse IP addresses (causing no end of confusion), mess up a subnet mask, or specify the wrong default router—all problems that can wreak havoc on your network installation and make you the butt of jokes at network integrator parties (should there ever be any).

Manual configuration also made reconfiguring an existing large network virtually impossible. If the idea of manually reconfiguring the IP addresses on every computer in your network between closing down on Friday and opening back up on Monday doesn't discourage you, there's always the fact that you simply won't be finished in time.

Oddly enough, it wasn't the pain of manual configuration that was the genesis of automatic IP configuration. The originators of the Internet protocols were real integrators who had no fear of manual configuration, and they knew that if the network didn't work on Monday, they wouldn't get fired, because no one else would be able to figure out how their hand-crafted network worked. But the challenge of the diskless workstation intrigued them.

Without a hard disk to boot from, a computer could not be permanently configured with an IP address. Booting from a floppy disk was too easily implemented to appease them, so they wrote a protocol that broadcast a plea for an IP address and created a service that provided it. They burned their protocol into the boot EPROMs of the network adapter cards; thus was born the automatic Boot Protocol (BootP) and the era of the network administrator who could be fired.

The original BootP protocol was somewhat limited in that it provided only an IP address, subnet mask, and default gateway. More complex networks require additional information, such as the address of a WINS server, or additional gateways. DHCP evolved from BootP to provide these (and any other) automatic configuration protocol addresses. DHCP can be forwarded by routers that forward BootP requests, thus removing the requirement that a DHCP server exist on each local network.

DHCP is a client/server protocol in that the booting client requests network information and a server provides that information. The DHCP server is responsible for allocating network numbers so that no two clients get the same IP address. If you have multiple DHCP servers, you must configure them so that no two servers can provide the same address to different clients.

DCHP supports three models of IP allocation:

- **Automatic allocation** assigns a permanent IP address to a host. Whenever a client boots, it will get the same automatically generated but permanently assigned IP address. The DHCP server identifies the client by its MAC address (usually an Ethernet address).

- **Dynamic allocation** assigns IP addresses for a limited period of time (lease duration) or until the client relinquishes the address.

This model does not guarantee that the same address will be provided to that client in the future.

- **Manual allocation** is used to assign a specific IP address to a specific host permanently. This model assigns IP addresses for resources whose IP addresses must be known because they provide some service to the network, such as a file or name server.

The three allocation methods can be used on the same network, as needs dictate. Dynamic allocation is often the most useful because IP addresses can be conserved. With dynamic allocation, IP address assignment is based on the number of clients actually attached, rather than on the number of clients that exist. In other words, dynamic allocation can reserve IP addresses for those clients that are actually using the network at any one time without reserving them for clients that are not in use.

DHCP will automatically avoid manually assigned addresses already in use on the network. If you have a router with an assigned IP address, DHCP will not assign that IP address. Proper implementations of DHCP provide service to BOOTP clients. (The Windows NT implementation of DHCP currently does not. Microsoft has committed to fixing this problem.)

IP addresses are assigned in ranges called *scopes*. A scope is simply a range of IP address that the DHCP server is allowed to assign, along with the DHCP options that go along with that range. DHCP options are IP parameters that would normally be manually assigned, such as the default gateway, WINS server, and DNS server. These parameters can also be set as global DHCP options if the same parameters apply to each of your DHCP scopes. That way, you only have to set up the parameter information one time. Figure 15.3 shows the DHCP Manager with reserved IP addresses.

You can also specifically exclude IP addresses or ranges when you set up a DHCP scope. Exclusion prevents DHCP from assigning IP addresses in the excluded range. This is useful for situations when more

F I G U R E   15.3

The DHCP Manager

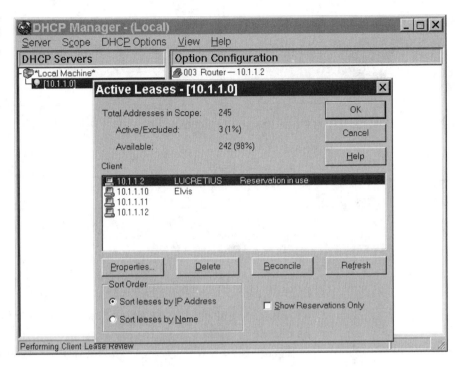

than one DHCP server may assign the IP address or when you want to reserve a range for future expansion.

As with most other protocols, it is technically possible for an illicit DHCP server attached to your local network to respond to DHCP requests from clients before the normal DHCP server responds to assign them bogus IP addresses. In combination with an illicit router, it would technically be able to deny clients service on the normal network and route them onto a fake network. This fake network could simulate normal network services in order to obtain passwords, encryption keys, or data from client computers.

This attack would be so difficult to actually implement and then hide as to be nearly impossible. Only sites with an espionage threat should consider DHCP as a security risk.

WARNING DHCP is not in itself a security threat, but it could potentially be an enabler of other security attacks.

Policies: IP Addresses

- Consider manually assigning IP addresses if your organization is a potential espionage target.

Internet Control Message Protocol

Internet Control Message Protocol (ICMP) is an integral part of all TCP/IP implementations. It is used specifically to send messages between Internet hosts about the routing of datagrams, as the name implies. Essentially, ICMP is the error messenger of the Internet protocols.

ICMP communications are transmitted between gateways (routers) and hosts (servers) under the following circumstances:

- When a gateway cannot reach a destination because a route path does not exist or because the time-to-live indicator of a packet has expired *en route*.

- When a packet has been discarded because its header information is erroneous.

- When a gateway can't buffer as much information as the host is sending. This is a flow control mechanism that throttles the rate at which a host transmits TCP/IP information.

- When a shorter route exists.

- When an echo reply has been requested, as in a ping request.

It's important to note that ICMP messages are only transmitted regarding fragment zero of a fragmented IP packet. Hackers can prevent ICMP error messages from being sent about bad packets by creating fragmented packets that have no zero fragment. Until the release of Windows NT 4 Service Pack 3, NT did not check for a zero packet, and simply reassembled packets in order until a fragment with the final fragment flag set arrived.

ICMP is defined by RFC 792.

Since ICMP has no authentication capability, hackers are able to exploit it for a number of denial-of-service attacks. ICMP redirection messages can be hacked to hijack an existing TCP/IP connection, but this is difficult to accomplish seamlessly, and the data must be sent along generally the same route. Inordinately large ICMP ping packets (about 64K) will crash most TCP/IP implementations by overrunning buffers, especially on Intel-based computers. These attacks are explained below in the *Hacking TCP/IP* section. Service Pack 3 fixes most of these problems (except ICMP redirection, which is necessary for the proper operation of TCP/IP and can't be fixed).

ICMP attacks are difficult to prevent because many of these messages are crucial to the proper operation of TCP/IP. You should set up your firewall to block any access to machines not specifically involved with the external Internet, however, and make certain you are running the latest version of the TCP/IP software on all your equipment.

Hacking TCP/IP

TCP/IP is the communications medium between computers on the Internet. That makes it an obvious target for exploitation as a method for gaining unauthorized access to Internet-connected systems. TCP/IP itself cannot provide access to useful information on target systems; it must carry higher-level protocol information in order to be useful.

TCP/IP hacks therefore fall into the following categories:

- Impersonation (IP spoofing)

- Implementation-specific exploitation

- Hijacking

- Denial of service

- Eavesdropping

Most useful TCP/IP hacks require special TCP/IP modules or user-level applications that directly generate TCP/IP packets. As such, these hacks are very difficult to perpetrate and are exploited only by the *crème de la crème* of hackerdom.

Impersonation

The goal of an impersonation attack is to be perceived as a computer that is authorized to access the system. Hackers use impersonation attacks because packet filters and firewalls simply drop packets that come from unknown or unauthorized machines. By impersonating authorized computers, hackers can sometimes gain access through these defenses.

The only way to overcome packet filtering based on source IP addresses is to spoof the source address. This is easy enough—the hacker can assign any computer any IP address they want. This probably won't be useful, however, since an IP address outside the hacker's local domain won't be routed back to their computer.

Bidirectional IP communications require that the end systems both be reachable by their address—so spoofing an address is about as worthless as calling for pizza delivery and giving someone else's address. You don't get the pizza, and for the same reason, return packets aren't routed back to your computer.

Remember that the end systems are not the only computers involved in a communication stream. Intermediate systems (routers/gateways) also handle those packets. A hacker working on a gateway between the system being hacked and real holder of the spoofed address can intercept the spoofed packets correctly and establish bidirectional communications with a spoofed address. This is a man-in-the-middle attack, similar to the one described in Chapter 3. This would be something like a postal worker writing letters and pretending to be you—that postal worker could intercept return mail destined for your address and respond to it.

Assuming that a hacker gains access to your Internet service provider's network, that hacker could impersonate virtually any host on the Internet—or any host on your own network. This makes it relatively easy to pass through firewalls that are open to certain hosts, as long as the hacker knows which hosts the firewall will pass or simply scans your entire domain for a source address that your firewall did pass.

These full-duplex spoofing attacks are very difficult to perpetrate, however, because they require physical access to your network or to a router between your computer and the end system being spoofed. For instance, if you perform a trace route between your computer and another host on the Internet, a hacker could spoof an attack using that address from any host on the same subnetwork (such as Ethernet) as any of the intermediate systems listed, but no others. That's actually quite specific and provides a relatively strong measure of inherent security.

There is another possible way to perform a spoofing attack: redirection. It is possible to use a routing update protocol like RIP or OSPF to add routing entries to intermediate systems so that the packets will be routed correctly back to the hacker's machine, or to use the ICMP redirect message to reroute traffic immediately to a new intermediate system. Routing protocol updates will cause a denial of service for a number of other computers, however, so it should cause alarms to go off at your service provider's network operations center. ICMP redirects may be transparent, because they don't permanently update the routing tables of intermediate systems.

Finally, full duplex connections are not necessarily the only useful spoof attacks. It is possible to send IP packets to a host and claim to be anyone. The hacker won't get anything back, and they won't be able to create a TCP connection, but they may be able to perform some useful mischief, especially in the form of denial-of-service attacks.

Implementation-Specific Exploitation

Implementation-specific exploitation refers to any exploit that works only with specific implementations of the TCP/IP protocol stack. For instance, Windows NT 4 prior to Service Pack 3 would reassemble a fragmented IP packet regardless of whether or not all the ordered packets had arrived. If the buffer had been filled correctly and the last fragment had its final fragment flag set, the packet would be forwarded. Under normal circumstances that's no problem and even conforms to the TCP/IP principle of robustness: Be conservative in sending and liberal in receiving.

Unfortunately, all packet filters that reject packets based on TCP port numbers rely upon the 0th fragment of an IP datagram containing the TCP header. This is because TCP/IP is embedded in the data payload of an IP packet, and, when fragmented, only the first fragment contains the TCP header. So, these filters check the 0th fragment only and let all other fragment numbers pass, confident that no system will reassemble a packet missing the 0th fragment.

Policies: External Connections to the Network

■ Limit the number of external hosts allowed to connect through your firewall to the absolute minimum possible. Take measures to make sure the IP addresses of those hosts are difficult to determine by using proxy servers or IP masquerades as detailed in Chapter 17.

■ Consider using an alternate protocol like IPX to provide the connection between an Internet mail server and hosts inside a firewall, if your mail server is capable of using different transports. (Microsoft Exchange Server is.) This allows your firewall to block all inbound TCP connection attempts, but still keeps the mail flowing through in a manner that can't be exploited from the Internet. Your mail server receives mail from the Internet via TCP/IP, but only allows client attachment via IPX.

■ Avoid using one of the smaller Internet service providers. Hackers frequently target them as potential employers because they often have less security awareness and may use UNIX computers, rather than dedicated machines, as gateways and firewalls—making spoof attacks easy to perpetrate. Ask your service provider if they perform background checks on technical service personnel, and reject those that say they do not.

So hackers simply transmit fragmented IP datagrams that start with the 1st fragment rather than the 0th fragment, but that contain within the set of fragments an entire valid TCP packet. The datagrams pass through the packet filter because no nonzero fragments normally contain TCP headers; so they can't be checked for validity and must be allowed to pass if any traffic is allowed to pass to that specific host.

The fragments are then reassembled on the Windows NT multi-homed server, which doesn't care that there's no 0th fragment as long as the datagram reassembly buffer is completely filled with valid data and a final fragment is received. The NT host then forwards that datagram to the target system. This hack allows TCP/IP traffic to flow freely to the target end system, completely bypassing the filter with no adverse effects. This is obviously a serious problem and one reason why packet filters don't provide as much security as application-level firewalls.

Of course, no normal TCP/IP module on an end system will transmit fragmented IP packets—fragmentation normally occurs only on intermediate systems, if at all. To exploit this vector, the hacker must have access to a custom TCP/IP module. Since Linux is distributed with the full source code, it's a reasonably trivial matter to customize the behavior of the TCP/IP module to generate all IP packets as fragment 1 datagrams rather than normal IP packets. When operating with this custom TCP/IP module, the packet filter between the hacker and the target system simply disappears.

Other implementation-specific exploits have been developed for the various TCP/IP modules of different operating systems. Very few are specifically hardened to verify header information robustly, simply because checking takes time and therefore lowers overall throughput of the router or end system. This is counter to the normal development of software systems, which usually emphasizes speed at all costs.

Policies: Operating System-Specific Security

- Stay abreast of hacking developments for the software you run.

- Update your service software as soon as you receive validated service pack releases.

- Do not use simple packet filtering or packet-filtering services from your Internet service provider as a replacement for application-layer firewalls. They are not as secure.

Hijacking

Hijacking is a specific type of IP spoofing. Using hijacking, a hacker takes over an active TTCP session, rather than creating a new forged connection.

Why hijack when you can just spoof? Because authentication has already been performed before the hijacking takes place. Passwords, authentication keys, and digital signature hashes have already been sent and confirmed. So this specific TCP connection is available without the need to log in. The benefits are obvious, but hijacking is a little more difficult to pull off than simple spoofing because, by definition, service is denied to the original client—so the client knows something has happened.

Since the Internet isn't completely reliable, however, most users will see their connection time-out as data begins passing to another end system, and will attempt to re-establish their connection. When the attempt fails, they will probably simply assume that the remote host or an intermediate system has a problem, and try again later.

Policies: Denial of Service

- As a part of security training, make sure users know to report all instances of denial of service whether they seem important or not. If you can't correlate a specific denial of service to known downtime or heavy usage, or if a large number of service denials occur in a short time, you may be under siege.

Terminology

- **Flooding**: A denial-of-service attack wherein a large number of nuisance connections are made to a specific host in order to waste its processing time.

- **Fragments**: Portions of a datagram that has been broken into smaller segments to facilitate routing.

Denial of Service

Service denial attacks are the easiest of all hacks to perpetrate because there are so many potential vectors. Shutting off power to a building will most certainly cause the denial of service to resources located inside. Physical destruction of equipment or communication paths also causes service to be denied. Eliminating intermediate systems either physically or by spoofing bad routing updates will cause a loss of connectivity for remote hosts. A flood of meaningless connection attempts can needlessly tie up TCP/IP resources, thus reducing the number of legitimate hosts that can connect.

Preventing TCP/IP denial-of-service attacks is mostly the responsibility of Microsoft. Windows NT 4 Service Pack 3 is hardened against the infamous ping-of-death attack, and against the 0th fragment problem. However, the extra boundary condition and parameter checking take more time, thus reducing the number of TCP/IP connections that can be handled by a hardened TCP/IP stack in the same time period. This unfortunately makes the host even more vulnerable to denial-of-service attacks based on flooding.

A good firewall is your best defense against TCP/IP-based denial-of-service attacks—but you'll have a hard time defending Web servers and other machines that must expose services to the public. Strong monitoring and alerting is the best defense for these machines.

Policies: Preventing Denial-of-Service Attacks

- Set up monitoring software that can alert you to the presence of flood attacks against your network. Record the IP addresses of the source computers (assuming they look valid) and try to determine the source of the attacks so you can take legal measures to stop the problem.

- Set up your firewall to discard ICMP echo and to redirect messages to interior hosts.

Eavesdropping

Eavesdropping on TCP/IP connections is quite easy if you are between the sender and the receiver. Any computer that can IP spoof your system is also capable of examining the contents of your Internet messages. The obvious fix for this problem is encryption.

Eavesdropping is performed in two ways. The eavesdropper can use network monitoring software like packet sniffers. Or they may choose to listen in with customized TCP/IP modules that can strip away the IP and TCP headers, order the packets correctly, and present both sides of the data stream without interfering in the communications themselves.

How well encryption solves the problem of eavesdropping depends on the strength of the encryption. It also depends on how the recent wave of proposed encryption laws now being considered by lawmakers turns out. It is conceivable that the government may force commercial encryption vendors to build in escrow keys that will allow the government to decrypt communications streams in order to provide a wiretapping capability for law enforcement. Unfortunately, opening encryption to law enforcement by definition weakens the encryption. It also provides the government or anyone who steals the key from the escrow agency with the ability to decrypt your private communications without your knowledge.

The problem with these laws is that they assume that encryption software must be written by commercial organizations. Unfortunately, any hacker worth their salt can write very strong encryption software bypassing any legal restrictions. This means that if the government forces key-escrow encryption, only criminals and hackers will have encryption software that the government can't easily crack. Pretty Good Privacy, an e-mail encryption package written by Phil Zimmerman, illustrates this quite clearly. This simple logic is lost on lawmakers, who don't understand the issues about which they legislate.

Policies: Encryption

- Always use encrypted communications for data that flows over public networks like the Internet.

- Use all legal means to resist attempts by the government to restrict the use or effectiveness of encryption software.

Summary

TCP/IP is the communications medium of the Internet. It was designed with simplicity and functionality in mind, and it has no serious security measures built in. Nearly all security inherent in TCP/IP is due to the fact that bidirectional communications must be routed correctly between end systems, making address spoofing inherently difficult.

TCP/IP hacks therefore fall into the following categories:

- Impersonation (IP spoofing)

- Implementation-specific exploitation

- Hijacking

- Denial of service

- Eavesdropping

These hacks range from extremely difficult (hijacking) to easy (denial of service). Your ability to defend against TCP/IP hacks is based on a solid firewall setup, good fault tolerance measures, encryption, monitoring, and a policy of upgrading service software using the latest security packs. In short, you'll benefit from doing all the things you have to do anyway to keep your systems secure.

CHAPTER

16

Client Security

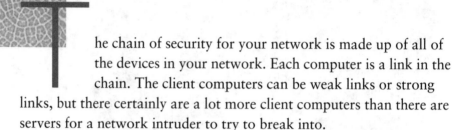

The chain of security for your network is made up of all of the devices in your network. Each computer is a link in the chain. The client computers can be weak links or strong links, but there certainly are a lot more client computers than there are servers for a network intruder to try to break into.

It is easier to attack a network from the inside than from the outside. Any unprotected client computer can serve as a base from which a hacker can attack the rest of your network; so while you take great pains to ensure that your servers are secure, don't ignore the client computers.

In order to make client computers secure you must understand how they are used. You can then draw up a general client security policy, and take specific actions for particular client operating systems and software packages. This chapter describes client security in general and then outlines some network policies for client security. It provides a brief introduction to the security issues of each of the most popular client operating systems. Finally, in this chapter we cover the security issues for software run on client computers.

Users Just Want to Have Fun

Computers exist to help people do their jobs. Computer security protects the information stored in the computers. But if security measures prevent users from using the computers to do their jobs effectively then the computers are useless—or worse than useless, because they take money and time to maintain. The system administrator must balance the organization's need to protect the data on the computers with the users' need to work without too much hindrance from computer security.

Users need to be able to run programs on the client computers. The type of programs a user must have access to depends on what the user does. A data entry clerk may only need access to one database program while the financial controller, in contrast, will need access to a wide range of tools, such as spreadsheets, word processors, presentation packages, and accounting packages. The network administrator must provide each user with sufficient access for them to perform all the functions of their jobs.

The more open a network environment is, the easier it is to use the network. If users don't have to remember passwords and don't have to change the permissions of files to allow other users to access them, then they are free to a certain degree to concentrate on their job. Without security, if a certain user is not around and a coworker needs a file the user has been working on, that coworker can simply access the file. On the other hand, in a very security-conscious environment, it can sometimes be difficult just to transfer a document from one user to another.

A security policy that is too rigid can paralyze a network, but judicious application of security mechanisms can keep a network safe while still allowing users to get work done. The key to securing client computers is to select the level of security that is appropriate for the user of the client computer.

An individual that requires a flexible computer configuration is usually someone in whom the company places greater trust. For example, the financial controller of your company probably needs access to a wider set of programs and resources than a data entry clerk, but the controller is probably more trusted as well. How you configure security for the controller and the clerk should reflect the level of trust the organization has in each individual.

Usually, the programs that network users use run on the client computer. File servers, print servers, application servers, and database servers all provide services to the client computers. The user typically runs programs on the client computer that communicate with these services instead of running programs directly on these server computers. Since users seldom need to directly access servers it is easier to make these servers secure than it is to make client computers secure.

Securing the client computers in your network involves the following (see Figure 16.1):

- Creating a secure client environment

- Securing the individual client operating systems

- Securing the application software

Terminology

- **Application software:** Software such as word processors, spreadsheets, Computer Aided Drafting (CAD) packages and desktop publishing packages that run on the client computer.

- **Internet client software:** Software that enables users of client computers to access Internet services such as the World Wide Web, FTP, and Internet mail.

- **Network client:** A computer used by an individual or by individuals (as opposed to a network server, which is shared by all users on the network).

- **Policy document:** A printed document describing the appropriate use of the network and the services that network support individuals will provide.

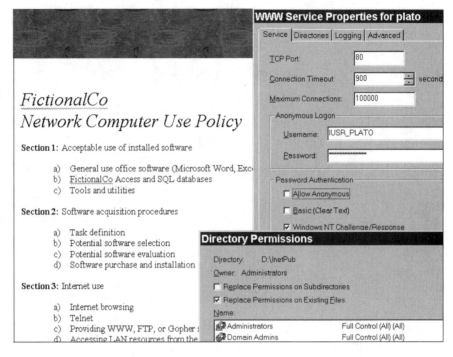

Creating a Secure Client Environment

The things you need to do to create a secure client environment are an extension of what you do to secure your Windows NT servers. The passwords should be the same, the access policies should be administered from the server computer, and the shared resources that the users will access from the client computers should all reside on servers. It is a good idea to store application software on the servers and to administer client operating systems from a central server using tools such as Microsoft's System Management Server.

Security tasks you can perform at the file server include:

- Creating network user accounts

- Managing users and groups

- Setting privileges for and taking ownership of files and directories

- Establishing and modifying system policies

- Administering network service security for services such as e-mail and group scheduling

- Establishing dial-in, Internet gateway, and intranet connection security

- Monitoring network activity

- Monitoring file and directory access

- Configuring network transport protocols

- Establishing network services such as DHCP and DNS

- Configuring server-based application software

Security actions that you must perform from the client computers include:

- Installing and configuring the client operating systems

- Installing application software that is stored on the client computers

- Installing and maintaining virus scanning software

- Configuring Internet client software

- Configuring mobile clients (laptops)

- Configuring clients for secure LAN access over the Internet

Part of making client computers secure is instructing client computer users in safe computing practices. Chapter 2 introduces a number of practices that are essential to client security. By collecting those practices that make sense for your network into a policy document, you have an unambiguous reference you can distribute to network users.

Once you have a policy document, network users will know what network behavior is allowed and expected of them. They will also know which services you will provide for them (installing networking adapters, for example, if users are not allowed to modify their hardware and operating system software) and which services you will not provide for them (such as installing personal software brought from home if the software is not on the approved list).

The practices you should consider including in a computer use and administrative policy document for your network include:

Policies

- Install only approved operating system software: A network administrator can only secure those operating systems that they understand. A naive installation of any operating system almost certainly leaves the operating system open to network attack.

- Restrict who can modify hardware settings: Both from a security point of view and an ease-of-administration point of view, it is a good idea to limit those who may modify operating system parameters to those whom the Administrator can trust to do so securely and properly.

- Require users to log on to their personal workstations or to shared-use computers: Limiting who can log onto a particular computer provides a second line of defense against both internal and network attack, as well as helping narrow the range of suspects when a network user causes trouble.

- Discourage file storage on local hard drives: Client computers seldom have the file and directory security that Windows NT servers do, so it is a good idea to get users in the habit of storing data on the file server.

■ Discourage sharing files from local hard drives: Most client operating systems provide only rudimentary security for remote computers connecting to shared resources, so users should place files for sharing in a shared directory on the file server.

■ Require approval for new application software installed on network client computers: Trojan horse software can provide a network intruder with all of the access that the user running the Trojan horse has. Restricting users from downloading and installing software alleviates this threat.

■ Require long and hard-to-guess passwords: This aspect of network security cannot be stressed enough. A weak password will be cracked by a hacker in hours or even minutes. (See Chapter 2 for details about password policy.)

■ Establish screen saver timeouts with passwords: A screen saver with a password will stop casual opportunistic use of a computer that is logged on and left unattended.

■ Never leave computers logged on and unattended: A computer left logged on is an open invitation to someone to do those things that their own account is not permitted to do or that they wouldn't want to do using their own account (such as sending incriminating e-mail to the company president).

■ Require network logon: An easy way to circumvent network security (at least for the local computer) is to cancel the network logon process and just use the services of the local computer (a hacker could then capture the local password list and crack it to get network passwords). Requiring network logon makes it a little more difficult for a hacker to get at the local computer's resources.

■ Do not use Domain Admin accounts on client computers and do not allow non-admin accounts to log on to the file servers: This restriction keeps the administrator accounts from appearing in the password lists of client computers.

- Create a domain user account that has administrative privileges on the client computers but may not log on interactively to the file servers: Use this account to administer the client computers instead of the Domain Admin account.

- Establish BIOS passwords on the computers in your network and disable the ability to boot from a floppy disk in the BIOS: This makes it more difficult (but not impossible) to bypass the client operating system and get directly at data stored on the client computer's hard disk.

WARNING   Be especially careful never to turn your back on a computer that is logged on to the network using the Administrator account.

Once you have established a computer use policy for your network you can mandate many aspects of that policy by configuring the client operating systems and application software appropriately.

Reality Check: Leaving Computers Unattended

A common pastime in many offices is to abuse a colleague's computer that has been left unattended with the account holder still logged on. People play pranks like leaving rude mail to the coworker from the coworker's own account, hiding files, reconfiguring the computer to use strange colors, and instructing the computer to make strange noises when the coworker uses it.

Sometimes the actions go beyond simple pranks. At a university where I worked (but not from the network I administered) a student found another student's account which had been left logged on. That student sent threatening e-mail to the president of the United States. Response from the Secret Service was immediate and severe. The unwitting victim was almost deported. Only compelling evidence that the student could not have sent the message kept him in the United States (he was seen elsewhere at the time by a number of reputable individuals). The "prankster" was never identified.

Client Operating Systems

Windows NT Server supports many kinds of client operating systems (see Figure 16.2). Each client operating system provides the administrator with a different set of requirements for security and a different set of tools to meet those requirements.

Some client operating systems (DOS, for example) are very simple and therefore don't provide much in the way of security—the network security provided by the file server will have to do (fortunately, if you don't allow any information to be stored on these computers with simple operating systems, the Windows NT Server security will suffice). At the other end of the spectrum is Windows NT Workstation, which is a client operating system every bit as complex as Windows NT Server and which provides the security administrator with a plethora of tools to facilitate or inhibit the user's use of the operating system.

FIGURE 16.2

Windows NT Server supports Windows NT, Windows 95, Windows 3.11, DOS, Macintosh, NeXT, UNIX, and OS/2 network client computers.

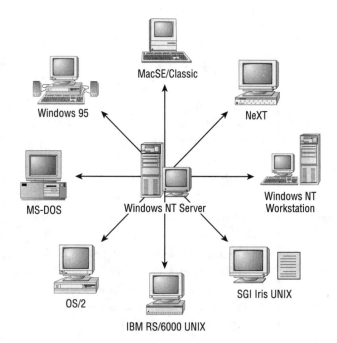

Microsoft Clients

Microsoft client operating systems (DOS, Windows 95, and Windows NT Workstation) integrate well into networks based on Windows NT, and Microsoft provides many tools to help you secure Microsoft network clients. It is also easier to control security on a network that uses the same interface on the client computers as it does on the server computers.

Each of the Microsoft operating systems differs in the amount of security it provides a network. In decreasing order of security provided they are as follows:

- Windows NT Workstation

- Windows 95

- Windows 3.11

- DOS

Windows NT Workstation

If you can secure a Windows NT Server computer then you know how to secure a Windows NT Workstation computer as well, because they are essentially the same operating system. Windows NT Server is optimized for file and print service, while Windows NT Workstation is optimized for application performance; NT Server includes some services that Workstation does not have, but the two operating systems are otherwise identical.

When you configure the Windows NT Workstation on the client computers in your network you should configure them the same way you configure the servers. The list of policies in the following sidebar should seem familiar, because many of these actions are ones you should also take to secure your Windows NT Server computer.

Policies: Windows NT Workstation Client Configuration

- Configure the computer to participate in domain security: This requires that passwords be validated by a central file server (the Primary Domain Controller) that you can secure more effectively than a client computer.

- Establish roaming profiles for users you wish to allow to customize their own Desktop environment and mandatory profiles for users who do not require flexibility: This provides a uniform view of the computers and the network-to-network users and provides a way to control which programs are available for less trusted or less sophisticated users to run.

- Configure a password-protected screen saver: This protects the computer when the user walks away momentarily.

- Do not create local user accounts on the computer: Local accounts allow users to bypass domain security for the local machine.

- Use NetBEUI or NWLink for NetBIOS communications: This segregates LAN and Internet communications.

- Remove the NetBIOS to TCP/IP binding if TCP/IP is installed: This keeps shared files and printers from being accessible over the Internet. (See Chapter 20 for instructions on how to disable NetBIOS on TCP/IP.)

- Use NTFS on the computer's mass storage volumes: This enables NTFS security for data stored on the Workstation computer.

- Give the Administrators group full control of the computer's volumes: This allows administrators to control access to the volumes when the Everyone/Full Control permission is removed.

- Remove the Full Control for Everyone permission on the computer's volumes (see the procedure detailed in Chapter 8): The default setting allows any user to install and modify software.

- Place each domain user's home directory on a file server: That way user data will be available from any workstation and will be protected by server security.

- Establish appropriate system policies: With a system policy you can limit the uses to which a computer can be put.

- Do not allow network logons to display the logon name of the last logged-on user: This keeps a valuable bit of information (a valid account name) from hackers attempting to log on.

Windows 95

Windows 95 does not have the formidable security mechanisms that Windows NT has. One fundamental security weakness in Windows 95 is that you can always boot to DOS (also known as the command prompt) and access the hard disk without there being anything Windows 95 can do about it.

You can make breaking into a Windows 95 computer more difficult by establishing system policies that limit what can be done from the Windows 95 interface, and by making it difficult to bypass the Windows 95 interface (by setting a BIOS password and disabling floppy disk booting as described at the start of this chapter). Figure 16.3 shows configuration settings for the Windows 95 System Policy Editor.

The Windows 95 system policy is virtually the only security the Windows 95 computer has, so you should be very familiar with what you can do with it. See Chapter 7 for an in-depth look at system policies for Windows 95.

Since Windows 95 cannot provide any real protection for files stored on the local computer's hard drive from a malicious user, and because the FAT file system used by Windows 95 does not recover well from operating system crashes and the system shutting down unexpectedly, the system administrator should not count on the client computer's hard drive remaining in a consistent state.

FIGURE 16.3

You can restrict what a user may do with a Windows 95 computer using the Policy Editor program.

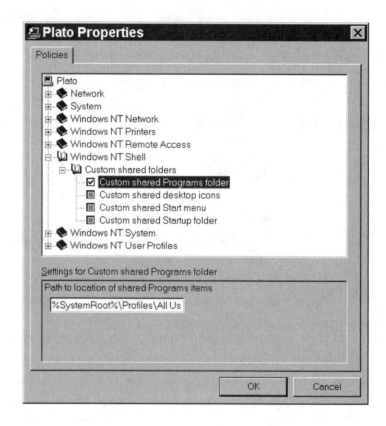

One way to overcome this limitation in Windows 95 is to locate all storage on the fileserver, including the Windows 95 operating system files for that client computer. This solution significantly increases the load on the file server. Another solution is to copy a safe image of the client computer's hard drive, including the operating system files, from the file server to the client computer when the client computer starts up. This increases the startup time of the client computer but then takes advantage of the local storage space efficiently. The sidebar that follows lists steps you can take to enhance the security of your Windows 95 computers.

Policies: Windows 95 Client Configuration

- Install virus scanning software: The Windows 95 operating system is vulnerable to virii that can be transferred via floppy disk or that can be downloaded from the Internet. The virus scanning software can detect and stop the virii it has been programmed to recognize.

- Configure a password-protected screen saver: This protects the computer when the user walks away momentarily.

- Use the System Policy Editor for Windows 95 to create mandatory user profiles for users that do not require flexibility in their Desktop environment: This provides a uniform view of the computers and the network-to-network users and provides a way to control which programs are available for users to run.

- Require network logon: This makes it so that the user must be authenticated by the PDC before they are allowed to run programs under Windows 95.

- Use NetBEUI or NWLink for NetBIOS communications: This segregates LAN and Internet communications.

- Remove the NetBIOS to TCP/IP binding if TCP/IP is installed: This keeps shared files and printers from being accessible over the Internet.

- Require user-level access control to shared resources in Windows 95: This ties Windows 95 share security into the domain security managed by the Primary Domain Controller.

- Do not allow network logons to display the logon name of the last logged-on user: This keeps a valuable bit of information (a valid account name) from hackers attempting to log on.

- Disable password caching: Cached passwords put other computers in the network at risk because if the client computer is compromised the cached password list can be cracked in a few hours.

- Disable access to executables: For dedicated-use computers (computers that have only one purpose, such as scanning or data entry), disable the run command, the Desktop Explorer, and the My Computer and network icons. Disable the MS-DOS prompt and disallow the running of single-mode (that is reboot-to-DOS) applications. This makes it more difficult to run other programs such as one to copy the password file to a floppy disk.

- Restrict the control panel from all users except administrative accounts: Only administrators should be able to change system settings.

- For a specific-use computer, set the shell to run that program rather than running the Desktop Explorer: The application can run without the Desktop Explorer.

- Disable registry editing tools: This protects configuration settings and user account names and passwords.

- Allow only necessary applications to run for users that don't need access to a wide variety of tools: This system policy setting is useful for public-use computers that need a word processor, spreadsheet, and presentation package but little else.

Windows 3.11

Windows 3.11 doesn't even have the system policies that are the only real security you get in Windows 95. The best way to secure a Windows 3.11 computer is to refrain from storing anything important on the local hard drive. If everything is stored on the file server (including operating system files) then the file server can protect the files. Another option (as with Windows 95) is to copy an image of the hard drive to the client computer every time the computer starts up. The sidebar that follows lists some things you should do to secure Windows 3.11 computers.

Policies: Windows 3.11 Client Configuration

- Install virus scanning software.

- Configure the computer to participate in domain security: This requires passwords to be validated by a central file server (the Primary Domain Controller) that you can secure more strongly than a client computer.

- Configure a password-protected screen saver.

- Use NetBEUI or NWLink for NetBIOS communications.

- Remove the NetBIOS to TCP/IP binding if TCP/IP is installed.

DOS

The only security advantage (if you can call it that) that DOS has over Windows 3.11 and Windows 95 is that there is less you can do with DOS, therefore there is less you need to secure. As with Windows 3.11 and Windows 95, you can make a DOS client computer more secure and ensure that the hard drive contents are safe by downloading the hard drive contents each time the computer starts up. You'll want to configure the computer to participate in domain security (see Figure 16.4 for a view of the DOS configuration file). Some steps you can take to secure a DOS client computer are listed in the sidebar that follows.

Policies: DOS Client Configuration

- Install virus scanning software.

- Configure the computer to participate in domain security: This requires that passwords be validated by a central file server (the Primary Domain Controller) that you can secure more strongly than a client computer. Configure a password-protected screen saver.

- Use NetBEUI or NWLink for NetBIOS communications.

- Remove the NetBIOS to TCP/IP binding if TCP/IP is installed.

FIGURE 16.4

The DOS and Windows 3.1 network configuration file contains the network logon settings.

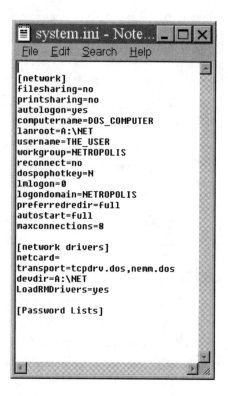

```
system.ini - Note...

File   Edit   Search   Help

[network]
filesharing=no
printsharing=no
autologon=yes
computername=DOS_COMPUTER
lanroot=A:\NET
username=THE_USER
workgroup=NETROPOLIS
reconnect=no
dospophotkey=N
lmlogon=0
logondomain=NETROPOLIS
preferredredir=full
autostart=full
maxconnections=8

[network drivers]
netcard=
transport=tcpdrv.dos,nemm.dos
devdir=A:\NET
LoadRMDrivers=yes

[Password Lists]
```

Non-Microsoft Clients

Many networks include non-Microsoft operating system clients attached to a Windows NT Server-based network. Network administrators can cope with this baffling behavior by learning the security requirements of these operating systems and configuring each in the appropriate manner.

Apple

The Apple Macintosh is a popular platform for companies or departments of companies that work in graphics, audio, or video media. The Macintosh is flexible and powerful, but unfortunately it does not lend itself well to a secure environment. Fortunately, the graphical interface of the Macintosh also makes it difficult to take remote control of a Macintosh computer if you don't install remote control software. So the primary security threat for a Macintosh network client is from unauthorized use of the computer inside your network.

Although the operating system does not come with access control for files and directories, there are several third-party software products (such as Folder Bolt) that add the capacity to the Macintosh. This kind of software can make it more difficult for users to modify their system settings or circumvent network security.

A Macintosh will use AppleTalk over Ethernet (EtherTalk) to communicate with a Windows NT Server computer running Services for Macintosh, so Internet and LAN communications for Macintosh computers are already separated by protocol. When connecting a Macintosh to your Windows NT network, you should also follow the policies outlined in the sidebar about Macintosh configuration.

Policies: Macintosh Client Configuration

- Install virus scanning software.

- Install folder control software.

- Configure a password-protected screen saver.

UNIX

UNIX computers in a network are more often servers than clients, but many companies that need high-powered workstations for animation, engineering, or simulation require the power that UNIX workstations traditionally provide. These UNIX computers can also store files on

Windows NT servers using the NFS protocol (and an add-in product for Windows NT) or using NetBIOS client software for UNIX (SAMBA is one such product).

UNIX computers can be very secure network clients when properly configured, but they are very complex and are often difficult to configure properly. UNIX computers use TCP/IP exclusively for networking services so the file service traffic and Internet traffic cannot be differentiated by transport protocol (you cannot use NWLink for file and print services and TCP/IP for Internet services such as Telnet, FTP, and WWW because UNIX does not support NWLink).

Most UNIX operating systems (HP-UX, Solaris, SCO UNIX, etc.) are at least as difficult as Windows NT for a hacker to exploit to attack your network, but Linux and the various free descendents of BSD UNIX (NetBSD, FreeBSD, etc.) are a different matter. These versions of UNIX come with source code that hackers can modify to make better tools to attack a network.

If someone wants to install Linux on your network, make sure that person has a good reason to do so. (The fact that it's free is a very good reason. Just make sure you trust the individual installing the software.) One security advantage of Linux and the various versions of BSD is that security fixes often appear for these operating systems mere hours after the discovery of a security weakness. That kind of responsiveness is almost inconceivable from commercial operating system providers.

NOTE   How you secure a UNIX computer as a client on a Windows NT network greatly depends on the version of UNIX installed. UNIX users and groups are managed separately from NT Domain users and groups, so an administrator will have to keep the information in sync manually.

Client Software

Once you instruct users on safe network behavior and you secure the client computer operating systems, you can turn your attention to the client software that runs on those client computers. Some software products present more of a security risk than others, and Internet client software is harder to secure than LAN client software.

LAN Software

Client computers, even with operating systems installed, aren't very useful (unless, of course, your users' job descriptions include playing Solitaire or Minefield). The computers require application software in order to be useful—spreadsheets to track financial or numerical information, word processors to aid in the creation of documents, as well as graphics programs, presentation software, CAD packages, and database software to automate or expedite other business processes.

Standard Applications

When you evaluate a software product for installation on your network there are several aspects of the software that you should pay particular attention to:

- Where does it store its configuration settings and user data? If the configuration settings or user data are stored in a common shared directory, then the user must have access to that directory. If that directory is the system directory, then the user will need write access to that sensitive portion of the operating system. You should create a group to assign the necessary rights to, and only assign users who need access to the program to that group.

- What direct hardware access does it require? A program that requires direct hardware access (to a video frame buffer or digitizer for example) may be able to affect the operation of other programs or even crash the computer.

- What kind of automation does it support? If the application supports a macro programming language, then that application can be vulnerable to macro virii.

- What Internet or networking features does it support? If the application supports documents with hyperlinks then the user can be tricked into clicking on a hyperlink that will launch a Web browser and download a hostile applet or control. You should disable or instruct users on how to deal with any such feature. If the application can accept and respond to documents via e-mail, then you should evaluate the feature to determine the extent of the remote control the feature provides.

Network Applications

Applications that support collaborative work over the network deserve special attention. LAN e-mail, database programs, workflow automation, scheduling, group discussion, and teleconferencing are examples of network applications that convey important data. Data, after all, is what network intruders are usually after, so these are the prime targets of hackers. Steps you can take to secure the network applications include:

- Require difficult-to-guess passwords on network applications that require passwords (e-mail, scheduling, database programs, and teleconferencing packages usually require a separate logon from the network logon).

- Consider requiring that users select a different password for the network application than they use for network logon—the network applications often store passwords in insecure locations and these password lists can be recovered and cracked by resourceful hackers. Be aware that users will resist memorizing a lot of passwords, however.

- Even when network applications require accounts and passwords in order to run, you should limit user access to the directories that contain network applications—a user that doesn't have an account name and password for the application might otherwise simply access the directory in which the network application stores its data. Create groups with access to these directories and then assign account membership to these groups for users that need access to the network applications.

Internet Software

The Internet poses a significant risk to any network attached to it, and the software that uses the Internet provides the most easily exploited vector into your network from the outside. Each Internet service introduces a different set of security problems: for example, e-mail lacks authentication, Telnet passwords can be intercepted, and Web browser controls can crash your system.

E-Mail

Most LAN administrators use a LAN e-mail package such as Microsoft Exchange or CC:Mail for their local LAN e-mail. They use a gateway product such as Microsoft Exchange Server or the CC:Mail Internet Connector (or Lotus Notes) to move e-mail between the LAN and the Internet.

Despite hysterical warnings and repeated rumors from easily excited people, your computer cannot catch a virus when you just read incoming e-mail if you are using one of the currently popular e-mail packages, such as Microsoft Exchange and CC:Mail, or if you are using an Internet mail package, such as Eudora Pro and Pegasus Mail.

In order for a virus to activate, the computer must pass control to commands provided by the virus, either as executable code or as macro commands. Since current e-mail packages merely display the contents of e-mail messages, the virii have no way to insert themselves in your computers. A virus may reside in an attached file, however, so be careful about files that are *attached* to e-mail messages.

In the future, when you will be able to include HTML with Java programs or ActiveX controls in your e-mail, you should worry about virii.

One security issue related to e-mail packages, however, is the use of POP to connect to e-mail from locations outside your network. Since POP passes the account names and passwords in the clear, you should never use the same account names and passwords that you use for your LAN. In fact, if you can establish some other method of retrieving mail (such as via an encrypted PPTP connection), you should not use POP at all.

The two other e-mail security issues are the lack of authentication for e-mail (it is easy for anyone to forge e-mail) and the lack of a standardized encryption mechanism for e-mail that crosses the Internet. Because any intermediate computer can scan e-mail traversing the Internet, you should never use Internet e-mail to send important information without encrypting the message before you send it. (You will, however, have to install an encryption software package that works with your e-mail software or purchase an e-mail software package that supports encryption.) You can also overcome the authentication issue by using a digital signature on the e-mail you send to others and by requiring that important messages sent to you to be digitally signed.

Browsers

It seems that every release of a Web browser introduces new security holes. Both Internet Explorer 3.02 and Netscape 4.0 contain severe security problems—Internet Explorer will transmit your user name and password to Web sites without your control, and Netscape's JavaScript implementation allows a malicious Web server to retrieve information from the hard drive of the computer the browser is installed on.

Since the Web is too useful to ignore, you simply must be aware of the weaknesses of whichever type of Web browser you use and plan accordingly.

The problem with Web browsers is not in their basic functionality (except for the password issue), which is simply to ask a Web server for an HTML page and then to display that page. Rather, the problem is with the *extensibility* of Web browsers. The browsers don't do much by themselves, but users can extend them with plug-ins that they download from the Internet. The plug-ins can allow the browser to accept realtime audio, display PDF files, show animations, or upload all of the contents of the user's hard drive to the Internet.

Internet users must be informed about the danger of downloading plug-ins from untrusted sources. Newer Web browsers (including Internet Explorer and Netscape) support digital certificates, which certify that the plug-ins you are about to download come from a reliable software provider. Of course, the certificate is only as trustworthy as the certificate authority that provided it. See Figure 16.5 for a view of a digital certificate.

FIGURE 16.5

A digital certificate informs you that a software component comes from a reputable source.

Java applets are a trickier security proposition—a properly written Web browser will not allow a Java applet to access resources on the client computer without the user's permission. The writers of browsers have been having difficulties getting all of the bugs out, however, so you should keep track of browser vulnerabilities as they are discovered. You should also disable local file storage access for the Web browsers on the client computers in your network.

Telnet

The trouble with Telnet is that it does not encrypt user names or passwords when transmitting them to the remote computer. For this reason users should be cautioned never to use the same user name or password on a remote computer that they use on your LAN, and you should be hesitant to allow users to Telnet in to computers on your LAN.

Policies: Client Software

- Use different passwords for applications than for network logon.

- Restrict access to directories that contain shared applications.

- Do not use POP to access e-mail across an unsecured network.

- Only download software with digital certificates from a certificate authority you trust.

- Limit the browser extensions used in your network.

- Disable ActiveX control and Java applets.

Summary

As a network administrator, you must satisfy three aspects of client security in your network: user behavior, which you can guide through education and an appropriate network policy manual; operating system configuration, which will be different for each kind of client operating system in your network; and software installation and configuration.

Windows NT Workstation is the client operating system that provides the best integration with Windows NT Server security because it uses exactly the same security mechanisms that Windows NT Server uses. System policies are your best tool for securing a Windows 95 computer because Windows 95 does not use NTFS to protect locally stored files. You can only clean up changes made to Windows 3.11 or DOS computers after the fact—copying a disk image to the client computer's hard drives may be the best option.

Security for network applications is as important as any other aspect of network security. Don't leave security up to the applications, however; assign access permissions to the files and directories for those applications, so users can't bypass the application security.

Be especially careful of how Internet client software is used in your network. Do not allow POP or Telnet logons to your computers over the Internet. Encrypt and apply digital signatures to important e-mail. Disable Java access to local file storage and do not download plug-ins from dubious sources.

CHAPTER

17

Border Patrol:
Firewalls, Proxies, and Filters

Nations without controlled borders cannot ensure the security and safety of their citizens, nor can they control piracy and theft. Networks without controlled access cannot ensure the security or privacy of stored data, nor can they keep network resources from being exploited by hackers.

The efficiency provided by the Internet has caused a rush to attach private networks directly to it. Direct Internet connections make it easy for hackers to exploit private network resources. Prior to the Internet, the only widely available way for a hacker to connect from home to a private network was direct dialing with modems and the public telephony network. Remote access security was a relatively easy problem to solve.

The Internet is an entirely different matter because when you connect your private network to the Internet, you are actually connecting your network directly to every other network attached to the Internet directly. There's no inherent central point of security control. Figure 17.1 shows what unrestricted access to the Internet looks like.

Firewalls are used to create a central point of security control. By providing the routing function between the private network and the Internet, firewalls inspect all communications passing between the two networks and either pass or drop the communications depending on how they match the programmed policy rules. If your firewall is properly configured and contains no serious exploitable bugs, your network will be as free from risk as possible.

There are literally hundreds of firewall products available, and there are different theories from different security experts on how firewalls should be used to secure your network. This chapter will explore the

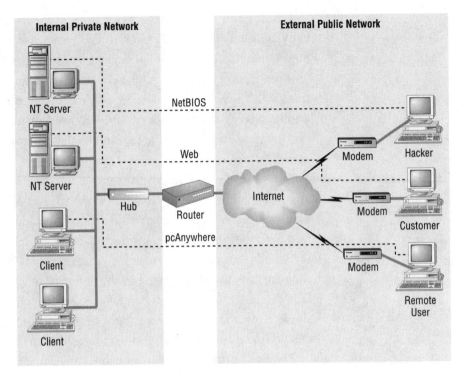

FIGURE 17.1

Unrestricted Internet
access

operation of a generic firewall in detail, outline the important features
you need in a firewall, and discuss how firewalls should be deployed in
networks of any size.

Understanding Firewalls

Firewalls keep your Internet connection as secure as possible by
inspecting and approving or rejecting each connection attempt made
between your internal network and external networks like the Internet.
Strong firewalls protect your network at all software layers—from the
data link layer up through the application layer.

Firewalls sit on the borders of your network—at those gateways that provide access to other networks. For that reason, firewalls are considered border security. The concept of border security is important—without it, every host on your network would have to perform the functions of a firewall themselves, needlessly consuming compute resources and increasing the amount of time required to connect, authenticate, and encrypt data in local area, high-speed networks. Firewalls allow you to centralize all external security services in machines that are optimized for and dedicated to the task.

By their nature, firewalls create bottlenecks between the internal and external networks because all traffic transiting between the internal and external networks must pass through a single point of control. This is a small price to pay for security. Since external leased-line connections are relatively slow compared to the speed of modern computers, the latency caused by firewalls can be completely transparent. Figure 17.2 shows how a large company might implement border security. Notice that in this example every connection to the Internet has a firewall.

Firewalls primarily function using three fundamental methods:

- **Packet filtering** rejects TCP/IP packets from unauthorized hosts and rejects connection attempts to unauthorized services.

- **IP masquerading** translates the IP addresses of internal hosts to hide them from outside monitoring.

- **Proxy services** make high-level application connections on behalf of internal hosts to completely break the network layer connection between internal and external hosts.

Most firewalls also perform two other important security services:

- **Encrypted authentication** allows users on the public network to prove their identity to the firewall in order to gain access to the private network from external locations.

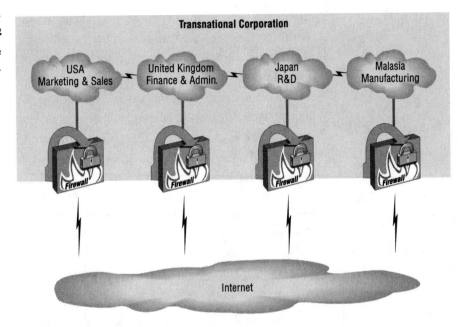

FIGURE 17.2

Multiple firewalls provide
border security.

- **Encrypted tunnels** (virtual private networking) establishes a secure connection between two private networks over a public medium like the Internet. This allows physically separated networks to use the Internet rather than leased-line connections to communicate.

These basic methods are used by nearly all firewalls to provide a security service. There are literally hundreds of firewall products on the market now, all vying for your security dollar. Most are very strong products that vary only in superficial details. The remainder of this section covers the five primary functions that most firewalls support.

You can use devices or servers that perform only one of the above functions—for instance, you could have a router that performs packet filtering, and then a proxy server in a separate machine. This is not nearly as secure as using a single firewall that performs both functions in one place because either the packet filter must pass traffic through to the proxy server, or the proxy server must sit outside your network without the protection of packet filtering. Both are more dangerous than using a single firewall product that performs all the security functions in one place.

This chapter doesn't discuss the installation or implementation of any specific firewall products, nor does it attempt to compare existing products to each other. Rather, it explains the fundamental operation of firewalls, their role in your network, and architectures that support proper network security.

Terminology

- **Encrypted tunnel:** A private connection between two networks created by encrypting data flowing over a public medium like the Internet.

- **Firewall:** A security control device that connects two networks and determines which traffic should be allowed to pass between them. Firewalls incorporate the functions of packet filtering, IP masquerading, and application proxy to perform their function.

- **IP masquerade:** A device that translates IP addresses from inside a network to appear as if all network traffic comes from a single host. IP masquerades hide the identity of internal clients.

- **Packet filter:** A device used to discard undesired network traffic based on its source address, destination address, or by the type of data specified by the TCP port number.

- **Proxy:** A service running either on a server or a firewall which receives service requests from clients and then reissues them as if the request originated from the proxy server. This hides the identity of the client and provides the ability to cache often requested data on the proxy to reduce bandwidth on lower-speed connections to the Internet.

Packet Filters

The first Internet firewalls were just packet filters. Filters compare network (such as IP) and transport protocol packets (such as TCP) to a database of rules and forward only those packets that conform to the criteria specified in the database of rules. Filters can either be implemented in routers or in the TCP/IP stacks of servers (see Figure 17.3).

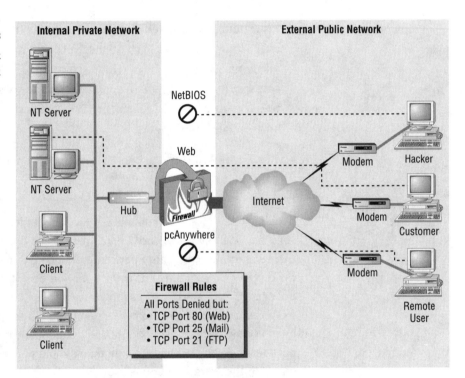

FIGURE 17.3

Filtered Internet connections block undesired traffic.

Filters implemented inside routers prevent suspicious traffic from reaching the destination network, whereas TCP/IP filter modules in servers merely prevent that specific machine from responding to suspicious traffic. The traffic still reaches the network, and could target any machine on it. Routing filters protect all the machines on the destination network from suspicious traffic. For that reason, filtering in the TCP/IP stacks of servers (such as that provided by Windows NT) should only be used in addition to routed filtering, not instead of it. Filters typically follow these rules:

- Dropping inbound connection attempts but allowing outbound connection attempts to pass.

- Eliminating TCP packets bound for ports that shouldn't be available to the Internet (such as the NetBIOS session port) but allowing packets that should (such as SMTP) to pass. Most filters can specify exactly which server a specific sort of traffic should go to—for instance, SMTP traffic on port 25 should only go to the IP address of a mail server.

- Restricting inbound access to certain IP ranges.

WARNING   Simple packet filters or routers with a packet filtering function that requires opening ports above 1023 for return channels are not effective security devices. These packet filters do not prevent internal users or Trojan horses from setting up a service on a client station in the port range above 1024 and simply listening for connection attempts from the outside. Firewalls only open channels for servers that have been invited back in by a connection attempt from inside the security perimeter—choose them rather than simple packet filters that can't maintain the state of a connection.

Sophisticated filters use proprietary algorithms to examine the states of all connections that flow through them, looking for the telltale signs of hacking, such as source routing, ICMP redirection, and IP spoofing. Connections that exhibit these characteristics are dropped.

Internal clients are generally allowed to create connections to outside hosts, and external hosts are usually prevented from initiating connection attempts. When an internal host decides to initiate a TCP connection, it sends a TCP message to the IP address and port number of the public server (for example, www.microsoft.com:80 to connect to Microsoft's Web site). In the connection initiation message, it tells the remote server what its IP address is and on which port it is listening for a response (for example, localhost: 2050).

WARNING Older FTP clients and servers may only work correctly if the remote server is allowed to establish the data channel on TCP port 20, which violates the general rule that all inbound connection attempts are dropped. More recent FTP implementations support passive connection, which allows the client to establish the command channel (21) and the data channel (20). It usually isn't worth compromising security to support older FTP software.

The external server sends data back by transmitting it to the port given by the internal client. Since your firewall inspects all the traffic exchanged between both hosts, it knows that the connection was initiated by an internal host attached to its internal interface, what that host's IP address is, and on which port that host expects return traffic on. The firewall then remembers to allow the host addressed in the connection message to return traffic to the internal host's IP address only at the port specified.

When the hosts involved in the connection close down the TCP connection, the firewall removes the entry in its state table that allows the remote host to return traffic to the internal host.

NOTE Unfortunately, filtering does not completely solve the Internet security problem. First, the IP addresses of computers inside the filter is present in outbound traffic, which makes it somewhat easy to determine the type and number of Internet hosts inside a filter, and to target attacks against those addresses. Filtering does not hide the identity of hosts inside the filter.

Filters cannot check all the fragments of an IP message based on higher-level protocols like TCP headers because the header exists only in the first fragment. Subsequent fragments have no header information and can only be compared to IP level rules, which are usually relaxed to allow some traffic through the filter. This allows bugs in the destination IP stacks of computers on the network to be exploited, and could allow communications with a Trojan horse installed inside the network.

Windows NT's Built-In Filtering

You might not be aware that Windows NT Server includes packet filtering in the TCP/IP protocol interface. You can use this filtering in addition to a strong firewall to control access to individual servers; you can also use this filtering to provide an additional measure of internal security without the cost of firewalls inside your organization. Just as filtering alone is not sufficient to protect your network entirely, Windows NT's internal filtering is not sufficient to create a completely secure environment.

Policy: NT Protocol Filtering

- Do not rely upon Windows NT's built-in filtering alone to protect your network.

- On each Windows NT server inside your network, establish filters to pass only those protocols you explicitly intend to serve. This prevents software from working in ways you don't expect.

The basic filtering in Windows NT allows you to define acceptance criteria for each adapter in your computer for incoming connections based on:

- IP protocol number
- TCP port number

■ UDP port number

The filtering does not apply to outbound connections (those originating on your server), and is defined separately for each adapter in your system. Enabling filtering in Windows NT is easy. To enable TCP/IP filtering in Windows NT follow these steps:

I. Right-click the Network Neighborhood icon and click Properties, or open the Networking control panel program.

2. Select the Protocols tab and double-click TCP/IP.

3. Click Advanced.

4. Check Enable Security, then click Configure.

5. Select the adapter connected to the network from which you would like to control access.

6. Under the TCP ports header, select Permit Only.

7. Click Add to allow a protocol to pass.

8. Enter the port number for the allowed protocol. Refer to the Internet Assigned Numbers Authority (IANA) or RFC 1700, which is included on the companion CD-ROM for a comprehensive list of protocol assigned numbers.

9. Click OK a few times (until all dialog boxes are closed). Click Yes to restart your computer and enable TCP/IP port filtering.

A typical Windows NT server sets up services to listen on the following ports. These ports must be open through your filter for these services to work correctly.

Simple TCP/IP services listen on the following ports:

■ 7: Echo

■ 9: Discard

- **13:** Daytime

- **17:** Quote of the Day

- **19:** Character Generator

Internet Information Server services listen on the following ports by default:

- **21:** File Transfer Protocol

- **70:** Gopher

- **80:** World Wide Web

The Windows NT networking services (browser, server) listen on the following ports:

- **53:** Domain Name Service (DNS service, if installed).

- **135:** NetBIOS Locator Service (Browse masters listen for browse requests on this port—used by the computer browser service).

- **137:** NetBIOS Name Service (Name requests are resolved by servers listening on this port—used by the WINS service and by NetBIOS).

- **138:** NETBIOS Datagram Service (NetBIOS datagrams are received on this port).

- **139:** NETBIOS Session Service (NetBIOS sessions are established on this port—used by the NetBIOS interface service).

- **515:** LPR is used by the TCP/IP print service, if installed.

- **530:** Remote Procedure Call (RPC connections are used by the WinLogon service as well as many other high-level network applications).

Exchange Server is usually configured to listen on the following ports:

- **25:** Simple Mail Transfer Protocol (Mail server-to-server exchanges).

- **110:** Post Office Protocol version 3 (Server-to-client mail exchanges).

- **119:** Network News Transfer Protocol.

If you install other Microsoft or third-party service software, you must make sure your server's filter is set up to listen on the ports required by the service—otherwise the service will not work. Find out from the software manufacture what ports are required for that service. This does not apply to border firewalls, which should only be configured to pass a service if you intend to provide that service to the public.

Policies: Packet Filtering

- Disallow all protocols and addresses by default, then explicitly allow services and hosts you wish to support.

- Disallow all connection attempts to hosts inside your network. Allowing any inbound connections provides a mechanism hackers might be able to exploit to establish connections to Trojan horses or by exploiting bugs in service software.

- Filter out and do not respond to ICMP redirect and echo (ping) messages.

- Drop all packets that are TCP source routed. Source routing is rarely used for legitimate purposes.

- Drop all external routing protocol (RIP, OSPF) updates bound for internal routers. No one outside your network should be transmitting RIP updates.

- Consider disallowing fragments beyond number zero, since this functionality is largely obsolete and often exploited.

- Place public service hosts like Web servers and SMTP servers outside your packet filters rather than opening holes through your packet filters.

- Do not rely upon packet filtering alone to protect your network.

Using IP Masquerades

IP masquerading, also known as *Network Address Translation (NAT)* solves the problem of hiding internal hosts. Masquerading is actually a fundamental proxy: A single host makes requests on behalf of all internal hosts, thus hiding their identity from the public network. Windows NT does not provide this function—you must use a third-party firewall if you want IP masquerading.

IP masquerades hide internal IP addresses by converting all internal host addresses to the address of the masquerade (see Figure 17.4). The masquerade then retransmits the data payload of the internal host from its own address using the TCP port number to keep track of which public-side connections map to which private-side hosts. To the Internet, all the traffic on your network appears to be coming from one extremely busy computer.

An IP masquerade effectively hides all TCP/IP-level information about your internal hosts from prying eyes on the Internet. Address translation also allows you to use any IP address range you want on your internal network even if those addresses are already in use elsewhere on the Internet. This means you don't have to register a large block from InterNIC or reassign network numbers from those you simply plugged in before you connected your network to the Internet.

Finally, IP masquerades allow you to multiplex a single IP address across an entire network. Many small companies rely upon the services

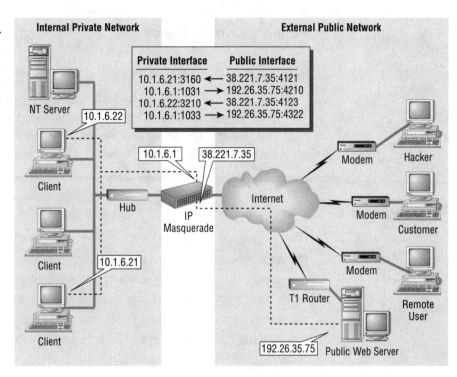

FIGURE 17.4

An IP masquerade keeps track of which clients on the private network equal which port numbers on the public network.

of an upstream Internet service provider that may be reluctant to provide large blocks of addresses because their own range is relatively restricted. Or, you may want to share a single dial-up or cable modem address without telling your ISP. These options are all possible using IP masquerades.

On the down side, IP masquerades are implemented only at the TCP/IP level. This means again that information hidden in the data payload of TCP/IP traffic could be transmitted to a higher-level service and used to exploit weaknesses in higher-level traffic or to communicate with a Trojan horse. You'll still have to use a higher-level service like a proxy to prevent higher-level service security breaches.

Policies: IP Masquerades

- Use IP masquerades to hide the identity of hosts inside your network.

- Set up your internal network within the reserved 10 class A domain. Most Internet routers do not route this domain. Use network translation to map your internal hosts to routable addresses. You can also use the reserved 192.168 class B domain if you so desire.

Proxies

IP masquerading solves many of the problems associated with direct Internet connections—but it still doesn't completely restrict the flow of datagrams through your firewall. It's possible for someone with a network monitor to watch traffic coming out of your IP masquerade and determine that it is translating addresses for other machines. It is then possible for a hacker to hijack TCP connections or to spoof connections back through the IP masquerade.

Enter the application-level proxy. Application-level proxies allow you to completely disconnect the flow of network-level protocols through your firewall, and restrict traffic only to higher-level protocols like HTTP, FTP, and SMTP.

Proxies stand in for outbound connection attempts to servers, and then make the request to the actual target server on behalf of the client. When the server returns data, the proxy transmits that data to the client. Proxies essentially perform a benign man-in-the-middle attack—and they're a good example of how any router between you and another end system could potentially perform any sort of processing without your permission.

Application proxies (like Microsoft Proxy Server) are unlike IP masquerades and filters in that the Internet client application is (usually) set up to talk to the proxy. For instance, you tell Internet Explorer what the address of your Web proxy is, and Internet Explorer sends all Web requests to that server rather than resolving the IP address and establishing a connection directly.

Without a filter or IP masquerade, there's nothing to prevent users from bypassing the application proxy by simply disabling the proxy settings in Internet Explorer.

Application proxies don't have to run on firewalls—any server can perform the role of a proxy either inside or outside your network. Without a firewall, you still don't have any real security though, so you need both. And, if the proxy doesn't run on the firewall, you'll have to open a channel through your firewall one way or another. Ideally, your firewall should perform the proxy function. This keeps packets from the public side from being forwarded through your firewall (see Figure 17.5).

Some firewall proxies are more sophisticated than others. Because they have the functionality of an IP filter and masquerade, they can simply block outbound connection attempts (on port 80 in the case of HTTP) to remote hosts rather than having the client software configured to address the proxy service specifically. The firewall proxy then connects to the remote server and requests data on behalf of the blocked client. The retrieved data is returned to the requesting client using the firewall's IP masquerade functionality to look just like the actual remote server. This method has the advantage of not requiring any set-up on the client application and that it can't be circumvented by reconfiguring the client application.

Sophisticated proxies are even capable of performing application-level filtering for specific content. For instance, some firewall HTTP proxies look for tags in HTML pages that refer to Java or ActiveX embedded applets and then drop them, which prevents the applet from executing on your client computers and eliminates the risk that a user will accidentally download a Trojan horse. This sort of filtering is extremely important because filtering, proxying, and masquerading can't prevent your network from being compromised if your users are lured into downloading a Trojan horse embedded in an ActiveX applet.

FIGURE 17.5

The difference between
proxy servers and direct
Internet connections

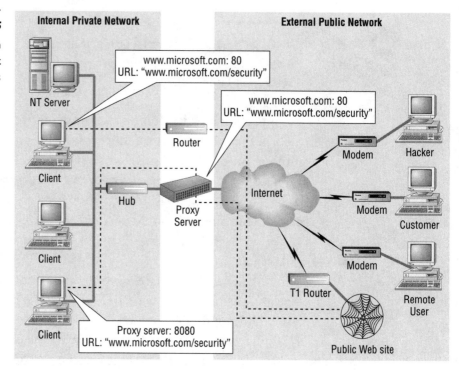

FIGURE 17.5

The difference between proxy servers and direct Internet connections

You may have noticed that as we have climbed the networking layers, the security services have gotten more specific. For instance, filtering is specific to IP and then to TCP and UDP. Applications that use IP with other protocols like Banyan Vines must use special high-cost or unusually robust firewalls.

Proxies are extremely specific because they can only work for a specific application. For instance, you must have a proxy software module for HTTP, another proxy module for FTP, and another module for Telnet. As these protocols evolve (HTTP is particularly fast moving) the proxy module for that protocol will have to be updated.

Even more problematic is the fact that many protocols exist for which there is no proxy service. Proxies don't exist for proprietary application protocols like Lotus Notes, so those protocols must be filtered. And since you aren't using proxies for all your protocols, you must allow filtered TCP/IP traffic from the Internet onto your local network, thus exposing it to greater risk.

Policies: Proxy Servers

- Whenever possible, use proxy servers for all application protocols.

- Consider disallowing services for which you do not have proxy servers.

- Use high-level proxies capable of stripping executable content like ActiveX and Java from Web pages.

Encrypted Tunnels

Encrypted tunnels (also called virtual private networks) allow you to securely connect two physically separated networks over the Internet without exposing your data to monitors. Encrypted tunnels on their own could be subject to redirection attempts, spoofed connection initiation, and all manner of hacking indignity while the tunnel is being established. But when implemented as an integral part of a firewall, the firewall authentication and security services can be used to prevent exploitation while the tunnel is being established (see Figure 17.6).

Once established, the tunnels are impervious to exploitation so long as the encryption remains secure. And, since firewalls sit at the Internet borders, they exist at the perfect terminal points for each end of the tunnel. Essentially, your private networks can pass traffic as if they were two subnets in the same domain.

Encrypted tunnels also allow you to address remote internal hosts directly by their hidden IP addresses. IP masquerades and packet filters would prevent this if the connection attempt came directly from the Internet.

The Point-to-Point Tunneling Protocol provides an encrypted tunnel using the security services of the Remote Access Server.

FIGURE 17.6

Two compatible firewalls create an encrypted tunnel.

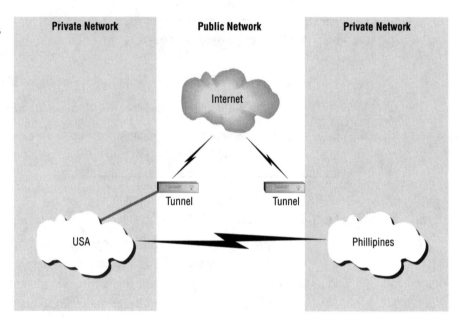

Policies: Encrypted Tunnels

- Use leased lines rather than encrypted tunnels whenever practical.

- Use encrypted tunnels for all communications over the Internet between organizational units if leased lines are not available or are cost prohibitive.

- Never communicate between organizational units over the Internet without using some form of encryption. Unencrypted packet headers contain valuable nuggets of information about the structure of your internal network.

Encrypted Authentication

Encrypted authentication allows external users on the Internet to prove to a firewall that they are authorized users and thereby open a connection through the firewall to the internal network. The encrypted authentication might use any number of secure authentication protocols. Once the connection is established, it may or may not be encrypted depending upon the firewall product in use and whether additional software has been installed on the client to support tunneling.

Using encryption authentication is convenient because it occurs at the transport level between a client software package and the firewall. Once the connection is open, all normal application software and operating system logon software will run without hindrance—so you don't have to use special software packages that support your specific firewall.

Unfortunately, encrypted authentication reduces the security of your firewall. By its nature, it causes the following problems:

- The firewall must respond on some port because it listens for connection attempts. This can show hackers that the firewall exists.

- The connection could be redirected using ICMP after establishment, especially if it's not encrypted. (ICMP redirection is explained in Chapter 15.)

- A hacker who monitored the establishment might be able to spoof the address of the authorized client to gain access inside the network without redirecting any existing connections.

- A stolen laptop computer with the appropriate keys could be used to gain access to the network.

- Work-at-home employees could become a target for breaking and entering because their computers are able to access the private network.

- The authentication procedure could be buggy or less than completely secure, thus allowing anyone on the Internet to open holes through the firewall.

All of these risks are not really all that likely to actually occur. Adminstrators of medium- to low-risk environments should not feel uncomfortable using encrypted authentication as long as the connection is encrypted for the duration.

Effective Border Security

Controlling your border security using firewalls that perform all three of the basic firewall functions (packet filtering, IP masquerading, and high-level service proxy) is the absolute minimum level of effective Internet security. Your firewalls must also be dedicated to the firewall functions: Avoid the temptation to run other services such as mail, Web, or other public services on the firewall unless the service software comes from the firewall software vendor. Even in this case, be aware that you are increasing your risk because a bug in any of the high-level services running on your firewall might be exploited to bypass the firewall completely.

Minimize the services running on the firewalls. This reduces the complexity of the software running on the machine, thereby reducing the probability that a bug in the operating system or security software will express to allow a security breach. In the case of Windows NT, none of the services in the service control panel are needed for a computer running only as a firewall. Turn off all services that the server will allow you to shut off and set them to start manually. Normally, you won't have to deal with this because the firewall software installation program will shut down all unnecessary services for you. If it doesn't, look elsewhere for firewall software.

It's always tempting to pile services like HTTP, FTP, Telnet, Gopher, and mail onto the same machine you use as an Internet router and firewall because it's cheaper and because that machine probably has a lot of spare compute time and disk space. Unfortunately, few operating systems, Windows NT included, are both secure enough and bug-free enough to guarantee that services can't interfere with each other or that a service can't crash the firewall. It's also quite probable that a high-level service running on the firewall, even if it didn't affect other security services, could provide a way to circumvent the security services of the firewall. And lastly, as we mentioned earlier in this chapter, many services contain logon banners or automatically generated error pages that identify the firewall product you are using. This could be dangerous if hackers have found a weakness in your specific firewall.

You must also enforce a single point of control in your firewall policy. If you have more than one firewall in your company (perhaps one firewall attaching each remote office to the Internet), you need to make absolutely certain they are all configured the same way.

WARNING   A lapse on any of your firewalls can compromise your entire network, especially if you use secure tunneling or private leased lines to connect offices. Hackers can be relied upon to use the path of least resistance.

Policy: Firewalls

- Dedicate a machine to be a firewall. Don't run other services on it, and disable all unnecessary service features that may be included in the firewall package.

- Make sure there's no way for a hacker to tell which firewall product you are using.

Comparing Firewall Functionality

There is a common misconception among network administrators that a firewall has to be based on the same operating system as the network file servers—UNIX firewalls for UNIX-based networks and NT fire-walls for Windows NT-based networks. In fact, there's no functional reason why the operating system used by a firewall should be the same as that used by the network, since except in very special circumstances, you'll never run any other software on the firewall computer.

All firewalls filter TCP/IP traffic, and in most cases you'll set them up once and leave them to do their job, with minor tweaks as security policies and work habits change in the organization. Some firewalls run proprietary operating systems that aren't related to UNIX or Windows NT—they are just as appropriate on any network.

The second most important factor in choosing a firewall operating system (after security, of course) is familiarity—the administrator should be familiar with the user interface and know how to configure the firewall correctly. Most Windows NT-based firewalls are far easier to set up than UNIX-based firewalls, but many UNIX-based firewalls are catching up by using Java-based graphical interfaces that run remotely on the administrator's PC.

Some firewall vendors claim that their products are superior to fire-walls based on Windows NT or standard versions of UNIX because they are based on a "hardened" implementation of the TCP/IP protocol stack or a theoretically more secure operating system. They also claim that bugs in Windows NT or UNIX releases can be exploited to get past the firewall software of their competitors. While this may be true, those vendors can't prove that similar bugs don't exist in their own software. In fact, there's no practicable way to prove that complex code is bug-free, and firewall vendors are no more likely to get it absolutely right than are large vendors like Microsoft, Sun, or Digital.

One major advantage of using a widely available operating system as the foundation of a firewall is that the code is put through its paces by millions of users. Bugs are more likely to be found and corrected, and patches are available far sooner and with greater regularity than is true for proprietary products provided by smaller vendors who usually don't have the programming resources to throw at problems as they arise.

Most firewall products that are based on a standard operating system don't rely on the standard TCP/IP stack or higher-level services that ship with the operating system anyway; they implement their own TCP/IP stack so that they can have absolute control over its operation. The base operating system is used for little more than booting, multi-tasking, and user interface.

Firewall products vary in the following ways:

- **Security:** Some firewall products are fundamentally flawed because they rely too heavily on the host operating system, because they contain bugs that can be exploited, or because there is a flaw in the authentication protocol used for remote authentication.

- **Interface:** Some firewalls are very difficult to configure because you must administer them via Telnet or an attached console and learn some cryptic command line interface. Others use very intuitive graphical interfaces that make configuration easy and obvious.

- **Enterprise functionality:** Some firewalls are fortresses unto themselves, while others use a centrally maintained security policy that is replicated among all firewalls in the enterprise.

- **Security features:** Many firewalls offer important security features such as virtual private networking and encrypted authentication to allow remote office networking with a high degree of security.

- **Service features:** Some firewalls include services such as FTP, Telnet, HTTP, and so forth so that you don't have to dedicate a machine to those functions. These features can be convenient, but they're often somewhat obsolete in functionality and can reduce the security of the firewall if they aren't properly implemented. Also, many services reveal a copyright that tells hackers exactly which firewall product you are using and allows them to target any weaknesses it may have.

Your primary criterion for firewalls should be security. The next most important feature is ease of use for you—you must be able to correctly configure a firewall for it to work correctly. Flashy features and services galore are tertiary to these primary requirements.

Problems Firewalls Can't Solve

No network attached to the Internet can be made completely secure. Firewalls are extremely effective, they will keep the hacking masses at bay, but there are so many different ways to exploit network connections that no method is entirely secure. Many administrators mistakenly assume that once their firewall is online and shown to be effective, their security problem is gone. That's simply not the case.

For example, let's say that the only thing you allow through your firewall is e-mail. An employee gets a message from a branch office asking him to e-mail a CAD file to them. So the employee looks at the From address, verifies that it's correct, clicks reply, attaches the file, and unknowingly sends the CAD file to the hackers that forged the e-mail request because the Reply-to address isn't the same as the From address. Your firewall can't realistically do anything about this type of exploitation because many typical users have different From and Reply-to addresses for very valid reasons.

There is another serious threat to the security of your network: the hidden border crossing. Modems provide the ability for any user on your network to dial out to their own Internet service provider and completely circumvent your firewall. Modems are cheap and they come in most computers sold these days. All Microsoft operating systems come with the software required for setting up modems to connect to a dial-up Internet service provider. And it's a good bet that most of your computer-savvy employees have their own dial-up networking accounts they could use from work.

Most users simply don't understand that all IP connections are a security risk. Modem PPP connections to the Internet are bidirectional just like leased lines. And there's a good chance that their client has file sharing turned and can be exploited directly from the Internet.

It's quite common for businesses with firewalls to allow unrestricted file and print sharing among peers because it's an easy and efficient way for users to transfer files. If one of those users is dialed into the Net, it's also an easy and efficient way for hackers to transfer your files.

Why would a user choose a dial-up modem connection when they have a faster secure Internet connection? Reasons include:

- Your firewall doesn't pass Internet Relay Chat and they want to talk to their friends.

- So they can use NetPhone to talk to their mother for free.

- So they can work from home using pcAnywhere.

- Because AOL uses a port your firewall doesn't pass and they want to check their personal e-mail.

- Because you filter FTP and they want to download a file.

- Because your network is configured to block pornography sites.

Users dial out so they can circumvent your security policy without your knowledge. To control border security, you must control all the border crossings; it must be impossible to establish a new border crossing without your permission. Exceptions to this rule endanger the security of your entire network.

Policies: Internet Connections

- Reduce the number of connections to the Internet to the minimum number possible: one per campus. Many large organizations allow only a single link to the Internet at headquarters and then route all remote offices to that point using the same frame relay lines used to connect internal networks.

- Don't allow dial-up connections to the Internet. Remove modems and all other uncontrolled network access devices. Disable free COM ports in the BIOS settings of client computers and password-protect the BIOS to prevent users from overriding your security settings.

- Don't allow unrestricted file sharing. Use file sharing with user-based authentication or, at the very least, passwords.

- Don't install file and print sharing on clients unless absolutely necessary. Encourage users to store all files on network file servers, and create server pools of resources like CD-ROM or modems that can be centrally controlled.

- Configure internal clients with IP addresses in the 10 domain, which is not routed by most Internet routers. Use an IP masquerade to translate these internal addresses to routable external addresses. This may prevent hackers from exploiting modem connections into your network beyond the computer which established the connection.

Border Security Options

Once you've got your firewall running on the border between your private network and the Internet, you're going to run into a problem. How do you provide the public services your customers need while securing your internal network from attack? There is more than one answer to this question, and which one is right depends entirely upon your security posture and the level of service you need to provide.

Methods used by companies to protect their networks range from the simple to the complex, the risky to the very secure. These methods (in order of security risk from highest to lowest) are:

1. Filtered packet services

2. Single firewall with internal public servers

3. Single firewall with external public servers

4. Dual firewalls or multilevel firewalls

5. Enterprise firewalls

6. Disconnection

The following sections discuss each method in detail, along with relative risks and issues.

Filtered Packet Services

Most Internet service providers provide packet filtering as a value-added service for leased-line customers. For a small monthly charge, (generally about $100) your ISP will probably set up their own firewall to filter traffic into and out of your network. Some ISPs also offer proxy servers and IP masquerades, but you may still be at risk from security attacks by other customers served by that ISP. Remember that all hackers have an ISP somewhere along the line. Figure 17.7 illustrates how filtered packet services work.

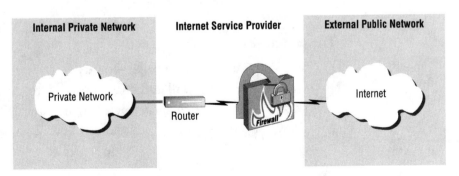

FIGURE 17.7

Filtered packet service

There are a number of problems with filtered firewall services:

- Packet filters can be exploited more easily than complete firewalls.

- Your security is in the hands of a third party. Their motivations may not always coincide with yours, especially if a legal dispute arises between your company and theirs.

- The responsibility for reliability isn't controllable.

- There's no provision for alarming and alerting.

- Configuration is a difficult and error-prone administrative hassle. Reconfiguration is also a pain in the neck if the ISP doesn't have a strong customer support ethic.

- You are probably vulnerable to the ISP's other subscribers, who are usually inside the same firewall.

Packet filters have the following advantage:

- No up-front capital expenditure is required.

Even if the firewall service provided by an ISP were complete, it's still never a good idea to put the security of your network in the hands of another organization. You don't know anything about your ISP's employees, and you don't know what measures your ISP might take if for some reason a dispute arose between your company and theirs. Add to that the simple fact that most people who can hack do so at least occasionally, and that many good hackers work for the people who can get them closest to the action.

The Single-Firewall Approach

The simplest complete border security solution is that of the single firewall. With one firewall and one connection to the Internet, you have a single point of management and control. Figure 17.8 shows a single firewall border security solution.

FIGURE 17.8

A single firewall with
public servers exposed to
the Internet.

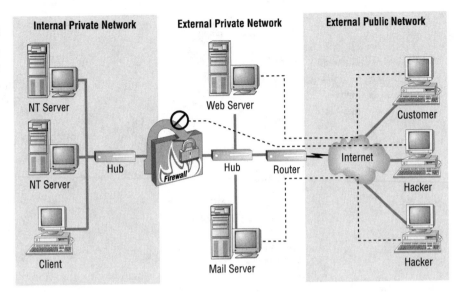

You also have a problem if you intend to provide public services like a Web or FTP site, or if you want to operate a mail server. You must either open a connection through your firewall to an internal host, or you must expose your public server to the Internet without the protection of a firewall. Both methods are risky.

The problem with putting public servers, like mail servers, outside your firewall is that they are at risk for unrestricted hacking. You can set these computers up so that they don't contain much useful information, but hacking attempts could easily cause denial of service if your servers are crashed, or embarrassment if hackers modify your Web pages. Figure 17.9 shows public servers inside the firewall.

The problem with opening a path through your firewall for external-source connection attempts is that inappropriate packets could potentially make their way onto your internal network if they look like packets that conform to the rules used by your packet filter. It also means that a hacker who manages to exploit a bug in high-level service software might gain control of a computer inside your network—a very dangerous situation. For this reason, most organizations put public servers outside their firewalls and simply do not allow external connections in through the firewall at all.

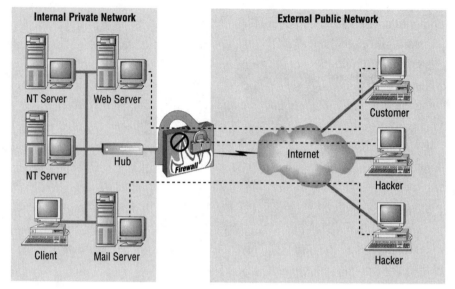

FIGURE 17.9

A single firewall with public servers protected but allowing external traffic in through the firewall.

Reality Check: Filtered Packet Services

A customer of mine relied on a filtered packet service from their Internet service provider for security. Since the client runs a very small startup business strapped for cash, I didn't put up too much resistance to this initially.

As part of my services for them, I made periodic hacking attempts against their server to make sure no easily exploitable methods could be used to gain access. After having verified the service a number of times, one scan showed that the service had suddenly failed, exposing the NetBIOS session ports of their NT server to the Internet. I mapped a drive connection right to their server over the Internet!

A panic call to their ISP verified that for some reason the filter had been turned off. The ISP could not explain why or how this had happened, and did not know how long the filter had been down. They simply turned the filter service back on and apologized. Needless to say, that client now uses a locally controlled and administered firewall.

Policies: Security Services

- Locally control and administer all security services for your network.

- Don't put responsibility for the security of your network in the hands of an external organization.

- Don't rely solely on packet filters for security protection from the Internet.

Reality Check: External Public Servers

Hackers love to embarrass organizations, especially the federal law enforcement bureaus. For security reasons, most government agencies put their Web servers outside firewalls—where they are exploited mercilessly by hackers. The Web sites of the FBI, the CIA, the U.S. Department of Justice, and NASA have all been hacked and modified to cause embarrassment to the agency in question. Check out www.2600.com for details on these and other Web hacking exploits.

Dual Firewalls and Virtual Dual Firewalls

You can reduce the risk of having exposed public servers with two firewalls and two levels of firewall protection. Basically, you put the first firewall at your Internet connection and secure your Web servers behind it. It provides strong security, but allows connection attempts from the Internet for the services you want to provide.

Between that network and your internal network, you place a second firewall with a stronger security policy that simply does not allow external connection attempts and hides the identity of internal clients. Figure 17.10 shows a network with two firewalls providing two levels of security.

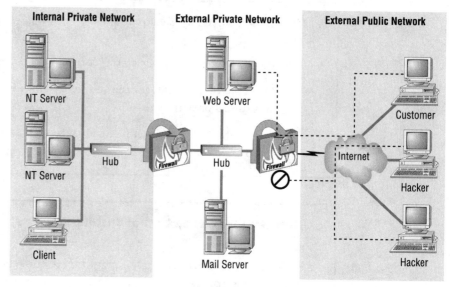

Some firewall products allow the use of dual virtual firewalls by providing a different security policy for each attached interface in the firewall. With three interfaces—external network, internal network, and public server network—you can customize your security policy to block connection attempts to your internal network but pass certain protocols to your public server. This allows you the functionality of two firewalls using a single product. This is sometimes referred to as a *demilitarized zone* or *trihomed firewalls*. Figure 17.11 shows a trihomed firewall with different security settings for each network.

Dual Firewalls (or trihomed firewalls that provide different security settings for each adapter) are the best bet. Keep in mind that both firewalls don't have to be of the same type—the front firewall can be a simple packet filter, but the back firewall should be a strong enterprise-quality firewall that provides the utmost in security.

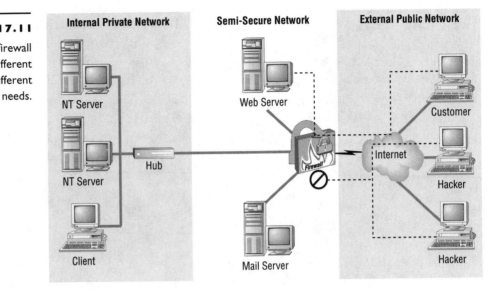

FIGURE 17.11

A trihomed firewall provides different security for different needs.

Enterprise Firewalls

Enterprise firewalls are those products that share a single centralized firewall policy among multiple firewalls. Enterprise firewalls allow you to retain central control of security policy without having to worry about whether or not the policy is correctly implemented on each of the firewalls in your organization. The firewall policy is usually defined on a security workstation, and then replicated to each firewall in your organization using some means of secure authentication.

Disconnection

The most secure way to provide service on the Internet and access for internal users is not to connect your internal network to the Internet at all, but to have a separate network used only for Internet-related services. Figure 17.12 shows a network that is disconnected from the Internet.

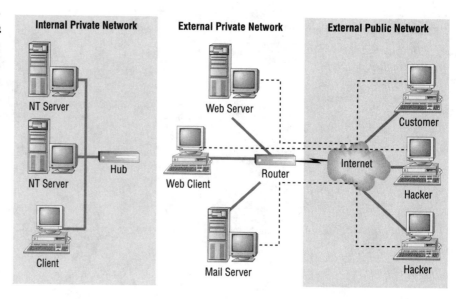

FIGURE 17.12

The disconnected security model provides the most protection from Internet intrusion.

This method is absolutely impenetrable from the Internet because no connection exists between the internal and the external networks. The public access servers for Web, FTP, and mail are located on a small network segment that is attached to the Internet along with a few clients. The client stations contain e-mail, news, and Web readers but no sensitive information. Employees travel to the external clients to check their e-mail, browse the Web, or perform any other Internet-related task.

This model has three very important benefits:

- The private network is absolutely secure. Data can't flow freely between the external and internal networks. You may consider putting a high-capacity removable media drive on one of the clients to facilitate large file transfers when necessary—but this can be a security problem!

- It's free. It doesn't require esoteric software or sophisticated hardware, and you can use outdated computers for the client stations.

- It provides a natural disincentive for employees to waste time surfing the Web randomly or downloading content that could cause legal liability problems.

And of course, there is one very important detractor: Employees hate it. They have to travel to access stations, which are typically located in one central area. Transferring files becomes problematic. It can cause a work bottleneck if there aren't enough access stations. Many employees simply won't use it, which reduces the efficiency of e-mail and other such important business tools.

In a nutshell, disconnection is the most secure and the least efficient way to connect your employees to the Internet.

WARNING

The disconnected security model provides the most incentive for an employee to blow off your security policy and dial up the Internet with his modem. Make sure your security policy can prevent that and that your users understand why you've chosen this model.

Policies: Disconnected Networks

- Don't attach your network to public networks if that can possibly be avoided. Use the disconnected network model to provide Internet access to your users rather than to your network.

- Use a Web and FTP hosting service rather than computers on your own network to provide your customers with information about your company. This puts the Web hosting agency at risk rather than your own network, and allows you to provide no public services.

Summary

Firewalls are the only reasonably secure way to attach a private network to the Internet. But they cannot guarantee security, and they should be used with the understanding that you must remain vigilant about security on your network.

Firewalls have three basic functions:

- **Packet filtering** allows or rejects connections based on network and transport layer information such as IP address or TCP port number.

- **IP masquerading** hides the identity of internal clients from the external network.

- **Proxy services** stand in for applications by intercepting application requests, fulfilling them on behalf of the client, and providing the results. Proxies allow you to prevent network layer traffic from passing between the private and public networks.

Additionally, most firewalls also provide two convenience functions:

- **Encrypted authentication** allows remote users to prove their identity to the firewall to gain access to internal resources without involving the client or server applications.

- **Encrypted tunnels** establish secure and private links between remote offices over public networks.

Single firewalls can make it difficult to provide complete security because some protocols must either be passed through the firewall or Internet servers must be placed outside the firewall. Dual firewalls, or virtual dual firewalls, solve this problem by allowing two levels of firewalls: one for public servers and a second higher level for private computers. Enterprise firewalls make establishing a uniform security policy easy by replicating the same rule and policy base among all firewalls.

Disconnection makes your private internal network completely secure but far less convenient for internal users.

As with all other security policies, the right method for you depends entirely upon the value of the information you are protecting, the risk of attack, and your budget for securing resources. No single method is correct for every situation.

CHAPTER

18

BackOffice Back Doors

A Windows NT Server computer that is part of your network can do more than just provide file and print services. Additional software packages can run on the file server and support such services as WWW, FTP, e-mail, SQL Database storage, SNA connectivity to mainframes, and network monitoring and management. Microsoft's versions of these server-based applications are bundled in a product called BackOffice, which encompasses any Microsoft product that runs on the Windows NT Server computer (including the Windows NT operating system itself).

Every network service must have a protocol that allows client computers to access that service, and every access point (or protocol) can be used appropriately or misused. It is by misusing protocols (impersonating other users, supplying data in unexpected formats, coercing a service to reveal more than it should) that network intruders gain access to your network. Adding these services to your network by installing BackOffice products therefore potentially increases your network's vulnerability to hackers.

The purpose of this chapter is not to tell you how to install or even how to use the BackOffice products. Instead, this chapter guides you through each of the products from the viewpoint of which features are tools to help secure your network and which features are potential targets for network intruders to attack. Some specific recommendations for how to install each product are included here and will help you make your network more useful, while also keeping it secure from network intrusion.

The Essentials of Microsoft BackOffice

What is Microsoft BackOffice? To answer that question you can look at Microsoft's other popular "office" product. Microsoft's Office suite of applications provides the essential tools needed for individual productivity in most business environments. All of the Office programs run on the client computer. In comparison, Microsoft's BackOffice suite of applications provides the essential tools needed for group productivity in most business environments, and BackOffice software runs on a network server computer. Figure 18.1 illustrates the difference between Office and BackOffice software.

Application Software

Word Processors

Spreadsheets

Presentation Packages

Computer-Aided Design Software

Graphics and Illustration Software

E-Mail Clients

Web Browsers

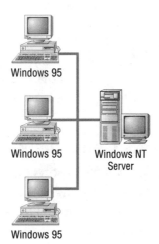

Windows 95

Windows 95

Windows 95

Windows NT Server

Network Service Software (BackOffice)

File Server Software

E-Mail Storage and Forwarding Software

HTTP, FTP, and Gopher Servers

Network Monitoring Tools

SQL Databases

Network Border Security Tools

BackOffice is not just one software product or one collection of software products. It is the name for all Microsoft software that runs on a Windows NT Server computer, including the Windows NT Server operating system itself. This is true regardless of whether the software is bundled with other BackOffice software, as is the case for BackOffice 2.5. SMS Server, BackOffice 2.5, Internet Information Server, and Index Server are all BackOffice products.

> **Terminology**
>
> - **BackOffice:** A suite of Microsoft software packages that run on Windows NT Server computers and provide network services such as e-mail exchange, WWW hosting, network monitoring, and relational data storage.
>
> - **BackOffice 2.5:** The set of BackOffice software collected and distributed as one product in 1996 by Microsoft.

All of the BackOffice software packages provide services over the LAN or Internet to client software on client computers. BackOffice includes Windows NT Server, which provides file and print services for a network, as well as server software for e-mail, WWW, FTP, Gopher, databases, mainframe connections, and network monitoring and control.

 BackOffice 2.5 contains a complete set of the server software. However, many of these software products have been updated or added to since the BackOffice 2.5 collection was assembled into one product.

BackOffice 2.5 Components

In 1996 Microsoft collected the software packages that fell under Microsoft's BackOffice product category and bundled them to sell as one product: BackOffice 2.5. The software packages included in that product (and their version numbers) are as follows:

- **NT Server 4:** All of the BackOffice packages run under Windows NT Server, which also provides file and print services for the network.

- **Internet Information Server 2.0:** IIS provides WWW, FTP, and Gopher services on the Internet or on an intranet or extranet.

- **FrontPage 1.1:** FrontPage helps a Web site administrator or creator manage Web content.

- **Index Server 1.1:** This software package creates a catalog of the information stored on a WWW server and provides a friendly, Web-based interface for searching that information.

- **Proxy Server 1.0:** Proxy Server increases security by hiding the identity of Internet clients on a network from the Internet. It also improves performance by caching frequently accessed HTML pages.

- **Exchange Server 4.0:** Exchange Server routes mail in to and out of a LAN. It also stores mail for LAN e-mail clients and supports network scheduling using the Schedule+ package.

- **SQL Server 6.5:** SQL Server hosts database information and performs database operations directly on the server that stores the actual database files. An SQL Server-based database can support many more users than a LAN-based database such as Microsoft Access.

- **SNA Server 3.0:** This product mediates connections between PCs on a LAN and IBM mainframes and minicomputers.

- **Systems Management Server 1.2:** SMS provides the network administrator with tools for monitoring network activity and managing desktop operating systems over the network.

What's New with BackOffice Products

As we mentioned earlier, Microsoft has updated many of the BackOffice 2.5 software packages since their inclusion in the BackOffice 2.5 package. The following list is not exhaustive because Microsoft continues to update and improve their products, but some changes to the BackOffice products are:

- **Internet Information Server 3.0:** This update to IIS 2.0 includes new features, not the least of which is support for dynamically generated content with Active Server Pages.

- **FrontPage 97:** This product has additional features for directly managing HTML pages stored on WWW servers using FrontPage Server Extensions.

- **Proxy Server 2.0:** Additional packet filtering capabilities as well as WinSock proxy support make it possible to use Proxy Server 2.0 as a firewall as well as an HTTP proxy server.

- **Site Server 1.0:** This product helps an administrator of multiple WWW sites manage Web content.

- **Exchange Server 5.0:** Version 5.0 of Exchange Server includes support for Internet News. Support for SSL provides for secure access to mailboxes and news from Web browsers over the Internet.

Evaluating BackOffice Services

Every server-based software package (including any of the BackOffice products) must be examined before you install it on your server to evaluate its impact on security. Otherwise, you may leave your network open to attack even if you have implemented strong Windows NT user account, file, and directory security on your server computer.

You must exercise caution with BackOffice services because information you might want to protect (such as e-mail or FTP files) flows through these services, and these services must often use administrator-like privileges to perform their functions. The danger is that a hacker could subvert a server-based package and use those administrator privileges to compromise your network security.

In general, the more powerful and useful a network service is the more vulnerable that service is to network attack. With e-mail, for example, all you can do is send messages from one computer to another; so the most mischief a hacker can do with e-mail is to snoop on other people's e-mail, intercept e-mail, and forge new e-mail.

Internet Information Server, on the other hand, accepts requests for FTP, HTTP, and Gopher data, processes those requests, runs programs on the server computer (CGI, ISAPI, or ASP) to generate the desired results, and sends the results to the network client. Since IIS can do so much more than a simple e-mail server, a hacker can trick an improperly secured IIS into running unauthorized programs, sending private files, deleting files, storing illicit data, or even crashing the server.

In order to secure each of the BackOffice services, you have to be familiar with how the service works and what its security weaknesses are. The location of the service in relation to your network (principally whether the service is hosted inside your LAN, outside your LAN, or on the firewall) determines the types of attacks the service must be able to withstand.

An Internet Information Server, for example, must be able to repel any kind of Internet attack because IIS servers are often set up outside of a company's firewall. On the other hand, SQL servers are most often implemented inside the firewall on the company's LAN. Therefore, they are more likely to be attacked by users who already have network accounts (either by employees attempting to get around access permissions or by intruders from the Internet who have circumvented firewall security and have most likely obtained some network account names and passwords).

Policies: Server Location

- Install Internet servers outside your firewall (or between your outer and inner firewalls), but install SQL Servers and other BackOffice products inside your firewall.

- Don't use Proxy Server (as a firewall) on the same server as other services (for example, SQL or Exchange, or as the PDC). The more different services you have running on the firewall, the more possible targets a hacker can attack. The firewall should serve a single purpose: to be the firewall. See Chapter 17 for more information on firewalls.

Windows NT Server 4

The Windows NT Server operating system is an important part of Microsoft's BackOffice suite of software. In fact, all of the other BackOffice software runs on top of it and uses NT security. Windows NT must therefore be set up securely for any of the services that run on top of it to be secure. The rest of this book is devoted to describing how to set up NT securely; the following list summarizes a few important NT security principles.

Policies: NT Security

- Choose passwords that are difficult to guess.
- Use NTFS security on all volumes.
- Create domain accounts for users.
- Assign permissions to groups rather than to individual users.
- Remove default Full Control for Everyone permission on volumes.
- Use NetBEUI or NWLink for NetBIOS connectivity.
- Remove NetBIOS binding to the TCP/IP transport protocol.

Microsoft Internet Information Server

Internet Information Server is the most flexible of the BackOffice services because it is the most extensible. IIS is also the platform on which several of the other BackOffice products are built (Microsoft Commercial Internet System and Microsoft Site Server are two examples). IIS comes on the installation CD along with Windows NT Server.

NT Server is a popular platform for hosting Internet sites, so IIS is used very commonly to provide WWW, FTP, and Gopher services on the Internet.

Because IIS is complex and powerful, you must take great care to set it up securely. Figure 18.2 shows the Internet Service Manager program used to configure most of IIS security. When you configure IIS to be secure, you should pay particular attention to the following areas:

- Authentication

- User account rights and privileges

- Directory accessibility

- Client IP address restrictions

- CGI, ISAPI, and ASP safety

Some things you can do to detect security problems or otherwise make your IIS installation more secure include:

- Logging

- Profiling

Authentication

IIS supports three modes of authentication for users accessing IIS via the HTTP protocol. The three modes are anonymous, clear text, and Windows NT Challenge/Response. Which mode browsers of your site will use depends on the kind of Web site you have set up.

If you've set up a Web site to advertise your company's products or services, most of the people who access your site will access it anonymously, because they most likely will not have visited your site before and will not have an account set up for them.

If you are providing an Internet service via your Web site (such as information delivery or e-mail hosting), you must support clear text

FIGURE 18.2

You configure IIS security
from the Internet Service
Manager program.

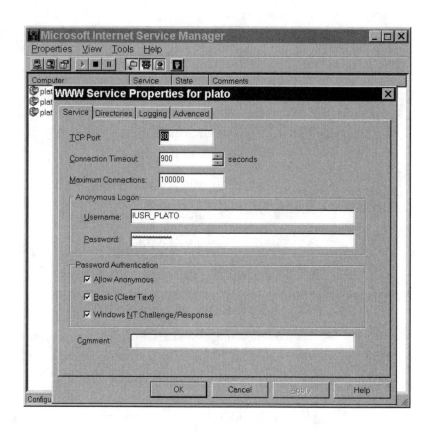

authentication. This is because the user must give a user name and password, but the user may be using a Web browser that does not support Windows NT Challenge/Response. If you are creating a Web site that is primarily for people in your organization to use—and you need the best security you can get—you can use Windows NT Challenge/Response authentication and require your users to connect to your site using Internet Explorer.

The following list contains the modes of authentication and a description of the security issues related to each:

- **Anonymous:** The primary concern with anonymous logon is to make sure that the anonymous account does not have access to any information that you don't want the world to know. The WWW, FTP, and Gopher services use the anonymous account to perform all file access for users that log on anonymously, so you should configure the NTFS permissions for that user to limit access to only public files and directories.

- **Clear Text:** The biggest problem with this method of logon authentication is that the user names and passwords can be *snooped* by computers on networks between the client computer and the server computer. Do not allow users to have the same user names and passwords that are used on your LAN.

- **Windows NT Challenge/Response:** This authentication method is secure, but only a few Web browsers support it (Microsoft's Internet Explorer, primarily). If you require Windows NT Challenge/Response authentication, then you are limiting who may access your Web site.

Because authentication is done using Windows NT account information, the Windows NT Server computer running IIS should be configured as a standalone server outside your firewall (not participating in domain security) or as a member server inside your firewall (participating in but not controlling domain security). This way the user accounts used to authenticate IIS logons can be local accounts rather than domain accounts. The reason the accounts should be local rather than domain accounts is explained in more detail in the next section.

Policies: IIS Authentication

- Install your Internet Information Server for Internet use on a standalone server outside your inner firewall.

User Account Rights and Privileges

Internet Information Server uses Windows NT security mechanisms to control user access to information. Because the accounts authenticated by IIS using clear text are regular Windows NT accounts, a user with an Internet account on your Web server could log on to your network as well. (This is why you *must* disconnect NetBIOS from the TCP/IP transport protocol for that computer.)

For Internet users, you should create only local computer accounts on the Windows NT server hosting IIS. If you create domain accounts for the Internet users you place your entire domain at risk; by creating only local accounts you reduce the risk to just the Windows NT Server computer hosting your Internet site.

While these accounts must have the user right to log on locally (so that IIS can access data on behalf of the user) you should not give these accounts user rights that you might give to regular domain users. You should also be careful about the groups that you make these users a part of, because groups can have user rights associated with them. Remove them from the Domain Users or Users groups, as appropriate; those groups convey user rights that allow network access for user accounts.

From the point of view of the operating system, access via IIS is not really network access. According to Windows NT, network access is access that occurs via NetBIOS, such as file sharing or printing.

Policies: Internet Information Server User Accounts

- Do not make Internet Information Server user accounts members of the Users or Domain Users groups. Avoid making these accounts members of groups that would grant these users additional rights or access permissions.

WWW and FTP Service Directory Accessibility

When you create your Web or FTP site you'll need to establish appropriate service security on the directories for those services. Regular Web directories containing HTML pages, images, and sound files, as well as binary files or application-specific files for downloading, should be marked with only the Read permission in the service's directory properties page for that directory. You should not place scripts in the same readable directories where you place HTML files. Instead, scripts should be placed in a separate directory.

IIS creates a default place for scripts called InetPub\Scripts. To keep scripts organized you can create subdirectories to the Scripts directory or even place your scripts elsewhere.

You should enable the Execute option for directories containing scripts but not the Read option, so that hackers can't read the scripts in order to find security weaknesses in them.

Policies: Internet Information Server Directory Accessibility

- Do not make script virtual directories readable, and do not make other virtual directories executable.

NTFS Directory Accessibility

You should create a Windows NT group for Internet accounts using the User Manager program, and then assign all accounts created for your Web site to that group. You can craft the NTFS permissions for that group to allow access only to the areas of your volumes that you want

Internet users to be able to access. You can create more than one group and give each group different access permissions; this is a good way to provide for (and enforce) different levels of service to different kinds of Internet users.

For example, you could make one set of Web pages accessible to anonymous visitors to your Web site, another set with more information available to regular subscribers, and an even wider range of material available to premium subscribers. NTFS security would ensure that even if an Internet user knew the URL to a restricted HTML page, that user would not be able to access it without being a member of the appropriate Windows NT group.

While IIS independently controls Read and Execute permissions to WWW service directories as well as Read and Write permissions to FTP directories, you should not rely on the IIS permissions to control access to your server for Internet accounts. Hackers can circumvent IIS security by using bugs in IIS or by exploiting naively written CGI scripts, ISAPI applications, or Active Server Pages programs. By maintaining strict NTFS security on your NT server's hard drive you minimize the damage that a hacker can do to your system.

If you want users of your network to be able to create and edit their own Web pages you have two options: You can create a subdirectory in the WWW tree and give the user's regular networking account full control of it or you can create a subdirectory of the user's home directory and use the WWW service's virtual directory capability to make that directory a part of the WWW tree.

If you create user-managed WWW directories in either of the manners described here, do not allow scripts to be executed from that directory. The user might create a script that could be exploited by a hacker to gain entrance to your system.

> **Policies: Internet Information Server Account NTFS Permissions**
>
> ■ Create a group for Internet users; apply permissions to that group account.
>
> ■ Do not allow users to place scripts in their own WWW service virtual directories.

Client IP Address Restrictions

You can deny access to your Internet server for specific computers or ranges of computers using the IP address restrictions of IIS. This feature is most useful when you are creating Web sites for organizational use only—presumably you know the IP addresses from which authorized users can access your site. Since customers may reside anywhere on the Internet, the IP restriction feature is less useful for general access Web sites, although you can use it to deny access to sites or Internet subnets from which you detect a large number of hacking attempts coming.

CGI, ISAPI, and ASP Safety

The most difficult aspect of securing an IIS-based Internet site is ensuring that the CGI, ISAPI, and ASP programs for the Web site don't compromise your Web server security. Unfortunately, the only way to make sure a CGI, ISAPI, or ASP program is safe to put on your server is to examine the program line by line. You must understand the effects of the program and how both IIS and NTFS protect the data on your server.

A carefully written program can provide a useful service such as generating a Web page from a database or storing user comments in a file without leaving your server defenseless on the Internet. A poorly written (or maliciously written) program can give hackers the equivalent of a command line interface to your server.

The Command Line as a CGI Executable

Version 2.0 of IIS included the command-line batch interpreter as a CGI executable. That way, scripts could be written in the batch file language. Unfortunately, it is relatively easy to fool the command-line batch interpreter. By passing extra information in the URL, a hacker can instruct the command-line interpreter to perform undesirable operations. Later versions of IIS have not included the batch file interpreter as a configured CGI executable.

The Security Side of Logging

As we've said throughout the book, security is more than just locking doors or setting NTFS permissions. Security is also watching to see if anybody is trying to get in. The IIS logging features can provide important clues to help you detect an Internet attack in progress, as well as help you tune your Web site for maximum performance and let you know which pages of your site are the most popular.

You can log IIS activity to a text file or to an ODBC database. Logging to the text file is a little faster, but logging to the ODBC database gives you more flexibility in examining the data. You can use the Crystal Reports software that comes with IIS to examine data stored in either manner. In either case, the primary thing you should look for in the log data is a high proportion of unauthorized, forbidden, or not found access attempts coming from one Internet site or user. If the behavior persists and you perceive a threat to your server, you can deny access to the IP address of the client computer of that user.

Policies: Internet Information Server Logging

- Use the logging facilities of IIS to watch for a high proportion of unauthorized, forbidden, and not found access attempts.

Profiling Suspicious Activity

With the Windows NT Performance Monitor you can profile the behavior of the IIS service on your Windows NT Server computer. Because IIS uses the Windows NT security mechanisms, you will actually be monitoring Windows NT counters that are affected by IIS users.

The Server object contains the counters most useful for detecting network attacks. You can instruct the Performance Monitor to write an event to the event log and/or send a message to the administrator when a threshold is exceeded. You should first monitor the counters to determine the normal settings and then instruct the Performance Monitor to send an alarm when a threshold above that value is exceeded. The counters you should watch are a part of the System object and are as follows:

- **Errors Access Permissions:** The user attempted to access a file they did not have permission to access.

- **Errors Granted Access:** The file was opened successfully but the user then attempted to perform an access not permitted to them.

- **Errors Logon:** The user did not have sufficient permission to log on or presented bad credentials.

- **Logons per Second:** A large number of these may indicate that a hacking attempt is in progress.

Microsoft FrontPage 97

FrontPage 97 is the software package from Microsoft that makes it possible for regular users who neither know nor care about how WWW sites are structured or how the data is stored to create and maintain complex Web pages. FrontPage 97 consists of four components—an Explorer, an Editor, a Server, and Server Extensions. Figure 18.3 shows the FrontPage 97 Explorer and Editor.

F I G U R E 18.3

FrontPage 97 enables
you to manage Web
sites remotely.

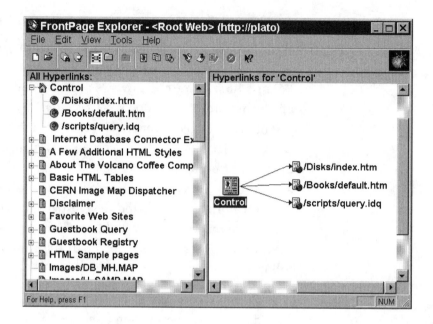

Like Microsoft Word and Microsoft Excel, the FrontPage 97 Explorer and FrontPage 97 Editor programs are just applications that run on the client computers. The security implications for the Explorer and Editor are the same as for other applications—the software will be installed on the client computers and must have space to store files and configuration data.

The FrontPage 97 Server and FrontPage 97 Server Extensions are another matter—FrontPage 97 Server is a simple Web server that provides the FrontPage 97 Explorer with a realistic server environment (which can be accessed by other computers on the Internet). The Server Extensions enable FrontPage to directly manage HTML pages on other WWW servers such as IIS or Netscape Enterprise Server. The extensions also contain software (CGI scripts or ISAPI DLLs) that can be referenced by HTML pages created by FrontPage.

FrontPage 97 Server

FrontPage 97 Server gives users who create and edit WWW pages on their client computers a realistic environment to preview that content in. The server allows the user to preview the Web pages using Web browsers other than the FrontPage 97 Editor. A thorough Web page designer will make sure that the Web pages show up correctly using all of the common browsers—and each browser has its own quirks that affect how it displays information.

The problem with the server part of FrontPage 97 is that, in addition to serving HTML pages to the Explorer, it can also serve HTML pages to other computers in the LAN or even over the Internet. The ephemeral nature of client/server software and the built-in limitations of the FrontPage 97 Server make casual use of FrontPage 97 Server a small security risk. This is especially true if your firewall blocks incoming HTTP traffic to computers other than your Web server. Avoid using FrontPage 97 Server as your permanent Internet server, because it does not provide all the security features that IIS does.

Policies: FrontPage 97 Server

- Do not use FrontPage 97 Server to serve HTML data to users outside your LAN's firewall.

FrontPage 97 Server Extensions

FrontPage 97 makes administering HTML Web sites easy because it allows you to directly edit the HTML pages stored on a WWW server that supports FrontPage 97 Server Extensions. The old-fashioned way to manage a WWW site is to download the HTML page you need to edit from the WWW server computer to the client computer via FTP, edit the page with an HTML editor, and then upload the HTML page to the WWW server.

With FrontPage 97, you can just connect to the WWW server and make the changes to the page with the FrontPage 97 Editor. The Save menu item in the FrontPage 97 Editor's File menu can save the HTML directly to the WWW server. FrontPage 97 also allows you to download entire Web sites, edit offline, and then publish the changes back to the WWW server without requiring you to use FTP or other tedious utilities.

Microsoft supplies FrontPage 97 Server Extensions for other WWW service platforms, including UNIX WWW servers. The Server Extensions packages on these platforms consist of complex CGI scripts that implement the same functionality as do the ISAPI DLLs for server extensions under Internet Information Server.

WARNING The CGI scripts for UNIX Web servers are more limited in their security implementation than the ISAPI DLLs are, and hackers have exploited weaknesses in Server Extensions for UNIX Web servers. (Two such weaknesses are the requirement for any Web administrator to be able to write to the configuration files, and the ability of a Web administrator of one virtual Web to be able to modify the content of another virtual Web.) FrontPage Server Extensions for IIS is not without its own security problems, but the problems are different from the Server Extensions for UNIX Web servers problems.

Although the FrontPage 97 Server Extensions for IIS doesn't have the same problems Server Extensions for UNIX does, Server Extensions for IIS can still pose a significant security risk to your network. If you use the Server Extensions package you must install it properly on your Windows NT Server computer, and you must constantly update the version of Server Extensions on your server to counteract bugs that hackers know how to exploit.

The following sections cover the two biggest concerns with FrontPage Server Extensions for IIS.

Administer, Author, and Browse Rights

When you install the server extensions you'll be asked which account you'll use to administer the FrontPage webs (FrontPage calls any distinctly managed portion of a Web site on a Web server a "web"). This account must exist on the Windows NT server and it must have NTFS permissions to write to the WWW service's virtual directories. You should not use the Windows NT server's Administrator account or your network's domain Administrator account to administer your FrontPage web—a regular user account is sufficient if it has the necessary file permissions for the WWW service's directories.

Rather than giving content developers complete control of your Web site you should give their accounts Author rights to Web content. You can enforce restrictions on what the users may edit by assigning NTFS permissions for those user accounts on the directories corresponding to WWW service virtual directories.

Web Bots

Web bots are FrontPage 97 components that perform commonly used functions in Web pages, such as presenting confirmations for submitted HTML forms, creating automatic tables of contents for Web sites, counting the number of times a page has been accessed, and presenting timestamp information about the page. You don't have to create CGI scripts or ASP programs to perform these tasks; Microsoft has already done it for you. These bots can save a Web administrator a lot of time and effort, but sometimes they introduce new security holes in the process.

Two areas where hackers have found weaknesses are the Save Results web bot and the Discussion web bot. Both bots accept text from the user and store the text to a results file. Neither web bot scans the text for HTML tags, so a user can insert tags that will present forms or even program scripts to the next browser of the saved data. A program thus embedded could exploit other server or browser bugs to give the hacker greater control over the server or client computer. You should update your server to the latest version of the FrontPage Server Extensions software to avoid these and other security problems.

Policies: FrontPage 97 Server Extensions

- Do not use the Windows NT Administrator account as the FrontPage Administrator account.

- Grant Author privileges to Web page designers rather than creating Administrator accounts for them.

- Use the latest version of FrontPage 97 to avoid security problems.

Microsoft Index Server

You can make it easy for people on the Internet to browse your Web site by installing Index Server on your Internet Information Server computer. Index Server is an ISAPI DLL (a linked executable file that Internet Information Server can call quickly and efficiently). It periodically scans the data stored in WWW service virtual directories and creates a catalog of the words in all of the documents and which files those words can be found in.

When a user queries Index Server, the server looks up the queried words in the catalog and returns an HTML page that contains references to the documents that contain those words. You control Index Server from Web pages that are installed when Index Server is installed. Figure 18.4 shows the top level Index Server page.

Index Server operation is automatic; you don't have to do any configuration beyond simply installing the software to allow users to query your site. The default configuration may not be what you want, however; Index Server may return references to documents that you don't

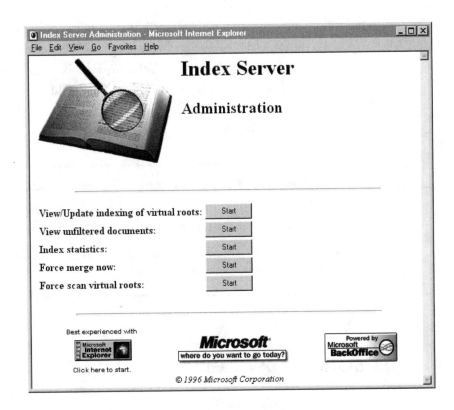

FIGURE 18.4

You manage Index Server's operation from the Index Server administrative pages.

want Internet users to see. By default, Index Server indexes all of the WWW service virtual directories published by IIS, and it will return references to documents other than HTML or text files.

When you install Index Server you should use the Index Server administrative Web pages to update the indexed virtual roots. You should prevent Index Server from scanning virtual roots that contain scripts. You can also configure Index Server to index only files that Index Server can read (other files are just indexed by file name and file attributes). Indexing by just certain file types can speed up queries. It will keep Index Server from returning program scripts and other security-sensitive files that are not specifically recognized by Index Server as files containing textual data.

Index Server indexes all of the virtual directories of your Web site, but it respects the browsing user's NTFS permissions when returning the list of files that match their query. Because only those files that the user would be able to access directly will be returned in the query results page, you can use NTFS permissions for users and groups to restrict the data returned to the user.

Policies: Index Server

- Limit the virtual directories indexed by Index Server.

- Use NTFS permissions to limit the results that will be returned in response to a user's query.

Microsoft Proxy Server

Most services running on Windows NT Server (such as Internet Information Server, FrontPage Server Extensions, and Exchange Server) provide back doors that must be securely locked and watched by the system administrator. However, Microsoft Proxy Server is more of a checkpoint through which all other traffic must pass.

True security is never automatic, so you must still be alert for network intrusion, but Proxy Server gives you a place to concentrate your attention and therefore makes securing your network easier. Proxy Server also makes it more difficult for hackers to know what your network contains by making your entire network appear to be just one computer attached to the Internet. Figure 18.5 shows the Proxy Server administrative tool.

Microsoft Proxy Server does more than just proxy HTML content. It can also be a proxy server for other kinds of Internet traffic, including SMTP, POP, FTP, Gopher, and Telnet.

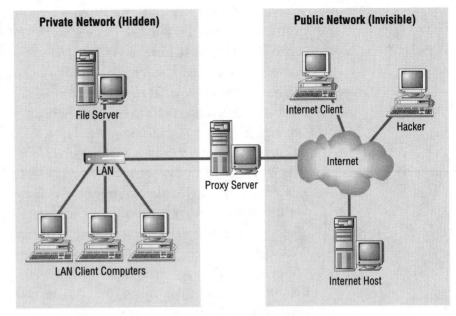

FIGURE 18.5

Using Proxy Server you can hide your entire network behind a single Windows NT Server computer connected to the Internet.

Chapter 17 describes how to use proxies, packet filters, and firewalls. Refer to that chapter for guidelines about what a proxy server can do for you and what ports to allow through the Proxy Server packet filter.

In networks where all of the client computers are Windows 95 computers, your Windows 95 computers can redirect all of their WinSock traffic to the Proxy Server. (WinSock is the Internet programming interface for Windows software.) You can select which ports you will allow in and out of your network, and the network traffic for your Windows 95 clients will appear to come from the Proxy Server computer, rather than from the client computers inside your network.

This feature even makes it possible for your Windows 95 computers to use Internet client software. This includes the America Online client and any other proprietary client that expects to connect directly to the network and cannot be configured to pass through a regular proxy server. Since the WinSock traffic is sent to the Proxy Server using a Net-BIOS connection, the Windows 95 clients that use the WinSock proxy service do not have to have the TCP/IP transport protocol installed, and that makes your LAN even more secure from attacks from the Internet.

You can use the Virtual Hosting feature of Microsoft Proxy Server to move your Internet servers inside your firewall. Proxy Server can accept connections from external computers (such as Web browsers from elsewhere on the Internet) and pass the connections through to the internal WWW, FTP, or Gopher servers.

Virtual Hosting provides greater protection to your Internet servers, but they are still at risk due to the security implications inherent in allowing Internet users to interact with programs on them, especially CGI, ISAPI, or Active Server Pages programs on a WWW server. A compromised Internet server is more dangerous inside your firewall than outside it, which is why so many security-conscious companies leave their Web servers "out in the cold."

Proxy Server 2.0 provides many of the features traditionally associated with firewall products, including a packet filter (see Chapter 17 for more information on packet filters and firewalls). If you decide to use Proxy Server as your firewall software, you should disable all of the nonessential services provided by Windows NT Server, especially the NetBIOS binding to the network adapters, so that hackers do not exploit them to gain entrance to your network.

Policies: Proxy Server

- Use Proxy Server to hide the size and nature of your network, as well as to speed up Internet access and to enforce network security.

Reality Check: Address Laundering

As always, you should watch for the latest versions of operating system and service software, because software venders fix security problems by releasing new versions of their software. An earlier version of Proxy Server had a weakness that meant a user on the Internet could Telnet in to the Proxy Server service and then Telnet back out to elsewhere on the Internet. The security hole did not compromise LAN security, but it did allow external users to "launder" their Internet traffic, because the IP header information would point back to the Proxy Server rather than to the Internet user.

A hacker used this bug to send harassing e-mail in response to senders of bulk e-mail (also called *spammers*). Only carelessness on the part of the e-mail sender allowed the system administrator to determine what was going on. Because the Internet traffic led back to the Proxy Server, the proprietors of that LAN could have been held responsible for the actions of the hacker (rightly or not). That's why it is important to keep even relatively minor security problems like this, which do not threaten LAN security, under control.

Microsoft Site Server and Microsoft Commercial Internet System

Microsoft Site Server and Microsoft Commercial Internet System both consist of ISAPI extensions to Internet Information Server. They also have other software packages that make developing Web content easier, managing Web servers less tedious, or interpreting Web server activity less difficult. The ISAPI extensions also extend the functionality of Internet Information Server, providing the capability to use services such as Internet Chat, Internet News, Web personalization for individual Internet users, and Internet shopping.

These two software bundles contain components that are far too complex for a comprehensive overview here. A complete security analysis of all of Microsoft Site Server and Microsoft Commercial Internet System deserves a book of its own. However, we do have space for a note on what you should be aware of about each product. At the time of this writing, the components of the two software products are as follows:

- Microsoft Visual InterDev

- Microsoft Posting Acceptor

- Microsoft Content Replication System

- Internet Locator Server

- Microsoft Site Analyst

- Microsoft Usage Analyst

- Chat

- Mail

- News

- Membership

- Address Book

- Merchant Server

- Personalization

We look at each of these components briefly in the following sections.

Microsoft Visual InterDev

Microsoft Visual InterDev is a client software component that helps you develop Web content, including ASP scripts and other server-based programs. So your primary security concern with it is with the scripts and server-based programs you can develop, not with Visual InterDev itself.

Any server-based program, whether it uses CGI, ISAPI, or Active Server Pages, is only as secure as its creator knows how to make it. The program components that come with Visual InterDev have been tested carefully by Microsoft, but you should be careful about how you use these programs, because an otherwise secure program installed improperly (such as with NTFS permissions or IIS virtual directory permissions that are too broad) can open up your IIS server to outside control.

Microsoft Posting Acceptor

This ISAPI DLL for IIS extends your Web server to support the industry standard POST options (used by Netscape browsers and by Microsoft's Content Replication System) to place HTML pages and other Web content on a WWW server. Since the Posting Acceptor requires the posting user to use IIS authentication, and since IIS uses the NTFS permissions of that user to restrict where a user may store files, it is vitally important that you implement strict NTFS security to protect your Web site content.

Posted data is placed on your server in the context of the virtual directory specified by the URL of the POST request or in a subdirectory of that virtual directory, rather than in the context of the server's hard drives and volumes. You can limit your Web server's vulnerability by never making program file directories or the system directory a part of your Web server's virtual directories.

You should also carefully control which users have NTFS permissions to write to any virtual directories that have the WWW Execute permission set, including the Scripts directory and subdirectories. With this permission, an Internet user could upload a script and have it executed on the server.

Microsoft Content Replication System

A large part of an Internet server administrator's job is to see that the Web content of the server is moved from where it is developed on the LAN to the server and that it is updated regularly. As the volume and scope of a Web site's content increases, the process of moving data, maintaining the consistency of the data, and making sure that the correct versions of the Web data are in the right places on the Web server can consume all of an administrator's time.

Using the Microsoft Content Replication System (CRS), you can automate the process of transferring data from Web developers to the Web site (or sites). This allows the administrator to concentrate on that most important aspect of the network: its security (what else?).

There are a few things to keep in mind when using CRS. The first is that CRS requires a service account with a user name and password on the Windows NT server that the data will be replicated to. This account should not be the administrative account for the Windows NT computer, or for the Windows NT domain. The account should have just the sufficient NTFS permissions to store data to the content areas of the server that that data will be replicated to. An account with permissions on the server that are too broad could be exploited to gain control of the Windows NT server.

CRS uses the concept of projects to manage replication. A CRS administrator can create projects that describe the source(s) and destination(s) of a replication event. The replication event for that project can then be configured to take place automatically, periodically, or when initiated by a CRS user. While a CRS administrator can control all of the aspects of CRS activity, a CRS user can merely start, stop, query, and roll back replications.

WARNING You should make sure when creating CRS projects that a user cannot create CGI scripts, ISAPI DLLs, or ASP programs that will be uploaded via CRS (using the permissions of the service account) to an area that the user would not ordinarily be able to place scripts. This compromises your system's security.

Policies: Microsoft Content Replication System

- Verify that CRS will not allow a developer of Web content to place a script in a location on the Web server that the developer would otherwise not be able to access.

- Do not use the Windows NT administrative account as the service account for CRS.

Internet Locator Server

Internet Locator Server can help to build a sense of community among the users of your Internet site by allowing them to "see" when and where other people are accessing your site. Using the Chat, Mail, and Address book services, Internet users on your system can communicate with other users in real-time or via e-mail.

The only real security problem with Internet Locator Server (that has been discovered as of this writing) is that it gives a hacker more information to go on in attempting to penetrate your network security. You should weigh the benefit of your Internet users being able to find each other against the drawback of hackers being able to discover the names of your users and then attempt to guess their passwords.

Microsoft Site Analyst

You can use Microsoft Site Analyst to view how your own site is structured and you can use it to analyze other sites over the Internet. If you set up proper security on your server, the Site Analyst package will have little impact on the security of your network.

The most dangerous use the Site Analyst software could be put to is to scan your site for script files in directories for which you have neglected to remove the IIS Read permissions. The purpose of Microsoft Site Analyst is simply to automate browsing operations any Internet user can perform using browser software such as Internet

Explorer or Netscape. But just as a spreadsheet package automates operations an accountant can perform with a pencil and calculator, Site Analyst makes gathering the information so much easier.

Microsoft Usage Analyst

Microsoft's Usage Analyst software can help you secure your Internet Information Server. Usage Analyst can profile the Internet traffic to your Web site, revealing access patterns that can indicate a network attack in progress. Microsoft Usage Analyst will report on information logged by standard IIS services as well as the additional services provided by the Microsoft Site Server and Microsoft Internet Commerce System ISAPI packages.

You should configure Usage Analyst to watch for an unusual amount of requests for the same page on your site, especially from the same IP address. You should also configure Usage Analyst to look for too many GUID create messages (messages to create Internet commerce accounts) in relation to the number of GUID changes (updates to the status of Internet commerce accounts). Too many messages asking to create accounts can indicate that a user is attempting to find accounts that have already been created in order to try to break into them.

Policies: Microsoft Usage Analyst

- Use Microsoft Usage Analyst to watch for GUID proliferation.

Chat

When you create a Microsoft Commercial Internet System site with Chat, Mail, and News, you are creating the equivalent of an online service like America Online or CompuServe. When you do so, you face the same problems that your larger online service cousins face. One such problem is users attempting to convince other users to give them their user names and passwords. Users may pretend to be sysops (system operators), network technicians, or account and billing operators.

You should establish a policy of never asking a customer for their user name and password. Make sure that the users of your system know that no authorized individual from your organization will ask for a user name and password. (Chapter 2 contains details of strategies to ensure password security.) A logon banner or an introductory e-mail message that is sent to the user when they subscribe to your site can inform new users of your policy and warn other users against attempting that sort of a scam.

Policies: MCIS Chat

- Inform users that system operators will never ask for the user's user name or password over the chat or mail system.

Mail

The problem with Mail service provided by the Microsoft Commercial Internet System is the same problem any Internet mail system faces: You can't be sure exactly who sent any particular e-mail message. E-mail sent over the Internet can be read by any host on any network between the sender and the recipient. If you use a client e-mail package that supports encryption and authentication to connect to MCIS e-mail, then you can use the security features of the client. MCIS does not provide those features for you.

News

Your primary concern when using the News feature of MCIS should be to ensure that newsgroups you create for the internal use of your organization or for use of subscribers to your site don't get out to the Internet at large. Network administrators commonly use the News feature of MCIS to host Internet News (brought in via NNTP) on the Internet server, and then use the same server to host private newsgroups. This is a perfectly acceptable configuration, but only if you establish security correctly.

Microsoft Commercial Internet System uses NTFS security features to protect news articles. So you should make sure the file system directories that contain private newsgroups are configured with NTFS Read permission for only the authenticated users and groups that should be privy to the information (in addition to the Full Control permissions for the Administrator and MCIS accounts). Within an organizational intranet using MCIS, news articles are transferred via the Microsoft Content Replication System, so you should take care that CRS is configured properly.

Membership

You can extend the number of users your Web site can support without bloating the user database on your Windows NT Server computer with the Membership component of MCIS. A Membership back-end component for IIS uses an SQL database to store user information, and there is a Lightweight Directory Access Protocol (LDAP) interface for other components of the MCIS package to use to access membership information.

One useful feature of the Membership back-end services is that you can configure one back-end component on one IIS server to trust membership information from a back-end service on another IIS server. The security implication is that you must trust the administrator of that other server not to compromise your security. You must also be careful about how you configure the SQL server with which the back-end service will be communicating. You should use the same precautions you use when configuring SQL to talk to Merchant Server (which is covered a bit later in this section).

Address Book

The Address Book component of MCIS has the same security implications that the Internet Locator Server component has: namely, the more information a hacker can get about your system's users, the easier it is for them to break into your system. You can use the Address Book's administrative features to limit what information is given out about your users, and users can also select what information they want to make available.

Merchant Server

Merchant Server is what puts the commerce in Microsoft Commercial Internet System. Merchant Server presents the Internet user with a catalog of options, allows them to select from the options, tabulates the results, accepts payment options, confirms orders, and can even accept and check credit card numbers if the right software components are in place. You can build a complete and secure Web-based business around Merchant Server, or put whatever business you do offline on the Web.

Because Merchant Server handles such important information as people's credit card numbers and personal data (shipping addresses, phone numbers, etc.), it is a prime target for hackers that break into systems for financial gain. Fortunately, Microsoft has provided a host of tools to protect that information, and Merchant Server is constructed in a manner that emphasizes security.

Customer information is stored on a SQL server that can be run on a computer other than the one hosting Internet Information Server. In addition, Merchant Server uses IIS's Secure Socket Layer support to keep transactions between the server and customers secure. It uses NTFS permissions to restrict access to Web server information.

As with any other service you run on your server computer, there are many details involved in configuring Merchant Server so that it is secure against network intrusion. We list some of the specific details on which Merchant Server security hinges.

Policies: Merchant Server

- Do not configure the ODBC data source to use trusted connections. Instead use the Auth_include.asp to configure the database account to use a specific account that has SELECT permissions on product tables and SELECT/INSERT permissions on shopper, basket, and receipt tables. Do not configure the database account to be a Computer or Domain Administrator account.

- Keep sensitive information out of the shopper table, because that information is accessible to a Web browser. Use both a secure port (HTTPS) and Secure Socket Layer encryption, and use strong NTFS permissions restrictions on WWW service virtual directories.

- Use the VerifyWith method to ensure that Web page content (hidden fields) are not modified between being sent to the browser and received back from the browser. (Modified content may indicate a man-in-the-middle attack on the information exchange between the server and the browser.) Use POST rather than GET to transmit information from the clients to the server.

Personalization

One way to make your Web site more useful to clients who access it over the Internet is to allow them to choose which types of information it will present to them. The MCIS Personalization system can store a user's preferences so the next time that user browses the Web site they are shown information that matches their interests.

However, the Personalization system requires that all users have full access to the User Property database files on the IIS computer. For this reason if you use the Personalization system you should scrutinize all other aspects of your Internet server security. You should make sure that Internet users can't place files not related to the Personalization system into the directory containing the User Property database files, and you should regularly scan that directory for inappropriate files.

Microsoft Exchange Server

One of the key components of Microsoft BackOffice is Microsoft Exchange Server. The primary use for Exchange Server is to support LAN e-mail and to route e-mail into and out of the LAN.

Exchange Server does more than just store e-mail for LAN user accounts, though. It converts e-mail from one standard to another; provides for distribution lists, public folders, encryption, key management, and replication between Exchange servers (even over WAN links); and integrates with other client software packages such as Schedule+ and Outlook 97. Exchange Server also supports several ways of accessing the e-mail and other services it supports, including connecting to the server using MAPI, SMTP, HTTP, and POP. Figure 18.6 shows the Microsoft Exchange Server administration tool.

One characteristic that makes Exchange Server different from most BackOffice products is that Exchange user accounts are not the same as Domain or Windows NT Server user accounts. Users must have a separate account name and password for Exchange Server. Exchange client software can store a user's Exchange account name and password so the user doesn't have to remember them, but allowing the client software to store the passwords is a bad security practice. Any other user could use another user's computer (if it were left logged onto the network) to access exchange, and would then be able to access Exchange mailboxes and other services as that user.

Sometimes e-mail cannot be delivered to the user it is addressed to—either because the user account has been deleted, or because the account does not exist. (This is often the case when the sender of an e-mail message misspells the recipient's e-mail account name.) E-mail of this nature must go somewhere, so when you set up a Message Transfer Agent you specify a Dead Letter account. This account will receive all mail sent to your system that cannot be delivered to a valid account.

F I G U R E 18.6

You can add and remove
user e-mail accounts, as
well as configure the
users' environments,
from the Exchange Server
administrative tool.

Because e-mail that cannot be delivered may contain important and sensitive information, the owner of this account should be someone you trust. The owner of this account is usually the system administrator, because the system administrator needs to know when there is a problem delivering e-mail.

Since the POP protocol does not encrypt user names and passwords, you should discourage or disallow users from using POP over the Internet to read their mail. You should instead help them establish secure, encrypted communications (using PPTP or SSL) over which they can safely check their mail.

When you install Exchange Server you'll be asked for a Windows NT account that will serve as the service account for Microsoft Exchange. You should not use a domain or Windows NT Server administrative account as the service account. Instead you should create an account with sufficient permissions to manage Exchange Server data but nothing more.

If you install a Key Management Server, your Exchange Server can encrypt and digitally sign e-mail sent between Exchange Server mailboxes. This provides considerably more security to e-mail sent over the Internet or other insecure networks (otherwise there is none at all). Once the Key Management Server is installed and configured properly, the Microsoft Exchange and Outlook e-mail clients will have a new button that instructs Exchange to encrypt the message being sent. Exchange Server will encrypt the message rather than requiring the user on the client computer to encrypt it.

Policies: Exchange Server

- Caution users about client software that remembers passwords, or disable the remember password feature.

- Do not use POP over an unencrypted Internet connection.

- Install Key Management Server.

- Select someone you trust to be the recipient of Dead Letter e-mail.

Microsoft Systems Management Server

The applications of Microsoft Systems Management Server to network security are so vast that the topic deserves a book all to itself. In fact, there are a number of books you can buy that show you how to use Systems Management Server in your network. You can also refer to the software documentation for instructions on setting up and using SMS. In this section we cover a few basic guidelines and suggestions for using SMS to secure your network. Figure 18.7 shows the SMS packet sniffer.

FIGURE 18.7

Using Microsoft Systems Management Server's packet sniffer you can monitor your network traffic directly.

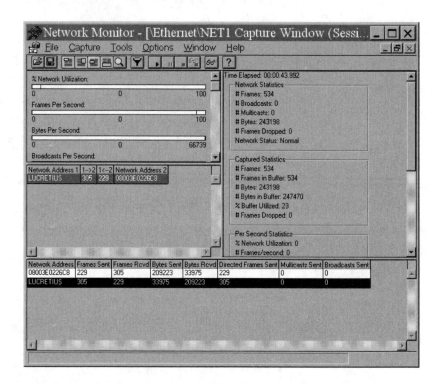

Systems Management Server is comprised of several software components, including the SMS services that run on a Windows NT Server computer, the SMS Administrator program from which you control SMS activity, and the SMS client components which run on client computers in the network. General uses for SMS include:

- Automatic inventory of computer hardware and software
- Remote diagnosis

- Software distribution

- Server-based software management

- Network diagnosis

- Network monitoring

When you install SMS you will be asked for an SMS system administrator account name and password. This account should not be confused with the Windows NT system administrator account, and you should not leave it with the default (blank) password.

WARNING Since SMS can configure client computers to run arbitrary log-on scripts when the users log on to the domain, you should carefully guard the administrative account privileges.

SMS also requires a service account for Windows NT, under which the server program performs all of its file and object access on the local computer. You should create a sufficiently privileged account for SMS rather than just using the Windows NT account for the domain administrator or server administrator. By creating a separate account you limit somewhat the damage that can be done if a user gains control of SMS.

Once you have SMS installed, you can use it for a number of security-related purposes. You can use the inventory feature to watch for changes in client computer configuration—a change in operating system, identification, network configuration, installed software, or supported services can indicate a computer that is being reconfigured to circumvent LAN security.

You can use the Network Monitor features of SMS to watch the network traffic on your LAN. Some specific things you should look for include: unusual use of protocols, such as NWLink traffic coming from your Internet router, or TCP/IP traffic coming from your file and print servers if you have disabled TCP/IP on those computers; inordinate network traffic to or from a particular computer on your network; and other (unauthorized) computers running SMS network monitoring software.

Policies: Systems Management Server

- Do not use a Windows NT administrative account as the service account for SMS.

- Use SMS to track changes in client computer and operating system configuration.

- Use SMS to watch for unusual protocol activity.

- Use SMS to watch for unusual network traffic patterns.

Microsoft SQL Server

The security of SQL Server depends a great deal on the use to which it is put. You will configure an SQL database for use by a Merchant Server Web site differently than you would an SQL database for storing Systems Management Server data, for example. You should establish your security requirements for SQL Server before you install the server software, because your security needs (such as whether you will use Standard, Integrated, or Mixed security) will affect the installation process.

When you install SQL server, you will have the choice of using standard, integrated, or mixed security. With standard security, SQL Server will maintain its own list of users and their passwords, independent of the Windows NT operating system and domain. With integrated security, SQL Server will accept Windows NT account authentication. The integrated authentication will be performed automatically when the user accesses the SQL server database—the user doesn't have to type a user name and password again. Mixed security uses both methods: The user's NT account or a different account independent of Windows NT may be used.

Because Windows NT accounts used to support IIS user activity are more at risk of being compromised by Internet users, you should not use integrated authentication for an SQL Server that is used in support of an Internet Information Server Web site. For a Microsoft Access database or other custom LAN software that uses SQL server to store information, you should use integrated authentication. Domain accounts for your network users are secure (if you have established good security practices in your network) and users will be less likely to share their one account name and password, or use simplistic passwords, if they have just one to remember.

One way to deter connections to your SQL server from the Internet is to use a network stack other than TCP/IP. If you do use SQL Server over the Internet using the TCP/IP network stack, you should use the option to encrypt the link. Encrypted links will require more processing power and bandwidth, but they will protect your data from eavesdropping by intermediate computers in the Internet.

The interactions of a firewall, Internet Information Server, and SQL Server make it difficult to secure an IIS- and SQL-Server-based Web site properly. For maximum protection, the SQL server should reside inside your network firewall.

For an intranet site, the configuration is simple: Both the IIS server and the SQL server will reside inside your firewall because they will only be used by authorized network users. For an Internet site, you have several options:

- Place the SQL server inside your network and place the IIS server outside your firewall. Configure SQL Server to use TCP/IP, and open the ports necessary to allow the SQL server and the IIS server to communicate. Configure the firewall to allow only the IIS server to communicate with the SQL server.

- Locate both the SQL server and the IIS server inside your firewall. Use the Virtual Hosting feature of Proxy Server to allow WWW requests from outside your firewall to reach your IIS server. Configure all of the computers inside your network to use NWLink for file and print services, and configure your servers to use only NWLink in order to reduce their susceptibility to attack from a compromised IIS server inside your LAN.

- Locate both the SQL server and the IIS server outside your firewall. Configure the SQL server to use only NWLink and configure the IIS server to use NWLink to communicate with the SQL server. Configure your router not to pass IPX/SPX packets. The NWLink-only SQL server will therefore not be visible to Internet computers.

Since SQL Server uses the NTFS permissions of the Database Owner Windows NT account, that account must have sufficient permissions to support SQL Server but should not be a Windows NT administrative account. If it were an administrative account, a user who gained control of SQL Server could then affect the operation of the server computer that is hosting the SQL server. Finally, you should not leave the SQL Server system administrator account password in its default (blank) state.

Policies: SQL Server

- Use Standard SQL security for a SQL database accessed by IIS.

- Select a strong password for the SQL Server system administrator account.

- Do not use the Administrative account of Windows NT as the SQL Server administrative account.

Microsoft SNA Server

In this brave new computer world of the Internet, LANs, and Windows 95 you may not expect to have to deal with a mainframe or minicomputer, but many companies still use these large, powerful, and expensive computers. Microcomputers may have taken over all of the individual-sized computing tasks such as word processing and spreadsheet use, but the big computers are still very useful for big computing tasks such as complex mathematical simulations and immense database operations.

IBM has led the business market for a long time in minicomputer and mainframe applications. IBM has its own network architecture, called the Systems Network Architecture (SNA), for connecting to these large computers.

SNA Server is a networking service that runs on a Windows NT Server computer and allows networking clients on a Windows LAN to masquerade as SNA client devices such as TN3270 terminals and printers. The client computers can use the LAN networking media and protocols (Ethernet and NWLink, for example) to communicate with the SNA Server computer, which will translate the data streams to use the standard SNA protocols and network link types in order to maintain the connection with the AS/400 computer or other IBM SNA target computer.

SNA acts both as a gateway to the IBM world of SNA and as a place to enforce security, because a user must have permission from the SNA Server in order to use the SNA gateway.

When you install SNA Server you should install it to an NTFS volume so that Windows NT can control access to the SNA configuration files. Otherwise any user could modify the configuration files and gain access to SNA network services that the user shouldn't be able to use. You should also limit access to the SNA administrative utilities.

You should caution users about their client software's ability to remember passwords. It may be more convenient for the user not to have to remember SNA passwords, but it makes the SNA network vulnerable to a computer left unattended or a client computer whose password file has been cracked. Similarly, the APPC single-sign-on feature can put the SNA network at risk.

Policies: Systems Network Architecture

- Install SNA Server to an NTFS partition.

Summary

The Microsoft BackOffice family of products extends the functionality of your Windows NT Server computers far beyond just file and print services. Each software product has its own security requirements, and as a rule the more useful and flexible a software product is, the more difficult it is to make that product secure.

In many cases the interactions between the BackOffice products (such as between IIS and SQL Server, or SMS and SQL Server) can also present security risks. Only a good understanding of the software product and of Windows NT Server will enable you to create a secure BackOffice environment.

CHAPTER

19

High-Level Service Holes

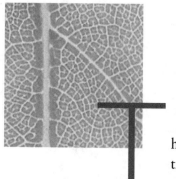

The advantage of a server-based (domain) network is the centralization of administration and security. With the network properly secured and clients configured correctly, there should be little users can do to compromise the network's security.

Unfortunately, it's not that simple. Occasionally a bug is discovered that allows hackers to exploit an innocuous application (such as a Web browser) and gain vital information about the network—or even a password. Unfortunately, a wide variety of bugs of this nature have been discovered recently.

This chapter is a compendium of information about security holes in application software, such as Web browsers, and in the Windows NT operating system. These include accessible copies of passwords, bugs in applications and the NT kernel itself, and denial-of-service attacks, which are designed to crash the Windows NT server.

In general, the security holes described in this chapter are complex and aren't the sort of thing that the average network will be subject to. However, these exploits are well-known in the hacker community, and networks connected to the Internet are particularly vulnerable. Although these aren't the most common security threats to your network, it's a good idea to plan for them just in case you confront them. Fortunately, it's simple to prevent most of these problems before they happen.

This chapter isn't meant as a comprehensive list of bugs that cause security holes—if it were, it would be obsolete by the time you read it. Rather, it's an introduction to some of the most well-known and most dangerous holes. If you learn nothing else from this chapter, you should learn that any application can be a potential security risk. Be sure to keep track of the applications in use on your network.

New security holes are always being found. See the Web site resources listed in Appendix C for sites that will inform you of the latest bugs and security holes in Windows NT and applications.

Password Issues

With Windows NT's password encryption, in theory it should be very difficult for hackers to obtain passwords. While a password can be compromised by a complex brute-force or dictionary attack, you would not expect there to be any way to simply grab a password. Unfortunately, there are several ways to do this, each useful only in certain circumstances. The following sections examine these security holes.

There are also bugs in Internet Explorer that can make passwords accessible, either in encrypted or plaintext form. See the *Web Browser Problems* section later in this chapter for details about these issues.

The Password Cache

Windows 95 includes a password cache feature, which stores encrypted copies of recently used passwords in a file in the Windows directory called USER.PWL, where USER is the user's name. In a system with several user profiles, a separate cache is included for each user.

Unfortunately, the encryption used in these files is not very secure, and has in fact been broken. A public-domain utility called Revelation gives the user the ability to display the passwords in the cache.

To prevent passwords from being cached in Windows 95, change this key in the registry to 1:

```
HKEY_LOCAL_MACHINE\SOFTWARE\Microsoft\Windows\CurrentVersion\
Policies\Network\DisablePwdCaching
```

This vulnerability may not be a major issue if users at Windows 95 workstations have limited privileges. Be sure the Administrator account or other powerful accounts are not used from Windows 95 workstations without first disabling the password cache.

Tweak UI

Tweak UI is an unofficial Microsoft utility that allows extra control of registry parameters in Windows 95 and Windows NT. This utility allows you to do such things as customize the Desktop and control the appearance of shortcuts. The latest version of this utility also includes a Network tab, shown in Figure 19.1.

As the dialog box shown in Figure 19.1 warns, the password you enter here is stored as ASCII text in the registry. Since the registry can

FIGURE 19.1

Tweak UI allows entry of a user name and password.

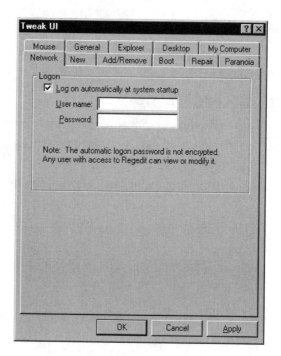

easily be accessed by any user, you should not enter a password in this tab except in systems where security is not a concern. Be sure your users are aware of this issue.

Security Loopholes

Despite programmers' best efforts to make a system secure, security holes deep within the system can surface. For example, a Russian programmer created a program called getadmin.exe that is available on the Internet. When this program is run from a command prompt, it adds the user you specify to the Administrators group. It can be run by any user, and it's completely undetectable.

Needless to say, this is a serious security hole, and it makes many NT servers susceptible to compromise. Microsoft released two hot fixes to address this issue, and it is said to have been fixed. These fixes are included in Windows NT Service Pack 3.

The one thing history teaches us about security holes is that you can never find the last one, so although this hole has been patched, an equally nasty one is certain to pop up in the future. This is why it's important to keep track of the latest hot fixes and service packs.

See Appendix C for a list of online resources, including Microsoft's list of hot fixes and updates.

Denial of Service

Windows NT is susceptible to a wide variety of denial-of-service attacks. These are attacks that, rather than attempt to obtain information or access to the network, simply attempt to crash (or otherwise make inaccessible) the NT server.

Most denial-of-service attacks concern the TCP/IP protocol, and many of them can also affect other systems (such as UNIX) that support these protocols. The most common types of denial-of-service attacks are described in the sections below.

The Ping of Death

The ping utility is a simple UNIX utility that sends a TCP/IP packet to a remote host requesting a response. It's an easy way to diagnose network problems or verify if a host is online. Windows NT also includes an implementation of the ping command, which can be used at the command prompt.

If you think this utility sounds harmless, you're right—except for one recent discovery. It turns out that many machines (including Windows NT and some UNIX servers) don't handle large packets correctly. The ping utility includes an option to vary the size of packets. For example, this command sends a 64K packet to a host:

```
PING -1 65527 -s 1 hostname
```

This command will crash Windows NT 3.51 or 4, or even Windows 95. Microsoft's implementation of TCP/IP doesn't properly fragment large packets such as this one (which rarely occur in normal networking) and the attempt results in a crash. This technique is known on the Internet as the *ping of death*.

Microsoft has created a fix to prevent ping of death attacks, included in Windows NT Service Pack 2. Be sure you have installed this fix on all Windows NT servers, particularly those accessible from the Internet. A fix is also available for Windows 95; see Microsoft's Web site for details.

Ping Storm Attacks

A more severe version of the ping of death attack was recently discovered, and Windows NT 3.51, Windows NT 4, and Windows 95 are all vulnerable to it. In this variation, instead of a single huge packet, several huge packets are sent at once. This is referred to as a *ping storm* or *ping flood* attack.

As with the original ping of death, this causes a server crash. The fix for the above attack does not correct this one, however. A new fix for this type of attack is included in Windows NT Service Pack 3.

SYN Flood Attacks

Another common attack on the Internet is the SYN flood. Windows NT 3.51 and 4 are both vulnerable to this attack. SYN is the message name that a client sends requesting a TCP/IP connection from a server.

This attack works by repeatedly sending SYN requests with an invalid (spoofed) IP address. Each of these requests causes Windows NT to repeatedly attempt to acknowledge the request, with each attempt failing because the address is invalid. This attack is illustrated in Figure 19.2.

F I G U R E 19.2

A SYN flood attack overwhelms a Windows NT server.

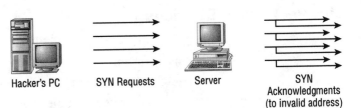

Hacker's PC   SYN Requests   Server   SYN Acknowledgments (to invalid address)

After enough SYN requests are received, the outgoing acknowledgments use all of the available TCP connections, and the server is no longer accessible to the outside world. This attack is prevented by the fixes in Windows NT Service Pack 3.

Telnet Attacks

TCP/IP port 135 supports RPC (Remote Procedure Call), a service that allows remote execution of commands. This sounds like a service that might be able to be exploited, and there's a surprisingly simple way to use it for a denial-of-service attack.

This attack is simple: A hacker just connects to this port and sends some bogus characters, causing the service to lock up. You can easily demonstrate this with the Telnet utility from the NT command prompt or from a UNIX system:

```
telnet host 135
```

After connecting to the host, type a few characters and press ↵, then disconnect. The RPC service will begin to hog the CPU. If you monitor it with System Monitor, you'll see usage as high as 100%. The NT server may become unresponsive or crash entirely.

Windows NT 4 is the only version vulnerable to this attack. You can prevent this attack by disabling port 135 on the network, or by installing Microsoft's hot fix. This fix is included in Windows NT Service Pack 3.

Simple TCP/IP Services

Windows NT includes Simple TCP/IP Services, a simple service that can be installed as a test for TCP/IP networking. This supports four simple services, including one called chargen (port 19), which echoes characters sent to it. This service is vulnerable to a denial-of-service attack.

The attack is similar to SYN flooding. A series of packets are sent to port 19 with spoofed IP addresses. Windows NT attempts to send responses, and retries when it fails. These responses quickly use up the resources of the server and make it unavailable.

A hot fix for this problem is available from Microsoft, and is included in Windows NT Service Pack 3. Also, since these services are rarely needed, you may want to disable Simple TCP/IP Services using the Services control panel.

Mail Bombing

A *mail bomb* is a particularly malicious type of denial-of-service attack. Unlike other attacks, it's often personal—not aimed at a particular company, but at a particular person.

A hacker sends a mail bomb by sending a large number of messages to the same e-mail address. This annoys the recipient and can cause mail client programs to crash. More importantly, it can overwhelm the mail server and cause serious network problems.

There's no way to prevent mail bombs completely. However, you can limit their effects by placing restrictions on the disk space used by e-mail messages (see your mail server's documentation for ways to do this).

It's also important to inform your users about mail bombs. If they notify you quickly when they suspect that this has occurred, you can minimize the damage.

Terminology

- **Denial of service:** A type of attack that attempts to disable the server rather than obtain information or access.

- **Mail bomb:** A denial-of-service attack that involves sending a large number of e-mail messages to the same address, overwhelming the mail server.

- **Password cache:** A file used in Windows 95 workstations to keep track of users and their passwords.

- **Ping:** A TCP/IP utility included with Windows NT and most UNIX systems that tests network connections by sending a packet and requesting an echo.

- **SYN:** The messages sent when a client attempts to initiate a TCP/IP connection with a server.

Web Browser Problems

Connecting your corporate network to the Internet creates a whole new list of security problems. While the typical problems involve deliberate attacks across the Internet and can be prevented by firewalls, there are a variety of attacks that can be performed over the Web, by exploiting holes in browser software.

In this section we'll look at the languages built into Web browsers that can be exploited by hackers. We'll also look at some more obscure problems caused by browser bugs.

As always, these aren't the only security holes that exist—new ones are discovered regularly. Since dealing with potential security holes in several different browsers can be an administrative nightmare, we recommend that you choose a single, up-to-date, reasonably secure browser, and install it on all of the workstations that require Web access. Also watch the Web for news of new security holes in that browser.

Client-Side Languages

The World Wide Web has been revolutionized in recent years by client-side languages such as Java, JavaScript, and ActiveX. Programs written in these languages can be embedded in Web pages and used for anything ranging from animation to full-scale order entry systems.

Of course, with any new language comes a new set of security holes. We'll look at each of the common client-side languages and their security strengths and weaknesses in the sections below.

Java

Java was developed by Sun Microsystems, and is currently all the rage on the Web. Java is a full-scale programming language that is platform-independent; in theory, a Java applet can run equally well on Windows, UNIX, and Macintosh systems without being recompiled.

Java was built with security in mind. Java applets on the Web execute in a *sandbox:* They're limited to their own area of memory and do not have access to the file system or other running applications. This makes Java a secure language—but nothing's perfect. Bugs in certain implementations of Java have allowed applets to reach outside the sandbox and access local files.

While security holes have been discovered, Java is still relatively safe. No one has found a way to access network passwords with it, or cause real damage. However, many network administrators restrict users' access to Java. Applets can be disabled within the browser or blocked entirely with a firewall.

JavaScript and JScript

JavaScript was originally called LiveScript. It was developed by Netscape Communications as a simple alternative to Java. While it uses a Java-like syntax, it is a simple scripting language that is embedded within a Web document. Microsoft's implementation in Internet Explorer is called JScript.

As with Java, JavaScript has very limited capabilities and is thus reasonably secure. No JavaScript program can format a disk or obtain a network password. However, bugs in JavaScript implementations have caused several security holes. These have included the following:

- A method of reading local files if the name is known

- Ways to read the browser's history, or otherwise obtain a list of sites the user has visited

- A way to send e-mail when a user accesses the page, or to obtain the user's e-mail address invisibly.

While the known bugs have been fixed, there is always the possibility of new ones. Since JavaScript is rarely used for anything but cute scrolling messages and animation, you may consider disabling it, or at least keeping browsers updated with the latest security fixes.

ActiveX

ActiveX is Microsoft's answer to Java. This is a full-scale programming language—as a matter of fact, ordinary Windows applications can be compiled to act as ActiveX controls, that can be embedded in a Web page. Few will argue that although it's limited to Windows machines and Internet Explorer, ActiveX is a powerful language.

Unfortunately, ActiveX is a bit too powerful. Unlike Java, it doesn't use a sandbox—an ActiveX program can do anything the programmer wants it to. It can read files, send them over the network, execute other programs, and even format your hard disk.

ActiveX is not completely without security, however. Microsoft has built an authentication system into the ActiveX specification. This uses encryption to add signatures to ActiveX controls. When you download a control, you can be sure of who it came from and that it hasn't been modified.

When a Web page includes an ActiveX control from a source you haven't received one from before, Internet Explorer prompts you before executing it. You can then indicate whether to trust any other controls signed by that provider.

Microsoft claims that this is a secure approach, but it doesn't really prevent problems. The best you can hope for is to find out just who created the control that formatted your hard drive. We recommend that you disable ActiveX or use system policies to restrict its use.

Specific Browser Security Holes

We've looked at languages built into browsers that add capabilities but can create security problems. In this section we'll look at a more serious type of problem: security holes that exist due to bugs in browsers, and may not even be known to the browser manufacturers.

Internet users are almost always the ones to discover these bugs, and hackers often know about them before the general public does. Be sure

---

Reality Check: The Web Page That Steals Your Money

Many Internet users have created Web pages that demonstrate the security deficiencies of ActiveX. One of the first of these was a page that used the power management features of Windows 95 to turn off your computer when you accessed it. This is a relatively harmless demonstration, but it could just as easily have formatted your drive.

A much more dangerous attack was demonstrated by some German hackers. They created a page that could add transactions to an electronic banking program, which would be executed the next time the user used it. Their demonstration was harmless, but it could easily have collected money from a few unknowing Web users before they knew what was going on.

---

that you install security fixes issued by the browser makers, and don't allow users to use out-of-date browsers known to have security problems.

We can't list all of the security holes—by the time you read this, new versions of Netscape and Internet Explorer will be available, with new undiscovered security holes. The following sections describe some of the better-known problems of this nature, most of which have been fixed by updated browsers.

See the browser manufacturers' sites for the latest security news and fixes:

- Netscape (`http://www.netscape.com`)

- Microsoft (`http://www.microsoft.com/ie/security`)

NTLM Negotiation (IE)

Internet Explorer supports a Windows NT authentication system called NTLM. Using this system, remote sites can request an authentication to allow you access to their files. When this happens, IE sends your user name, domain name, and host name to the host. (It does this without notifying you.)

The host then sends a challenge code, and IE encrypts your hashed password with this code and returns it. While this is intended to allow remote sites to be more secure, it ends up making your own network less secure. Knowing user names gives a hacker a head start, and a dictionary attack can be run on the encrypted passwords.

This problem affects Internet Explorer versions 2.*x* and 3.*x*, and has been fixed in Internet Explorer 4.0. You can prevent this problem by using the new version. You can also use the Services control panel to stop the NTLM service.

SMB Negotiation (IE and Netscape)

Internet Explorer isn't the only browser with security bugs. A bug in both IE and Netscape allows remote sites to request an SMB (Server Message Block) negotiation, another type of authentication.

The browser responds to the SMB request with your user name and hashed password. This gives hackers all they need to run a dictionary attack and obtain access to the network, all without even connecting to your system.

As with the previous method, this can be done without the knowledge of the user. By the time the security problem is discovered, there's no way to figure out just which Web site snagged the passwords.

At this writing, there is no known fix for this problem. It's a complicated process for a hacker to set up a system to grab passwords this way—but there are at least two Web sites that harmlessly demonstrate this technique, and there may be others that aren't so polite.

URL Executable Code (IE)

Internet Explorer supports .lnk and .url files, two types of Internet shortcut files. A bug in IE 3.0 allows malicious sites to post a link to one of these files. When the user clicks on the link, it can execute a remote program, or a local one (such as FORMAT.EXE).

Microsoft has posted a fix at the site mentioned earlier for this problem. It is also fixed in Internet Explorer 4.0.

Viewing Text and HTML Files (IE)

A bug in Internet Explorer 4.0 allows a malicious site to load a local text, graphic, or HTML file into a frame. The site can then use Jscript to read the contents of the file. The name of the file must be known for this to work, but some names (such as the password cache file mentioned earlier) are the same on most systems.

A patch for this problem is available from the Microsoft site mentioned at the beginning of this section.

Buffer Overrun (IE)

At this writing, the latest IE security discovery is a bug in Internet Explorer 4.0 that allows sites to send executable code to be executed on the user's computer. It involves sending a URL beginning with `res://` and containing too many characters.

This type of URL overflows IE's buffer and overwrites part of the executable code. Thus, code could actually be included in the URL that would be executed when the browser attempts to load the URL.

Microsoft has posted a fix for this problem at the site mentioned earlier.

Policies: Avoiding Attacks

- Install the latest service packs and hot fixes from Microsoft.

- Disable the password cache in Windows 95 workstations.

- Don't allow users to use the Network feature in the Tweak UI utility.

- Be sure you have the latest versions and fixes for applications. Microsoft applications are particularly vulnerable—not because of anything wrong with them, but because they tend to access high-level features of the operating system more than other applications.

- Install the fixes in Service Pack 3 to prevent SYN flood attacks. If practical, disable outside access to port 135 on servers to prevent Telnet-based denial-of-service attacks against the RPC service.

- Remove Simple TCP/IP Services using the Services control panel, unless you need one of its components.

- Configure your mail server to minimize the impact of mail bombs.

- If users are allowed access to the Web, use the same browser on all workstations.

- Avoid using untested browsers. Download the latest patches from Microsoft or Netscape to keep browsers secure.

Summary

In this chapter, we've looked at various types of high-level attacks that can cause problems with Windows NT servers.

Windows NT passwords can be compromised by access to the Windows 95 password cache, by applications that store the password as clear text, or by more complex attacks that obtain access to the password.

Windows NT and applications running under it may have bugs that provide unintended access to resources. The getadmin program is a particularly good example of the kind of damage that a hacker can do by manipulating these bugs.

Denial-of-service attacks are some of the easiest attacks to carry out—a ping of death attack, for example, can be done with one simple command from UNIX or Windows NT. These attacks are commonly used against World Wide Web servers, so these machines should be carefully guarded.

By installing the latest hot fixes and service packs, you can avoid the issues described in this chapter. New security holes are always being discovered, so be sure to watch for news of them. With any luck, someone else will be the victim when the attack is first discovered, and you can install the fix to save your network.

CHAPTER

20

Network and Data Link Security

etwork layer and data link layer security are both key parts of creating a defense in depth for your network.

Defense in depth is a concept used by military strategists who arrange the defense of a location—whether it is a camp, a fort, a city, or a nation—against an external threat. The military definition of defense in depth is to establish defensive measures that reinforce each other, that prevent the enemy from observing the defender's activities, and that allow the defender to respond quickly and effectively to an enemy attack.

Network administrators can use the defense-in-depth strategy to effectively defend their networks from attack from the Internet, from dial-up connections, or from internal agents.

A defense in depth strategy does not rely solely on any one security mechanism for protection. You should not rely just on Windows NT logon security to control access to your servers and NTFS security to protect your application data. You should also use firewalls to guard your link to the Internet, and proxy servers to hide the structure of your network, as well as network and data link security software and hardware to guard your LAN's data as it crosses the LAN's network connections.

Network layer and data link layer security protects the network connections between computers. The type of data that flow over the secure network connections does not matter to the network and data link layers—the purpose of these layers is to transport the data from one computer to the other quickly, reliably, and securely.

Modern networks are complex assemblies of hardware and software components that interact to link computers together. Every component of the network is a potential security problem. Hackers will leave no potential security weakness untried; in order to stay one step ahead of them and keep your network secure, you must know how hackers exploit network protocols. With that understanding you can develop strategies and install products that will secure the network and data link layers of your network.

Some of the topics of this chapter are also covered in other chapters. This chapter, however, ties together the information contained elsewhere and provides additional information about how to protect your network. The purpose of this chapter is to help you build a defense in depth for your network by showing how hackers attack the network protocols that your network is based on, and how you can defend your network against a hacker's tactics.

How Hackers Exploit Network Protocols

In order to defeat hackers you have to think like a hacker and see your network from the hacker point of view. Information is everything to a hacker, and specific pieces of information about your network can be leveraged to obtain more information. However, when a typical network intruder attempts to penetrate your network security they are at a disadvantage for the following reasons:

- The intruder is usually physically located outside your network (although this is not always true, as you will see).

- The intruder does not know the Internet names or NetBIOS names of your computers (except perhaps for those of your Internet server computers).

- The intruder does not have a valid account name and password for your network (if the attacker *does* have this information, your network is already compromised).

- The intruder does not know the physical or logical layout of your network.

Your job as a network administrator is to keep network intruders in this state of ignorance. The hacker will attempt to find out more about your network, subvert network security measures, gain account name and password information, and ultimately gain full control of network resources. Hacker activity can be broken down into the following areas:

- Eavesdropping and snooping
- Denial of service
- Impersonation
- Man-in-the-middle attacks
- Hijacking

Once you evaluate your network infrastructure and find weaknesses that a hacker can exploit to gain entrance, you can take measures to shore up your network's defenses.

Eavesdropping and Snooping

The first and easiest things a hacker does to obtain information about your network is simply to listen, and then to ask your network computers information about themselves. The hacker may not even contact your computers directly but may instead communicate with other computers that provide services your computers rely on (Domain Name Service computers on the Internet, for example).

Chapter 15 contains a more general discussion of eavesdropping as a hacker tactic; this section describes specific eavesdropping and snooping activities a hacker might pursue in an attempt to compromise your network. Networked computers will volunteer a remarkable amount of information about themselves and how they are configured, especially if you leave them in the default configurations set up by the operating system vendors who supply them. Figure 20.1 shows a hacker listening in on network data.

FIGURE 20.1

A hacker between a network client and a network server can listen in on the data being exchanged.

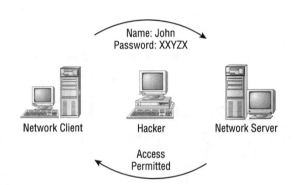

Name: John
Password: XXYZX

Network Client   Hacker   Network Server

Access
Permitted

Hackers will attempt to exploit any data or network service that is exposed to their view. Common hacking practices include (but are by no means limited to) the following activities:

- Password capture

- Traffic analysis

- Network address scanning

- Port scanning

- Finger, Whois, NSLookup, and DNS range grabbing

- SNMP data gathering

Password Capture

Most hacker activities carry some risk that the activities will be detected and traced back to the hacker. One that does not is eavesdropping on the local networking medium for logon information. Many networking protocols do not encrypt passwords, allowing any computer on the path between the client and the server to "overhear" the user name and password. Not all encrypted logon procedures are safe from eavesdropping either, because if the logon procedure is naïve, a hacker can record the user name and encrypted password to send to the server later in a *replay attack.*

Eavesdropping requires software that will listen to all of the communications that flow over a network medium (such as Ethernet) rather than just listening to communications that are sent specifically to the hacker's computer. An eavesdropping hacker must have access to a computer situated on a network link that has network traffic flowing over it (such as a campus Ethernet or a computer in the server room of an Internet service provider). The more data that flows over the link, the more likely the hacker will capture passwords sent in the clear.

The physical location of computers on the network will not restrict the eavesdropping ability of a hacker who has penetrated other computers on the same network, because the hacker can install software on those computers that will allow them to snoop. The hacker may be typing at a computer in New York while a compromised computer in San Francisco records everything that goes over that remote network for the hacker's later perusal.

A determined network intruder may even physically intrude on an otherwise secure LAN and connect a snooping device to the network cable. Casual hackers, more interested in network "joy riding" or in finding a place to store their pirated software, will seldom exhibit this level of effort (or brave this degree of risk), but other network intruders who might target your network for financial gain could easily do so if you don't take precautions.

Network eavesdropping is a technique hackers can use regardless of which technology is used to implement the network. An NWLink wide area network is just as vulnerable to someone eavesdropping on network connections as the Internet or an intranet that uses TCP/IP.

Policies: Countering Password Capture

- Do not send unencrypted passwords over insecure network links.

- Do not use network client software that sends passwords over external networks in the clear.

- Do not allow unauthorized individuals to install hardware or software that can "snoop" on your internal networks.

- Regularly check your network for physical devices or software modifications that might be installed by a network intruder.

- You can provide further security for your local area network or wide area network by encrypting the network links.

- You can provide further security for an intranet by encrypting the data that is tunneled over a nonsecure network such as the Internet.

Network Traffic Analysis

Passwords aren't the only things a determined hacker will listen for when eavesdropping on network traffic. Quite a bit of information about your network can be obtained just from watching the nature of the traffic in and out of your network (or within your network if the hacker has compromised a computer within your security boundary). Some things a hacker will look for include:

- The IP addresses of the source and destination computers of network traffic

- The locations of gateways and routers

- The amount of traffic originating from, being sent to, or flowing through computers identified by the hacker

- Particular kinds of network traffic going to or from a computer, which might identify the computer's function (DNS requests to one computer, or FTP responses from another, for example)

- Network service availability broadcasts (such as NetBIOS browse list updates) that are external to a private network and indicate a network security hole, or that are within a network and indicate targets for further attack

A firewall is the best tool for keeping traffic analysis from revealing too much about your network. The firewall will make all of the Internet (or other public network) traffic appear to come from one computer. A hacker from outside will not be able to determine the true extent of your network behind the firewall. You must also configure your firewall or packet filter not to pass service availability broadcasts beyond your network boundary.

Policies: Countering Traffic Analysis

- Install a firewall on a gateway computer between your firewall and the Internet (or any other public network that allows firewall technology).

- Configure the gateway or packet filter not to pass service availability broadcasts.

Network Address Scanning

Hackers who are more active in finding targets to penetrate often use a technique called *network address scanning*. The hacker will specify beginning and ending addresses to scan, and then the hacker's computer program will attempt to establish a connection to a computer on each of those network addresses in turn. If a computer answers from any one of those addresses, then the hacker has found another target.

All network technologies that specify an address of one kind or another for each computer on the network are vulnerable to this kind of attack. TCP/IP (the transport protocol used on the Internet) is the network technology most often scanned by hackers, and tools to scan TCP/IP are widely available. But other technologies such as NWLink, X.25, and FDDI are equally susceptible if the hacker is willing to find or create the tools necessary to perform the scan.

The best way to foil this kind of attack is to watch for it. A security administrator who determines that this kind of attack is in progress can take steps to halt it, including configuring gateways or routers to discard network traffic from the offending host(s). A firewall will also prevent scanning attacks.

Policies: Countering Network Address Scanning

- Configure gateways, packet filters, and routers to log connection requests to hosts that do not exist on your network.

- Periodically examine log data for network address scanning, and if the logging software supports it, configure a network alert that will signal if a scan is in progress.

Port Scanning

Once a hacker has identified a target computer, they will attempt to determine what operating system it is running and what services it is providing to network clients. On a TCP/IP-based network (such as the Internet), services are provided on numbered connections called ports. Which ports a computer responds to often allow the hacker to identify the operating system and supported services of the target computer.

There are a number of tools available on the Internet that a hacker can use to determine which sockets are responding to network connection requests. These tools try each port in turn and report to the hacker which ports refuse connections and which do not. The hacker can then concentrate on ports corresponding to services that are often left unsecured or that have security problems.

The defense against port scanning is the same as that against network address scanning—watch for connection attempts to unsupported ports and then deny access to the computers doing the scanning.

Policies: Countering Port Scanning

- Configure computers that provide services on the Internet to log port connection requests to inactive ports.

- Periodically examine log data for port scanning, and if the logging software supports it, configure a network alert that will signal if a scan is in progress.

Finger, Whois, NSLookup, and DNS Zone Transfer

There are a number of network services that hackers will use to find out more about your network if those services are enabled on your Internet host. The Finger and Whois services are favorites of hackers because they give account name and personal contact information for users of network computers. This is a useful service for people who need to contact members of your organization or who need to find an e-mail address for a network user, but hackers will take user names returned by these services and then try to break into those accounts by trying commonly used passwords.

By default, Windows NT does not support Finger or Whois. If you support UNIX computers in your network, however, you should either disable these services or curtail the information they return. You can install software for Windows NT that provides these services, but you probably shouldn't.

Few network users will miss the Finger and Whois services, but the same cannot be said for the DNS service. The DNS service is required by Internet client software to convert human-friendly Internet names such as www.microsoft.com into computer-friendly IP addresses such as 10.1.1.2. Without the DNS service, many Internet client tools such as Web browsers, FTP clients, and Telnet clients will not work as the user expects.

Windows NT Server does support the DNS service. (It is included on the installation CD-ROM and may be installed after you install the operating system.) Most networks that support the use of Internet tools within the network, rather than just the use of Internet tools to connect to services on the Internet, will include support for DNS. A small network can rely on an external DNS server to provide Internet name service translation for its clients, but a large IP network or an IP network behind a firewall is unwieldy to manage without a DNS server of its own.

Hackers can use a DNS service to attempt to discover the structure of your network. Since DNS records the IP addresses and Internet names of all of the computers that client computers need to be able to look up via Internet name, a hacker who can get the DNS data will have a list of the most important computers in your network.

The NSLookup tool is a standard Internet program for interrogating DNS servers, and a hacker can craft a program that makes the hacker's computer appear to be a peer DNS server that needs DNS information from your DNS server.

NOTE Your task is to configure security so that clients from within your network security perimeter can access the DNS server and get the information they need, but so that computers from outside your network security perimeter cannot get that information.

The security problem is compounded by the fact that DNS is a hierarchical service. If one DNS server does not have the answer to a query, it will ask the next server up or down the DNS tree. This means that in a traditionally configured network, a DNS service within your firewall will need to be able to communicate with DNS servers outside the firewall.

DNS servers are configured to transfer blocks of Internet name and address data using a feature called *zone transfer*. In addition, many Internet services will not respond to Internet requests from client computers that don't have DNS reverse mappings. Those Internet servers must be able to connect to your DNS server to verify that the DNS reverse mapping exists.

Since part of network security is keeping the enemy from knowing how your network is configured, you should not allow client computers to connect directly to servers on the Internet. Instead you should require all external connections to go through a proxy server.

The proxy server computer through which you route connections should be registered with an external DNS server (and be reverse IP mapped as well). But the Internet names and IP addresses of client computers on your network should not be exported.

Perhaps your network requirements mandate that computers external to your network be able to resolve IP addresses for computers inside your firewall or vice versa (if you must use a software package that does not support use of a proxy server, for example). In that case, you should configure your firewall to disallow connections to your DNS server for all external computers except the DNS server "up" the tree from yours. You should also disable zone transfers for all DNS servers except those within your security domain.

Policies: DNS Security

- Require all network connections to services outside your network security to go through a proxy server whenever possible.

- Configure your DNS server to exchange information only with computers within your network security perimeter and with the DNS server "up" the network tree from yours.

SNMP Data Gathering

The Simple Network Management Protocol (SNMP) is an essential tool for managing large TCP/IP networks. SNMP allows the administrator to remotely query the status and control the operation of network devices that support SNMP. Unfortunately, hackers can also use SNMP to gather data about a network or (as described in the next section) interfere with the operation of the network.

Policies: Preventing SNMP Data Gathering

- Your first defense against SNMP data gathering on your network should be a gateway or packet filter.

- Do not allow SNMP to travel into or out of your network.

- Configure those SNMP devices that provide for security to allow connections only from authorized user accounts.

Terminology

- **Defense in depth:** The use of reinforcing defensive measures to prevent information gathering and to defend against attack.

- **Denial-of-service attack:** Causing a computer or network service to be unavailable to authorized client computers.

- **DNS cache pollution:** Sending misleading or nonsense Internet name and IP address updates to a DNS server.

- **Eavesdropping:** Gathering information about a target network or computer by listening in on transmitted data.

- **Impersonation attack:** A hostile computer masquerading as a trusted computer.

- **Out-of-band attack:** Sending extraneous command information to a TCP port.

- **Ping of death:** An ICMP packet that violates the rules of ICMP packet construction.

- **Snooping:** Gathering information about a target network or computer by interrogating the targeted computers.

- **Zone transfer:** Transferring a block of DNS data (typically an entire IP subnet) from one DNS server to another.

Denial of Service

After eavesdropping, the easiest thing for a hacker to do to your network is to disable some aspect of it or even to bring the entire network down. Chapter 19 describes many reasons why a hacker might attempt a denial-of-service attack; this section shows some specific attacks a hacker might attempt, especially in support of other hacking efforts, such as an *impersonation attack*. The hacker may merely be interested in inconveniencing your organization, or they may have a more sinister goal. It is much easier for one computer to impersonate another computer if the other computer is disabled (see the following section on impersonation). Figure 20.2 shows some denial-of-service activities a hacker can undertake.

There are a number of methods a hacker can use to disable a computer or a service provided by a computer. Most of these methods affect computers using TCP/IP; not because TCP/IP is less secure that other protocols such as NWLink or X.25, but because TCP/IP is the most widely used internetwork protocol and the most pressing hacker threat is from the Internet. Methods hackers can use to disable computers or computer services include:

- Ping of death

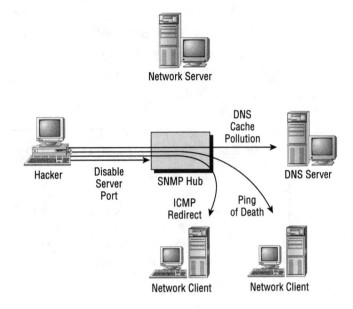

FIGURE 20.2

A hacker can cause havoc in your network by sending bad packets, attacking specific network services, redirecting network traffic, or reconfiguring network devices.

- SYN attacks and ICMP flooding

- Service-specific attacks

- DNS redirection

- Route redirection (RIP, BGP, ICMP)

- SNMP reconfiguration

Ping of Death

Perhaps the most ominous sounding of network layer attacks is the aptly named *ping of death*. A specially constructed ICMP packet that violates many of the rules for constructing ICMP packets can cause the computer to which it is sent to crash (if that computer's networking software does not check for invalid ICMP packets).

The only solution for protecting computers outside your gateway (or the gateway computer itself) from the ping of death is to use a version of the operating system that is not susceptible to it. You can shield computers inside your network by not passing ping (ICMP) packets through your firewall.

Policies: Stopping the Ping of Death

- Use operating system software on Internet-accessible machines that are not susceptible to the ping of death. For Windows NT 4, apply Microsoft's icmp-fix patch (found at ftp.microsoft.com/bussys/ winnt/winnt-public/fixes/usa/NT40/hotfixes-postSP3/ icmp-fix/ on Microsoft's FTP site.

- Configure your gateway not to pass ping (ICMP) packets.

SYN Attacks and ICMP Flooding

Another way hackers disable the networking capability of computers is by overloading the network protocol software of the target computer with connection attempts or information requests. (Chapter 19 also discusses this hacker activity.) The initial IP packet of a TCP connection attempt is simple and easy to generate (a distinguishing characteristic of these packets is that they have the SYN bit set).

Responding to a connection attempt takes more compute time and memory space than does generating the packet because the receiving computer must record information about the new connection and allocate memory for connection data. An attacker can send one SYN packet after another to a target computer, and that target computer will then be unable to process connection attempts from legitimate users because all of its available time and memory will be spent processing SYN requests.

A similar network protocol attack is *ICMP flooding*, in which the hacker sends a constant stream of ICMP echo requests to the target computer. The target computer then spends most of its time responding to the echo requests instead of processing legitimate network traffic.

At the time of this writing, the latest service pack for Windows NT 4 protects NT from a SYN attack and from ICMP flooding. You should configure your router to log SYN attacks and ICMP flooding in order to protect operating systems within your firewall that may be vulnerable to these attacks.

Policies: Defending Against SYN and ICMP Attacks

■ Install the latest version of the operating system software.

■ Your best defense against SYN attacks and ICMP flooding within your network is to log network activity and to have the log software signal an alert when a SYN attack or ICMP flood is in progress. You can then deny access to the computer or network that originates the attack and take measures (such as calling or sending an e-mail message to the administrator of the offending network) to stop the malicious behavior.

Service-Specific Attacks

Sometimes a hacker may not want to crash your computer. The hacker may be more interested in shutting down one of the services supported by your network-connected computer (perhaps in order to impersonate that service, as described in the next section, *Impersonation*.)

Although any service provided by your computer may be the target of a service-specific attack, there are four services that hackers are particularly attracted to because they are either fundamental components of a TCP/IP network or are fundamental components of Windows networking. The four services are RPC, NetBIOS, DNS, and WINS. Hackers will also attempt to use other services such as HTTP or FTP to break into your computer, but these are application-level services rather than network layer or data-link layer services and are discussed in Chapters 18 and 19 .

Services such as Chargen or Time do not provide a sufficiently rich environment for a hacker to have any real chance of using them to break into or take down your computer.

Network clients connect to specific ports for each network service, and each service expects the network client to send the data to the service in a specific format. The DNS service, for example, expects data that is sent to the DNS port from the client to be formatted in a different manner than is the case for WINS requests, and DNS will not be able to respond properly to WINS requests sent to it. This is much like (sur)real world services such as the Department of Motor Vehicles and the Social Security Administration, each of which need different information from you in order to perform their services, and each of which have different forms for you to fill out. You could send a form requesting a duplicate social security card to the DMV, but you would get neither a social security card nor a driver's license in return. You must send the right form to the right service.

While the repercussions of sending misleading or incorrect information to government institutions can be severe for the perpetrator and will have negligible effect on the operation of the government service, sending incorrect or nonsense messages to network services can crash them. Such actions are difficult to track back to the hacker, especially if the hacker is using obfuscatory techniques, such as source routing (described later in this chapter), or has suborned another computer into being a relay for hacker activity.

DNS, RPC, and WINS are vulnerable to random information being sent to their ports. A recently released Widows NT service pack (along with a hot fix for WINS) performs better data checking and protects your services against these attacks. DNS will also crash if it receives a

DNS response without having first sent a DNS request. You can protect against unsolicited DNS responses by only allowing authorized external hosts to communicate with your DNS server.

The NetBIOS service is vulnerable to an *out of band attack*, which is a specific kind of message sent to the NetBIOS ports. Service Pack 3 with an additional hot fix will prevent this denial-of-service attack, but the NetBIOS ports should not be accessible to computers outside your network at all, so the best solution to this problem (after installing the latest version of the operating system software) is not to bind NetBIOS to network adapters that can be reached from outside your network.

Policies: Thwarting Service-Specific Denial-of-Service Attacks

- Install the latest service pack for Windows NT Server as well as these Microsoft hot fixes for denial of service attacks: `ftp.microsoft.com/bussys/winnt/winnt-public/fixes/usa/nt40/hotfixes-postSP3/winsupd-fix` and `ftp.microsoft.com/bussys/winnt/winnt-public/fixes/usa/nt40/hotfixes-postSP3/icmp-fix`.

- Unbind NetBIOS from Internet-accessible network adapters. Allow only authorized hosts outside your network to connect to your DNS servers.

DNS Cache Pollution

Another DNS service attack that deserves special mention is *DNS cache pollution*. A hacker can observe a Windows NT computer that provides DNS service (using techniques described in the previous section, *Eavesdropping and Snooping*) and determine the sequence used by the NT server to provide query IDs for recursive DNS queries. The hacker can then forge a response that contains invalid information or information that will redirect Internet traffic to a computer the hacker has already suborned. (The hacker may have to perform a denial-of-service attack on the DNS server being queried in order for the substitution to be accepted by the querying, targeted DNS server.)

This sort of attack can cause client computers that rely on the DNS server to be unable to resolve Internet names into valid IP addresses. That in itself can cause problems on a TCP/IP network. More dangerous, however is when a hacker populates the DNS server with valid IP addresses that are different from the correct IP addresses, especially if the hacker controls the computers at those addresses. This means a DNS cache pollution attack can be the beginning of an impersonation attack on computers in your network.

Policies: Foiling DNS Cache Pollution Attacks

- Install the Windows NT Server 4.0 hot fix found at `ftp.microsoft.com/bussys/winnt/winnt-public/fixes/usa/nt40/hotfixespostSP3/dns-fix`, which makes the sequence numbers more difficult for a hacker to predict. This hot fix also fixes other bugs in Microsoft's DNS implementation.

Route Redirection (RIP, BGP, ICMP)

A hacker can cause a great deal of havoc in your network if they can get control of your network's routers. Routers direct the flow of information within your network, as well as in and out of it, from information stored in their routing tables. By making changes to those routing tables a hacker can isolate parts of your network and direct network traffic out of it.

Routers must adapt to network conditions in order to maintain network functionality in the face of slowdowns or failures in network links. The routers in your network will exchange information about routing conditions, will accept routing updates from network administrative programs, and will communicate with routers outside your network if you allow them to. These routing updates are transmitted using a routing protocol, usually either RIP, OSPF, or BGP.

RIP has no authentication capability. If a hacker can communicate with a router that uses RIP to update its network information, then they can easily reconfigure the router to deny service to computers in your network or redirect the network traffic from computers in your network. OSPF provides more security than does RIP, and BGP is fairly secure about who it will communicate with in order to update routing tables.

Another way a hacker can get your computers to send data to the wrong address is to send ICMP redirect packets to the computer. An ICMP redirect packet instructs the computer that an IP packet is being sent to the wrong router and that there is another route to the destination address that is either more efficient or faster, or that avoids a network problem. It is difficult to forge ICMP packets, however, because they must appear to come from the router closest to the originating computer.

Policies: Routers

- Use BGP on routers between your network and the Internet, and configure those routers to only accept route updates from computers you trust.

- Use OSPF or BGP within your network.

- Filter out RIP traffic at the gateway.

- Filter out ICMP traffic at your Internet gateway.

SNMP Reconfiguration

Many network devices, including Windows NT Server computers (if you install the SNMP service for them) can be managed remotely using SNMP. In addition to data snooping, a hacker can use SNMP to reconfigure your network to deny service to network computers or even to route data out of your network, depending on the SNMP features of the device that the hacker gains control of.

Policies: Preventing SNMP Reconfiguration of Devices

- Configure your gateway or packet filter not to pass SNMP traffic.

- Configure those SNMP devices that provide for security to only allow connections from authorized user accounts. (This includes Windows NT computers with SNMP services installed.)

Impersonation

Impersonation is the next step for a hacker to take if they still don't have access to your network computers. The goal of a hacker is to penetrate your network security and get at the information or resources on the computers in your network. Figure 20.3 shows a hacker computer impersonating a trusted computer.

Merely snooping on your network traffic may give the hacker enough information to log on to your network. If that does not work, the hacker may reduce the functionality of your network via a denial-of-service attack, causing computers on your network to reveal enough information to allow the hacker to break in. (The hacker might also pursue a denial-of-service attack just to inconvenience users of your network.)

FIGURE 20.3

A hacker computer can
impersonate client
computers on your
network.

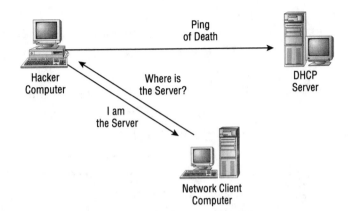

By impersonating another computer that the computers on your network trust, the hacker's computer may be able to trick your computers into revealing enough information for the hacker to get through your network security. Alternatively, by impersonating another computer, the hacker's computer may be able to trick one of your computers into executing a command that weakens your security enough to let the hacker in. The tactics a hacker may use depend on the computer or service that the hacker may attempt to impersonate, as follows:

- Source routed attacks

- DHCP, WINS, and DNS service impersonation

- Password playback, server impersonation, and password capture

Source Routed Attacks

The TCP/IP protocol suite includes a little-used option for specifying the exact route a packet should take as it crosses a TCP/IP-based network (such as the Internet). This option is called *source routing,* and it allows a hacker to send data from one computer and make it look like it comes from another (usually more trusted) computer. Source routing is a useful tool for diagnosing network failures and circumventing network problems but it is easily exploited by hackers, so you should not allow source routed packets into your TCP/IP network.

The hacker can use source routing to impersonate an already connected user and inject additional information into an otherwise benign communication between a server and the authorized client computer. For example, a hacker might detect that an administrator has logged on to a server from a client computer. If that administrator is at a command prompt, the hacker could inject a packet into the communications stream that appears to come from the administrator and that tells the server to execute the change password command, locking the administrator account and letting the hacker in.

The hacker also might use source routing to impersonate a trusted external DNS server and send DNS updates to your DNS server. The hacker could thereby redirect all of the network clients that rely on the DNS server to translate Internet names into IP addresses so that the client computers' Internet name-to-IP address translation requests would go instead to a hostile server under the control of the hacker. The hacker could then use the hostile server to capture passwords, as described below in *Password Playback, Server Impersonation, and Password Capture*.

Policies: Stopping Source Routed Attacks

- Configure your gateway or packet filter to discard all IP packets that use the source routing feature.

DHCP, WINS, and DNS Service Impersonation

Another tactic a hacker can use to penetrate your network is to impersonate a service that your client computers get configuration information from when they boot. Microsoft network clients can be set up to get their configuration (including the location of the default gateway,

DNS, and WINS servers) from a DHCP server, so a hacker that can impersonate a DHCP server can redirect your network clients to talk to almost any hostile host. By impersonating a WINS server the hacker can return invalid or hostile IP addresses for NetBIOS computer names, and by impersonating a DNS server the hacker can return invalid or hostile IP addresses for Internet names.

In order for a hacker to impersonate a DHCP, WINS, or DNS server, the hacker must get control of one computer within your network and then initiate a denial-of-service attack against the legitimate DHCP, WINS, or DNS target computer. Once the target computer goes down, the computer controlled by the hacker can begin satisfying DHCP, WINS, or DNS requests in its place. This is one way that a hacker can use one compromised computer in your network to further penetrate your network security and gain control of other computers in your network.

A DHCP, WINS, or DNS impersonation attack on your network by a hacker is dependent on other attack methods to succeed. The hacker must first gather information about your network in order to identify targets. The hacker then must cause a denial-of-service on the service being impersonated. The hacker then must either gain control of at least one computer in your network to take the place of that server or redirect network traffic to an external computer that can take the place of that server.

The defensive measures you put in place to stop denial-of-service attacks and to restrict information about your network will help prevent an impersonation attack as well. You should also watch your network traffic for DHCP, WINS, or DNS services being hosted by unauthorized computers in your network, and you should take swift action to shut down any unauthorized servers.

Policies: Watch for DHCP, WINS, and DNS Service Impersonation

■ In addition to taking measures to prevent disclosure of network configuration and to foil denial-of-service attacks, you should also use network traffic analysis tools to watch for unauthorized DHCP, WINS, or DNS servers on your network. Move swiftly to shut down any such services you detect.

Password Playback, Server Impersonation, and Password Capture

If the hacker has observed an encrypted logon session to one of your computers, they may not know the user name and password being used to log on, but they may be able to fool your system anyway. The hacker might simply record the encrypted log-on credentials and send those same credentials to your computer later. Your computer won't detect that the hacker doesn't know what the unencrypted password is.

Older networking protocols are vulnerable to this kind of attack. The way to defeat this sort of network attack is to use a protocol that uses challenge and response for password authentication.

Challenge and response means that the server computer does not ask for the user name and password immediately, but does so instead when a remote computer begins the logon process and the server sends back a number to the client computer (the challenge). The client computer's response is to encrypt that number along with (or as the key to) the user's password. The purpose of the number is to make the encrypted result different each time. Figure 20.4 compares the challenge and response authentication method to the traditional method of encrypted authentication.

Since a different challenge is issued by the server for each log-on request, a simple replay of a captured encrypted password will not work. To determine the validity of a password, the server encrypts the

FIGURE 20.4

Challenge and response
authentication foils
replay attacks by making
the encrypted result
different each time.

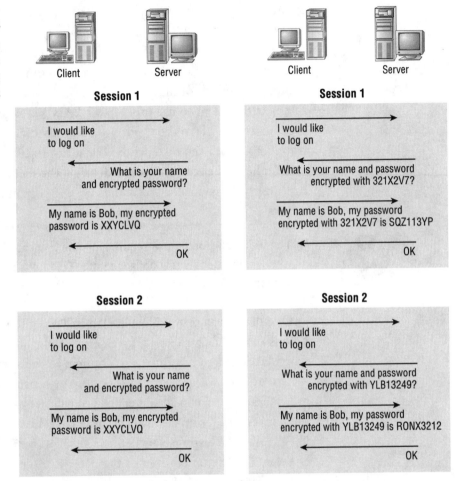

user's password that is stored on the server with the same number and
then checks the encrypted result it has computed with the encrypted
result it receives from the network client. If the results match, the client
is authenticated.

Windows NT uses this sort of password encryption and authentication by default for NetBIOS connections from network client computers. Unfortunately, Windows NT also supports an older LAN
Manager authentication protocol, which networking clients may elect

to use if they inform Windows NT that they do not support the Windows NT Challenge/Response protocol.

Hackers can exploit NT's support for this weaker protocol by forging a response packet that appears to come from the server (using source routing, rerouting, or a man-in-the-middle attack) and that instructs the client to use the weaker LAN Manager protocol. This way the hacker can make the client use an easily cracked password encryption method or even instruct the client not to use password encryption at all. The hacker can then eavesdrop on the resulting log-on traffic and capture the password used by the client to log on to the server.

> The best solution to the security problem created by support for this weaker protocol is to configure your Windows NT computers not to accept LAN Manager authentication.

One limitation of the NT Challenge/Response protocol as it exists now is that a hacker can set up a server computer for capturing passwords and either entice users to connect to the server or use denial-of-service attacks to redirect network connections to a computer that is masquerading as a valid server for your network. (In the first scenario, the hacker can set up a Web site, for example, that accepts Windows NT Challenge/Response authentication.)

When the hacker configures the deceptive server, they don't have the passwords for the user accounts that will attempt to connect to it. The hacker can specify one number that the server will always send to the client computers as a challenge, however, and can precompute passwords encrypted with that seed from dictionary files.

If an unsuspecting client computer sends an encrypted password that matches a computed dictionary value the hacker has calculated, then the hacker has found a new user name and password to use to get into your network. Currently the best solution to this kind of network attack is for network users to never select passwords that might show up in a dictionary, that might be easily guessed, or that contain less than eight characters.

> ### Policies: Foiling Password Playback and Password Capture
>
> - Install the service pack found at `ftp.microsoft.com/bussys/winnt/winnt-public/fixes/usa/nt40/hotfixes-postSP3/lm-fix` after installing Service Pack 3 on your NT 4 server.
>
> - Require users to select passwords that cannot be found in a dictionary and that are eight characters or longer.

Man-in-the-Middle Attacks

A special case of the impersonation attack is the man-in-the-middle attack. In this type of attack the hacker operates between one computer and another on your network, or between a client computer on the Internet or other WAN network and your server computer in your secure LAN. You may recall that we talked about this technique in Chapter 3.

When the client computer opens a connection to the server computer, the hacker's computer intercepts it (perhaps via a DNS or DHCP impersonation attack, or by rerouting the IP traffic from the client to a compromised computer). The hacker's computer opens a connection on behalf of the client computer to the server computer. Ideally (from the hacker's point of view) the client will think it is communicating with the server, and the server will think it is communicating with the client. The hacker computer in the middle will be able to observe all of the communications between the client and the server and will be able to make changes to the data sent between them. Figure 20.5 shows a man-in-the-middle attack.

Depending on the nature of the communications, the hacker computer may be able to use a man-in-the-middle attack to gain greater access to

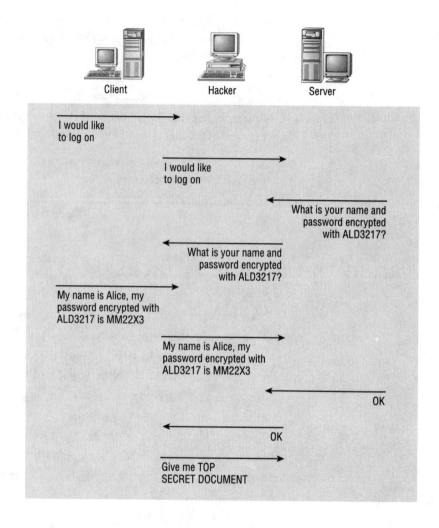

FIGURE 20.5

In a man-in-the-middle attack, the hacker computer appears to be the server to the client computer, and also appears to be the client to the server computer.

your network. For example, if the connection is an administrator-level Telnet link into a server computer from a client computer, the hacker computer in the middle could download the password file from the server to the hacker computer instead of uploading HTML pages that the administrator may wish to place on the server computer. (In this case, the hacker's computer would have to pass through the log-on credentials to gain entry to the server).

NOTE On an insecure network such as the Internet it is difficult to defend against a man-in-the-middle attack. Fortunately, it is also difficult to construct a successful man-in-the-middle attack.

The measures you take to protect your network against data gathering, denial-of-service, and impersonation will also help protect you from a man-in-the-middle attack. Nevertheless, you should never connect to your network using an administrative account over an insecure network. You can use encryption to create secure communications links over a TCP/IP network (PPTP is an excellent example). You can use third-party authentication packages such as S/KEY provided by Bellcore and SecureID provided by Security Dynamics to ensure that your client computers are communicating directly with a trusted host computer (and vice versa).

Hijacking

One last hacker trick is the hijacking of an already established and authenticated networking connection. In a Windows NT network this can happen at two layers of the networking protocol: at the TCP connection layer and at the SMB session layer. In order for a hacker on the Internet to hijack a network share connection, the hacker will have to compromise both, because SMB uses TCP ports to make the connection.

In order to hijack an existing TCP connection, a hacker must be able to predict TCP sequence numbers, which the two communicating computers use to keep IP packets in order and to ensure that they all arrive at the intended destination. The hacker must also be able to redirect the TCP/IP connection to their computer and launch a denial-of-service attack against the client computer so that the client computer does not indicate to the server computer that something is wrong. In order to hijack an SMB session (such as a drive mapping to a NetBIOS share), the hacker must also be able to predict the correct NetBIOS Frame ID, Tree ID, and the correct user ID at the server level of an existing Net-BIOS communications link.

The details of how a hacker might hijack a TCP and a NetBIOS session may interest a hacker or the developers of new networking protocols, but there is little a system administrator can do about them. Any changes to these protocols would make the computers using the new protocols incompatible with computers using the old ones. (That is why Microsoft hasn't just removed the deficiencies from NetBIOS.)

While an exploit of this nature is theoretically possible, tools for hijacking SMB connections are not readily available to the garden-variety hacker (as opposed to TCP hijacking tools, which can be downloaded from the Internet). However, if you have a properly secured Internet site it will not expose NetBIOS to the Internet anyway.

Policies: NetBIOS Hijacking Avoidance

- Do not allow NetBIOS connections to be made over the Internet.

Summary

Protecting the network layer and the data link layer of your network require that you understand how a hacker looks at your network and take steps to keep the hacker from learning enough about your network to penetrate the security you establish.

Securing your network begins with keeping the hacker from learning too much about it. Use a proxy server to hide your client computers from prying eyes, configure your firewall to not allow service advertisement packets to leave your network, and only allow your DNS server to talk to trusted DNS servers "up" the DNS tree from it.

You should also watch for IP address snooping and port snooping and take steps to stop such activity. Don't support services on your network (such as Finger and Whois) that tell hackers who your users are and what computers exist in your network. Keep hackers from accessing network monitoring tools via SNMP or ICMP.

You should always know what the latest versions of your software are so you can install fixes for security holes in your network. Install the security fixes for Windows NT that stop denial-of-service attacks, and monitor your network for denial-of-service attacks in progress. If you detect an attack in progress take swift action to stop the attack.

Foil impersonation attacks by using software that uses Windows NT Challenge/Response or equal (or greater) security. Use monitoring software to watch for unsanctioned DHCP, WINS, or DNS servers. Install the LAN Manager fix that disables the Windows NT feature of accepting LAN Manager authentication.

You should also recognize that the security measures you implement on your network should change depending on how your network is used. They should change depending on both the operating system software you have and with the tactics being used by hackers. You should always keep up to date on the service pack and hot fix software provided by Microsoft, and you should conscientiously apply fixes that close networking holes in software you use. The price of network security is vigilance.

CHAPTER

21

The Secure Server

By now you've read a number of times in this book that without physical security there is no security. This simply means that network security and software constructs can't keep your data secure if your server is stolen. And some organizations face the possibility that their servers may be seized by the government as evidence in a criminal case—it can happen even if the organization isn't the defendant.

Many hacks rely upon the hacker logging on locally to the server. Removing data is rarely the objective of an intruder at a server console. Adding a small Trojan horse or running a password-cracking tool often is, because it provides a vector for them to exploit the server from the network at their leisure later on. Or, the hacker may want to change security settings or reboot the server to implement a change they've managed to make remotely.

Centralization is axiomatic to security, and physical security is no exception. It's far easier to keep server and compute resources physically secure if they are located in the same room or are clustered in rooms on each floor or in each building. Distributing servers throughout your organization is a great way to increase overall bandwidth, but you need to be sure you can protect workgroup servers adequately from penetration before you decide to use a distributed architecture.

Despite the value of the data stored on servers, many small- to medium-sized companies don't understand the need to protect their computing resources. Many stuff servers in facilities closets, telephone distribution frames, or in someone's office. Without realizing it, they're compromising the security of their organization's data. This chapter covers ways you can protect your servers from being exploited by protecting access to them or by making exploitation difficult even when intruders do have access to them.

Physical Security

Physical security seems pretty simple: At one extreme, you can put your servers in one room, lock the door, and voilà! Your servers are secure. If it were that easy, this chapter would be finished. Banks don't keep money in the manager's office, even with the door locked, because that's simply not secure. Anyone with a ladder can pop a few ceiling tiles, crawl over to the room, and drop down inside. Normal offices do not provide real security.

At the other extreme, many military installations actually put mainframes and servers in room-sized vaults similar to bank vaults. There's a small hole for ventilation, power cables, and fiber-optic network links. There's no serious possibility of intrusion of any sort, and the computers are very physically secure. While this works well, those vaults are extremely expensive and they make administration difficult.

As with all things, you've got to assess the value of your data against the risk of intrusion and determine where in this spectrum you belong. There are a number of secure options that are far less expensive than room-sized vaults and far more secure than your office.

Locks and Alarm Systems

Physical security relies upon locks. The benefits of a strong lock are obvious and don't need to be discussed in detail, but there are some subtle differences between locking devices that are not immediately apparent. For the purposes of this discussion, locks are divided into the following broad categories:

- **Mechanical key locks:** Very experienced locksmiths can usually pick mechanical key locks given a few hours—but it is a very specific skill that even very serious intruders usually don't possess. And, some mechanical key locks are simply too difficult to bother with. It's also possible for a pilfered key to be copied. Remember to retrieve keys from people who no longer require access to a secure facility.

- **Mechanical combination locks:** Skilled individuals can also pick mechanical combination locks, but combination locks suffer from a more serious problem: The distribution of a combination cannot be controlled because combinations are the same things as passwords, and they suffer from all the same problems. They can be written down, told to people for the sake of convenience, or simply tried repeatedly. Unlike the distribution of physical key locks, there are no inherent limitations to the distribution of a combination. If you use mechanical combination locks, you'll have to change the combination every time an employee who knows the combination leaves the company. Many secure facilities require combination changes with the same frequency as network password changes.

- **Mechanical magnetic locks:** Mechanical magnetic locks are rare. They are similar to mechanical locks, but they use a key that has permanently embedded magnets in a specific pattern to pull the tumblers in the lock mechanism. This hides the shape of the key from obvious disclosure, but the pattern can be discerned with iron filings and sometimes duplicated with small permanent magnets.

- **Electronic key locks:** Electronic key locks take a number of forms, but they usually consist of a magnetic swipe card similar to a credit card or a plastic card with a specific pattern of holes. These keys range in complexity from simple magnetic signals to encrypted private keys. These keys are usually used in combination with a security system that logs each time a key is used to open a door—valuable information when reconstructing an intrusion. They can also be integrated into an employee ID tag system that logs which employees have opened doors.

- **Electronic combination locks:** Electronic combination locks consist of a numeric pad upon which a user enters their access code. These locks may or may not log the code that opens a door, but most are capable of being integrated into an alarm system. These locks suffer from the same problem as mechanical combination locks: uncontrolled combination distribution.

- **Digital encrypted signal locks:** Digital signal locks are unlocked by the reception of a radio (or sometimes infrared or ultrasonic) signal containing a digital combination number. These keys can vary from simple single code keys that can be picked up by a scanner and taped, to sophisticated challenge/response signature keys that can't be forged. These keys are usually embedded in identity tags or small keychain devices with a button that can be pressed to identify the user and open the door.

A secure space has secure lock mechanisms on each door, locks that can't simply be removed from the door, doors that can't be removed from outside the space, and no available access except doors. A secure space doesn't have glass windows, a drop ceiling adjoining other rooms, flimsy walls, or ventilation ducts large enough to crawl through.

Alarm systems add to the functionality of electronic locks by integrating them into a system capable of detecting unauthorized entry and alerting a monitoring agency. They can cause horns to sound, lights to flash, or otherwise announce the presence of intruders.

Most alarm systems are enabled and disabled with a keypad based on a combination—avoid these. Combinations are no more secure for alarm systems than they are for locks, and since most companies outsource their alarm monitoring, they're even less secure since at least one other agency has access to your codes.

Good alarm systems can automatically call the police, integrate with fire alarms, and page responsible employees when alarms go off. Alarm systems add considerably to the security of a secure facility.

Policies: Locks

- Do not use combination locks or alarms that are activated or deactivated by codes.

- If you use combination locks, change the combinations at least once a year.

- Always use physical lock devices with keys that can't easily be duplicated.

- Consider using electronic locks that log the time and (if possible) the identity of the person accessing the space. Integrate locks into your alarm system.

- Don't use alarm systems that can be deactivated by a combination.

- Retrieve physical keys from individuals when access is no longer appropriate.

- Change combinations when individuals who know them should no longer have access.

- Don't post signs or stickers that name your security alarm provider. Use generic alarm warnings instead.

Computer Rooms

In the early days of computing, the computer room had one really big computer in it. The room's cooling system was the computer's cooling system, and the walls of the room were the computer's case. These days, computer rooms contain many computers and network devices, each of which maintains its own cooling system and secure design. Computer rooms are now the nucleus of your network because:

- They protect all of your servers in one central location.

- They are the cortex of your network wiring.

- They have uninterruptible power circuits for mission critical servers and network devices.

- The temperature is lowered to keep other employees from hanging out. (Some claim this is good for computers, but they're generally fine up to about 120 degrees, and circulation inside the computer's case is far more important than the ambient temperature in the room.)

Consider all six sides of a space before declaring it secure. Check above drop ceilings, below false floors, and through duct systems to make sure no unexpected access is possible.

If you have a computer room, securing it is pretty easy. Strengthening interior walls and ceilings with steel plates is not particularly difficult, and adding heavy-duty keyed locks isn't too expensive. If you have a central computer room, physical security won't be much of a problem.

Closets and Racks

Many large companies centralize computing resources in computer rooms. Unfortunately, there are only 500 Fortune 500 companies. Most security administrators work for small- to medium-sized businesses that aren't interested in spending hundreds of thousands of dollars on cabinet-sized uninterruptible power supplies and extra HVAC equipment to cool a computer room.

These smaller companies tend to go in the opposite direction—they put in a network without planning for computing facilities. So servers sit on the floor in the back of the broom closet, or in the telephone distribution frame, or under someone's desk.

Networks for these companies may have been designed for maximum bandwidth and minimum cost, which means that servers also perform the routing function, and they are distributed throughout the organization—usually with a server near each work group. Although well designed for their purpose, distributed networks can be difficult to physically secure because network resources aren't centralized.

If you can't move servers to improve security, you can improve the physical security where the server sits. Put strong locks and doors on closets (even mop closets) where network products are located. Don't give the keys to these closets to employees who have equipment or other items located in the same closet as network equipment—have them get a network administrator to gain access to the closet when they need it.

You can also solve the physical security problem closer to the server, even if you can't get control of the room where the server is located. Secure racks of the usual 19-inch variety for network and telephony equipment can be used in place of strut racks or nonsecure case racks. Be careful though—just because a rack has a locking door doesn't mean it's secure. Make sure you can't disassemble the rack easily before using it to secure network equipment. Many three-foot rack cabinets come with strong secure doors—they are perfect for securing distributed networks.

If you really can't spend much money on the problem, get a large safe at a military surplus auction and have two holes cut in the back. Put your server with its UPS, keyboard, and mouse in the safe; run power, network, and video cables out one hole; and put a vent fan on the other. Fill the rest of the safe with something heavy to make it hard to steal, or bolt it to something (with the bolt heads inside the safe, of course). Make sure any destructive attempt to open the safe will destroy the server, so you won't have to worry about your data being compromised.

Reality Check: Secure Racks

A client of mine once showed me the secure locking racks they used in their computer room. The front Plexiglass door locked, as did the rear panel, thus keeping the server secure from intrusion. The side panels could be unscrewed with a dime, however, providing ample access to the devices inside.

Some computers come with cases that can't be opened without a key, or with screws that can only be removed using a keyed screwdriver that comes with the case. These locks are effective against being opened casually by unauthorized personnel, but they won't keep a serious intruder out, and they won't keep your computer from being stolen.

Policies: Secure Containers

- If servers are not located in secure rooms, put them in secure containers. Safes or strong enclosed racks with locks can be used.

Peripherals

Generally, you should remove most peripheral devices from servers when local access to the server is not required. A computer does not need a keyboard, mouse, or monitor to operate, and all of these devices can be hot-plugged into a server while it's running to provide access whenever necessary. Some PS/2 mice (Microsoft brand mice, for example) won't work after being reattached. Test your PS/2 mouse by unplugging it and then plugging it back in before you assign it to your server. Serial port mice always work after reattachment.

Removing peripheral devices makes it difficult for casual intruders like employees to mess around with your servers, but it won't keep a serious intruder away since they could easily bring their own equipment.

Switch boxes that allow you to switch a single keyboard, mouse, and monitor among different servers can also be used to provide a modicum of security if the switchbox is secured in a lock box. Simply switch to an unused port when you've finished configuring your servers and lock the switch to keep prying fingers away from your servers.

Terminology

- **Basic Input/Output System (BIOS):** The default low-level operating program, built into computers, that identifies the hardware present in the system and controls a mass storage device long enough to read and execute the bootstrap program that loads the operating system.

- **Combination:** A password consisting (usually) of numbers and used to gain physical access to a locked security device.

- **Mass storage controller:** A device which interfaces mass storage devices like hard disks to a computer. Often, mass storage controllers like SCSI adapters have their own BIOS installed so they can perform the bootstrap process.

- **Physical security:** Security of actual things, rather than information security or human security. In this context, physical security means controlled access to the actual network devices.

- **Security container:** A locked room, a safe, or any other space with completely controlled access.

- **Uninterruptible power supply (UPS):** A device that guarantees power will be available to all devices attached to it for a certain period of time, regardless of the condition of the power mains.

Environmental Security

Securing your server's environment is an integral part of preventing denial-of-service attacks. Servers are sensitive to four environmental factors:

- Electrical

- Temperature

- Humidity and moisture

- Shock

We'll discuss each of these factors individually in the sections that follow.

Electrical

All computers contain internal power supplies that convert AC line power to DC power and step down the voltage to that required by the low-power internal computer components. These power supplies can normally operate over a rather wide range of power current and electrical conditions, providing a reasonable level of immunity from brownouts (voltage drops), over-voltage conditions, and some spikes. But their primary purpose is not power protection, so they don't protect against lightning strikes and blackouts.

NOTE   Abnormal conditions like brownouts and spikes also tend to wear out electrical components in the power supply and that increases the probability of power supply failure over time.

Protection against lightning strikes requires a power supply capable of "clamping" high voltage by automatically shorting to ground when an extreme over-voltage condition occurs. Protection against blackouts requires rechargeable batteries that provide power when the main power fails. An uninterruptible power supply (UPS) uses both techniques to completely protect high-value equipment from electrical disturbance. (See Figure 21.1.)

There are two types of uninterruptible power supplies: those that switch from main power to battery backup when main power drops below a certain threshold, and those that use main power to charge batteries constantly and constantly generate protected power from the batteries. Of the two types, the second provides better power protection since the protected

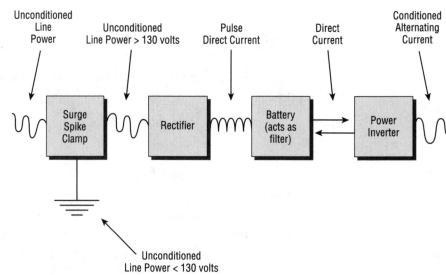

F I G U R E 21.1

An uninterruptible power
supply works to protect
your server.

equipment is isolated from all electrical disturbances on the power mains—but the batteries wear out far faster and must be replaced with greater frequency. Typically, large cabinet-sized UPS devices are of the first type, and small desktop UPS devices are of the second.

Reality Check: When a UPS Can't Help

I designed a small network for a client that included a smart UPS with plenty of battery power for the server. The network was originally designed for 25 users, but the company grew rapidly and soon over 70 computers were logged on to the same server most of the time. Despite the growth, the server was well designed and still within its service capacity. The UPS however, had been outgrown—but not due to additional load.

One day the janitor had noticed a flickering light in the server room, and decided to shut off the power circuit to the room to change the bulb. The UPS signaled the server that power was lost, and that it had not been restored within the allowed maximum time. The server then began a shutdown—which at that time took over 20 minutes due to the number of logged-on users and the fact that Windows NT tries to close each connection gracefully as it goes down. The UPS battery probably lasted about half that time, and the server lost power before it had shut down normally.

When power was restored, the server failed to boot normally and locked up, prompting someone to call me in a panic. I had failed to think about the additional UPS capacity that would be needed as the network grew, due to the additional time it takes a busy server to shut down. The company promptly replaced the UPS and the janitor with higher capacity models.

It is possible that an attacker could cut power to cause a denial of service, although this sort of attack normally only happens in horror films. More likely it will be caused by an electrician who cuts power to a circuit for repair without realizing that your mission-critical servers are on it. Instituting good UPS policy will give you time to restore power before your servers go down.

Policies: Uninterruptible Power Supplies

- Protect all data storage equipment with uninterruptible power supplies.

- Use UPS equipment that can communicate with your servers, and use the server's UPS monitoring software to shut the server down gracefully if power is not restored before the UPS battery loses power.

- Consider protecting all computer and network equipment with uninterruptible power supplies.

- UPS equipment should be located close to protected equipment and use the shortest possible circuit paths to reduce the probability of electrical disturbance created between the UPS and protected equipment.

- Limit the number of devices on the protected side of a UPS to reduce the chance that a device that short circuits will affect other devices on the same circuit. For instance, you don't need to protect your server's monitor with UPS since it doesn't store anything.

- Test UPS facilities at least once every six months by simulating a normal user load and pulling main power. It's important to be under normal load conditions. Make sure most computers are logged on and have an unimportant file open on the server. Inactive servers shut down much faster than active ones. Make sure your server has enough time to close connections gracefully and completely power down on battery power. Do this only when you can tolerate a server crash.

Temperature

There exists a persistent myth in the computing sciences that cold equipment operates better, or more safely, than warm equipment. While this is true in an absolute sense, computers have a far wider comfort zone than human beings, so if a room is comfortable for you, it's more than comfortable for your computers. All semiconductors operate normally up to 150°F (66°C), as do hard disk drives and all other computer components. That's about the temperature that you can handle a hot component, so if you can keep your hand on a device comfortably, it's operating within normal thermal bounds.

But certain components inside computer cases heat up far more than other components. Without proper circulation, these components become overheated quickly and fail. Three components in computers normally create heat above 100°F (38°C):

- Power supplies

- Microprocessors

- Hard disk drives

Of the three, only power supplies must by their nature create this much heat. Power supplies invariably have fans built into them to dissipate the heat they generate.

Microprocessors that raise the temperature enough to require fans and heat sinks are relatively new: Pentium and PowerPC processors are the first mass-market microprocessors to require fans as part of a normal operating specification. Heat is generated because the processors now have far more junctions and operate at faster speeds (thus consuming more power, and more power equals more heat) than earlier processors.

Hard disks are simply easier to manufacture using components and techniques that generate more heat. Thus, more expensive drives from better manufacturers run cooler than cheaper drives from manufacturers less concerned with quality. For computers with only one hard disk, heat isn't much of an issue.

Drives with multiple drives placed close together (such as in RAID packs) frequently suffer from heat problems. When hard disks operate at temperatures exceeding 150° for extended periods, the spindle-bearing lubrication oil breaks down, causing the spindle bearings to wear out faster, which in turn leads to mechanism seizure and disk failure.

Unfortunately, you can't tell by the manufacturer or model whether or not a drive will run hot. Good manufacturers sometimes make cheap drives, and some of the largest names in hard disks have become large because they make cheap disks. It is an unfortunate fact that some of the best manufacturers no longer make hard disks because they can't compete against crappy drives from some mass-market vendors.

You should do research on the Internet about a specific hard disk manufacturer before specifying their product in your server.

Reality Check: Hard Disks and Heat

To protect mission-critical biomedical application servers, a client of mine used two identical servers configured to fail-over to one another in the event of the total failure of either machine. Each had RAID packs of six drives configured to tolerate the failure of two individual disks. The systems were built by one of the largest manufactures of computers in the world.

About six months after the servers went on line, a disk failed. We ordered a replacement and installed it. Mere weeks later, another disk failed in the same machine, so we replaced that one and began to suspect that the RAID controller might be too intolerant of drive spin-up time or that perhaps the SCSI cable wasn't performing up to specification. A few months later, two disks in the other machine failed. At this point, we became seriously concerned about the ability of these servers to perform consistently. The disks ran at a temperature that made them too hot to handle, and they were stacked with approximately 1/4 inch between disks with no fan drawing air past them.

In the course of the next few months, nearly every one of the twelve original disks failed and was replaced—in one instance, three disks went down at the same time and caused a failover to the redundant server. When the replacement disks started showing up with a new warranty disclaimer on the disk that specifically excluded heat-related damage, it was obvious that the manufacturer was receiving a large number of heat-related warranty returns. The drives simply weren't of high enough quality to handle the server environment.

I contacted the server manufacturer and demanded replacement drives from a different manufacturer for both servers. Since the drives were replaced with a higher quality disk, no further failures have occurred.

All moving parts eventually wear out. In computers, this means that you can count on the eventual failure of fans and disk drives. Although fans keep heat-generating components cool, they introduce a failure component. When a processor fan fails, the processor fails shortly after. The same applies to fan-protected power supplies and hard disk drives.

Unfortunately, there's usually no indication that a fan inside a computer case has failed until the component it protects fails and the computer crashes. For this reason, you should choose computers that use passive heat sinks on processors rather than fans, as long as the case has a fan that keeps air circulating inside. (It's easier to tell that a case fan has failed than that a microprocessor fan has.)

Policies: Temperature

- When storing critical data, always use high-quality disks designed for operating in server environments.

- Budget for server cases with good ventilation rather than spending money on extra air conditioning for computer rooms.

- Install alarming temperature sensors or fans with failure indicators in your mission-critical servers.

- Don't put servers or computer equipment in rooms that don't have adequate ventilation or that have equipment that generates excessive heat. Any room that's not comfortable for humans should be avoided.

Humidity and Moisture

Almost everyone knows that computers *shouldn't* get wet. What's less obvious is ways that computers *can* get wet.

Excessive humidity (above 80%) can cause moisture to condense inside computer equipment, which can lead to short circuits and other electrical damage. Removable media can be warped by excessive moisture. Normal air conditioning will prevent these problems.

Check the space above the ceiling panels in the drop ceiling above your computer room. If you see any steam, water, sewage, sprinkler, or HVAC condensation return pipes, move your equipment to ensure a pipe rupture won't leak water onto your equipment.

Reality Check: Unexpected Water Sources

While working at a fiber optic networking company, an employee noticed that water seemed to be dripping from the ceiling above the server rack. The drop-ceiling tile was soaked with water and threatening to burst at any time. We hurriedly draped the equipment in plastic tarps, got buckets, and lifted the bulging tile out. Water drenched my coworker and myself. Apparently, the HVAC equipment for the floor above our office was located directly above our server in the ceiling, and the condensation return had clogged and began to leak.

In another instance, I happened to be working on a client's server (replacing one of the hard disks mentioned in the earlier sidebar, actually) when I felt a drop on my head. Looking up, I noticed quite a bit of water beginning to stream down the wall and pooling on the floor near me. Within minutes, the entire area was soaked, and the facility administrator and I hurriedly downed the servers and got them out of the way.

It had been storming all day, and a portion of the roof had just given way while I was there. Normally the room was unmanned (it was also a Sunday), and had someone not been there when the ceiling gave way both servers would probably been complete losses.

Shock

Hard disk drives are extremely sensitive to shock. The drives themselves usually contain inherent vibration dampening hardware (that's the rubber seal between the top and the bottom) to combat minor vibration effects, but a sharp jar to a server from an earthquake, from being dropped, or from intentional sabotage can cause hard disk failure.

Hard disk platters have considerable rotational inertia when in use and will resist changes in horizontal attitude. Hard disks on moving platforms such as ships or aircraft will wear out faster for this reason, and because they are usually exposed to severe vibration as well.

To protect against shock, use shock absorbing hard disk mounts, rubber feet on the bottom of your case, and install rack-mounted equipment in racks with vibration and shock absorbing pedestals.

You can shock mount any piece of equipment easily. Make a 2-inch diameter coil out of a 24-inch length of 1/4-inch steel cable. Clamp it tightly to the bottom with clamping bolts (the kind available at hardware stores). Bolt the bottom clamp to a floor or shelf, and the top clamp to the bottom of your equipment or rack. If you can't clamp it tightly enough to keep the coils from falling over, weld the coils to the clamp. Figure 21.2 shows how shock mounts can be constructed from common hardware.

FIGURE 21.2

Do-it-yourself shock mounts

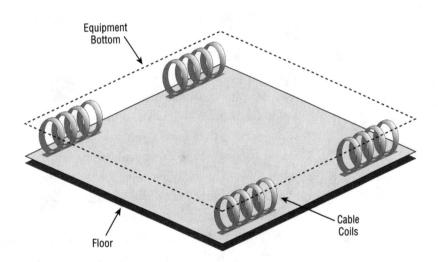

Equipment Bottom

Floor

Cable Coils

Boot Security

Windows NT File System (NTFS) security is a veritable fortress when set up correctly. Users logged on locally or coming in from the network have very little chance of circumventing your security settings if they are correctly implemented.

Reality Check: Shock Mounting

While aboard ship when I served in the U.S. Navy, I could not keep server disks operational for more than about a year at a time. That was before I adapted the shock mounting method described above from mounts used for military equipment racks. After I implemented it for servers, no disks failed for the remainder of my tour of duty. I now recommend it for all my customers in California.

That is unless they insert a DOS boot floppy and hit the reset button on your server. Windows NT can't protect the files on your disk drives if it's not running. Encryption is not a part of the file system, so nothing keeps another operating system from accessing hard disk sectors at a low level and returning the information they contain to a user. The NTFS system structures are not difficult to track down, and utilities already exist that will mount NTFS-formatted volumes as read-only volumes under MS-DOS and under Linux. This is all an intruder needs to copy your data onto a removable media drive (they can even mount a driver for your tape drive and use your own equipment to copy the data) and walk away with it.

Controlling this aspect of security means controlling the boot process of your computer. Whenever an intruder can boot a removable media device or an operating system on another partition or disk, they can potentially steal data from your server.

On the other hand, you're safe if your server:

- Invariably boots the proper Windows NT installation every time it's started

- Never looks for (or doesn't have attached) removable media drives during the boot process

- Has a BIOS that is strongly password protected

- Has a case that can't be opened

Intruders can cause denial of service by resetting your machine, but they can't steal data because they can't boot another operating system.

Booting Removable Media

All modern motherboards support booting some form of removable media. Floppies are always supported, and most new computers can boot at least IDE CD-ROMs. SCSI mass storage controllers can usually be configured to boot nearly any attached SCSI device: CD-ROMs, removable cartridge hard disks, and even tape drives. Each of these boot media options represents a different vector that can be exploited to gain access to the data on your server.

Floppy Disks

All computers will boot floppy disks—in fact, early PCs could only boot from floppy disks. It wasn't until MS-DOS 2.11 and the PC XT that PCs supported booting from hard disks. Booting from floppy disks is an important restorative and diagnostic feature. If your hard disk fails to boot, you probably don't have many other options except a floppy boot. You may also need to boot from a floppy to install your computer's operating system unless you can boot from CD-ROM.

Booting from a floppy is too useful for us to seriously recommend removing floppy drives from your servers, but most BIOS configuration programs will allow you to disable the Boot from Floppy feature. Even in those that can't, you can remove the floppy setup information completely so the computer won't recognize a floppy that is attached and can't boot from it. Set up another floppy drive as the B: drive to allow floppy access for installing drivers and other software while the system is running. This is safe since you can't normally boot from the B: drive.

By protecting your BIOS configuration page with a password, you can prevent unauthorized access to your server via the floppy boot vector.

If your server's BIOS doesn't support password protection, get a new motherboard.

Policies: Boot Floppies

- Disable the Boot from Floppy feature in your BIOS configuration program.

- If your BIOS doesn't support disabling the Boot from Floppy feature, disable the A: (bootable) floppy drive by removing its configuration data.

- Protect your BIOS floppy disk settings with a strong password.

- Make certain your server's case can't be breached to reset the motherboard BIOS password.

CD-ROM Readers

Servers with SCSI CD-ROM drives or newer IDE CD-ROMs may support booting from CD-ROM. Booting a CD-ROM to install an operating system is far faster than setting it up with floppies, so it can be a real convenience when you need it. But you should never leave CD-ROM booting set in your operating system because it provides another vector for access to your hard disk drive.

By booting the Windows NT CD-ROM, an attacker could install a fresh version of Windows NT, set the administrative password, mount your disks, and take ownership of all the files contained therein. Of course you'd find out the next day, but by then it would be too late.

Removable Cartridge Hard Disks

Most SCSI adapters support booting from any SCSI device, which means an intruder could potentially set your server's BIOS to boot from a removable cartridge hard disk like a Zip, Jaz, SyJet, or even from tape in some cases.

Policies: Bootable CD-ROMs

- After installing your operating system, always disable the boot from CD-ROM setting in your motherboard's BIOS.

Most servers have an external SCSI port to which one of the new portable cartridge hard disks like Zip or SyJet drives can be attached. An intruder can bring their own drive, attach it to your server's external SCSI port, modify your SCSI adapter's BIOS (which is separate from your computer's BIOS and not protected by the same password) and boot their own operating system. Even small removable cartridge hard disks have more than enough room to boot sophisticated operating systems like Linux, Windows 95, NT, or other versions of UNIX.

Policies: Mass Storage Controller BIOS Configuration

- Make sure your mass storage controllers that have their own BIOS configuration programs also support password protection so that they can't be exploited to circumvent the normal boot process. Most SCSI controllers have their own separate BIOSs—make sure those you use support password protection!

Securing the BIOS

Protect your server's boot process by configuring your servers not to boot from any source but the primary internal hard disk. Most BIOS configuration programs allow you to specify exactly which disks can be booted from and in what order. Avoid those that don't.

Each BIOS configuration program is different (even those from the same manufacturer vary significantly from version to version) so we can't really show you how your BIOS configuration program works. You should have received a manual with your server or motherboard that explains the BIOS features in detail, or you can call the manufacturer's tech support line or visit their Web site for more information on exactly how to secure your BIOS.

BIOS settings on all computers can be erased by shorting a jumper somewhere on the motherboard. This prevents the computer from being worthless if you forget the BIOS password. You'll need to have a secure computer case to prevent intruders from getting access to this jumper and erasing your BIOS password. Storing servers in safes or locked cabinets can help prevent this.

Policies: BIOS Configuration Programs

- Use only BIOS configuration programs that support strong password protection. Most modern motherboards come with BIOS configuration programs that support this feature.

- Disable the BIOS feature that displays which key to press to enter the BIOS configuration program during boot, if possible.

- Make sure servers can't be disassembled to gain access to the BIOS erasure jumper.

Alternate Boot OS

Intruders won't have to go through all the hassle discussed above to boot removable media if you conveniently provide a bootable DOS volume on your server for them. It's very convenient to use Windows NT's dual boot feature to provide a small DOS partition with hardware configuration software—for you and for intruders. They won't need to circumvent your boot security if they can simply boot your DOS partition.

NTFSDOS and Friends

Programs like NTFSDOS, which allows MS-DOS access to NTFS partitions irrespective of Windows NT's security settings, can simply be run from a floppy disk. Or NTFSDOS can be downloaded directly off the Net if your partition contains enough software to establish a TCP/IP connection and run an FTP client (most Windows 95 installs meet these criteria).

NTFSDOS is currently available for both MS-DOS and Linux. It provides read-only access to a server's NTFS partition and completely bypasses all security settings normally enforced by Windows NT. If your computer can be booted to MS-DOS, you are potentially vulnerable to an intrusion via NTFSDOS. The MS-DOS version of NTFSDOS is described in detail in Appendix B and is provided on the companion CD-ROM for your inspection.

Policies: Dual Booting

- Do not configure your server to dual boot to any operating system other than Windows NT. Other operating systems can exploit their low-level access to hard disk drives to circumvent NTFS security permissions.

- Keep MS-DOS-based hardware configuration utilities in a secure locked location away from your server.

- If you use an alternate installation of Windows NT for software testing and repair operations, make sure it has identical security settings to the degree that is practicable.

Driver and Service Security

Now that your server is booting securely, it's time to step up the software ladder to the next vector: drivers and services. Drivers are trusted by the Windows NT kernel, which means that they operate inside the kernel's boundary security layer. They have full access to each other's memory regions, and they don't have to go through the normal secure methods to pass information from one to another.

This lack of strong interdriver security is a speed optimization that Microsoft chose to allow early in the development of Windows NT. Security checking at the driver and service level would make Windows NT an even bigger CPU hog than it already is, and would keep it from competing favorably against highly optimized but nonsecure systems like NetWare.

This means that drivers are the tools for achieving hacking nirvana—if hackers can get a driver installed, they can do anything they want inside Windows NT's kernel space. That includes hooking into the logon process to record passwords or installing a Trojan horse that will wait for connection attempts.

NTFS file permissions prevent this, unless the administrative account is compromised. But NTFS permissions can't prevent it if they're not in use. For this reason, Windows NT is totally nonsecure when booted from a FAT volume.

Because FAT volumes don't support security, you can't keep people from adding files to the Windows NT boot process.

Because drivers and services operate inside Windows NT's security boundaries, due to oversight in their design they can circumvent security. This has already happened a few times with Microsoft services like IIS, and it will probably happen more often in the future as more vendors begin writing software for Windows NT.

Services That Can Circumvent Security

The scheduler service is a good example of a service that causes a security loophole. When you use the AT command to schedule the regular execution of a command (or one of the numerous graphical front-ends for the scheduler service) you are adding a task that is executed by the system—not by you, the logged-on user. This means that the service runs with all the permissions allowed to the system account, not the permissions allowed to your account.

For instance, the following command:

```
AT 12:10 /interactive "c:\winnt\system32\taskmgr.exe
```

Will launch the Task Manager for interactive use at the server's console at 12:10 p.m. with the security permissions of the system. Anyone at the console at that time has even greater control over the system than an administrator, because the system will not disallow any activity. You could even shut down the cursor service (`csrss.exe`, the service that provides that little white pointing thing on the screen) if you so desired.

Windows NT retains a modicum of security by reserving use of the scheduler service for administrators. Only administrators can add or delete tasks. And, unless specifically allowed by the interactive switch, there's no way the logged-on user can interact with the scheduled service.

Reality Check: Internet Information Server

IIS is another example of a service that can accidentally circumvent security. Early versions of IIS (1.0) contained a bug that allowed users to browse down through the server's hard disk below the level of the IIS root directory. The bug did not circumvent NTFS security, but a number of Internet servers used FAT as their file systems, making the servers completely vulnerable to exploitation by Internet hackers.

The Batch File Problem

Unfortunately, most administrators actually execute batch files using the scheduler service rather than executable programs, because batch files can be easily modified without changing the schedule list. This means that anyone with write access to the batch file can modify it to run any program they want, with the permissions allowed by the system. They could make themselves an administrator, copy a file to a new location, or perform any other mischievous operation to gain further access to the system.

Policies: Scheduler Service

- Disable the scheduler service.

- If you use the scheduler service, execute the desired command directly rather than through a batch file, and don't allow interactive access.

Application Security

Some popular server applications, including Lotus Notes and a number of fax servers, are designed to be run as user-mode applications through a logged-on user account on a Windows NT server instead of as a service. They also usually want full access to the server through an Administrator account or its equivalent.

Quite simply, this means that your server already has someone logged in, so there's no need to attempt a password. An intruder can just walk right up and start hacking.

WARNING Password-protected screen savers are no substitute for the WinLogon service. A hacker can use the `netstat` command to determine the Net-BIOS name of the account logged in at the server from over the network, thus deobfuscating your renamed Administrator account.

Finally, these server applications won't come back up automatically when your server is restarted unless you configure the server to automatically log on at boot. Configuring your server to log on automatically is another major security problem because a password-protected screen saver won't kick in as long as someone at the console is moving the mouse after they've reset your server—a good reason why you shouldn't rely on password protected screensavers for security.

Server software written to execute as user-mode applications is simply poorly designed and poorly implemented. Software companies that can't figure out how to write a server application as a service can't be trusted to write bug-free software anyway. Don't use these applications; use a competing product with similar functionality that runs as a service.

NOTE The Windows NT Resource Kit contains a software utility that allows a user-mode application to run as a service. This can be used to secure user-mode applications when you must use them.

Storage Security

Since this has been a breezy and somewhat optimistic book so far, let's assume the worst for a moment about your data security. Consider the following scenario: Your pager goes off in the middle of the night—it's the building alarm system indicating a breach. You arrive at work before daybreak to find a few police officers writing vigorously on their

---

Policies: User-Mode Service Applications

- Never leave a logged-on server unattended. If service software requires this, don't use it.

- If you must use server applications that normally require a logged-on account, use the Microsoft utility in the Windows NT Resource Kit to configure them as a service.

- Never configure a Windows NT computer attached to a network to log on automatically.

- Don't rely on screen savers to secure a computer console.

---

notepads about the truck-sized hole in the exterior wall of your computer room. Your server is gone.

You know that the perpetrator can simply mount your server disks in their system and take ownership of all of your files. What could you have done to prevent the loss of data?

Disk Encryption

Yep, disk encryption. Windows NT does not natively encrypt data on your hard disk, but there are a number of utilities available that will. Typically, these utilities create a large file on your disk and implement an encrypted partition inside. Good ones operate at a low enough level that the encrypted partition existing inside the file can be NTFS formatted to allow the use of normal NFTS security for logged-on users.

The great thing about disk encryption is that it can be entirely seamless. You simply create the secure volume, tell users to put all secret documents there, and you're safe. You have to enter your password or present your encryption key to mount the volume for the first time, so no third party can exploit your disk by installing it in another server—or by using tools like NTFSDOS to gain low-level access to your disk.

Use disk encryption only for sensitive documents. Encrypting mundane data like applications, NT system files, or routine data just wastes compute time and makes your server harder to use.

Your secret encrypted volume should only be used for files that aren't required for the proper operation of your server, since you might not be around to provide the secure key when the server is rebooted.

Create the encryption volume with a name that sounds routine and could explain the large file. I recommend placing it in the root directory of a non-system volume and naming it pagefile.sys. Few thieves (or government agents, if that's the threat you fear) familiar with Windows NT would look twice at a large file with this name. Hide the disk encryption software deep in the bowels of your system directory and remove shortcuts to it in your start menu to keep its presence obfuscated. You may even want to name the application files something else (like excel.exe for instance).

Disk encryption has three drawbacks:

- It takes time. Encryption is CPU intensive, so you may need to buff up your server if you intend to make heavy use of disk encryption.

- It's not automatic. Obviously, if your secure volume mounted automatically, it would be worthless. So you won't be able to automatically remount the volume after a server boot. This is a small price to pay for security, however.

- If you forget your password or lose your key, you're screwed. There's no recovery here, except from backup media.

Backup Media

If you're a good network administrator, you back up your server daily, and you keep at least one full system backup copy off site in the event that your primary facility is somehow destroyed. That off-site facility is most likely your house. By now, you can probably see where this discussion is going: That tape contains the entire contents of your servers, and is far easier to steal and exploit than a server.

Microsoft's backup software (written by Arcada and closely related to Backup Exec, by the way) doesn't provide for security or encryption in any real respect. Although a backup set can be configured to require a password, the data on the tape is not encrypted. That password is the security equivalent of a car lock—it only keeps honest people honest. You've got to physically protect your backup media if you use Microsoft's backup software.

Keep your backup tapes in a vault—or at least in a room with as much physical security as your computer room. Number them so that you can easily tell if one is missing. Keep a catalog of tape sets that includes when the tape was run and who the backup operator was. Never leave a backup tape sitting in the tape drive.

Reality Check: Backup Media

I was once commissioned to attempt to decrypt the contents of a server that had been seized by a government agency as evidence in a criminal case. I examined the server and determined that it had been properly secured, that the encryption software in use was strong, and that the encryption key existed nowhere on the server or on the floppies that had been seized with the machine.

I didn't have the compute resources to even attempt a brute force decryption, so I decided to call the person who had given me the assignment and have the machine picked up. As I was dialing, the tape drive caught my eye. I pressed the eject button and, sure enough, a 4mm DAT tape ejected.

The tape contained all the evidence the government needed to prove their case. So remember: Any flaw in your entire security policy invalidates all other efforts.

Summary

If your servers are not physically secure, neither is your network. Physical security is the basis for all other Windows NT security, since without physical security you cannot ensure that Windows NT's secure architecture is running to protect your data. Securing servers requires implementing a number of otherwise unrelated aspects of security:

- Physical security includes strong building security, computer room security, and the security provided by storage racks and cabinets.

- Environmental security includes electrical power stabilization, normal temperature control, protection from moisture and humidity, and protection from physical shock and vibration.

- Boot security includes securing the boot process against the use of alternate boot methods such as floppy disks, CD-ROMs, and SCSI devices.

- Driver and service security includes protection against virii and Trojan horses, as well as against normal Windows NT services that can be exploited to gain control of a secure system.

- Application security is implemented by making sure no user logon is required to run service applications.

- Storage security includes server disk encryption, and the security and protection of backup media.

Properly implementing these aspects of security will protect your servers from exploitation whether or not an intruder gains physical access to them.

C H A P T E R

22

Physical Layer Security

he physical layer is made up of the actual media used to transmit data on the network. This media is usually copper or optical fiber wiring, but sometimes it consists of radio signals (used by microwave transceivers) or light signals (used by infrared diode and laser systems) cast through free space.

Security at the physical layer consists of those measures that ensure that access to the actual cabling or signaling in a network is secure from intrusion or penetration. The physical layer can be penetrated in the following ways:

- **Wiretapping:** Directly connects an extra "listen only" communications connection to an existing connection to allow eavesdropping.

- **Inductance amplification:** Exploits the radiation from electrical signals by placing an inductance amplifier next to a cable (without penetrating it) to receive the signal running through the cable.

- **Covert attachment:** Unauthorized equipment is simply attached to normal unused ports in a communication system.

Federal law enforcement agencies routinely use wiretaps (about a thousand times a year in the United States) to gather evidence in criminal cases. These wiretaps are exploitations of the fundamental lack of physical layer security in telephone systems: Anywhere along the line between callers in a telephone conversation, the telephone wires can be tapped for eavesdropping.

Inductance amplification is commonly used in cable installation to trace out which cable in a bundle runs to a specific port. In fact, you can purchase an inductance amplifier (called a *toner*) capable of directly eavesdropping on a telephone conversation through any phone cable at any electronics store for about $25. These inductance amplifiers are sufficient for extracting the data stream of a modem conversation, which can then be decoded by running it into another modem that uses the same protocols. There are also inductance amplifiers that show how much network traffic is running over a twisted pair cable by detecting the presence or absence of a network signal. High quality inductance amplifiers of this type may be able to discern the data stream running through the cable.

Covert access occurs when an unauthorized computer or network sniffer is plugged into an unused hub port on your network. It's also possible for someone to put a hub where a client computer is located to easily break out more access points—without your knowledge. And in coaxial networks (especially 10Base-5) an intruder can simply clamp a vampire tap around an existing cable to create an access point without interrupting anyone's service.

But why would anyone bother with a physical layer intrusion, especially since such intrusion must be performed locally? Because you've got strong Internet security that they couldn't get past, and because your wide-area data links are encrypted, so they couldn't tap them usefully. Put simply: because the rest of your security is strong, so physical layer security is now the weakest link.

Except in special circumstances, physical layer security problems are related either to espionage or to theft. Few hackers are tenacious enough to bother leaving their lair to perpetrate a hack, and few have any serious criminal intent. Physical layer intrusions are performed mostly by foreign competition eager to gain information, by the government in criminal cases, or by serious criminals attempting to perpetrate a large theft of assets (usually against financial institutions).

Reality Check: Uncle Sam or Big Brother?

Recent legislation requires telephone switch manufacturers to install wiretapping ports on digital telephone switches so that the federal government can wiretap automatically and without the cooperation of a telephone company. Proposed legislation seeks to require an infrastructure that will allow federal law enforcement to wiretap 1 percent of all telephone communications simultaneously.

This infrastructure will allow the government to "browse" for illegal activity being conducted over the telephone system using voice recognition technology that automatically records conversations that include key words like "bomb," "FBI," and "drug"—or for any other purpose. Although it is currently illegal for the federal government to use technology in this manner, this browsing capacity will be in place for a future government to use as the legal climate dictates.

The federal government is also actively seeking the power to restrict the use of encryption inside the United States, because encryption reduces their ability to effectively wiretap criminal activities. Unfortunately (for the government), strong encryption algorithms are well known and easy to create. Strong encryption technology is already in the hands of most criminals, so these restrictions will actually only affect the business use of encryption for privacy.

As of this writing, the federal government is using an antiquated World War I era munitions export restriction law to restrict software manufacturers from exporting strong encryption—by classifying encryption software as a weapon. This law also keeps us from including strong domestic-grade encryption software on the companion CD-ROM of this book because some copies of the book are being exported.

If you would like to keep your right to use strong network encryption for network privacy, make sure you and your company oppose the government's attempt to restrict the freedoms we currently enjoy.

Network Media and Their Vulnerabilities

Each of the several network media has certain specific vulnerabilities. Each medium requires specific expertise to exploit. Certain media are readily exploited; others are practically impossible to exploit. Each medium is presented in order of its presently installed base.

All electrical signals generate electromagnetic radiation (radio signals) congruent to the data transmission on the wire—in other words, copper wires are radio antennas that broadcast the data they carry. Fortunately, the radiation is very low power and easily clobbered by the other electromagnetic interference that usually coexists, such as power wiring, fluorescent lighting, electric motors, and most other electrical devices. Signals from low voltage systems like networks are not useful beyond about six inches from the wire, but a device placed on the wire or clamped around it can extract useful data from the wire without penetrating the cable sheath.

Reality Check: Electromagnetic Interference and Signal Induction

Have you ever heard someone else's faint conversation while you were on the phone? Their conversation radiates from the wire pair it's being carried on and induces an analogous signal in the wire pair carrying your conversation. Somewhere along the line, the wire pair carrying your conversation is next to the wire pair carrying their conversation.

This effect is called *cross talk,* and it can occur in data systems as well as voice systems. Cross talk is usually presented as simple interference that reduces the distance that a signal can be transmitted, but with a sensitive receiver, data flowing on one pair can be read off the pair next to it in the cable. Regular 10Base-T and 100Base-TX Ethernet over twisted pair wire have two unused pairs in a regular Category 3, 4, or 5 cable. With sensitive equipment, data can be read off the unused pairs at either the station side (from a tap located in the wall-plate) or in the wiring closet at the patch panel side.

Terminology

- **Coaxial:** A type of cable consisting of a solid wire conductor shielded by a coaxial wire mesh. Coaxial cable is capable of carrying a wide spectrum of broadcast radio frequency (generally 500MHz in bandwidth). Typically used for bus topology networks and for video.

- **Cross talk:** The inductance of radio frequency signal in adjacent wires.

- **Inductance:** An aspect of the fundamental electromagnetic property in which a moving current in a conductor creates a magnetic field proportional (and analogous) to the current in the cable. This magnetic field is capable of then inducing current in other conductors present in its domain. Inductance can be exploited by sensitive amplifiers to read signals off of electrical conductors.

- **Inductance amplification:** The amplification of the inductance field of a conductor for the purpose of obtaining useful information.

- **Media:** A material used to convey information. In computer networks, media consists of copper wiring, optical fiber, broadcast radio signals, or light signals.

- **Optical fiber:** Thin glass filaments used to conduct light between two distant points. Usually light in the infrared 850nm, 1310nm, or 1550nm wavelengths is used, depending upon the budget allowed and the distance required. The light may be incoherent, as when generated by light-emitting diodes, or coherent, as when generated by laser diodes.

- **Shielded twisted pair:** A cable consisting of (for networks) four pairs of individually foil-shielded pairs of 24-gauge solid or stranded copper wire, enclosed in another foil-shielded cable sheath.

- **Toner:** A small portable inductance amplifier used to identify a specific cable in a bundle by receiving a special tone presented on that cable by a tone generator. Also useful for wiretapping.

- **Unshielded twisted pair:** A cable consisting of (for networks) four pairs of 24-gauge solid or stranded copper wire. Each pair is twisted together to make certain they are always within the same magnetic domain, which affords a high degree of noise cancellation and immunity compared to nontwisted wires.

Twisted Pair Cable

Unshielded twisted pair (UTP) wiring for networks consists of four pairs of 24-gauge wire. Each wire in a pair transmits the opposite signal as the other wire, so that in sum the transmitted power is zero for each pair—this tends to flatten the electromagnetic transmission and increase immunity to induced signals from adjacent pairs (cross talk). Figure 22.1 shows how this works. At the receiving end, the negative wire is inverted and summed with the positive side to produce the strongest possible received signal.

FIGURE 22.1

Differential signaling over twisted pair

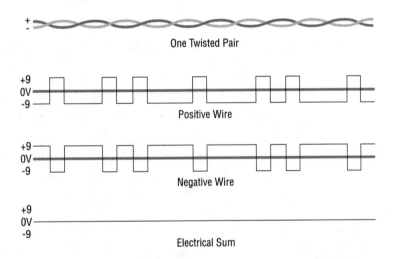

Twisted pair wiring comes in levels (or categories) according to its information carrying capacity. Information carrying capacity in twisted pair wiring is a function of its quality of manufacture and the strictness of control of the rate of twist in the wire while it's being manufactured. Twisted pair wiring radiates radio waves based on the length of a single twist. A pair that twists once every four inches will generate primary interference waves within a four-inch period.

If the various pairs in a cable are twisted at the same rate, they will cause radio interference with each other. So by ensuring that each pair in a cable is twisted at a rate that does not form harmonics (multiples) of the wave periods generated by other pairs, the pairs interfere less with each other. The categories established for twisted pair are:

- **Level 1:** Legacy voice applications

- **Level 2:** New voice wiring, legacy serial data applications

- **Level 3:** 10MB/sec, sufficient for Ethernet or 4MB Token Ring

- **Level 4:** 20MB/sec, sufficient for 16MB Token Ring

- **Level 5:** 100MB/sec, sufficient for Fast Ethernet or CDDI (FDDI over copper)

- **Level 6 (Proposed):** 155MB/sec sufficient for ATM-155

Category 3, 4, and 5 unshielded twisted pair wiring is designed not to interfere with itself to various degrees, but is not immune to external interference sources, nor is the data transmitted immune from being received by other devices. Signals on twisted pair wiring can be readily received by inductance amplifiers external to the cable or by reading induced signal (cross talk) off unused pairs. It's a simple task to decode data being read off wires using a network sniffer.

Shielded twisted pair wiring (STP) provides a measure of electrical immunity from outside sources similar to Category 4. However, since its rate of twist is not well controlled, it still suffers from cross talk. Due to it's high cost compared to UTP, it is not commonly used in the United States, but it is required by building codes in many European countries.

Unshielded twisted pair wiring is rarely used outdoors or between buildings, so if you are comfortable with the level of physical security at your site and the loyalty of your coworkers, you shouldn't have many twisted pair security problems.

Policies: Twisted Pair Wiring

- Choose optical fiber to the desk instead of twisted pair wiring where security requirements are high and budgets allow. Currently, optical fiber wiring is only about twice the price of twisted pair wiring to the desk, and optical fiber network devices are between four and 10 times the cost.

- Make certain all twisted pair wiring outside wiring closets and drop ceilings or false floors is enclosed in nonmetallic pipe, conduit, or plastic network raceway (like Panduit). Put breaking tape or paint on the seams of pipe and raceway joints to show if they've been opened.

- Paint the seams of drop ceiling tiles to show when they've been removed. Repaint them after routine authorized access.

- Consider running all network wiring in the ceiling in cable trays that can be closed and sealed. This can be very expensive, so you may want to consider optical fiber as an alternative.

- Lock all wiring closets with the same level of protection you afford your computer rooms.

Coaxial Cable

Coaxial cable is far more resistant than twisted pair wiring to the effects of electromagnetic interference in cabling systems. This is because the center conductor is completely shielded by a coaxial ground sheath that essentially absorbs most electromagnetic inductance coming into or out of the cable. This makes the interior environment (the center conductor) essentially free from the effects of electromagnetic interference. Inductance amplifiers must be very powerful to read a useful signal from a coaxial cable, if it's possible at all.

But that doesn't mean coaxial cable is secure. Many coaxial network devices simply pierce the cable sheath and ground shield with a pin that reaches the center conductor. (This is called vampire tapping because the devices usually have two triangle-shaped pins that resemble vampire teeth.) These devices are then able to receive and transmit data on the cable. Unless your cable runs are secure through their entire length, your network could be vulnerable to such wiretapping by an unauthorized user.

Since coaxial networks are designed for multiple devices to exist on a single cable, there's no good way to tell that this sort of penetration has occurred. The intruder doesn't even have to remain in your building. They can simply run a cable from the vampire tap to a wireless bridge on the roof of your building, and then read (or transmit) data on your network from miles away. So a single physical penetration of an hour or less could open your network to routine exploitation if so desired.

Coaxial cable (especially 10Base-5) is often used to connect buildings that are close to each other, so it's quite possible that either aerial or buried coaxial cable exists at multibuilding sites. This cable could be accessed without anyone's knowledge if security at your premises is enforced only inside buildings.

Policies: Coaxial Cable

- Enclose all coaxial cable runs in pipe or conduit that is painted so that it will show intrusion attempts.

- Enclose all outdoor-buried cable in metal conduit whether the cable requires it or not.

- Consider pressurizing sealed conduit that runs between buildings and putting alarmed pressure sensors at each building entry point. When pressure suddenly drops in the conduit, an intrusion or a break in the conduit has occurred.

- Ensure that aerial coaxial cable runs are not easily accessible from the tops of buildings or from telephone poles.

Optical Fiber

Optical fiber is the most secure cable type because it relies on light signals rather than electrical signals for data transmission. No electromagnetic signals permeate the sheath of the cable, so there's nothing to be detected. The light does not induce signals in other fibers in the same bundle, so there's no cross talk effect.

Light travels through a mirrored path created by the interface between slightly different types of glass. Light in the center (or core) of the optical fiber reflects off the boundary to the next type of glass, so it stays coupled inside the core of the glass even when the fiber bends around corners. (The sidebar that follows, called *Testing Light Coupling at Refractive Boundaries,* describes this refractive mirror effect in more detail.)

The smaller the difference between the refractive indexes of two materials, the smaller the angle of incidence must be for light to reflect. Two materials that are very close to one another in refractive index will only couple light with a small angle of incidence to the boundary, as shown in Figure 22.2.

FIGURE 22.2

Light coupling in optical fiber

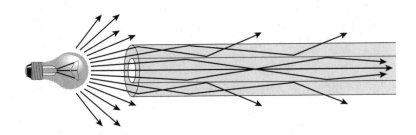

Because the types of glass used in optical fiber are very close in refractive index, only light that strikes the boundary with a relatively low angle of incidence remains coupled. In fact, optical fiber tends to shed light for tens or hundreds of meters down the fiber at bends. The point at which all light that will eventually decouple under normal bending circumstances has been reached is called *equilibrium.* After this point, no further light is lost through the cable due to initial incoherence.

You can force equilibrium just after signal launch by wrapping your fiber cables at their bend radius (usually one inch, or about the diameter of a coffee cup) a few times right where the fiber leaves the source equipment. In any case, the light shed through normal coupling loss isn't strong enough to penetrate the cable sheath or to be usefully detected.

It is theoretically possible to bleed a signal off of an optical fiber without breaking the fiber by stripping away the cable and all plastic cladding to reveal just the glass fiber, and then bending it beyond the normal bend radius and placing a sensitive receiver on the glass cladding. Because the acceptance aperture has been exceeded, a significant amount of light will decouple and could be detectable. Figure 22.3 shows this process.

In reality it's nearly impossible to strip the plastic cladding of an optical fiber cable away without breaking the fiber. Optical fiber is about the same diameter as coarse hair, and it is considerably more fragile. Any mechanical stripping process is certain to destroy the fiber.

FIGURE 22.3

Tapping an optical fiber cable

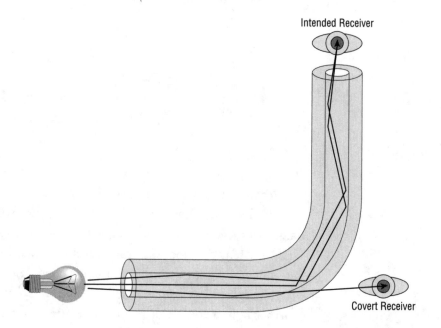

It is possible to burn the plastic cable components away without damaging the fiber as long as both ends of the fiber are anchored so as not to stress the unprotected fiber. At that point, the intruder must bend the fiber enough to ensure a detectable signal without causing enough attenuation that the light falls below the receiver's threshold, which would cause link loss.

In any case, if you think that this sort of intrusion is possible, you can easily use an optical splitter at the receiving end of your link. By plugging one split connection into your receiver and the other into an optical fiber attenuation meter you can alarm on any sudden decrease in signal strength—thus making optical fiber virtually penetration proof.

Testing Light Coupling at Refractive Boundaries

You can see the refractive mirror effect yourself by comparing the index of refraction between water-glass boundaries and air-glass boundaries. Try this:

1. Plunge your head into a fish tank. If you don't have a fish tank, use one at the house of a friend or at a seafood restaurant.

2. Notice that from inside the fish tank, you can't see out. Rather, the walls of the tank appear much like a mirror.

This is because the refractive index of water and glass is higher than the refractive index of air (that is, light travels faster through air than it does through glass or water, so the light reflects back at certain angles of incidence). This may explain why fish never seem to notice that they're actually trapped in a small tank in a living room.

Wireless

Wireless connections are inherently nonsecure. The only way to totally secure a wireless connection is by using encryption at higher layers. Highly directional wireless connections like microwave and laser are more secure than typical broadcast technologies like packet radio or cellular, but there really isn't any way to absolutely secure a wireless connection without using encryption at a higher layer.

You may have heard that spread spectrum technology is an encryption device. It is not. It does obfuscate a signal and make it far harder to detect and reliably receive, but it doesn't eliminate the possibility that it could be surreptitiously received.

WARNING   If you can receive a wireless signal, so can someone else.

Highly directional wireless systems like microwave or laser will require all receivers to be within line of sight along the same direction—but a microwave signal doesn't stop at your receiver, and a laser signal doesn't necessarily stop there either.

Spanning Tree

Spanning tree radio networking technology allows multiple transceivers to participate in a wireless network—more than the two allowed by point-to-point radio communications. This makes the ad-hoc setup of local area networks very quick and easy and works well for mobile workgroups or situations where network nodes need to be moved around a small area. This technology also makes it possible for an intruder to secretly establish a link to your spanning tree wireless network simply by using a compatible adapter in range. Newer models of network adapters require security identifiers to begin networking, but these security identifiers are sometimes not very secure.

Infrared and Laser Point-to-Point

Wireless infrared light-emitting diode technology (the same technology used in television remote controls) is used on occasion for short distance network links, either for workgroup connections in a single room or for point-to-point connections between adjacent buildings. Indoor infrared connections are reasonably secure since they won't penetrate walls (although there is a small possibility that a highly focused receiver could receive useful data through a window). Outdoor laser and infrared LED links are susceptible to intrusion by another receiver located near your receiver. This additional receiver would be rather difficult to hide, so routine inspection can keep these links secure. Optical wireless links are far more difficult to intrude upon than radio links since they only work when line of sight between the transmitter and receiver exists.

Policies: Wireless Networking

- Use cabled systems instead of wireless transmission whenever possible.

- Always encrypt data transmitted over wireless links.

- Never use spanning tree technology for interbuilding links. If you use spanning tree technology for intrabuilding links, be sure that the technology you use is distance limited to the intended radius of operation and that your company controls all property within the potential reception area.

- Choose optical point-to-point systems over microwave radio systems for short distance building-to-building links if weather conditions are usually favorable.

Network Topologies and Security

In addition to the media type used, topology can have a dramatic effect on network security. Many of the various media types are typically associated with the topology they support most often—but there's no hard and fast rule that a specific media must conform to a certain topology. The four common network topologies are:

- Point-to-point (as in wide area links)

- Bus (as in Ethernet 10Base-2 and 10Base-5)

- Star (as in Ethernet 10Base-T and 10Base-F)

- Ring (as in Token Ring and FDDI)

Each topology is discussed based on its security merits irrespective of the topology's popularity or installed base. In reality, the vast majority of networks are Ethernet, and of those the majority are star-wired twisted-pair networks.

Terminology

- **Bus:** A network topology in which all transceivers are connected to a single shared wire, usually coaxial.

- **Hub:** The central access point at which the individual segments of a star-wired network are combined into a single shared media broadcast domain. Hubs can be active (powered), in the case of copper hubs and repeating optical hubs; or passive (non-powered), in the case of optical hubs, which are really just complex splitters.

- **Ring:** A network topology in which data is transmitted from one transceiver to the next in round-robin fashion.

- **Star:** A network topology in which all network stations are directly attached to a central hub by a cable on which that station alone communicates. Stars are typically implemented using twisted pair wiring or optical fiber.

Point-to-Point

Point-to-point communications links are generally used in medium and wide area networks to connect two distant shared media networks such as a bus or a star. Because two, and only two, end systems participate in a point-to-point link, it's nearly impossible to introduce a new device on a point-to-point link. Security intrusions on point-to-point links must then take the form of a wiretap. If data is to be introduced covertly on a point-to-point link, it must appear to come from the other participant on the network.

Wide Area Security

Security in wide area links is problematic because you don't own the media, nor do you control how well secured it is. Although the telephone companies have come a long way from the days when hackers could reroute calls with ease, the fact remains that if you assume your wide area links are secure, you are putting your security in the hands of a third party that you cannot control.

For that reason, you should assume that all wide area links, no matter how secure they seem, should be secured in the same manner as a broadcast wireless medium (in other words, a public medium); they should be secured with encryption. Chapter 20, on data link security, covers a number of ways to secure wide area data links.

Policies: Wide Area Network Security

- Always encrypt data traveling over wide area data links or over any other data links which your company does not completely control.

Bus

Bus networks are the simplest forms of shared media broadcast networks. Used only in coaxial networks, bus networks allow any computer to simply tap the coaxial wire to begin communicating on the network. In a theoretical sense, bus networks are the cabled analog to radio broadcast networks. There are limitations to the length of coaxial cable that can be used and the number of computers that can be attached to each cable segment, but to allow for a margin of error most correctly operating networks don't approach these limits.

The problem with bus networks stems from the fact that there's no inherent way to prevent the attachment of an additional station to the bus network. At any point along the cable, a sniffer or computer can simply be vampire tapped onto the cable to add a station without providing any indication of what has happened. For this reason, bus networks can only be considered secure if the cable is contained in secure spaces for its entire length. Figure 22.4 shows the covert attachment of a computer to a bus network.

FIGURE 22.4

A covert attachment
to a bus network

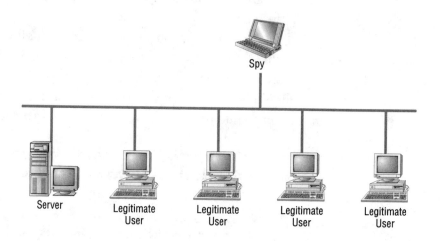

It's tempting to consider 10Base-2 networks more secure than 10Base-5 networks. A 10Base-2 cable is typically cut and T-tapped to add stations—rather than vampire tapped—so it's logical to think that cutting the cable would cause the entire segment to go down, thus providing at least an indication that something is wrong. But T-tapping is not a firm requirement of 10Base-2, it is merely the common practice. 10Base-2 networks can be vampire tapped as well, making them no more secure than 10Base-5 networks.

Policies: Bus Networks

- Upgrade bus networks to more secure topologies as quickly as budgets allow.

- Never specify bus networks for new installations. The security risk, unreliability, and management inconvenience is not worth the cost savings even in very small networks.

Star

Star networks are the most common topology in use today. Usually, star networks use twisted pair, although they may also be optical fiber. Star networks mandate that each cable attach directly to a computer and to a hub—in that sense, stars are much like a series of point-to-point links. No more than one computer can participate on the network from each physical cable (although hubs can be attached to cables to break out additional attachment points).

The problem with star networks comes from unsecured network ports on the hub or from the clandestine attachment of a hub where a computer should be attached. In both cases, a fully functional computer can be added to the network without the knowledge of the security administrator. You can control the unused hub port problem by strictly controlling access to wiring closets, but you cannot control the attachment of clandestine downstream hubs except at higher layers with monitoring software—or by mandating that all computers stay on at all times and then monitoring for link loss. Figure 22.5 shows the clandestine attachment of a hub where a computer is supposed to be.

Ring

The ring topologies used by Token Ring and FDDI have lost the popularity battle to Ethernet and Fast Ethernet because Ethernet equipment is cheaper and easier to manage. For security purposes, this is a shame, because ring networks are the easiest topology to keep secure.

There's no way to add computers to a ring topology without causing some noticeable disturbance in network services that's easy to monitor. This is because the ring must be momentarily broken to attach the new computer.

FIGURE 22.5

A clandestine attachment
of downstream hubs
in a star

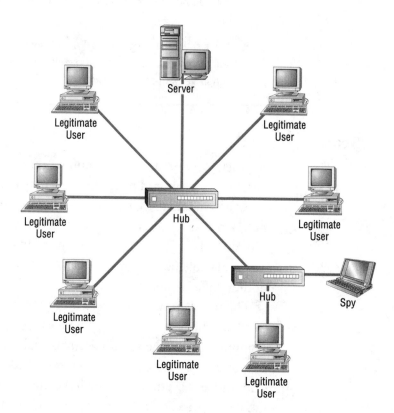

Policies: Star Networks

- Ensure strong physical security for all wiring closets.

- Leave all computers attached to stars running whenever servers are running to indicate when a link is lost. Monitors should remain shut off when not in use. Your company's energy policy may prohibit leaving computers running.

> **Policies: Ring Networks**
>
> - Where possible, choose ring topologies for highly secure networks.

Securing the Physical Layer

Physical layer security builds upon the other security precepts outlined in this book, especially facility security and encryption. Effective physical security for the premises makes it impossible to exploit physical layer vectors except when the physical layer extends beyond the facility security perimeter, as it would for wide area links and for wireless communication links. By encrypting all wireless and wide area links, you effectively close those vectors of attack.

When you can't use those methods or you don't have effective facility security (such as in an academic environment, where nearly every computer science student is a practicing hacker) you can use other means to increase the security of your physical layer. Most of these methods rely upon monitoring and alarming to detect security penetration attempts rather than attempting to prevent them all together. With rapid detection and response, you can keep your network safe even when you can't keep your physical layer secure. These alternate methods include:

- Link loss detection

- Wiring enclosure penetration detection

- Network device port security

- Network layer monitoring

We look at some of the details of these methods in the sections that follow.

Link Loss Detection

Whenever a point-to-point cabling technology such as optical fiber or twisted pair is broken, the devices on both ends are able to detect that the link has gone down. Unmanaged network devices are not capable of doing any more than blinking an LED to show a status change when a link is lost.

If you must use unmanaged hubs, you can use dark detecting optical alarms (a very simple circuit any electronics student could devise) attached to the LEDs on the hub to signal an alert when a link is lost.

It's much easier simply to use SNMP-managed hubs and switches to determine when a link is present on each port. Most SNMP-managed hubs are capable of reporting link status for each port, so you can set up alarming software whenever a port status changes.

Be sure your SNMP-managed equipment is properly secured, so that you are the only one who can "manage" it. If you think this might be a problem in your environment, use unmanaged hubs.

Unfortunately, the normal action of shutting off an end-user computer will report as a link loss detected. For link loss detection to be 100 percent effective, all network-attached devices must remain on at all times. This may not be possible for all users, but where security is more important than energy costs, it should be considered.

Securing Unused Ports

Since anyone can simply attach a device to an unused port on an Ethernet hub, you must secure unused ports on these hubs either through facility security or through alarming based on an SNMP port

> ### Policies: Link Loss Monitoring
>
> - Where security is important, use SNMP-managed network devices that are capable of detecting and reporting all port state changes. Use SNMP monitoring software that is capable of immediately alerting you to SNMP events.

status change. If you've set up your SNMP-managed hubs to alarm on a port state change, this feature is already in place.

Securing unused ports doesn't just need to take place at the hub. As networks are reconfigured, it's quite common for station wall drop locations near computers to be abandoned but left attached to the hub. Be sure you disconnect all station locations that are not in use so you can prevent clandestine attachment to your network in areas that are not locked up.

> ### Policies: Unused Attachment Ports
>
> - Always disconnect physical premises wiring when they are not in use. Make sure that whenever a computer is moved, the network outlet that corresponds to it is disconnected from the hub.

Security Network Monitoring

Security network monitoring is the constant monitoring of your network for new Ethernet addresses, protocol addresses like IP addresses, or any other information that indicates that a new and unauthorized device is operating on your network. This will usually catch any normal hacking activity—but spies and serious espionage agents will use read-only equipment that doesn't make its presence known on your network, so network monitoring can't cover all the security bases for you.

Summary

Physical layer security is based primarily on the security layer below (facility security) and the security layers above (especially data link and network layer encryption). Simply assuming that your network wiring is impenetrable because it would require effort to attach to your local area network does not ensure security.

Wireless links are the least secure connections you can use for your physical layer, followed by copper (twisted pair and coaxial) wiring, and finally by optical fiber which is the most secure. Most installations will prefer twisted pair wiring (which affords at least link loss detection) for intrabuilding wiring, and optical fiber for wiring between buildings.

APPENDIX

A

Security Doctrine

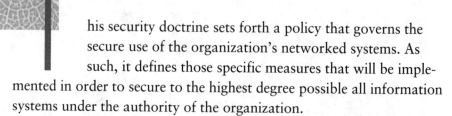

his security doctrine sets forth a policy that governs the secure use of the organization's networked systems. As such, it defines those specific measures that will be implemented in order to secure to the highest degree possible all information systems under the authority of the organization.

This doctrine is the ultimate authority on all aspects related to network security—it is not to be superseded except by amendment, and system users are not to circumvent it. The scope of this doctrine includes:

- All computing resources attached to the network

- Network devices and equipment that make up the network

- Cabling, media, and interfaces used to create the connected network

- Software that runs on any of the above equipment

- Users of the above equipment, while they are engaged in its use, or in respect to information required in determining their eligibility to use the system

- Facilities in which such equipment is maintained to the degree necessary to protect the systems from unauthorized access

This doctrine represents the networked systems policy of the organization as determined and promulgated by the recognized authority. The information security staff under the direction of the security administrator is primarily responsible for implementation of policy details. All users of the networked system are responsible for implementing policy details that are within their area of control.

Security Classifications

All networked facilities, systems, and data are classified according to their sensitivity to disclosure and their mission criticality. The following security classifications are to be used when determining to what level a specific resource will be classified for security purposes:

- **Unclassified:** Distribution of this material is not limited. This includes marketing information, sales materials, and information cleared for release to the public. Data on public Internet servers are Unclassified. Unclassified systems are not specifically restricted by this security doctrine.

- **Confidential:** Disclosure of this information could cause measurable damage to the organization as a whole, and includes market strategies, plans for marketing campaigns, bid documents, or other factors that could cause the loss of an individual contract or customer. Confidential material should be safeguarded at all times, but trusted employees are permitted to take Confidential documents home. All networked systems are assumed by this document to be Confidential or higher.

- **Secret:** Disclosure of this information would cause serious damage to the organization as a whole, and includes trade secrets, blueprints or schematics for proprietary equipment, or information that, if released to competitors, could cause the loss of many contracts or customers. Secret material should not leave the company facilities or be left unattended in an open space.

- **Top Secret:** Disclosure of this information would cause grave and irreparable harm to the organization as a whole, and includes legal documents, high-level strategies, proprietary secrets upon which the company is based, and any information which, if released to competitors, could cause the downfall of the organization. Top Secret information should be controlled using distribution lists, sign-out sheets, and inventories.

For each of the classifications beyond Unclassified, specific policy recommendations are presented in each of the security zones. Policy recommendations are cumulative. Confidential installations should implement those policies listed as Confidential. Secret facilities should implement those policies listed as Confidential and those policies presented as Secret. Top Secret installations should implement all presented policies.

It is possible for a facility or a networked system to have various security classifications—however, mixed security classifications on the same network should only be implemented when the security policies of the highest implemented security classification are in place throughout the network. Areas with lower classifications may then be downgraded to permit greater freedom of use and convenience where appropriate.

Security Zones

This doctrine is divided into security zones and each is covered in detail by a section in this doctrine. The security zones begin with the potential human user, broaden to include system users, their client computers, the network to which they are attached, network servers, the data stored on servers, methods used to remotely access the network, and finally the Internet and other public networks. These security zones are:

- **Human Security:** Defines those security policies that regulate non-users or potential users prior to their contact with the system. The intent of these policies is to prohibit or limit the extent of unauthorized access to networked systems.

- **User Policy:** Defines those security policies that regulate the normal use of networked systems by authorized users. These policies seek to limit the extent of damage that can be caused accidentally or otherwise by authorized users.

- **Client Security:** Defines those practices that secure client computers from either authorized or unauthorized use.

- **Network Security:** Regulates the software used to connect network clients to network servers, including networked file systems, user accounts, and logon methods.

- **Server Security:** Regulates the services and applications that run on servers.

- **Data Security:** Protects the data stored on servers through fault tolerance and account-based permission security.

- **Physical Security:** Defines those procedures that secure the containers, spaces, facilities, and campuses in which networked systems are housed.

- **Remote Access Security:** Protects networked systems from unauthorized access via direct remote attachment.

- **Internet Policy:** Protects the networked system from unauthorized intrusion from public networks such as the Internet.

The security zones concept, shown in Figure A.1, is intended to structure the security effort. Security should be approached in the order presented, since security lapses in the inner areas tend to cause widespread collapse of further security perimeters.

Human Security

Human security regulates the assignment of access to networked systems. It is the specific goal of human security to deny access to unauthorized users, to make difficult the compromise of secured systems, and to provide criteria upon which potential users are judged as to whether access will be granted or revoked.

Security at its core is dependent upon the unfailing and unified effort of the employees. All employees must actively pursue security in their

FIGURE A.I

Security zones

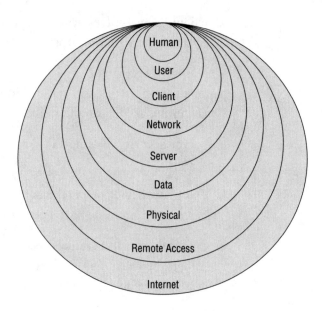

activities and must understand that organizational security is in their personal interest. Comfort is a basic tenet of human security. The organization recognizes the additional burden shouldered by employees to enhance security by making the workplace as pleasant as possible for employees. Positive reinforcement will help employees make a habit of security without adversely affecting their attitudes.

Confidential

1. Access to information will rise with pay and with proven loyalty.

2. Employees are paid commensurate with their value to the organization—and their value to the competition.

3. All candidate users must demonstrate that they understand the risks of intentionally circumventing security for the sake of convenience.

4. Security personnel are sensitive to personal problems that might make employees easy targets for recruitment by the competition. These include debt, drug use, loneliness, and animosity towards the organization.

Secret

1. Nonemployees are not allowed to move through the premises unescorted.

2. Employees are not responsible for the damage or loss of networked systems in their custody unless they clearly acted with malice in the loss or damage.

3. Employees are responsible for immediately reporting lost, misplaced, or unaccounted for networked system components.

4. When audit policy monitoring reveals that an employee is a security risk, that employee's access to sensitive information will immediately be downgraded.

5. Assignment of portable systems is limited to those who require portability to perform their work. Portable equipment is not perquisite due to the inherent security risk and the cost of replacement.

6. Sudden changes in demeanor that might indicate an external risk factor at work in the employee's life are noted and monitored by security personnel. Sudden changes in lifestyle, apparent income, or attitude may necessitate a security reevaluation.

7. All out-sourced service personnel must be escorted by an employee at all times while on the premises. No account password information will be granted to nonemployees. Escort personnel can log on for out-sourced service personnel.

8. Security check in/check out and name tags are required for all personnel on the premises. Employees will be issued permanent badges. Visitors will be issued temporary badges for the duration of their visit only.

9. Employees will not have access to secret or higher systems or information for a period of 90 days from their initial employment. The purpose of this policy is to make the employment of spies from competing organizations prohibitively expensive.

10. Animosity, aggression, or violence towards the company, its assets, or its employees is an indicator of serious security risk. Audit policy is used to monitor the behavior of suspect individuals without alerting them to the fact that they are under observation. Instances of sabotage or other security violations are grounds for immediate dismissal.

Top Secret

1. It is the policy of the organization that any and all networked systems may be used to monitor the work of employees. Specifically reserved is the right to monitor the contents of suspect employee's company e-mail. Employees will be warned that this policy is enforced.

User Policy

User policy encourages proper use of networked systems and discourages activities that may in part or in sum decrease the effectiveness of security measures. User policy should be enacted through systematic modifications to software and hardware rather than through human behavior and habit modification where possible for three reasons:

- Systematic changes cause natural barriers to incorrect use, which are easier to implement and properly enforce than regulating human behavior.

- Systematic policy is seen as a natural characteristic of the system rather than as a specific restriction, which encourages acquiescence rather than circumvention of security policy.

- Machines are unceasing in their vigilance and are therefore more constant in their application of policy.

Confidential

1. Update networked systems regularly with the latest vendor patches for all software executed on servers.

2. Select passwords that cannot be found in a dictionary and that are of sufficient length that the probability of determining the password over a network would take at least 160 hours. Currently, this is at least eight characters but shall be automatically increased as technology allows.

3. Immediately change all user passwords attached to a network when a compromise has occurred or is suspected.

4. Enable client operating system (Windows 95) user profiles so that specific users and groups have their own security settings that reflect their level of trust in the network.

5. Force password changes often. Passwords should be valid for no longer than 30 days.

6. Make sure coworkers understand that no one else needs to know their password. If files are stored securely on a server, with proper group accounts set up to allow coworkers access to the same files, there should never be a need for users to supply their passwords for use when they are absent. If users have to have a specific individual's password to access a resource, account security has not been correctly enacted. Correct the account security settings rather than compromising a password.

7. Select the Hide Share Passwords with Asterisks in order to keep share passwords from being seen by casual users of a computer or by passers-by.

8. Train users to prevent mishaps, by doing things such as turning off a workstation that holds shared data when it is not required.

9. Execute a virus scanner automatically whenever a user logs onto the computer.

10. Use workstation user accounts and system policies to prevent individual users from controlling the security of their workstations.

Secret

1. Disable password caching so passwords do not accumulate on client computers.

2. Client computers shall be restricted such that their network settings may not be modified by non-administrative personnel. In the case of Windows 95, implement the following specific policies:

- Disable the network control panel for all users except administrators and trusted knowledgeable users.

- Disable the registry editing tools for all users except system administrators.

- Enable all of the policy options for the Windows 95 System control panel for all users except administrators.

- Enable the Require Validation option. This will keep people from bypassing security by selecting the Close or Cancel button in the Windows 95 logon screen.

- Enable the shell restrictions for accounts that serve a particular purpose, such as public e-mail accounts, public wordprocessing accounts, process control, etc.

- Hide the general and details pages for printers in the network, disable deletion of printers, and disable the addition of printers.

- Hide the remote administration page and the user profiles page for all users except administrators.

- Disable single-mode MS-DOS applications on Windows 95 computers.

- Hide the Windows 95 display settings page from everyone except administrators.

- Set the workgroup name as a policy so that it will be reset to the correct value every time the computer logs on. Since changing the workgroup name requires a reboot, this (along with requiring network authentication) will ensure that the workgroup is not changed.

- Use the Run Only Allowed Windows Applications option to restrict the programs that can be run by users who are security risks.

3. Disable booting the A: drive in the BIOS and apply a password to the BIOS to keep the user from using a DOS boot floppy.

4. Limit the rights of default Administrators group members, and create a separate group with full access.

5. Provide periodic security training for new and established employees alike. A periodic refresher keeps users aware of security problems.

6. Require alphanumeric passwords so that a hacker cannot quickly determine the password to a user account simply by performing a "dictionary scan."

Top Secret

1. Modify the client operating system to boot directly to the allowed application or a menu restricted to allowed applications. For Windows 95, use the Run Only Allowed Windows Applications option to restrict the programs that users who are security risks may run.

Client Security

Client security secures the individual machines that are used by network account holders to perform their work. These machines typically do not store information, but because they are connected directly to the network and its servers, they are potential vectors into the network. As such, their use should be restricted as appropriate to the security posture.

Confidential

1. If attachment via the Internet is allowed, be absolutely certain that home users who attach via the Internet do not have file sharing turned on. For Windows clients, use automatic scanning software across the range of IP addresses attached to the network to make sure that no clients respond on TCP/IP port 139.

2. Instruct users to avoid inappropriate local access and not to create or modify shares.

3. Remove the remote access and dial-up connection services from clients on the network. There should be no need for remote access outbound connections from computers on networks that are connected to the Internet.

4. Company-owned computers used by work-at-home telecommuters cannot be connected to the Internet or used by any family member other than the employee. Employees shall use their own computers at home for entertainment or personal interests.

Secret

1. Carefully review the company's work-at-home policy in light of the security breaches that sharing removable media can cause. Consider providing laptop computers to employees who work at home rather than using removable media devices.

2. Do not allow client computers to be configured to use any sort of remote access software.

3. Clients should not be configured to answer dial-in security connections.

4. Do not allow users to install software on their clients. Take removable media drives like floppy, CD-ROM, and Zip drives out of client computers since all authorized software installations can occur over the network.

5. Do not install file and print sharing on clients unless absolutely necessary. Encourage users to store all files on network file servers, and create server pools of resources like CD-ROM or modems that can be centrally controlled.

6. Require user-level access control for Windows 95 resources.

7. Remove all modems and other alternative access devices from client computers. Each client computer should have one—and only one—possible connection to any data network.

8. Restrict logon access to the network to the computers that an employee normally uses. This makes it impossible to exploit an account name and password from anywhere other than the user's regular computer.

Top Secret

1. Disable all unused I/O ports, especially parallel ports that are not attached to printers, since many alternate access devices are capable of attaching through the printer port.

2. Do not allow attachment of clients over the Internet, even when using IP-encrypted tunnels. Encrypted tunnels only provide security for the socket between the home user and the server—they do not protect the home user from attack. Force home users to dial in directly despite the cost.

3. Disable unused serial ports in the BIOS of client computers. Put strong administrative passwords in the BIOS setup pages of client computers to maintain central control of network security.

Network Security

Network security comprises those devices used to connect networked computers together. It defines policy for the operation and use of intermediate systems such as routers, bridges, encryption tunnels, and other connectivity devices. Protocols used at these layers are also covered.

Confidential

1. Never communicate between organizational units over the Internet without using some form of encryption. Unencrypted packet headers contain valuable nuggets of information about the structure of the internal network.

Secret

1. Always use encrypted communications for data that flows over public networks like the Internet.

2. Don't allow special access to inside lines or telecommunication lines that originate from remote offices. Treat all inbound telephone lines the same regardless of their origin.

3. Limit the number of computing devices (those that actually contain microprocessors which run an operating system) on the network to the extent possible.

4. Locally control and administer all security services for the network.

5. Make telecommunications security an integral part of the network security if the network can be accessed via modems.

6. Tunneling encryption software does not protect the server and client from other connections coming in from the Internet. Be certain no client attaching from the Internet is listening for connections on any port.

7. Use encrypted tunnels for all communications over the Internet between organizational units if leased lines are not available or are cost prohibitive.

8. Use leased lines rather than encrypted tunnels whenever practical.

Top Secret

1. Data encryption over standard telephone lines is necessary only for companies that might be espionage targets. Encryption is easy to implement as an extra security measure, but it limits the types of clients that can attach to the network. In itself, this limitation may provide an extra measure of security in homogenous networks.

2. Use the NWLink IPX transport for the internal network. Install TCP/IP only on those workstations that need access to the Internet and those servers that serve data to the Internet (and exist outside the firewall). Servers that aren't running TCP/IP are reasonably secure against Internet attacks.

3. Encrypt any communications containing sensitive or proprietary information that go over an insecure medium such as radio, telephone networks, or the Internet.

Server Security

Server security embodies those methods required to keep servers and the data they contain secure from compromise, including the administration of accounts, permissions, and other server-related security structures.

Confidential

1. Have a strict rule (such as a 10-user limit) about when to use workgroups and when to use domains.

2. Limit the number of protocols in use throughout the network to the extent possible.

3. Use connection-monitoring software like the performance monitor to alert the network administrator to potential intrusion attempts.

4. Add trust relationships between domains only when several users need access.

5. Create groups based on natural associations in the organization. Assign file permissions by groups. Make user accounts members of the groups that need access to certain files.

6. Don't allow unrestricted file sharing. Use file sharing with user-based authentication or, at the very least, passwords.

7. Limit the rights of Guest and Anonymous accounts.

8. Never enable the Guest account.

9. Try to arrange data so that as few user accounts as possible are required for users to access it.

10. Install Internet servers outside the firewall (or between the outer firewall and the inner firewall), but install SQL Servers and other BackOffice products inside the firewall.

11. Install the Internet Information Server for Internet use on a standalone server outside the inner firewall.

12. Do not make Internet Information Server user accounts members of the Users or Domain Users groups. Avoid making these accounts members of groups that would grant these users additional rights or access permissions.

13. Do not make script virtual directories readable; do not make other virtual directories executable.

14. Create a group for Internet users for IIS; apply permissions to that group account.

15. Do not allow users to place scripts in their own WWW service virtual directories.

16. Use the logging facilities of IIS to watch for a high proportion of unauthorized, forbidden, and not found access attempts.

17. Do not allow NetBIOS connections to be made over the Internet.

Secret

1. Replace the default Everyone, Full Control permission with a Domain Users, Change permission on all drives except the system and boot volumes.

2. On each Windows NT server inside the network, establish filters to pass only those protocols that are explicitly served. This prevents software from working in unexpected ways.

3. To make administration easier and leave less possibility for error, use several shares on one workstation rather than scattering them among several workstations, if possible.

4. Use different names for e-mail accounts than those used for network account names.

5. Use the No Access permission only when necessary to override other permitted access.

6. Grant permissions for a share to a specific group or set of users, rather than using the Everyone group and attempting to restrict users at the subdirectory level.

7. Use NTFS volumes for file sharing whenever possible, and use file-level security rather than share-level security when possible.

8. Keep sensitive information out of the shopper table because that information is accessible to a Web browser. Use both a secure port (HTTPS) and Secure Socket Layer encryption, and use strong NTFS permissions restrictions on WWW service virtual directories.

9. Require all possible network connections to services outside the network security to go through a proxy server.

10. Configure the DNS server to exchange information only with computers within the network security and with the DNS server "up" the network tree from them.

Top Secret

1. Disable the automatic NetWare logon on the network if there is no NetWare server on the network. It is conceivable for a computer to masquerade (or actually be) a NetWare server on the network in order to gain access to user names, passwords, and other sensitive information.

2. Remove all instances of the Everyone, Full Control permission. Do not set a default permission to replace it so that all subdirectories from the root do not by default inherit permissions. Add permissions only where specifically required.

3. Use third-party permissions auditing software to manage permissions in complex environments.

4. Use SMS to track changes in client computer and operating system configuration, to watch for unusual protocol activity, and use SMS to watch for unusual network traffic patterns.

Data Security

Data security is the term that covers those methods and procedures used to ensure the integrity of stored data and includes such measures as fault tolerant storage, backup, and recovery.

Confidential

1. Create a backup strategy and test backups regularly.

2. Create separate partitions to store the Windows NT system files and the volume the server will share. Then don't share the system/ boot partition; share only the empty volume created for file storage.

3. Implement strong permission-based security for all files stored on the server.

4. Never use the FAT file system on the hard disk of a Windows NT computer when security is a concern.

5. Remove default assignments to the Everyone group.

6. Repair damaged drives in mirror or stripe sets as soon as possible.

7. Store backup tapes in a waterproof, flameproof safe in the server room. If tapes must be moved off site, make certain security measures are in place to prevent their being compromised while off site.

8. Use disk mirroring or duplexing for critical data. Use duplexing when possible.

Secret

1. Consider using hardware RAID, which is faster and is independent of the operating system.

2. If there are three or more drives in a server, use a stripe set with parity for added speed and reliability.

3. If the server's physical security could be compromised in any way, and the data on the disk warrants protection, use file system encryption.

4. Use file system encryption to protect sensitive data when operating system features are not effective (when the hard drive has been removed or the operating system has been replaced).

Top Secret

1. For extreme fault tolerance, consider using a third-party server replication system.

2. Test file-system encryption candidates for robust operation with voluminous file copies of complex files. Test the encrypted file system's performance characteristics. Be familiar with the encryption technique used, and try to find out from the vendor what method is used to generate random numbers. Avoid encryption techniques that use the real-time clock as random number seeds, as these are frequently far less secure than they seem.

Physical Security

Physical security seeks to keep all networked resources safe from theft or unauthorized physical access. Physical security is the foundation upon which all other security measures depend.

Confidential

1. Keep the domain controllers physically secure.

2. Make sure building security is adequate to prevent walk-up access to the workstations.

Secret

1. Employ a security officer or an "attack receptionist" to guard the front desk, and don't allow nonemployees access beyond that point.

2. Make certain all servers are located in locked and secure rooms. Restrict access to administrative personnel.

3. Make certain the servers are stored in an area that is secure from physical compromise under all reasonable circumstances. Make sure all guests have an escort when they are in the room.

4. Remove the keyboard and monitor from servers if possible. They can be reattached when administration is necessary. Certain mouse devices will not reset properly when reattached; they should be left attached.

Remote Access Security

Remote access security covers privately-owned or leased direct connections to the network from off campus, as well as connection over public networks when the connection is encrypted and considered secure.

Confidential

1. RAS (Remote Access Server) provides the most secure method for remote access to the network if it is required.

2. Never allow client computers on the network to answer remote access connections. Organize all remote access servers in a centrally controlled location.

3. Servers have no need to originate dial-out connections (except when using telephone lines as low-cost WAN connections, but those connections should be relatively permanent).

4. To simplify security administration, allow only one method of remote access into the network.

Secret

1. Carefully consider the wisdom of providing cellular telephones and modems for use with laptop computers. This technology isn't

usually justified considering the relatively modest increase in productivity compared to the cost and the security risk of a lost laptop.

2. Consider using only the NetBEUI protocol for remote access to limit the extent of intrusions on the network.

3. Control the distribution of remote access software on the network. Never allow client computers to run remote control software. If remote control software is necessary, run the software from centrally controlled computers or thin-client servers.

4. Disable dial-in networking, except in the cases of trusted individuals or to special computers, because dial-in networking can bypass regular network security.

5. Encourage an easy-to-use (but secure, of course) method for users to indicate when they need remote access, for how long, and to which phone number. Base the dial-in permissions on these requests. Always verify the request verbally with the user to ensure that it's not a spoof.

6. Favor ISDN over analog modems for remote access connections within the local toll area. ISDN equipment is far less prevalent than modems are, so it provides a measure of security through obscurity.

7. Gather contact information for the telephone companies as soon as possible so that it is on hand if dial-up hacking attempts are discovered.

8. If possible, use external modems to answer RAS connections. They can be powered off when no RAS activity is anticipated, and they allow manual disconnection if necessary.

9. If remote access is required only occasionally, set the Remote Access Server service to start manually, then use the Services

control panel to start the service when needed and to stop it when it is no longer in use.

10. Multiport serial tunnels are inherently more secure than terminal servers because they concentrate the management problem on the Windows NT servers. Use them rather than terminal servers when possible.

11. Revoke dial-in permissions for users during periods when they are not necessary, and invoke them when the user is away from the office or working from home for a period.

12. Thin-client and remote control software can be more secure than remote access software in certain circumstances. For instance, an entire database could be copied using remote access software, but that same data would be extremely difficult to extract using remote control software configured to disallow file transfers.

13. Tightly control user-based remote access permissions. Allow only those users who have an immediate need to log on remotely to do so.

14. Use alarming software to detect numerous attempts at password guessing over dial-up networks. Use the standard performance monitor to detect this activity, or purchase third-party alarming software.

15. Use callback security. Without callback security, tracing RAS-based intrusion attempts is very difficult.

16. Use external modems that have on/off switches for those machines that have remote access software installed. Turn on a modem only when a user calls in and requests a remote control connection.

17. Use frame-relay-dedicated circuits for telecommuters outside the local toll area. Frame relay connections are more secure than dial-up connections like ISDN.

18. Use hard-coded callback security for all remote users that don't normally travel, to prevent their account from being exploited from unknown locations.

19. Use Microsoft encryption when possible.

20. Use the Point-to-Point Tunneling Protocol for all Internet connections allowed into the network, or use some third-party software that performs the encrypted tunnel function in concert with the firewall.

Top Secret

1. Consider a constantly connected 56Kbps frame relay as an alternative to long-distance ISDN for distant telecommuters. Frame relay has a fixed monthly cost, and it is available to home users in many metropolitan areas.

Internet Policy

Internet policy controls security relating to the attachment to public networks, especially (but not limited to) the global Internet. This includes direct network connections and dial-up connections by any computing resource attached to the networked system.

Confidential

1. Dedicate a machine to be a firewall. Don't run other services on it, and disable all unnecessary service features that may be included in the firewall package.

2. Disallow all connection attempts to hosts inside the network. Allowing any inbound connections provides a mechanism hackers might be able to exploit to establish connections to Trojan horses or by exploiting bugs in service software.

3. Disallow all protocols and addresses by default, then explicitly allow supported services and hosts.

4. Disallow fragments beyond number zero, since this functionality is largely obsolete and is often exploited.

5. Divide provided services using Internet tools into public services and private (organizational) services. Place the public services on an Internet site (or sites) external to the Internet firewall and provide the private services on an intranet site (or sites) on the protected LAN.

6. Do not rely upon packet filtering alone to protect the network.

7. Do not depend upon Windows NT's built-in filtering alone to protect the network.

8. Do not use simple packet filtering or packet-filtering services from the Internet service provider as a replacement for application-layer firewalls. Those services are not as secure.

9. Don't rely solely on packet filters for security protection from Internet-based attacks.

10. Drop all external routing protocol (RIP, OSPF) updates bound for internal routers. No one outside the network should be transmitting RIP updates to internal routers.

11. Filter out and do not respond to ICMP redirect and echo (ping) messages.

12. Limit the number of external hosts allowed to connect through the firewall to the absolute minimum possible. Take measures to make sure the IP addresses of those hosts are difficult to determine using proxy servers or IP masquerades.

13. Make sure there's no way for a hacker to tell which firewall product is in use.

14. Never publish a list of user or employee names on the Web site. Publish job titles instead.

15. Reduce the number of connections to the Internet to the minimum number possible: one per campus. Many large organizations allow only a single link to the Internet at headquarters and then route all remote offices to that point using the same frame relay lines used to connect internal networks.

16. Respond immediately to intrusion attempts when they are detected. Collect as much information about the attacker as possible. Use their IP domains to determine who the higher-level service providers are.

17. Set up the firewall to discard ICMP echo and to redirect messages to interior hosts.

18. Unbind NetBIOS from all servers outside the firewall. Set the TCP/IP stacks on those machines to accept connection only on ports for services that the machine specifically provides.

19. If there is only one connection to the Internet, hard code that connection in the router connected to the service provider's network. Use RIP or other automated routing protocols to manage routing inside the network.

20. Do not allow SNMP to travel into or out of the network.

21. Use operating system software on Internet accessible machines that are not susceptible to the ping of death. For Windows NT 4, apply Microsoft's icmp-fix patch.

22. Configure the gateway not to pass ping packets.

23. Install the latest version of the operating system software.

24. Log network activity and have the log software signal an alert when a SYN attack or and ICMP flood is in progress. Deny access to the computer or network that originates the attack, and take measures (such as calling or sending an e-mail message to the administrator of the offending network) to stop the malicious behavior.

25. Unbind NetBIOS from Internet-accessible network adapters. Allow only authorized hosts outside the network to connect to the DNS servers.

26. Filter out RIP traffic at the gateway.

27. Filter out ICMP traffic at the Internet gateway.

28. Configure the gateway or packet filter not to pass SNMP traffic.

29. Configure those SNMP devices that support Windows NT security (Windows NT computers with SNMP services installed included) to allow connections only from authorized user accounts.

30. Configure the gateway or packet filter to discard all IP packets that use the source routing feature.

Secret

1. Configure internal clients with IP addresses in the 10 domain, which is not routed by most Internet routers. Use an IP masquerade to translate these internal addresses to routable external addresses. This may prevent hackers from exploiting modem connections into the network beyond the computer that established the connection.

2. Consider using an alternate protocol like IPX to provide the connection between an Internet mail server and hosts inside a firewall, if mail server is capable of using different transports. (Microsoft Exchange Server is.) This allows the firewall to block all Inbound TCP connection attempts, but still keeps the mail flowing through in a manner that can't be exploited from the Internet.

3. Disallow services for which there are no proxy servers.

4. Don't allow cleartext-password authentication.

5. Do not use the Routing Information Protocol (RIP) or other automated routing protocols. Statically assign the routing tables and disable RIP updates unless the network is too large to manage manually. This makes them impervious to RIP-based denial-of-service or spoofing attacks.

6. Don't allow dial-up connections to the Internet. Remove modems and all other uncontrolled network access devices. Disable free COM ports in the BIOS settings of client computers and password protect the BIOS to prevent users from overriding the security settings.

7. Drop all packets that are TCP source routed. Source routing is rarely used for legitimate purposes.

8. Log all public access to servers, and check the logs often. Use alerting software to detect hacking attempts against the exposed machines.

9. Place public service hosts like Web servers and SMTP servers outside the packet filters rather than opening holes through the packet filters.

10. Set up monitoring software that can alert on flood attacks against the network. Record the IP addresses of the source computers (assuming they look valid) and try to determine the source of the attacks so legal measures can be taken to stop the problem.

11. Set up the internal network within the reserved 10 class A domain. Most Internet routers do not route this domain. Use network translation to map the internal hosts to routable addresses. Use the reserved 192.168 class B domain if desired.

12. Set up a firewall to protect the organization from the public network. Place Web and FTP servers outside it, and mail servers on the inside. Pass only SMTP and POP3 traffic from external sources. Run no other services or software on mail, Web, FTP, or firewall servers.

13. Use a port scanner periodically (about once a month) from outside the network to check the status of the firewall, packet filter, and NetBIOS bindings. This is especially important when servers are maintained by more than one person or when retaining outsourced security services. Shareware port scanners are included on the companion CD-ROM and discussed in Appendix B.

14. Use high-level proxies capable of stripping executable content like ActiveX and Java from Web pages.

15. Use IP masquerades to hide the identity of hosts inside the network.

16. Whenever possible, use proxy servers for all application protocols.

17. Use IP address assignment, in combination with an internal firewall and IP selection on servers, to further control and partition the access allowed to remote users.

18. Use a Web and FTP hosting service rather than computers on the organization's own network to provide the customers with information about the company. This puts the Web hosting agency at risk rather than the organization's own network, and allows the provision of no public services from internal servers.

Top Secret

1. Don't attach the network to public networks if it can possibly be avoided. Use the disconnected network model to provide Internet access to the users rather than to the network.

2. As a part of security training, make sure users know to report all instances of denial of service whether or not they seem important. If a specific denial of service can't be correlated to known downtime or heavy usage, or if a large number of service denials occur in a short time, a siege may be in progress.

3. Avoid using one of the smaller Internet service providers. Hackers frequently target them as potential employers because they often have less security awareness. Hackers find them attractive because they may use UNIX computers (rather than dedicated machines) as gateways and firewalls—making spoof attacks easy to perpetrate. Ask the service provider if they perform background checks on technical service personnel, and reject those that say they do not.

4. Consider using the disconnected Internet security model if the services required by the users can be made available from a single machine.

5. Manually assign IP addresses if the organization is a potential espionage target.

APPENDIX

B

Security Utilities

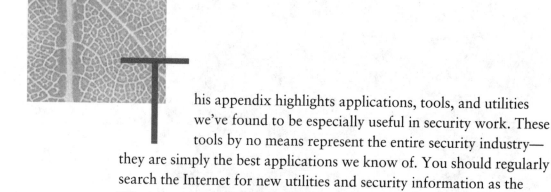

This appendix highlights applications, tools, and utilities we've found to be especially useful in security work. These tools by no means represent the entire security industry— they are simply the best applications we know of. You should regularly search the Internet for new utilities and security information as the Windows security environment changes.

Although it is possible to secure Windows NT very well against attack without using any third-party tools, there's no good way to monitor your security environment completely with the tools provided by Microsoft. For that, you must rely upon third-party security vendors.

Windows NT Applications

Windows NT applications are graphical interface applications that ship with Windows NT and have an express security purpose. These utilities are:

- Event Viewer

- Performance Monitor

- Network Monitor

Use these utilities regularly to monitor your security environment.

Event Viewer

Profile

Name	Event Viewer
Vendor	Microsoft
Cost	$0 (Included with Windows NT)
Use	Graphical utility for displaying system, security, and application logs
Issues	None

The Event Viewer utility displays system logs and allows you to filter the display to show certain types of events. The security log includes security violations, such as account lockouts. Any auditing you turn on with User Manager's Audit Policy dialog box also causes events to be written to these logs.

Event Viewer is located in the Administrative Tools menu under the Start menu. When you first run the Event Viewer utility, a list of events in the system log is displayed, as shown in Figure B.1. An icon indicating its significance precedes each entry.

The menus of the Event Viewer utility provide these functions:

- You can use Log ➢ System, Log ➢ Security, or Log ➢ Application to choose the log to display.

- You can use Log ➢ Save As to save a copy of the current log, or Log ➢ Open to open a saved log file.

- Log ➢ Clear All Events allows you to clear the current log.

FIGURE B.I

Event Viewer displays
system log information.

- Log ➤ Log Settings allows you to configure settings for the current log. This dialog box allows you to limit the size of the log to a maximum value.

- Log ➤ Select Computer allows you to view the log file for a different computer you have access to.

- View ➤ Filter Events allows you to view log items for a particular user, a particular event type, a date range, or other options.

- View ➤ Find allows you to search for events in a log.

- View ➤ Detail displays detailed information about a log entry.

- View ➤ Refresh updates the display with the current log entries.

Network Monitor

Profile

Name	Network Monitor
Vendor	Microsoft
Cost	$0 (Included with Windows NT)
Use	Graphical utility for monitoring network use
Issues	None

Network Monitor allows you to capture network packets and display information about them. This can be a useful tool for monitoring the usage of the network, as well as searching for specific packets to track down security problems.

Before Network Monitor can be used, you must install the Network Monitor Agent on one or more computers, and the Network Monitor Tools and Agent service on the computer you will do the monitoring from.

To install these services under Windows NT, open the Network control panel. Select the Services tab, then click Add to add a service. Select the appropriate service (either Network Monitor Agent or Network Monitor Tools and Agent) and click OK. You must then restart the computer.

Once the service is installed, you can run the Network Monitor utility from the Administrative Tools menu. The utility's main screen is shown in Figure B.2.

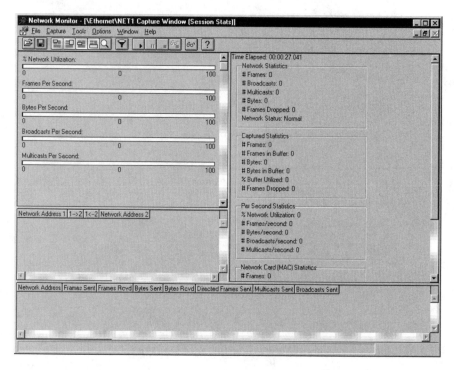

Once Network Monitor has started, select Capture ➤ Start to begin capturing packets. After a period of network activity, select Capture ➤ Stop. You can then display a detailed list of packets captured.

The version of Network Monitor included with Windows NT can only capture packets coming from and going to the current server, which limits its use as a packet sniffer. A version included with Microsoft SMS (Systems Management Server) can capture all packets. This version may be more useful for diagnostics or just for getting an idea of the type of information a hacker could obtain by packet sniffing.

Performance Monitor

Profile

Name	Performance Monitor
Vendor	Microsoft
Cost	$0 (Included with Windows NT)
Use	Graphical utility for tracking system performance and errors
Issues	None

The Performance Monitor utility is one of Windows NT's most useful utilities for optimizing and monitoring performance, and it also has a few uses relating to security. To run this utility, select Administrative Tools ➢ Performance Monitor.

Performance Monitor deals with individual parameters, called *counters*, relating to the system. You can use the View menu to switch between four methods of monitoring these counters:

- **Chart:** Displays a running graph of selected counters, as shown in Figure B.3.

- **Alert:** Allows you to set minimum and maximum values for one or more parameters. You are alerted when a counter crosses one of these values.

- **Log:** Creates a log of specified counters to a disk file.

- **Report:** Allows you to create a customized report based on counter information.

FIGURE B.3

Performance Monitor displays a running graph of system information.

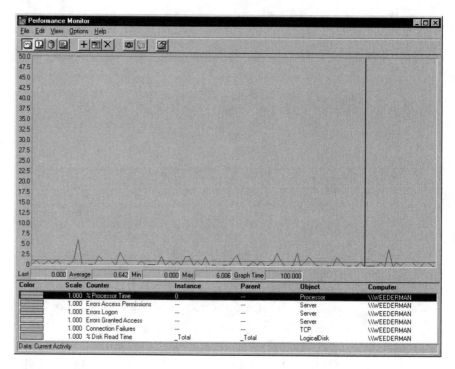

In Performance Monitor there are a wide variety of counter categories, each of which includes several counters. The Server category includes several counters relevant to security:

- **Errors Access Permissions:** The number of times users have attempted to access files without proper access. A high number might indicate that a hacker is searching for accessible files.

- **Errors Logon:** The number of invalid logon attempts. A dramatic increase in this counter may indicate that a hacker is attempting to guess a password or is running a program to try passwords in succession.

- **Logon/sec:** The number of logons per second. A change in this value may indicate that an intruder is repeatedly logging in and out, perhaps trying different default accounts.

Depending on your needs, other counters may be useful. For example, you can monitor network use and errors for the TCP/IP protocol.

Windows NT Command Line Utilities

Command line utilities are small programs that ship with Windows NT and provide minor security functionality or perform a network troubleshooting function. They are:

▪ ARP	▪ NSLookup
▪ AT	▪ Ping
▪ CACLS	▪ RCP
▪ Finger	▪ Route
▪ IPConfig	▪ RSH
▪ NBTStat	▪ Telnet
▪ Net	▪ TFTP
▪ Netstat	▪ TraceRT

Use these utilities whenever you need the functionality they provide. It's important to be familiar with their operation, but you probably won't use them very often.

ARP

Profile

Name	ARP
Vendor	Microsoft
Cost	$0 (Included with Windows NT)
Use	Command line utility used to show the mapping between physical adapter addresses and IP addresses
Issues	None

ARP (Address Resolution Protocol) is used to display the mappings between physical (usually Ethernet) media access control (MAC) addresses and the IP addresses assigned to those ports. ARP requests are transmitted on the network, and some proprietary TCP/IP devices like print servers are assigned their initial TCP/IP address using the Address Resolution Protocol.

When you type in ARP with no command line parameters, you'll see the instructions shown in Figure B.4.

F I G U R E   B.4

ARP command line options

Most of the functionality of ARP is described by the commands in Figure B.4.

AT

Profile

Name   AT

Vendor   Microsoft

Cost $0 (Included with Windows NT)

Use   Command line utility used to add scheduled jobs to the scheduler service

Issues   None

Using the AT command you can control the entry of commands into the scheduler service's execution list. When you type in AT with the help (/?) switch, you'll see the instructions shown in Figure B.5.

FIGURE B.5

AT command line options

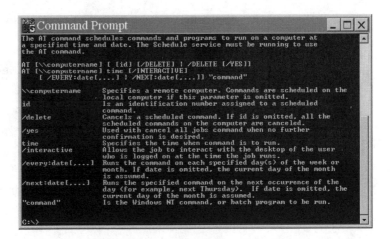

When you type **AT** with no parameters, a list of the currently scheduled jobs appears. Schedule entries have the following parameters:

- Computer that should run the job (defaults to local computer if not specified)

- ID number used to refer to the job (defaults to next number for adds, required for deletion)

- Time at which the command should be run

- Dates or days of the week when the command should be run (optional)

The AT command uses the following switches to control job entries:

- /delete: Deletes the specified job. If no job is specified, all jobs are deleted.

- /delete /yes: Deletes all jobs without individual confirmation.

- /interactive: Specifies that the program should interact with the logged-on user. If you do not specify interactive, you will not be able to answer alerts or dialog boxes that the executing program may raise.

- /every: Specifies that the command should be executed on every date or day of the week specified.

- /next: Specifies that the command should be executed on the next date or day of the week specified, but not thereafter.

You must specify the full path and command name—including the extension—to any command you specify. The Scheduler service cannot use path information to find a command.

The AT command is most commonly used to schedule tape backup sessions using the NT Backup tape backup utility. To schedule NT Backup to back up the entire contents of the C: and D: drives every weekday night, use the following command:

```
C:\>at 01:00 /EVERY:T,W,TH,F,SA
"c:\winnt\system32\ntbackup.exe backup c:\ d:\ /v /r /b /
hc:on /t copy
```

Of course you'll have to modify the path to your NTBACKUP.EXE command to match your computer and change the parameters specified to match the way you want backups performed. If you don't include the /interactive switch, a logged-on user will have no indication on the screen that a command is running in the background and will not be able to interact with the command. In the case of NTBACKUP, this means that if an error occurs that causes NT Backup to raise an error window, the NTBACKUP command will hang. You won't be able to use the task manager to shut down the command even if you are logged in as the administrator.

WARNING Avoid the temptation to use the AT command to schedule the execution of a batch file. If the file system security on that file is somehow compromised, an unauthorized user could use a text editor to change the contents of the batch file to gain access to your computer as the system.

If you need to act as the system to shut down a malfunctioning process, you can schedule an interactive task manager session. When the task manager appears, it will have the permissions of the system so you won't get any "access denied" messages. Watch out though—if you shut down system critical processes, your server may crash. You can schedule an interactive task manager session like this:

```
C:\>at 12:05 /interactive "c:\winnt\system32\taskmgr.exe
```

Of course, you'll have to change the time specified to a minute or so after you type the line, and you'll have to change the path to match your Windows NT installation.

CACLS

Profile

Name	CACLS
Vendor	Microsoft
Cost	$0 (Included with Windows NT)
Use	Command line utility used to change access control lists
Issues	None

CACLS (Command-line Access Control ListS) is a command line utility that provides fine control over the assignment of permissions to files and directories. Since CACLS is a command line utility, you can use it in batch files to perform mass changes to the permission structure of your drives.

 WARNING   Be careful of the order in which you perform permission changes so that you don't deny yourself access before you can grant it! Always add new access permissions first, then delete inappropriate permissions.

When you type in CACLS with no command line parameters, you'll see the instructions shown in Figure B.6.

F I G U R E B.6

CACLS command line
options

Most of the functionality of CACLS is described by the commands described earlier, but there are a few things you should be aware of that are not immediately apparent:

- If you type CACLS with the name of a file or directory, the permissions for that file or directory are displayed. This is useful for showing exactly who has permission to what before you change anything. It's also possible to save this information as a text file that you could parse using a command interpreter like qbasic.exe to rebuild permissions later on.

- If you don't include the /E (edit) switch, the access control list is completely replaced: The access control list for an object is created anew. You should usually include the /E switch.

- Accounts (user or group) with spaces in their identifiers (like "Domain Users") must be preceded by a single " character, as below. Accounts without spaces do not require a quote.

  CACLS . /E /R "NETROPOLIS\Domain Users

- You can use a period to specify the current directory. Wild cards will show all files in the current directory.

- Use the /T operator to show or change permissions from the current location and in all subdirectories thereafter. The command below will record permissions for every file on your hard disk to a text file.

```
CACLS C:\*.* /T >C:\PERMIT.TXT
```

You can use batch files to control the functionality of CACLS; otherwise, there is little advantage to using it rather than the Desktop Explorer to change permissions on an NTFS volume.

Finger

Profile	
Name	Finger
Vendor	Microsoft
Cost	$0 (Included with Windows NT)
Use	Command line utility used to show the directory names of users on remote systems
Issues	None

Finger is used to access directory information such as e-mail addresses, user names, and telephone numbers for users of remote network systems. Most new networked systems no longer support the Finger protocol due to its usefulness to hackers.

When you type **Finger** with no command line parameters, you'll see the instructions shown in Figure B.7.

To get information about a user, enter the following command:

```
Finger user@host.com
```

To get information about all users on a host, enter this:

```
Finger@host.com
```

F I G U R E B.7

Finger command line options

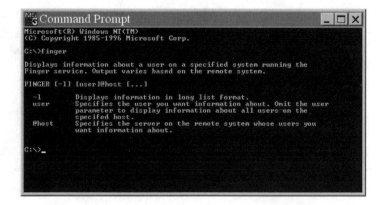

Very few computers actually still serve Finger requests. Usually, you'll get a "connect refused" error or a "connection timed out" error.

IPConfig

Profile	
Name	IPConfig
Vendor	Microsoft
Cost	$0 (Included with Windows NT)
Use	Command line utility used to show IP addresses
Issues	None

IPConfig (Internet Protocol Configuration) is used to display IP addresses assigned to ports on your system.

When you type **IPConfig** with no command line parameters, you'll see the instructions shown in Figure B.8.

```
Command Prompt                                            _ □ ×

C:\>ipconfig /?

Windows NT IP Configuration

usage: ipconfig [/? | /all | /release [adapter] | /renew [adapter]]

       /?        Display this help message.
       /all      Display full configuration information.
       /release  Release the IP address for the specified adapter.
       /renew    Renew the IP address for the specified adapter.

The default is to display only the IP address, subnet mask and default gateway
for each adapter bound to TCP/IP.

For Release and Renew, if no adapter name is specified, then the IP address
leases for all adapters bound to TCP/IP will be released or renewed.

C:\>ipconfig /release Elnk31

Windows NT IP Configuration

IP address 204.210.33.166 successfully released for adapter "Elnk31"

C:\>
```

IPConfig is used to determine configuration information about the various TCP/IP adapters installed in your system. It is comparable to the winipcfg.exe program for Windows 95. Typing **IPConfig /all** at the command prompt provides information like that shown in Figure B.9.

```
Command Prompt                                            _ □ ×

        Host Name . . . . . . . . . : lucretius
        DNS Servers . . . . . . . . :
        Node Type . . . . . . . . . : Hybrid
        NetBIOS Scope ID. . . . . . :
        IP Routing Enabled. . . . . : Yes
        WINS Proxy Enabled. . . . . : No
        NetBIOS Resolution Uses DNS : No

Ethernet adapter Elnk31:

        Description . . . . . . . . : ELNK3 Ethernet Adapter.
        Physical Address. . . . . . : 00-20-AF-9F-BF-BB
        DHCP Enabled. . . . . . . . : Yes
        IP Address. . . . . . . . . : 0.0.0.0
        Subnet Mask . . . . . . . . : 0.0.0.0
        Default Gateway . . . . . . :
        DHCP Server . . . . . . . . : 255.255.255.255

Ethernet adapter NE20002:

        Description . . . . . . . . : Novell 2000 Adapter.
        Physical Address. . . . . . : 00-00-E8-2C-47-BA
        DHCP Enabled. . . . . . . . : Yes
        IP Address. . . . . . . . . : 10.1.1.2
        Subnet Mask . . . . . . . . : 255.255.255.0
        Default Gateway . . . . . . :
        DHCP Server . . . . . . . . : 10.1.1.1
        Lease Obtained. . . . . . . : Thursday, October 30, 1997 8:54:15 AM
        Lease Expires . . . . . . . : Monday, January 18, 2038 7:14:07 PM

Ethernet adapter NdisWan6:

        Description . . . . . . . . : NdisWan Adapter
        Physical Address. . . . . . : 00-00-00-00-00-00
        DHCP Enabled. . . . . . . . : No
        IP Address. . . . . . . . . : 0.0.0.0
        Subnet Mask . . . . . . . . : 0.0.0.0
        Default Gateway . . . . . . :

Ethernet adapter NdisWan5:

        Description . . . . . . . . : NdisWan Adapter
        Physical Address. . . . . . : 00-00-00-00-00-00
        DHCP Enabled. . . . . . . . : No
        IP Address. . . . . . . . . : 0.0.0.0
        Subnet Mask . . . . . . . . : 0.0.0.0
        Default Gateway . . . . . . :

C:\>_
```

In addition to returning the status and configuration of your network adapters, IPConfig can be used to renew or release DCHP-assigned IP addresses. In a network that is functioning normally this occurs automatically, so you won't need to worry about it; but you can use the functionality to test a DHCP server or other network link if you suspect a problem.

NBTStat

Profile

Name	NBTStat
Vendor	Microsoft
Cost	$0 (Included with Windows NT)
Use	Command line utility used to show the mapping between NetBIOS names and IP addresses
Issues	None

NBTStat (NBT status) is used to display the mappings between Net-BIOS network names and IP addresses.

When you type in **NBTSTAT** with no command line parameters, you'll see the instructions shown in Figure B.10.

Most NBTStat functions are provided for the purpose of trouble-shooting—but one of them can be exploited by hackers to gather information about your host if you aren't careful. NBTSTAT –a [*ip address*] will return the NetBIOS name of the logged-on user if your Internet-connected computer has NetBIOS bound to the TCP/IP stack. This means that a hacker can type in **NTBSTAT** [*ip address of your machine*] and find out the name of at least one account holder—even the administrator, if logged in! Figure B.11 shows the name table returned by NBTStat. Notice that in this case, the administrative account has not been renamed and is logged on.

F I G U R E   B.10

NBTSTAT command line
options

F I G U R E   B.10

NBTSTAT command line
options

F I G U R E   B.11

The NetBIOS name table
contains information
about the logged-on user.

WARNING

Never leave the administrative account logged on for machines connected to the Internet, especially if NetBIOS is bound to TCP/IP. Hackers can determine the name of your administrative account and use automated password guessing tools to determine your password.

Net

Profile

Name	Net
Vendor	Microsoft
Cost	$0 (Included with Windows NT)
Use	Command line utility used to control NetBIOS networking resources
Issues	None

The Net command is capable of performing nearly all NetBIOS networking functions.

The Net subcommands are:

- Accounts
- Computer
- Config
- Continue
- File
- Group
- Help
- Helpmsg
- Localgroup
- Name
- Pause
- Print
- Send
- Session
- Share
- Start
- Statistics
- Stop
- Time
- Use
- User
- View

Accounts

The net accounts command is used to control account password policy. The functionality of the net accounts command is provided by the User Manager for Domains in the Account Policy window. Figure B.12 shows the net accounts syntax and a sample response.

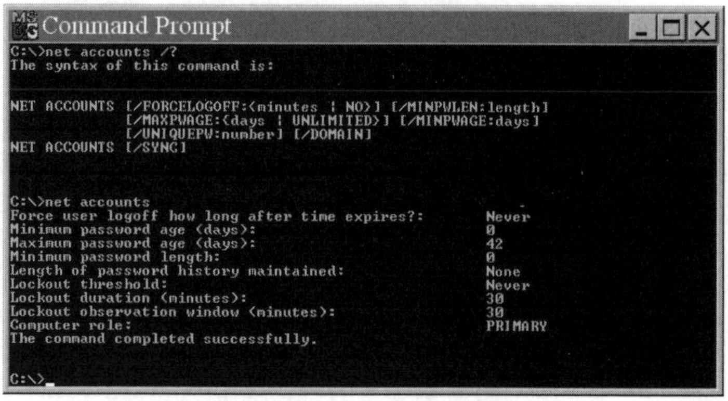

FIGURE B.12

The net accounts command

```
Command Prompt                                          _ □ X
C:\>net accounts /?
The syntax of this command is:

NET ACCOUNTS [/FORCELOGOFF:{minutes | NO}] [/MINPWLEN:length]
             [/MAXPWAGE:{days | UNLIMITED}] [/MINPWAGE:days]
             [/UNIQUEPW:number] [/DOMAIN]
NET ACCOUNTS [/SYNC]


C:\>net accounts
Force user logoff how long after time expires?:        Never
Minimum password age (days):                           0
Maximum password age (days):                           42
Minimum password length:                               0
Length of password history maintained:                 None
Lockout threshold:                                     Never
Lockout duration (minutes):                            30
Lockout observation window (minutes):                  30
Computer role:                                         PRIMARY
The command completed successfully.


C:\>
```

Computer

The net computer command is used to add or remove Windows NT computers from the domain security structure. The syntax of the command is:

NET COMPUTER *COMPUTERNAME* ADD

NET COMPUTER *COMPUTERNAME* DELETE

Config

Net config provides a generic interface through which Windows NT network services can be controlled. A default Windows NT installation has two services which can be controlled using the net config command:

- **Net config server** shows various server-related information such as the adapters to which the server service is bound, user and file maximums, and whether or not the server shows up in browse lists. You can change some of these parameters with this command.

- **Net config workstation** provides information about the configuration of various workstation-related network parameters, such as the bound network adapter, domain association, and communication device timing parameters. You can also change the various communication device timing parameters with this command. Use `Net help config workstation` for more information about this command.

Continue

Net continue is used to continue a service which as been paused with the net pause command. The syntax is:

```
NET CONTINUE SERVICENAME
```

File

Net file is used to control files that have been opened by users on the server. Typing **net file** provides a list of opened files. Net file with a file ID number (provided by the net file command) provides additional information about the file in use, and Net file id/close closes the file.

Group

The net group command is used to display, add, delete, and change membership in domain group accounts. Typing **net group** at the command line provides a list of global groups on the primary domain controller. Net group groupname/add creates a new group, and /delete removes a group. Net group *groupname accountname*/add makes the account specified a member of the group specified, and /delete removes account membership from the group.

Help

The net help command provides detailed information about all of the various net commands. For instance, typing **net help config workstation** provides the information shown in Figure B.13.

FIGURE B.13

Getting Help with the net commands

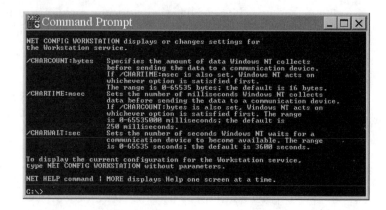

HelpMSG

Net helpmsg decrypts Windows NT message numbers that can be received during installation or during abnormal conditions. For instance, typing:

```
C:\>NET HELPMSG 0021
```

Returns the following message:

```
The device is not ready.
```

Use this command whenever you see a Windows NT error message that you don't understand.

Localgroup

The localgroup command works the same way the group command does, but it specifies groups local to the computer rather than domain groups.

Name

Net name displays and changes the net names that are currently accepting messages from the messenger service at that computer. Normally, the net name list will include the logon name of the individual using the computer (unless it's already in use somewhere else) and the net name of the computer.

You may add any net name for which you wish to receive messages, and you can delete any net names except the computer name.

Pause

Net pause is used to pause services running on the computer. Pausing a service makes it unavailable to service clients but does not deallocate memory or unload the service.

Print

Net print provides a command line interface that allows you to control print jobs, much the way the Explorer does when you double-click on a printer. Figure B.14 shows the syntax of the net print command and a sample queue.

FIGURE B.14

Controlling print jobs with
the net print command

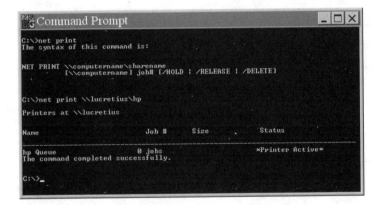

Send

Net send sends a message to another user or computer using the messenger service. Net send is a great way to provide immediate alerting from monitoring programs that will only run a command line program when some abnormal event has occurred—for instance, the UPS monitor control panel or the Performance Monitor. Figure B.15 shows the UPS power monitor control panel configured to send a message to all domain users when the UPS on the server reports a power fail condition.

You can also embed net send commands in a batch file to alert you that long processes (such as a tape backup) have completed.

FIGURE B.15

The net send command sends a message using the messenger service.

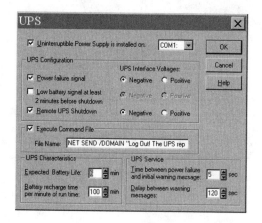

Session

Net session lists and controls the service session established between the server and its clients. Net session is a command line interface similar to the functionality provided by the Server control panel.

Share

Net share controls NetBIOS shares provided by your server. The functionality is similar to the Sharing window provided by the Desktop Explorer. Use the net share command to see a list of shares provided by a server, or to control access to those shares. Figure B.16 shows the command line parameters of the net share command and a sample share listing.

Start

Net start is used to start a service that is set to start up manually or that has been stopped with the net stop command. Net start supports only one command line parameter: Net start *servicename*. If the service name consists of more than one word, it must be enclosed in quotes. This functionality is also provided by the Services control panel.

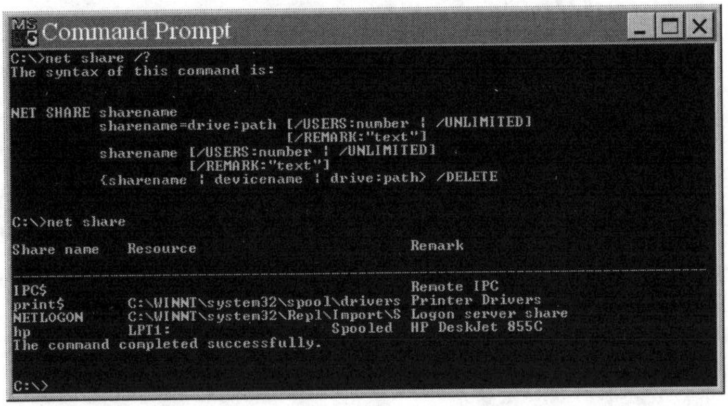

FIGURE B.16

The net share command

```
MS
C  Command Prompt                                          _ □ ×
C:\>net share /?
The syntax of this command is:

NET SHARE sharename
              sharename=drive:path [/USERS:number ¦ /UNLIMITED]
                                   [/REMARK:"text"]
              sharename [/USERS:number ¦ /UNLIMITED]
                        [/REMARK:"text"]
              {sharename ¦ devicename ¦ drive:path> /DELETE


C:\>net share

Share name    Resource                        Remark

IPC$                                          Remote IPC
print$        C:\WINNT\system32\spool\drivers Printer Drivers
NETLOGON      C:\WINNT\system32\Repl\Import\S Logon server share
hp            LPT1:              Spooled      HP DeskJet 855C
The command completed successfully.

C:\>
```

Statistics

Net statistics displays statistics for the server and workstation services such as number of connections, bytes sent and received, errors, hung or failed sessions, and other statistics that might be useful in determining whether an excessive number of network errors are occurring. The Performance Monitor can track all these statistics, and it is much easier to use.

Stop

Net stop is used to stop a service that is currently running. The net stop command is used like this:

```
C:\>NET STOP "COMPUTER BROWSER"
```

The service name only needs to be quoted if it consists of more than one word. The Services control panel also provides this functionality.

Time

Net time is used to synchronize the time between a time server and a time client. Unless correct time synchronization is extremely important in your environment (for instance, to match lab samples or for process control) there's little reason to use this command. You can synchronize your computer's time with that of the domain server using the following command:

```
C:\>NET TIME /DOMAIN /SET
```

Use

Net use is one of the most useful net commands. With it, you can map local identifiers, like drive letters and printer ports, to shared network resources. Normally, when you net use a resource, the mapping is persistent across booting and logging on. You'll only have to do it once, and the mapping will persist until you delete it. Although you can change this functionality, there's little reason to do so. Figure B.17 shows the parameters and use of the net use command.

FIGURE B.17

Net use command line options

User

Net user allows you to manage user accounts for Windows NT local and domain accounts. With the net user command, you can create and delete user accounts and set the various account policy options that are available in the user manager for domains. Use net user whenever you need to add a large number of accounts with very similar options because the net user command can be included in a batch file. Figure B.18 shows the user information provided by the net user command.

F I G U R E B.18

Information for a user account provided by net user

The following text dump of the net help user command provides the syntax of this command:

```
NET USER     [username [password | *] [options]] [/DOMAIN]
             username {password | *} /ADD [options] [/DOMAIN]
             username [/DELETE] [/DOMAIN]
```

NET USER creates and modifies user accounts on computers. When used without switches, it lists the user accounts for the computer. The user account information is stored in the user accounts database.

This command works only on servers.

username	Is the name of the user account to add, delete, modify, or view. The name of the user account can have as many as 20 characters.
password	Assigns or changes a password for the user's account. A password must satisfy the minimum length set with the /MINPWLEN option of the NET ACCOUNTS command. It can have as many as 14 characters.
*	Produces a prompt for the password. The password is not displayed when you type it at a password prompt.
/DOMAIN	Performs the operation on the primary domain controller of the current domain. This parameter applies only to Windows NT Workstation computers that are members of a Windows NT Server domain. By default, Windows NT Server computers perform operations on the primary domain controller.
/ADD	Adds a user account to the user accounts database.
/DELETE	Removes a user account from the user accounts database.

Options   Are as follows:

Options	Description
/ACTIVE:{YES | NO)	Activates or deactivates the account. If the account is not active, the user cannot access the server. The default is YES
/COMMENT:"text"	Provides a descriptive comment about the user's account (maximum of 48 characters). Enclose the text in quotation marks.
/COUNTRYCODE:nnn	Uses the operating system country code to implement the specified language files for a user's help and error messages. A value of 0 signifies the default country code.
/EXPIRES:{date | NEVER}	Causes the account to expire if date is set. NEVER sets no time limit on the account. An expiration date is in the orm mm/dd/yy or dd/mm/yy, depending on the country code. Months can be a number, spelled out, or abbreviated with three letters. Year can be two or four numbers. Use slashes(/) (no spaces) to separate parts of the date.
/FULLNAME:"name"	Is a user's full name (rather than a username). Enclose the name in quotation marks.
HOMEDIR:pathname/	Sets the path for the user's home directory. The path must exist.

PASSWORDCHG: {YES | NO}

Specifies whether users can change their own password. The default is YES.

/PASSWORDREQ: {YES | NO}

Specifies whether a user account must have a password. The default is YES.

/PROFILEPATH[:path]

Sets a path for the user's logon profile.

SCRIPTPATH:pathname

Is the location of the user's logon script.

/TIMES:{times | ALL}

Is the logon hours. TIMES is expressed as day[-day][,day[-day]],time[-time][,time [-time]], limited to 1-hour increments. Days can be spelled out or abbreviated. Hours can be 12- or 24-hour notation. For 12-hour notation, use am, pm, a.m., or p.m. ALL means a user can always log on, and a blank value means a user can never log on. Separate day and time entries with a comma, and separate multiple day and time entries with a semicolon.

USERCOMMENT:"text"

Lets an administrator add or change the User Comment for the account.

WORKSTATIONS:{compu tername[,...] | *}

Lists as many as eight computers from which a user can log on to the network. If /WORKSTATIONS has no list or if the list is *, the user can log on from any computer.

View

Net view shows the network shares provided by a specific computer. You can use net view from any Windows-based network computer to see the shares on another computer, which is especially handy if your network browsing is not operating correctly or is temporarily unavailable. The following command will return a list of shares provided on the addressed server:

```
C:\>NET VIEW \\LUCRETIUS
```

Net view without command line parameters displays a list of computers in the current domain or network. With parameters, you can view a specific computer or domain. Use net help view at the command prompt to see more details about this command.

Netstat

Profile

Name	Netstat
Vendor	Microsoft
Cost	$0 (Included with Windows NT)
Use	Command line utility used to show the status of IP connections.
Issues	None

Netstat (network status) is used to display current TCP/IP connections and their status.

When you type **netstat** with a **/?** (help) parameter, you'll see the instructions shown in Figure B.19.

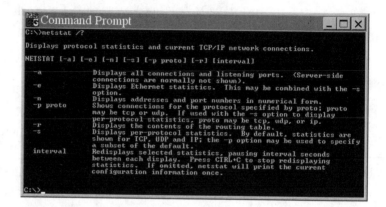

When you type **netstat** with no parameters, the command returns the status of all current TCP/IP connections. Including a **-a** parameter will show all server-side connections. You can use this information to quickly determine which services are running on your server—make certain you know what each listening service is! (Ports starting just above 1024 are usually the return channels for sessions established by user-level applications or proxy servers.) Figure B.20 shows the ports a typical proxy server might use.

You can use the interval setting to periodically refresh the netstat display automatically if you want a continuous listing of running sessions. For instance:

```
Netstat -a 5
```

will display all TCP/IP sessions (including server listening ports) every five seconds until you press Ctrl+Break. This can be useful for continuous monitoring. Other functions of the netstat command are useful mostly for troubleshooting.

FIGURE B.20

FIGURE B.20

Typical TCP/IP service
ports for a proxy server

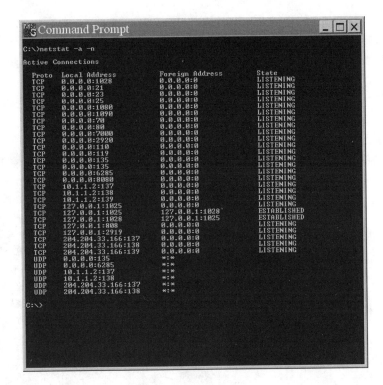

NSLookup

Profile	
Name	NSLookup
Vendor	Microsoft
Cost	$0 (Included with Windows NT)
Use	Command line utility used to find IP addresses from Internet names, or Internet names from IP addresses
Issues	None

NSLookup (Name Server Lookup) is used to resolve Internet names to IP addresses. When you type **nslookup** with no command line parameters, and then type **?** at the greater-than (>)prompt, you'll see the instructions shown in Figure B.21.

```
Command Prompt                                          _  □  ×

C:\>nslookup www.ibm.com
Server:  tas5-fddi.san.rr.com
Address:  204.210.7.21

Non-authoritative answer:
Name:    www.ibm.com
Address:  204.146.17.33


C:\>nslookup
Default Server:  tas5-fddi.san.rr.com
Address:  204.210.7.21

> ?
Commands:   (identifiers are shown in uppercase, [] means optional)
NAME            - print info about the host/domain NAME using default server
NAME1 NAME2     - as above, but use NAME2 as server
help or ?       - print info on common commands
set OPTION      - set an option
    all         - print options, current server and host
    [no]debug   - print debugging information
    [no]d2      - print exhaustive debugging information
    [no]defname - append domain name to each query
    [no]recurse - ask for recursive answer to query
    [no]search  - use domain search list
    [no]vc      - always use a virtual circuit
    domain=NAME - set default domain name to NAME
    srchlist=N1[/N2/.../N6] - set domain to N1 and search list to N1,N2, etc.
    root=NAME   - set root server to NAME
    retry=X     - set number of retries to X
    timeout=X   - set initial time-out interval to X seconds
    querytype=X - set query type, e.g., A,ANY,CNAME,MX,NS,PTR,SOA
    type=X      - synonym for querytype
    class=X     - set query class to one of IN (Internet), CHAOS, HESIOD or ANY
server NAME     - set default server to NAME, using current default server
lserver NAME    - set default server to NAME, using initial server
finger [USER]   - finger the optional NAME at the current default host
root            - set current default server to the root
ls [opt] DOMAIN [> FILE] - list addresses in DOMAIN (optional: output to FILE)
    -a          - list canonical names and aliases
    -d          - list all records
    -t TYPE     - list records of the given type (e.g. A,CNAME,MX,NS,PTR etc.)
view FILE       - sort an 'ls' output file and view it with pg
exit            - exit the program

> exit

C:\>
```

Typically, you use NSLookup to resolve an IP address given a name, as in:

```
C:\>Nslookup www.ibm.com
```

This command will return the IP address of IBM's Web server. Unlike most command line utilities, NSLookup has two modes of operation. If you type **nslookup** *name* and press ↵, NSLookup will resolve the address using your default name server, return the results, and exit back to the command prompt.

If you provide no parameters when you launch NSLookup, it will run as a UNIX-style command line program, complete with its own prompt and list of commands. You can then use these various commands to perform all sorts of name-server related functions, such as changing your default name server. The use of most of these commands is esoteric and usually not necessary except for troubleshooting.

Ping

Profile

Name	Ping
Vendor	Microsoft
Cost	$0 (Included with Windows NT)
Use	Command line utility used to send ICMP echo messages to a remote host
Issues	None

Ping is used to send ICMP echo messages (pings) to a remote host to determine if the host is available for further TCP/IP traffic. Ping is so often used to test for the existence of hosts and for the proper operation of network clients that it is commonly used as a verb among TCP/IP network integrators, as in, "Did you ping the server?"

When you type in **ping** with no command line parameters, you'll see the instructions shown in Figure B.22.

Most of the functionality of ping is described by the commands in Figure B.22. You can control the various ICMP message parameters of the generated ping packet using the available parameters. Most of these options are used only during esoteric troubleshooting sessions.

```
MS Command Prompt                                              _ □ X
Microsoft(R) Windows NT(TM)
(C) Copyright 1985-1996 Microsoft Corp.

C:\>ping

Usage: ping [-t] [-a] [-n count] [-l size] [-f] [-i TTL] [-v TOS]
            [-r count] [-s count] [[-j host-list] ! [-k host-list]]
            [-w timeout] destination-list

Options:
    -t              Ping the specifed host until interrupted.
    -a              Resolve addresses to hostnames.
    -n count        Number of echo requests to send.
    -l size         Send buffer size.
    -f              Set Don't Fragment flag in packet.
    -i TTL          Time To Live.
    -v TOS          Type Of Service.
    -r count        Record route for count hops.
    -s count        Timestamp for count hops.
    -j host-list    Loose source route along host-list.
    -k host-list    Strict source route along host-list.
    -w timeout      Timeout in milliseconds to wait for each reply.

C:\>_
```

The success of a simple ping request can be used to determine exactly how a malfunctioning client is operating. If a ping to another computer succeeds, you know that the physical layer, data link layer, and network layer are all functioning correctly and that any communications problems you may be experiencing must be occurring in higher layers.

Figure B.23 shows how hosts normally respond to ping requests, and the sorts of error messages you can expect when there is a communications problem between hosts.

```
MS Command Prompt                                              _ □ X
C:\>ping sybex.com

Pinging sybex.com [209.1.78.150] with 32 bytes of data:

Reply from 209.1.78.150: bytes=32 time=110ms TTL=20
Reply from 209.1.78.150: bytes=32 time=31ms TTL=20
Reply from 209.1.78.150: bytes=32 time=31ms TTL=20
Reply from 209.1.78.150: bytes=32 time=32ms TTL=20

C:\>ping www.microsoft.com

Pinging www.microsoft.com [207.68.156.52] with 32 bytes of data:

Request timed out.
Request timed out.
Reply from 207.68.145.53: Destination net unreachable.
Request timed out.

C:\>_
```

Hackers also use ping for various purposes that are detrimental to networks. For instance, you can use ping to cause "floods" of useless data by transmitting large numbers of long ping packets, as in:

```
Ping 10.1.1.1 -l 65000 -n 1000
```

Although a single host won't tie up a server this way, as few as 10 hosts transmitting this command to the same server can generate so much useless traffic that actual users won't be able to get through. This is a denial-of-service attack.

"Ping of death" attacks, wherein exceptionally large (>64K) and mal-formed ICMP echo requests generated by custom ping programs are transmitted to hosts that have delicate TCP/IP stacks, cause many TCP/IP implementations to crash when they can't decipher an ICMP message correctly. These "ping of death" attacks can be used to crash some TCP/IP servers remotely. Windows NT was susceptible to various "ping of death" attacks prior to Service Pack 3.

RCP

Profile

Name	RCP
Vendor	Microsoft
Cost	$0 (Included with Windows NT)
Use	Command line utility used to copy files among hosts that support the remote copy protocol
Issues	None

RCP (Remote Copy Protocol) client is used to transfer files between hosts that support the remote copy protocol service (daemon in UNIX parlance). The Remote Copy Protocol is largely obsolete because its functionality is usually provided by the FTP service. Although Windows NT provides an RCP client, it does not support the RCP service.

When you type in **RCP** with no command line parameters, you'll see the instructions shown in Figure B.24. Most of the functionality of RCP is described by the commands in Figure B.24.

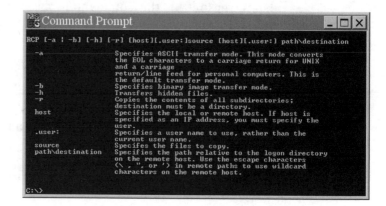

Route

Profile

Name	Route
Vendor	Microsoft
Cost	$0 (Included with Windows NT)
Use	Command line utility used to control the TCP/IP routing table of a server
Issues	None

Route is used to add and delete routing entries in a static routing table. When you type in **route** with no command line parameters, you'll see the instructions shown in Figure B.25.

F I G U R E   B.25

Route command line
options

F I G U R E   B.25

Route command line
options

You can use the route command to manually create and remove
routing table entries for a Windows NT server. You can also use the
route command to display the current status of the routing table as
shown in Figure B.26.

F I G U R E   B.26

The routing table of a
typical Windows NT
server

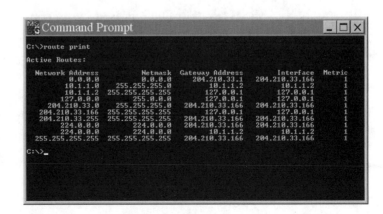

For security purposes, consider disabling RIP requests and using manually assigned routing tables if your network is small enough to support the additional administrative burden.

> If you will be converting a RIP-enabled server to a manually assigned routing table, be sure to take a snapshot of the RIP routing table before you disable it, using this: C:\>**route print >router.txt**. You can then use this text file as a guide for creating your own manual routing table.

RSH

Profile

Name	RSH
Vendor	Microsoft
Cost	$0 (Included with Windows NT)
Use	Command line utility used to launch shell commands on remote UNIX hosts
Issues	None

RSH (Remote Shell) is used to run commands on remote UNIX hosts. Although Windows NT includes an RSH command line utility, it does not support the RSH server service. When you type **RSH** with no command line parameters, you'll see the instructions shown in Figure B.27.

Most of the functionality of RSH is described by the commands in Figure B.27. Very few Internet servers support the RSH protocol due to the inherent danger of allowing anonymous users the ability to execute programs remotely.

F I G U R E B.27

RSH command line
options

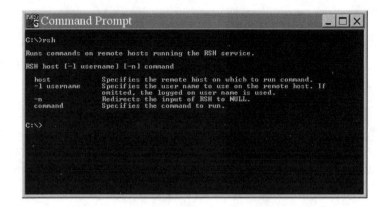

F I G U R E B.27

RSH command line
options

Telnet

Profile

Name   Telnet

Vendor   Microsoft

Cost $0 (Included with Windows NT)

Use   Client for hosts running the TELNET service

Issues   None

Telnet is a graphical client that allows you to remotely attach to
servers running the telnet service (daemon). Windows NT comes with a
telnet client but does not support the telnet service.

Telnet takes one parameter from the command line: the Internet
name of the host to which you wish to attach. Alternatively, you can
launch telnet and then provide the host name or IP address and the
TCP/IP port to which you wish to attach. Telnet then provides a char-
acter-based console that you can use to control the host.

Many routers, switches, firewalls, and print servers are configured by opening a connection via telnet to their IP address.

Many routers, switches, firewalls, and print servers can be configured remotely by hackers who open a connection via their telnet ports to their IP addresses. Block inbound telnet connections through your firewall.

TFTP

Profile

Name	TFTP
Vendor	Microsoft
Cost	$0 (Included with Windows NT)
Use	Command line utility used to copy files among hosts that support the Trivial File Transfer Protocol
Issues	None

TFTP (Trivial File Transfer Protocol) is used to transfer files between hosts using the Trivial File Transfer Protocol. TFTP is largely obsolete because its functionality is normally provided by the FTP service. Although Windows NT provides an TFTP client, it does not support the TFTP server service.

Tracert

Profile

Name	Tracert
Vendor	Microsoft
Cost	$0 (Included with Windows NT)
Use	Command line utility used to show the route taken between two Internet hosts
Issues	None

Tracert (Trace Route) is used to display the routers between two communicating Internet hosts. Figure B.28 shows the command line parameters of the Tracert command and a sample route traced between two Internet hosts.

Since most Internet service providers use meaningful names on their router interfaces, you can often determine quite a bit about the route taken between two hosts. From the example shown in Figure B.28, we can determine the following:

1. The first router interface is listed as `tas5-hfc3.san.rr.com`. Since we know from other hops on this service provider that they usually include the protocol for the interface, we can assume that hfc3 is some sort of physical port technology. It may stand for "High Frequency Cable modem channel 3" which would indicate that the end user is using cable modem technology to connect to the Internet. This line also indicates that the router is probably located in a city beginning with the letters "San," or that the naming convention is following the common router practice of identifying a city by its three letter airport designator, which in this case would be San Diego, CA.

```
Command Prompt                                                    _ □ X

C:\>tracert

Usage: tracert [-d] [-h maximum_hops] [-j host-list] [-w timeout] target_name

Options:
        -d                      Do not resolve addresses to hostnames.
        -h maximum_hops         Maximum number of hops to search for target.
        -j host-list            Loose source route along host-list.
        -w timeout              Wait timeout milliseconds for each reply.

C:\>tracert www.ibm.com

Tracing route to www.ibm.com [204.146.17.33]
over a maximum of 30 hops:

  1     16 ms     15 ms     32 ms  tas5-hfc3.san.rr.com [204.210.33.1]
  2    <10 ms      *        <10 ms  tas5-fddi.san.rr.com [204.210.7.21]
  3    <10 ms     16 ms     15 ms  7507-atm.san.rr.com [204.210.0.254]
  4     16 ms     16 ms     15 ms  bordercore1-hssi5-0-2.Bloomington.mci.net [166.4
8.172.13]
  5     16 ms     46 ms     16 ms  core7.SanFrancisco.mci.net [204.70.4.93]
  6     31 ms     31 ms     32 ms  mae-west3-nap.SanFrancisco.mci.net [204.70.10.24
6]
  7    344 ms     78 ms    172 ms  mae-west.ibm.net [198.32.136.20]
  8     94 ms     78 ms     63 ms  sf33-16-br2.ca.us.ibm.net [165.87.33.18]
  9    422 ms     94 ms     78 ms  chi36-0-br2.il.us.ibm.net [165.87.36.2]
 10     94 ms    110 ms     93 ms  scha34-16-br2.il.us.ibm.net [165.87.34.18]
 11    109 ms    141 ms    109 ms  scha34-48-fddi1.il.us.ibm.net [165.87.34.62]
 12     78 ms     78 ms     94 ms  www.ibm.com [204.146.17.33]

Trace complete.

C:\>
```

2. The next line is another interface on the same router, this time using fiber distributed data interface (FDDI), a 100Mbps token ring over optical fiber technology.

3. The next line indicates that the next higher router is using Asynchronous Transfer Mode (ATM) technology. This technology operates at bit rates varying from 25Mbps to 2200Mbps. As routers get closer to the Internet backbone, they (should) use increasingly faster data link technologies. This probably means that the ATM link is either 155, 622, or 2200Mbps.

4. The next line indicates that the next higher router uses High Speed Serial Interface (HSSI) technology, that it is located in Bloomingdale, and that it is operated by MCI.

5. The next line indicates that we've reached the Mae West Network Access Point (NAP) in San Francisco. This network access point is one of four commercial Internet exchanges in the country that forms the backbone of the Internet. So far, the route includes only very high-speed protocols and is relatively close to the Internet backbone—lucky user!

6. The next line indicates a switch from MCI's network to IBM's. This indicates that IBM has a presence on the Internet backbone directly, and so would be a good candidate for consideration as an Internet service provider, as would MCI.

7. The next router is still in San Francisco and still on IBM's network.

8. The next router appears to be in Chicago (another NAP location).

9. The next router is in some city abbreviated "scha"—perhaps Schenectady, NY?

10. The next router indicates a shift down to FDDI.

11. The final hop is the destination server.

With practice and a strong knowledge of data link technologies you can determine quite a bit about the identity of remote hosts on the Internet.

Windows NT Resource Kit

Windows NT Resource Kit utilities come with Microsoft's Resource Kit for Windows NT Server, which is available for about $150 at bookstores. The Resource Kit contains a number of useful administration utilities beyond those shown here and is well worth the investment. The security-related utilities are:

- C2Config

- Dumpel

- Passprop

C2Config

Profile	
Name	C2Config
Vendor	Microsoft
Cost	N/A (Included with Windows NT Resource Kit)
Use	Checks system security
Issues	None

One of Windows NT 4's much-hyped features is its support for the National Computer Security Center's C2 Security specification. Although it may not be wise to fully secure your system to this specification—particularly since it requires disabling networking—this utility does provide many useful pointers about potential security problems.

The C2Config utility is shown in Figure B.29. This utility is self-explanatory: When first run, it displays a list of potential security problems found in your system. The entries with the red (locked) icon are already secure; those in blue are possible causes for concern.

Double-click one of the entries for a detailed description. The description window also offers a way to automatically make the recommended changes for many of the settings.

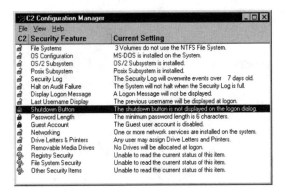

Dumpel

Profile	
Name	Dumpel
Vendor	Microsoft
Cost	N/A (Included with Windows NT Resource Kit)
Use	Command line tool to convert event log to other formats
Issues	None

Dumpel is a simple utility to convert Windows NT event logs (the same logs displayed by Event Viewer) to ASCII files. This allows you to import the logs into a spreadsheet, database, or report-generating program.

The main options of this utility are **-s** to specify a server, **-l** to specify a log (system, application, or security), and **-f** to specify the output file name. For example, this command dumps the security log from server WEST1 to the file LOG.TXT in the current directory:

```
DUMPEL -S WEST1 -F LOG.TXT -L SECURITY
```

Type **DUMPEL /?** to display a list of other options.

Passprop

Profile

Name	Passprop
Vendor	Microsoft
Cost	N/A (Included with Windows NT Resource Kit)
Use	Command-line tool to enforce complex passwords
Issues	None

Passprop is a useful command-line tool for enforcing more complex passwords than arenormally possible on Windows NT. Without this utility, you can only enforce the minimum length of passwords.

You only need to run passprop once at each server to set up the type of password enforcement you want. Type this command:

```
PASSPROP /COMPLEX
```

This turns on complex passwords. This means that passwords either have to include numbers, mixed case, or punctuation characters in order to be valid. To turn this feature back off, use this command:

```
PASSPROP /SIMPLE
```

Another function of passprop is to control whether the Administrator account can be locked out. Normally, this is the one account that can't be locked out. If you turn on this feature, you can still log in when Administrator is locked out, but only at the server's console. Type this command to activate administrator lockout:

```
PASSPROP /ADMINLOCKOUT
```

To disable administrator lockout (the default) use this command:

```
PASSPROP /NOADMINLOCKOUT
```

Security Vendors

These utilities are either demonstration versions of commercial applications, shareware distributed applications, or applications that the vendors have provided free of charge for inclusion in the CD-ROM that comes with this book. Evaluate these utilities and determine where in your security environment they belong. Perform regular checks of the software industry on the Internet through search engines to find more security applications as they become available. Security applications included in this appendix are:

- ERDisk
- FileAdmin
- Internet Scanner
- Kane Security Analyst
- NetXRay
- NTFSDOS

- NTRecover
- Red Button
- RegAdmin Pro
- ScanNT
- Suck Server
- WS-Ping

ERDisk

Profile

Name	ERDisk
Vendor	Midwestern Commerce, Inc.
Cost	$0 (Demo)
Use	Creates emergency repair disks
Issues	None

It's a good idea to have an emergency repair disk handy for every Windows NT computer on your network. However, this can be time-consuming with a large network. ERDisk is a useful utility that can create an emergency repair disk for any computer in the network. You must have Administrator access to use this utility.

This utility is shown in Figure B.30. To create an emergency repair disk, select a computer and click the Go button. You can also select a directory to create emergency repair disk files in, rather than using a floppy disk.

FIGURE B.30

ERDisk creates
emergency repair disks.

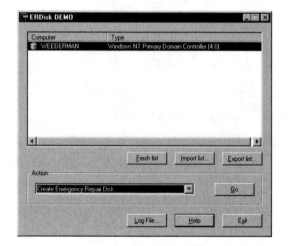

 The version of ERDisk included on the CD accompanying this book is a demo and is limited to five computers to a network. For information about the full version, see MWC's Web site at http://www.NTsecurity.com/.

FileAdmin

Profile

Name	FileAdmin
Vendor	Midwestern Commerce, Inc.
Cost	$0 (Demo)
Use	Controls access to files and directories
Issues	None

FileAdmin allows you to modify user permissions for files and directories, and provides a few features missing from the dialog boxes that Windows NT uses for this purpose.

To use FileAdmin, select a file or directory at the top of the dialog box. You can then modify the list of users that have permission for the file. This utility functions similarly to the Windows NT utilities, and it is easy to use.

This is a demo version of FileAdmin that is limited to modifying single files or directories. The full version can propagate changes to an entire directory tree. See the Web site mentioned above for information.

Internet Scanner

Profile

Name	Internet Scanner
Vendor	Internet Security Systems
Cost	(unknown)
Use	Command line utility used to show the mapping between physical adapter addresses and IP addresses
Issues	Installation requires reboot

Internet Security System's Internet Scanner is the most comprehensive security checking utility we've found for Windows NT. It checks a vast array of common security problems and ranks them according to the risk they present. The security scanner is client/server-based so you can scan systems remotely. Figure B.31 shows the results of a security scan against an NT server.

Installing IIS Internet Scanner is straightforward, but you will have to install a raw packet driver manually and reboot your system. Once it is installed, you simply launch the application and select whether you want a light, medium, or heavy scan. These various grades indicate the depth (and time) Internet Scanner will devote to uncovering security problems in your system.

When finished, you'll see each problem listed in a display window. The Internet scanner can generate a report in HTML or text format that

FIGURE B.31

A security scan reveals weaknesses.

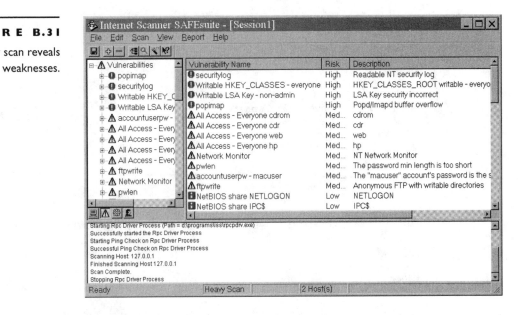

delineates each problem found and its effects. This report is very useful in determining what measures you'll take (if any) to correct the problems found.

A number of the problems turned up by the scanner (especially in the low-risk category) can't be avoided because they are inherent risks in providing service to clients. You should concern yourself mostly with correcting those risks shown as high or medium risk.

Never rely too heavily upon a single tool for security administration. No tool can check for problems its creators weren't aware of, so tools go out of date quickly. Update security analyzers often.

Kane Security Analyst

Profile

Name	Kane Security Analyst
Vendor	Intrusion Detection
Cost	(unknown)
Use	Scans registry settings to determine potential vulnerabilities and grades security settings
Issues	None

The Kane Security Analyst scans through the registry to determine which security-related settings are weaker than they should be. As an analytical tool, KSA is not capable of determining security vulnerabilities other than those listed in its database.

Installing and running KSA is straightforward, but you will have to contact Intrusion Detection for a free evaluation key. Once you've got KSA up and running, you can scan your system for vulnerabilities. KSA will grade your system, pointing out specific areas where security is especially weak.

KSA's interface is rather cheesy, bespeaking an obvious Visual Basic background. But it's a fast way to check security on a system for which you've become responsible to quickly point out where you need to make immediate changes.

NetXRay

Profile

Name	NetXRay
Vendor	Cinco Networks (Network General)
Cost	$995
Use	Sophisticated packet sniffer with graphing and charting functionality
Issues	Installation requires rebooting

NetXRay is a protocol analyzer (commonly known as packet sniffers) that runs under Windows NT and provides a very easy to use graphical user interface. (Figure B.32 shows NetXRay's easy to use performance gauges.) Like all modern packet sniffers, NetXRay provides features for packet capture and decoding. But unlike many others, it can provide graphical charts pinpointing exactly where in your network heavy traffic congestion is occurring.

FIGURE B.32

NetXRay's performance gauges

Installing NetXRay is straightforward, but you do have to manually add its analysis network service after you install the software and reboot your server.

Figure B.33 shows an Ethernet frame and the data contained within it. The top window is the frame buffer; it shows each captured Ethernet frame. Selecting a frame allows you to view the contents in the two content viewers below. The content viewers show you the raw (bottom) data and the decoded (top) information represented by that data. Reading from top to bottom in the Decode button is like reading up the OSI stack, from the data link layer (Ethernet) to the network layer (IP) to the transport layer (UDP) and finally to the session layer (DNS). Since this packet doesn't actually carry user data, it stops at the session layer.

F I G U R E   B.33

Decoding an Ethernet frame

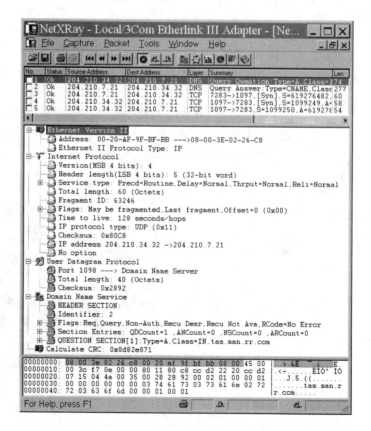

NetXRay is far too complex for us to detail its use here, but we can browse through a list of its major features:

- Client/server architecture allows you to attach to other copies on other machines for remote monitoring.

- Triggers alert you to conditions that you specify based on errors, utilization, or any other network characteristic.

- Packet Generator allows you to load your network very specifically so you can test its ability to deal with heavy conditions. You can also use the packet generator to transmitted custom (or forged) packets.

NTFSDOS

Profile

Name	NTFSDOS
Vendor	Winternals
Cost	$0 (freeware)
Use	DOS disk driver for NTFS
Issues	Does not support striped volumes

NTFSDOS is a read-only NTFS file system driver for MS-DOS. With it, you can boot a DOS floppy disk and mount the NTFS volumes of a Windows NT computer. NTFSDOS does not respect NTFS security settings, so there's no security restriction for the logged-on user.

WARNING NTFSDOS provides read access to NTFS file systems from DOS. Make certain your server is physically secured to prevent improper use of this software.

NTFSDOS is easy to use: Simply run the NTFSDOS.EXE program from the DOS command prompt. NTFSDOS will scan all available hard disk partitions looking for NTFS volumes, and assign drive letters as it finds them.

Keep a copy of NTFSDOS on a DOS boot floppy. It's an invaluable tool for fast data recovery when NT servers fail. Keep it locked up, though!

NTRecover

Profile

Name	NTRecover
Vendor	Winternals
Cost	$189
Use	Mounts NTFS-formatted hard disks from other computers as local drives via an RS-232 serial connection
Issues	None

NTRecover is a unique utility that allows you to connect an NT machine that can't be booted correctly for whatever reason to another operational NT machine through the serial ports on both machines. By running the NTRecover utility on the operational computer and booting the NTRecover client disk on the dead machine, you can mount the dead computer's NTFS volumes as if they were located inside the operational machine.

Functionally, this is identical to removing the dead computer's disk and physically attaching it to the operational computer, but it doesn't require you to open either computer and works even when you don't have an interface available for the other computer's drive.

Once mounted, you can perform whatever recovery operations you need to either restore the dead computer or retrieve necessary information. The function and operation of NTRecover is fairly obvious from the opening dialog box. Remember that both computers must have the same serial port settings.

An associated program called NT Locksmith, available at http://www.winternals.com, allows you to overwrite the administrative password of an NT computer attached by NTRecover. That's about $238 ($189+$49) to gain access to a machine that you've lost the administrative access. It's a small price to pay compared to the loss of function and the high price of NT password recovery services.

WARNING   A hacker with NTRecover, NT Locksmith, a laptop NT machine, and physical access to your server could extract any information stored on the machine regardless of your NTFS security settings.

Red Button

Profile

Name	Red Button
Vendor	Midwestern Commerce, Inc.
Cost	$0 (Freeware)
Use	NT security flaw demonstration
Issues	Demonstrates a serious bug in NT; fix available from Microsoft

The Red Button program is a demonstration of a serious security hole in Windows NT. This is a bug that allows remote access to more of the registry than should be available; the net result is that access can be obtained remotely without a password.

Run the Red Button program to display its simple screen. You can then press the big red button to attack a remote computer.

This program is useful as a demonstration of the danger a minor bug can present; it's also useful to make sure your computers are not vulnerable to this attack. A hot fix is available from Microsoft for this problem.

RegAdmin Pro

Profile

Name	RegAdmin Pro
Vendor	Midwestern Commerce, Inc.
Cost	$0 (Demo)
Use	Controls access to the registry
Issues	None

RegAdmin Pro is a utility that allows you to control access to registry keys. It gives you more control over the registry than Windows NT's built-in functions. This utility is shown in Figure B.34.

To use this utility, choose a registry key at the top of the dialog box. You can then modify the list of users who have access to that key. You can add a user, modify a user's permissions, or delete an existing user's access.

The version of RegAdmin provided here is a demo version, and it is limited in its ability to propagate changes. See the Web site for information about the full version.

FIGURE B.34

RegAdmin allows you to control registry security.

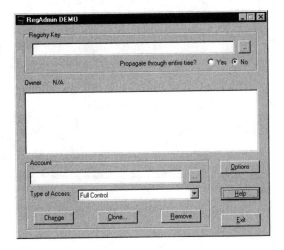

ScanNT

Profile

Name	ScanNT
Vendor	Midwestern Commerce, Inc.
Cost	$0 (Demo)
Use	Checks for easy-to-crack passwords
Issues	None

ScanNT is a useful utility for checking the passwords on your Windows NT workstation or server. It checks for easy-to-crack passwords, and even checks passwords against a dictionary to find common words used as passwords.

This utility is shown in Figure B.35. To scan the passwords, use the Add button to add one or more users to the list, then press the Scan button. A log file will be created with information about crackable passwords.

ScanNT checks for easily crackable passwords.

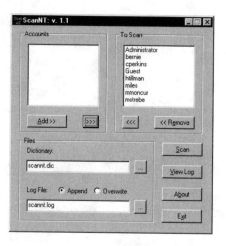

The version of ScanNT included on the CD is a demo version. The full version runs faster and provides more information about crackable passwords. See http://www.NTsecurity.com/ for information.

Suck Server

Profile

Name   Suck Server

Vendor   Matthew Strebe

Cost $0 (Included with Windows NT Network Security)

Use   Server application that records connection attempts to TCP/IP ports that would otherwise be unused

Issues   Application does not run as a service

Suck Server lets you establish port suckers on unused TCP/IP ports on your public Internet servers. Port suckers are server programs that simply record all the data sent to a specific port along with the IP address of the attached client.

This enables you to tell when hackers are attempting to attach to your computer for services it does not provide, and lets you tell when your server has been port scanned by tools like Ping Pro. For instance, if you have a Web server that only allows connections on ports 21 (FTP) and 80 (Web), you could run port suckers on otherwise unused ports that invite attack—like the NetBIOS session port (139) that hackers use to gain access to Windows computers. Suck Server will log the connection attempt and the data sent to these ports, so you can tell exactly what the hacker is trying to do by looking at the data recorded in the log.

Suck Server is also capable of launching an external application each time a new hacking connection is established. You can use this facility to alert you over the network using the net send command or to run a program capable of paging you. Both the port being attacked and the IP address of the attacker are sent to the external application. This facility alerts you to attacks when they first commence, so you can respond to them as they happen. It's the best chance you'll have of actually catching someone in the act.

WARNING According to data collected by one well-known security company, 79 percent of all companies that have been hacked never find out that anything happened. Using a tool like Suck Server is often the only way to find out when your server is under siege.

Ports with port suckers established appear as normal services to a hacker when they perform a port scan. Then, when they attempt to establish a connection (with, for instance, the NetBIOS Auditing Tool or with a Telnet client) the service simply doesn't respond—it looks like a slow connection or a connection with broken routing. Nothing gives away the fact that it's actually a countermeasure tool.

Suck Server automatically drops connections (freeing up the memory and compute resources a connection uses) after 60 seconds to keep hackers (who may realize what's happening) from flooding your server with connection attempts in order to tie up memory resources to crash your server. Suck normally requires about 5MB of RAM, and we've been unable to allocate more than 20MB under very serious automated attacks. Figure B.36 shows the Suck Server monitor during an attack.

FIGURE B.36

Suck Server showing a port scan and a Web browser attempting to connect

Suck Server is written in the Java programming language for a few very important reasons: Java makes creating multithreaded TCP/IP server applications very easy, and it automatically deallocates memory resources that are no longer needed. Both of these complexity-reducing factors lower considerably the chance that a bug in the application will cause problems on your server. Suck Server is an application that runs on your server—security issues that affect Java applets that are loaded through Web browsers do not apply in this environment. Suck Server has been compiled to run native in the Win32 environment. It does not require the installation of any Java Runtime Environment.

Using Suck Server

Suck Server is normally launched by double-clicking the `suck.exe` file. When Suck Server starts, you'll see the dialog box shown in Figure B.37. With this dialog box, you can choose to monitor a port by selecting the well-known port in the Port pick box or by typing a port number in the Port input box and clicking Add. Select ports appear in the Port list box. To remove a selected port, double-click its entry in the Selected Ports list box.

You can save a group of port settings as well as your log and alarm file settings by clicking Save and giving the port group a name. You can use the Load button to load any number of port groups. This allows you to create port groups to simulate specific services. For instance, ports 21, 70, and 80 could be saved in a port group called `IIS.SUC` to simulate IIS services. Ports 25, 110, and 119 could be saved in a port group called `EXCHANGE.SUC` to simulate an exchange server. You can load both groups to simulate an NT server running those services. Figure B.38 shows the same NT server before and after establishing port suckers on ports 21, 70, and 80 to simulate an IIS server.

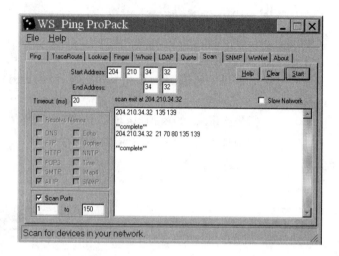

Although our example simulates a Web server, this usually isn't a good idea. You'll get hundreds of benign connection attempts to a simulated Web server from people who are simply checking to see if you have a Web site at this address. Instead, you should monitor ports like 23 (Telnet), 25 (SMTP), 57 (DNS), 110 (POP), 135 (NetBIOS browser), and 139 (NetBIOS session). These ports would normally show up on an unprotected server, are common targets of hackers, and aren't normally connected to by benign users.

Avoid establishing suckers on ports that don't normally provide services, because hackers will immediately recognize a large number of uncommon ports as an indication that you are using monitoring software. If you want to establish a number of port suckers to make port scan detection easier, use 7, (Echo), 9 (Discard), 13 (Daytime), 17 (Quote of the Day), and 19 (Character Generator). These services are provided by simple TCP/IP services and are commonly seen on servers.

Once you've selected the ports you want to monitor, you can select a log file and an application to launch when connection attempts are made (called the alarm application). If you don't select a log file, the program will default to SUCK.LOG in the current directory. If you don't select an alarm application, Suck Server will not launch a program when connection attempts are made.

Suck sends two parameters to the alarm application: the port being attacked and the IP address of the source. You can use a batch file to send these parameters to any application that accepts command line parameters as shown by the LAUNCH.BAT application that comes with Suck Server.

When Suck Server is operating, you'll see a screen similar to Figure B.39, which shows a port scan and a Web server attaching to port 80. The same data displayed on the screen is written to the log file.

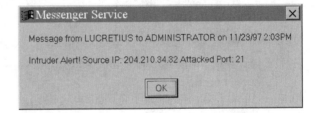

You should leave Suck Server operating constantly to monitor your public servers—but since it's an application, you'll have to be logged on to use it. This violates a very important security principle, but there *is* one way to get around the problem. Using the AT command to establish an interactive scheduled session allows you to log out without interrupting the operating program.

WS-Ping

Profile

Name	WS-Ping
Vendor	IpSwitch
Cost	$24
Use	An IP scanning tool used for a variety of IP administration and hacking purposes
Issues	None

WS-Ping is the "best of breed" TCP/IP administration tool available. It provides a number of other TCP/IP client services to help you administer your network. The very services that make it useful to administrators also make it useful to hackers, so it's likely you'll run into hackers using it if you have monitoring software installed on your public servers.

Installing WS-Ping is simple—just run the install program included with it, and it does all the rest. You then launch it using the Start menu. WS-Ping provides the following services, which can be selected by clicking the appropriately named tab:

- **Ping** allows you to ping a host automatically with any sized packet for any duration.

- **TraceRoute** performs a TCP/IP trace route.

- **Lookup** performs normal or reverse DNS name lookups.

- **Finger** performs the Finger function to get user details from Internet hosts.

- **Whois** attaches to servers running the whois services to resolve e-mail names.

- **LDAP** allows you to attach to servers running the Lightweight Directory Access Protocol to glean account information.

- **Quote** is a Quote of the Day client.

- **Scan** allows you to automatically ping across a range of IP addresses to find responding hosts. It also allows you to scan TCP ports to determine which port are accepting connections, and that indicates the services running on a server and often allows you to identify the operating system running on the host.

- **SNMP** is an SNMP MIB browser that lets you get low-level SNMP information from managed network devices and hosts.

- **WinNet** is a NetBIOS probe that will return Windows Networking information about hosts on the local network.

- **About** provides information about your local host's TCP/IP configuration.

The Scan tab is the most useful for hackers, as it identifies for them targets of opportunity within a specific IP address range.

Hackers

Hacking utilities are programs written by hackers or hacking groups for the purpose of exposing security problems with an operating system. The two included here are useful for this purpose. They are:

- NetAlert

- NetBIOS Auditing Tool

NetAlert

Profile

Name	NetAlert
Vendor	Christopher L. T. Brown
Cost	$10)
Use	Command Line Utility used to monitor the state of TCP/IP services.
Issues	Command Line Utility, requires constant logon, requires additional software for some features.

NetAlert constantly monitors the state of TCP/IP services by periodically attempting to attach to them. When the port state changes (goes up or down) NetAlert will send you e-mail or a page informing you of the change.

You can launch NetAlert by typing **NetAlert** at the command prompt. NetAlert takes its configuration data from three configuration files, which must be located in the same directory as the executable. Notes on installation as well as the format of the configuration files are explained in the readme.txt file that accompanies the program. NetAlert requires an e-mail program called Blat1.2 in order to use the e-mail functionality.

NetBIOS Auditing Tool

Profile

Name	NetBIOS Auditing Tool
Vendor	GNU Software Foundationt
Cost	$0 (Subject to the GNU CopyLeft)
Use	Command line utility used to expose security flaws in NetBIOS networks
Issues	Command Line Interface

The NetBIOS Auditing Tool (NAT hereafter) is technically a Net-BIOS security auditing tool. Its purpose is to expose security flaws in NetBIOS networks. To that end it is somewhat practical, but there are tools that are better suited to that task. One of NAT's features, auto-mated password checking, makes it a favorite of hackers. Using NAT, you can launch an automated attack against an NT server from over a network and attempt to attach via NetBIOS (which allows the remote user to map a drive, for instance) by repeatedly trying passwords against accounts. NAT accepts a list of accounts and a list of pass-words, and then tries each password against each account in the order presented.

NAT accepts three command line parameters:

```
usage: nat [-o filename] [-u userlist] [-p passlist]
<address>
```

- –o specifies a log file to redirect output to.

- –u specifies a text file of account names, one per line, to attack.

- –p specifies a text file of passwords to attempt against each account.

A few security measures normally prevent NAT attacks. If user accounts are set to time out after a few password attempts, these sort of hacks will never work against them. But the NT Administrators account cannot be locked out. Since this is the account hackers are after, NAT is still an excellent tool.

Foiling NAT attacks can be accomplished by renaming the Administrator account and by restricting Administrator account logons from the network. You can then create another administrative account (that can be locked out) and use that for network administration.

APPENDIX

C

Online Resources

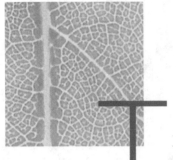

The Internet is a really big place. There are literally thousands of resources you can use to help you solve your security problems. We've listed the few sites here that we find especially useful for one reason or another—many more exist, and many are linked from these pages. You can use a search engine, such as `http://www.altavista.digital.com` to search for other security-related sites using keywords like "+windows +nt +network +security"—about 50,000 sites contain all four of those words.

We haven't included any newsgroups here because, sadly, Usenet news has become a morass of idiots selling "get rich quick" schemes and new users asking obvious questions of each other. Most useful information there is now lost in the din of the teeming millions. Most good advisory sources have abandoned Usenet for the Web, where all content is at least edited by someone. You can try searching the `http://www.dejanews.com` site for stored news archives by a specific topic.

Many of the sites below do have security-related mailing lists you can sign up for. They are excellent sources of breaking news on security.

Microsoft

Microsoft's Web site is a phantasmagoria of marketing information about their products. Wedged in the nooks and crannies of this massive site is a lot of useful information and some really compelling software.

`http://www.microsoft.com/ntserver` is Microsoft's support site for NT Server. A lot of NT-specific software is found here, especially the latest service packs and security hot fixes. The site is oriented more towards marketing than support, so you'll probably want to click through to the support or download sections to get to the good stuff. Stay up to date by checking this site often.

`http://www.microsoft.com/ntworkstation` is Microsoft's support site for NT Workstation. Most of the information on this site also applies to NT Server.

`http://www.microsoft.com/security` is Microsoft's security-specific site. Details about newfound holes in all of Microsoft's software usually appear here. This is a great place to catch up on the latest fixes for client software, especially if you don't have time to wade through all the product-specific sites. It is a vendor-run site, so Microsoft does try to calm security fears and sidestep some issues. Check this site often!

`http://www.microsoft.com/support` is Microsoft's tech support home page. This site lets you search all of Microsoft's online resources for specific troubleshooting or security information on any Microsoft product. It's also the location of Microsoft's Knowledge Base, which can quickly help you solve those nit-picky problems—especially if they're caused by a bug in Windows NT. There's also easy access to Microsoft downloadable betas and evaluation software, as well as a simple known problems link.

BackOffice

BackOffice is the family name for Microsoft server applications—that is, applications that run on a server and form the server side of a client/ server application. There is also a Microsoft product called BackOffice that is a bundle consisting of NT Server, Exchange Server, SQL Server, SMS Server, and a few other miscellaneous packages. The most popular BackOffice titles are listed below, others are similar or are available from the BackOffice home page.

http://backoffice.microsoft.com/ is the home page for BackOffice. It has links to all BackOffice products. This site has links to Microsoft's huge site of downloadable files that has evaluation versions of almost all BackOffice products.

http://www.microsoft.com/sql is the home page for SQL Server.

http://www.microsoft.com/iis is the home page for Internet Information Server. Stay up to date on this site if you use IIS—there have been a bunch of security patches available here in the past.

http://www.microsoft.com/exchange is the home page for Exchange Server. It seems like there's a new version of Exchange every six months or so, so be sure to check here often. The current version of Exchange (5.0—5.5. is in beta at this writing) is vulnerable to certain types of mail bombs, so stay up to date with the service packs available here.

Security Software Vendors

Security software vendors beat a different drum about NT than does Microsoft. They tend to overemphasis security threats that most users will never face. The reality of the Internet threat is somewhere between Microsoft's downplaying of it and the security software vendors hype—exactly where varies depending upon your security needs.

Monitoring and Analysis

There's a dearth of strong monitoring software out there for Windows NT (any programmers listening?). We've scoured the Net but have only come up with a few decent candidates for good security software.

http://www.iss.net is the home page for Internet Security Systems, a group with some really cool monitoring and analysis software. Their site is also a great place to get up to date on theoretical security problems. They've got some interesting links to other NT security sites as well. There's too much there to spend much time talking about—just check it out!

`http://www.intrusion.com` is the home page for Intrusion Detection Inc., makers of the Kane Security Analyst. They have security software and links to other security-related sites.

Utilities

These utilities take two forms: utilities used to attack networks and utilities used to defend against attack. They are all small and do not run as services.

`http://www.ntinternals.com` isn't really a hacker's Web site—in fact, it's put together by two research computer scientists who have Ph.D.s from Carnegie Mellon—but it has the tools hackers use. NTFSDOS, the utility that mounts NTFS-formatted volumes as read-only volumes under DOS, is here, as are some utilities that make it easy to bypass all of Windows NT's security systems if you have physical access to a server.

`http://www.ipswitch.com` is the Web site for IPSwitch, Inc., makers of WS Ping ProPack, as well as a few other Internet clients and utilities.

`http://www.ntsecurity.com` is the site for Midwestern Commerce's NT security products. These are small but somewhat useful security-related products. This is a major source for links to other security-related sites.

`http://www.somarsoft.com` has a number of small security-related NT tools on their site, as well as links to other NT security sites. Not as pretty as most, but a good source of information.

Firewalls and Proxies

Firewalls are your most important line of defense against intrusion from the Internet. Windows NT is well represented in the firewall market. These firewall products are the strongest of the batch. The two proxies presented are the high and low ends—and functionally they are not much different.

`http://www.altavista.software.digital.com` is the home page for AltaVista Software's Firewall and Tunnel, one of the best NT-based firewalls available. AltaVista firewall does not offer all types of content screening (ActiveX, for example), but of the serious firewalls available it is probably the least expensive and offers the best performance.

`http://www.raptor.com` is the Web site for Raptor Systems Inc., a firewall vendor and maker of perhaps the easiest to use firewall ever made, the WALL. It is based on a simple "no management" concept that simply assumes anything can go out and nothing can come in. That covers it for many corporate firewalls.

`http://www.checkpoint.com` is the Web site for Checkpoint Software Technologies, Ltd., makers of Firewall-1. Firewall-1 is probably the best NT-based firewall solution on the market—and far from the cheapest. Firewall-1 offers the ability to put firewall modules in many brands of routers, and then control them all from a single policy database residing on a Windows NT machine.

`http://www.microsoft.com/proxy` is the home page for Proxy Server, Microsoft's pseudo-firewall product. You can download an evaluation version of Proxy Server from this site. (Microsoft wouldn't let us include it on the CD-ROM.) Despite Microsoft's use of the word *firewall* in their product literature, Proxy Server is not a firewall in the modern sense of the word. While it offers proxy and filtering services, it does not disable packet forwarding at the IP layer, so it can't guarantee that no network-layer traffic passes through your router the way that application firewalls like Firewall-1 and AltaVista can.

`http://webnz.com/qbik` is the home page for Qbik's WinGate, perhaps the most popular proxy server around. WinGate is not a security product *per se*—it is not a firewall and does not protect your proxy computer from Internet attack. But it is a true proxy, and, as such, it can completely disconnect your internal network from the Internet.

Since there need not be any routing between your internal network and the Internet, you'll be relatively safe—as long as you don't run WinGate on your server. We've included WinGate because it's extremely cost effective even for (and especially in) small networks, and it's way better than nothing when attaching your network to the Internet. You can customize your own TCP and UDP proxy services too. It also runs on Windows 95.

Encryption

There's a surprising amount of disk encryption software available for Windows NT. Most of these products support disk-based or smartcard-based encryption keys. Check out their Web sites for all the details.

`http://www.softwinter.com` is the Web site for SoftWinter, producers of Sentry 2020 (formerly Shade), my favorite disk encryption software. It's easy to use and it works very well.

`http://bpdconsulting.com/TorDisk/` is the U.S. mirrored home page for TorDisk, a disk encryption package written by Alex Tormasov, a Russian citizen. It's not as mature as Sentry 2020, but we like to support rogue programmers. You should take a look if you're interested in security.

`http://www.soundcode.com` is the home page for Soundcode, Inc., makers of Point 'n Crypt which offers file encryption on a file-by-file basis.

`http://www.maedae.com/encr95.html` is the home page for MaeDae, producers of Encrypt-It, a file-by-file disk encryption package that works under both Windows NT and 95.

`http://www.pgp.com` is the Web site for Phil Zimmerman's Pretty Good Privacy encryption package. You may download the Pretty Good Privacy software at no charge for individual (non-commercial) use. The PGP software can be used with most e-mail packages, including CC-Mail, Pegasus Mail, and Microsoft Exchange. You can learn more about PGP at the company's Web site: `http://www.pgp.com`.

Fault Tolerance

Fault tolerance is an aspect of security, and these two tools provide the ultimate in server security: real-time fail-over to a replica server.

http://www.vinca.com is the Web site for Vinca, purveyors of Stand-byServer for a variety of platforms including Windows NT. Standby-Server performs real-time hard-disk mirroring to an offline server on a disk sector-by-sector basis. When your primary server fails, the standby server automatically assumes its identity providing a high degree of fault tolerance.

http://www.octopustech.com is the Web site for Qualix Group, the makers of Octopus for NT. Octopus is another fault tolerance product similar to StandbyServer but replicated on a file-by-file basis.

Security Special Interest

These sites are not about NT—they're about the Internet and Internet security. They are applicable to all operating systems that interface to the Internet.

http://www.cs.purdue.edu/coast/ is the Web site for Purdue University's Computer Operations, Audit, and Security Technology project. There isn't a whole lot here that's NT specific, but it's an excellent backgrounder for security in general and has a links page that can't be beat.

http://www.cert.org is the Web site for Carnegie Mellon University's Computer Emergency Response Team, the oldest and best-known Internet security advisory system. COAST is probably larger and better organized now, but CERT is still the original, and an excellent source of practical information on Internet-based intrusions.

http://globecom.net/ietf/index.shtml is by far the best-linked and best-indexed RFC repository I know of. It's got all the Internet Engineering Task Force Requests for Comment in an easy-to-use indexed HTML format. You can read the RFCs that define all of the Internet protocols in complete detail here.

Hacking Tools

Hacker Web sites are heavy on attitude and light on actual information. Browsing through them is like taking a walk through the seediest parts of town. Unfortunately, if you're going to protect yourself from hackers, you've got to know what they're doing. Watch out though—it doesn't take long before you run into pornographic ad banners and clearly illegal software piracy sites.

You should be extremely careful about your firewall settings and your choice of Web browser—turn off all automatic content downloading except pictures and text, and be sure your security level is set very high. All those gnarly Web browser hacks (where they extract your network password or run executable content on your computer) show up on these pages.

We recommend dialing in from a computer used only for this purpose that's not attached to your network. Be prepared to reinstall your operating system on a regular basis. If you want to find hacker sites other than the few listed here, you'll have to do your own searching with AltaVista or Excite. We can't really recommend others due to their questionable value and frequent disappearance.

`http://www3.10pht.com` (that's a zero in l0pht) is the Web site of l0pht Heavy Industries, where the best U.S. hackers still willing to make themselves known hang out. These guys have plenty of room to brag, though—they produced l0phtcrack, the slickest and fastest NT password crack tool out there. There's a really good security advisory that stays on top of the latest NT security issues—required reading. They've got a lot to say about just about everything, and the print media seems to be listening. You should too.

http://www.2600.com is the granddaddy of hacking sites. There's no software here, but it is a hacker advocacy site so you can get a good look at who hacks and why. Based on the printed *2600* hacker zine, this site shows you just how easy it is to hack most Web sites with its *Hacked Sites* link. By the way, 2600 hertz is the frequency produced by the infamous toy whistle distributed free in Cap'n Crunch cereal. It ushered in telephone phreaking in the '70s when a hacker figured out it produced the exact tone necessary to take control of a telephone switching computer to route their own calls.

APPENDIX

D

Glossary

Access Control Entries (ACE)   Permission elements of an ACL that enumerate specific permissions for a specific user or group account. *See* Access Control List.

Access Control List (ACL)   Lists of security identifiers contained by objects that allow only those processes identified in the list as having the appropriate permission to activate the services of that object. *See* Object, Permissions, Security Identifier.

access token   An object containing the Security Identifier of a running process comprised of the combined Security Identifiers for a user account and the group accounts that the user is a member of, along with the LUID for the user. A process started by another process inherits the starting process's access token. The access token is checked against each object's ACL to determine whether or not appropriate permissions are granted to perform any requested service. *See* Access Control Entries, Access Control List, object, permissions, process, Security Identifier.

account lockout   Used to specify how many invalid logon attempts should be tolerated before a user account is locked out. Account lockout is set through User Manager for Domains. *See* security, User Manager for Domains.

account policies   Account policies are used to determine password and logon requirements. Account policies are set through User Manager for Domains. *See* User Manager for Domains.

accounts   Containers for security identifiers, passwords, permissions, group associations, and preferences for each user of a system. A user name and password you create to give a user access to the network (or to a single machine). Along with the name and password, an account includes other information about the user, such as groups the user belongs to, and directories and files the user can access. The User Manager for Domains utility is used to administer accounts. *See* Groups Security Identifier, permissions, passwords, preferences.

ACE   *See* Access Control Entries.

ACL   *See* Access Control List .

Active Directory   Windows NT 5's system of large-scale network management. Rather than using domains, Active Directory presents the entire network as a hierarchy of objects.

Active Server Pages (ASP)   An extension to Internet Information Server that provides the ability to run server-side scripts written in JScript or VBScript that return dynamically created HTML documents based on user input or other variables. *See* Internet Information Server.

ActiveX   Microsoft's control plug-in technology for Web browsers that allows compiled controls to be referenced from HTML documents, and automatically downloaded and installed if they are not already plugged into the Web browser.

adapter   Any hardware device that allows communications to occur through physically dissimilar systems. This term usually refers to peripheral cards permanently mounted inside a computer that provide an interface from the computer's bus to another media such as a hard disk or a network. *See* Network Interface Card, SCSI.

adaptive speed leveling   A modem technology that allows modems to attempt a change in the bit rate at which data is transmitted to optimize for changing telephone line conditions. For instance, a connection initially made at 33.6 might drop to 28.8 if the error rate exceeds a certain threshold that indicates a transient line problem.

Address Resolution Protocol (ARP)   An Internet protocol for resolving an IP address into a physical layer address (such as an Ethernet media access controller address). *See* Internet Protocol, physical layer.

Administrator account   A special account in Windows NT that has the ultimate set of security permissions and can assign any permission to any user or group. The Administrator account is used to correct security problems. *See* Permissions.

administrator   Any user who is able to perform administrative tasks, such as creating or modifying other user accounts. By default, Windows NT includes an account called Administrator with these privileges.

administrators   Users who are part of the Administrators group. This group has the ultimate set of security permissions. *See* Administrator account, groups, permissions.

Advanced Projects Agency Network (ARPANET)   Predecessor to the Internet that was developed by the Department of Defense in the late 1960s.

algorithm   Detailed steps for performing a function.

alias   The reference name of a virtual directory, which appears as a subdirectory in the www root directory. *See* virtual directory.

applet   A small application (typically written in Java) that runs inside another application, such as a Web browser. *See* Java.

application layer   The layer of the OSI model that interfaces with user-mode programs called applications by providing high-level network services based upon lower-level network layers. Network file systems like named pipes are an example of application layer software. *See* application, named pipes, OSI Model.

Application Programming Interface (API)   A set of related procedures built into Windows NT that are called by applications to perform a specific function.

applications   Large software packages that perform a specific function, such as word processing, Web browsing, or database management. Applications typically consist of more than one program. *See* Programs.

ARP   *See* Address Resolution Protocol.

ARPANET   *See* Advanced Research Projects Agency Network.

ASP   *See* Active Server Pages.

asymmetrical multiprocessing   A multiple processor architecture in which certain processors are designated to run certain threads or in which scheduling is not done on a fair-share basis. Asymmetrical multiprocessing is easier to implement than symmetrical multiprocessing, but does not scale well as processors are added. *See* microprocessor, symmetrical multiprocessing.

Asynchronous Transfer Mode (ATM)   A wide area transport protocol that runs at many different speeds and supports real-time, guaranteed packet delivery in hardware, as well as lower-quality levels of service on a bandwidth-available basis. ATM will eventually replace all other wide area protocols, as most worldwide PTSN providers have declared their support for the international standard. *See* Public Switched Telephone Network, wide area network.

ATM   *See* Asynchronous Transfer Mode.

attack   Measures taken to undermine the security of a system either to force a denial of service or to gain unauthorized access.

audit policy   Audit policy determines which user events you wish to track for security reasons. Audit policy can track the success or failure of specified security events; it is set in the User Manager for Domains. *See* Security, User Manager for Domains.

auditing   The process of logging certain events on the network, such as accesses to a certain file or directory. Windows NT's auditing feature can be left on continuously to monitor critical areas.

authentication   The process used by Windows NT to recognize a user and grant privileges based on user account name and password. The authentication process is designed to avoid storing passwords as text or sending them over the network.

BackOffice   A suite of software packages from Microsoft that run on Windows NT Server computers and provide network services such as e-mail exchange, WWW hosting, network monitoring, and relational data storage.

back up   The process of writing all the data contained in online mass-storage devices to offline mass-storage devices for the purpose of safe keeping. Backups are usually performed from hard disk drives to tape drives. Also referred to as archiving. *See* Hard Disk Drive.

back-end   The server side of a client/server application.

backup browser   A computer on a Microsoft network that maintains a list of computers and services available on the network. The master browser supplies this list. The backup browser distributes the browsing service load to a workgroup or domain. *See* master browser.

Backup Domain Controller (BDC)   In the domain security model, servers that contain accurate replications of the security and user databases; servers can authenticate workstations in the absence of a Primary Domain Controller. *See* Primary Domain Controller.

backup   A copy of files on a network written to a storage device, usually a tape drive.

baseline   A snapshot of a computer's current performance statistics that can be used for analysis and planning purposes.

Basic Input/Output System (BIOS)   A set of routines in firmware that provides the most basic software interface drivers for hardware attached to the computer. The BIOS contains the bootstrap routine. *See* boot, driver, firmware.

Bindery   A NetWare structure that contains user accounts and permissions. It is similar to the Security Accounts Manager in Windows NT. *See* Security Accounts Manager.

binding   The process of linking network services to network service providers. The binding facility allows users to define exactly how network services operate in order to optimize the performance of the system. By default, Windows enables all possible bindings. The Network control panel is used to change bindings. *See* network layer, data link layer.

BIOS   *See* Basic Input/Output System.

bit   A binary digit. A numeral having only two possible values, 0 or 1. Computers represent these two values as high (voltage present) or low (no voltage present) state on a control line. Bits are accumulated in sets of certain sizes to represent higher values. *See* byte.

block cipher   A cipher designed to operate on fixed-size blocks of data.

boot   The process of loading a computer's operating system. Booting usually occurs in multiple phases, each successively more complex until the entire operating system and all its services are running. Also called bootstrap. The computer's BIOS must contain the first level of booting. *See* Basic Input/Output System.

boot partition   The boot partition is the partition that contains the system files. The system files are located in C:\WINNT by default. *See* partition, system partition.

BOOTP   *See* Bootstrap Protocol.

Bootstrap Protocol (BOOTP)   Predecessor to the DHCP protocol. BOOTP was used to assign IP addresses to diskless workstations. *See* Dynamic Host Configuration Protocol.

border   A security perimeter formed by natural or logical boundaries that can only be passed at defined locations called border gateways.

border gateways   Routers that attach a private network to the Internet. They are usually used in a system as security checkpoints that force all traffic into and out of a secured system through a single point of access control. Traffic passing through the border gateways is security tested before being passed through to the secure system. Firewalls are an example of border gateways. *See* firewalls.

bottlenecks   Components operating at their peak capacity that restrict the flow of information through a system. Used singularly, the term indicates the single most restrictive component in a system.

breach   A loss of security due to a successful attack.

breakable A cipher that, given a reasonable amount of time and resources, can be compromised by a competent cryptanalysist.

bridge A device that connects two networks of the same data link protocol by forwarding those packets destined for computers on the other side of the bridge. *See* router, data link layer.

browser A computer on a Microsoft network that maintains a list of computers and services available on the network. Also used to refer to Web browsers. *See* Web browsers.

browsing The process of requesting the list of computers and services on a network from a browser.

brute force attack The process of checking passwords in a password file against every possible password generated sequentially. This hack will reveal all the passwords of all users on a system, and takes approximately two days to run against Windows NT (with the default LAN Manager security provider installed) on a modern Intel Pentium-based computer. Also called a *keyspace attack*.

caching A speed optimization technique that keeps a copy of the most recently used data in a fast, high-cost, low-capacity storage device rather than in the device upon which the actual data resides. Caching assumes that recently used data is likely to be used again. Fetching data from the cache is faster than fetching data from the slower, larger storage device. Most caching algorithms also copy the data that is most likely to be used next and perform write caching to further increase speed gains. *See* write-back caching, write-through caching.

CD-ROM *See* Compact Disk-Read Only Memory.

cellular Radiotelephony that works by establishing a radio link with a "cell site," or fixed radio transceiver connected to the telephone network. This radio link can be handed off to other closer cell sites as the radiotelephone moves, thus enabling (in theory, anyway) truly mobile permanent telephone connections.

central processing unit (CPU)   The central processing unit of a computer. In microcomputers such as IBM-PC-compatible machines, the CPU is the microprocessor. *See* Microprocessor.

certificates   Encrypted electronic documents that attest to the authenticity of a service, provider, or vendor of a product. Forgery of certificates is unfeasible, so the information they contain may be trusted. To require connection using secure socket layer, a key with a valid certificate must be installed. *See* key, secure socket layer.

CGI   *See* Common Gateway Interface.

channel service unit/digital service unit (CSU/DSU)   A device used to interface a digital telephony trunk to a serial I/O port.

checkpointing   The process of moving transactions from the transaction log to their permanent location on disk.

checksum   The result of a mathematical function applied to a data payload which will remain the same as long as no errors have crept into a datagram between end systems.

cipher   Protects a message by permuting its text (by rearranging it or performing modifications to the encoding, rather than the meaning, of the message).

ciphertext   An encrypted message that requires a cipher and a key to decrypt.

CIX   *See* Commercial Internet Exchange.

Class A domain   Large networks on which the first byte specifies the network number and the last 3 bytes specify the local addresses.

Class B domain   Medium networks on which the first 2 bytes specify the network number and the last 2 bytes specify the local addresses.

Class C domain   Small networks on which the first 3 bytes specify the network number and the last byte specifies the local address.

classless addressing   A subnet mask that splits the network number and the host number without regard for byte boundaries.

cleartext   The message to be sent from the sender to the receiver. This is what must be protected from being intercepted and understood. *See* plaintext.

Client Services for NetWare (CSNW)   A service provided with Windows NT that connects a NT client to NetWare file servers. *See* NetWare.

client   A computer on a network that subscribes to the services provided by a server. *See* server.

client/server   A network architecture that dedicates certain computers, called *servers,* to act as service providers to computers called *clients* that users operate to perform work. Servers can be dedicated to providing one or more network services such as file storage, shared printing, communications, e-mail service, and Web response. *See* peer, share.

client/server applications   Applications that split large applications into two components: compute-intensive processes that run on application servers and user interfaces that run on clients. Client/server applications communicate over the network through interprocess communication mechanisms. *See* client, interprocess communications, server.

cluster The basic unit of allocation in a file system, equal to a number of sectors fixed when the volume is formatted.

code 1. An agreed-upon way of keeping a secret between two or more individuals. *See* cipher. 2. Synonymous with software but used when the software, rather than the utility it provides, is the object of discussion. *See* software.

codebook Contains meanings assigned to words; a code word replaces the word that it stands for.

COM Port Communications port. A serial hardware interface conforming to the RS-232 standard for low-speed serial communications. *See* modem, serial.

Commercial Internet Exchange (CIX) Locations where top-tier ISPs maintain routers to route IP packets between their respective networks. CIX locations connect ISPs together to form the Internet from discreet TCP/IP wide area networks. *See* Internet.

Common Gateway Interface (CGI) A standard for starting programs on the Web server computer that return dynamically created HTML documents to the HTTP service for transmission to the remote client. A new instance of the CGI application is started each time a connection is made, which can put excessive load on an Internet server.

Compact Disk-Read Only Memory (CD-ROM) A media for storing extremely large software packages on optical read-only discs. CD-ROM is an adaptation of the CD medium used for distributing digitized music. CD-ROM discs can hold up to 650MB of information and cost very little to produce in large quantities. *See* hard disk drive.

components   Interchangeable elements of a complex software or hardware system. *See* module.

compression   A space optimization scheme that reduces the size (length) of a data set by exploiting the fact that most useful data contains a great deal of redundancy. Compression reduces redundancy by creating symbols smaller than the data they represent and an index that defines the value of the symbols for each compressed set of data.

computationally secure   A cipher that, given all the computational power that will be available to the most powerful governments over the next hundred years is unlikely to be compromised.

computer   A device capable of performing automatic calculations based upon lists of instructions called programs. The computer feeds the results of these calculations (output) to peripheral devices that can represent them in useful ways, such as graphics on a screen or ink on paper. *See* microprocessor.

computer name   A 1–15-character NetBIOS name used to uniquely identify a computer on the network. *See* Network Basic Input/Output System.

control panel   A software utility that controls the function of specific operating system services by allowing users to change default settings for the service to match their preferences. The registry contains the Control Panel settings on a system and/or per-user basis. *See* account, registry.

cooperative multitasking   A multitasking scheme in which each process must voluntarily return time to a central scheduling route. If any single process fails to return to the central scheduler, the computer will lock up. Both Windows and the Macintosh operating system use this scheme. *See* preemptive multitasking, Windows for Workgroups 3.11.

countermeasures Actions taken to eliminate security vulnerabilities.

CPU *See* microprocessor.

crack An attempt to determine a password or gain access to a system using a programmatic method.

cryptanalysis The examination of codes and ciphers.

cryptographer An individual who studies codes and ciphers. *See* cryptologist.

cryptography The study of codes and ciphers.

cryptologist *See* cryptographer.

crystal reports A drill-down data reporting tool used to extract and report on disparate information contained in many documents. A version is included with IIS to report on IIS log data.

CSNW *See* Client Services for NetWare.

CSU/DSU *See* Channel Service Unit/Digital Service Unit.

Data Link Control (DLC) An obsolete network transport protocol that allows PCs to connects to older IBM mainframes and HP printers. *See* TCP/IP.

data link A hardware protocol used to connect computers. Usually Ethernet in local area networks or frame relay in leased telephone line connections.

data link layer   In the OSI model, the layer that provides the digital interconnection of network devices and the software that directly operates those devices, such as network interface adapters. *See* physical layer, network layer, OSI model.

database   A related set of data organized by type and purpose. The term can also include the application software that manipulates the data. The Windows NT Registry (a database itself) contains a number of utility databases containing information on topics such as user accounts and security. *See* registry.

datagram   A discreet packet of information that is not a part of a larger data stream. Individually addressed packages of data. *See* packet.

DDE   *See* Dynamic Data Exchange.

decryption attack   An attempt to discover the key or plaintext of a ciphertext.

decryption   The process of turning ciphertext into plaintext using a cipher and a key.

default document   The HTML document returned when no specific page is referenced on a Web server.

default route   The router to which a host (end or intermediate system) will forward packets to if its routing table has no better information.

default shares   Resources shared by default when Windows NT is installed. *See* resource, share.

defense in depth   The use of reinforcing defensive measures to prevent information gathering and to defend against attack.

denial of service   An attack that attempts to eliminate or reduce the ability of a system to provide a service. A denial-of-service attack is far easier to perform than an unauthorized access attack because access to the system is not required and because far more vectors for it exist.

Desktop   A directory that the background of the Windows Explorer shell represents. By default the Desktop contains objects that contain the local storage devices and available network shares. Also a key operating part of the Windows GUI. *See* Explorer, shell.

DFS   *See* Distributed File System.

DHCP   *See* Dynamic Host Configuration Protocol.

dial-up connections   Data link layer digital connections made via modems over regular telephone lines, thus providing network connections (analog or digital) that can be made to any receiving station in the world by specifying (dialing) the receiver's unique address. The term *dial-up* refers to temporary digital connections, as opposed to leased telephone lines that provide permanent connections. *See* data link layer, modem, Public Switched Telephone Network.

dictionary attack   The process of checking passwords in a password file against a list of words likely to be chosen as passwords, or against the entire language lexicon. This hack will reveal all passwords that are contained in the dictionary and takes less than five minutes to run against Windows NT on a modern computer.

differential backup   A type of backup that backs up all files changed since the previous full or differential backup.

digital key system   Small switches that usually use proprietary digital telephones to provide internal switching of inbound telephone lines (rather than trunks) to internal extensions. Generally used in installations with between 10 and 100 internal extensions and less than 24 outside lines.

directories   In a file system, directories are containers that store files or other directories. Mass storage devices have a root directory that contains all other directories, thus creating a hierarchy of directories sometimes referred to as a *directory tree*. *See* file, file system.

directory replication   The process of copying a directory structure from an import computer to an export computer(s). Anytime changes are made to the export computer, the import computer(s) is automatically updated with the changes.

Discretionary Access Control List (DACL)   Lists services users are permitted to access.

Disk Administrator   Graphical utility used to manage disks.

disk duplexing   A type of disk mirroring that uses multiple disk controllers along with multiple drives, providing for increased security. *See* disk mirroring.

disk mirroring   The process of creating one volume that stores the same data on two partitions on separate drives. If one drive fails, the volume contents can be read from the surviving drive. *See* disk duplexing.

disk striping   Data that is stored across partitions of identical size on different drives. Also referred to as RAID 0. *See* Redundant Array of InexpensiveDrives.

disk striping with parity Disk striping with redundant parity information distributed across the stripe set that can be used to regenerate the contents of any one missing disk. Also referred to as RAID 5. *See* Redundant Array of InexpensiveDrives, stripe set.

distributed file system A method for aliasing directory shares on a network so they show up as subdirectories of other shares in Windows NT.

DLC *See* Data Link Control.

DNS cache pollution Sending misleading or nonsense Internet name and IP address updates to a DNS server.

DNS *See* Domain Name Service.

domain 1. In Microsoft networks a domain is an arrangement of client and server computers referenced by a specific name that share a single security permissions database. *See* Workgroup. 2. On the Internet a domain is a named collection of hosts and subdomains, registered with a unique name by the InterNIC. *See* InterNIC.

domain controllers Servers that authenticate workstation network logon requests by comparing a user name and password against account information stored in the user accounts database. A user cannot access a domain without authentication from a domain controller. *See* backup domain controller, domain, primary domain controller.

domain name The textual identifier of a specific Internet host. Domain names are in the form of: *server.organization.type* (as in www.microsoft.com) and are resolved to Internet addresses by domain name servers. *See* domain name server.

domain name server   An Internet host dedicated to the function of translating fully qualified domain names into IP addresses. *See* domain name.

domain name service (DNS)   The TCP/IP network service that translates textual Internet network addresses into numerical Internet network addresses. *See* domain name, Internet, TCP/IP.

drive   *See* hard disk drive.

drive letters   Single letters assigned as abbreviations to the mass storage volumes available to a computer. *See* volumes.

driver   A program that provides a software interface to a hardware device. Drivers are written for the specific device they control, but they present a common software interface to the computer's operating system, allowing all devices (of a similar type) to be controlled as if they were the same. *See* data link layer, operating system.

Dynamic Data Exchange (DDE)   A method of interprocess communication within Microsoft Windows operating systems.

Dynamic Host Configuration Protocol (DHCP)   A method of automatically assigning IP addresses to client computers on a network.

eavesdropping   Gathering information about a target network or computer by listening in on transmitted data.

electronic mail (e-mail)   A type of client/server application that provides a routed, stored-message service between any two user e-mail accounts. E-mail accounts are not the same as user accounts, but a one-to-one relationship usually exists between them. Because all modern computers can attach to the Internet, users can send e-mail over the Internet to any location that has telephone or wireless digital service. *See* Internet.

emergency repair disk   A floppy disk created by the RDISK.EXE program that contains a backup of critical Windows NT registry data, such as the configuration of NTFS volumes and the Security Accounts Manager database.

encrypted tunnel   A private connection between two networks created by encrypting data flowing over a public medium like the Internet.

encryption   The process of obscuring information by modifying it according to a mathematical function known only to the intended recipient. Encryption secures information being transmitted over nonsecure or untrusted media. The process of turning a plaintext into a ciphertext using a cipher and a key. *See* security.

end system   A host that either initiates or receives a datagram.

enterprise network   A complex network consisting of multiple servers and multiple domains over a large geographic area.

environment variables   Variables, such as the search path, that contain information available to programs and batch files about the current operating system environment.

Ethernet   The most popular data link layer standard for local area networking. Ethernet implements the carrier-sense-multiple-access-with-collision-detection (CSMA/CD) method of arbitrating multiple computer access to the same network. This standard supports the use of Ethernet over any type of media including wireless broadcast. Standard Ethernet operates at 10 megabits per second. Fast Ethernet operates at 100 megabits per second. *See* data link layer.

Exchange   Microsoft's messaging application. Exchange implements Microsoft's mail application programming interface (MAPI), as well as other messaging protocols such as POP, SNMP, and faxing, to provide a flexible message composition and reception service. *See* electronic mail, fax modem.

Explorer   The default shell for Windows 95 and Windows NT 4. Explorer implements the more flexible Desktop objects paradigm rather than the Program Manager paradigm used in earlier versions of Windows. *See* Desktop.

external security   Measures taken to prevent intrusion from outside the security perimeter of the system.

FAT   *See* File Allocation Table.

fault tolerance   The set of systems and software for preventing or recovering from data loss caused by hard drive crashes, system crashes, virii, and other problems. Any method that prevents system failure by tolerating single faults, usually through hardware redundancy. *See* backup, stripe set with parity.

fax modem   A special modem that includes hardware to allow the transmission and reception of facsimiles. *See* exchange, modem.

FDDI   *See* Fiber Distributed Data Interface.

Fiber Distributed Data Interface (FDDI)   A data link layer that implements two counter-rotating token rings at 100 megabits per second. FDDI was a popular standard for interconnecting campus and metropolitan area networks because it allows distant digital connections at high speed, but ATM is replacing FDDI in many sites. *See* asynchronous transfer mode, data link layer.

File Allocation Table (FAT)   The file system used by MS-DOS and available to other operating systems such as Windows (all variations), OS/2, and the Macintosh. FAT has become something of a mass storage compatibility standard because of its simplicity and wide availability. FAT has few fault tolerance features and can become corrupted through normal use over time. *See* file system.

file attributes Bits, stored along with the name and location of a file in a directory entry, that show the status of a file, such as archived, hidden, read-only, etc. Different operating systems use different file attributes to implement such services as sharing, compression, and security.

file system A structure used to store data in named capsules, called *files,* on a storage device. File systems impose an ordered database of files on the mass storage device (called volumes) that use hierarchies of directories to organize files. *See* database, device, directories, files, mass storage, volumes.

file system driver A software component that manages the storage of files on a mass storage device by providing methods to create, read, write, and delete files. *See* database, directories, files, mass storage device, volumes.

File Transfer Protocol (FTP) A simple Internet protocol that transfers complete files from an FTP server to a client running the FTP client. FTP provides a simple no-overhead method of transferring files between computers but cannot perform browsing functions. You must know the URL of the FTP server to which you wish to attach. *See* Internet, Uniform Resource Locator.

files A set of data stored on a mass storage device identified by a directory entry containing a name, file attributes, and the physical location of the file in the volume. *See* directory, file attributes, mass storage device, volume.

filter 1. In Index Server, a program (DLL) that can parse documents of a specific format to return a list of index terms for that document. 2. In ISAPI, a program (DLL) used to extend the capabilities of IIS. *See* Internet Information Server, ISAPI.

firewall   A security control device that connects two networks and determines which traffic should be allowed to pass between them. Usually implemented as a dual-homed computer attached to both the Internet and an intranet that protects the computers on the intranet from intrusion by blocking connections from untrusted sources and on specific protocols. Firewalls are the strongest form of Internet security yet implemented. Firewalls incorporate the functions of packet filtering, IP masquerading, and application proxy to perform their function.

firmware   Software stored permanently in nonvolatile memory and built into a computer to provide its BIOS and a bootstrap routine. Simple computers may have their entire operating system built into firmware. *See* BIOS, Boot, Software.

flooding   A denial-of-service attack wherein a large number of nuisance connections are made to a specific host in order to waste its processing time.

flow control   The handshaking signals to moderate the speed at which data is transmitted to make the best of data link conditions.

form   A collection of input fields processed by a scripting language or passed to a back-end service.

format   The process of preparing a mass storage device for use with a file system. There are actually two levels of formatting. Low-level formatting writes a structure of sectors and tracks to the disk with bits used by the mass storage controller hardware. The controller hardware requires this format, and it is independent of the file system. High-level formatting creates file system structures such as an allocation table and a root directory in a partition, thus creating a volume. *See* mass storage device, volume.

formatting   The process of creating a volume in a partition.

fragments   Portions of a datagram that has been broken into smaller segments to facilitate routing.

frame relay   A telephony protocol that routes digital trunk circuit data over the telephone network in a manner similar to packet-switched networks like IP. Frame relay simply provides for virtual permanent circuits with various levels of guaranteed service referred to as *Committed Information Rates (CIRs)*.

frame   A data structure that network hardware devices use to transmit data between computers. Frames consist of the addresses of the sending and receiving computers, size information, and a check sum. Frames are envelopes around packets of data that allow them to be addressed to specific computers on a shared media network. *See* Ethernet, FDDI, Token Ring.

front-end   The client side of a client/server application.

FrontPage   Microsoft's Web site organization and Web page content-creation application.

FTP   *See* File Transfer Protocol.

gated daemon   An early UNIX routing service. Gated is no longer in widespread use.

gateway   1. A computer that serves as a router, a format translator, or a security filter for an entire network. 2. General-purpose computers that are used as routers and perform no other function.

Gateway Services for NetWare (GSNW)   A NT Server service used to connect NT Servers and NT clients to NetWare resources via a gateway service. *See* gateway, NetWare, Client Services for NetWare.

GDI *See* Graphical Device Interface.

global account   A user or group account defined on a primary domain controller that may be used from all computers that participate in the Windows NT domain.

global group   A group that exists only on domain controllers. A global group can only contain members from within its domain. *See* local group.

Gopher   An Internet service that provides text and links to other Gopher sites. Gopher predates HTTP by about a year, but has been made obsolete by the richer format provided by HTTP. *See* Hypertext Transfer Protocol.

graphical device interface (GDI)   The programming interface and graphical services provided to Win32 for programs to interact with graphical devices such as the screen and printer. *See* programming interface, Win32.

graphical user interface (GUI)   A computer shell program that represents mass storage devices, directories, and files as graphical objects on a screen. A cursor driven by a pointing device such as a mouse manipulates the objects. Typically, the objects are represented by icons that can be opened into windows that show the data contained by the object. *See* shell, Explorer.

group account   A record, maintained by Windows NT, of user accounts that are assigned access permissions as a group.

group identifiers   Security Identifiers that contain the set of permissions allowed to a group. When a user account is part of a group, the group identifier is appended to that user's Security Identifier, thus granting the individual user all the permissions assigned to that group. *See* accounts, permissions, Security Identifier.

groups Security entities to which users can be assigned membership for the purpose of applying the broad set of group permissions to the user. By managing permissions for groups and assigning users to groups, rather than assigning permissions to users, security administrators can keep coherent control of very large security environments. *See* accounts, global group, local group, permissions, security.

GSNW *See* Gateway Services for NetWare.

GUI *See* graphical user interface.

hacker A person who attempts to obtain illegitimate access to computer systems.

HAL *See* Hardware Abstraction Layer.

hard disk *See* hard disk drive.

hard disk drives Mass storage devices that read and write digital information magnetically on discs that spin under moving heads. Hard disk drives are precisely aligned and cannot normally be removed. Hard disk drives are an inexpensive way to store gigabytes of computer data permanently. Hard disk drives also store the installed software of a computer. *See* mass storage device.

Hardware Abstraction Layer (HAL) A Windows NT service that provides basic input/output services such as timers, interrupts, and multiprocessor management for computer hardware. The HAL is a device driver for the motherboard circuitry that allows different families of computers to be treated the same by the Windows NT operating system. *See* driver, interrupt request, service.

Hardware Compatibility List (HCL)   The listing of all hardware devices supported by Windows NT. Hardware on the HCL has been tested and verified as being compatible with NT. You can view the current HCL at `http://microsoft.com/ntserver/hcl`.

hardware profiles   Used to manage portable computers which have different configurations based on their location.

hash   An algorithm that converts a string of text (such as a password) to a number. If the number can be converted back to the original text, it is referred to as a two-way hash. In a one-way hash, such as that used by Windows NT's password authentication process, the number cannot be converted back to text.

HCL   *See* Hardware Compatibility List.

High Performance File System (HPFS)   The file system native to OS/2 that performs many of the same functions of NTFS when run under OS/2. *See* file system, new technology file system.

hijacking   A hack wherein an established TCP session is redirected in mid-communication to an unauthorized host.

home directory   The root directory of a Web server or virtual server that contains the default document or home page. *See* default document, World Wide Web.

home page   The default page returned by an HTTP server when a URL containing no specific document is requested. *See* Hypertext Transfer Protocol, Uniform Resource Locator.

host   1. Any computer attached to the Internet with at least one unique IP address. 2. An Internet server. Hosts are constantly connected to the Internet. *See* Internet.

hot fixing The automatic detection, recovery, and marking "out of use" of bad disk sectors.

HotJava A Web browser written entirely in the Java programming language and designed to show the capability of the language. HotJava was the first browser to support Java applications.

HPFS *See* High Performance File System.

HTML *See* Hypertext Markup Language.

HTTP *See* Hypertext Transfer Protocol.

hyperlink A link embedded in text or graphics that has a Web address embedded within it. By clicking on the link, you jump to another Web address. You can identify a hyperlink because it is a different color from the rest of the Web page. *See* World Wide Web.

Hypertext Markup Language (HTML) A textual data format that identifies sections of a document as headers, lists, hypertext links, etc. HTML is the data format used on the World Wide Web for the publication of Web pages. *See* Hypertext Transfer Protocol, World Wide Web.

Hypertext Transfer Protocol (HTTP) Hypertext Transfer Protocol is an Internet protocol that transfers HTML documents over the Internet and responds to context changes that happen when a user clicks on a hypertext link. *See* Hypertext Markup Language, World Wide Web.

icon A graphical representation of a resource in a graphical user interface that usually takes the form of a small (32 x 32) bitmap. *See* graphical user interface.

IDE *See* Integrated Device Electronics.

IIS *See* Internet Information Server.

impersonation attack A hostile computer masquerading as a trusted computer.

incremental backup A type of backup that backs up all files changed since the previous full backup.

index server A search engine ISAPI extension to IIS that indexes all the documents stored on a Web site. Users can then query the indexes to return Web pages that match the query. *See* IIS, ISAPI, search engine.

Industry Standard Architecture (ISA) The design standard for 16-bit Intel compatible motherboards and peripheral buses. The 32/64-bit PCI bus standard is replacing the ISA standard. Adapters and interface cards must conform to the bus standard(s) used by the motherboard in order to be used with a computer.

Integrated Services Digital Network (ISDN) A direct, digital dial-up PSTN data link layer connection that operates at 64KB per channel over regular twisted pair cable between a subscriber site and a PSTN central office. ISDN provides twice the data rate of the fastest modems per channel. Up to 24 channels can be multiplexed over two twisted pairs. *See* data link layer, modem, Public Switched Telephone Network.

Intel architecture A family of microprocessors descended directly from the Intel 8086, itself descended from the first microprocessor, the Intel 4004. The Intel architecture is the dominant microprocessor family. It was used in the original IBM PC microcomputer adopted by the business market and later adapted for home use.

Integrated Device Electronics (IDE) A simple mass storage device interconnection bus that operates at 5Mbps and can handle no more than two attached devices. IDE devices are similar to, but less expensive than, SCSI devices. *See* Small Computer Systems Interface, mass storage device.

interactive user   A user who physically logs on to the computer where the user account resides is considered interactive, as opposed to a user who logs in over the network. *See* network user.

intermediate system   A host that forwards datagrams between networks but is not interested in the content of those datagrams.

internal security   Measures taken to prevent unauthorized access from inside the security perimeter of the system.

Internet   A voluntarily interconnected global network of computers based upon the TCP/IP protocol suite. TCP/IP was originally developed by the U.S. Department of Defense's Advanced Research Projects Agency to facilitate the interconnection of military networks and was provided free to universities. The obvious utility of worldwide digital network connectivity and the availability of free complex networking software developed at universities doing military research attracted other universities, research institutions, private organizations, businesses, and, finally, the individual home user. The Internet is now available to all current commercial computing platforms. *See* FTP, TCP/IP, Telnet, World Wide Web.

Internet Database Connector   An extension to IIS that returns a database table formatted as an HTML document based on a query from the Web client. *See* Database, IIS.

Internet Explorer   A World Wide Web browser produced by Microsoft and included free with Windows 95 and Windows NT 4. *See* Internet, World Wide Web.

Internet Information Server (IIS)   Serves Internet higher-level protocols, like HTTP and FTP, to clients using Web browsers. *See* File Transfer Protocol, Hypertext Transfer Protocol, and World Wide Web.

Internet Protocol (IP)   The Network layer protocol upon which the Internet is based. IP provides a simple connectionless packet exchange. Other protocols such as UDP or TCP use IP to perform their connection-oriented or guaranteed delivery services. *See* Internet, TCP/IP.

Internet Relay Chat (IRC)   An informal Internet protocol for multi-user simultaneous conversation via relayed text strings between an IRC server and multiple IRC clients.

Internet Server Application Programming Interface (ISAPI)   A specification to which extensions to IIS are written in order to expand its functionality or the services it provides.

Internet server   A server computer connected to the Internet or an intranet that serves Internet protocols like HTTP, FTP, and Gopher based on the TCP/IP protocol suite. *See* FTP, Gopher, Internet, HTTP, TCP/IP.

Internet Service Provider (ISP)   A company that provides dial-up connections to the Internet. *See* Internet.

Internetwork Packet eXchange (IPX)   The network and transport layer protocol developed by Novell for its NetWare product. IPX is a routable, connection-oriented protocol similar to TCP/IP but much easier to manage and with lower communication overhead. *See* IP, NetWare, NWLink.

Internetwork   A network of networks, usually based on a packet-switching scheme.

InterNIC   The agency that is responsible for assigning IP addresses. *See* Internet protocol, IP Address.

Interpreter   A program that executes the commands read from a script. *See* Script, Scripting Language.

interprocess communications (IPC)   A generic term describing any manner of client/server communication protocols, specifically those operating in the application layer. Interprocess communications mechanisms provide a method for the client and server to trade information. *See* local procedure call, mailslots, named pipes, NetBIOS, NetDDE, remote procedure call.

Interrupt Request (IRQ)   A hardware signal from a peripheral device to the microcomputer indicating that it has I/O traffic to send. If the microprocessor is not running a more important service, it will interrupt its current activity and handle the interrupt request. IBM PCs have 16 levels of interrupt request lines. Under Windows NT, each device must have a unique interrupt request line. *See* Driver, Microprocessor, Peripheral.

intranet   A privately owned network based on the TCP/IP protocol suite. *See* Transmission Control Protocol/Internet Protocol.

intruder   Anyone who has accessed a secure resource without authorization.

IP address   A 4-byte number that uniquely identifies a computer on an IP internetwork. InterNIC assigns the first bytes of Internet IP addresses and administers them in hierarchies. Huge organizations like the government or top-level ISPs have class A addresses, large organizations and most ISPs have class B addresses, and small companies have class C addresses. In a class A address, InterNIC assigns the first byte, and the owning organization assigns the remaining three bytes. In a class B address, InterNIC or the higher-level ISP assigns the first 2 bytes, and the organization assigns the remaining 2 bytes. In a class C address, InterNIC or the higher-level ISP assigns the first three bytes, and the organization assigns the remaining byte. Organizations not attached to the Internet are free to assign IP addresses as they please. *See* Internet, InterNIC, IP.

IP masquerade   A border system that translates IP connections for an internal network into requests from itself, thus protecting the identity of internal systems at the network layer rather than at the application layer as with Internet proxies.

IP   *See* Internet Protocol.

IPC   *See* interprocess communications.

IPX   *See* Internetwork Packet eXchange.

IRQ   *See* interrupt request.

ISA   *See* Industry Standard Architecture.

ISDN   *See* Integrated Services Digital Network.

ISP   *See* Internet service provider.

Java Virtual Machine   A fictitious machine language to which all Java applications are compiled. Java runtime environments can either interpret or compile JVM code to execute it on any computer or inside an application like a Web browser.

Java   A compiled object-oriented cross-platform language based on the syntax of C++ that uses the interpreted Java virtual machine as its machine language. Since Java applications and applets can be run on any platform, it is a natural candidate for Web-based programs.

JavaScript A scripting language based on the syntax of Java that can be embedded in HTML documents to provide simple client-side active content. *See* scripting language, script.

Kerberos The basis for the new security features that will be available with Windows NT 5. Like the Windows NT domain model, Kerberos is a trusted authentication system for large-scale networks. Kerberos keeps a database of the private keys of its users and network services.

kernel The core process of a preemptive operating system, consisting of a multitasking scheduler and the basic services that provide security. Depending on the operating system, other services such as virtual memory drivers may be built into the kernel. The kernel is responsible for managing the scheduling of threads and processes. *See* drivers, operating system.

keys A value (usually a number or a string of characters) that is used with a cipher to encrypt a message. The key must be kept secret in order for the message to remain private. Often, keys are paired codes used to encrypt data in communication streams. One part of the keys is kept private on the server, while the other (public) part of the key is transmitted to Web browsers. Web browsers can then encrypt data using the public portion, which can only be decrypted using the private portion of the key. The process is called public key encryption and is used in Secure Socket Layer mechanism, as well as most other common public forms of encryption. *See* encryption, Secure Socket Layer.

keyspace The range of all possible keys for a cipher. A cipher with a large keyspace is harder to crack than one with a smaller keyspace because there are more keys (numbers or combinations of letters) to try.

LAN Manager   The Microsoft brand of a network product jointly developed by IBM and Microsoft that provided an early client/server environment. LAN Manager/Server was eclipsed by NetWare, but was the genesis of many important protocols and IPC mechanisms used today, such as NetBIOS, named pipes, and NetBEUI. Portions of this product exist today in OS/2 Warp Server. *See* interprocess communications, OS/2.

LAN Server   The IBM brand of a network product jointly developed by IBM and Microsoft. *See* LAN Manager.

LDAP   *See* Lightweight Directory Access Protocol.

LAN   *See* local area network.

Lightweight Directory Access Protocol (LDAP)   An open standard for storing user and group information independent of the operating system that hosts the WWW service.

Linux   A free 32-bit version of the UNIX operating system developed on the Internet and frequently used by hackers to attack Internet systems.

local account   A user or group account that only exists on the local Windows NT computer.

local area network (LAN)   A network of computers operating on the same high-speed, shared media network data link layer. The size of a local area network is defined by the limitations of high speed shared media networks to generally less than 1 kilometer in overall span. Some LAN backbone data link protocols, such as FDDI, can create larger LANs called *metropolitan* or *medium area networks (MANs)*. *See* data link layer, wide area network.

local group   A group that exists in a NT computer's local accounts database. Local groups can reside on NT Workstations or NT Servers and can contain users or global groups. *See* global group.

Local Procedure Call (LPC)   A mechanism that loops remote procedure calls without the presence of a network so that the client and server portion of an application can reside on the same machine. Local procedure calls look like remote procedure calls (RPCs) to the client and server sides of a distributed application. *See* Remote Procedure Call.

local security   Security that governs a local or interactive user. Local security can be set through NTFS partitions. *See* interactive user, network security, New Technology File System, security.

LocalTalk   A data link layer standard for local area networking used by Macintosh computers. LocalTalk is available on all Macintosh computers. The drawback of LocalTalk is that it only transmits at 230.4 kilobits per second (as opposed to Ethernet which can transmit at 10 megabits per second). *See* data link layer, Macintosh.

log   A database of time-based security and service-related information stored in text format.

logging   The process of recording information about activities and errors in the operating system.

logical port   Printers can be attached to a network through a logical port. A logical port uses a direct connection to gain access to the network. This is done by installing a network card on the printer. The advantages of using logical ports are that they are much faster than physical ports and that you are not limited to the cabling limitations imposed by parallel and serial cable distances allowed when connecting a printer to a PC's parallel or serial ports. *See* printer, printing device.

logoff   The process of closing an open session with a server. *See* logon.

logon   The process of opening a network session by providing a valid authentication consisting of a user account name and a password to a domain controller. After logon, network resources are available to the user according to the user's assigned permissions. *See* domain controller, logoff.

logon script   Command files that automate the logon process by performing utility functions such as attaching to additional server resources or automatically running different programs based on the user account that established the logon. *See* logon.

long file name (LFN)   A file name longer than the eight characters plus three-character extension allowed by MS-DOS. In Windows NT and Windows 95, long file names may be up to 255 characters.

LPC   *See* Local Procedure Call.

Macintosh   A brand of computer manufactured by Apple. Macintosh is the only successful line of computers that is not based either on the original IBM PC or on running the UNIX operating system. Windows NT Server supports Apple computers despite their use of proprietary network protocols.

MacOS   The operating system that runs on an Apple Macintosh computer. *See* Macintosh.

mailslots   A connectionless messaging IPC mechanism that Windows NT uses for browse request and logon authentication. *See* interprocess communications.

mandatory user profile   A profile that is created by an Administrator and saved with a special extension (.man) so that the user cannot modify the profile in any way. Mandatory user profiles can be assigned to a single user or a group of users. *See* user profile.

mass storage device   Any device capable of storing many megabytes of information permanently, but especially those capable of random access to any portion of the information, such as hard disk drives and CD-ROM drives. *See* CD-ROM drive, hard disk drive, IDE, SCSI.

master browser   The computer on a network that maintains a list of computers and services available on the network and distributes the list to other browsers. The master browser may also promote potential browsers to be browsers. *See* backup browser, browser, browsing, potential browser.

member server   A server that participates in a security domain but does not act as a domain controller and does not store domain user accounts. Member servers can be used for shared data, but users must authenticate with a PDC or BDC to access them.

memory   Any device capable of storing information. This term is usually used to indicate volatile semiconductor random access memory (RAM) capable of high-speed access to any portion of the memory space, but incapable of storing information without power. *See* mass storage device, random access memory.

message   Information sent from the sender to the receiver, usually encrypted by the sender and decrypted by the receiver.

microprocessor   An integrated semiconductor circuit designed to automatically perform lists of logical and arithmetic operations. Modern microprocessors independently manage memory pools and support multiple instruction lists called threads. Microprocessors are also capable of responding to interrupt requests from peripherals and include onboard support for complex floating point arithmetic.

Microprocessors must have instructions when they are first powered on. These instructions are contained in nonvolatile firmware called a BIOS. *See* BIOS, operating system.

Microsoft Disk Operating System (MS-DOS)   A 16-bit operating system designed for the 8086 chip that was used in the original IBM PC. MS-DOS is a simple program loader and file system that turns over complete control of the computer to the running program and provides very little service beyond file system support and what is provided by the BIOS.

Microsoft Services for NetWare   Software for NetWare servers that allows NetWare clients to access Windows NT services.

Migration Tool for NetWare   A utility used to migrate NetWare users, groups, file structures, and security to a NT domain. *See* NetWare.

Modem   Modulator/demodulator. A data link layer device used to create an analog signal suitable for transmission over telephone lines from a digital data stream. Modern modems also include a command set for negotiating connections and data rates with remote modems and for setting their default behavior. The fastest modems run at about 33Kbps. *See* data link layer.

Module   A software component of a modular operating system that provides a certain defined service. Modules can be installed or removed depending upon the service requirements of the software running on the computer. Modules allow operating systems and applications to be customized to fit the needs of the user.

MPR   *See* MultiProtocol Router.

MS-DOS   *See* Microsoft Disk Operating System.

multihomed host   General-purpose computers that perform some other function in addition to routing packets, such as file service or Internet site hosting.

multilink   A capability of RAS to combine multiple data streams into one network connection for the purpose of using more than one modem or ISDN channel in a single connection. This feature is new to Windows NT 4. *See* Remote Access Service.

Multimedia Internet Mail Extensions (MIME)   A specification for the content types of files transmitted over the Internet. Web servers identify the type of file being sent to Web browsers using MIME types.

multiprocessing   Using two or more processors simultaneously to perform a computing task. Depending on the operating system, processing may be done asymmetrically, wherein certain processors are assigned certain threads independent of the load they create, or symmetrically, wherein threads are dynamically assigned to processors according to an equitable scheduling scheme. The term usually describes a multiprocessing capacity built into the computer at a hardware level in that the computer itself supports more than one processor. However, *multiprocessing* can also be applied to network computing applications achieved through interprocess communication mechanisms. Client/server applications are, in fact, examples of multiprocessing. *See* asymmetrical multiprocessing, interprocess communications, symmetrical multiprocessing.

MultiProtocol Router (MPR)   Services included with NT Server that allow you to route traffic between IPX and TCP/IP subnets. MPR also allows you to facilitate DHCP requests and forward BOOTP relay agents. *See* Bootstrap Protocol, Dynamic Host Configuration Protocol, Internetwork Packet Exchange, Transmission Control Protocol/Internet Protocol.

multitasking The capacity of an operating system to rapidly switch among threads of execution. Multitasking allows processor time to be divided among threads as if each thread ran on its own slower processor. Multitasking operating systems allow two or more applications to run at the same time and can provide a greater degree of service to applications than single-tasking operating systems like MS-DOS. *See* multithreading, multiprocessing.

multithreading *See* multitasking.

named pipes An interprocess communication mechanism that is implemented as a file system service, allowing programs to be modified to run on it without using a proprietary application programming interface. Named pipes were developed to support more robust client/server communications than those allowed by the simpler NetBIOS. *See* file systems, interprocess communications, OS/2.

NDIS *See* Network Driver Interface Specification.

NDS (NetWare Directory Services) NetWare's directory of network resources, stored as NDS objects. NDS keeps a single database for the entire network and allows single-login access.

NDS *See* NetWare Directory Services.

NetBEUI *See* NetBIOS Extended User Interface.

NetBIOS *See* Network Basic Input/Output System.

NetBIOS Extended User Interface (NetBEUI) A simple network layer transport developed to support NetBIOS installations. NetBEUI is not routable, and so it is not appropriate for larger networks. NetBEUI is the fastest transport protocol available for Windows NT.

NetBIOS gateway A service provided by RAS that allows NetBIOS requests to be forwarded independent of transport protocol. For example, NetBIOS requests from a remote computer connected via NetBEUI can be sent over the network via NWLink. *See* NetBEUI, NetBIOS over TCP/IP, Network Basic Input/Output System, NWLink.

NetBIOS over TCP/IP (NetBT) A network service that implements the NetBIOS IPC over the TCP/IP protocol stack. *See* interprocess communications, NetBIOS, TCP/IP.

NetBT *See* NetBIOS over TCP/IP.

NetDDE *See* Network Dynamic Data Exchange.

NetWare Directory Services (NDS) In NetWare, a distributed hierarchy of network services such as servers, shared volumes, and printers. NetWare implements NDS as a directory structure having elaborate security and administration mechanisms. The CSNW provided in Windows NT 4 supports the NDS tree. *See* Client Services for NetWare, Gateway Services for NetWare, NetWare.

NetWare Link (NWLink) A Windows NT transport protocol that implements Novell's IPX. NWLink is useful as a general purpose transport for Windows NT and for connecting to NetWare file servers through CSNW. *See* Client Services for NetWare, Gateway Services for NetWare, Internetwork Packet eXchange.

NetWare NetBIOS Link (NWNBLink) NetBIOS implemented over NWLink. *See* NetBIOS, NetBT, NWLink.

NetWare A popular network operating system developed by Novell in the early 1980s. NetWare is a cooperative multitasking, highly optimized, dedicated-server network operating system that has client support for most major operating systems. Recent versions of NetWare include graphical client tools for management from client stations. At one time, NetWare accounted for more than 70 percent of the network operating system market. *See* Client Services for NetWare, Gateway Services for NetWare, NWLink, Windows NT.

network   A group of computers connected via some digital medium for the purpose of exchanging information. Networks can be based on many types of media, such as twisted-pair, telephone-style cable, optical fiber, coaxial cable, radio, or infrared light. Certain computers are usually configured as service providers called *servers*. Computers that perform user tasks directly and that use the services of servers are called *clients*. *See* client/server, network operating system, server.

Network Basic Input/Output System (NetBIOS)   A client/server interprocess communication service developed by IBM in the early 1980s. NetBIOS presents a relatively primitive mechanism for communication in client/server applications, but its widespread acceptance and availability across most operating systems make it a logical choice for simple network applications. Many of the network IPC mechanisms in Windows NT are implemented over NetBIOS. *See* client/server, interprocess communication.

Network Client Administrator   A utility within the Administrative Tools group that can be used to make installation startup disks, make installation disk sets, copy client-based administration tools, and view remote boot information.

Network Driver Interface Specification (NDIS)   A Microsoft specification to which network adapter drivers must conform in order to work with Microsoft network operating systems. NDIS provides a many-to-many binding between network adapter drivers and transport protocols. *See* transport protocol.

Network Dynamic Data Exchange (NetDDE) An interprocess communication mechanism developed by Microsoft to support the distribution of DDE applications over a network. *See* DDE, Interprocess Communication.

Network Interface Card (NIC) A physical layer adapter device that allows a computer to connect to and communicate over a local area network. *See* adapter, Ethernet, token ring.

network layer The layer of the OSI model that creates a communication path between two computers via routed packets. Transport protocols implement both the network layer and the transport layer of the OSI stack. IP is a network layer service. *See* Internet Protocol, Open Systems Interconnect Model, Transport Protocol.

Network Monitor A utility used to capture and display network traffic.

Network News Transfer Protocol (NNTP) A protocol for the transmission of a database of topical message threads between news servers and newsreader clients.

network operating system A computer operating system specifically designed to optimize a computer's ability to respond to service requests. Servers run network operating systems. Windows NT Server and NetWare are both network operating systems. *See* NetWare, server, Windows NT.

network printer A network printer can use physical or logical ports. By defining a printer as a network printer, you make the printer available to local and network users. *See* local printer, printer, printing device.

network security   Security that governs a network. Network security can be set through share permissions. *See* local security, network user, security.

network user   A user who logs on to the network using the SAM from a remote domain controller. *See* interactive user.

New Technology File System (NTFS)   A secure, transaction-oriented file system developed for Windows NT that incorporates the Windows NT security model for assigning permissions and shares. NTFS is optimized for hard drives larger than 500MB and requires too much overhead to be used on hard disk drives smaller than 50MB.

newsgroups   Internet-wide threads of topical discussion implemented using the NNTP protocol. *See* newsreader, NNTP, Usenet.

NFS (Network File System)   The UNIX standard for file sharing.

NNTP   *See* Network News Transfer Protocol.

nonbrowser   A computer on a network that will not maintain a list of other computers and services on the network. *See* browser, browsing.

NT Directory Services   The synchronized SAM database that exists between the PDC and the BDCs within a domain. Directory Services also controls the trust relationships that exist between domains. *See* backup domain controller, primary domain controller, security accounts manager, trust relationship.

NTFS   *See* New Technology File System.

NWLink   *See* Internetwork Packet eXchange, NetWare Link.

NWNBLink   *See* NetWare NetBIOS Link.

object   1. A software service provider that encapsulates both the algorithm and the data structures necessary to provide a service. Usually, objects can inherit data and functionality from their parent objects, thus allowing complex services to be constructed from simpler objects. The term *object oriented* implies a tight relationship between algorithms and data structures. 2. A Windows NT resource that may be shared and which has a list of services that user accounts may be permitted or denied access to. *See* module.

object counters   Containers built into each service object in Windows NT that store a count of the number of times an object performs its service or to what degree. You can use performance monitors to access object counters and measure how the different objects in Windows NT are operating. *See* object.

ODBC   *See* Open Database Connectivity.

Open Database Connectivity (ODBC)   A standard for the connection of database clients to database servers irrespective of the vendors or systems involved.

Open Graphics Language (OpenGL)   A standard interface for the presentation of two- and three-dimensional visual data.

Open Systems Interconnect Model (OSI Model)   A model for network component interoperability developed by the International Standards Organization to promote cross-vendor compatibility of hardware and software network systems. The OSI model splits the process of networking into seven distinct services. Each layer uses the services of the layer below to provide its service to the layer above. *See* application layer, data Link layer, network layer, physical layer, presentation layer, session layer, transport layer.

OpenGL *See* Open Graphics Language.

Operating System 2 (OS/2) A 16-bit (and later, 32-bit) operating system developed jointly by Microsoft and IBM as a successor to MS-DOS. Microsoft bowed out of the 32-bit development effort and produced its own product, Windows NT, as a competitor to OS/2. OS/2 is now a preemptive, multitasking 32-bit operating system with strong support for networking and the ability to run MS-DOS and Win16 applications, but IBM has been unable to entice a large number of developers to produce software that runs natively under OS/2. *See* operating system, preemptive multitasking.

operating system A collection of services that form a foundation upon which applications run. Operating systems can be simple I/O service providers with a command shell, such as MS-DOS, or they can be sophisticated, preemptive, multitasking, multiprocessing applications platforms like Windows NT. *See* kernel, network operating system, preemptive multitasking.

optimization Any effort to reduce the workload on a hardware component by eliminating, obviating, or reducing the amount of work required of the hardware component through any means. For instance, file caching is an optimization that reduces the workload of a hard disk drive.

OS/2 *See* Operating System 2.

OSI Model *See* Open Systems Interconnect Model.

out-of-band attack Sending extraneous command information to a TCP port.

owner   Used in conjunction with NTFS volumes. All NTFS files and directories have an associated owner who is able to control access and grant permissions to other users. *See* New Technology File System.

packet filter   A device used to discard undesired network traffic based on its source address, destination address, or the type of data specified by the TCP port number.

packet   A datagram.

page file   *See* swap file.

parity   Extra information used to recover data when portions are missing.

partition   A section of a hard disk that can contain an independent file system volume. Partitions can be used to keep multiple operating systems and file systems on the same hard disk. *See* hard disk drive, volume.

password   A secret code used to validate the identity of a user of a secure system. Passwords are used in tandem with account names to log on to most computer systems.

PBX   Private Branch eXchange. A PSTN telephone switch owned and operated by a private corporation other than a telephone company (telco). PBXs allow large corporations to use trunk lines directly from the telephone company rather than individual telephone lines, and to pay for telephone service at wholesale prices by switching telephone extensions themselves. Generally used only in installations with 100 or more internal telephone extensions and 24 or more external lines.

PC   *See* personal computer.

PCI *See* Peripheral Connection Interface.

PCS Personal Communication Service. Digital cellular that digitizes the radio signal in the radiotelephone to allow lower transmission powers, light encryption, and loss-less transmission.

PDC *See* primary domain controller.

peer A networked computer that both shares resources with other computers and accesses the shared resources of other computers. A nondedicated server. *See* client, server.

peer-to-peer network A network that does not have a dedicated server. Individual workstations can share files, printers, and other services. Windows NT setups using the workgroup model are peer-to-peer networks.

Performance Monitor A utility provided with NT that provides graphical statistics that can be used to measure performance on your computer.

Peripheral Connection Interface (PCI) A high speed 32/64-bit bus interface developed by Intel and widely accepted as the successor to the 16-bit ISA interface. PCI devices support I/O throughput about 40 times faster than the ISA bus.

peripheral An input/output device attached to a computer. Peripherals can be printers, hard disk drives, monitors, and so on.

Perl A scripting language commonly used in CGI scripts to parse user input from Web pages and dynamically create HTML documents. *See* scripting languages.

permissions   Assignments of levels of access to a resource, made to groups or users. Security constructs used to regulate access to resources by user name or group affiliation. Permissions can be assigned by administrators to allow any level of access, such as read only, read/ write, delete, etc., by controlling the ability of users to initiate object services. Security is implemented by checking the user's security identifier against each object's access control list. *See* Access Control List, Security Identifier.

personal computer (PC)   A microcomputer used by one person at a time (that is, not a multiuser computer). PCs are generally clients or peers in an networked environment. High-speed PCs are called *workstations*. Networks of PCs are called *LANs*. The term PC is often used to refer to computers compatible with the IBM PC.

phreaking   The act of hacking telephone systems, whether by computer or other means. The term comes from "phone freak."

physical layer   The cables, connectors, and connection ports use to connect a network. The passive physical components required to create a network. *See* OSI Model.

physical port   Printers can be connected directly to a computer through a serial (COM) or parallel (LPT) port. If a printer is connected in this manner, it is using a physical port. *See* print device, printer.

ping   A protocol used to check the connected route between two systems on an IP network. Also the name of the utility used to generate ping traffic. *See* IP.

ping of death   An ICMP packet that violates the rules of ICMP packet construction.

plaintext   The message to be sent from the sender to the receiver. This is what must be protected from being intercepted and understood. *See* cleartext.

plug-ins   Compiled components that extend the functionality of Web browsers, usually by interpreting specific types of data such as sound or video. *See* Web browser.

Point-to-Point Protocol (PPP)   A network-layer transport that performs over point-to-point network connections such as serial or modem lines. PPP can negotiate any transport protocol used by both systems involved in the link and can automatically assign IP, DNS, and gateway addresses when used with TCP/IP. *See* domain name service, gateway, Internet Protocol.

Point-to-Point Tunneling Protocol (PPTP)   A protocol used to connect to corporate networks through the Internet or an ISP. *See* Internet, Internet service provider.

policies   General controls that enhance the security of an operating environment.

policy   A specification for your network's approach to security. In Windows NT, policies affect restrictions on password use and rights assignment and determine which events will be recorded in the security log; these can be managed with the User Manager utility, and they specify general security options that apply to all users.

POP, POP3   *See* Post Office Protocol.

port   A TCP connection number used to determine which service a specific datagram should be sent to on a host.

Post Office Protocol   A protocol used for offline mail readers to manage the contents of their inbox on a mail server.

potential browser   A computer on a network that may maintain a list of other computers and services on the network if requested to do so by a master browser. *See* browser, master browser.

PowerPC   A microprocessor family developed by IBM to compete with the Intel family of microprocessors. The PowerPC is a RISC-architecture microprocessor with many advanced features that emulate other microprocessors. PowerPCs are currently used in a line of IBM computers and in the Apple Power Macintosh. Windows NT is available for the PowerPC.

PPP   *See* Point-to-Point Protocol.

PPTP   *See* Point-to-Point Tunneling Protocol.

preemptive multitasking   A multitasking implementation in which an interrupt routine in the kernel manages the scheduling of processor time among running threads. The threads themselves do not need to support multitasking in any way because the microprocessor will preempt the thread with an interrupt, save its state, update all thread priorities according to its scheduling algorithm, and pass control to the highest priority thread awaiting execution. Because of the preemptive nature, a thread that crashes will not affect the operation of other executing threads. *See* kernel, operating system, process, thread.

preferences   Characteristics of user accounts, such as password, profile location, home directory, and logon script.

presentation layer   That layer of the OSI model that converts and translates (if necessary) information between the session and application layers. *See* OSI Model.

primary domain controller (PDC) The domain server that contains the master copy of the security, computer, and user accounts databases and that can authenticate workstations. The PDC can replicate its databases to one or more backup domain controllers. The PDC is usually also the master browser for the domain. *See* backup domain controller, domain, master browser.

print server Print servers are the computers to which shared printers are attached. Print servers queue print jobs coming in from clients on the network and print them sequentially. *See* print device, printer.

priority A level of execution importance assigned to a thread. In combination with other factors, the priority level determines how often that thread will get computer time according to a scheduling algorithm. *See* preemptive multitasking.

private key The key in public key encryption that is kept private.

process A running program containing one or more threads. A process encapsulates the protected memory and environment for its threads.

processor A circuit designed to automatically perform lists of logical and arithmetic operations. Unlike microprocessors, processors may be designed from discrete components rather than be a monolithic integrated circuit. *See* microprocessor.

program A list of processor instructions designed to perform a certain function. A running program is called a process. A package of one or more programs and attendant data designed to meet a certain application is called software. *See* application, microprocessor, process, software.

programming interfaces   Interprocess communications mechanisms that provide certain high-level services to running processes. Programming interfaces may provide network communication, graphical presentation, or any other type of software service. *See* interprocess communication.

protocol   An established communication method that the parties involved understand. Protocols provide a context in which to interpret communicated information. Computer protocols are rules used by communicating devices and software services to format data in a way that all participants understand. *See* Transport Protocol.

proxy server   A server dedicated to the function of receiving Internet Web requests for clients, retrieving the requested pages, and forwarding them to client. Proxy servers cache retrieved Web pages to improve performance and reduce bandwidth, and also serve the security function of protecting the identity of internal clients.

proxy   A service running either on a server or a firewall which receives service requests from clients and then reissues them as if the request originated from the proxy server. This hides the identity of the client and provides the ability to cache often-requested data on the proxy to reduce bandwidth on lower-speed connections to the Internet.

pseudorandom   Numbers created by a deterministic means (that is, given identical starting conditions, identical numbers will be produced). Good pseudorandom numbers have a long periodicity and satisfy the other conditions of random numbers, such as incompressibility and having an even distribution.

PSTN   *See* Public Switched Telephone Network.

Public Switched Telephone Network (PSTN)   A global network of interconnected digital and analog communication links originally designed to support voice communication between any two points in the world, but quickly adapted to handle digital data traffic when the computer revolution occurred. In addition to its traditional voice support role, the PSTN now functions as the physical layer of the Internet by providing dial-up and leased lines for the interconnections. POTS (Plain Old Telephone Service) is another common acronym for the PSTN. *See* Internet, modem, physical layer.

public key algorithm   An algorithm in which a different key is used for encryption than for decryption. For this reason, the encryption key can be made public without compromising security because it cannot be used to decrypt the ciphertext.

query   A request to an index or database server for a specific set of information.

RAID controllers   Hard disk drive controllers that implement RAID in hardware. *See* Redundant Array of Inexpensive Disks.

RAID   *See* Redundant Array of Inexpensive Disks.

RAM   *See* random access memory.

random   Unpredictable (a series of random numbers cannot be reproduced, even from identical starting conditions). Truly random numbers also satisfy other criteria, such as incompressibility and having an even distribution.

random access memory (RAM)   Integrated circuits that store digital bits in massive arrays of logical gates or capacitors. RAM is the primary memory store for modern computers, storing all running software processes and contextual data. *See* microprocessor.

RARP   *See* Reverse Address Resolution Protocol.

RAS *See* Remote Access Service.

real-time application A process that must respond to external events at least as fast as those events can occur. Real-time threads must run at very high priorities to ensure their ability to respond in real time. *See* process.

receiver The receptor and decryptor of a message.

redirector A software service that redirects user file I/O requests over the network. Novell implements the Workstation service and Client services for NetWare as redirectors. Redirectors allow servers to be used as mass storage devices that appear local to the user. *See* Client Services for NetWare, file system.

Reduced Instruction Set Computer (RISC) A microprocessor technology that implements fewer and more primitive instructions than typical microprocessors and can therefore be implemented quickly with the most modern semiconductor technology and speeds. Programs written for RISC microprocessors require more instructions (longer programs) to perform the same task as a normal microprocessor but are capable of a greater degree of optimization and therefore usually run faster. *See* microprocessor.

Redundant Array of Inexpensive (or Independent) Disks (RAID) A collection of hard disk drives coordinated by a special controller or file system driver that appears as one physical disk to a computer. RAID takes advantage of the inherent speed and/or fault tolerance afforded by using more than one disk. RAID disk storage has several levels, including 0 (striping), 1 (mirroring), and 5 (striping with parity). RAID systems are typically used for very large storage volumes or to provide fault-tolerance features such as hot swapping of failed disks or automatically backing up data onto replacement disks.

registry A database of settings required and maintained by Windows NT and its components. The registry contains all of the configuration information used by the applications and services running on the computer. It is stored as a hierarchical structure and is made up of keys, hives, and value entries. You can use the Registry Editor (REGEDT32 command) to change these settings.

Remote Access Service (RAS) A service that allows network connections to be established over PSTN lines with modems. The computer initiating the connection is called the RAS client; the answering computer is called the RAS host. *See* modem, Public Switched Telephone Network.

remote access A suite of related technologies that allow the extension of private networks over dial-up circuits.

remote control Software that allows remote users to control the functionality of a distant computer over a low-bandwidth connection.

remote procedure calls (RPC) A network interprocess communication mechanism that allows an application to be distributed among many computers on the same network. *See* local procedure call, interprocess communications.

remoteboot A service used to boot diskless workstations over the network by attaching to a remoteboot server which provides the operating system.

replication Any system that duplicates data between servers. This can include simple replication, supported by Windows NT, or full server replication via third-party software.

Requests for Comments (RFCs) The set of standards defining the Internet protocols as determined by the Internet Engineering Task Force and available in the public domain on the Internet. RFCs define the functions and services provided by each of the many Internet protocols. Compliance with the RFCs guarantees cross-vendor compatibility. *See* Internet.

resource   Any useful service, such as a shared network directory or a printer. *See* share.

restricted algorithm   An algorithm that is kept secret to make it more difficult to break.

Reverse Address Resolution Protocol (RARP)   The TCP/IP protocol that allows a computer that has a physical layer address (such as an Ethernet address) but does not have an IP address to request a numeric IP address from another computer on the network. *See* TCP/IP.

RFC   *See* Request For Comments.

RIP   *See* Routing Information Protocol.

RISC   *See* Reduced Instruction Set Computer.

roaming user profile   A user profile that is stored on and downloaded from a server. Roaming user profiles allow a user to access their profile from any location on the network. *See* user profile.

roll back   The process of regressing to a consistent and error-free prior state.

route   The list of intermediate systems between two specified end systems.

routed daemon   A UNIX routing service that uses the Routing Information Protocol (RIP).

router A network layer device that moves packets between networks, usually implemented by specially designed computers optimized for routing packets. Routers provide internetwork connectivity. *See* network layer.

routing The process of forwarding datagrams among end systems to reach a specified end system.

Routing Information Protocol (RIP) A protocol within the TCP/IP protocol suite that allows routers to exchange routing information with other routers. *See* Transmission Control Protocol/Internet Protocol.

routing tables Lists of routes maintained by a router to determine which router is the next closest in the route to a specific end system.

RPC *See* remote procedure calls.

SAM *See* Security Accounts Manager.

Samba Server Message Block (SMB) client for UNIX developed without Microsoft's help. Since the source code is freely available, Samba is frequently modified into a NetBIOS hacking engine.

scheduling The process of determining which threads should be executed according to their priority and other factors. *See* preemptive multitasking.

script A list of commands to be executed by an interpreter. Web browsers can be interpreters for scripts embedded in HTML documents. *See* interpreter, scripting language, Web browser.

scripting language A specific syntax and structure for commands in scripts. *See* interpreter, script.

SCSI   *See* Small Computer Systems Interface.

search engine   Web sites dedicated to responding to requests for specific information, searching massive locally stored databases of Web pages, and responding with the URLs of pages that fit the search phrase. *See* Universal Resource Locator, World Wide Web.

sector   The basic unit of physical storage on a mass storage device.

Secure Socket Layer (SSL)   An encrypted transmission protocol that uses TCP/IP to implement a secure public key encrypted data channel between a client and a server. *See* encryption, TCP/IP.

Secure   A cipher that, even given a reasonable amount of time and resources, most likely cannot be compromised by a competent cryptanalysist.

security   Measures taken to secure a system against accidental or intentional loss, usually in the form of accountability procedures and use restriction. *See* security accounts, Manager Security Identifiers.

Security Accounts Manager (SAM)   The module of the Windows NT executive that authenticates a user name and password against a database of accounts, generating an access token that includes the user's permissions. *See* access token, security, Security Identifier.

Security Descriptor   The portion of the object containing the Owner, Group, and Access Control List information.

Security Identifiers (SID)   Unique codes that identify a specific user or group to the Windows NT security system. Security identifiers contain a complete set of permissions for that user or group.

Security Reference Monitor (SRM)   The portion of the Windows NT operating system that checks each object access made by a process to ensure that that access is allowed in the object's DACL. It initiates an audit event if that access is being audited in the object's SACL.

sender   The originator and encryptor of a message.

Serial Line Internet Protocol (SLIP)   An implementation of the IP protocol over serial lines. SLIP has been obviated by PPP. *See* Internet Protocol, Point-to-Point Protocol.

serial   A method of communication that transfers data across a medium one bit at a time, usually adding stop, start, and check bits to ensure quality transfer. *See* COM Port, modem.

Server Manager   A utility in the Administrative Tools group used to manage domains and computers.

Server Side Include (SSI)   A generic term for Web services that use embedded HTML tags to dynamically create HTML documents based on the contents of many different HTML documents.

server   A computer dedicated to servicing requests for resources from other computers on a network. Servers typically run network operating systems such as Windows NT Server or NetWare. *See* client/server, NetWare, Windows NT.

server-based network   A network that uses one or more central, dedicated server. Also referred to as a client/server network. The Windows NT domain model is server-based.

service   A process dedicated to implementing a specific function for other processes. Most Windows NT components are services used by user-level applications.

Services for Macintosh Service available through NT Server that allows Macintosh users to take advantage of NT file and print services. *See* Macintosh.

servlet A server side application written in Java.

session layer The layer of the OSI model dedicated to maintaining a bidirectional communication connection between two computers. The session layer uses the services of the transport layer to provide this service. *See* OSI Model, transport layer.

share A resource (such as a directory, printer, etc.) shared by a server or a peer on a network. *See* peer, resource, server.

share-level security The security system that allows you to set permissions for shared directories. Share-level security works on FAT or NTFS systems. It includes a smaller list of permissions than file-level security, which can be used on NTFS volumes for greater security.

shell The user interface of an operating system; the shell launches applications and manages file systems.

SID *See* Security Identifier.

Simple Mail Transfer Protocol (SMTP) An Internet protocol for transferring mail between Internet hosts. SMTP is often used to upload mail directly from the client to an intermediate host, but can only be used to receive mail by computers constantly connected to the Internet. *See* Internet.

Simple Network Management Protocol (SNMP) An Internet protocol that manages network hardware such as routers, switches, servers, and clients from a single client on the network. *See* Internet Protocol.

site   A related collection of HTML documents at the same Internet address, usually oriented toward some specific information or purpose. *See* Hypertext Markup Language, Internet.

SLIP   *See* Serial Line Internet Protocol.

Small Computer Systems Interface (SCSI)   A high-speed, parallel-bus interface that connects hard disk drives, CD-ROM drives, tape drives, and many other peripherals to a computer. SCSI is the mass storage connection standard among all computers except IBM compatibles, which use SCSI or IDE.

SMTP   *See* Simple Mail Transfer Protocol.

sniffer   A software or hardware troubleshooting device used for the low-level analysis of network protocols.

SNMP   *See* Simple Network Management Protocol.

snooping   Gathering information about a target network or computer by interrogating the targeted computers

software   A suite of programs sold as a unit and dedicated to a specific application. *See* application, process, program.

spooler   A service that buffers output to a low-speed device such as a printer so the software outputting to the device is not tied up waiting for it.

SQL   *See* Structured Query Language: SQL Server

SQL Server   Microsoft's relational database server based on SQL syntax. *See* SQL.

SSL *See* Secure Socket Layer.

standalone server A Windows NT server that does not participate in any domain. These servers can be accessed locally, or can be configured to form a workgroup.

stream cipher A cipher designed to operate on a continuous stream of data.

stripe set A single volume created across multiple hard disk drives and accessed in parallel for the purpose of optimizing disk access time. NTFS can create stripe sets. *See* file system, NTFS, volume.

striped set with parity A stripe set that includes redundant data in the set for fault tolerance. *See* RAID, stripe set.

strong cipher A cipher that, given the computational power that may reasonably be brought to bear on it any time in the near future, is unlikely to be compromised.

strong password A password that is difficult to guess. Strong passwords always include punctuation or numbers, and are longer than eight characters.

Structured Query Language (SQL) An open syntax for the transmission of queries between clients and servers. Database servers interpret SQL to return the data described by the query.

subdirectory A directory contained in another directory. *See* directory.

subnet mask A number mathematically applied to Internet protocol addresses to determine which IP addresses are a part of the same subnetwork as the computer applying the subnet mask. *See* Internet Protocol.

subnet   A single broadcast network defined by the fact that no routing need occur for any two computers in the subnet to communicate.

subnetwork   A broadcast network wherein all clients can communicate directly on a shared medium. *See* internetwork, network, subnet.

substitution cipher   Replaces each character (or other small unit such as a byte) of the message with a different character (or byte) according to the cipher algorithm.

surf   To browse the Web randomly looking for interesting information. *See* World Wide Web.

swap file   The virtual memory file on a hard disk containing the memory pages that have been moved out to disk to increase available RAM. *See* virtual memory.

symmetric algorithm   An algorithm in which the same key is used for encryption and decryption.

symmetrical multiprocessing   A multiprocessing methodology wherein processes are assigned to processors on a fair-share basis. This balances the processing load among processors and ensures that no processor will become a bottleneck. Symmetrical multiprocessing is more difficult to implement than asymmetrical multiprocessing as certain hardware functions, such as interrupt handling, must be shared between processors. *See* asymmetrical multiprocessing, multiprocessing.

System Access Control List (SACL)   Lists services for which user access will be audited.

system partition   The system partition is the active partition on an Intel-based computer that contains the hardware-specific files used to load the NT operating system. *See* boot partition, partition.

System Policy Editor   A utility found within the Administrative Tools group used to create system policies. *See* system policies.

system policies   Used to control what a user can do and the user's environment. System policies can be applied to a specific user, group, a computer, or all users. *See* registry, System Policy Editor.

T0, DS0   The basic digital telephone trunk that carries a single voice conversation at a data rate of 56Kbps (64Kb/s in Europe, Central and South America). DS refers to the data rate, T refers to the trunk itself. Also commonly used as a low-speed dedicated connection to an Internet service provider.

T1, DS1   A high-speed circuit that multiplexes 24 DS0 circuits onto a single 1.5Mb/s circuit. These circuits are also commonly used as a medium-speed connection to an Internet service provider.

T3, DS3   An aggregate of 30 T1 circuits onto a single 45Mbps circuit. Also commonly used as a high-speed transport to Internet service providers.

Task Manager   An application that manually views and closes running processes. Task Manager can also be used to view CPU and memory statistics. Press Ctrl+Alt+Del to launch the Task Manager.

TCP/IP   *See* Transmission Control Protocol/Internet Protocol.

TCP   *See* Transmission Control Protocol.

Telnet   A terminal application that allows a user to log into a multiuser UNIX computer from any computer connected to the Internet. *See* Internet.

TFTP   *See* Trivial File Transfer Protocol.

thin client   A computer designed to remotely control a user session on a more powerful multiuser computer.

thread   A list of instructions running in a computer to perform a certain task. Each thread runs in the context of a process, which embodies the protected memory space and the environment of the threads. Multithreaded processes can perform more than one task at the same time. *See* preemptive multitasking, process, program.

throughput   The measure of information flow through a system in a specific time frame, usually one second. For instance, 28.8Kbps is the throughput of a modem: 28.8 kilobits per second can be transmitted.

time-to-live indicator   A metric used to determine when a packet should be discarded.

token ring   The second most popular data link layer standard for local area networking. Token ring implements the token passing method of arbitrating multiple-computer access to the same network. Token ring operates at either 4 or 16Mbps. FDDI is similar to token ring and operates at 100Mbps. *See* data link layer.

transaction   A write-to-disk operation.

Transmission Control Protocol (TCP)   A transport layer protocol that implements guaranteed packet delivery using the Internet Protocol (IP). *See* Internet Protocol, TCP/IP.

Transmission Control Protocol/Internet Protocol (TCP/IP)   A suite of Internet protocols upon which the global Internet is based. TCP/IP is a general term that can refer either to the TCP and IP protocols used together or to the complete set of Internet protocols. TCP/IP is the default protocol for Windows NT.

transport layer   The OSI model layer responsible for the guaranteed serial delivery of packets between two computers over an internetwork. TCP is the transport layer protocol for the TCP/IP transport protocol.

Transport Protocol   A service that delivers discreet packets of information between any two computers in a network. Higher-level connection-oriented services are built upon transport protocols. *See* Internet IP, NetBEUI, NWLink, TCP, TCP/IP, transport layer.

transposition cipher   Rearranges the text of the message according to the cipher algorithm.

Trivial File Transport Protocol (TFTP)   A simple file transport protocol often used during the booting of diskless workstations. FTP is more robust and therefore more common. *See* FTP.

Trojan Horse   A malicious software program (or an attachment to another benign program) designed to look harmless in order to entice a user to install it. Once installed, the Trojan horse software opens a vector for further attack, such as answering the modem or listening on a TCP/IP port and vectoring inbound data to the console.

trunk   Digital high-speed circuits that aggregate individual telephone lines for transport between telephone company central offices (CO) and PBXs.

trust   A relationship between domains that allows users of one to access the other without separate authentication.

trust relationship   Administrative link that joins two or more domains. With a trust relationship users can access resources in another domain if they have rights, even if they do not have a user account in the resource domain.

trustee   In NetWare, a user (or other object) that has been given access to a file, directory, or NDS object.

tunnels   Secure encrypted links created over nonsecure public mediums like the Internet.

UDP   *See* User Datagram Protocol.

UNC   *See* Universal Naming Convention.

unconditionally secure   A cipher that, given an unlimited amount of time and an infinitely powerful processor, cannot be compromised.

Uniform Resource Locator (URL)   An Internet standard naming convention for identifying resources available via various TCP/IP application protocols. For example, `http://www.microsoft.com` is the URL for Microsoft's World Wide Web server site, while `ftp://gateway.dec.com` is a popular FTP site. A URL allows easy hypertext references to a particular resource from within a document or mail message. *See* HTTP, World Wide Web.

UNIX   A multitasking, kernel-based operating system developed at AT&T in the early 1970s and provided (originally) free to universities as a research operating system. Because of its availability and ability to scale down to microprocessor-based computers, UNIX became the standard operating system of the Internet and its attendant network protocols and is the closest approximation to a universal operating system that exists. Most computers can run some variant of the UNIX operating system. *See* Internet, multitasking.

Usenet News   A distributed news database implemented on NNTP, divided into topical discussion threads called *newsgroups* which are distributed among news servers. Clients using newsreaders can subscribe to specific newsgroups and have them automatically downloaded when they open their newsreader.

user account   A security record maintained by Windows NT that records your user name, password, logon permissions, home directory, and other information pertaining to your individual use of the computer and the network.

User Datagram Protocol (UDP)   A nonguaranteed network packet protocol implemented on IP that is far faster than TCP because of its lack of flow-control overhead. UDP can be implemented as a reliable transport when some higher-level protocol (such as NetBIOS) exists to make sure that required data will eventually be retransmitted in local area environments. At the transport layer of the OSI model, UDP is connectionless service and TCP is connection-oriented service. *See* Transmission Control Protocol.

User Manager for Domains   A Windows NT application that administers user accounts, groups, and security policies at the domain level.

user profile   Used to save each user's Desktop configuration. *See* mandatory profile, roaming profile.

User Rights Policies   Used to determine what rights users and groups have when trying to accomplish network tasks. User Rights Policies are set through User Manager for Domains. *See* User Manager for Domains.

user name   A user's account name in a logon-authenticated system. *See* security.

VBScript   A variant of Visual Basic used as a scripting language in Internet Explorer and Active Server Pages. *See* scripting language.

VDM   *See* Virtual DOS Machine.

vector of attack (vector)   A method (or a point of entry) used to exploit vulnerability.

virtual directory   A directory accessible to Internet Information Server which has a registered alias so that it appears to be a subdirectory of a service root directory.

Virtual DOS Machine (VDM)   The DOS environment created by Windows NT for the execution of DOS and Win16 applications. *See* MS-DOS, Win16.

Virtual Machine   A fictitious machine language that can be interpreted on a number of actual machines. Programs compiled to the Virtual Machine specification can then be run on any computer that can interpret that Virtual Machine specification. *See* Java.

virtual memory   A kernel service that stores memory pages not currently in use on a mass storage device to free up the memory occupied for other uses. Virtual memory hides the memory-swapping process from applications and higher-level services. *See* kernel, swap file.

Virtual Reality Modeling Language (VRML)   A syntax that describes the position of three-dimensional objects in a space, which can be transmitted from a server to a client and rendered on the client.

virtual server   A set of directories that simulate the functionality of a WWWROOT directory in that they appear to be Web servers unto themselves. IP addresses are unique to each virtual server and serve as the selection factor between them on the same machine. One actual server can embody many virtual servers.

virus   A malicious program that copies itself between computers, and occasionally damages data. Virii can infect disk boot sectors, executable files, and documents for applications (such as Microsoft Word) that support macro languages.

volume   A collection of data indexed by directories containing files and referred to by a drive letter. Volumes are normally contained in a single partition, but volume sets and stripe sets extend a single volume across multiple partitions.

vulnerability   A specific weakness in a system that can be exploited to gain unauthorized access to a system.

WAN   *See* wide area network.

weak password   A password that is easy to guess, such as a word or number relating to the account holder, a single letter, or words appearing in a word processor's spellcheck dictionary.

Web browser   An application that makes HTTP requests and formats the resulting HTML documents for users. The preeminent Internet client, most Web browsers understand all standard Internet protocols and scripting languages. *See* Hypertext Markup Language, Hypertext Transfer Protocol, Internet.

Web page   Any HTML document on an HTTP server. *See* Hypertext Markup Language, Hypertext Transfer Protocol, Internet.

Webmaster   The administrator of a Web site.

well-known ports   Common port assignments for services that listen for public connections. Well-known ports are used when no prior information about how to connect to a specific host is known.

Wide Area Information Service (WAIS)   An Internet-based distributed database connection protocol that allows the simultaneous query of multiple separate databases.

wide area network (WAN)   A geographically dispersed network of networks, connected by routers and communication links. The Internet is the largest WAN. *See* Internet, Local Area Network.

Win16   The set of application services provided by the 16-bit versions of Microsoft Windows: Windows 3.1 and Windows for Workgroups 3.11.

Win32   The set of application services provided by the 32-bit versions of Microsoft Windows: Windows 95 and Windows NT.

WinCGI   The Windows adaptation of the CGI specification for UNIX computers.

Windows 3.11 for Workgroups   The current 16-bit version of Windows for less-powerful, Intel-based personal computers; this system includes peer networking services.

Windows 95   The current 32-bit version of Microsoft Windows for medium-range, Intel-based personal computers; this system includes peer networking services, Internet support, and strong support for older DOS applications and peripherals.

Windows Internet Name Service (WINS)   A network service for Microsoft networks that provides Windows computers with Internet numbers for specified NetBIOS names, facilitating browsing and inter-communication over TCP/IP networks.

Windows NT   The current 32-bit version of Microsoft Windows for powerful Intel, Alpha, PowerPC, or MIPS-based computers; the system includes peer networking services, server networking services, Internet client and server services, and a broad range of utilities.

Windows Sockets   An interprocess communications protocol that delivers connection-oriented data streams used by Internet software and software ported from UNIX environments. *See* interprocess communications.

WinLogon process   The process that presents the logon window to the user, and that coordinates the logon authentication and the user's logon process creation.

WINS   *See* Windows Internet Name Service.

workgroup   A peer-to-peer network. In Microsoft networks, a collection of related computers, such as a department, that doesn't require the uniform security and coordination of a domain. Larger networks should use the *domain* model. *See* domain.

workstation   A powerful personal computer, usually running a preemptive, multitasking operating system like UNIX or Windows NT.

World Wide Web (WWW)   A collection of Internet servers providing hypertext-formatted documents for Internet clients running Web browsers. The World Wide Web provided the first easy-to-use graphical interface for the Internet and is largely responsible for the Internet's explosive growth.

write-back caching   A caching optimization wherein data written to the slow store is cached until the cache is full or until a subsequent write operation overwrites the cached data. Write-back caching can significantly reduce the write operations to a slow store because many write operations are subsequently obviated by new information. Data in the write-back cache is also available for subsequent reads. If something happens to prevent the cache from writing data to the slow store, the cache data will be lost. *See* caching, write-through caching.

write-through caching   A caching optimization wherein data written to a slow store is kept in a cache for subsequent rereading. Unlike write-back caching, write-through caching immediately writes the data to the slow store and is therefore less optimal but more secure.

WWW   *See* World Wide Web.

X.25   A telephony protocol that routes digital trunk circuit data over the telephone network in a manner similar to packet-switched networks like IP. X.25 is a more robust older protocol than frame relay and provides more error correction and addressing for the establishment of temporary circuits.

X.25   The standard that defines packet-switching networks.

zone transfer   Transferring a block of DNS data (typically an entire IP subnet) from one DNS server to another.

Index

O

S